W9-AEC-085

FRENCH
LITERATURE
from 1795 to our era

FRENCH LITERATURE

from 1795 *to our era*

BY

ALBERT THIBAUDET

Translated by Charles Lam Markmann

FUNK & WAGNALLS
New York

CONTENTS

PART TWO: The Generation of 1820

PART THREE: The Generation of 1850

PART FOUR: The Generation of 1885

del — Romantic Revival: Rostand; The Last Verse
Comedies — Ibsen's Influence; The Theater of
Ideas: Curel; Hervieu; Brieux; The Theater of Agi-
tation and Mirbeau — *Théâtre d'Amour* — Bataille;
Bernstein — The Life of Paris — Courteline; Renard;
Bernard

PART FIVE: The Generation of 1914

NOTE

Albert Thibaudet did not conceal from himself, but rather exaggerated in his own mind, the difficulties and the element of the arbitrary that were entailed in a classification by generations: it was undoubtedly because of this that he rewrote certain chapters of this *History* at least three or four times—sometimes altering the span of the generations themselves, sometimes attempting new transitions from one generation to another; and, in every case, leaving the various versions of a given chapter mingled among his papers and disordered in their pagination.

Only "The Generation of 1914" escaped these revisions. It is also the shortest part of the work. "I feel thwarted face to face with the present period," Thibaudet told us. "It is literature that has not been sorted out; the perspective changes constantly. I shall confine myself to a mere diagram."

We have had to unravel what was left. What would have been only a game for Albert Thibaudet has required assiduous study on our part. At least the outlines and the tables prepared by our friend have made it possible for us to select with certainty among the various versions. The *History* that you are about to read is the authentic volume that Albert Thibaudet was preparing for publication when he was interrupted by death.

LÉON BOPP; JEAN PAULHAN

PREFACE

"The critic," Sainte-Beuve said, "is only a man who can read and who teaches others to read." But he is first of all a man who loves reading, who loves to get things read by others. Criticism is stillborn when the love of letters is lacking in its inception and its progress. There is a love of letters for themselves, both in their spirit and in their substance, without which there can be no living criticism or literary history, just as there is a physical love of the theater without which there can be no real dramatic literature; as there is a love of the state without which, in a man of politics, there can be no political soul. It would be gratifying to view this picture of French literature as in another time Sébastien Mercier's *Tableau de Paris* was regarded: the author wrote it first of all as a citizen, a townsman, a lounger in the republic of letters, occupying a place on the terrace of the café where it conducted its business, adjusting his gait to its military bands, proud of the monuments of his city and diligent in his attendance at the meetings of the society concerned with their preservation, taking his morning stroll among the newest works and carrying one of them home under his arm like a carefully chosen melon, sheltering under his umbrella the charming idea that he had followed in the street, in the approximate phrase of Denis Diderot, and quite resigned, furthermore, to the fact that his idea might already have been followed by Diderot or someone else. And I am quite aware that there are more heroic, more spectacular, forms of the love of letters. But these transcend criticism. They belong no longer to the burgher in the town, but rather to the conqueror of the citadel. That impersonation of the Pericles of the republic of letters to which Ferdinand Brunetière aspired is not in our program.

Such a love of letters, however, is the foundation of criticism only in that it is the lowest level of criticism. One might say of letters what King Edward VII remarked of a great French wine to a man who was drinking it too quickly: "A wine like that is to be gazed upon, to be breathed, to be savored, to be drunk—and to be talked about." One must not only learn to love, to savor letters. They reach full growth only in that moment when, according to the hierarchy formally defined by the sagacious sovereign of Great Britain, they are talked about. As soon as one begins to talk about them, one moves from letters, in which one takes pleasure, to literature, which has a historical continuity. Letters are a republic; literature is a state.

To speak of letters is to contemplate them, to know them, and to celebrate them, endowing them with order, observing their changes, espousing a continuity in them. There is a style in literature that meets the definition of Georges-Louis Leclerc de Buffon; the order and the movement that we put into the thoughts of that literature that are works and men.

That we put into them . . . Somewhat of the arbitrary is to be found in every order and every movement of this nature: they belong to the world of what Montaigne called the Discourse; their course is a course with which we endow them by tracing in the world of the real their half-sketched or incipient articulations. We may choose among many systems of discourses and of outcomes.

The model of the purest partisan Discourse, the type most opposed, in its prejudgment on the side of order, to the spirit of Montaigne, is Bossuet's *Discours sur l'histoire universelle*. It would seem that its three sections—*Les Epoques, La Suite de la religion, Les Empires*—offer us the types of the three systems of order applied to a living continuity, and especially to the life span of a literature.

The division by Epochs is used (and with obvious satisfaction christened with a name taken from Bossuet) by Brunetière in his *Manuel d'histoire de la littérature française*. The Literary Epochs are dated by literary events, or, better, by literary advents, those of Montaigne's *Essais, L'Astrée Les Précieuses ridicules, Le Génie du christianisme*. Here we have so many new kingdoms, with their retinues, their actions, their responsibilities. Writers are important and deserve a place to the extent that they create an epoch, as is the case with Honoré d'Urfé and Pierre Bayle. And the logic of this system both demanded and made certain that in this *Manuel* Brunetière should not speak of Mme. de Sévigné and Claude-Henri de Saint-Simon, for the simple reason that, since the letters of the one and the memoirs of the other did not appear until 1726 and 1834 respectively, "their influence cannot be felt at all in history," and therefore Saint-Simon has no more right to an epoch than the Duke of Burgundy to a kingdom. A delaying influence was not contemplated in the plan of the Epochs. From 1850 on, *Adolphe* exerted infinitely more influence than *Le Génie du christianisme*, and the richness of the influence of the Marquise de Sévigné and the Comte de Saint-Simon is justified and affirmed in Marcel Proust. Too bad for them! Periods of transition do exist (and Brunetière gives them a great deal of attention). There are no periods of retrieval.

The second system of *Discours*—an Effect of Religion, so to speak—consists of organizing a history in conformity to some dominant thesis, some higher idea that it is called upon to realize, with a certain degree of freedom and certain intrinsic and extrinsic difficulties, so that sometimes it succeeds and sometimes it fails, sometimes seeks the good and sometimes bows before the bad, without any statute of limitations on the rights of the good. Thus each of our political systems has had and still has an official history, of which it is the culmination, and we know the systems of the middle third of the century that made the history of France a kind of Effect of the Middle Class or Effect of the French Revolution. These are the time and the theme to which Désiré Nisard's *Histoire de la littérature française* belongs. Nisard established, if not a definition, at least a nature and a duty for the French spirit, which searches for itself, finds itself, achieves itself, deceives itself, misleads itself, accuses itself, and learns to know itself through literature. This course found its institution in the classical seventeenth century, as the *Suite de la religion* found its in Christ and the Apostles. A discourse on literary history would sustain that institution, rescue its perpetuity, restore its authority, denounce its heresies, shape new generations on this best of the past, and Nisard, not only a professor but the director of the Ecole Normale, could pass for the tutor of a hundred-headed heir to the throne, responsible for the welfare of literature as the tutor of the prince was responsible for the welfare of the state. These successions, however, are doctrines of a school, which for sixty years have beguiled the most varied minds and which are one with the oratorical spirit. One meets them again in the systems classification that we owe to Victor Cousin. One encounters them in the doctrine of race, environment, and time, the foundation of Hippolyte Taine's *Histoire de la littérature anglaise*, with this difference—which, however, is fundamental—that Taine's course is determined and determining, while Nisard's is inspired by a very firm idea of human freedom.

Dogmatism, choice, spirit of government—after Nisard and also after Brunetière, these tendencies have grown singularly weak. If a name were required to be found for the aspect under which the order of French literature appears most naturally and most normally today, we should borrow the title of the last section of the *Discours sur l'histoire universelle: Les Empires*. French literature seems to be a succession of empires, each of which has been overthrown by a literary war or a revolution and succeeded by a new empire. The four empires of the Assyrians, the Persians, the Macedonians, and the Romans can be found again in the great sequential *climates* of the Christian Middle Ages, humanism, classicism, and romanticism—these last two, the civilizing empires, still continuing, in a parallelism that recalls the Greeks and Romans of Plutarch, to form two competing and complementary languages of the mind and of letters. Histories of literature written in the first third of the twentieth century, whether individually like that of Gustave Lanson or, especially, collectively, would readily tend toward that syncretism that we offer here *cum grano salis*. In the collective histories that appear to be a necessity of the present, whether lay, like that of the school of Joseph Bédier and Paul Hazard, or Catholic, like that of the Calvert school, each of these empires is guided by its own specialists through its own particular function:

medievalists for the Middle Ages, "sixteenthists" for the sixteenth century (to adapt the current French label), which some would gladly supplement with "seventeenthist" while waiting to be able to reach "twentiethist"; the links in time and space are made by "comparativists." The collective histories have brought French literature under the influence—or, as they say, under the sign—of these groups based primarily on erudition. At the same time they correspond to that general idea that we have expressed in terms of empires or climates. In the body of French literature as a whole one can identify four major literary characters, those of the sixteenth, seventeenth, eighteenth, and nineteenth centuries, within which there have been extended revolutions of taste, each of which has indeed been born by a kind of rupture and absolute beginning. The progression by periods of a development and that by the consequences of an idea would then be followed here by a progression by the replacement of a whole, analogous to the order of succession of the philosophic systems, the four empires of the Scholastics, the Cartesians, the Kantians, and the post-Kantians; a progression, too, by dialogue and conflict among these four literary orders, none of which ever wholly disappears any more than the philosophies, and all of which are still present today in the conflicts of forms and of ideas.

✓   Each of these three discourses—Epochs, Effect, Empires—is a possible method, each corresponds to certain turns of literary reality, to certain necessities of literary history: explanatory, didactic, organizational. For our own part, we shall adopt an order the disadvantages and arbitrariness of which we do not try to deny, but which seems to us to offer the advantage of more closely following the natural progression, of more faithfully coinciding with unpredictable change and living continuity, of better adapting the reality and the production of a human activity to the ordinary dimensions of human life: in other words, the order of generations.

The composite, Leibnitz said, symbolizes the simple. The history of a literature is symbolized by the elementary fact of the history of an individual: a fact so elementary that it could be made part of his civil and religious vital statistics along with life, birth, marriage, and death.

ALBERT THIBAUDET

PART ONE

The Generation
of 1789

THE GENERATION OF 1789

The Generation of Napoleon

We are amazed at the stubbornness with which René de Chateaubriand, who was born in 1768, always took a year off his age; it was assumed that he did so only in order to have a common birth year, 1769, from which to launch the parallelism that it pleased him to trace between Napoleon Bonaparte's career and his own. Let us accept this thumb on the scale of the years and recognize it as the intention of creating a reality: the generation of Napoleon. Mme. de Staël, Chateaubriand, and Napoleon were born in three different years between 1766 and 1769: the Genevan, the Breton, the Corsican belonged to the twenty-year-olds of 1789, Napoleon literally, Germaine and René approximately. We shall take this synchronization as a point of departure for the new era.

In the early years of the nineteenth century these three names were almost to create a vacuum around themselves; they were to serve France as official witnesses before the world. They constitute a link in the succession of the generations. When we compare them with the other links in the French chain, a remarkable characteristic impresses us.

Two of them were foreigners. And the third was an eternal exile. Germaine Necker was the daughter of the controller general, the foreign technician; after Jean-Jacques Rousseau and her father, Jacques Necker, she was to represent the third wave of that conquest by Geneva whose story did not end with her. Bonaparte, another of our conquerors, was an Italian, as truly Italian despite his French citizenship as Mme. de Staël was truly Genevan despite her Swedish nationality. And, if Chateaubriand was a Breton, he launched a new fashion of being Breton. Brittany, in the eighteenth century, had joined the mainstream of French culture: Duclos (Charles Pinot) and Pierre-Louis Moreau de Maupertuis were French writers of whom we know, though we attach no importance to the fact, that they were born in Brittany. But Chateaubriand, although he had early and forever left Brittany, to return there only in a celebrated coffin, was personally, tenaciously Breton, as Félicité-Robert de Lamennais and Ernest Renan were to be after him. A Breton as Rousseau was a Genevan or Bonaparte a Corsican, this pure Frenchman became, through his position as a decorative, stylized exile, eccentric to his time, a kind of honorary alien.

The Fall of the Republic of Letters

These three initially extraordinary appearances of quasi-foreigners seem more ordinary and almost necessary to us if we see in them the counterpart of an absence: the absence of everything that, in this generation of the twenty-year-olds of 1789, had been prevented by the Revolution.

Prevented to a certain extent, undoubtedly, for demographic reasons. This generation had barely begun to live when the ruinous wars began. Did they subject the world of letters to equal or greater loss than that inflicted on it by the revolutionary tribunals? Did some André Chénier die at Wattignies or at Eylau? It was so, probably, in a proportion only inferior to that of the 1914 war. The slaughter of the elite that swept away the generation of the twenty-year-olds of 1914 remains today a fact unique in history, and in any case we can derive from such hazardous speculations on possibilities nothing that can become part of a chain of explanatory causes.

The absence that prevailed when that earlier generation came to manhood was not that absence of individuals of which we can know nothing: it was the absence of a literary condition, of a literary climate. The proclamation of the French Republic, in fact, coincided with the abolition of the republic of letters.

The republic of letters, that ancient state that gave literature its atmosphere, its customs, its problems, its rhythms, its domestic economy, its foreign relations, was destroyed by the very revolution that it had nurtured. No more Académies, no more *salons*, no more "society." At the origin of the literature of any period, of any generation, there are usually one or two million young minds with the idea of creating an interesting life for themselves by "making literature," and a hundred thousand persons with the idea that it is interesting, pleasant, or important that people "make literature." Then for a few years this idea is forgotten or obscured. The generation that has experienced that oblivion and that obscurity is permanently marked and wounded.

Success in the republic of letters meant pleasing the respectable, as success in the political republic means pleasing the voters. Chateaubriand had nothing else in mind when, as a young officer, he used to write for the *Almanach des muses*. And what was meant by pleasing the respectable had been learned by Germaine Necker sitting on her stool in her mother's *salon*. While the Revolution included many respectable people, it never-theless destroyed or scattered the respectable. What public—or, rather, what publics—could replace that one for this generation? There were three possibilities, and all three were to play their parts in a literary revo-lution.

The New Publics

1. First of all, the public of those who were not respectable, the men in the street and the new rich—that is, in the one case as in the other, the public of the crowd. But this public had no effect on the twenty-year-olds of 1789. They were growing up with an already fixed education, that of the old society. They could not repudiate it. The Revolution had a revo-lutionary literature; it did not have a literary revolution. From the literary point of view, it was more conservative, more pedantic, more *elementary* than any other period. In poetry and the theater the wheels of the old machinery went on turning mechanically. The generation that would make a literary revolution, that would incorporate the popular forms into literature in the theater and the novel, was not to be the generation that, from desire or duress, had had to swallow the French Revoluiton: it would be the generation that had digested it—in other words, the next generation.

2. But, while the respectable public was no longer in Paris, it could re-group its forces elsewhere, and literature could go there with it. The essential literary event for this generation was emigration. Most of the new values were created in exile, or through it, or by life abroad: Chateau-briand, Mme. de Staël, Xavier de Maistre, Louis de Bonald, Antoine de Rivarol. The length of this exile seems to have been proportioned by an artistic destiny, like the floods of the Nile, to the needs of literature. It lasted about ten years. Had it ended sooner, as the emigrants hoped in 1792, the exile would not have had sufficient time to steep itself in the alien, to set up its table of comparisons, to flex, broaden, and enrich its capital of ideas and sensations. Had it persisted for a generation or more, like the Protestant emigration of the seventeenth century, it would have been swallowed up abroad, it would have enriched the literature of other lands, not that of France. The Revolution and the emigration collaborated to transform the generation of the twenty-year-olds of 1789 into a gen-eration that would see and experience much in a few years, that was to accumulate a capital of experience and of diversity far greater than that of any period since the sixteenth century, and that would provide the next generation with an open-hearted, eager public: it was to be the *salons* of the one-time emigrants that would first make the literary fortunes of Al-phonse de Lamartine and Victor Hugo. Such was the second public pos-

sible to literature between 1792 and 1802, and, from another point of view, between 1792 and 1815—in short, a return of the traditional public of the republic of letters.

3. But, especially after Rousseau—the *Confessions* and the *Rêveries*—one can easily imagine a third public: that absolutely minimal public that consists of the author himself, writing for himself. In 1793 the best work of living writers was all in manuscript: the poems of Chénier, the chest full of papers brought back from America by Chateaubriand. When the presses were restored to letters, the monologues of solitude would appear —Chateaubriand's *René*, Etienne Pivert de Sénancour's *Obermann*.

This generation was to furnish the inner life with a master, though unknown to his contemporaries: Marie-François-Pierre Maine de Biran. The obvious, external emigration, to foreign countries, was balanced by an inner emigration, the nomad tent by the secret temples. The man least qualified for such a life, Antoine-Nicolas de Condorcet, writing his *Tableau des progrès* in his hiding place after the second of June, said of it: "For me this contemplation is a quiet refuge where the memory of my persecutors cannot reach me." The Revolution drove many souls into such refuges.

Thus the generation that was twenty years old in 1789 was forced into a mode of life and of literary works other than those that it would have followed if the times had taken a normal course. Undoubtedly this generation was shaped at the expense of a purely French literary movement that would have been the direct, the delicate, perhaps the enfeebled product of the dying eighteenth century. We know toward what horizon and for what voyage the curve of the literary current was turning on the eve of the Revolution. That departure was more or less countermanded by the Revolution. In the eight preceding years, from 1782 to 1788, there had appeared *Les Liaisons dangereuses*, *Le Mariage de Figaro*, *Paul et Virginie*. It is indeed worth noting that their respective authors, Choderlos de Laclos, Caron de Beaumarchais, Bernardin de Saint-Pierre, all three witnesses of the preceding generation, though in their prime, and having all three survived the Revolution, having joined it, having been employed by it, as writers did not survive the old order and produced nothing more of merit.

THE SECOND EMIGRATION

The Departure of the Elite

Whether it be centripetal or centrifugal, the European character that was assumed by French literature at the end of the seventeenth century and at the end of the eighteenth was dependent on two tides of emigration which had the same cause, a single-minded fanaticism, and which led to the same result, the emigration of an elite. In 1789 the Parisians of the Faubourg St.-Antoine destroyed the Bastille with the same enthusiasm that their grandfathers had manifested in demolishing the Protestant church in Charenton. Similarly, as Albert Sorel has shown, the jurists of the Revolution simply applied against the emigrants and the clergy the same law that the jurists of Louis XIV had created in order to despoil the Protestants and destroy their families. From the time of Pierre Bayle the Protestant emigration had produced a French literature abroad, and even a style that was called the refugee style. The great difference between the first emigration and the second was that the emigrants of the Revolution went back to their homes after an interval that was more or less the length of the Trojan War—that at the end of their Odyssey there was a return—and that the literary influence of the emigration made itself less felt abroad by its sojourn than in France by this return.

When the people of the ancient cities came into conflict with the aristocracy, they encountered this stumbling block: the fact that the noble families held the key to religion, to the rituals, to the sacrifices, to the auspices, and that, even if the people could take over the exercise of power, they lacked not the initiative but the initiation required to establish contact between the city and the gods. In what concerned arts and letters in 1789, the various aristocracies possessed those customs, that initiation, that taste that cannot be improvised. They took them away when they left, but they denaturalized them and themselves.

The Literature of the Emigration

Only one great writer had not emigrated—and he was then unknown: that was André Chénier. His brother, Marie-Joseph, could be taken as the type and the leading figure of those stragglers who went on repeating the empty gestures of eighteenth-century poetry in France. But for a quarter of a century, from 1793 to 1820, all the writers who counted were foreigners, like Mme. de Staël, Benjamin Constant, Xavier de Maistre, even, after all, Bonaparte, or emigrants, like Chateaubriand, Bonald, Etienne de Sénancour, Rivarol. Whatever had not undergone the ordeal or the sacrament of the frontier, whatever said, with Emmanuel-Joseph Sieyès, "I have lived!" was in decline. Regardless what political or moral judgment one may risk on the emigration, regardless whether one repeats in this connection such a remark as that of Father Jean-Nicolas Loriquet in his *Histoire de France* concerning the Protestants who, after the revocation of the Edict of Nantes, "did not blush to carry abroad the secrets of our industry," it was a benefaction to literature. It brought about new experiences. It enriched French sensibility. It mingled European tendencies. It provided a counterweight of autonomy and freedom to the official conformism under which the Revolution and Napoleon threatened to crush and sterilize letters. It laid the foundations for Restoration Parisian society, the first fires of romanticism, the most delicate forms of intellectual liberalism and esthetic intelligence, the peaceful, harmonious, tolerant, and cultivated Europe of the years from 1815 to 1848.

The exiled elite lived tragically. They were compelled to an existence of danger, solitude, humiliation. Exile and ordeals led them to revise their values and to learn or to create new ones. The gods that they had taken out with them made contacts and alliances with the foreign gods. Charles-Augustin Sainte-Beuve, pointing out that Chateaubriand's originality was due to his uprootedness, said: "Revolutions are good for that, at least; they triumph by uprooting, they smash what follows too closely, and they start the great mixture all over again. There is always the chance that out of all this something original and new will be produced."

There are those emigrants who lose their own country and there are those who discover other countries. There are those emigrants who find themselves without a society and there are those who create a new one for themselves. There are those emigrants who have no youth and there are those who create a youth. Three antitheses, each of which strikes its spark of literary life.

The Discovery of Europe

In losing France, other emigrants, children of the eighteenth century, did not have too accurate a notion of their own state, and they regarded their solitary lives hardly otherwise than in the pleasant, humorous guise of Xavier de Maistre's *Voyage autour de ma chambre*. On the other hand, they discovered Europe. In the witticism of Jacques Mallet du Pan, they became cosmopolitans in spite of themselves. The range of their dispersion was vast. Of the three Bourbons who were to follow Louis XVI, Louis XVIII lived in Russia, Charles X in Scotland, and Louis-Philippe, who sojourned in Scandinavia just below the Arctic Circle, and then in America, was a passionate traveler. The bibliography of emigrants' travel books, whether published abroad or, after their return, in France, is considerable. They discovered England, Germany, Scandinavia, Russia, Spain, the United States, not as in other times through journeys of exploration or diplomatic missions or the sojourns of men of letters in refined company, but in the harsh reality to which they were harnessed by hard lives, association with the populace, journeys on foot, the work that they had to do in order to live, the languages that they had to learn. Their exile lasted long enough for them to learn the world but not long enough to make them forget France.

The welcome that they received in British society laid the groundwork for that Anglo-French life of the political and literary spirit that took shape after 1815. It was among emigrants from Lyon that Sir Walter Scott met the woman he married. It was from England that Chateaubriand brought back, along with his enthusiasm for Milton, his recognition of the Christian literary genius. In Germany, Hamburg and the surrounding area housed the most compact and the most brilliant of the emigrant colonies. Forty thousand exiles lived there; they had their own theater, their own café and their French newspapers, their magazine, *Le Spectateur du nord;* they also had Rivarol, and Charles-Julien de Chênedollé, and Beaumarchais, and Abbé Jacques Delille, and Mmes. de Genlis and de Flahaut-Souza and the men of the Constituent Assembly of 1789, in contact with the poets Friedrich Gottlieb Klopstock, Hans Heinrich Voss, and Hans Georg Jacobi, and the historian Berthold Georg Niebuhr. It was in Hamburg that a bookseller called Fauche entrusted Rivarol with the task of preparing a *Dictionnaire de la langue française* for the Germans. In Ansbach, Adalbert de Chamisso and Jean-Baptiste Suard were the intimates of Prince von Hardenberg. From Mme. de Staël's Geneva to Mme. de Charrière's Neuchâtel, French Switzerland, which had become one of the crossroads of the emigration, was preparing to provide a living center, a *salon* of Europe, for the new cosmopolitanism. For literature, from the time of the Consulate, Coppet would become almost a French Hamburg.

L'Emigré

Since the emigration lasted only ten years, its literary life was merely a corridor, a passage. Hence we shall meet its principal characters in other chapters, as well as specific works—the various memoirs—all written long afterward. Nevertheless we must make an exception. The only important novel published between *Paul et Virginie* in 1787 and *Valérie* in 1803 not only was written by an exile but was called *L'Emigré*. Written by Gabriel Sénac de Meilhan, it was published in Brunswick in 1797 and did not have the slightest success. It is a novel told in "letters written in 1793," which the author insisted were real and which in any event describe a situation that must have existed often enough: a young German woman, married but not too seriously, has taken a wounded young emigrant into her Rhenish castle. The love story of the exile, deliberately portrayed as a French type, and the intelligent care with which the author writes of German minds and society give *L'Emigré* the aspect of a less decorative but more living, more moving and more authentic cosmopolitan novel than Mme. de Staël's *Corinne*. The difference between *L'Emigré* and *Corinne* is like that between *Obermann* and *René*. The two books by Sénac and Sénancour, absolutely ignored by the generation of their contemporaries, have found a public in direct proportion to the degree that of the two famous books, like squeezed lemons, have lost one, until these now barely survive as relics of literary history.

REVOLUTIONARY LITERATURE

The Revolution smashed, overthrew, or scattered the literary generation of 1789. Remarkable invention and creation in the sphere of action
were purchased at the literary price of the disappearance of taste, the
penury of forms, the sterility of the theater and of books.

The Debauch of Popular Literature

At the same time that the eighteenth century sustained and in many
ways perfected a literature for people of taste, for the citizens and invited
guests of the republic of letters, it had created or suggested a popular,
even a populist, literature with the novels of Nicolas-Edmé Restif de la
Bretonne and the plays (and the theories) of Sébastien Mercier. By sack-
ing, exiling, or muzzling the citizens of the republic of letters, the French
Republic opened a broader avenue to this popular literature. The republic
of letters became a democracy of letters: the people sang, the people read,
the people listened. And that might have produced results. Unhappily, the
age-old habits of French literature had congealed, a transition was lacking
and, though romanticism would later profit thereby, the result during the
revolutionary period was nil.

Song

The people sang, and authentic revolutionary poetry was in effect, or
should have been, sung poetry, such as the popular festivals called for.
Marie-Joseph Chénier's *Chant du départ*, not too unworthy of Etienne-
Nicolas Méhul's noble music, is the most beautiful of the revolutionary

hymns. The sublime soaring of the *Marseillaise,* unfortunately, is dragged
down by awkward words. Let us not mention the *Carmagnole* and *Ça ira.*

Newspapers

The people read. They read newspapers above all. The newspapers are
certainly the most living part of the literature of the Revolution. They
attained this position as early as the States General of 1789, which came
together already borne on the tide of a curious spontaneous literature,
that of the *Cahiers* which were written in little towns and villages by
prosecutors, schoolmasters, priests, and in which there was no lack of picturesque and individual accents, touching and sincere. These notebooks of
the electorate sometimes had their counterpart in the accountings rendered
by their representatives, such as Honoré-Gabriel de Mirabeau's *Lettres à
mes commettants,* which were real journalism. And in Paris especially,
the opinions to be defended, the causes to be furthered, the relaxation and
later the disappearance of censorship of the press set off a grapeshot fire
of fervid leaflets, often of periodical pamphlets, edited by one or two men
and issued sporadically.

The best and in any event the most famous of the newspapers of 1789–
1791 was *Les Actes des apôtres,* published by Jean-Gabriel Peltier, Rivarol, the Chevalier de Champcenetz, Mirabeau, and François-Louis
Suleau: a conservative pamphlet that addressed itself first of all to cultivated society, or to what was left of it: whence came a more refined
literature. To read it, however, has become disappointing. It is difficult
for us to understand all these hidden meanings and allusions to forgotten
persons. It is much easier for us to understand Jean-Paul Marat's *L'Ami
du peuple,* which began to appear in September 1789, and the *Révolutions
de France et de Brabant,* which Camille Desmoulins started to publish in
November 1789. But Desmoulins' forceful talent was made known above
all in 1793, with *Le Vieux Cordelier.* The issues of the latter that immediately preceded his death are regarded with reason as the masterpieces
of the journalism of the Revolution, because then he was in mortal combat. In the same manner, *L'Ami du peuple* owes to the force of its con-
victions, the ferocity of its hatreds, its direct contact with the passions of
the street the vigor that still dazzles in those of its pages to which we retain a thread of connection. In popular literature it stands beside Jacques-
René Hébert's *Le Père Duchêne.* Hébert had a true journalist's temperament; he created a popular and powerful style of remarkable dash and
savor, which the Goncourts admired and from which Jean Jaurès, when
he published his *Histoire socialiste* in installments, enjoyed quoting long
passages for the renewed entertainment of his popular readers of 1900.

Eloquence

And, finally, the people listened. Spoken literature, in sum, remains the best of what was produced in the Revolution, even though it was often written and read in the three Assemblies. The eloquence of the Constituent Assembly was not a popular eloquence. In the body of Mirabeau's speeches his celebrated apostrophes, exhortations, surges of pathos, tides of lava, shakings of the head occupied only a small place, and indeed, as in the oration on the hideous bankruptcy, they were capable of coinciding with gaps in the good sense of which he had an ample supply. The speeches of Mirabeau, Joseph Barnave, Jacques de Cazalès, Jean-Siffrein Maury, Maximilien de Robespierre (when he was in the Constituent Assembly) were generally discussions of ideas and of business in hand, in which pathos was only a kind of foam and which were sustained by the accomplishments and the logic of the speakers' experience and their culture. The same qualities are not to be found in the orators of the Legislative Assembly, who had acquired the habit of speaking less for the Assembly than for the gallery, who loved eloquence for itself, but who had the poetry of youth and who presented, in a monumental movement like that of the *Horatii* in Jacques-Louis David's painting, the image of a new generation in its united uprush. It was Pierre-Victurnien Vergniaud, with that generous and egotistical romanticism in which we seem to hear already the lyric flights of his future historian, Lamartine; it was Maximin Isnard, the frenzied Provençal, who in a few speeches (written, moreover, with hard labor) before the Legislative Assembly and the Convention struck perhaps the sharpest notes before the most Pythian tripod that the Assemblies ever knew. Most of these orators met again and grew in stature in the Convention, where Robespierre, at least, reintroduced the full style and the upright, cogent effort of his beginnings in the Constituent Assembly. It is undoubtedly Robespierre who, with Mirabeau, has left behind him the greatest number of pages of oratory worth reading. He remains the colleague of whom Mirabeau said: "This man will go far because he believes what he says." Deep conviction, its roots strengthened by lonely meditation and by hatred for the enemy; an inexhaustible determination to force what he believed into every ear that heard him, by virtue of a consistent, clear, and vehement logic; and the goal, which, the farther the speaker went, fled the farther into the distance, because it was nothing other than the kingdom of righteousness: all these gave Robespierre what he alone was to have wholly for a time under the Revolution: authority. The authority of the definer, of the guide, of the policy-maker, the authority of the Incorruptible. If something remains of Robespierre's speeches, all that remains of Georges-Jacques Danton is a few gestures, phrases, outcries, fire, all of them the finest of the Revolution. It is probable that Louis de Saint-Just possessed something of genius, and some remarkable words of his, too, have been preserved. But his speeches themselves are stringy, dull; and, when his reasoning turns down the road of the absurd, the delirious fanaticism with which he pursues it to its end seems no longer a strength but a curse of nature.

Writings

But it is not only, nor particularly, because of their oratory that the important men of the Revolution have survived in literature. The best of Mirabeau is in other productions: not so much his *Histoire secrète de la cour de Berlin*, the hasty and ill-ripened fruit of his diplomatic mission in Prussia, as in his *Lettres* of volcanic love to Sophie de Monnier, and less in his love letters than in his political letters—that is, the secret notes written (for a price) to Louis XVI. Above Mirabeau the orator stands Mirabeau the minister.

By this I mean Mirabeau as an aspirant for a ministry, Mirabeau thinking and writing like a minister; the Mirabeau teeming with ideas who wept to see the state abandoned, through the king's "nill" (it was Mirabeau's coinage: *nolonté*), to the mad mob of Paris or to the stodgy Genevan bookkeeper; the Mirabeau who knew what must be done and who, alert to all the dangers that faced the monarchy, wanted to rescue it and wept at the vices, the debts, the whole legend attached to its burdening past that deprived it of any action for the better. When the States General of 1614 withdrew, it left the Bishop of Luçon, the future Richelieu, on the shore of the court. The dynasty of the Bourbons could have been saved by a great minister who had the ability to consolidate and systematize in terms of the monarchy what came out of the States General of 1789. Mirabeau alone could have been that minister at that time, but he was forced aside by the king, the Assembly, fate, and the debility of a spent life. He has left his testimony of all this, and it belongs to letters: the *Correspondance* between Mirabeau and Count de La Marck. But La Marck figures here rather as a straw man. These three volumes, published in 1851, are a dialogue between Mirabeau and the throne, or a monologue by Mirabeau before the throne, and, to borrow the language of Bossuet, an *Avertissement politique*.

The essence of this *Correspondance*, because of its substance, of the correspondents, and of the consequences, is the fifty notes written by Mirabeau between June 1790, and his death ten years later. A foreigner without ideas, Necker, and a brainless weathercock who veered with the wind, the Marquis de La Fayette, were the two consuls of irresolution and conceit; they held the reins. Mirabeau, compelled to attend in the wings, offered a proposal while he waited for something better. These fifty notes were written diabolically, with more genius, perhaps, than common sense. They are still worth reading, especially in periods of crisis, when a government is tottering and must be shored up, when the spirit of revolution is resurgent, when, since the evils and the perils are the same, the remedy is also the same in its major outlines: a vigorous synthesis, active rather than passive, of the new exigencies and the old order. Like the writings of Napoleon, these notes became part of literature because they comprised not only arguments and ideas but also a personality, a character, a man: therefore a style.

There has also been preserved a certain body of the powerful thinking of that mystery, Saint-Just. This, his licentious but flat poem, *Organt*, and his cold, venomous discussions of the *Institutions républicaines*, studded with flashes of genius and the light of a great soul, seem to belong to three different individuals. Marie-Jean Hérault de Séchelles, a real writer, was a part of the same group and the same period as Laclos. But it is as a moralist, not as a political writer, that the ironic and intelligent author of the *Voyage à Montbard* and the *Discours sur l'ambition* is ranked.

The many memoirs on the revolutionary era that began to appear after 1815 constitute a very special literature, which will be discussed in its proper place. Nonetheless one must take account here of the *Notes* of Baudot, a member of the Convention—virtually the only memoirs written at the very time that they report, which bring views of exceptional penetration to bear on the principal authors of the Revolution, and which, utilized by Edgar Quinet in his *Révolution*, were not published until the end of the nineteenth century. Then there were the *Mémoires* that Mme. Roland wrote in her prison while Condorcet was writing *L'Esquisse* in his refuge. These two books by authors under the ban, the one projected through the raging storm on the past, the other toward the future, would be enough to save the honor of the literature of the Revolution.

The Theater

The division of the literature of the Revolution, which we have shown, into a literature that followed tradition but lacked health and a popular literature that made little headway is to be found again in the theater.

Tragedy dragged its feet stubbornly in the muddy thaw of the eighteenth century. Being republican did not make the tragedies of Marie-Joseph Chénier any the better or the worse. They deserve the most honored position in the funeral procession of the art.

Comedy did a better job of adjusting itself to mediocrity. In 1790, not without skill or success, Philippe Fabre d'Eglantine's *Philinte de Molière* presented Alceste in the character that would later belong to the good Jacobin, Philinte in that of a monarchist or an aristocrat. In the same way, the respectable Antoine-Marin Lemierre's *Guillaume Tell*, a tragedy a quarter-century old, owed a new success to a subtitle that was a brainstorm: *Guillaume Tell ou Les Sans-culottes suisses*. *Philinte*, moreover, found itself flanked between the two successes of Jean-François Collin d'Harleville, *L'Optimiste* in 1788 and *Le Vieux Célibataire* in 1793; Fabre launched a campaign against *L'Optimiste* and optimism, which he denounced as a counterrevolutionary doctrine, and in those days it was only one step from counterrevolution to the guillotine. Or from the Revolution, for that matter: Fabre made the step.

Logically it was a time neither for comedy nor for tragedy, but for drama, on the stage as in the street. Denis Diderot and Mercier had already prepared the way, creating for the drama an agitated style chopped up by exclamations and "natural movements." Then the Comédie-Française had yielded: on 2 September 1793 its twenty-eight actors had been imprisoned for having presented a *Paméla* in vassalage to William Pitt and Duke Friedrich von Saxe-Coburg, and so the way was open for republican authors and actors. But "open" is a figure of speech: *Jean sans terre* could not be presented in the Théâtre de la République because that good *sans-culotte*, Antoine-Joseph Santerre, the commander of the Garde Nationale, would have been offended by it. Nor would the censorship under the Directory allow the name of Louis to be given to a virtuous character in a play by François-Benoît Hoffmann. In spite of everything, the crowd went to see plays, and in the end the need created the organ: in 1798 Guilbert de Pixérécourt staged his first melodrama, *Victor ou L'Enfant de la forêt*. It alarmed the authorities: "The vital principle of never portraying bloodshed on the stage," an official decree asserted, "has been absolutely thrust aside, and the play continually presents the repugnant spectacle of robbery and murder. It is to be feared that the young, if they become accustomed to such spectacles, may be emboldened to put them into practice and abandon themselves to behavior that could lead to their own destruction and the despair of their families." Theaters have always made trouble for governments. Nevertheless the cake mold of tragedy rode out the storm without damage. It was enough that Napoleon stood guard over the mold and that François-Joseph Talma (Napoleon's favorite actor) sold the cakes: the art was reprieved for a generation.

The Novel

The revolutionary theater was rich in quantity, at least: a thousand plays in ten years. One cannot say even this of the novel. Between *Les Liaisons dangereuses* and the beginning of the nineteenth century, the literary interregnum continued. It is true that the subliterary world teemed with the successes of François-Guillaume Ducray-Duminil, author of *Victor,* and those of Pigault-Lebrun. And, outside France, there was to be a novel of the emigration: the art form of the future had crossed the border with the best of the literature.

IV

NAPOLEON

Adolphe Thiers, statesman and historian, has said—and Sainte-Beuve has endorsed the statement—that Napoleon was the major writer of his time; others have advanced the paradox that his true calling was that of the man of letters. One must not exaggerate, but certainly, from the most varied points of view, his personality dominates the literature of his time. Victor Hugo's comparison in *Les Orientales*—Napoleon on the horizon of the century like Vesuvius on the horizon of Naples—is as true of the literary as of the political century.

Like Louis XIV, though with more resolve and less success, he created a climate, the climate of a literature under supervision and control. But this system must not be held responsible for the mediocrity of letters under Napoleon. He killed only those who could not live! If the Empire was a period only of literary transition, that was for literary reasons only. In what fashion did the antagonism between the master and Chateaubriand and Mme. de Staël injure their work? On the contrary, it would seem that both sides found this state of affairs a tonic, the occasion for Chateaubriand's "Bonaparte and I."

The Empire was the only regime that placed a pure man of letters, Louis de Fontanes, at the head of the university, and he was in other ways a kind of permanent delegate to Napoleon for the university, whose cause he often served bravely. Napoleon's real influence on letters, however, was to be posthumous, when romanticism came into being and wrote a thousand variants of an *Imitation de Napoléon*.

His personal work is unique in the literature of royalty. Far superior to that of Frederick the Great, it can be compared only with what has been handed down to us of what Caesar dictated. It will be observed that French was no more the mother tongue of Napoleon than it was of Frederick the Great, but the clear, precise, pragmatic language of the eighteenth century, the language of Montesquieu and Voltaire, has never better expressed its universality, its mission of formulating thought as an algebra of action, than in affording this Corsican the style of their genius and the genius of their style.

In the long literary trail left by his actions, zones are to be distinguished.

First of all a "note for memory" should be made of a body of youthful personal writing, more or less inspired by Rousseau, that is similar to what any young officer might scribble in his barracks. Among the fragments that have been discovered, the dialogue of the *Souper de Beaucaire* is the best known. But we have no idea what a literary Bonaparte might have been.

Bonaparte's real entrance into the world of words that are written and endure was his proclamation in Nice to the Army of Italy: "Soldiers, you are naked . . ." This was the inauguration of what might be called the Napoleonic rhetoric. Indeed, there can be no oratorical action on men without rhetoric. In perspective, the proclamations, the appeals, the exhortations, the discourses of Napoleon may sound hollow beneath their platitudes. They were successful. They belong to a class of military movements that wins victories over souls and crowds. They cross commonplaces as if they were bridges. The power of this dynamic literature is not yet exhausted. "Victory will march with the speed of a charge. The eagle bearing our national colors will fly from belfry to belfry until it has reached the towers of Notre-Dame." That should be measured by its effect on "the population," and then it is as great as that expanse of the map of France that Jules Michelet, in his *Tableau,* saw unrolling from the peaks of the Jura.

On 12 March 1815, Marshal Ney, who had been dispatched to capture the Emperor and who had boasted (as Napoleon knew) that he would bring him back in an iron cage, received this letter: "Cousin, my chief of staff is sending you our order of march. I have no doubt that, as soon as you have learned of my arrival at Lyon, you will put your troops back under the Tricolor. Follow Bertrand's orders and come join me at Chalon. I will welcome you as I did the day after the battle of Moscow." Ney's first reaction was: "The Bourbons will never be able to speak like that." On the day after the farewells at Fontainebleau, discussing at Briare his speech to his Old Guard, Napoleon himself observed: "That is how one ought to speak." Who in the nineteenth century knew how to talk, in the whole sense of the word, to Frenchmen? Napoleon, Lamartine, Léon Gambetta. None of the lieutenants of Napoleon had the capacity. In 1808 he wrote to Marshal Murat: "Your order of the day to the troops on the Barjos matter is wretched . . . the Frenchman has too much wit not to make fun of such proclamations. You certainly did not learn that in my school."

Much the biggest monument to Napoleon's work, in terms of quantity, is the thirty thousand letters of his *Correspondance* thus far published.

Always dictated while he was standing, they give us like a phonograph the tone, the orders, the angers, the active intelligence of the Emperor. They belong more to the category of recorded remarks than to that of written literature. During his campaigns Napoleon continued to govern, receiving reports from his ministers every day, dictating answers to everything, often using at the same time several secretaries, who had difficulties in following him. Every reply is always pertinent, clear, direct. The man is in them, reprimanding, inveighing or praising, speaking his mind on everything, and often in flashes of fire.

To these directly dictated pieces in the *Correspondance* we must add the conversations reported by the participants—Pierre-Louis Roederer, Louis-Mathieu Molé, Prince von Metternich-Winneburg, and especially Napoleon's companions on St. Helena. His dominant strength was such that they could not help writing about Napoleon, and the remembered utterances always molded the written style of the recorder, a phenomenon that can be likened only to the dialogues of Socrates or the conversations of Blaise Pascal. But the stenographically preserved remarks are sometimes disappointing: such is the case with the reports of the sessions of the Council of State during which the Civil Code was developed, sessions which Bonaparte often attended. His contributions might have seemed as strange and ingenuous to the juridical experts as they do to us today. But this underbrush was less familiar to him than that of his native island, and, while he was the master in such subtle matters, he was no master of them.

Little importance is to be attached to the historical essays that he dictated on St. Helena expressly for posterity. And their fundamental authenticity might also be questioned. He is least believable when he recounts the events of his time and his reign in perspective. What he says of his intentions and his plans was constructed on St. Helena, and generally it is given the lie by contemporary documents. His arguments for the defense are arguments that history does not very often uphold. He seems, moreover, to have always labeled "truth" the statement that could best be transformed into action. Out of imagination, out of necessity, out of his position as a maker of opinion, a maker of truth, he must have lied a great deal: he was a pragmatist, and he must be read as such.

With all that, the *Mémorial de Sainte-Hélène*, or, rather, the three works of Emmanuel de Las Cases, Charles de Montholon, and General Gaspard Gourgaud, is among those books of his century that had the greatest effect on the imagination. First of all as a narrative; then, and particularly, by its abundance of phrases marked by the lion's claw. Many of its pages are of an inexhaustible beauty. A sharp challenge sent to Chateaubriand from St. Helena is the equal of the finest pages of the *Mémoires d'outre-tombe*.

If Bonaparte's political destiny had not revealed itself, if he had followed the career of a man of letters, it is most unlikely that such a career would have produced a body of literary work equal to what has been handed down to us by his career as a Caesar.

V

CHATEAUBRIAND

Between Two Centuries

Like Napoleon and Mme. de Staël, Chateaubriand was a child of the eighteenth century, reaching his majority in 1789 and maturing with the spirit of the new century. He was to become much less the father than the classic of the romantic poets. A great deal of his work has been forgotten. But nevertheless the prestige of his personality is greater than would seem to be authorized by the reading of what has survived. Inner movements, rhythmic alterations, general themes of French life and letters are transmitted by him and explained by him. They would have been otherwise, and so should we have been, if Chateaubriand had been born a few years earlier or a few years later, if, on this even scale of two centuries and two spirits, one side had been burdened either with the Parisian attitudes of 1780 or with romanticism, whether inclined toward Jacques-Henri Bernardin de Saint-Pierre or toward Lamartine.

Side by side with his obdurate will to afford posterity the idea of "Napoleon and I" he suffered the dread of offering that of "Rousseau and I." He did everything in his power to distract us from it. In vain. Following and resembling Rousseau, he imposed on French literature the type of the public life of the great writer, of a body of work designed as a historic residence, a residence imbued with the personality of its owner, like the Versailles of Louis XIV—invested with a sensitivity and an atmosphere emanating from him to display and impose his reign—with the official position of a lord of climate. And in this way, indeed, he does become paired with Napoleon for posterity. He was to bequeath us the slogan, "Be the Napoleon of something." General Léopold Hugo's adolescent son Victor was to write in one of his notebooks: "I want to be Chateaubriand or nothing."

His Vocations

There is still much discussion of the vast designs of Napoleon. Those of his contemporary in letters were not more immune to setbacks and miscalculations, even less devoid of imperialism. But they emerge with sufficient clarity. He had three of them, all of which helped the imaginative Breton to make his life, and only one of which was literary. The two others will help us to isolate and rank the third.

THE SON OF THE SEA

The first great project of the man of Saint-Malo, as befitted his race, was that of a seaman. He was a seaman's son—a corsair's, in fact—and through him the sea was to come into literature. He dreamed of going to America, of discovering its Northwest Passage, of becoming a kind of Magellan of the north who would join the Atlantic and the Pacific by means of his voyage through the ice. A schoolboy's idea. His sister-in-law's grandfather was Chrétien-Guillaume de Lamoignon de Malesherbes. From him Chateaubriand got a bundle of navigation maps. Observe the child in love with maps and prints at the poetic moment, the moment when the world is huge in the lamplight. He did not discover the Northwest Passage any more than Columbus discovered the Indies. But, like Columbus, he discovered America. He brought back a vision of the picturesque, exactly like another viscount, also a relative of Malesherbes: Alexis Clérel de Tocqueville. The package of 2,383 manuscript pages, if he is to be believed, was his American plunder—was his great project, which, begun as soon as he had reached the New World, burst into an eruption of literary froth. Moreover, let us not think that literature had ever been lacking from this project. "You should paint that," René was told by his sister Lucile, when they stood together enraptured at Combourg before the pool, the moor, and the forest. Together with the maps for his grand design he took to America a plenitude of paper on which to describe it, and, for lack of the journal of the man who fulfills his plan, he was to write the journal of the man who does not fulfill it.

THE MAN OF LETTERS

His second great project was purely literary. But in how many ways it resembled the first! His invincible vocation was that of the man of letters. It was inevitable that his religious conversion, like his travels in America, should be immediately turned into literature. He had gone to America to seek there, and he had brought back from there, the literary "genius" of America. Driven into exile by the Revolution, he had flung

himself on his pen and written a "genius" of revolutions in his *Essai* of
1797. His conversion to Christianity would not proceed without a literary version of that conversion: that was to be *Le Génie du christianisme*,
which was only the first part of a vast project of literary architecture.
The second part was to be the proof in fact, the proof of the literary superiority of Christianity through the Christian epic of *Les Martyrs*. The
third part would be his voyage to the Orient, the theater and the setting
of that epic.

THE BELIEVER

The *Essai sur les révolutions* was filled with the philosophy of the
eighteenth century, which the emigration had carried in its luggage. Above
all, for a born writer, pledged to the calling of literature, that philosophy
remained the mother house of literature. For Chateaubriand it had meant
emancipation; besides, this Breton had the vocation of belief in his blood,
and in him it was as imperious as it was theatrical. In July 1798 he learned
through his sister, Mme. de Farcy, that their mother had died; not much
later, the sister herself died. They had died, he said, from the sufferings
that they had endured in the prisons of the Revolution and from grief for
the errors of the French people. That it was the supreme summons of
these two women that finally converted him there can be no doubt. His
famous remark is typical: "By no means, I grant, did I give way to great
supernatural illuminations; my conviction comes from my heart; I wept
and I believed." There indeed is Chateaubriand's real religion. He was no
theologian (what there is of theology in *Le Génie* is veneer, and borrowed
at that). He had no private little religion of his own. No one has indulged
less in dogma than he. If he had been asked what he believed, he would
perhaps have said, like Brunetière, "Go ask Rome." And, if he had been
asked what he was, he would have replied, "A simple believer."
    The whole of Chateaubriand's religion is in fact embraced in one word:
belief. Belief in the women of his family made him a Christian, as belief
in the men of his race made him an exile and a royalist. What is *Le Génie
du christianisme?* A system of loyalties, and loyalty is the knightly synonym of tradition.

Chateaubriand's Religion

It is not a very intimate religion, and there is no difficulty in understanding that the theosophical Louis-Claude Saint-Martin found at least
as much ground as the philosopher, Pierre-Louis Ginguené, for criticizing
Le Génie. Without giving the subject too much of his attention, Chateaubriand, in sum, remained a Christian quite easily, in spite of everything.

The clergy, which had not taken *Le Génie* seriously as an *apologia*, did not question the religious sincerity of its author. The priests knew this kind of Christian professionally and by way of the confession box: they had no reason not to admit the good faith and the real faith of such believers, whereas they were easily skeptical of the religious sincerity of Lamartine and Hugo. The Catholicism of belief is integral in the French tradition: it was that of Montaigne. It keeps the greater number of Christians within a minimum of religion; and the reversibility of merit, the intentions of prayer, the delegation of some to the salvation of others are so many indications in Catholic dogma that more or less tend to ratify it. It is true, however, as Saint-Martin observed, that *Le Génie* seems to be much more a *Génie du catholicisme* than a *Génie du christianisme*.

Sainte-Beuve, deliberately emphasizing the description, has called Chateaubriand "an Epicurean who had a Catholic imagination." But this is to confuse him somewhat unjustly with the author of *Volupté* himself. One must look or seek higher.

Virtue Ripened by Time

The Breton gentleman will not be forgotten. Certainly the nobility has contributed much to French literature, but chiefly by way of its memoirs—that is, through family literature, a flowering on the genealogical tree that is sometimes, as in Saint-Simon, miraculous. In Chateaubriand we find one of the rare authors—the only great French author—who have merged the traditional life of the nobility, and even a puritanism of caste, with the career, the profession, the virtues, and the defects of the man of letters.

The free-thinking, pagan Chateaubriand was the Chateaubriand uprooted by exile. For him, his Christianity coincided with his return to his country, to his old order, to his way of life. Before he had a Catholic imagination he had the Catholic tradition. His poetic imagination marked that tradition as rows of poplars mark the course of an underground stream. *Le Génie du christianisme* is the genius of tradition, of all traditions; the sense of a *continuum*, familiarity with continuity. It is not the function of a priest to write such a *Génie*, for the priest would emphasize the actual presence of dogmas, their timeless truth, their character as foundations. What was needed was a nobleman, indoctrinated in the veneration of inherited wealth, of estates enhanced by time. One has only to compare this trait of *Le Génie* with the feeling for religious "antiquity," the "defense of tradition," the "train of religion" in Bossuet. Obviously we encounter in Bossuet values that are analogous to and that harmonize with those of *Le Génie* to explain the Catholic customs of France. But there is still a great difference. For Bossuet the virtue of "antiquity" lies in the guaranty against change that it provides, in the preservation of an intact presence, of something that endures. For Chateaubriand it lies in antiquity's pact with life, retaining, like life, a permanence underlying change, embracing the shadings and the needs of the moment: the majesty of age after the graces of childhood and the vigor of youth, the thing that endures like a family tree.

Lack of Religious Imagination

Imagination arrives only later, and awkwardly. It will be observed that Chateaubriand was never successful with a work of imagination, that there is no creative force in any of his fiction, that he lacks to a remarkable degree that appropriately Catholic imagination so abundant in a Pascal, a Bossuet, a Fénelon,* that enables the letter of Scripture or dogma to create a ceaseless lightning of spiritual symbols on which to feed the life of the soul. *Le Génie du christianisme* lacks this Christian genius. It finds its compensation, indeed, by way of tradition, it reworks what has already been thought, felt, digested by Christian imagination. *Le Génie*, which was a pioneering book in the order of art, is a follower's book in the train of religion, the book of a disciple.

Moreover, its original title, when it was begun in London in 1799, was less poetic but more explicit: *Des Beautés poétiques et morales de la religion chrétienne et de sa supériorité sur tous les autres cultes de la terre.* He had discussed the plan for it with Fontanes, who was also a convert and was in exile at the time, and who, appropriately to the future grand master of the university, had the institutional mind. The work was destined less to display, to expound, Christianity than to serve it by revealing some of its still unsuspected riches—and to serve the author by proving to himself that his conversion could not impair his vocation of letters or the vocation of letters in general; quite the contrary!

What Is Dead and What Survives in
Le Génie du christianisme

Of the twenty-two books of *Le Génie du christianisme*, more than half represents dead tissue. What may be properly called the apologetic, without theology, without philosophy, woven of emotions, impressions,

* François de Salignac de La Mothe-Fénelon was his full name—Translator.

allusions, falls to pieces. The bravura passages on the sacraments, the poetry of the Days of Rogation or the cloisters, after their fleeting brilliance collapse into the bric-à-brac of oratorical commonplaces. *Le Génie* suffers from the same disease as that "génie de l'hellénisme" represented by *Télémaque*. It wears itself out in imitation. What was new in its time has become a platitude; consider for a moment the effort that is required, and that very few make, to cleanse this tarnish of time from Athalie's dream!

Le Génie could hardly rouse us to more than the emotion of history that is evoked by a date if there were not its third part: *Beaux-Arts et littérature*, in which Chateaubriand inaugurated a part—the best part—of modern criticism. To find other pages of such vibrancy, such divination from within, such re-creative sympathy as Chateaubriand devotes to Homer, to Vergil, to Racine, one must plunge back into the past as far as Montaigne or forward into the future to the post-1830 Sainte-Beuve. *Le Génie* initiated a fresh literary feeling. Its banknotes of sumptuous rhetoric are convertible into the gold of a taste that is sure, tested, authentic. And it created in part, it popularized and gave life to, three qualities which were to renew the meaning of works and of men in the nineteenth century, and by which we still live.

First of all, it did for time what Rousseau had done for space. Rousseau had opened the sluices of nature. *Le Génie* opened those of history. With this book time became what the philosophers call an essence. Under the Christian banner, history made its entrance into the new century supercharged with poetry.

Next, following Jean-François La Harpe but better than he, Chateaubriand gave a voice, a style, to a dialogue that was to be one of the great intellectual themes of the nineteenth century: the dialogue of the seventeenth and the eighteenth centuries, with the reasons and the sentiments that made Chateaubriand take the side of the seventeenth, a dialogue of the two centuries no longer in their continuity, as this had shown itself in Voltaire, but in their contrast, in their incompatibilities, in the necessity for choice that they imposed, in their capacity to determine families of minds, currents of ideas, religious, philosophical, political, literary parties. This dialogue was to go far: it still governs us.

Finally, with the most conscious, the most luminous, the most artistic style, Chateaubriand restored its rights to what was seemingly most discordant with, most opposed to, this style: abstruse ideas. Just as Voltaire has been called a "chaos of clear ideas,"—a debatable characterization—Chateaubriand would have to be called a dazzling system of obscure ideas. Against the seventeenth century, in the manner of Leibnitz and Maine de Biran, he declared the rights of obscure perceptions. Poetry, of which these are the source of nutriment, profited thereby, and so did religion—especially religion.

Religion, which was an array of clear ideas to Bossuet and an array of

simple ideas to Fénelon, had encountered and passed through the world
of pure feeling with Rousseau; it had gone from a solid state to a fluid
state. *Le Génie* embellished this fluid state with marvels, incorporated the
dimension of time into it, attuned it to the voices of history.

The most penetrating of analysts, a man of the eighteenth century encountering these obscure ideas eighteen years after *Le Génie*, was to view
them as being of necessity linked to the whole religious and poetic life of
man. "If I were to be accused here," Benjamin Constant wrote about 1820,
"of not giving a sufficiently precise definition of religious feeling, I would
ask how it is possible to define with precision that vague and profound
part of our moral sensations that by its very nature defies every effort of
language. How would you define the impression of a dark night, of an
old forest, of the wind that howls through ruins or over graves, of the
ocean that runs out beyond our vision? How would you define the emotion that is aroused by the songs of Ossian, the church of St. Peter, the
contemplation of death, the harmony of sounds or that of shapes? How
would you define revery, that inner tremor of the soul where all the forces
of the senses and of thought come to meet and, as it were, to lose themselves?" Here we have the Constitutional Charter proclaimed in favor of
obscure ideas by the analyst himself, the liberal heir of the philosophers:
Le Génie had passed that way.

The Epic of the Natural Man
in the Man of Letters

Behind the vague grand design of the American voyage there was a
more definite grand design, which was to derive from it the epic of the
natural man. Chateaubriand had sketched this in America and written it
in London; he did not publish it until 1826; it was *Les Natchez*, still
strange in epic costume, more Telemachean than Odyssean. Extremely
shrewd, well counseled by his friends, he hesitated to enter the field of
the epic unless with a new *Pucelle*, a new *Incas*, and he preferred to try
a new *Paul et Virginie*, presented, moreover, as an episode of the *Génie*
in preparation: this was *Atala ou Les Amours de deux sauvages dans le
désert*, in 1801. Atala and Chactas are just about as "savage" as the characters of *Télémaque* are Greek. *Atala* succeeded with the public and was an
object of mockery for the critics. This controversy over *Atala* in 1801 is
extremely instructive as an indication of the movements of taste, if not of
revolutions. The charm of this Indian romance has vanished for us. But
the flagship opened the course for the majestic vessel of *Le Génie* and
prepared its triumph of 1802.

Le Génie was intended to fecundate the novel and the epic alike. This typical book of the literature of the returned emigrants was pregnant at once with a *Werther* and a *Messiade.*

RENÉ

René is to *Werther* what *Atala* is to *Paul et Virginie.* For, when it came to art forms, no one was less the inventor than Chateaubriand, who rejuvenated anything only through his style, the style of a spirit and the style of a form. *René,* published in the body of *Le Génie* itself in 1802, contributed to its triumph. To portray the donor in the best-lighted corner of the immense altar painting (which was a triumph) in the new Church of the Concordat—what a fine idea! It was a matter of illustrating and keeping alive an illness "almost wholly unknown to the ancients, insufficiently studied by the moderns," a *melancholy,* attached to existence, in a young man filled with powerful imprecise passions, caught in the certainty that life would always disappoint the magnitude of his desires. The intimate, tragic adventure, the incestuous destiny of René and Amélie, invested women's imaginations with an inspired and inspiring image of the author. There was René as there was Jean-Jacques. For a half century *René* emanated an extraordinary poetic fever, which abated little by little after Chateaubriand's death but especially because *René* had been relieved and supplanted by the *Mémoires.*

LES MARTYRS

Chateaubriand's *Werther,* however—and in this he saw a great injustice —had better luck than his *Messiade. Les Martyrs* was not only the point of culmination of the second of his great designs, but the greatest conception of his reign. These great conceptions end badly. The best thing in *Les Martyrs* to Chateaubriand was this conception itself, the studied, ingenious elaboration of his poem, of this proof of *Le Génie,* and that voyage to Greece and Jerusalem that he undertook in order to bring its setting to life. When the book appeared, it was not a success, and it became less and less one.

René, which created the short autobiographical given-name novel in France, was directed, like the novel form itself, toward the future. *Les Martyrs* was directed, like the epic itself, toward the past. It was a return to the seventeenth century, but to a European, French-English seventeenth century (note the consequence of the emigration), in which a Milton would triumph over a Nicolas Boileau-Despréaux. In the seventeenth century there appears to have been a pure classicism, broken and divided in space into three sections, or three languages: with Claude Lorrain in Rome, with Milton in England, with Racine in France. Everything occurred as if the ambition of the author of *Le Génie* and *Les Martyrs* consisted of refashioning this lost unity in a composite prose, steeping the Christian epic of Milton in the poetry of Racine and enveloping both in the golden light of the Roman landscape.

Time, unfortunately, had moved forward, and it was no longer possible to erase the scientific attainments of the eighteenth century. "Go rebuild a firmament," Sainte-Beuve said, "with all the scaffolding of thrones and domination, when you are the contemporary of La Place!" * Chateaubriand had assembled his epic machines at the very moment when real machines were about to transform the world. Thirty years after him, Lamartine introduced an airship into *La Chute d'un ange.* There was the fracture.

It is true that Chateaubriand published his tragedy of *Moïse* one year after Hugo's *Hernani* was produced. His loyalty to the seventeenth century was a loyalty to the elder branch of literature. Nevertheless, when *Les Martyrs* has been subjected to a cleaning process, admirable fragments emerge in fresh colors. Certainly it is an *Aeneid* whose grand design no longer touches us, in which the pious Eudorus goes to rejoin the pious Aeneas in our indifference, and to the epic setting and miracle formulary of which we submit in gloomy torpor. But in many pages we feel that Chateaubriand, like Vergil, is a living genius, superior to his task, a delicate amalgam of antiquarian, artist, and creator. The beginning of *Les Martyrs,* when Eudorus is with Lasthenes, is fresh and simple like the opening of *Mireille;* Eudorus encamped on the Rhine, the famous sunrise over Naples, the battle of the Franks, the episode of Velleda, are far from having used up their poetic quality, and in 1809 that poetry was admirably new. Even that eternal combat of hell against heaven, that Hierocles who reminds us of Joseph Fouché †—all that spoke significantly to the noble audience that had left so many kinsmen under the guillotine, for which Chateaubriand wrote, and which backed *Les Martyrs* against criticism to the best of its ability.

The Political Writings

The third of the grand designs that distracted Chateaubriand from René's sickness was the vocation of politics from 1815 to 1830. Minister, ambassador, publicist, pamphleteer, he was assuredly one of those who had the greatest influence, for good and for evil, on the destinies of the Restoration. On the very subject of his politics, opinions clash. What we shall note is the importance and the interest of his political writings, which

* Pierre-Simon de La Place was a noted mathematician, physicist, and astronomer—Translator.
† A member of the Convention, a repressive Empire minister, who later betrayed Napoleon.—Translator.

are too much ignored. *De Buonaparte et des Bourbons* was the strongest and the most successful pamphlet that had been written since the *Satire Ménippée:* it erupted in 1814 like a thunderclap: but how much the prestige of this "*Napoléon le Grand*" would have gained if it had been written three years earlier in exile like "*Napoléon le Petit!*" *La Monarchie selon la charte* is a strange mixture of ultra-ism and rare and far-sighted intelligence. And the fact that Chateaubriand made himself impossible as a minister to Louis XVIII, that in his struggle with the ultra-royalist Joseph de Villèle it is difficult to take sides with the proud writer, in no way detracts from the power of his style, the magic of his images, the blended play of irony and eloquence that can be admired in his newspaper articles. His political ambition was perhaps the strongest ambition in his life. His disappointments fed his zest.

The Personal Writings

It might be said that in Chateaubriand the writer there were two natures, which, furthermore, accommodated very well to each other: a Chateaubriand who was a man of letters and a Chateaubriand who was a descendant of Montaigne, a Joseph Joubert in three dimensions, who wrote for himself and of himself. Not only did they accommodate to each other; they constantly blended, since Eudorus is often Chateaubriand and the Chateaubriand of the *Mémoires* is a stylized Chateaubriand. Nevertheless we shall devote ourselves here to Chateaubriand's work to the degree to which it is oriented in the second direction.

In his personal writings one can identify a group of essays and a group of memoirs.

ESSAYS

By essays we mean those books of Chateaubriand that were made from his notes on his reading, from the author's dialogues with himself and with books: the *Essai sur les révolutions*, the essays on the *Histoire de France* or on *Littérature anglaise*. They are often worth as much or as little as the derivative works the reading of which inspired them in the author. Though they are sometimes mere business chores, it almost never happens that one reads three pages in them without finding an epitome, a maxim, or an image of luminous genius.

The most curious is still the "pourâna" of Chateaubriand's youth, written in London during the hectic years of the emigration, which is called *Essai sur les révolutions anciennes et modernes, considérées dans leurs rapports avec la Révolution française.* It might also be called a "Génie des Révolutions," precursor of the other *Génie*. It explains the revolutionary condition as a historical, chronic condition, whose manifestations are not new, and this would afford the subject for what we should call today the study of comparative revolutions. The Abbé René Aubert de Vertot had already specialized in the eighteenth century (apparently, for the titles have little resemblance to the works) in this field with his three histories of the *Révolutions de la République romaine*, the *Révolutions de Suède*, the *Révolutions du Portugal*. The young Chateaubriand took advantage of these, achieved an enormous amount of reading in a few months, and spread out all of it pell-mell, transfiguring it in a simmer of invention, fantasy, and genius, composed at the same time of extracts from his reading and reflections of his own: hence the incoherence of a book that had not yet taken the public into consideration, hence too the interest that it offered when in 1826 he republished it in his collected works with notes in which he interrupts himself, contradicts himself, makes fun of himself, or corroborates himself. All that is already in the spirit of the *Mémoires d'outre-tombe:* an intimate journal of thoughts, but also the intimate journal of a stylist and a public man who is always ill at ease when he is alone with himself, and who requires at least that deputy of the public, the mirror.

LES MÉMOIRES

In 1811 Chateaubriand began his *Mémoires*. With intervals, he worked on them, recast them, tested them, during more than thirty years. He had admired the idea of Cheops spending his life in the erection of his own pyramid. Similarly he wanted a monumental tomb for himself. The Muse of his destiny guided him naturally and nobly toward that stylization whose Pharaoh-like character he enhanced by making it posthumous.

The *Mémoires d'outre-tombe* should not be separated from a great mass of autobiographical material, of which some was published by Chateaubriand during his life. First of all, the travel books, which themselves have a greater place in Chateaubriand's work than would seem to be indicated by the volumes that are expressly consecrated to them. He shifted a large part of the writings on the voyage to America in order to place fragments in the *Essai sur les révolutions, Les Natchez, Atala, René, Le Génie. L'Itinéraire* retains only those travel pages that were not used in *Les Martyrs*. He cut out the most beautiful part of his journey to Italy in order to make it into the *Lettre à Fontanes* on the Roman Campagna. Other fragments were inserted in the *Mémoires*. Conversely, the *Voyage d'Italie* contains letters to Joubert that he borrowed back. It must not be forgotten that Chateaubriand's processes of composition were those of a mosaic maker and an arranger. *L'Itinéraire* in the form in which it was published is a pleasant book, where there are some fifty admirable pages that could serve to exemplify modern descriptions of historic landscape, as well as, especially in the case of the Holy Land, much padding and fabrication. Chateaubriand was bored by this journey, which was a literary chore on behalf of his epic and his fame, and which he was eager to finish with the meeting that the romantic Mme. de Mouchy had promised him in Granada. He was going, he said, "in quest of glory in order to be loved." To use the expression that he applied to someone else, at the Holy Sepulcher he remounted himself for literature and provisioned himself for love. It was clever, but in addition he had himself armed as a knight. Was there any occasion for this? Similarly, his description of the plain of Sparta is one of the most beautiful in *L'Itinéraire*. But he felt obliged to cry aloud: "Leonidas!" and he marveled that no one responded. "It may be sublime," Jules Lemaître said, "but what if it were not sublime?" The same question mark might be inserted at several other stages of this stylized journey.

The *Mémoires d'outre-tombe* may similarly be paired with the very interesting political memoirs that he extracted from it under a title that should not turn away readers: *Congrès de Vérone*. The greater part of the *Mémoires d'outre-tombe*, however, is political. It is not what most attracts us. Protracted reading of the huge monument is arduous, and the political justifications of a man who was as often wrong as the others, and more often, the spiteful portraits of his antagonists, the long accounts of plots to which historians alone know the clues, cause the final volumes, in a private library, to be less often disturbed than the earlier ones.

Stylizations

But many pages, and all the recollections of youth and exile, contain an inexhaustible charm. Chateaubriand made no mistake. When the generation that had been influenced by *René* disappeared, the *Mémoires* gave posterity a new René, the real René. For with the *Mémoires* Chateaubriand had introduced a new reality into literature, and it had its consequences: the stylized man. Stylized first of all by style itself. Buffon's aphorism was to be reversed by this: the man is the style. In this there is a mechanism—an autonomous dynamism, if you will—of style. Chateaubriand never really thought except with a pen in his hand, carried on by the motion of his tractable phrase, as Marshal Joachim Murat was never himself except on horseback. But on the other hand his life was stylized by the same dash, the same nature, as his phrases and his books. Molé was astonished that public opinion conspired with so much pleasure and loyalty in keeping up his mask, in accepting him in the flattering self-portrait that he created for himself, and, even when, as Paul-Louis Courier said, he held the mask in his hand, in bidding him: "Monsieur de Chateaubriand, cover yourself!"

Chateaubriand's style is connected with the roots of good French prose. It is the style of Jean-Baptiste Massillon, secularized and naturalized by Rousseau, then imaged and colored by Bernardin de Saint-Pierre, to which, bringing it to perfection, Chateaubriand added the created expression, the final curve, and the detached image.

He stylized his life on the model of that image and that same movement. He contemplated his life (rather than lived it, for in the daily business of life he was simple, charming, and never pontifical), he contemplated it and wrote it with the primary purpose of making it expressive and significant, of having it mark a great luminous arc, of silhouetting its attitudes against an eternal horizon. Thinking of the careers of Alexander and Napoleon, he wrote: "The destiny of a great man is a Muse." The *Mémoires d'outre-tombe* represents the most potent and in sum the most successful effort that a familiar of the Muses has ever made to incorporate one of them into his destiny. The poet here has attained to her and he has triumphed, far more than the lover ever possessed his sylph.

We strive today, as his contemporaries did, to keep that august smoke rising above an ancient altar in the Chateaubriand landscape. That desire for a scene, that tension of a within toward a without have succeeded. They have succeeded because the within is genuine, and, with a certain key, we can feel its life. And, if they have succeeded with us, they succeeded even more with his heirs.

Radiations

Chateaubriand created a style of the romantic genius as Louis XIV created a style of royalty. And the two styles resemble each other. With Voltaire's Ferney, the monarchy of a man of letters had clothed the body of a house in the Versailles manner. All that remained was to give it the outlook, the habits, and the soul of a king. With Voltaire, Chateaubriand, Lamartine, and Hugo—or, more accurately, from the arrival of Voltaire at Ferney until the funeral of Victor Hugo—the heart of French literature contained a problem, a setting, a destiny of literary monarchy.

If Voltaire had given it, like Henri IV, its lust for battle, its fighting blood, its *pathos*, Chateaubriand created for it, like Louis XIV, its stage, its style, its *ethos*.

And it was not for nothing that this literary royalist was the contemporary of Napoleon. He played an imperial part. His voyage to America, if not his journey to the Orient, had been enough to annex a new world to letters. With *Le Génie du christianisme* he signed the Concordat between the two antiquities. One may smile at the Napoleon-Chateaubriand parrallelism sustained without a quiver through the whole length of the *Mémoires*. The fact remains that one of the glories of romanticism is just that reference to the destiny of Napoleon that is to be found in a Lamartine, a Balzac, a Hugo, that ambition of the poet to find his own Saint Helena, whether at the Grand Bey or on Guernsey, that inscription under Balzac's Napoleon: "What he attempted by the sword I will accomplish by the pen," and romantic letters, as a workroom of destinies, competing with the registry in Ajaccio.

Chateaubriand reproached Rousseau for having dishonored Mme. de Warens as a reward for her hospitality. What a fine witticism! One of the charms of the *Confessions* for us is that Rousseau's loves are not missing from it. Chateaubriand's, on the contrary, are absent from the *Mémoires d'outre-tombe*. The pages on Mme. de Beaumont are very beautiful, but they would not have been very much different if Pauline and René had not loved each other. Three-quarters of the *Mémoires*, of Chateaubriand's political recollections, are more or less recollections of others, even sometimes, when he cloaks himself in a disguise, recollections of another. The recollections of his emotions would be lost to us without the pages, published much later, on the woman of Provence, without the allusions of the remarkable book that he wrote at the age of sixty-five on the *Vie de rancé*.

It is from asides, however, rather than from his work itself (virtually all his love letters are missing from his magnificent *Correspondance*), that we obtain the picture of the Chateaubriand who loved, garbed in the official costume of the eternally disappointed, the eternally bored.

Let us not say, with Jules Lemaître, that this constantly proclaimed boredom is only affectation. The tone does not deceive, and the measure of the happiness of a great man is not to be found in the fact that his destiny would have more than satisfied a mediocrity. Congenital boredom is a proclivity, a fatal attribute, an absolute beginning in the nature of a man. Chateaubriand carried it with him, and his remark, "Life was inflicted on me," really issued from the depths of the man. In 1797, before his conversion, he wrote: "Let us die absolutely wholly, lest we suffer elsewhere. This life should cure the mania for living."

On the other hand, Sainte-Beuve, particularly by way of the confidences of Hortense Allart, a young friend of Chateaubriand when he was in his sixties, presents him as the great lecher: "He was the *man of desire*, in the Epicurean sense, desire prolonged and always renewed for an earthly Eve." So be it. But "man of desire" does not mean what would be more "Epicurean": man of satisfaction. Even less, however, a man of scruples. When Sainte-Beuve, vulgarly, calls Chateaubriand a man favored by luck, Sainte-Beuve is looking at him through his own wishes. Desire, in Chateaubriand's character, like style, like boredom, should be taken as an essence proof against every possible satisfaction. The *Sylphide* is not only the decent periphrasis of his adolescence but the ideal woman, the projection of his desire, whom he sought through all the real women.

It was through this desire that his spirit rose toward life, and ceaselessly that drive fell back on the soil that was his country: the thick grass that covers the dead. The vocation of his heart was contested by that of his genius, and the vocation of his genius was to terminate a past, to conduct an obsequy, to live in a castle of ideas, of feelings, of forms of which he was the ultimate inheritor. The leitmotiv of "I am the last to . . ." or "I shall be the last to . . ." runs through the whole course of his work. *Le Dernier Abencérage*, a tale built on his romance in Granada with Mme. de Mouchy, gives us indeed one of his pseudonyms, and Lucile and René meet again in Bianca and Carlos: "Don Carlos, I feel that we are the last of our race, we are too much outside the common run for our blood to bear fruit after us: the Cid was our ancestor, he will be our posterity." It was natural for the viscount and his noble friend to love each other beneath a family tree. This love of Abencérage will serve as a luminous myth for the nostalgic genius of Chateaubriand, for his vocation for history, for his invocation of the ancient powers of time, for his romanticism of death.

THE PROTESTANT
SCHOOL

The Literary Return of the Protestants

The official persecution of the reformed religion having persisted, on the whole, until the end of the reign of Louis XVI, the first generation of Protestants that could freely breathe the air of France was that of François Guizot, who was two years old in 1789. Again at the age of six he had occasion to wish for the soldiers of the king whose bullets had lodged in his grandmother's skirts during the gatherings in the Wilderness, for the Revolution guillotined his father and confiscated his property, and his mother had to flee with him to Geneva, where he was educated. Guizot, then, will hardly constitute an exception if we say that, aside from Rousseau, the return of Protestantism to French intellectual life, the literary revocation of the revocation of the Edict of Nantes, began in French Switzerland, in Geneva and Vaud—the work of that nucleus of Protestant culture that had maintained itself all along the Jura between Gallican France and ultramontane Savoy.

Lyon, French Switzerland, and Savoy formed a great literary region in another sense: a provincial and foreign culture partly removed from the influence of Paris—patrician, but not parliamentary—and, in spite of Ferney, the conservator of that spirit and those religious forms that Paris, the Académie Française, the culture of the Encyclopedists, and the language of analysis had momentarily stricken from the rolls at the end of the eighteenth century.

The Neckers

JACQUES NECKER

At that time in French Switzerland a great family gained renown: the Neckers. Jacques Necker was the son of a Prussian who had resettled in

Geneva. Necker moved to Paris in his youth; as a banker, an ambasador, comptroller general, the husband of the woman who maintained the chief *salon* under the monarchy, he remained in France until he was in his sixties. And yet he might be called the very earliest of the strictly Genevan writers, with the virtues and the vices that marked all the branches of that literary family: *Considérations* in the style of his daughter, Mme. de Staël (essay on *L'Importance des opinions religieuses*); the sermons of a pastor who had learned the refinements of style in Thomas Aquinas (*Cours de morale religieuse*); somewhat labored humor, but pleasant and elevated like that of Rodolphe Töpffer and Petit-Senn (*Le Bonheur des sots*). He was, in short, the man of whom it was said by the Swiss, Meister, that, "during his early years in Paris, it happened a hundred times that he would sit more than a quarter of an hour in his carriage trying to decide what house he should have himself driven to first," and who wrote hundreds of intimate pages wholly in the spirit of Henri-Frédéric Amiel. We shall not speak of his writings on finance, administration, and politics: they are the work of a patrician who wanted to run the affairs of France as he had run the business of his bank and as he would have run the affairs of his little republic if he had stayed there. The Neckers and their descendants never learned really to know the French.

He was the second citizen of Geneva to exert a tremendous influence on France. Some historians have called his term in office the major cause of the fall of the monarchy. Let us leave that aside. To us it is only the fifteen volumes of his *Oeuvres* that are important—those and, above all, his place as the founder and leader of a great literary family which, through the de Broglies and the d'Haussonvilles, lasted into the twentieth century.

SUZANNE NECKER

If we have fifteen volumes of diverse works by Necker, we have also six volumes of *Mélanges* by his wife, born Suzanne Curchod. The daughter of a pastor, with no dowry beyond the freshness of her beauty and her conversation, bearing with sober grace what was called a high mind, queen of the Vaud countryside, she had married the Genevan banker as a shepherdess marries a king. The rural bridal songs which told every girl that her May-queen time would end with the wedding and that the work of running a farm would begin at four o'clock the next morning were not as true for any peasant girl as they were for Mme. Necker, when suddenly, through the political fortunes of her husband, the pastor's daughter from Crassier had to conduct a *salon* of Encyclopedists, of philosophers, of cynics. She managed it by an effort of will that aged her rapidly. The serious character of her works, all moral and moralizing, was at once weighed down and made more touching thereby. Like the shepherd in the fable, the shepherdess of Vaud had saved the wreath of pastoral flowers in her cupboard. And, moreover, the best of her work is her pages on life, on marriage, and on the religious feeling inspired in her, after the comptroller general's retirement to Coppet, by the regained peace of her native place; she wrote of it in words that embodied all the Calvinism of the region: "It seems that here the Supreme Being has given more concern to his creature, whom he compels constantly to elevate his thoughts to him."

ALBERTINE NECKER DE SAUSSURE

The genius of their daughter, Germaine, burst all the retaining bonds; the family estate became the *salon* of Europe. But the literary vigor of that lively, potent blood did not stop with Mme. de Staël. Genevans said that the most Genevan book in their literature was the *Education progressive* of her cousin and biographer, Albertine Necker de Saussure. Its ponderous style did not afford it any great circulation beyond Bellegarde. But there was no other book of that family to which Joubert's remark could be more appropriate: "M. Necker's style is a language that is not to be spoken but that demands close application for its understanding if one does not wish to be deprived of the knowledge of a host of useful, important, great new thoughts." The *Education progressive* completely lived up to its subtitle, *Etude du cours de la vie*. A thoroughly Genevan upbringing, that of the wealthy families, the elect, elevated in sentiment, bound to the history, the countryside, the soul of that nation that a city is, is relived here, beneath the lushness of a dense style, with the freshness of a Töpffer novel (and besides, when the question of the most Genevan book is raised, many reply, though out of the same source as the others, by naming *Le Presbytère*). For all its demonstrated reasonableness, the psychology of the *Education progressive* seems no less new, alert, and subtle, strong in the experience of a preaching and pedagogical society— that of the rue des Granges. The Genevan matron did not move her reader of either sex as did the Genevan gentleman, but she educated him better.

ALBERTINE DE BROGLIE

Mme. Necker de Saussure was in every way a Necker; she had none of the adventurous spirit of the Saussures. In similar fashion a great French literary and political family, the Broglies, was to remain as much Necker as Staël and Broglie, if not indeed more so. In 1816 that liberal patrician duke, Victor de Broglie, married into the mother house of French-Swiss liberalism, his bride being Necker's granddaughter, Albertine de Staël. The posthumous works of the duchess might very well be added as a seventh volume to her grandmother's *Mélanges*. Here, in a woman of society, in the third generation of glittering *salons*, were the same Protestant spirituality, the same great marital destiny, the same ardent, generous nature, the same radiant virtue. One would gladly add the word "mind," which was also a Necker mind, if Mme. de Broglie's social diary, largely unpublished, were known to us otherwise than through the somewhat arranged fragments that Duke Victor excerpted from it for his *Mémoires*.

The children of Victor and Albertine de Broglie, having been born or having become Catholics, not without some religious drama, Protestanism apparently disappeared among Mme. de Staël's descendants. But, like the Jansenist Pierre-Paul Royer-Collard and the Protestant Guizot, the Catholic Broglie-Staëls were always the incarnation of doctrinaire liberalism. On 14 July 1789 the "conquerors of the Bastille" carried the busts of Necker and the Duc d'Orléans. In July 1830, with the accession of the Orléans monarchy, when the doctrine became a spiritual political power, the establishment of the new order took on the appearance of a sort of return of Necker, and the Guizot experiment, which collapsed in 1848, was in a way a continuation of the Necker era. The history of literature consists not only of the history of forms but also of the history of formulated, active ideas: therefore Mme. de Staël must be considered, on the one hand, in that family of flesh and spirit that was her environment, that set her off, that preceded her and enlarged her—and, on the other, in the group of her friends in Coppet. She exists less as a producer of books than as the guiding heart and the moderator of a vast dialogue.

❧ ✤✤✤✤ VII ✤✤✤✤ ☙

MME. DE STAËL

The Salon School

Mme. de Staël's mother, Suzanne Curchod, was considered the most accomplished girl in the whole Vaud region, and as a reward, like the shepherdess in the stories, she became the dowerless bride of the opulent Genevan banker who made her Mme. Necker. Through will power, thought, study and common sense, she succeeded, or almost, in becoming a Parisian and in maintaining in the banker's, the comptroller general's, residence a famous *salon*, the most serious and the most popular with men of letters. A teacher, she made the Neckers a family of pedagogues. Contrary to French custom, little Germaine was allowed to sit on a stool in the comptroller general's *salon*, and she profited by it. From the age of ten she lived in the ambience of great men and great ideas. Having made her entrance there as a mascot, for a quarter of a century she was the commanding general or the Napoleon of the world of *salons*. The ladies of the eighteenth century had ruled their *salons* by their wit. Mme. de Staël was the first to rule hers by genius, but a genius that she drew from it as the sky draws from the earth the waters that are rained down again.

All Mme. de Staël's books were talked before they were written. No one found more inspiration in others than did she, and yet the problem of her "sources" would never be posed, for they were superseded by innumerable streams, by a watercourse at ground level, by the reflections of men and the passage of their words.

The Revolution was directed against tyranny, the upper classes, the life of "society." Yet, of the three great figures of the Revolution, the first, Napoleon, imposed on France a tyranny of which her kings had never given even the faintest indication; the second, Chateaubriand, was the outstanding example of an aristocratic man of letters in France; the third, Mme. de Staël, was the first model of the career of a great writer defined by the amenities of a *salon*.

Her Criticism

Her books of criticism could be more aptly called manifestos. Hers was a passionate intelligence and, to flower, her ideas required the heat of enthusiasm. Since in addition she spoke and made others speak of the events and the ideas of the moment, since she lived in the present, since Jacques Necker's daughter aspired to be the comptroller general of ideas in France as long as she lived there, and since all this in her was governed by genius, she was able to write two manifestos of great compass, *Littérature* and *L'Allemagne*. The full title of the first, *De la Littérature considérée dans ses rapports avec les institutions sociales*, in itself marks a date. Such a title, the promises of which were virtually all kept, carried the idea and the method of Montesquieu into literature, prepared the way for an *Esprit des lois* of literature. Although its style is labored, congested, and heavy, exactly the opposite of Montesquieu's, the modern reader makes his way to the end of Mme. de Staël's book with considerably less effort than to the end of the *Esprit des lois*. He is kept interested by the movement of a conversation. The first part, which deals with the past, is often venturesome or challengeable, even absurd, Mme. de Staël having read little and knowing books principally through the people who talked about them. But the second part introduces us into the heart of the literary consciousness of that generation of 1789, into the problems that were posed to them.

Literature, according to this book, is a function of society: whence the differences in literature on the basis of climates—the literature of the north, the literature of the south—and on the basis of political systems—the literature of authoritative systems, the literature of libertarian systems. Mme. de Staël proclaims progress—the superiority of the moderns—the advent and the future growth of a great new literature. It is not difficult, in this work so rich in ideas, to recognize the successive strata of these ideas, those that she acquired from the philosophers when at the age of ten she sat on her stool, those of her father too, above all those of her friends in the Directory and the Consulate, and, in sum, the union of Mme. Necker's *salon* with her daughter's in the rue du Bac, the whole made living by a burning, illuminating intelligence.

Politics

The great interest of her *Littérature*, even today, consists less in its wealth of vistas, ancient or new, than in this quality of a manifesto, which is bound up with Mme. de Staël's drive to preach (this is quite Genevan), and in the conjunction of her ideas with the politics of the republic.

Beginning in the Year VIII (1799)—that is to say, the same year in which the book appeared—France was drawn into the orbit of Bonaparte's genius, and the Republic was finished. Neither the long-prevailing belief according to which a beneficent *coup d'état* in the month of Brumaire brought down a government that was nothing but corruption and ruin, nor the idea of Albert Sorel that Napoleon was driven to his policy of imperial and imperialistic conquests by the necessity of preserving the conquests of the Republic, seems an inevitable conclusion to us today. A durable peace with the Continental powers, given pledges of compensation, on the principles of Basle, was not only possible but was anticipated in Europe. The inevitable intervention of the army, whether directed by Bernadotte, Moreau, or Bonaparte, was prepared for and looked forward to only as intervention in defense of the Republic. The man most highly regarded was Washington. To the same degree as the return of the Bourbons, the re-establishment of the Catholic church and a massive homecoming of the emigrants were rejected—that is, the two unforeseen factors, growing out of the personality of Bonaparte, which had so great a consequence for literature and which brought on romanticism. A society had been refashioned in Paris, and in its own *salons* the new republican order was discussed and even planned. Or, rather, there were two societies: that of Auteuil, where the ideologists, the members of the Institute, the direct heirs of the eighteenth century and the Convention gathered round Antoine-Nicolas de Condorcet's beautiful widow, and that of the Saint-Germain quarter, of which the major *salon* was Mme. de Staël's in the rue du Bac. Her affair with Benjamin Constant had begun in 1794. Her political-manifesto literature dated from 1796 with her book, *De l'Influence des passions sur le bonheur des individus et des nations.* Her reputation and her entourage served as the intellectual laboratory of a system in the process of formation, which would be liberal, egalitarian, deist, pacifist, already "internationalist," intellectual, influenced and indeed represented by writers, an eighteenth-century philosopher come back from Geneva, a whole kingdom of luminaries, for whom, naturally, she would be the Egeria. The Auteuil group, for its part, looked mistrustfully on deism and foreign influences. But really this dualism of Paris and Geneva was a legacy of the eighteenth century, of the opposition between Voltaire and Rousseau. Such as it was, the literate society of the decline of the Directory and the rise of the Consulate re-established a regime of the mind with republican habits and on this double note. It was an attempt at an alliance or a fusion between the French Republic and the republic of letters under the aegis of the re-emerging *salons* and of the Institute, which supplanted the Academies. When *Littérature* appeared, in the Year VIII, this hope of a consistent evolution of the Republic in the fresh republican tradition had just vanished. Three months earlier, Bonaparte had turned the explosions of his anger against the *salon* of the rue du Bac, the occasion being a speech by Benjamin Constant, that not without reason, Napoleon thought had been inspired by Mme. de Staël. And the baroness's manifesto was launched in a world, a political atmosphere, a society, in which for fifteen years to listen to it would be forbidden.

From then on the air of the rue du Bac became unbearable to that ardent, masterful heart. A part of *Littérature* had already been written at Coppet. Beginning in 1803 the author was forbidden to approach within sixty miles of Paris. For ten years, basing herself on Coppet as her home port, creating the *salon* of Europe there and forever mourning, beside the lonely lake, the gutter of the rue du Bac, she led a feverish, restless, disappointed life of travel. Out of this, in 1810, the second and the more resounding of her manifestos, *De l'Allemagne*, exploded—or would have exploded if the entire edition had not been destroyed by Napoleon and if Mme. de Staël, in order to avoid prison, had not had to pledge herself not to publish it on the Continent. The manifesto did not appear until 1813, when it was published in London; it circulated everywhere and until the fall of Napoleon, it was the most talked-of book in Europe.

The Cosmopolitan

De l'Allemagne is the record of her journey to Germany in 1804, of her sojourn in Weimar, beyond which she did not go and where Germany came to her; it is also the record of her *salon* at Coppet, where August Wilhelm von Schlegel had accompanied her on her return from Germany and where he was the past master of Germanics. The greatest injustice that could be committed toward *L'Allemagne* would be to judge it on itself, to demand of it inherent and lasting truths and beauties. It must be judged (and it was also from this point of view that Napoleon judged it) as a manifesto, for its capacity to excite, and as we judge Voltaire's *Lettres anglaises*. Friedrich Schiller said that he found more flashes than light in it, and we may add that the fire contained even more motive power than flashes. What was that motive power?

It is not to be found in the first part, *Le l'Allemagne et des moeurs des allemands*. The Germans have never liked Mme. de Staël's convention of the German spirit or the platitudes that it has engendered. But the three other parts—*De la Littérature et des arts, La Philosophie et la morale, La Religion et l'enthousiasme*—though they abound in errors and trivialities, created or brought to light for the French a land of romanticism, or a climate of romanticism. That literary and philosophical Germany was to remain the Germany of literary and philosophical romanticism.

Of literary romanticism, Mme. de Staël's judgments came not so much from her own reading as from the opinions she heard expressed in Weimar circles. Now, at that time and in that place the great literary subject was the theater. There was not only a Hamburg dramaturgy but also a Weimar dramaturgy. And the great dramatist of Germany was Schiller. And the most popular plays were those of Zacharias Werner. Hence their place in *L'Allemagne*. Goethe's dramatic work was less highly regarded. On *Faust*, which appeared in 1808, Mme. de Staël gives us the general opinion that had been reached at Coppet, since she read German badly. Goethe, a part of whose work still lay ahead of him, had not yet gained the stature that he was to have for posterity. Schiller, with the help of theatrical acclaim, had achieved all of his, and more than he deserved. Klopstock and Christopher Martin Wieland were considered Germany's great poets. Everything that Mme. de Staël said about them was good current information that did not go beyond its own time, that would go on being accepted until 1830 and later, and that played its part in the passionate discussions comparing the French theater with those of Shakespeare and Schiller. This was not a waste of motive power.

The importance that France and Weimar gave to the question of the theater had a natural counterpart in the importance that Mme. de Staël attached to everything that concerned social life. The parallel between social life in Paris and in Germany, between German individualism and the urbanism or urbanity of French civilization, became for Mme. de Staël a commonplace that she carried over, furthermore, into *Corinne ou l'Italie*, which dealt with the socialized Frenchman and the spontaneous Italian. Stendhal, who was to have occasion to corroborate these observations, was to make great use of them. *L'Allemagne* and *Corinne* (to the extent that *Corinne* is *l'Italie*) would become the basic works of the French cosomopolitanism that was to flourish with the traveler-writers of the Restoration.

The third part, on *La Philosophie et la morale*, is necessarily superficial, and Charles Villiers presented Kant to the French reader better than did the mistress of Coppet. The Germans have made considerable mock of her conversation with Johann Gottlieb Fichte, whom she asked to explain his philosophy to her in fifteen minutes. Mme. de Staël did not understand German well, Fichte's system was developed in the very entrails of the German language, and he had to explain it in French, which he spoke badly. That did not prevent her from exclaiming after ten minutes: "I understand!" This famous anecdote is an invention, but it is not necessarily so risible. After all, the essential conclusions of an original system should become intelligible to a cultivated mind in a period of one to three quarters of an hour. Fichte could have learned that from Mme. de Staël as Mme. de Staël could have learned the dialectical philosophy of consciousness from Fichte. This is the value of the establishment of a European clearinghouse of the intellect. This third section of the work did indeed fulfill the function of such an exchange (thanks in particular to Schlegel).

Without much deceiving herself or being deceived on their metaphysics, Mme. de Staël, like a true Genevan, understood the German philosophers and caused them to be understood from the point of view of their contributions to moral doctrine and to religious life or the substitutes for religious life. This third section leads naturally into the fourth, *La Religion et l'enthousiasme*, the last chapter of which is without doubt the most characteristic, and perhaps marks the summit, of all Mme. de Staël's work.

Once it had been used, *De l'Allemagne* was less and less read. It was the bridge of boats across the Rhine that was dismantled when the army had crossed. Until 1806 Napoleon undoubtedly would have allowed it to be published. In 1810 he could no longer afford to. Not so much because the emperor is not named in it or because it contains no lack of disobliging allusions, but because *L'Allemagne* established Europe as a binomial, designating Germany at the head of one of the two terms of the binomial, of the dualism of the classical and the romantic, the social and the individual. "We have not been so far debased," the Minister of Police wrote, "as to seek our models in the peoples whom you admire. Your latest work is not French." That, furthermore, is why the Empire had no literature and why Napoleon did wish literature to have an empire.

The Novelist

Mme. de Staël maintained her empire over minds, which was then quite real, more through her novels than through her books on ideas. *Delphine* and *Corinne* enjoyed tremendous success and popularity. Today it requires a serious effort, and above all a professional obligation, in order to read them through to the end.

Delphine, which appeared in 1802, belongs to the long succession of great novels told in letters, derived from *Clarissa Harlowe*, with the extenuating circumstance that it is the last of them. Like all Mme. de Staël's books, it is given life by a central problem that is an integral part of the author's life, with its inner tragedies: the ordeals and the struggles that public opinion imposes on a woman who loves outside the norm. It is the theme that, thirty years later, George Sand would draw from the same source, from the same interests of her sex. In this respect *Delphine* initiated a whole department of feminine literature. The origin of public opinion lies in society (in the caste sense), and *Delphine* is the first society novel, written by a woman who lived at the center of society. When one has the key to the novel, *Delphine* can still imbue one's reading of it with something of the interest that the public of 1802 took in it. In contrast, though *Delphine* takes place from 1790 to 1792, in the midst of events that were already pitting one France against another, there is only a meaningless portrayal of political feelings and events. The length of the often languishing letters, the confusion of characters and adventures, the heavy and abstract style are all discouraging. It is remarkable, however, that Mme. de Staël's own letters, of which her cousin, Mme. Necker de Saussure, said that for fire and spirit they did not match her talk, are diametrically opposite in form to the artificial letters of *Delphine;* they leap out in spontaneity, disorder, vehemence, immediate sincerity, turmoil, and inaccuracy. The epistolary form, which was not natural to the author, certainly spoiled *Delphine.*

Equally deserving of being read, *Corinne* is of better workmanship. It was long considered Mme. de Staël's great book, and, from a certain decorative point of view, this opinion can be supported. The paths of her genius cross in it, and they are the same that crossed in Geneva. Just as, in *Delphine*, she had written the first novel that could be called "un Coeur de femme," so in *Corinne* she wrote the first "cosmopolis," the first novel of that cosmopolitan life that she lived and that made Geneva a way station for Britons and Frenchmen on the road to Italy. Geneva itself is absent from it, but the spirit of Geneva is in it.

Two subjects, but perfectly fused: this novel of cosmopolitan life and the novel of the woman of genius.

Obviously the backdrop is Italy. Mme. de Staël's journey to Italy gave birth to its book in 1807, as her journey to Germany bore its in 1810. Its characters appear in it as representatives of their countries, and this is new. The temporary Italians are well drawn. Lord Nelvil stands for the liberal aristocracy of England with the ideal features that it easily assumed for a Genevan. In Comte d'Erfeuil, the author sought, in a rather heavy but often accurate fashion, to paint the portrait of the frivolous and charming French nobility. The descriptions of Italy and especially those of Northumberland are quite beautifully drawn. And the great theme of Coppet, the literary contrast between north and south, between Catholicism and Protestanism, takes on its full dignity of an eternal dialogue on this classic soil.

As for Corinne herself, she is not only a character, she is also a theme, on which Mme. de Staël constructs variations on her destiny, her loves, her genius. Corinne and Germaine could claim the same device: enthusiasm unprepared. Representing genius by her place in Italian poetry and her coronation at the Capitol, Corinne represents reason in her English birth and ties. When Mme. de Staël excerpts from the papers of Necker in order to write the moral testament of Lord Nelvil's father, she seems to be trying to give her Genevan wisdom British naturalization. And that was not likely to ease matters with Napoleon, who refused to go to Geneva on the pretext that he did not know English.

Corinne ou l'Italie could also be "Corinne ou la Poésie." Unfortunately nothing is more lacking from Mme. de Staël's book than poetry. The granddaughter of Brandenburgers, Corinne travels in Italy in order to be educated, to "profit"; French by culture, she travels there in order to talk in the country and about it. But she does not travel in order to feel: a feeling for nature and a taste for the arts are foreign to her. She would have traded the Bay of Naples, she says, for a quarter of an hour of conversation. But for her the interest of the place is precisely the quarter of an hour of written conversation that it can suggest. Between the sensual sweep of the shore, the very lines of which the prose of *Les Martyrs* embraces, and the Neopolitan poetry of Lamartine, Corinne spreads out only a desert of ideas. Mme. de Staël has defined the genius of a woman as the splendid mourning of happiness. *Corinne,* in a certain way, is the thinking mourning of poetry.

And yet we can restore that poetry to her, or give it to her. This book that seems dead to us today was one of the most glorious of its time. When Lamartine read it in his adolescence, he was overwhelmed by it. Stendhal, with *La Chartreuse de Parme* has made us unfair to this novel of Italy. But that required a generation or two. *Corinne* established the prestige of cosmopolitan life and of the international dialogue of ideas. It added to Europe's civilization. Corinne at the Cape of Miseno, inspired by that invented Plato at the Cape of Sunium of Abbé Jean-Jacques Barthélemy, belongs for us to the ingenuity of an Empire clock. But for thirty years, in Chateaubriand's circle, the friends of Mme. Récamier gathered beneath that portrait by François Gérard; an idealized Germaine, abandoned to enthusiastic prophecy, personified the grip of the mind and of letters on that romantic generation, and one is reminded of those altar paintings, with their two levels, in which the circle of the earth is dominated by the circle of glory. Perhaps all the poetry of *Corinne* has retreated from that name and that presence. But she remains, and she will endure.

The Mother of the Doctrine

Mme. de Staël died in Paris in 1817, having lived barely six decades, and, what is tragic in such an end, before she could enter into a promised land that was no longer distant and that would have been the glorious, overflowing road of her seventh decade and of the triumph of her ideas. Her memoirs, reduced to the *Dix ans d'exil,* which are obviously not the equal either of the *Mémoires d'outre-tombe* or of the *Mémorial* of her two rivals, remained unfinished. She was working then on her *Considérations sur les principaux événements de la Révolution française,* which she was able almost to complete.

It is one of her most important books, the testament of her political life, and again a manifesto: the manifesto of what would be called ten years later the doctrinaire school, of that royalist liberalism, with a Genevan tradition and English sympathies, that would come into power in 1830, that gave Benjamin Constant his splendid funeral in that same year and that would have given an even more splendid one to Mme. de Staël, the mother of the Doctrine and the mother-in-law of the doctrinaire duke.* While Corinne at her cape dominated the circle of Mme. Récamier, Mme. de Staël governed France. One day, when the young Guizot had passed through Coppet and recited a page of Chateaubriand in the drawing room in his beautiful, solemn voice, Mme. de Staël took his arm and said: "Monsieur, you must stay here and act plays with us!" These were her drawing-room plays, such as she enjoyed writing. (Is it known that the last act of *Sapho* is one of the most beautiful things that she wrote?) But M. Guizot, educated in Geneva and even more Genevan than Mme. de Staël, was going to act on the political stage in the face of risks and perils that would seem in 1848 to be the very drama of Mme. de Staël's political ideas. While Chateaubriand, after her death, perpetuated an old age and a life of the eternal exile in his solitude of Grand-Bey, she survived in her descendants, in a family of political and literary notables singularly bound to the history of the nineteenth century, the Broglies.

There is a remarkable disparity between, on the one hand, the paucity of modern readers of Mme. de Staël's books, which have not been kept, like her body at Coppet, in the incorruptible fluid of style, and, on the other hand, the rank, the prestige, the radiance of her name. Great values are still grouped round that name. She was a source, rather than a stage, of the nascent European consciousness. When today, in Geneva itself, such fine words are spoken as "League of Minds" or "League of Ideas," it may be observed that that league has thus far had only one great name, hers; one mother house, Coppet. The hegemonical Europe of Napoleon has crumbled. The grandeur of the duel between Napoleon and Mme. de Staël consists in this: that, in the realm of ideas, his Europe was opposed by a Europe of Mme. de Staël that, on the whole, was a success from 1814 to 1914, and perhaps even from 1914 to 1930. Today life and the greatness of the cause demand that the necessary effort be made to go back to its precedents, its claims, in a work of which one cannot deny that it has become ponderous.

* The Duc de Broglie.—Translator.

VIII

THE COPPET GROUP

Mme. de Staël's books are no longer familiar to anyone. But she retains the rank of a monument. From her pedestal she dominates a circle, a group. She cannot be understood without that society of minds that began in her salon, extended itself in time and space around Coppet, and created one of the world's intellectual climates on Lake Geneva. If the puritanism of Old Geneva had not imposed a long quarantine on Necker's daughter, one could envisage, on the shore of the lake, a somewhat high-flown monument of a forceful, emphatic woman, a turban wound around her head, as in a statue by James Pradier in the Place de la Concorde, under her crown of curls; and, amid the jets of fountains feeding on talk and life, four figures that, for various reasons, represent Mme. de Staël's company (the word could almost be used in the military sense) in letters: Constant, Léonard Sismondi, Charles-Victor Bonstetten, and Prosper de Barante.

Benjamin Constant

One of them, on Germaine's left, has every right to the given name alone. That is Benjamin. Nonetheless, if it were not essential to preserve in literature the character of an order, to respect the places attained, to refuse to abandon literature without ranks to the anarchy of personal tastes, Benjamin Constant might be given a more eminent place than that of his illustrious friend. He is closer to us, he is a much better writer, and, above all, more than any author of his time, perhaps more even than Chateaubriand, he is read: like Marie-Madeleine de La Fayette and Abbé Prévost, he wrote a timeless little book that survives the ages without a wrinkle or a speck of dust. He is the representative or the head of a family of the intellect that will always go back to his *Journal intime*, his *Cahier rouge*, when the Staël family has given up opening the books of its mother. We have exhausted Mme. de Staël, readers, but we have not exhausted Constant.

He knew, and more than anyone else, certainly more than Maurice Barrès, who with good reason ranks him among the "intercessors" of a free man, he taught us to know the interacting fusion, reinforcement, and fecundation of a poetic sensitivity, a critical intelligence, a political culture. He is the father of the analytical novel, created, obviously, without a mother. And he and Mme. de Staël are the father and mother of political liberalism, or rather its two creators, since in this instance the sexual characteristics are not too separate.

Adolphe comes to us today shored up by a posthumous literature of memoirs and correspondence that makes Benjamin even greater than he seemed to his contemporaries. The contrast between him and Chateaubriand is striking, and one cannot conceive a cleaner cleavage between the analysts and the orators. And we are far from Rousseau himself. When the Genevan paraded his sorrows, he did so with a great literary eloquence and a poet's deformations or transformations; the *Confessions* and the *Rêveries* have much more to do with the origins of the *Mémoires d'outre-tombe* than with those of the *Cahier rouge*. Besides, Jean-Jacques wrote for the public, oratorically, like Chateaubriand, while Benjamin wrote only for himself. He was the first to apply that insight without malice, far more merciless to himself than to others; he expressed it with the dry-point needle of a lucid style, the great style of the analyst. Before Amiel, and in a manner much more French than Amiel's the great Vaud writer exposed to the light of the written word the complex of intelligence and impotence that he desperately contemplated within himself.

Inability to organize his emotional life and find his place in the framework of social life did not imply in Benjamin, as it was to do in Amiel, an inability to organize and to create in literature. The mere desire to do so was enough to enable him, in a few days, to write in *Adolphe* the novel that would explain that passive and faltering life: the novel of a failed life, which is so diametrically the opposite of a failed novel that, for a half century, the psychological novel in France consisted in repeating, filling out, varying, modernizing this quiet, modest story that says everything, that awakens infinite echoes.

It would diminish *Adolphe* to reduce it to the anecdote that was its source: Benjamin's love for Anna Lindsay. *Adolphe* is that episode, and the character of Adolphe is Constant, but, in Ellenore, Constant merges almost all the women who were his loves or his wives, and above them all, of course, the most illustrious, in order to incarnate an eternal feminine character. As *Daphnis et Chloé* is the novel of the attraction and the harmony between the sexes, *Adolphe* is the novel of their battle, written by a compatriot of General Henri Jomini.*

* A Swiss who served Napoleon and, after 1812, Alexander I of Russia.—Translator.

And by a contemporary of Napoleon. For *Adolphe* is also the novel of an assent to slavery, and the analysis of that slavery by a man who had a taste for freedom. From childhood on, he had prized freedom above everything. Like Amiel or Charles Secrétan, the philosopher of liberty, he understood his freedom in its depth and in its essence. His passions and especially his impulsive acts are explained by a critical refusal to give himself. It was by rejecting that great golden chain that binds man to beings and things that he came to drag behind him all those shards of broken heavy chains, cut short and ridiculous.

For the same reason he was concerned with politics. His passion for inner freedom and the problems that it created for him imbued him with the passion for political liberty and led him to its problems. This is the Constant who knew his era, whose writings and speeches constituted a strong point of liberalism. They are no longer read, because those political problems, at their height in 1830, have been engulfed, assimilated, made obsolete, and the systems born of universal suffrage have imposed a new political language. And also because in Constant there was more of the explanatory than of the creative intelligence. This same creative current, that of the Chateaubriands and the Tocquevilles, is even more lacking in his great work on *La Religion*, which was to be his life work. Under the Restoration he was the apostle of freedom of the press, and it was for this apostle that Paris held a famous funeral four months after the Revolution of July 1830: but here again it was left to Paul-Louis Courier and Royer-Collard to pronounce the decisive words. Against the oblivion whose tide has closed over that work, the peak of *Adolphe* and his intimate manuscripts remains the more brilliant and indestructible.

It would be impossible to rank Mme. de Staël's three quasi-Genevan friends with Constant. Their names, with Schlegel's, are inseparable from the atmosphere and the activity of Coppet.

Sismondi, Bonstetten, and Barante

First of all there is Sismondi, to whom we are indebted for a library shelf of impartial, lackluster history, but above all for the important *Littérature du midi de l'Europe*, to which we shall return later. Bonstetten, who came from Berne, became bound to Geneva by the attraction of the *salon* of Coppet and the charm of French civilization, and there, through his simplicity and his good nature, he contributed to giving the city of Calvin that function as the *salon* of Europe that it fulfilled during the Restoration. His book on *L'Homme du nord et l'Homme du midi* is an important testimony to the current of Staëlesque ideas, and his archeological journey of *Latium* gave rise to a whole literature, from Jean-Jacques

Ampère to Gaston Boissier and Victor Bérard. But, since he came late to
the writing of French, his style is barbarous and inaccurate. Finally, there
was Prosper de Barante, whose father, that prefect of Mont Blanc who,
charged with keeping watch on Mme. de Staël, had himself dismissed, to
his credit, for professional inadequacy. Prosper, who was later to build a
brilliant career as a graphic historian, published a *Tableau du XVIII*ᵉ
siècle in 1809 under the influence of Coppet. It was intelligent and most
interesting, particularly in comparison and contrast to Marie-Joseph Chénier's *Tableau de la littérature française,* which covered the same period
and appeared a year earlier. Born in 1782, Barante represented the new
generation in opposition to Chénier, the generation that dropped the
ideologists, that accurately and normally assimilated the new values contributed by Chateaubriand and Mme. de Staël. This benjamin (without a
capital letter) of the mother of the Doctrine was to make a pleasing and
comfortable success among the doctrinaires.

IX

THE ROMANTIC

Literatures for Those Who Can Write Them

Mme. de Staël's *De la Littérature* may not be one of the monuments, but it is one of the most important milestones in criticism and the literature of ideas; it might still better have been entitled "Des Littératures," for it launched a problem of literary pluralism in France.

Just as French literature encompasses families of minds, as its styles fall easily into pairs of conplementary geniuses or series of oppositions (Corneille and Racine, Bossuet and Fénelon, Voltaire and Rousseau), so there are families and contrasts of literatures, between which a comparison, a dialogue, takes shape: ancient and modern literatures, northern and southern literatures, classical and romantic literatures.

As early as the Consulate, arguments on the subject had begun; magazines that gave a great deal of space to European intelligence carried *Le Spectateur du nord* and the periodicals of the emigrants to French soil. So there appeared *Le Journal de littérature étrangère, La Bibliothèque germanique, Les Archives littéraires, Le Magasin encyclopédique*, whose titles are programs. In an article in *Les Archives littéraires* for January 1804, *Des communications littéraires et philosophiques entre les nations de l'Europe*, Degérando—accepting both of them—defined the two possible directions of literary taste and judgment: "There are certain absolute beauties the feeling for which should be universal, because they have their origin in a necessary, though secret, relation with the needs of human nature. It is the universal testimony of men that must consecrate them, it is through the comparison of different literatures that one can learn to recognize them. There are also relative beauties, which are no less real for being peculiar to certain local circumstances, for having a special relation to the customs, the institutions, the tastes, and the usual emotions of a people. The study of these relative beauties is no less necessary."

The Function of Schlegel

Degérando was a philosopher: his differentiation between the absolute and the relative in the matter of taste and criticism lacked neither pertinence nor fruitfulness. It was another philosopher, the man who introduced Kant to France, Charles de Villers, who in 1806 published in Münster an *Erotique comparée*, or *De la Manière essentiellement différante dont les poètes allemands et français traitent l'amour*. Despite its title, it was read much less than Schlegel's celebrated dissertation given in Paris in 1807 in French—*Comparaison entre la* Phèdre *de Racine et celle d'Euripide*. This, violently attacking the French theater, provoked vehement replies in the *Journal de l'empire*, while an old forerunner of romanticism, Sébastien Mercier, backed Schlegel a year later with his *Satires contre Racine et Boileau*.

Definition of Romantic

Romantic, a vague epithet that had wandered since Rousseau between nature and literature, was made more precise at that time in a literary system called "the romantic," a translation of the German *die Romantik*. The German romantic, expounded in particular by Schlegel, could be taken for a literary racism. According to the romantic, the modern world had grown out of the triumph of the Germans and of Christianity. In their own country of Germany, but still more in the Roman lands where their genius fertilized and reinvigorated the decadent populations, German virtues, the love of freedom and justice, respect for women, culminated in the institution of chivalry. Chivalry gave life to a poetry dedicated to God, to bravery, to ladies, with an autochthonous setting of castles, forests, sorcerers, enchanters; a poetry that was long formless, that had at length developed—really with Dante—into a great romantic literature, but that on the greater length of its line had been blocked, turned back, diverted with the beginning of the Renaissance and its imitation of the Greeks and the Latins. Literary France, and Europe in so far as it imitated the French imitations, were the victims of that deviation. England and Spain, defended better by the sea and the mountains, gave birth to the best of that romantic in the genius of Shakespeare and Calderon, on the eve of the French classical invasion. Let the present carry on this effort! Let the Germans create for themselves a literature worthy of their own past! Let the Roman peoples renew their communications with the virtues, the art, the poetry, the legends of their Middle Ages! The romantic would even serve the cause of true Hellenism; it would bring about the rediscovery of a Homer, an Aeschylus, a Euripides that would be in both senses of the word "original," beneath and beyond the utilitarian distortions that had been imposed on them by their classical imitators.

Schlegel's romantic, which thus made Germany, England, and Spain the three peaks of true modern literature, and which seemed an aggressive act of encirclement of French classicism, could have no other effect in the France of the imperial period, ruled by the censor and the police, than to provoke the anger and the thunderbolts of the authorities. It penetrated in particular through the Swiss breach and the circle of Coppet. In 1812 Albert Stapfer gave it a sympathetic presentation to the French in his preface to the translation of Bontewerk's *Histoire de la littérature espagnole*. Here the Bernese author defined the romantic as "a style of poetry born of the very genius of modern peoples, having as its base the Bible, legend, the heroic and marvelous history of our ancestors, feeding on local spirit and inhering in the soil, and portraying the indigenous sufferings, adventures, and great deeds."

"Génie de la romantique" and Génie du christianisme

This was a matter of another *Génie du christianisme*, whose influence would replace and further that of Chateaubriand's *Génie*, but whose spirit was strongly opposed to it. Indeed, in his inventory and restorations of the values of the past, Chateaubriand is a classicist. His reaction against the eighteenth century expressed itself in the name of the seventeenth, the century of Corneille and Racine, of Bossuet and Fénelon. He himself, in *Les Martyrs*, affirmed his allegiance to the classic, Fénelonized Homer. He serves as the contact between *Télémaque* and Anatole France, a fact that puts him categorically at the opposite pole from Schlegel's romantic. But a "Génie de la romantique"—perhaps in two parts—surrounds the *Génie du christianisme:* the parts are *Littérature* in 1800 and *L'Allemagne* in 1810. Above all, around Mme. de Staël, the Coppet group, with its Germanic Genevan and French elements, represents the parade ground or the mother house of the romantic. On her return from Weimar, Mme. de Staël brought Schlegel to Coppet, where she established him as her children's tutor and also as her shop foreman in the construction of *L'Allemagne*.

In 1809 Benjamin Constant, who had traveled through Germany with Mme. de Staël, published (at her request) a rather strange adaptation of *Wallenstein* in a painful verse, with the unities of time and place imposed on Schiller's drama by force and with thirty-six of the forty-eight characters in the trilogy eliminated, but very interesting because of its preface, in which Constant shrewdly compared the two dramatic systems and announced his allegiance to the romantic, which he had so little honored in his labor of adaptation. In the same year, young Barante published his *Tableau de la littérature française au XVIIIe siècle*, which is a work of elevated synthesis in which the eighteenth century, still so much alive for the contemporaries of 1809, is not brought down in the world but classified like an era of past history.

In 1813 the Germanic romantic was rising on one horizon in direct proportion to Napoleon's decline on the other. That year, when Mme. de Staël was a fugitive and Coppet was shut up, was the year when the spirit of the Coppet circle spread through France in three works that created excitement and that were to have some influence.

The Three Books of 1813

First, in May and June, came the four volumes (Provençal, Italian, Spanish, and Portuguese literature) of Sismondi's *De la Littérature du midi de l'Europe*, which the author intended to complete with the *Littérature du nord:* a very Genevan book in its European spirit, its moral concern, its cosmopolitanism, its heaviness of style, and this thesis of northern and southern literatures, part of the stock in trade of Coppet. Schlegel's point of view on the romantic civilization of the Middle Ages is developed by Sismondi with conciliatory qualifications in favor of French classicism and with the reservations of a Genevan Calvinist: it was not to be forgotten that Schlegel was a Catholic, and so was his esthetic. Schlegel's thoroughgoing Hispanophilism was a discord in the house of the Neckers; on the contrary, it favored a union with Chateaubriand during the Catholic period of romanticism.

Sismondi's book (with the customary modifications) became a course, taught first in the Academy of Geneva. Similarly Schlegel's *Cours de littérature dramatique*, the translation of which by Mme. Necker de Saussure was also published in 1813, had been taught as a course in Vienna and published in German in 1808. In La Harpe's *Lycée* and the courses of Guizot, Victor Cousin, and François Villemain, in anticipation of *Port-Royal*, one observes the importance of a wholly new literary form: the published course.

Finally, it was also in 1813 that Mme. de Staël's *L'Allemagne* appeared in London. The entire 1810 edition, except two copies, had been destroyed; this time seventy thousand copies inundated Europe in a few weeks.

The Influence of the Romantic

So the romantic invaded France, in large part through what has been called the gap of Geneva and Coppet. It implied the dualism of north and south and their creative and critical synthesis. There was one sector of the romantic movement in which everything proceeded as if *romantique* were derived not from *romanesque* and *roman* (romance-like and romance) but from the Roman language, which, Sismondi contended, "was born of the mixture of Latin and ancient German. In the same fashion the romantic customs were composed of the habits of the northern peoples and the remnants of Roman civilization." Neither the French noun, *la romantique*, nor the ideas that it represented has been preserved.* But it can be credited with the whole current that from 1814 to 1830 ran through the Restoration under the name of the troubadour style. In 1818 appeared *La Gaule poétique*, by the future prosecutor, Louis-Antoine-François Marchangy, a romantic treatment of the Middle Ages whose influence would be much felt around 1820, until sentimental medievalism found another vehicle in Walter Scott.

The most interesting result of this interim movement between the pre-romantic and the romantic movements was the enthusiasm that it aroused among certain readers, if not for primitive poetry, at least for poetry that long ago in time or far away in space had been produced by national spirits. The style and the influence of Ossian were closely connected with the romantic. Of the thirty-nine chapters of Sismondi's work, only four deal with Provençal literature. It goes without saying that they are superficial. But he mentions it, gives it a place, directs attention to it, in such a manner that in 1816 François Raynouard published his *Choix de poésies* in Provençal and directed his studies toward the area from which, thanks primarily to him, a scientific *Romanism* was to arise. He was the first, Gaston Paris says, "to conceive the idea of encompassing the whole of the Romance languages in one grammar and one lexicon," whence the "Romanism" of the Germanic universities. What Raynouard did for philology was done more boldly for history and poetry by Claude Fauriel, one of the most learned, most cultivated, and richest minds of his time, in his *Histoire de la Gaule méridionale sous la domination des conquérants germains* and in his *Histoire de la poésie provençale*. Fauriel's theory, his super-Romanism that saw in the poetry of the troubadours the source of all modern poetry, has not stood up to time. But his teaching in the Collège de France, his irradiations, his luxuriant books are at the root of

* The modern masculine noun, *le romantique*, has the modern English meaning.—Translator.

the meridionalism and the Provençal renascence that were to flower in Frédéric Mistral. All roads lead to Rome, the devil adds his mite, the Geneva-Coppet gap opens on Maillane: a wholly unexpected conclusion for a chapter on Schlegel's romantic.

IDEOLOGISTS, ATTICS,
AND CHRISTIANS

The Frosts of May

The new era, but not the literature of 1789 and the nineteenth century, began with the twenty-year-olds of 1789. In fact, one must incorporate in that literature the greater part of the representatives of the previous generation who were about thirty-five years old and who would occupy a considerable place in the contacts, the dialogue, the debate between the two centuries. A man who had lived his youth under Louis XVI, his mature years under the Revolution, and his old age under the Restoration would have in his memory one of the most varied and most powerful time spans that history has provided.

This half-generation, born between 1753 and 1762, was marked by the eighteenth century but carried by a very lively movement toward the margins, the extremes. It considered Voltaire and Rousseau great geniuses, but more or less average and common, beyond whom and against whom something pure, naked, absolute, must be sought, refined, grasped. Here it would be a matter almost of an aristocratic romanticism, the absolute contrary of that popular pre-romanticism, made up of enthusiasm, intemperance, and outbursts, that was diffused by the Revolution. This aristocratic generation, or half-generation, would be more or less wounded, rejected, turned aside by the Revolution. In any case it could bear its fruits only in storms that destroyed a part of it, marked the rest, gave the best of this rest a strange aspect of paradox, unreality, and perfection. Three groups, moving in very different directions, can be identified: the ideologists, or analysts; the Attics, or artists; the Christians, or "thinkers."

The Ideologists

The eighteenth century was a century of ideas, it fermented ideas, it was caught up in a lightning, an ecstasy, and also a criticism of ideas. Thereafter it seems natural that it should have finished, on a full stop, with a science of ideas, that the clarity and the differentiation, the separation and the management, the individuality and the society of ideas should have become the highest exercise and the most fruitful method of the mind. The analysis of religious, political, moral ideas can play as valuable a part in the lives of societies, of states, of men, as mathematical analysis or the foundation of the sciences. Etienne de Condillac, the most acute and the most methodical, if not the most animated, of the minds of the eighteenth century, opened the way, created a method and a school. His philosophy prepared and sharpened the critical and constructive spirit of the Revolution, for which it seems natural that his disciples should have been working from the first moment, if not at the last.

CONDORCET AND GARAT

The most noted representative of these under the Revolution was Condorcet, who, born in 1743 and already an Academician under Louis XV, saw in the Revolution the logical sequel of all his science and his philosophy, and who adopted it as a human mechanism as valid for him as Newton's celestial mechanism. His work as a revolutionary journalist is of no literary interest, but it is important in that he attempted in it to give the Revolution a doctrine. *L'Esquisse des progrès de l'esprit humain,* which he wrote in hiding during the ban on the Girondists, before he committed suicide, derives from this circumstance a sublime aura, and Auguste Comte, who called Condorcet his spiritual father, ranked this book at the source of positivism and the positivist era. It is read today with thorough disillusionment: the ingenuousness of the mathematician in matters of human nature is abundantly demonstrated in it; the train of progress is as arbitrary in this book as the "train of religion" in Bossuet's *Discours sur l'histoire universelle;* one reaches the level at which the impetus of a great century is lost in a bare wilderness, where the stone of Sisyphus rolls to the bottom of a slope that must be climbed again. As for the ideologist Joseph Garat, who prepared himself for the sittings of the Convention by rereading Condillac, and who taught ideology in the Ecole Normale, all that was to be remembered of him was his useful *Mémoires sur Suard,* indispensible to an understanding of that time and that school.

FUNCTION AND LIMITS OF IDEOLOGY

The active generation that carried ideology into the nineteenth century was composed of Antoine-Louis-Claude Destutt de Tracy, born in 1754; Pierre Laromiguière, born in 1756; and Georges Cabanis, born in 1757. These were the ideologists against whom Napoleon was enraged. Nothing of theirs is read any longer, but they were valuable binding agents, and their disciples preserved or rediscovered the spirit of the eighteenth century and of analysis through romanticism. Tracy, who embodied the ideology in lucid and elegant manuals between 1804 and 1815, was read with enthusiasm by Stendhal and could be said to have been one of his masters. Cabanis, who was a physician, gave materialism one of its breviaries and psycho-physiology one of its starting points with his *Rapports du physique et du morale* in 1802. Laromiguière, a subtle, perspicacious, and judicious professor, who was the first to attract the great public to the philosophy courses of the Sorbonne, and whom Cousin pushed into the background, had his heir and almost his avenger in Taine.

These ideas, of which the ideologists made a science and for which they traced the outline of a course that the ideas themselves could not complete, were shadows. They glided elegantly through a world of two dimensions. The names of the two great disciples of the ideologists, Stendhal and Taine, are enough to show us that they could take shape, voice, a third dimension, only by drinking black blood, by incorporating a romanticism into themselves. Ideology had to be eaten and digested; not without resistance, for the lamb has difficulty understanding that he is enjoyed as a roast. When Stendhal sent *L'Amour* to his master, "M. de Tracy," said Tracy's daughter-in-law, "attempted to read the book, understood nothing of it, and told the author that it was absurd." Perhaps he would have thought the same of *L'Intelligence*.

The Attics

With ideology the eighteenth century, which was approaching its end, settled itself in precision, seeped out into the sand. In another direction, it grew thinner and chiseled itself into a fine needle of pure poetry. The flower of culture, in its last period, tends toward an Atticism, or, rather, through an inevitable Alexandrianism it regains certain more or less pure states of Atticism. These Attics belonged to exactly the same generation as the ideologists. Among them we see Rivarol, born in 1753; Joubert, born in 1754; Fontanes, born in 1757; and Chénier, born in 1762.

All four had highly intelligent minds that were touched by poetry, that had the desire for perfection and the feeling for light, that were terribly limited by their times. Fontanes, the only one who could show his full worth, was also the only one who had great areas of mediocrity. Under the Revolution, in the most natural way possible, Rivarol represented the emigration, Fontanes banishment, Joubert the life of hiding in the country, Chénier the scaffold. Joubert, who was the last to die, in 1824, carried French Atticism off with him.

RIVAROL

The flavor of poetry that was closely linked to Atticism makes it easily possible to distinguish between the spirit of Chamfort (Nicolas-Sébastien Roch) and that of Rivarol. Rivarol, an idler of genius who died prematurely just when he was about to gather all the brilliances of that genius into a book, is known to us better, as in the olden times, for what he said than for what he wrote. He looked down on the pen, "that sorry midwife of the mind, with its long, pointed, shrilling beak." With a vast wealth of learning ("Why should I subscribe to the *Encyclopédie?*" a great gentleman asked; "Rivarol comes to my house"), he had the gift of the brilliant formula, a depth of view, and a talent for imagery. In the realm of intuition he was what the ideologists were in that of logic. Or he would have been if the scattered seeds of his ideas had flowered. Even more than his celebrated *Discours sur l'universalité de la langue française*, a set piece, the *Discours préliminaire* of the *Dictionnaire* that he had undertaken in Hamburg, is the work of a real philosopher of language. The conversation reported by Chênedollé, which, however, was not improvised; the magnificent theory of poetry, the rain of judgments, like shooting stars, bring us, through the despised beak of the pen, what is left of his conversation and give us a presentiment of what would have been the great book of criticism, the gallery of French writers to which he expected to dedicate himself on his return to France(prevented by his death in 1801): *Les Vivants morts et les morts vivants.*

JOUBERT

Rivarol was an Attic of talk, Joubert an Attic of thought. The friend and mentor of Chateaubriand, with an irresistible vocation toward doubt and silence, he would have readily carried over to the press, that rolling mill of thought, the derogation that Rivarol directed toward the long beak of the pen. Timid, wounded, ailing, and coy, he did not publish a line. The *Pensées* and the *Correspondances* that were assembled from his papers after his death had their enthusiasts and their enemies like Amiel's *Journal.* Jean de La Fontaine's line, "The delicate are unhappy," seems to have been written for Joubert. In him this delicacy was quite compatible with precision of form and thought, but it excluded the normal conditions and the materiality of life. It was made for a country of happy shadows, and marvelously suited to a posthumous existence. Everything that Joubert wrote on poetry is beyond comparison. Such familiarity with the serpentine path of thought and with its light and shadow would not be encountered again until Stéphane Mallarmé and Paul Valéry. With close study and sympathy one can find a whole philosophy of life, and of his life, in his precious pages (precious in both meanings of the word) on modesty. His letters reveal a remarkable penetration, refined by the society of women, and such a secret portrait as his of Chateaubriand has never been surpassed in its intelligent intuition.

FONTANES

Rivarol and Joubert, neither of whom wrote verse—or so little!—were the familiars of the secret chambers of poetry, real critical forerunners of the subtler Sainte-Beuve. But Fontanes is the official representative of poetry in their group. Official . . . He was an honest man, quite intelligent and quite clever. Sainte-Beuve assigned to him the rank—equally official— of the last of the classics. This he was in his judgment and his delicacy, in the elegant correctness of his verses. To spend time with Fontanes, in the beautiful edition of him that Sainte-Beuve put together with a still more beautiful introduction, is amusing today in the sense in which oenophiles speak of an amusing wine. One laughs with Fontanes, while one laughs at Delille, who was not a bore either, but one of them was intelligent, the other was not. Unfortunately the poet Fontanes had not been endowed with the minim of poetry that was inherent in those two writers of prose, Rivarol and Joubert. He wrote good verses, but to him being a poet meant writing verses. To Montaigne, who used to ask about everyone: "How did he die?" a depressing answer would have to be given about Fontanes. For he died refusing audience to Les Méditations of Lamartine on the wonderful pretext, which is the testament of an era and which was to be repeated by Catulle Mendès after Victor Hugo by Charles Leconte de Lisle after himself: "All the verses have been written." Fontanes' most important work was his influence on that of Chateaubriand, who was very amenable to advice and who gave unlimited credit to that of his friend. Unhappily this Chateaubriand-Fontanes is the Chateaubriand of three-quarters of Le Génie and Les Martyrs, the Chateaubriand whom we no longer read. When Anatole France died, everyone concurred in pronouncing the same praise: "He stood fast!" Fontanes, who had got his instructions from La Harpe, stood fast, and he helped, he almost compelled Chateaubriand to stand fast. But we recognize this today more coldly than Sainte-Beuve did.

Of these four contemporaneous Attics, Rivarol was the spirit of poetry; Joubert was its soul, its Psyche; Fontanes was its material manifestation; but André Chénier, the last to be born and the first to die, was its genius.

ANDRÉ CHÉNIER

Like Rivarol and Joubert, he was published posthumously. He left mountains of manuscript that would not be printed until the next generation, and even later. Here the revolutionary interregnum of literature is patent, dramatic, like a fissure in a geological map. He did not emigrate—unfortunately. But, from the literary point of view, it might be said that his emigration was behind him. The son of a Greek mother, he was born in Constantinople, traveled in Italy, spent three years in London. He read the English and Italian poets in their own languages. But, above all, his acquaintance with Greek poetry was probably the most intimate of any modern man's. Much more than Pierre de Ronsard, he is our great philologist-poet. Homer and the Bucolics were as familiar to him as Racine was to Voltaire.

Greece to him was in no way an asylum, an alibi, as the country was to be for that anti-Chénier, Leconte de Lisle. He loved life, his time, the men of his time and, of course, the women of his time. The elegant materialism of the eighteenth century fused with that antique paganism that in him seemed to be a hereditary vocation. His conception of poetry did not go further beyond the eighteenth century, was no more romantic, than his political conception went beyond constitutional monarchy or was either Girondist or Jacobin.

In addition, every trend, every possibility is to be found in his papers, so that it is absolutely futile to wonder of what development, of what riches the execrable date of 7 Thermidor (Chénier was thirty-one years old) deprived French poetry. His great projects were his great poems: *L'Hermès, L'Amérique, L'Invention.* The considerable sections of them that were completed hardly stand out from the rest of the poetry of the waning eighteenth century. Since this didactic poetry was going to remain in favor under Napoleon, and since all that we know about André Chénier makes us suppose that he, as much as Fontanes and even more, would have found a perfectly agreeable arrangement with and under the Empire, we may suppose that, without any major profit to us, he would have had a great career in great poetry. The difference between the two Chéniers would have reminded us rather less than we might think of the difference between the poet-playwright Corneille brothers, Pierre and Thomas.

His *Elégies* surpassed Evariste-Désiré de Forge de Parny no more perceptibly than his poems surpassed Delille. Yet it was the poems and the elegies that undoubtedly seemed to Chénier the nearest to the quality and dignity of publishable works. The rest was chiefly exercises, outlines, sketches, whose potential rank we cannot know, as we cannot know whether that rank would have been considerable in a completed body of work by André Chénier. The immortal Chénier is the student Chénier; would the fruit have kept the promise of the blossom? A student of antiquity, a student of nature, a student of poetry.

The Student Poet

Student of antiquity, disciple of Philippe Brunck, whose *Analecta* was one of his bedside books, as the *Odes anacréontiques* were for the poets of the Pléiade. What he transmuted of the Greek verse of Theocritus or The Anthology into the structure of French verse is extremely difficult to estimate and does not go far; the more so in that he drew inspiration from it and did not translate, and, whatever he might have said, he would have preferred to write new verses on old themes. But, given the postulate that a literary Greece could exist for us only as it was transplanted into books and that we had to accept it as not only a necessary but a salutary substitute for the real Greece that is unknown to us, Chénier's poetry infused French poetry with what books have made us conceive of as the most Greek and even the most Athenian (let us not exaggerate the Alexandrian side): the proportion, the grace, the melody of life in an olive grove, the music of the creatures, their passage eternalized in monoliths, the capture of movements, of faces, of scenes, of humanity, through which poetry became a rival of painting—so that the image of the notebooks of sketches and the outlines of studies now presses hard on the reality. Shakespeare, Salomon Gessner, nature seen at first hand, the sources of books and of nature are transmuted in André Chénier into a plastic, diaphanous form that becomes a sort of general language of poetry as it was in Racine. But the masterpieces, naturally, are the purely Greek pieces, in subject and in appearance—*Le Malade, La Jeune Tarentine, Le Mendiant, Néère, Hylas, L'Aveugle*. Through them we find a school of Chénier as we find a school of David. The discovery of the school of Chénier in 1819 resembled, for the romantic generation, what the discovery of Herculaneum had been for the generation of Chénier himself: a world of forms arrested and immobolized by a catastrophe, suddenly brought to light, and becoming a school, or, rather, becoming a school again.

Student of nature. As much as nature is stylized in Chénier's didactic work, to the same degree it is portrayed freshly in his study notebooks. He loved, savored, evoked the countryside through verses that surged up from within, as La Fontaine did. Lamartine was to see Greece in his hills of the Mâconnais, Mistral in his rocks and his sea of Provence; so Chénier knew and felt an eternal nature, a Greece that was everywhere: the Ile-de-France, Versailles, Normandy suggested to him the same poetic sketches as did a text of Theocritus or Propertius. In that direction he found the classicism of the perfect grafting of nature and books, that of Ronsard and La Fontaine.

Student of poetry. Chénier's poetic ear was always as unsatisfied, as seeking, as David's pencil: sensual like the hand of a painter. He deliberately burrowed into the hidden musics of French verse, he sought out and patiently exploited their resources. In his work the beautiful line is by no means a lightning-flash passage, as in Lamartine and Hugo, but a pause, a possession, and, as in Mallarmé, a thing in which all things come to an end.

> *Le toit s'égaie et rit de mille odeurs divines*
> (Gay laughs the roof with thousand godlike scents)

was taken as an enigma in 1850, just as was, in 1900,

> *Trompettes, tout haut d'or pâmé sur le vélin*
> (Trumpets all gleam of gold aswoon on parchment).

He made few innovations in verse structure, which Delille and Jean-Antoine Roucher had ruptured with the same audacities as his: three-part cadences, dislocations, syllables carried over from one line to another—and the Racine of *Les Plaideurs* had already been there. But Chénier created another summit of pure poetry, the grace line, the ambrosial line, the element and aliment of the gods, breaking away from the significations of prose, as it was to pass on to Alfred de Vigny, to Hugo, to Mallarmé, to Valéry. On this subject there is a major text by Chénier. It is his commentary on *Les Larmes de Saint-Pierre*, the youthful poem of François de Malherbe, the poem of a student, a poem that later the established poet, a maker of forms and reforms, was to disavow, undoubtedly with reason, since this was the price of his future. But Chénier felt that, after this vast deviation, the time had come for poetry to receive a new trial, to accept baptism in the admirable and forgotten lines of *Les Larmes*. With all due allowances, we can recognize here the first contact between romanticism and Ronsard and the fact that Sainte-Beuve's *Tableau* and Chénier presage romanticism to exactly the same degree to which this *Commentaire* foreshadows the *Tableau*.

The four and a half months that he spent in the prison of Saint-Lazare caused Chénier's poetry to soar still higher. The voluptuous, graceful poetry that is crowned by *La Jeune Tarentine* lacked a cry, a bell tone. These it was given by the fragments of *Les Iambes*. In a powerful, uniform rhythm, created by Chénier, there is a unique fusion of enthusiasm, of invective, and of sculpture. These few couplets, which Auguste Barbier could do no more than imitate, were enough to make Chénier the greatest battle poet between Agrippa d'Aubigné and Victor Hugo.

It will be regretted that he did not emigrate, like Delille. Not only would he have saved his life, but the life and the surroundings of the emigration, the sojourn in London or in Hamburg, association with foreigners, with the philologists and the writers of Germany, would have provided him with the uprooting and the renewal that he more than anyone needed. The Revolution unleashed a movement of ideas against itself. It did not unleash a poetic movement. Its *Tragiques* and its *Châtiments* remained in their sheaths. *Les Iambes* makes us imagine what a swarm of golden arrows Chénier could have loosed on the Revolution. His lightning came, like Hugo's, from the hall of the gods. The movement of

> *Diamant ceint d'azur, Paros, oeil de la Grèce!*
>
> (Blue-girdled diamond, Paros, eye of Greece!)

is the movement of that fragment of *Les Châtiments, Juvénal,* and above all of *Stella.* Between Ronsard and Victor Hugo, and going by way of Racine and La Fontaine, the best of the fragments of Chénier seem to have strewed their seeds, like grains of corn or a sowing of gold, to cover the whole field of our poetry.

The Christians

Le Génie du christianisme was a successful book. But the Christian renascence in reaction against philosophy had not waited for it. Its Christianity of imagination and beauty crowned a sensitivity and corroborated a Christian rationale that had taken form and life from Rousseau. Unfortunately, the strong mystic movement of the end of the eighteenth century had no literary expression, unless perhaps in Saint-Martin, the unknown philosopher, the French Jacob Boehme whose style is difficult but who was more than a great soul—a soul, and who, in *Le Livre de désir,* wrote one of the beautiful books of the inner life. But the revolutionary upheaval gave being, a style, and a public to two men who turned forty years old at the same time in 1794 and who, as great writers, became the witnesses and the Christian judges of the Revolution, the prophets of the Restoration: Vicomte de Bonald and Comte Joseph de Maistre.

BONALD

Bonald belonged to one of the most solid of all structures, a structure at the base of the old France or, rather, of the old Europe: the families of the minor nobility, accustomed to military service, to discipline, to power over their holdings, to loyalty to the king—the same structure to which the Vignys and the Lamartines belonged. An emigrant at the age of forty, retreating into studious Heidelberg, where he educated his sons, this gentleman of the old Rouergue, thoughtful, tenacious, much given to ponderous logical deductions, took the road of the philosophers, but against the philosophers whose doctrine had destroyed authority and brought on revolutionary anarchy. He was of a race whose life had need of foundations. He became the philosopher of foundations.

He is generally called a theocrat, and this is not inexact. But God is external to him. The living basis of his philosophy, which he lived, is the reality of the family, the magisterial dignity of the father, and especially, and even only, of the land-owning and land-working father of a family. Bonald thinks in terms of the Roman *pater familias*. Toward luxury, elegance, individuality of mind he nourishes the same scorn that Cato had for the Greeks. He regards the individual, as Comte would later do, as a dangerous abstraction of society. Social reality is the family. True and just power is conferred by God, who is himself a king and a father, on the king in society and on the father in the family. Everything that does not adjust itself to the framework of this agrarian philosophy is evil and pernicious.

But it is astonishing to observe how much that is unexpected is brought in by Bonald's stubborn and inventive dialectic. He was one of the first to have thrown any illumination on the nature of society as a living organism that transcends individuals, that is created directly by God, whose organ is power. His well-known doctrine of language as a direct gift of God has a fine honest audacity. Few small works are more replete with insights than his comparison of the agricultural family with the industrial family.

He wrote much. He has the strength of masonry, but his country-gentleman style (even though he lived most often in Paris) lacks attraction. Nevertheless he is admirable at turning a maxim, a struck and striking phrase, that endures, that circulates, that is quoted. Few read M. de Bonald, but many write: "As M. de Bonald says . . ."

This man of authority was an authority. It was he, in sum, far more than Joseph de Maistre, who gave a philosophy to that very tenacious French social and political complex that is called *the reaction*. The new reactionary school, which was born of Frédéric Le Play and Taine in the second third of the nineteenth century, venerated Bonald as one of its sires; Paul Bourget and Charles Maurras quoted him often. For their disciples he makes rather rough reading, a tasty, healthful Auvergne peasant bread. In addition, there is an exaggeration, a caricature, of Bonald in a curious gentleman of the Auvergne, his contemporary, who had a touch of madness but also a picturesqueness as a writer and his own hour of celebrity: François-Dominique de Montlosier.

JOSEPH DE MAISTRE

Nevertheless the team of Bonald and de Maistre is much more valuable and instructive than that of Bonald and Montlosier. These are two dialects of the reaction, two Catholics, two emigrants, whose difference and even whose opposition were dictated by those of their country and their destiny.

Joseph de Maistre was no more a Frenchman than Rousseau was. As Rousseau was a citizen of Geneva, he was the loyal subject and functionary of the King of Sardinia. Until he was forty years old he had never thought of publishing: he was happy in his duties in the Senate of Savoy, in his family life, in his reading, in his conversations, for he was a remarkable conversationalist. By uprooting him, injecting tragedy into his life, into his ideas, into society, the French Revolution compelled him, as it compelled Bonald, to question himself, to think, to write.

Much more than Bonald, he is a thoroughbred writer. He had one of the best styles of his time, infinitely superior to that of his neighbor and enemy, Mme. de Staël, but clinging, like hers, to conversation, and pure, spirited, full of movement, of bite, of images.

Savoy lived under a rather paternal government. The entrance of the revolutionary armies led first to anarchy, to violence and, for the de Maistres, to ruin. The contrast between these two conditions, this transition from order to disorder, from a prosperous life to exile, were incorporated by de Maistre into a general theory of order and disorder. Besides, his thinking had long since taken a mystic turn. A convinced Christian, he had been initiated into Freemasonry. He was a reader and a fervent disciple of Saint-Martin. Above all, the training given by his mother, which had entirely shaped his emotions, had accustomed him to see God everywhere. And it must not be forgotten that he had been the pupil, and would always remain the disciple and the friend, of the Jesuits. For him the Revolution was the tremendous event that would illuminate the depth of human and social nature for the eyes of his generation. It illuminated it by demonstrating the presence and the will of God in it. When Bossuet appealed to Providence to explain the English revolution, he may have diminished the range of that idea by pointing to the salvation of Queen Henrietta as the purpose of the divine intervention. Beginning with his *Considérations sur la France*, which he published in 1796 in Neuchâtel, de Maistre raised this doctrine of a visible Providence to a breadth, a force, a spirited and almost *virtuoso* ingenuity that captured the imagination, all the more so because Bonald, a mind in other ways so different from Joseph de Maistre, published his *Théorie du pouvoir* in the same year in Constance, and de Maistre was justified in writing to him later: "Is it possible that nature should have amused itself by stretching two strings so perfectly attuned to each other as our two minds? This is strict harmony. It is a unique phenomenon."

Providence was visible, for him, in the disparity between the immensity of the fact of the Revolution and the wretched mediocrity of the men by whom it was achieved. De Maistre viewed the Revolution as a purifying punishment: whence a flamboyant theory of punishment, an eloquent theory of purification, which he was to take up again in still more brilliant fashion in his *Soirées de Saint-Pétersbourg*.

But, though he was a faithful servant of his king, Joseph de Maistre was by no means a Gallophobe. Quite the contrary, the Savoyard regarded France as the first nation of the world, the leading nation. The French Revolution, that universal phenomenon lacking any common measure with the insular revolution of the English, struck him all the more forcibly because it was called forth, chosen by God, for a greater mission. The elder daughter of the Church, France had betrayed her mother by her public sins. Among the public and political sins of France, de Maistre denounced the Ultramontanes and the disciples of the Jesuits, Gallicanism and Jansenism. His book *Du Pape*, published in 1819, and its supplement on *L'Eglise gallicane* had already been contained in *Les Considérations*, as had the most important of *Les Soirées*. This lightning play of ideas that is one of the great charms of reading Joseph de Maistre starts with a few simple principles, the presence and action of God and a theory of the demon—that is, of evil—and especially of pride as it is embodied by philosophy.

Care must be taken to avoid regarding the Savoyard count as a writer as foreign to France as his Alpine duchy governed by Turin. Joseph de Maistre was the great pupil of the Jesuits. Through him, and through him alone, the doctrine of that order which has exerted so great an influence on French youth entered into the great literature of France, took on an original, authentic literary expression. Taught with his own imagination, almost with his personal poetry, by a layman who committed only himself, his sword of paradox made it possible—a trick, moreover, that is always excellent in societies—to disavow the caustic gentleman as an extremist and an ultra. All things considered, de Maistre was to be to the Society of Jesus almost what Pascal (who was not of Port-Royal) was to Port-Royal. Laymen without mandates, free intermediaries, proxies in literature function in the relations between the Church and the great public not as polemicists (the clergy makes its own polemics—Antoine Arnauld, Gabriel Daniel, Barruel) but as journalists of the great religious parties. The qualities of Joseph de Maistre are precisely those of a great journalist: clarity, animation, the most common ideas expressed in the guise of paradox, challenge, mockery, movement, action, and a simplicity that arouses confidence. None of the pertinent replies that were made to Pascal's *Provinciales* in the seventeenth century succeeded with the pub-

lic, not because Pascal was right, but because he was a journalist (he invented journalism more assuredly than the wheelbarrow) and his adversaries were not. And read de Maistre's pamphlet on Jansenism. It is
unjust, admittedly absurd, rich in ignorance, but what fire, what wit, what
trenchant words that hunt out the human, the ridiculous, underneath the
conventions and the hagiography! What a rousing, lusty play at massacre!
It was by reviving the tradition and to a certain degree the manner and
the style of Joseph de Maistre that Louis Veuillot was to create the great
journalism of Catholicism.

The journalism without a journal that de Maistre practiced is an aggressive journalism, with a fire, a force, an effectiveness, even a swagger of
healthy madness, which took up opposition to the journalism of the prudent, the defensive journalism of *Les Actes des apôtres* of Rivarol, or
that of Peltier, or of the Genevan, Mallet du Pan. Its intransigence, its
wholeness were its strength, at least its literary strength. Rivarol and
Mallet were liberals: in the nineteenth century they would have written
for the *Journal des débats*. De Maistre, for his part, was of sufficient
stature to take proudly to his own charge the stigma that Mirabeau cast
on the Duc de Savoie, his master: "A bad neighbor for all freedom." Freedom of study in Geneva, freedom of the Gallican Church in Bugey or
Dauphiné, freedom of the French Republic, freedom of the philosophers,
and even, in the past, Athens as a civilization of freedom—he exhausted
his ink supply in battle against them all. He created the style of the fight
against freedom for the nineteenth century.

He remains one of the prose writers of his time who can be read again
with the greatest of interest and even of pleasure. He is never a bore. But
he lacks reliability. He lived on a solid education, on an abundance of
reading of antiquity that he hardly renewed. His errors of fact are many,
and, besides, the spirit of scientific truth is completely lacking in this pure
humanist and disciple of Saint-Martin who believes only in the truth of
feelings. To infer, to invent, to set off his fireworks—this whole business
of writing that he discovered at the age of forty amused him. But did he
always take it seriously? Educated by Italian Jesuits, did he not give full
course to the virtuoso in him or to the strain of theocracy? What was
really serious in life for him was duty, conscience, service to his king, the
care and the love of his family, all of which, fortunately, make their presence felt in his work in an abundant political and personal correspondence,
intelligent, full of shadings, and witty, which does not contradict his dogmatic writings but puts them in their proper place by classing them (and
perhaps too by demoting them) among life's values.

Without this *Correspondance* French literature would lack any evidence of a way of life that deserved to leave more: a gentleman of stature
at once local and European, for whom, however, nothing came by way of
Paris. De Maistre knew Paris only from a stay of a few weeks in 1817 on

his return from Russia (he was sixty-five years old), and he seemed something of a country cousin there. He thought not only outside Paris but
against Paris. Thus, through his Calvinist enemies in Geneva and Vaud,
a precious autonomous and anti-Parisian corner of French literature exists
for him in the first half of the nineteenth century.

THE BIRTH
OF LITERARY CRITICISM

The Nineteenth Century and Criticism

The nineteenth century may go down in history as the great century, the unique century, of literary criticism. In the eighteenth century criticism declined, even in Voltaire, to a dust cloud of feelings, tastes, discussions, formulas, which did more to parade intellects than to provide a legacy of lasting and original works. As for the twentieth century, its first third was far from having replaced the great critics who died in its early years.

The nineteenth century owes its advantage in part to the formation of a middle class, of a new society in which there was a rapid growth of the prosperity and the leisure that furthered reading and the pleasures of the mind, as well as to the revolution of the press, the creation of a literary press of newspapers and magazines (thus the history of dramatic criticism was centered for almost a century on the articles in the *Journal des débats*, in *le Globe* of 1824 and *Le Temps* of 1868, as well as the two *Revues* of 1830, and the career of Sainte-Beuve as a critic was governed by the life of a journalist). The climate also favored the new dwellers in the University, in its Faculty of Letters, in the Ecole Normale, who gave rise to a professorial criticism that was the not always friendly rival of the journalistic, and it favored the conflicts of ideas and literary forms, whose banners were carried and whose battalions were uniformed by criticism, as well as the almost new phenomenon of the renewal of literary tastes by the fashions of the hostile literary generations that, every thirty or forty years, as in music, pitted the taste of the fathers against that of the sons and that, being founded in and felt as emotion, exerted every effort to explain itself rationally.

As far as the early years of the nineteenth century, the years of Napoleon, are concerned, it should be added that for newspapers literary criticism was very nearly the only form of criticism, the sole subject for dogmatic considerations, that could be debated freely. The theater was not free, but technical criticism of the theater remained free. And, while the theater of that period was worse than nothing, Julien-Louis Geoffroy was able to found dramatic criticism, over which he exercised hegemony until 1814.

Geoffroy

Born in 1743, Geoffroy had been a Jesuit. After the suppression of the order, he taught rhetoric in the colleges of the University until the Revolution. At the same time he was an anti-Voltairean journalist for Elie Fréron's *L'Année littéraire*, and later an anti-revolutionary journalist for *L'Ami du roi*. During the Revolution he had to go into hiding. Extremely erudite, courageous, bellicose, at once pedantic and biting, he was perhaps the first practitioner of professorial criticism. On 18 Brumaire he did not go back into teaching, and at the age of sixty he made his first appearance as a dramatic critic in the *Débats*. The articles that he published there over the next fourteen years were collected into the *Cours de littérature dramatique*. At that time La Harpe, although a convert and the enemy of the philosophers, ranked Voltaire's tragedies at the summit of the French theater, placing them far above Corneille's, and his judgments on the art of the drama, popularized by *Le Lycée*, were becoming a peril to public taste. Geoffroy was the first to put the proper evaluation on *Zaïre* and *Tancrède*. The disciple of Fréron speedily and rightly triumphed over the disciple of Voltaire. That Geoffroy wrote as much nonsense about Shakespeare as did La Harpe was the fault of the spirit of the eighteenth century. But he had the feeling of the seventeenth century, that of classical literature, of the theater, of candor, even of style. He can hardly be said to have been replaced, from 1814 to 1830, by the feeble Duviquet, nor, from 1830 to 1874, by Jules Janin. Janin's success, which earned him the title of "prince of critics," a reign of forty-four years in the *Débats* in consequence of a bright, chattering humor that concealed a void, was to corrupt dramatic criticism for a half century. It is at once the most difficult and the easiest of all the forms of criticism. As far as its ease goes, it is open to everyone. On the side of its difficulty, of its true nature, Geoffroy had hardly any successor other than a second professor, Francisque Sarcey.

La Harpe

Geoffroy lorded it over the theater as he domineered over a college. While he was a professor who had become a critic, Jean-François La Harpe was a critic, a journalist, a jack-of-all-writing, who became a professor, and a great professor.

A guest at Ferney, an admirer of the master, he had been chosen by Voltaire as his disciple, and Voltaire had given the *imprimatur* to his judgments. But presence and authority had been withheld from this hooted dramatic author, the editor of *Le Mercure*, this dwarf at once very learned, intelligent, envious, pugnacious, peremptory, and hot-tempered, whose face, in the words of Alexis Piron, asked to be slapped, and who, as one of his colleagues put it, always arrived at the Academy with a bloody nose. Meanwhile, in 1786, at the corner of the rue Saint-Honoré and the rue de Valois, the first institute of fashionable lectures had been inaugurated. Very soon the lecturers were enjoying the same success among the ladies that the preachers of Louis XIV had had with their grandmothers. La Harpe launched a general course there in literature—Greek and Latin, but chiefly French—that lasted (with an interruption of three years at the end of the Revolution) from 1786 to 1798. In those nine years La Harpe founded the history of French literature in the form in which it would be carried on throughout the whole of the nineteenth century.

For the first time French literature became the subject of a living, sequential story, in which individual works took their places, were analyzed, were judged, less according to a code of pre-existing rules than on the basis of the literary experience of respectable people. Since such a history was concerned principally with works that had endured, the criticism of virtues (to adopt an expression of Chateaubriand, who was to employ the principle in *Le Génie*) received more attention than the criticism of defects. Othénin d'Haussonville has called Sainte-Beuve the Thomas Aquinas of France. But in truth it was *Le Lycée* that for a half century and more figured as the *Summmum* of French literature.

A sum that was anything but coddled when it came to subtracting from it. The Greek-Latin introduction did not amount to much, the Middle Ages were ridiculously treated; La Harpe had read nothing of the sixteenth century, but this did not prevent him from saying whatever he could about it: rubbish. To him Corneille was the great archaic poet, abounding in faults, of Voltaire's *Commentaire:* "Old monuments, sublime in some portions and in their whole insignificant, that belong to the birth of the arts" (the subject was *Horace* and *Cinna!*). Racine was presented and explained with judgment. As for the tragedies of Voltaire, to which La Harpe consecrated no less than two volumes, they were the work of "the greatest tragic writer of the entire world"! He was completely ignorant of the seventeenth century as a religious century. His picture of the eighteenth century, which encompasses more than half the work, is alive because contemporaries are explained by their contemporary, from the perspective and with the prejudices of custom, and because in its obsolete mass it gives us a foretaste of what our histories of French literature under the Third Republic will be to our posterity.

But there is also something else in this curious eighteenth century, according to La Harpe. The favorite child, the journalist and the deputy of the philosophers, of whom Voltaire wrote to Jean-François Marmontel: "He will be one of the pillars of our Church," La Harpe found his road to Damascus during the Revolution. He traveled a long way to find it. In 1792 and 1793 he had edited a Jacobin *Mercure* and on 3 December 1792 he had delivered his lecture while wearing a red cap. This masquerade did not save him, any more than others, from making acquaintance with the prison of the Luxembourg, an observation post from which the Jacobins and their fathers seemed monsters to him, and in which a reading of *The Imitation of Christ* converted him—quite sincerely, it is thought. Resuming his chair after 18 Brumaire, he made it a jousting ground against the philosophy of the eighteenth century, showered insults on Diderot, Rousseau, Claude-Adrien Helvétius, and revised his whole course in order to publish it in a new guise in 1799, three years before *Le Génie du christianisme*, on which the influence of *Le Lycée* and La Harpe is unmistakable. Almost all the professorial criticism in the nineteenth century, a criticism taking its position on the right, was to be of the seventeenth century against the eighteenth, their opposition cutting as deeply into literature as the conflict of right and left into politics. This originated in La Harpe's conversion and, curiously, ended in another conversion, Ferdinand Brunetière's.

Professorial criticism, we said. It was created, before Geoffroy, by the lecturer of *Le Lycée*. Thirty years later the sons and daughters of his audience would crowd into the courses of Cousin, of Villemain, of Guizot, who were to succeed through the same oratorical qualities as La Harpe's. For, as soon as he was at the lectern, this little man whom Pierre Le Brun's epigram shows us absurdly scrambling about the foot of the Pindus Mountains delivered his lectures and read his quotations like an actor, reminiscent of the manner of Lekain (Henri-Louis Cain) and Clairon (Claire Léris), impressing literature on his hearers like a physical force. His eloquence was fed the more by his anti-revolutionary and anti-philosophical fanaticism. Here criticism was at the source of a flood of oratory that would end with Brunetière.

Continued reading of *Le Lycée* is impossible today. But it has its place —in the attractive bindings in which it was clothed in the early nineteenth century—on the library shelf from which now and again one takes this or that volume of it: one of the early volumes in order to be amused and to

say with Flaubert: "What rot those people's antiquity was!"; or a volume
on Racine or even on Voltaire, which assists us to an excellent, meticulous
understanding of what tragedy was for those who had created it, to some
extent, but above all for those who fabricated it and for the public that
indefatigably flocked to see it; or one of the volumes on the eighteenth
century, preferably on its minor authors, like that of Louis-Petit de
Bachaumont or Friedrich Melchior von Grimm, evoke for us with exactitude the laws, the ideas, the literary customs of an era that we no longer
see except in a distant mass and through a glass of time.

The Real Creators

The other critics under the Consulate and the Empire, one of whom at
least, François-Benoit Hoffmann, was quite good, must be neglected here.
But we must point out again that the two major books that inaugurated
the nineteenth century, Mme. de Staël's *Littérature* in 1800 and Chateaubriand's *Le Génie du christianisme* in 1802, rejuvenated not the common
trade of criticism, as Geoffroy practiced it, but its general ideas, its stan-
dards of values, of comparisons. They added a further dimension to it.
What was diffuse and imprecise in opinion and talk they condensed with
genius. They hauled up in their nets a vast capital of European and historical ideas that were wholly foreign to Geoffroy and La Harpe. Mme.
de Staël in her criticism of ideas, Chateaubriand in his criticism of taste
left us the two creative books with that "divine element" of criticism
that is totally lacking in the two others.

XII

COURIER AND BÉRANGER

The Writers of the Left

In the eleven years between 1772 and 1783 Paul-Louis Courier, Pierre-Jean de Béranger, and Henri Beyle (Stendhal) were born. It is they, their work, their literary destinies that must be remembered when one seeks the origin of that remark of Barrès: "France is radical." In 1924 a radical politician launched the term "the average Frenchman." With these men an old French vine gave the end of the eighteenth century the fruit that the Revolution would ripen—an "average French" type of the nineteenth century who chose as his adversaries the king, the priests, and the nobility, who took cognizance of the Revolution and assimilated it, who carved out his independence in a bit of the national wealth, whom the political systems were to know, to manipulate, to use, to serve, and who was to come to power with the Third Republic.

There is a great literature of counterrevolution. There is a wretched literature of the official, rhetorical revolution. But by virtue of Courier, Béranger, and Stendhal there is a real literature of the true revolution. Let us take the word in its juridical sense: that of revolution in things, in property, revolution in depth, revolution learned and experienced at the age of twenty by Courier in the talk of soldiers, by the young Béranger in the countryside of Picardy or the rue Montorgueil, by Henri Beyle, a child of the left, in the daily battle of the rue des Vieux-Jésuites against those whom he called his natural enemies: his parents and his teachers. In 1816 Molé, attempting to present a common liberal list of candidates in the department of Seine-et-Oise to the big farmers who had bought government land and had voting rights, met this obstinate answer: "You are noble and we are not. We have government land and you have none." And he wrote: "There you have the whole of France, she is all summed up in the words of my ploughmen." Obviously, Courier was an heir of the time before the Revolution, Béranger was a citizen of Paris, and Beyle never owned a foot of land. But they explain, as they accompanied, the France that was discovered in the elections of 1816 by the aloof, perceptive vision of Mathieu Molé's descendant.

Courier

THE HELLENIST

Praised one day by Renouard as a leading Hellenist, Courier replied: "If I correctly understand that word, which I admit is new to me, you are saying *a Hellenist* as one might say *a dentist, a chemist, a machinist,* and, following that analogy, *a Hellenist* would be a man who displays Greek, who lives by it, who sells it to the public, to the bookshops, to the government. That is far from what I do. You are not unaware, monsieur, that I devote myself to these studies solely for my pleasure, or, to put it better, by fits and starts, and when I am not attracted to anything else, and that I attach no importance to them and derive no profit from them, that no one has ever seen my name on a single book."

This fine middle-class citizen would always be a M. Jourdain of independence. Therefore let us say that he was quite at home in Greek, since he did not trade in it for money, and that only small minds would call him a Hellenist.

At the same time, let us be among those small minds. And let us describe as an Atticist this writer who wanted to be Attic. The Atticist is an Attic plus the oil of his lamp. Paul-Louis was a contributor to the establishment of that expert Hellenism of style, that artificial simplicity toward which one must not be too harsh, first of all because one may say of it what Courier said of Chateaubriand, that it carries its mask in its hand and no longer deceives us; and then because, although of the left, it belongs to exactly the same vein as Chateaubriand's Hellenism of the right in *Le Génie* and *Les Martyrs;* and, again, because both, descended as they are from *Télémaque* and Abbé Barthélemy, lead to Anatole France, inasmuch as the Chavonnière and the Béchellerie of these two Parisians resemble each other foot by foot of their literary, political and regional Touraine landscapes; finally and particularly because this Atticist is still read, because, though he amuses us too consciously at the expense of his reactionary victims, he amuses us very unconsciously at the expense of himself, because the interest of the man equals and surpasses the interest of the style, because his work has substance, because it casts as much light on the political ideas of France, on political life in France—let us find a term of comparison that would have given Courier pleasure—as the poetry of Theognis affords on the intimate life of the Greek cities of his day.

THE TWO COURIERS

To consider his work is to find two Couriers. There is, first, the Courier of the Revolution and the Empire, the Hellenist officer, the horse artillery-man whose military life consisted mainly in translating Xenophon's *Cavalry Commander*, the sensual burgher, the cavalier wencher who had the good luck to edit and translate *Daphnis et Chloé* while revising and finishing Jacques Amyot. In addition there is the Courier of the Restoration, the suspicious protector of his own rights lying in wait for the nobleman and the priest, the master of the fearful firebrands that no court could extinguish—quite the contrary.

The first is known to us through his *Mémoires;* that is, through a book that you will hunt for in vain in his bibliography, since, like Pliny the Younger, he wrote it in the form of letters, those letters published in 1829 —in other words, ten to twenty years after they were supposed to have been written—and sometimes revised, sometimes completely redone. There is a world of difference between Courier's real letters, those autograph collectors' treasures that are usually rather dry, and these artificial and artful letters in which he imitates Mme. de Sévigné, obviously anthology pieces but intended to be such, and justifiably smelling of the oil of that Greek-rooted word, anthology . . . The other is the Courier of the *Pamphlets.* But letters and pamphlets are in the same style, the style is of the same man.

THE GRUMBLER

A man who loved Greek and style but who quarreled with everyone, who nursed solid rancors against all systems and avenged on the first government that would more or less allow him to express them all those that he had amassed against the governments under which he could say nothing. The horse-artillery officer Courier was a grumbler. With his astute genius Napoleon has made the word the synonym of soldier, of hero. And posterity understood little, if at all, that the grumbler really did grumble and that grumbling really did mean not being satisfied when, furthermore, there was no reason to be. The soldier of the Empire had no official voice, or had one only on condition that he enter into collusion with the setting and convention. Grumbling was taken to mean serving as the model for the jolly grumbler of Béranger, of Thiers, of the good citizen who puts on his tricolor slippers when he sits down to read *Victoire et conquête des français;* but grumbling was speaking out, stating one's resentments strongly, simply, accurately, saying that the announcements of the Grand Army were the announcements of the big lie, and that Plutarch was a liar.

This voice, under the Empire, had no written expression; it blew away with the smoke of the camp fires. Literature lived under the system that put covers on watches. The Empire was the golden age of this school of clockmakers. Even the key word of army grumbling was inscribed on a watch cover after Waterloo; it was considered sublime.

Now, Courier's military career was that of an acute, resourceful grumbler. He grumbled literarily in his letters. His experience as an officer was summed up thus in a letter to Silvestre de Sacy: "I have finally left my low calling—a little late, I regret to admit. But I did not altogether waste my time in it. I saw things that books tell all wrong. Plutarch makes me die laughing now; I no longer believe in great men."

With even better reason he no longer believed in the august house of the Bourbons, or in the clergy, or in the government ministers, or in the mayor. It is to be doubted whether the Restoration gave the French as many occasions to grumble as did the imperial Moloch, but it did give them the right to grumble. Courier used it as a permanent right of the human being, as a new Right of Man—his right as a natural tendency of the Frenchman, as an eternal defense of the property owner, as the privilege of one who had learned how to write from the Greeks, and as a refined pleasure of an erudite humanist.

THE INHERITOR

In the author of the *Pamphlets*, the Frenchman, the property owner and the humanist collaborate in a unique style. It is the style of an inheritor. The jealous heir of a good estate, Courier was the no less jealous heir of a literary patrimony in which he occupied two estates: the olive groves of Attica and the gardens of Touraine; more exactly, he intended to further, to represent, the double tradition of Xenophon and of Lysias, of the Pascal of the *Petites Lettres* and of Mme. de Sévigné. He did not produce but he inherited: he was an Alexandre Grimod de la Reynière or an Anthelme Brillat-Savarin of style. He did not, like that other hereditary master of style, M. de Chateaubriand, look to his literary heritage for the great, the poetic, the universal, but rather for the rare and the exquisite. The stylist behaved like a French gardener and vine grower.

He applied the style of the heir to the defense of his heritage: I mean the inheritance of his class, which was average middle. An average property owner, he tossed back and forth in his bed, hating on the one side the great noble proprietor, on the other the poacher. In his dealing with his neighbors and his servants, Courier behaved like a bad "big shot" (and that was his private life, which left no trace in his literature). But face to face with the official "big shots," this qualified voter put on the mask of the vine grower of the Chavonnière; that is, of a feigned "little man," and even of the husbandman of Naboth's vineyard. His political literature, far more than Chateaubriand's, marched under a mask. *Larvatus prodeo.*

THE PRIVATE DISTILLER

The author of the *Pamphlet des pamphlets* falls back on *Les Provinciales*, and his dialogue with M. Arthur Bertrand even imitates, in a rather labored manner, Pascal's with the good Father. There is, however, one difference, other than that of originality, and that is that *Les Provinciales* deals with vast spiritual matters, while the *Pamphlets* do not touch even average political matters such as those with which Royer-Collard concerned himself in the Chamber or that Constant treated in the press. Courier had the gift of grasping every question at its small end: this is indeed France seen from the village of Véretz, Courier's dealings with the mayor and the priest, whether the villagers should or should not dance. And Flaubert would not even have dared to put into the mouth of Homais the subdruggist's and subveterinarian's observations of Chambord's dissertation on the lubricities of royalty and the misdeeds of the black gang. Courier deserved his monument in the village square of Véretz, as close as possible to the Café du Commerce.

But in another way this provincial localism brings a French political microorganism to life for us. What happened and what was thought in Véretz were like what happened and what was thought in thousands of villages in France. Vine grower of the Chavonnière—the title is an omen! The vine was to become radical, and it created radicalism in strength in Véretz. The *Pamphlets* do not so much explain political reasons as interpret the states of feeling that prevented the majority of the middle class from having a common language with the Bourbons and with the order that they represented. Courier admired the Duc d'Orléans, a prince who sent his sons to religious boarding school; he wanted to see the duke on the throne, and no doubt the July Monarchy would have overjoyed him. But Courierism went farther than Courier; Courierism was not Orléanist; Courierism was the Third Republic—at least that of yesterday, anti-clerical and radical.

It was not a matter of radicalism in government but of radicalism in the individual, the critic defying authority, the citizen the powers. "In a well-made state," Courier said, "the nation would make the government do its job like a coachman whom one pays and who has to take one not where he likes, or as he likes, but where one wants to go and by the route that pleases his employer." In this the Hellenist Courier antedates the professor, Alain (Emile Chartier); the *Pamphlets*, as well as the later *Eléments d'une doctrine radicale*, can be treated as republican classics, their authors as classic republicans. With this difference: that Courier's political philosophy is the philosophy of a property owner rather than that of a militant (a poacher with the right to vote would have been as intolerable to this qualified voter as a king by divine right), of a solitary rather than of solidarity. To continue from Courier completely is to continue electorally, according to the formula of 1902, to be against the government of the priests and for the privileges of private distillers.

Therefore Paul-Louis should be read preferably during election campaigns, when he had a thousand echoes. And yet he is good in all seasons. All of him is in two volumes, since he went to great pains in order to write hardly anything that was not exquisite. Translations from Xenophon and Herodotus blend with his own short pieces, like Greek marbles brought from Italy in a white house in Touraine. The perfect pamphlet, that transient thing, is to be found only here, like real minced pork in Vouvray. The press killed it after 1830. One was a journalist, one was no longer a pamphleteer. A country squire, Louis de Cormenin, and a rustic, Claude Tillier, were to attempt pamphleteering without leaving anything lasting. Courier, furthermore, would never have accepted the hierarchy, the discipline, the regular schedule of a newspaper; the only thing that suits the grumbler, the solitary, the man who is always against, is this pamphlet, which he writes when the mood takes him, this brochure in which he is at home, this glass that is not big but from which he drinks the wine of his own grapes, the brandy that he has distilled.

Béranger

THE INTELLECTUAL UPSTART

The citizen-poet was educated in the schools of the Revolution; more accurately, in the *Ecole primaire* (the name dates from this period) founded in Péronne, in conformance with Rousseau's maxims, by a teacher who was a deputy in the Legislative Assembly. The children wore uniforms, celebrated victories, made speeches, wrote to their representatives —in short, they were a club of little Jacobins, of which little Béranger was the orator. Their studies suffered. But what is important is that Béranger, both as to his mind and as to his tendencies, and especially as to his poetry, can be said to be the first official primarian of our literature, the word being used without the slightest deprecatory meaning.

A mixture of limited rationalism, simple politics, ordinary common sense, and preaching, prosaic literature was given by Béranger exactly and fortunately the frame that suited it, the popular song.

THE MIDDLE-CLASS SONG WRITER

Béranger's glory is explained in part by the joy, the success, with which he became the leading figure of a class—the Voltairean lower middle class, carping, jingoistic, salacious—that from 1814 on formed a notable part of

Parisian public opinion. Literarily, the burgher of 1830 was a man who subscribed to *Le Constitutionnel*, bought the Touquet edition of Voltaire, sang Béranger's songs after dinner and contributed a couple of francs to the national fund-drive that paid the ten-thousand-franc fine that was imposed in 1828 on the equally national song writer.

The school of the popular after-dinner song, the sentimental romance, had flourished in that middle class since the eighteenth century, when Charles Collé, Charles-François Panard, the Caveau singing society were its debtors for a splendid celebrity. But the eighteenth-century song was to Béranger's what the hand-printed gazettes were to the press after 1815.

Béranger's songs were borne on the same current as the press. Like the press they were a product of the Charter of 1814, as caricature was to arise out of the Charter of 1830. The songs were poetic journalism, at that time infinitely more effective and more widespread than the other kind, circulating everywhere on the wings of their tunes. Political and religious journalism, or, rather, anti-religious. No product of the mind contributed more than Béranger's songs to the destruction of the government of the Bourbons. Few did better service in keeping alive the Napoleonic legend, the illusion of the Grand Army.

THE PENSIONER

Béranger's work had virtually ended by 1830. He recognized that his popularity, which meant so much to him, required his silence. If he had persisted in producing, against the strong tide that flailed and ridiculed the middle class, he would have become an out-of-fashion poet. He was simply a poet on pension, and the pensioner, like the private distiller, is an eminently French phenomenon. The glorious survivor was admired; he spent eighteen years in a tranquil, comfortable glory that the most hirsute of the romantics did not challenge, constituting with his friends Chateaubriand and Lamennais (also more or less pensioned off) a splendid trinity of old fighters and jogging gently on toward apotheosis: for the national funeral of Béranger in 1857 held in the annals of the Second Empire the rank given to the Return of the Ashes in those of the preceding reign and the status of Victor Hugo's burial in the regime that followed.

He has disappeared as completely as Jean-Jacques Rousseau from living literature. The terrible article that Renan devoted to him after his death has become a commonplace of opinion. The end of singing him meant the end of reading him, if it can be said that he was ever read otherwise than as a memento or a promise of song, of the chorus struck up over M. Poirier's roast goose. The flatness of language, the flatness of verse, the flatness of sentiment showed through equally in these songs that are today on the shelf; 1857, the year of Béranger's obsequies, was also the year of *Madame Bovary*, the year when Homais had just received the

Légion d'honneur. And in the landscape of ideas and names Homais and
Béranger merged. Béranger was not read and would not again be read.
But, just as Béranger's songs were sustained, even created, by their music
and their choruses, so they are still preserved by assistance from without:
the collection illustrated by Alfred and Tony Johannot and by Henry
Monnier, is leafed through like something out of a museum, an album of
1830; that middle-class world takes on dimensions and life. Neither the
theater of Eugène Scribe nor the fiction of Paul de Kock is classed as a
historic monument. Béranger's songs are. They are visited, even if they
are no longer read or lived in. They are the July Column of French poetry: a series of little sentimental, off-color, patriotic, anti-clerical pictures
throughout which, the one pinching the other, the shipping clerk and the
shop girl ascend toward an affected genius that is itself a theme for a song,
toward a platform from which one sees spread out a whole neighborhood
of popular history, that of July 1789, and July 1830.

XIII

THE ECONOMISTS:
SAINT-SIMON AND FOURIER

Quasi-Literature

The true generation of 1789 barely crossed the frontier of literature. It seemed destined to the most powerful explosion of life that had ever occurred in the progression of the generations of France. It was the generation of Napoleon, as once there had been a century of Louis XIV. But this generation had been given no literary shape. When it had a style, that was because it had sought it in the past, with Chénier and Chateaubriand, and a Genevan woman without a style could become the leader of the literature of her time. Genius in those days resided in a world of quasi-literature, analogous to the juridical concept of quasi-contract. The other French generations are generations of fully-paid-for literature; this was a generation of literature on credit. The note ran into the next generation, that of romanticism, which redeemed it splendidly, principal and interest.

In another place we should have hesitated at using these metaphors of commercial materialism. But now we are dealing with two contemporaries of Napoleon, of Mme. de Staël, and of Chateaubriand: Henri, Comte de Saint-Simon, born in 1760, and Charles Fourier, born in 1772. In 1789 the one was not yet thirty years old and the other was not yet twenty. It is not principally as leaders of a school, or even of religion, or because of the Saint-Simonian and Fourierist terminologies that they bequeathed to the French language that they are important to us here, but primarily as sources of revolutionary ideas, seized in the full course of the Revolution and incorporated into its being.

Henri de Saint-Simon

It is common knowledge that the Saint-Simon family claimed descent from Charlemagne. "One night during my imprisonment in the Luxembourg (1793)," Saint-Simon wrote, "Charlemagne appeared to me and told me: 'In the whole history of the world, no one family has enjoyed the honor of producing both a hero and a philosopher of the first rank. This honor, my son, was reserved to my race: your triumphs as a philosopher will be the equal of mine as a soldier and a statesman.' " And Napoleon was to write to the Pope: "Charlemagne, our august predecessor . . ." Let us bear in mind that this was an imperial generation. But one of these two Carolingianisms, Napoleon's, failed, and the other, Saint-Simon's, succeeded.

To be exact, it was not Saint-Simon the philosopher who gained the success of Charlemagne, but his philosophy, Saint-Simonism, of which his disciple, Prosper Enfantin, known as Father Enfantin, said: "The world will share out what we leave behind."

SAINT-SIMON'S FIRST IDEA

Two ideas dwelt in Saint-Simon. First, that what had begun with his generation was not a French political revolution but a world-wide economic and industrial revolution, the exploitation of the world by man. Saint-Simon was the visionary and the prophet of what, after Marx, would be called capitalism and what Saint-Simon's followers more accurately called industrialism. Just as there can be no industry without the plan of an industrialist, so there can be no industrialization without planning techniques. The late French word, *planisme,* is the word best adapted to Saint-Simon's doctrine, an orgy of plans, but of plans that were directed by an inspired vision of the world and the society of the nineteenth century and that, in contrast to those of our own time, were not the plans of a managed economy.

SAINT-SIMON'S SECOND IDEA

The second idea was based not only on plans of what was to be done but, in a static sense, on an especially needed plan that industrial society could not afford to be without, the spiritual plan. The idea of the new spiritual power necessary to humanity in the new life into which it was being thrust by the Revolution—that is Saint-Simon's real argument, handed on by him to Auguste Comte and Renan. The idea of the new power, and as a natural consequence the criticism of the past and the

present powers—of the one that was to be replaced with due acknowl-
edgment of services rendered, the power of religion fashioned thus far on
an obsolete world system; of the other, which was to be scorned and eliminated in all its forms, the power arrogated to themselves by the legalists
profiting by the Revolution as they had profited by the monarchy,
against whom Comte de Saint-Simon reiterated all the wrath of his great
cousin, the duke and peer of France. The house of Saint-Simon might be
called the general staff headquarters of anti-legalism. Industrialists detached from profit, scholars, artists, philosophers—Saint-Simon never precisely established the governing classes of the new spiritual power. He
was more adept in the idea of the social spirit than in the precise choice
of the social spirits.

Saint-Simon's publication was called *Le Producteur:* it stood as witness
to the proposition that material production could not dispense with a
spiritual direction of production. In order to establish contact between
these two hostile worlds of matter and mind, Saint-Simon wrote some
twenty disordered, heady works, sometimes in the fullness of folly, sometimes in the grandeur of genius—never, unfortunately, the genius of a
writer, except in a few pages like the famous parable, but interesting by
reason of the current that carried *Le Nouveau Christianisme* toward the
future and especially the 1814 memorandum on the *Réorganisation de la
société européenne*. To these, Saint-Simon's last remarks on his deathbed,
handed down by his disciples, add a sublime page.

The Saint-Simonians

It is more through his disciples than through his works that Saint-Simon
has survived. The *Exposition de la doctrine* (1829–1831) was a collective
labor by Rozand, Enfantin, Olinde Rodrigues, and Lazare Carnot. It is of
prime historical value, but this resolutely collectivist doctrine is no longer
that of Saint-Simon himself. And, unfortunately, the Saint-Simonians
never had any contact with letters. All that they wrote was trash, except
perhaps Michel Chevalier's *Lettres sur l'Amérique*. Sainte-Beuve was a
sympathizer for a few months: he professes to have nosed at the bait but
to have stayed out of the trap. Perhaps for lack of literary advocates, Isaac
Pereire's prophecy in *Le Globe* in 1831, "The name of Saint-Simon will
very soon resound throughout the whole world," was not fulfilled. But
the world of today cannot be explained without some reference to a latent
Saint-Simonism. It was in industry, in the Egyptian undertakings (the
Suez Canal was a Saint-Simonian idea), in political economy, in banking,
that Saint-Simonism bore its fruits. And this should be remarked as a fact

of importance to letters: Saint-Simonism was the first intellectual movement in which there was active participation by the autochthonous Jews,
whom the Revolution had just admitted into the French community. The
two Rodrigues brothers were Saint-Simon's most devoted disciples. His
following produced as well the Pereires, who always remained, and who,
in the current phrase, still are, Saint-Simonian characters. Positivism,
which originally was only a deviation, a kind of Saint-Simonism, and
which preserved the essence of it, maintained contact with the pure forms
of intelligence more rigorously than did the original. But all this can
hardly be expressed except on the religious and economic level, only
slightly on the literary.

Fourier

The literary level, apparently, was equally foreign to Fourier's genius;
he was a highly educated man of business who even had a certain dedication to the grocery trade, a trade much decried by romanticism, and
wrongly, for it demands (or demanded in those days) talents of method,
of classification, of ingenuity, of psychology, that Balzac knew how to
value. The heir to forty thousand pounds, Fourier was on his way to becoming a major grocer when he was ruined and almost guillotined by the
Revolution, which forced him (he was twenty years old in 1792) into
two years of service as a mountain cavalryman. He had always liked to
write, and, like Joseph Prudhomme, he admired nothing so much as the
well-made phrase. The genius that he had cultivated in the grocery trade
was that of the psychology of business or of the stock exchange. Observing in 1798 that an apple that cost fourteen sous in a restaurant was
being sold for half a farthing in the street, he was inspired to such a psychology and critique of mercantilism that (at least for him) Fourier's apple
came into being along with Newton's. In 1799, ordered by his employer
in Marseille to destroy a cargo of rice in order to keep the price high, he
promised himself that he would discover a system that could put an end
to the categorical imperative of profit.

That system was expounded in a certain number of works that repeated
themselves in different guises; the most complete was the *Théorie de
l'unité universelle*, previously contained in a *Traité de l'association
domestique* in 1822: a minutely detailed picture—we would call it today
chronometered or Taylorized—of a society, or, rather, of little societies,
of cells or phalansteries, in which each man would work with joy according to his skills and his desires. Every passion, according to Fourier, produces a social benefit when one knows how to make use of it. Part of the
interest of his books arises out of the ingenuity, the humor, the drollery

with which the subtle grocer stages (for he had a real feeling for puppetry and the theater) this world of human passions, idealized, plumed, wreathed, as in the *Supplément au voyage de Bougainville* or Rousseau's Swiss descriptions, both real forerunners of Fourier. Fourier's experience is the experience of the lewd, sensual Frenchman, the future drinker of *apéritifs* at the Café du Commerce, a fusion of the "little man" and the most unbridled utopian who ever lived (what is Victor Hugo's *Plein Ciel* beside the sea transmuted into lemonade by the miracle of sexual attraction, and that spontaneous birth of the third eye in the back of the head, from which the caricaturist, Cham [Amédée de Noé], drew the Fourierist tail with an eye at its tip?); and a *real* fusion, in harmony with a whole popular French romanticism of the nineteenth century that united Paul de Kock and François-Vincent Raspail. If the Saint-Simonian is often a great Jew, at once mystic and banker, the Fourierist is an "average," or, better, a "little," Frenchman. *L'Harmonie* is the sensual paradise of the "little man," of the Frenchman tending his garden or his trees. One must not overlook, in Fourier's work, that remarkable *Hiérarchie du cocuage* published long after his death, in which every man in the regiment of the *Coupe enchantée*, from colonel to lowest private, is given a certificate by the sergeant-major setting forth his rank and his duties: the whole experience that might have been acquired in the Battant section of Besançon (Fourier's birthplace as it was that of that other "little man," Pierre-Joseph Proudhon) by the corner grocer who gave honest weight, good nature, and credit, in return for pleasure. This curious lower-middle-class communism is the communism of a compatriot and contemporary of Béranger. Furthermore, Restif de la Bretonne had had the chance to prepare a popular audience for the para-literary style, the neologisms, the motley of an illiterate of genius that give Fourier's books their unique tone. When Emile Zola, in *Travail*, ran down the list of the great utopians, the designers of the future, it was Fourier at whose name he paused with the most sympathy; it was, in short, Fourier in whose favor the middle-class naturalist decided.

Say

The extra-literary, even extra-rational position held by the talents of Saint-Simon and Fourier helps us to rank the most eminent of their adversaries and their despisers, the defenders and the theoreticians of classical liberal political economy, the disciples of Adam Smith, the *laissez-faire, laissez-passer* mercantilists. The most important was Jean-Baptiste Say, who in 1803 published his *Traité d'economie politique*, which was literarily, as it was in substance, the opposite of the work of the two proph-

ets: an elegance and a clarity of exposition that have never been surpassed, a clear vision and a common sense alien to all romanticism, in
which we recognize a disciple of the idealogists, even a contemporary of
Stendhal.

PART TWO

The Generation
of 1820

THE GENERATION OF 1820

The Children of Their Time

The generation that was roughly twenty years old in 1820 reckoned its age more or less with the century's. Alfred de Musset, who was not born until 1810 but who first published at the age of nineteen and was famous at twenty, really belonged to it—indeed it was he who popularized the label, *enfants du siècle*. Also Lamartine, who was thirty in 1820 and for whom this was the year of *Les Méditations*. The breath of fresh air that excited a new literary France to life in those days lasted from Lamartine's thirtieth year to Musset's twentieth.

But these two names, and a certain Lamartine-Musset dialogue, have given rise to an ambiguity, have even occasioned a misunderstanding. The term *l'enfant du siècle* more or less symbolized the young man sick in body and soul, sick with the *mal du siècle:* Lamartine's *Le Poète mourant*, Sainte-Beuve's tubercular *Joseph Delorme*, Musset's suicidal *Rolla*, the lamentations of obscure poets who could not resign themselves to being *minores*. This fashion only brushed Lamartine, and did not even touch Hugo, or Sainte-Beuve as a critic.

Quite the contrary; here was much the most potent generation, the most saturated with life and work, that had existed in the fifteen literary generations of five centuries, the most gifted with creative force and genius. A brood of Rabelaisian giants—Balzac, Hugo, Dumas—was born in the hinge of the two centuries, the four years between 1799 and 1803. This brood of giants, with Lamartine, its precursor by a few years, and George Sand, the "mother" of these comrades, was to set the tone of the thirty years, from 1820 to 1850, that were the zenith of the great generation (as one speaks of the great century when one means the seventeenth, or the great man when one means Napoleon). Victor Hugo, undecided where to insert *Le Satyre* in *La Légende des siècles*, fixed at the last moment on a random title: *Seizième Siècle, Renaissance.* It would have been more fitting to call it "Dix-neuvième Siècle, Romantisme."

It is true that a certain part of its forces was dissipated and turned astray, as was true in the sixteenth century and in every period in which there has been an irruption of dynamism. What is important to us is the presence of this immense and remarkable energy and the succession of the most replete literary generation to the most hollow.

Fathers and Sons

The preceding generation had been hollowed, drained, by revolutions, wars, insecurity, a completely military situation that had weighed on France and Europe for a quarter of a century. It was peace that summoned the generation of 1820 to the life of the mind. This was not literally a generation of inheritors, for that quarter of a century had transmitted to it not a world all made but a world to be made and had not provided any models. The two protagonists of that preceding generation, the author of *Les Martyrs* and the author of *L'Allemagne*, while preparing a new spirit, had actually been prevented by a wise providence from writing anything that might become an express object of literary imitation. And yet the new generation indeed came into life with an inheritance, in the same way in which the farm laborer's children possessed a treasure in their fields: the heritage of energy, the energy that their fathers had expended in action and that the sons would transfer to thought. The symbol and the memory of Napoleon were to give the romantic generation a master of literary energy. The date of Napoleon's death, 1821, is the year in which the pure child of the century, born with it, came to his majority. And the dead man seized hold of the living.

A generation of war vested its energy in a generation of peace. The generation of 1820 was the last generation of the traditional monarchy; it would exactly fill the thirty years of solid, constructive, flourishing peace that coincided with the reign of the two branches of the Bourbon dynasty. The generation of security succeeded that of insecurity. The great careers in letters, that rich, powerful, and regular abundance of works that characterizes literature, that ease of production, that public breath of air, that general dynamism of a society engaged in remaking itself—all of literature was caught up in the pace of constructive rhythms.

The Enlistment of the Public

What is striking is the eager zest with which opinion, the public, threw itself into letters after the fall of the military regime. This was a phenomenon of decompression, like Thermidor.

Not that the literary public of 1820 was very large: the most noted writers were to achieve only modest sales. But it was a public of quality, alert, enthusiastic, rich in women of intelligence and taste. The success with which in 1820 it rewarded a slender book of lyric verse, Lamartine's *Méditations*, is still almost unique in literary history. The court, the *salons*, the newspapers, alike testify to this attention given to letters. It might be said that letters would take, for the generation of 1820, the place that theology and religion had held for the generation of 1661, and it was the congregations of Bourdaloue that were recalled by those of Villemain and Cousin at the Sorbonne. The sacrificial generation of the Revolution and the Empire was succeeded in letters by a generation crowned.

Security and Liberty

The generation of security, this was also the first generation with literary liberty. No generation had been more deprived of that than the generation of the Revolution and the Empire. The consequences have been demonstrated: for twenty-five years virtually the whole republic of letters lived in exile or in silent opposition; the official, approved literature never rose above the dregs. The Restoration gave the republic of letters its freedoms again. In large part that republic was one of opposition—political opposition, religious opposition, social opposition, nonconformity of every kind, balanced, however, by conformities as vigorous and as paradoxical. The ways of literary liberty were half foreign to the old monarchy, wholly so to the Revolution and the Empire. In the course of time they grew blunted and vulgarized by habit, and only recently they had to vanish from a great part of Europe in order to make us aware of their presence. But between 1825 and 1848 that comparison that we make in space was made in time, and liberty was still measured enough, sometimes restrained enough, to make it necessary to dedicate a certain art to making use of it, a certain suppleness to getting round its obstacles. Besides, it is almost a law in literature that the first generation that enjoys a benefit gets the better part of it and exhausts its original substance: first come, best served.

The Technical Revolution

Perhaps nowhere better than in this generation's privileged position with respect to techniques can one find a better illustration of that adage.

Two kinds of techniques are important to literature: those that are properly literary, and the material techniques that apply to the distribution and expansion of literature.

The revolution in literary techniques between 1820 and 1840 can be compared only to that of the sixteenth century. Although Victor Hugo's friends presented him with a magnificent copy of Ronsard inscribed: "To the greatest inventor of rhythms that French poetry has had since Ronsard," it is less the invention of new techniques than an exceptional and unmatched way of employing old techniques (to which there was not much to add) that constituted the creative superiority of romantic lyric poetry. As far as the novel is concerned, in contrast, this generation created its techniques entirely, with Balzac, Dumas, George Sand, Prosper Mérimée, to such a degree that it was to be by means of the lack or the rejection of techniques and construction, not by an impossible perfection of them, that the novel was to try later to change or to progress. While this generation may not have achieved full success in the theater, at least it did so in theatrical construction, in which Eugène Scribe, with Corneille, is the greatest French technician. The techniques of prose matched those of poetry in creative originality, and Chateaubriand, always a great, tractable, and skillful disciple, was not too proud to go to the prose school of the writers of 1830 in order to carry that of his *Mémoires d'outre-tombe* to its point of perfection. When the generation of the Parnassians, of the younger Dumas and Flaubert, raised the flag of technique, technique was to be precisely the area in which it would seem most like a generation of imitators.

The material techniques were those of the bookshop, the press, and the periodical. In another part of this book it will be seen how important for them were the dates of 1815, 1830–1834, how literature has been oriented and altered by the sudden augmentation of these means of distribution. The equivalent of this revolution in material techniques is to be found only in the history of two other literary generations: that of 1515, the first that was substantially touched and fashioned by the invention of printing, and that of 1914, which was destined to be marked by the cinema. Obviously not everything in this technical revolution constituted a net gain for literature, and in *Illusions perdues* Balzac has drawn a terrible, though exaggerated, picture of the ravages made by the newspapers even among the young authors of the Restoration.

The Mystique of the Revolution

The word that is most often spoken and written in the literature of this epoch is "revolution." Not that this generation was revolutionary as a whole, or even for the greater part. One can be at once counterrevolutionary and revolutionary. One can be a revolutionary in literature and a conservative in politics, or the reverse. But, whether it be imputed to God or the devil, the idea of revolution is to be seen at the end of every avenue of thought.

Revolution as an idea was thought about and spoken about all the more by those who had not personally known the French Revolution, who knew it only through their parents, who had thus already been separated from their parents by a gap wider than any created in any previous period. A contemporary made the observation that, during the few months that preceded the revolution of 1830, *Le Globe* and *Le National*, newspapers of and for young men who had not seen the Revolution of 1789, adopted in their opposition to the Prince de Polignac an anti-dynastic position that *Le Journal des débats*, owned by the Bertins, who had been among the twenty-year-olds of 1789, found itself stopped from adopting by its owners' experiences in their youth, which forbade them "to plunge with a kind of irresponsible familiarity into these terrible questions that affect the very existence of peoples and of kings." It was this familiarity that would lead the generation of the children of their time to the revolution of 1848, that would make them play at the French Revolution before 1848, as before 1830 they played at the English revolution, still more remote in time.

This generation's familiarity with the idea of political revolution is less important to us here than its familiarity with the ideas of literary revolution. Poetry, the theater, the novel, philosophy, history embarked on their courses between 1820 and 1830 with a more or less revolutionary program, breaking away from some tradition. The analogy between romanticism in literature and revolution in politics is a commonplace of the time, and the two movements, the two ruptures, determined analogous severances in the French future.

The Breach in the Center

The breath of fresh air from politics to literature is indeed a unique characteristic of this whole generation. Twice, in 1830 and in 1840, it made itself felt to the point of compromising and dethroning literature.

From a certain point of view the monarchy of 1830 was the monarchy of the professors. Not of the professors at their lecterns but of the professors away from their lecterns. It was from their university chairs that the three orators of the Sorbonne—Guizot, Villemain, Cousin—first launched themselves toward the speakers' platform and high office. Thus the place was open for a Sainte-Beuve, a simple journalist, and yet no one has deplored more than he "the sudden, massive withdrawal of all of the most distinguished and the most solid part of the already matured generations, the leaders of the critical school, who have abandoned literature for politics and business. The services that these enlightened men have rendered in politics can be admitted, but they are indisputably less than those that they would have rendered to society by keeping their posts in the sentry box of ideas. . . . Their withdrawal, to put it plainly, has made a *breach in the center*."

The poets, happily, had remained. From 1830 to 1840, the output of lyric and epic poetry surpassed in quality and importance, in those ten years, that of the preceding two and a half centuries of French literature. Already, however, Lamartine in the Chamber of Deputies and Victor Hugo in his social poetry were tracing for themselves a horizon beyond the book and the lyre. But, beginning in 1840, the breach in the center appeared in poetry, in its turn, in everyone's opinion, as it had ten years earlier, in Sainte-Beuve's opinion, in criticism: Lamartine had published his last book of verse, Hugo his last before going into exile. In 1843 he was to leave the theater, and, though he wrote the novel of *Les Misères*, he would keep it in his desk. The facts were that Lamartine was part of the "grand opposition," that Hugo was a peer of France like Cousin and Villemain, and like the Chateaubriand of the Restoration. The breach in the center, resulting from the race for the platform and power, was moreover accompanied by a yielding on the flanks. Vigny stopped publishing; soon Musset virtually ceased to write verse.

The literature of ideas in 1830, and poetry after 1840, then, lost those whom it had been the custom to regard as their leading figures. But the case was not the same with the novel. Novelists had never been so productive, and especially the outstanding ones, Balzac, George Sand, and Dumas. With Eugène Sue the revolution of the serial novel broke out. What Sainte-Beuve called the sentry box of ideas fell partly into the hands of these novelists, for it was the great period of the philosophical, ideological, and social novel; partly into the hands of the press lords, Emile de Girardin and Dr. Véron; partly into the hands of the social theorists. The breach in the center, the emigration of the elite into politics called into their place a light cavalry of ideas, or a cavalry of slight ideas, that from 1840 to 1848 never left off producing a literature which was interesting but which, compared to that of the preceding decade, lacks what is called class. Never, perhaps, had serious criticism spoken more of decadence. It had even—and this is one of its net gains—deeply analyzed the idea of decadence. The articles that Sainte-Beuve was writing then for *La Revue des deux mondes* came back to it incessantly. This was the period in which Nisard wrote his *Histoire de la littérature française*. In poetry, the fragile classical revival of 1843 should be taken as much, if not more, for the awareness of that sickness or that deficiency as for a positive reality.

The Three Decades

So the generation of the children of the century passed through three distinctly separable decades. From 1820 to 1830 it tested, defined, defended its ideas by arms and on the appropriate field of the intelligence and letters: books, newspapers, universities. From 1830 to 1840 it victoriously exploited the revolution—or, rather, the two revolutions—that it had made: the liberal political revolution, the romantic literary revolution; the professors won power, poetry won the theater, the novel won the public. From 1840 to 1850 the whole literary order, its sights fixed on temporal and spiritual power, kept pace with the professors, the critics, and the regents turned rulers. Poetry was on the ebb, ideas were in turmoil, ambitions were on the rise. Sainte-Beuve, who after 1830 deplored the insolvency of hypothecated criticism and intelligence, had warned as early as 1838 of the danger of industrial literature, at once the writer's triumph and his doom. Not only industrial literature but political literature, and writers' politics, and there went the Revolution. The generation of 1820 had entered letters with *Les Méditations* behind Lamartine. Thirty years later—that is, at the climacteric date in the life of generations—the same Lamartine concluded his revolution, the active life of the children of the century, the reign of the twenty-year-olds of 1820, with a political revolution.

Bilateralism

Through these three decades one can note the opposition between the two parts of this generation, the birth of a literary bilateralism comparable to that bilateralism of left and right that was born with the Restoration: both still control us today.

What was the generation of 1789, the Napoleon-Staël-Chateaubriand generation, if not that of the Revolution? The generation of 1820, literary, political, civil, social, economic, did not have to digest the Empire: the fallen Empire was only an adventure, a dazzling sport of history that would not recur, that no one except retired officers and malcontents even dreamed of bringing back. This generation had to digest another revolution, the revolution among the classes and the leaders, the revolution in property, the revolution in individuals, the revolution in minds. Was not Balzac's fiction the official transcription, the physiological description of that digestive process? And the career of Lamartine? And the life of Victor Hugo?

It was the generation of 1789 that had bequeathed this problem, this tragedy of the Revolution, to the literary nineteenth century. Just as the generation of 1636, that of Corneille, had imposed the point of view of the king, of thought centered, if not by, then at least on, the king, on the center of French civilization for a hundred and fifty years, similarly the generation of 1789 set up the fact of the Revolution on the high roads of literature like a sphinx on the road to Thebes. Bonaparte, Chateaubriand, Mme. de Staël had lived the Revolution, lived in the Revolution, having been borne and governed by it as by a force of nature. Only one of them was an artist, possessed the keys to the locks: Chateaubriand. He and he alone personified literature, the great literary essence. It was literature that had sailed to America with him in 1791, on the theme of "La Fayette and I," that had returned from exile in 1800 with "the Revolution and I" in Le Génie and L'Essai, and that, from the day in 1811 when he would start his memoirs, would adjust his past life to the theme of "Bonaparte and I." Already, then, the principle of revolution was incorporated into letters as the principle of authority had been after 1635. But in the end, with Chateaubriand and Mme. de Staël, that generation, even as it had lived the Revolution from within, had considered it and measured it from without. It had fallen in the Revolution. It was not born in it. The next generation of writers would be the first born during or after the Revolution. The literary revolution, having followed the political revolution by a generation, was to take that political revolution as a kind of Old Testament that would symbolize the revolution of the spirit, the revolution of letters, the revolution of taste.

It was in 1830 that this profound sentiment of a union between the literary revolution and the political revolution came to the foreground. Obviously the idea of this parallelism was old. In 1800 it had filled Mme. de Staël's Littérature; she found herself in agreement with Bonald in viewing in literature "the expression of society." But, under the Restoration, romanticism, revolutionary in its form, was conservative in the ideas of its poets, in their family traditions, the hospitality of the salons, the good will of the authorities, the prestige of M. de Chateaubriand, who kept it, as they say, on the right. On the other hand, the liberals and what Mme. Delphine de Girardin called the Touquet youngsters (from the name of the bookseller who launched the popular editions of Voltaire) were still loyal to the form and the ideas of their eighteenth-century masters, to the spirit of the ideologists; 1830 was to put an end to these surface contradictions and to fuse in the metal of Revolution with a capital "R" those three revolutions that were so diverse in their origins and their people: the French Revolution, the July Revolution, the Romantic Revolution.

Lamartine's ode on revolutions would put the great decorative stamp on this turning point. Victor Hugo's poetry would live by it. It is worth noting that on Sainte-Beuve's return from Lausanne he would choose this language and these metaphors of the Revolution to express his break with the enemy, the Mountain,* and to deliver his programmatic speech on classical moderatism. This fashion of revolutionary reference, which corresponded to a fashion of considering and experiencing literature, was to end somewhat later with the life of Chateaubriand (1848), who, strangely, would establish its boundary. Its end would also coincide somewhat with the end of literary romanticism, revolutionary after 1843, and later and above all with the end of the "acted out" political revolution, whose first act was *L'Histoire des Girondins*, whose second act was the February Revolution, whose third act was Lamartine's three months in power, whose fourth act was the presidency of the Prince and whose catastrophic fifth act was the *coup d'état*. The literary mythology of the Revolution disappeared in 1851. Therefore, when Victor Hugo wrote, on the Isle of Jersey in 1854, *La Réponse à un acte d'accusation* and *Quelques mots à un autre* in which this mythology is extracted and bottled in a kind of Hindu creation, he ingeniously dated them back twenty years to 1834 in Paris, to the height of the romantic battle, of which in effect they stand as the synthesis.

Sainte-Beuve was to endure the melancholy of his victory. The generation of the children of the century came to its sunken road of Ohain in the median year of the century, 1850. They had marched over the bodies of their comrades and the weakened, disorganized survivors. In the bilateral generation of 1820, one of the parties was the conquered party, the romantic party; but, though it might be vanquished, it was not destroyed. The eighteenth-century party, also wounded, held out better, even provided the next generation with part of its armor. Only perspective, the comparison between the generations that preceded it and those that have followed it, has since made it possible to classify, to judge, and to measure this generation of the children of their time. It was to be worthy to be called the great generation, as one speaks of the great century.

* The name given to the extremist group in the Convention, which occupied the highest seats.—Translator.

ROMANTICISM

Definition

The adjectives "classical" and "romantic" led an obscure, intermittent life
in the language until the beginning of the nineteenth century. Classical,
which was already being used in the sixteenth century, had two meanings:
one old, corresponding to the Latin meaning of *classicus*—that is, applied
to an author, a writer of the first class, or, as we would say, "of class," the
great listed vintage of literature—and the other rather pejorative—an author suitable for classes in secondary schools. It was in the first meaning
that La Harpe spoke of "the classical authors," and in the second that
Beaumarchais, in the *Essai* that serves as a preface to his drama *Eugénie*,
made it a synonym for pedantic. Romantic is later. An obscure usage had
been found for it as early as 1675: in the sense of "fabulous," "fictional,"
with an inflection that was then pejorative, like that of "fantastic." It did
not come into general usage until the third quarter of the eighteenth century, Rousseau having applied it to the Lake of Bienne (and indeed, for
him and Lamartine, lakes were to be the cradles of romantic poetry). It
was introduced into the *Dictionnaire de l'Académie* in 1798, with this
definition: "It is generally used of places and scenes that recall to the
imagination the descriptions of poems and novels." In a few years it came,
inversely, to designate the poems, the novels, the works of art that summon up in the imagination lonely landscapes, privileged places, the most
intimate presences of nature. In addition, as early as 1793, *La Chronique
de Paris* said: "The music of Méhul is romantic." Even more romantic,
obviously, was the autochthonous music of the mountains in 1800 for
Sénancour, who entitled a section of *Obermann: de l'expression romantique et du ranz des vaches.*
    But the two adjectives did not attain important literary existence until
the day when they became enemies. They acquired position by opposition. This opposition was a "message" from Germany, from the German

awakening. In 1814 Adolphe de Custine wrote to his mother from Germany: "The designations 'romantic' and 'classic,' which the Germans created several years ago, are used to identify two parties into which the human race will very soon be divided like the Guelphs and the Ghibellines long ago."

Resistance and Movement

In the first third of the nineteenth century the definitions of the romantic were naturally more numerous and more complete than those of the classic. *Le Globe*, an excellent example of the intelligence of that time, offered a dozen such definitions in succession from its editors. The simplest, the most moderate, the most accurate, and the supplest is probably that developed by Stendhal when he saw in contemporary romanticism the literary right and duty of a generation to express a new sensibility in a new form of art and in the classic a body of instruction that sought to impose art forms dictated by the sensibility of former generations on the sensibility of the present. Politics was to give these two tendencies a name in 1830, when it would oppose the party of resistance to the party of movement. Romanticism too was a party of movement. There is a romantic dynamism, but there is not a classic dynamism. Classical art, in the theater and in poetry—that is, in the art forms that depend on the sensibility of an epoch—preserves, reproduces, no longer creates, or creates with an eye-dropper and a bad conscience. It occupies inherited positions. It is a defender. It relies, like Jean Lapin, on custom and usage. The romantic is a demander; it intends to dislodge the classic and it does dislodge it. Primarily through the effect of a natural force, because romanticism is youth, and then because it is allied with the three natural enemies of the classic, of the French classic, of the classic of "common forms," of the classic of respectable opinion. These enemies are, first, the foreign (the literatures of north and south staffed and assisted romanticism, as the literatures of Rome and the sixteenth century staffed the classic); second, the solitary (isolation is the primary attitude of the romantic poet, as *L'Isolement* is the first poem in *Les Méditations*); third, the popular (its relations with the popular theater and poetry, its appeal to the people as a source and an audience, and the popular form of the novel gave romanticism its potentials for growth).

The Inventory of Romanticism

Historically and in the literary panorama of the century, the romantic movement, the romanticism of movement, coupled, in addition, with a literature of resistance, as Custine predicted, left in the life of the mind and of letters durable elements that are still in being. What are they?

THE PARTIES

At the very outset romanticism introduced a second dimension into our literary life. It accustomed us to think of the literary life in the form of a conflict, a contrast between two worlds that were formerly the classic and the romantic and that were able to change their names without changing their functions or their directions. More precisely, it created parties.

The republic of letters assumed an appearance analogous to that of the Republic itself—that is, the state, the life of politics. In general, since the Restoration, there has existed in our cities and villages a division into political parties, rival clans, that was unknown in France before 1789. One was white, or red, or blue. One was of the right or the left. In 1830 one belonged to the party of resistance or the party of movement. In short, parties were formed. Ideas that had not circulated previously—that of revolution, that of the Restoration—became habitual ways of thinking of political life. And it was the same in literary life. The struggle between the classic and the romantic took on the same character. Today there are antagonisms, differences, opposing camps, hostile essences where none existed in the past. A certain common taste, formed by the classic disciplines, has disappeared. A common romantic taste has never taken its place. The literary world has gained in diversity. There is no longer simply a public, there are publics. This diversity of tastes that prevails today, this distinctness, this liveliness of literary parties—all owe their origin to romanticism.

Having accustomed us to a contemporary pluralism of ideas and esthetic tendencies, it has accustomed us to an analogous pluralism in space and time.

PLURALISM

In space, we cannot say that romanticism has brought us to know foreign literatures, given the facts that, first of all, they are still known rather as an exception, and, second, in the seventeenth and eighteenth centuries the influence of Italian, Spanish, English literature was at least as strong as the influence of German or Russian literature could be in the days of romanticism or afterward. But, rightly or wrongly, romanticism has accustomed us to put these foreign literatures on a footing of equality not only with our own but with the ancient literatures, which classicism viewed as matchless models. This is what has led the twentieth century to speak of modern humanities and so to admit, after the educational reforms of 1902, that the foreign literatures of modern Europe have a value equal to that of the ancient literatures in the formation of the mind and of taste. Now this is a heritage of romanticism—that is, of the first French literary generation that put Shakespeare above everything.

In time, in the revelation and the exploration of time, the influence of romanticism has been no less strong. The sense of history, the revelation of the past as a third dimension have entered our ways of thinking and writing. Here we are dealing not only with the more or less successful effort by which the historical novel, the historical drama, Alexandre Dumas or Victor Hugo, have, through a picturesque manner, accustomed the public to be interested in the things of the past. We put no great value on that side of romanticism. It is much more a matter of the manner in which, over the last hundred years, we have contracted a certain habit of thinking historically, of viewing matters of literature, art, politics, science, philosophy in their consecutiveness and, as the Germans say, in their becoming. It has been accepted more and more, with more or less excess or moderation, that the great ideas, the great themes of art and politics, the programs of schools, the platforms of parties have value only for a time, for one or two generations, that they are very soon cast aside, that they become stumbling blocks to progress and delay it after they have initiated it. Lamartine's lines—

> *Marchez, l'humanité ne vit pas d'une idée,*
> *Elle éteint chaque soir celle qui l'a guidé,*
> *Elle en allume une autre à l'immortel flambeau*

> (March on, man does not live by one idea,
> Each night he quenches what led him that day,
> And lights another at the deathless torch)

—express that impulsion of the romantic spirit. Romanticism put movement into the world of the mind at the very moment when the discovery of new means of transport was tracing the paths of movement on our physical world.

AUTHORS AND PUBLIC

Romanticism profoundly changed the relations between the author and the reader. Much more is demanded of a book today than was demanded of it in the classic epoch: namely, direct communication by the reader with the personality of the author. We know what the mail of a fashionable author, a well-known poet, contains nowadays: the confidences of readers and admirers of both sexes, the moral or emotional counsel that is asked of him, the long-distance friendships, the contacts between two sensitivities. None of this was to be found in classic literature before Rousseau. It was *La Nouvelle Héloïse* that first stirred that current of air round a great popular writer. The demand is complemented by an abundant offer: this familiarity flatters the authors, the poets, the novelists, and they gladly collaborate in it. A Lamartine, a Hugo, a Balzac were the objects of love and hate for the men and women who read them, the objects of exclusive and extreme preferences, which until then had seemed to belong rather to the domain of personal relations than to that of literature.

GENERATIONS

This results in part from the fact that in the world of reading the young have played a part, gained an independence, exerted increasing pressure. Romanticism was a revolution made by the young. Today we speak readily of the young, of the place and the function of the young, of the right and the duty of the young in matters of the renewal of literary values. But that gap between the rising generation and the established generation, between yesterday's taste and tomorrow's, was virtually nonexistent in classical literature. It was only rarely to be seen emerging in the time of what is called the generation of 1661. Since romanticism it has been strongly bound to the rhythm of literary life. The young have their own authors, often unintelligible to the preceding generation, just as, the missionaries tell us, the languages of the American Indians developed so rapidly that the old could no longer understand what the young were saying.

THE NOVEL

Let us next consider the fact that in romanticism there is the novel, that the advent of romanticism coincided with the remarkable predominance of a form that sometimes seemed to absorb the others. Romanticism was a literary revolution less because of lyricism and the theater than because of the novel. There is not one great romantic writer or poet who did not feel obliged to sacrifice to the new divinity, who did not seek through it a great public success. Vigny, Hugo, Lamartine, Musset wrote novels without having any deep vocation for the form and because the very drive of the romantic era demanded it. For romanticism, success was complete, the road was free, only in two literary forms, lyric poetry and the novel. The public of the romantics, furthermore, became accustomed to demanding of the novel the same kind of emotion and clues that it sought in lyric poetry—that is, to understand it and feel it as a personal confession of the author: such was the case of the *Confession d'un enfant du siècle*, of

Volupté, of *Stella*, of *Raphaël*. This confession-novel of romanticism goes back to Rousseau, and we know what an abundant posterity it has today.

PERSONAL LITERATURE

In sum, it is a platitude to recognize in romanticism, born of Rousseau, the reign of personal literature. Its drawbacks could easily be pointed out. But we see them largely compensated for every day by the ceaseless renewal that it engenders. Today we accept the fact that the singular individuality of every man, of every woman, can become an element of literary value and interest. The confession of an unusual character, the expression of a sincere personality are even recognized as the essential value of literature. When, in contrast, a writer was required above all to conform to a model, to subject himself to the laws of a form, he soon arrived at the stage at which he could only duplicate what the earlier arrivals had discovered and done. From this point of view it is instructive to compare the two forms that are often reproached for their dominating character: the tragedy of the eighteenth century and the novel of the nineteenth.

Every beginner, it is often said, writes his novel today as in the eighteenth century he wrote his tragedy. But there is this difference, that the tragic mold, the tragic ideal, the personalities of Corneille and Racine crushed the author, reduced him to the rank of a copyist. In contrast, the much more supple novel form makes it possible for him to produce authentically a genuine and living character. In the hundred years during which the novel has developed among us, with an elemental potency and continuity, we can see in it nothing of the rapid impoverishment and the empty formalism that characterized the tragedy of the eighteenth century.

These are some of the traces that romanticism has left on our literary life today. It was the great modern literary revolution. There has been much talk of reactions against romanticism. This name has been given to such movements as that of the Parnassians, realism, naturalism, symbolism, neoclassicism. But it would not be difficult to show that these are much more decompositions or transformations of romanticism. Will some final reaction be the real one? In that case there would be reason to fear that in destroying romanticism it might destroy literature itself, that in getting rid of the disease it might get rid of the patient as well.

III

LAMARTINE

Lamartine did not publish *Les Méditations poétiques* until he was thirty years old. But their very weight and quality are composed of an authentic, slow, regular continuity of the seasons that lie behind them. Or, better, of two continuities that meet and harmonize.

The Poetic Tradition

The first is the continuity of a poetry. Lamartine began with the poetry of the eighteenth century, and he never wholly abandoned it. His ears would always echo with the verse of Voltaire and Parny. His own poetry would fall back into that form at those times when he was merely facile. Lamartine's elegy was a continuation of the plaintive elegy in long mourning garments, and there is a Parny-Lamartine connection that matches an Eléonore-Elvire connection. Thus the readers of 1820 were still in a family and a climate that they knew. And yet, in the face of *Les Méditations*, these overtures no longer count. A long-drawn-out poetic chrysalis became a winged poetry. That very thing that the genius of the Restoration aroused in society, that flower of endowed youth, that first poetry of the tradition that the July sun would vulgarize as it dried it out, was set down, idealized into the pure state by *Les Méditations*.

The Personal Tradition

The other continuity was that of a poet, of a poet in his domain—that is, in the world of continuity. Schools, longings—and, too, exalted sentiments, principles, a whole "what a young man should be" for the ladies—

and a great love, which, at the appointed time, worked this soil and sowed in it the supernatural teeth of the dragon, caused the miraculous harvest to rise out of the hereditary furrow. *Les Méditations* truly brought to French poetry a discovery of love that resembled the discovery revealed to a young man and a young girl, for the only beautiful verses of love lyrics, those of Ronsard or François de Maynard, which were three centuries old, had been forgotten.

Les Méditations

Has there existed since a protracted continuity that exactly corresponds to that continuity of 1820? Can *Les Méditations* still be for us what they were for their contemporaries? Let us point out first of all that *Méditations* must be understood to mean, not the arbitrarily confused collection, padded with mediocrities and desk-drawer fragments, that Lamartine later provided for the booksellers and that is always reprinted in its final form, but the twenty-four poems of the original volume. In a copy of *Les Méditations* into which he had inserted notes on cards that could be read at the auction of his effects, Paul Souday provided comments and evaluations on these twenty-four poems. Half of them died on the guillotine of one peremptory word: "Enough!" The super-critic's verdict coincides here with the median reaction of the Parisian of today. But median taste is not quite taste.

Let us acknowledge first that, of the twenty-four poems, there are only four that still bring to life for us, in intact purity, that note of pure poetry, that sound, as Lamartine himself wrote in a letter, "as pure as art, as sad as death, as soft as velvet," that connects the Lamartinian meaning of *Méditations* to a musical meaning (as the word is used in the program notes at concerts), and that, as soon as it is spoken, is evoked in everyone's memory by the famous title: these are *L'Isolement, Le Vallon, Le Lac de B . . .* (which later became simply *Le Lac*), and *L'Automne*, four themes in stanzas for love and loneliness. It is the fine point beneath which a less pure poetry has body and harmony. Lamartine, who as a judge of his own poetry was usually prejudiced against himself, always distinguished between the exquisite quality and the necessary quantity in his work. He always regarded true poetry, "poetry itself," as a precarious state of grace that it would be rash to consolidate into a habit.

From the opposite point of view, let us discard the insignificant pieces on which one is tempted to imprint Souday's brutal stamp—*Le Soir, Le Souvenir, La Gloire, La Prière, L'Invocation, Le Golfe de Baïa, Les Chants lyriques de Saül, L'Hymne au soleil*. This still leaves a dozen important poems that might be called the average *Méditations*, which are still far superior to any poetry published since 1700, which transport us into unquestionably the best atmosphere of 1820, and which were the major factors in Lamartine's success.

These are religious discourses, and precisely those religious discourses that had been waited for, those of a *Génie du christianisme* in the language of beautiful verse. On the one hand, the Voltairean form of the epistle and the discourse in verse; on the other, the sentimental and spiritual poetry of *Le Génie*—both brought together into a transfiguring fusion, the poetry of a restoration, the restoration of a poetry, in the dual historical dawn of the Restoration and of romanticism. Without hope, Heraclitus said, you will not encounter the unhoped for. The unexpected poetry of *Les Méditations*, without effort and in a single movement, put the seal to a great hope.

The Byron of the Salons

There was Voltaire, there was Chateaubriand, and, where their two currents met, there was, so to speak, Lyon in the form of Lamartine. But in 1820 another name soared to the zenith of poetry. There was a "poet's passage" in France: this poet was Byron. A few months had been enough to make his poetry the sole topic of everyone's talk. In 1818 his complete works had been published in Paris in English; in 1819 and 1820 they were translated. Four articles in the *Débats* in September and October 1818 had served as articles of initiation. One of the most intelligent and kindest of the children of the century, Charles de Rémusat, found the phrase for him: "He is the Bonaparte of poetry." And indeed the *salons* talked of the young poet as twenty years earlier they had talked of the young Bonaparte. The same thrill ran through the young. It was Mme. de Rémusat, the author of *Mémoires sur Napoléon*, who wrote to her son, Charles: "I have seen Lord Byron; he fascinates me. I wish I were young, beautiful and unattached; I think I would go and find that man so that I could try to bring him back to happiness and truth." And there we have the theme of the second of *Les Méditations*, *L'Epître à Lord Byron*, and also the theme of *Eloa*, two poems that the young Lamartine and the young Vigny (they had both married Englishwomen) had only to pluck like ripe fruit in the *salons* of the Restoration. To Hugo, Byron was always remarkably alien. But *Les Méditations* of 1820 can no more be understood without the Byron of 1820 than the romantic theater without Shakespeare.

The voice of the time, the voice of the women, the voice of the *salons* said: "We need a *Génie du christianisme* in poetry." Those voices said too: "If only Byron were a Christian! Then we should have a Christian

Byron." The arrangement of *Les Méditations* was very painstakingly planned: it was not by accident that *L'Homme*—that is, the epistle to Lord Byron—immediately followed *L'Isolement*, with its sweeping solitary view of the horizon. In *L'Homme* Lamartine imagined that repentant, Christian, French Byron that the *salons* demanded. It is no secret that it amused the real Byron.

Quite as aptly as the later *Harmonies, Les Méditations poétiques* could have included *et religieuses* in its title. It went to a religious public, and it contained all the religious turns of Lamartine's lyrics and epics. The theme of the fallen angel animated the whole poem *A Byron*. In the great treatises of *L'Immortalité, La Foi, La Prière, Le Temple, Dieu,* Lamartine (who had long since lost any positive faith) seemed to be writing for an audience as much as for himself, and no one will be astonished to find that *Poésie sacrée*, a dithyramb to M. Eugène Genoude that is the last of *Les Méditations*, is all formality, a chore. The true, alive religious tone of *Les Méditations* is nowhere better struck than in the fine poem, *Semaine sainte*, in which there is nothing of the ritual Christian emotion of a Holy Week, but rather an exquisite and very faithful picture of those retreats to which Edouard de Rohan, the future cardinal, invited the young conservatives of his generation in his chateau of La Roche-Guyon, where the exquisite chapel in the grotto seemed the perfectly designed oratory for *Le Génie du christianisme* and the ladies devoted to M. de Chateaubriand.

La Mort de Socrate

It might be said that with *La Mort de Socrate* Lamartine had set up in the philosopher's prison a chapel like that of La Roche-Guyon, or wound the swaddling of the Jesuit style around an Italian tenor Socrates. Let us view it as the first example of those poems in groups of lines set off by suspension points, in which Lamartine imitated (as the preface attributed to his publisher says) the clipped lyric tale of Byron. *La Mort de Socrate* is a very strange poem, first of all in that it shows us to the full the extent to which Lamartine, whom Jules Lemaître called a great Hindu, was alien to Greek art; then because, inspired by the translation of the *Phaido* that Cousin had just made, it joined that spiritual movement that excited Restoration society; and finally because its oratorical vigor is often magnificent, because these waves of blue shadow, of incense and music, this myth of Psyche, this prophecy of Socrates, though they may seem to us quite foreign to Greece, transpose into poetry the art of Pierre Prudhon, a man of Cluny like Lamartine's ancestors. And why does Lamartine's young Phédon remind us of Gian Lorenzo Bernini's Saint Theresa? Perhaps because, from 1820 on, Lamartine spent most of his time in Italy. A forceful, rich, harmonious and mellow Italianism was to run through his lyrics until 1830.

Les Nouvelles Méditations

It is manifest first in *Les Nouvelles Méditations*, which appeared at the same time as *La Mort de Socrate*. Obviously less original than their predecessors, they were more rich. The poet had gained and grown. *Le Lac* of *Les Nouvelles Méditations* was the bay of Naples: *Ischia*, the hazy softness of a Mediterranean evening, some hints of mandolin and water ice, but also the divine strophe and pure music. *Le Poète mourant* soars high above its old-fashioned, tearful title. *Bonaparte* is the first of those great solid odes whose every strophe, like a victory, marches with the ring of bronze sandals and that would constitute the finest chorus of Lamartine's lyricism after 1830. But *Les Etoiles* was already a *Harmonie*, a harmony of night. This nocturne of Lamartine's has the softness of the Milky Way above land and water, it is a vision taking place in a tender Elysian dew, the feeling of the cosmic dust in which we float, of the living space through which the planet whirls. As for *Les Préludes*, it is a shower of sparks, a triumph of pure virtuosity. Here the muse is naked under the Tuscan sun, in all the proud glow of her beauty: "a sonata in poetry," Lamartine called it; written in Florence, of course. The poet sings for the sake of singing. An inexhaustible nature at his side provides him with themes and pictures. He crystallizes one of those hours of well-being, of opulence, when life fills the poet to overflowing and makes him seethe with the intoxication of giving. It is not so much the sound of his lyre, it is the lyre itself that is offered to us to be touched and caressed. The opposite extreme is the masterpiece of *Les Nouvelles Méditations*— *Le Crucifix*. Much more vaguely religious than precisely Christian, Lamartine nevertheless reached the high point of Christian poetry here, he reached it before the Cross and by means of the Cross. This goes very far beyond *L'Immortalité* and *La Mort de Socrate*. The crucifix that is passed from one dying man to the next, handed down from Christ to humanity, the crucifix of Elvire's death, the future crucifix of the poet's own death, the fusion of heart with heart that is the life of the spirit as the fusion of seed with seed is the life of the body—*Le Crucifix* rises in a perfection of pure music; made of nothing, it encompasses everything.

Le Dernier Chant du pélérinage d'Harold

Le Crucifix, a Christian counterpart to *Le Lac,* is an evocation of the
original *Méditations.* But the Italian climate of Lamartine's poetry, which
luxuriates through *Les Préludes,* includes in general a strength, a vitality,
a thirst for active life in which there naturally continued to be a place
for that Byronian destiny that haunted Lamartine (one of his last works,
in his old age, was a *Vie de Byron*) and that this poet of the same breed
always envisaged as remotely possible for himself. On vacation at Saint-
Point, before he went back to Tuscany, he wrote *Le Dernier Chant du
pélérinage d'Harold,* a tribute to Bryon from a candidate to succeed him
in art and history. *Le Chant du sacre* (the anointing of Charles X at
Reims in 1826), which is curious in itself, Lamartine was later to call his
Fontenoy poem. *Le Dernier Chant* was in a way to be his *Henriade,*
eloquent and artificial. But these poems assume a peculiar worth as direction signs along his road: *Le Dernier Chant* already revealed his idea of
a European career as a poet-prophet and a commanding muse, and *Le
Chant du sacre* made an enemy of the future Louis-Philippe, whose family he insulted in this official poem with a frivolity as reckless as that with
which, in *Le Dernier Chant,* he insulted the Italy whose king he portrayed. After the irritations with which they had been plagued by the
Vicomte de Chateaubriand, his poetic rival boded no good to the Bourbons of either branch.

Les Harmonies

Lamartine's great book of those years, *Les Harmonies poétiques et
religieuses* (1830) was at the same time the peak of his Italian inspiration
and of the religious poetry peculiar to the Restoration.

Lamartine admitted in a letter to Virieu that of the fifty poems there
were only fifteen worth reading. But here even the padding helps to give
us the feeling of the aura of poetry, the diffuse and divine presence to
which he alluded when he said of *Les Harmonies:* "I wrote some of them
in verse, some in prose; thousands of others I heard only in my heart."
Those that were written in the four books of 1829 are islands, islands in
an Italian abundance and liquidity and light. *L'Invocation* at the beginning, written at Santa Croce, stamps this seal of an Italian church on the
whole volume. *L'Hymne de la nuit, L'Hymne du matin* seem Guido
Reni's *Night,* Francesco Albani's *Dawn.* With *La Hymne du soir dans
les temples,* dedicated to the Princess Borghese, the poet takes the key-
board of a vast organ and makes the vaults ring with a song that is rich
and empty. Not the Gothic vaults: "The (Gothic)) cathedral," the com-

mentary on the poem was to say later, "is nothing but a vast sepulcher, all within it is the tomb, there are only sobs, there is no song. The sonorous vaults of the Italian churches sing in themselves, they are the temples of the Resurrection." *Le Paysage dans le Golfe de Gênes, L'Infini dans les cieux, Désir, Le Premier Regret* display the flow and the light of nature in Italy with an exalted voluptuousness or a melodious melancholy. But the islands are indeed those fifteen poems whose number Lamartine established and that we can find without trouble.

La Bénédiction de Dieu dans la solitude, written at Saint-Point, is perhaps the fullest, the most exuberant of the poetry of Lamartine, of the landowner, the clan chief, and the poet, revealing his depths of salubrity and tradition: thick human roots under a cover of leaves that vibrates with the presence of centuries, the simple picture of a patriarchal day in the country, the act of living solemnized at length by a music without end, and the clearly perceived essence of the thousands of unwritten *Harmonies* beneath the *Harmonie* sung here. *L'Occident*—strophes of bronze and gold, the peace of the day over the earth and the spirit. *L'Hymne à la douleur*—a masterpiece of moral poetry and beautiful gnomic lines. *Jéhovah ou L'Idée de Dieu*—an oratorio that mounts slowly into the brilliance of a splendid ending. *Le Chêne*—in which the poetry follows the hidden, slow, long, vegetal life of the oak tree. *L'Humanité*—out of the great paintings of Bologna, with its marvelous portrait of the Virgin, its soft, stroked verses, the hymn to the Virgin Mother of whom spiritual man was born. *L'Idée de Dieu* and its ending of light and faith; *Le Souvenir d'enfance ou La Vie cachée*—faith full and abounding as a running stream, the height of the familiar epistle in the whole of French poetry, poetry of twilight years that is our *Vieillard du Galèse* and that embodies all that poetry of roots sunk deeply in the earth, that country gentility (as one would say probity) that would reappear in Mistral and also in Barrès' *Eternité de la nature, Brièveté de l'homme*—a pure ode surpassed in France by no other, Pascal's thinking reed enhanced by lyricism to the girth of the oak and the olive tree. *Milly ou La Terre natale*—another of those epistles of which Lamartine was the master, the only master (later he published a volume of *Epîtres* based on the poems, and still more of them were found among his papers: a whole unpublished packet addressed to his father-in-law, Montherot), an expanse of fertile land that naturally, with its many verses, took on the appearance of shaped parallel furrows. *Le Cri de l'âme*—genuine and vehement, it fulfills its title: it seems that in the sensuality of the Tuscan summer (almost all the *Harmonies* were written in the summer or the autumn) a love without women mounts in a mystic intoxication, burgeons in the vision of God and fuses in a pillar of light. *Le Tombeau d'une mère*, as poignant as *Le Crucifix. Pourquoi mon âme est-elle triste?*—a lyric meditation whose strength is given it not by its subject, which is poor, barren in language and poetry, but by its oratorical movement, its commonplace spirit having encountered one of the great tides of the human soul and ridden it with all sails spread. *Novissima Verba*, written at Montculot, Bossuet's sermon transposed into the lyric mode, a consideration of man by man, grave, cadenced, flowing like a river swollen and unleashed in a winter night, no rare or novel sentiments, but the royal road of the human heart. The cry to *L'Esprit saint*, the breathless conclusion of which is weak but in which it seems that, completing *Les Harmonies* and publishing them in the summer of 1830, the poet is demanding investiture and sanctification for the political prophet of tomorrow.

The two volumes of *Harmonies* are to Lamartine's work what the two volumes of *Contemplations* are to Hugo's—his summer, his poetic testament, his long, full dialogue with life, men, and God, and also a lyric accounting by which the poet dispenses with a part of himself in order to ascend to the full peak of maturity, to mount to the Homeric Acropolis, to fulfill himself in the epic, in an *Odyssey* of the soul and human destinies.

The Epic Poet

In contrast to Hugo, whose epic scheme was suggested to him by the voices of Jersey and Guernsey, the plan of an epic was an old one with Lamartine. Before 1820 his dream of great poetry consisted not in *Les Méditations* but in an epic poem of *Clovis*, this Petrarch's *Africa*. (He included a fragment of it in *Les Nouvelles Méditations*.) During his years in Italy this was succeeded by another epic project, the poem of *Les Visions*, of which he was later to publish the detailed outline and a few finished parts, a series of episodes in which, against historical backgrounds, the fallen angel, man, would be progressively rehabilitated by sacrifice. After 1830 he allowed this project to lie fallow in order to write a familiar, popular epic, that of the country priest, the model for which was supplied to him by his friend, Abbé Dumont, the curate of Buissières. This was the first version of *Jocelyn*, which he left unfinished in 1832 when he departed for the Orient. Contact with the Orient brought him back to his earlier plans for a great religious epic. When he returned, the extremely simple *Jocelyn*, in its four songs, was therefore transformed into a vast poem whose philosophic and religious echoes ranged far, and which was followed two years later by *La Chute d'un ange*, the basis and the first episode of the final cyclical poem. He planned to write further episodes, beginning with that of *Les Pêcheurs;* in all, he thought, sixty thousand lines, if God let him live long enough, "and we shall also have," he wrote to Virieu, "our Indian poems, as infinite as nature, of which every poem should be the vast and deep and living reflection."

But the concerns of his political life were also there: the plan of *Les Pêcheurs* was to be executed only ten years later, and in prose, and it would be *Graziella*. But *Jocelyn* and *La Chute d'un ange* are enough to rank Lamartine at the summit of French epic poetry.

JOCELYN

With *Jocelyn* Lamartine repeated the triumph of *Les Méditations*, a success of sentiment and tears that recalled (and perhaps aimed for) that of *Paul et Virginie*. Later *Jocelyn* went out of fashion—like all narratives in verse, and also because of the speed and the carelessness of the writing, especially in the second part, written after 1834. Its idealism seemed mawkish. And yet it was enough to save it that it unflaggingly hewed to the key word in the epigraph that Lamartine gave it: ψυχή (*Psyche*). It had soul. It was soul. Fulfilling every individual and social meaning of the word, it remains the poem of the soul.

However Lamartine strove to relocate it and idealize it in the Alps that, to his Mâconnais eyes, towered above Bresse, *Jocelyn*, which owed its origin to a revolutionary incident in the history of Milly, and whose hero was Dumont, M. de Lamartine's curate (and, let us not forget, no more a believer than he), remains the poem of that same earthy substance of local Christian tradition on which Lamartine's genius was borne (and into which he plunged huge roots). The poem of the soul becomes poetically human because it is also the poem of the man of soul in his most elementary, ordinary, and simple form, the guardian of souls in every village, the country priest as he exists ideally—and soul in action consists in the belief in an ideal existence. But soul is not given, or easily borne. Soul is created by sacrifice, by effort that toils again up a height, the same height from which one has fallen. Lamartine's epic takes as its theme the struggle against that very facility with which Lamartine had passed for hero and victim. In so far as it remembers heaven, the soul— the divine spark that returns to the flame—is Jocelyn the priest, not so much through his vocation of faith as through his vocation of sacrifice, sacrifice and expiation for Laurence, a militant love that sacrifices for the happiness of his sister, then an existence endured through suffering love to win to triumphant love. But the soul has a double meaning and it lives on a double level. There is the individual soul of man and there is the collective soul of humanity, and for the Christian that collective soul of humanity is called the Church. From this point of view the central scene of *Jocelyn* is that of the prison, the spark from cleric to cleric, from soul to soul (the theme of *Le Crucifix*), and, through a new sacrifice, the individual soul that rejoins the soul of the Church, of humanity, of the collective ascent toward God; except that all this symbolic grandeur, this epic and mystic substance of *Jocelyn*, is hardly more visible externally in the poem than the soul is in the body. The poet does not move us, does not seek to move us, otherwise than through individual living bodies, the people whom he depicts, the story that he tells, the tragedy in which he takes part. Jocelyn, in a letter to his sister, compares himself rather clumsily with Faust. The passage does not ring true, but the idea survives. The poem of *Jocelyn*, which Lamartine conceived as the conclusion and the final episode of the cyclical epic, does indeed include a Faustian conjecture on the nature and the destiny of man. But none of this Faustian conjecture violates the framework, the body, the feeling, the intimacy of a french *Hermann und Dorothea*. Lamartine achieved this balance without a trace of obviousness in his scheme, of exaggeration in his effort. "I never think," he used to say; "my ideas think for me." In *Jocelyn* he felt for an idea, and an idea thought for him.

LA CHUTE D'UN ANGE

Jocelyn was to conclude the human epic; *La Chute d'un ange* would be its beginning. The fate of this poem was remarkable. It was the only complete failure of Lamartine's poetry among his contemporaries, a Tarpeian rock two years after the Capitoline of *Jocelyn*. He himself, who was the first to extol *Jocelyn* (let us remember his visit to Mme. Récamier, as described by Sainte-Beuve), called his *Chute d'un ange* abominable, offering the excuse that it was necessary to the following episodes, in which one would see what was to be seen. Later the poem found admirers, who virtually discovered it, pre-eminent among them the leader of the anti-Lamartine reaction, Leconte de Lisle, who regarded it as the poet's masterpiece. And that opinion is very nearly shared today by those who might be called the far-left Lamartinians. Readers of substance prefer *La Chute* to *Jocelyn*, and since 1890 its rehabilitation by the critics has been a matter of fact.

One must admire the grandeur of the myth, the force and the importance of the ideas. Cédar, the angel who owes his fall to love but who, like the theologian, could say, "My love is my significance," realizes an idea of man, the idea that runs through Lamartine's life and poetry and that it was essential for him to express once in its totality. He had considered this idea religiously only during his journey through the land that was the cradle of religions. Standing before the stones of Balbek, he enlarged it with the vision of a materialistic humanity, the master of the forces of nature, which man uses only in order to oppress and to enjoy. A few persecuted men of worth, the keepers of the fragments of a revealed book, preserve a kingdom of God in hiding. These fragments of the *Livre primitif* are a masterpiece of gnomic poetry, strong, simple, classic, with a purity and a substance, a perfection of style unequaled elsewhere by Lamartine. But the famous chorus of the cedars of Lebanon is only a *Harmonie*, and inferior to the others.

La *Chute*, not *Les Martyrs*, is the epic specifically prepared for and announced by *Le Génie du christianisme*. The theme is that of the religiosity of the romantics, the battle against the spirit of the eighteenth century in its double aspect: encyclopedism and sensuality. Encyclopedism: man's domination of nature without a corresponding mastery over his own nature can lead only to a monstrous culture, and as early as 1838 the myth of *La Chute* had posed the anguishing problems with which Europe was wrestling a hundred years later. Sensuality: it is astounding what a factitious, ingenuous, and monster-ridden picture Lamartine drew of the lustful lives of these lords of nature. He simply copied it from the *cloaca maxima* in which the sensuality of the eighteenth century culminated, from the Marquis de Sade himself, whose works, read at the age of twenty by Lamartine with his friend, Guichard de Bienassis, terrified both young men.

Obviously one must not seek in *La Chute d'un ange* what is offered in *Jocelyn*—living humanity and individuals. Its people live only symbolically. But, whatever may be said of it, its poetic style is generally of a more consistent quality than that of *Jocelyn*. It is the style of an orator-poet. For four years Lamartine had been demonstrating his mastery of the art of the spoken word in the Chamber of Deputies. It shows in his poetry.

Les Recueillements and Les Psaumes

That mastery is revealed not only in the epic, which, unfortunately, he abandoned at this point, but in a lyric poetry that, more unusual than before, gained in harmony, in breadth, in substance, and that swelled and surged in the poems of *Les Recueillements*, written after 1830. The *Cantique sur la mort de la duchesse de Broglie* endowed the tomb of Albertine de Staël with the same sacraments that Bossuet provided for the grave of Henrietta of England. The odes to Wasp, to Guillemardet, the tribute *A l'Académie de Marseille*, *Gethsémani* opened the idealized home of family and parents to the tides of politics. The lyric masterpieces of Lamartine in this time were his great political odes. With *A Némésis*, *Le Toast des gallois et des bretons*, *Utopie*, *Les Révolutions*, *La Marseillaise de la paix* the flag of his parliamentary eloquence was flung out under the sky.

Lyric poetry in Lamartine had always matched a precarious state of grace. For a long time he thought that after *Les Méditations*, the fruit of his springtime, and *Les Harmonies*, the harvest of his summer, he would find the lyric sources of his autumn in *Psaumes*—that is, dialogues between the soul and God, closer to the Bible than those that Victor Hugo would conduct for several years on Guernsey but like Hugo's the testament of a way of thought that was always religious. The forced labors of journalism and the automatism of prose prevented him from writing them, except one day during the grape harvest at Milly in 1857, when, outside the house of his childhood, he wrote *La Vigne et la maison, Psaumes de l'ame*, the last warm golden cluster from the stripped trellis. No poet has been able to equal this poetry written at the age of sixty-seven. It is on the level of *Le Crucifix*. And, furthermore, opening the twenty-eight volumes of the *Cours familier de littérature* at random is enough to show that, if the poetic spring no longer pours forth, it survives under ground. Two years later, giving *Mireille* the investiture of the poet of *Jocelyn*, the Quarantième Entretien marked a golden date in the history of poetic genius.

The Destiny of Poetry

In effect, Lamartine's function from 1820 on was to sustain poetry in France as an essence and as a climate. He was not so much a force of nature as a presence of nature, not so much a date as a season. In 1820, catching fallen poetry by the hand, he gave it a kingdom over a heart, over many hearts, and then over all the rest, over politics, over history, over criticism. This enemy of Napoleon was the Napoleon of a poetic imperialism. Like the Empire of 1811, Lamartine's poetry of 1847 and 1848 committed inordinate political sins that inevitably brought on reaction. The reaction began as early as the autumn of 1848. It was to last forty years and to end only with the end of the nineteenth century.

But the term poetry has another meaning besides that of "essence": namely, the meaning of art, of technique. This is the meaning that it assumes when we speak of Malherbe, of Racine, of Charles Baudelaire, of the Parnassians, of Paul Valéry. Then a whole hemisphere of poetry has to group itself, learn to know itself, test itself, fortify itself against Lamartine. In the society of minds that is formed by French poetry, Lamartine cannot be separated from the anti-Lamartine reaction that was to create the original poetry of the Second Empire. The poet must be accepted with his impossibilities and with his enemies. There was a time when he was unanimously acclaimed the victor. There was a time when he was unanimously branded obsolete. Lamartine's triumph and his rejection today no longer belong to generations that succeeded and contradicted one another but to coexistent and necessary categories of the complex called poetry, the category of inspiration and the category of technique.

IV

ALFRED DE VIGNY

Alfred de Vigny's Place

There were two periods at which, among a select group, Vigny was ranked as the greatest of the romantic poets. The first was approximately 1826: then less than thirty years old, he was producing glorious master-pieces to which, for the rest of his life, he did not add another book of verse. This handsome, proud, reserved officer had taken up the poetic rev-olution where André Chénier had left it, breaking at the same time with the ode and the rhymed dissertation of the eighteenth century, in which the early works of Lamartine and Victor Hugo were still caught; adding —the first to do so—Biblical inspiration to classical inspiration; re-creating "the poem," after *L'Aveugle* and *Le Malade*, by incorporating into it what was lacking in Chénier, the symbol and the idea; achieving almost at once, like Keats, a poetry that was intellectual in its design, sensual in the substance of its lines; evoking in his own person, for the poetic imag-inations of young men and women, those figures of swans and angels of which he sang; the first and finest love of the blonde Muse, young Del-phine Gay; the prince charming of romanticism between Lamartine and Musset. Again, at the end of the nineteenth century, thirty years after his death, when Lamartine was still barely emerging, with infinite effort, from oblivion, when Hugo was still trapped in the vulgarities of his of-ficial apotheosis, when, in the phrase of Jules Lemaître, the finest tastes found that the one was "too nyah-nyah" and the other was "too boom-boom," when Armand Sully-Prudhomme, to a certain degree the heir of Vigny, was becoming the poet of "sensitive youth" in the universities: then the author of *Eloa,* and above all of the posthumous book *Les Destinées,* appeared once more as the poet of quality, of substance, of spirit, of analysis, of idealism; the thinking poet; the poet with ideas, backed by a *Journal intime* the equal of those of Maine de Biran and Amiel; the poet who, with a romantic soul, had discovered the principle of what was then called symbolism beneath a classic form; the poet pure of all oratorical taint, in whom the poetic life and the inner life were joined under a double illumination, that of Psyche's lamp and that of the lonely lighthouse of *La Bouteille à la mer* and *L'Esprit pur* swept space and time. Later the strong glare that fell on his imitators of 1830 burned away some of that rank of watcher and thinker; Baudelaire's *Les Fleurs du mal* tended to replace Vigny's poetry as a volume of unique verses; admiration was sometimes diluted to respect; but he remains great, and his influence on minds is by no means exhausted. Two peaks of poetry bear his name: a pleasant Brocken, that of the ballad, and the highest summit, that of the myth.

The Ballad Poet

Before 1830 the romantic ballad had been in fashion for some time. The Germans were imitated as Chénier had imitated the Greeks. The troubadour school found its lance and its wings in the ballad. It did not go very far with Emile Deschamps. In *Les Ballades* Victor Hugo diverted himself with his own virtuosity, but *La Fiancée du timbalier* degenerated and *La Chasse du Burgrave* has always been a trifle. This good-humored romanticism ended with the *Ballade à la lune*. Vigny alone had the good fortune to strike a serious note here. From this Middle Ages of romantic ballads there are still *La Neige* and, especially, *Le Cor*. Obviously the form of these stanzas has nothing to do with that of the ballad. In addition, it seems that the alternation of masculine couplets with feminine couplets is ill adapted to the group of four Alexandrines, Vigny having been almost alone in using this pattern. And yet it is these alternated couplets, this false distich, this apparent artlessness that offer the means of making the tone of the ordinary tale accord with the stanza imposed by the lyric spirit of the ballad. *La Neige* and *Le Cor* are impressions, exactly those that their titles and their first strophes evoke, and at a single stroke these impressions burgeon into narratives. The ballad is not put together in a workshop, as Hugo does it; it is created in and of an essence, as the reader watches; rich in power, the lines leap into the memory like the finest lines of La Fontaine, of Racine, or of Chénier. Perhaps it was because, with the substance and the ivory of his verse, Vigny had transported the magic horn of German romanticism into French lyricism that, a thousand years after the battle of Roncevaux, Victor Hugo made it resound again in the battle of *Hernani*.

The Myth Poet

But what is much more important in Vigny's poetry is that it must be marked in history as the date of the discovery of myths. Myth, introduced into art by Plato as the epic was by Homer, is an idea carried by a story, an idea that is a soul, a story that is a body, and each inseparable from the other. The poetry of the French classics ignored it: it left myth confounded with fable, from which, for that matter, the Greeks did not clearly distinguish it, since they had only one word to designate both, and the Socrates of Plato, who turned the fables of Aesop into verse in his prison, certainly intended in the myths of the *Phaedo* only to recount fables. But these fables were philosophical, and this word philosophical is for us the definition of the myth. The esthetic meaning of the myth, in sum, was discovered by Goethe for the first time since the Greeks. It will be observed that, in the article that she devoted to *Faust* in *L'Allemagne*, Mme. de Staël judged the poem by the rules and the taste of the eighteenth century and apparently understood nothing of its mythic character. From La Fontaine's *Psyché* to the allegorical utilization of the myth of Psyche by Lamartine in *La Mort de Socrate* (even though the latter is rather weak), one feels the transition from a poetry without myth to a poetry fertilized by myth. But these observations only help us better to grasp the strong originality, the creative power, the indestructible brilliance of *Moïse* and *Eloa*, and Vigny's right to declare in 1829: "The only virtue in these compositions that has never been challenged is that of having been the very first of all such in France, in which a philosophic thought is almost always brought on stage in an epic or dramatic form." The masterpieces of myth, *La Chute d'un ange* and *Le Satyre*, were to be born later.

Moïse is the myth of the genius. Written perhaps in the Pyrenees, it tells of the man meditating on the mountain, and we should note that it was intended to be placed at the van of *Poèmes antiques et modernes* as *L'Isolement* was placed at the beginning of *Les Méditations*. Two Solitudes—Lamartine's a sentimental solitude, Vigny's the solitude of genius; Lamartine's in the direct light of lyricism, Vigny's in the reflected light of myth. If all is barren around the first, it is because a single being is lacking. If a being, if another heart, is lacking to the second, it is because it is surrounded by a people, because the genius is marked with solitude for the service and the illumination of this people. No choice was more felicitous for the incarnation of the myth of genius, for the casting in gold of the seal of the ministry, than that of Moses, the prophet of the promised land who did not enter in because he had to live, like Plato's wise man, not in realities but in their ideas.

Eloa is the myth of evil. From a tear of Christ a woman angel is born.

A vocation for pity causes her to love the angel of evil, who seduces her by his lies and her truth, through her and through himself, and who carries her off. In principle the couple is purely human: the eternal theme of the virgin and the seducer, Marguerite and Faust, and Vigny in *Eloa*, like Musset in his *Rolla*, unrolls his youthful poem, the classic theme of the humblest romance. But by poetic multiplication, by the space in which it grows in geometric progression, the theme becomes myth. Born of Christ's pity, not of his wrath or his justice or his sacrifice, Eloa confronts the evil of the world and knows only the feeling of Christ before human evil: his pity. Evil is not absolute cold; it is a climate. It has its flowers, those of which Baudelaire would sing, that Satan evokes:

> *Les voluptés des soirs et les biens du mystère*
> (Delights of nights and riches of the void).

It is wrought of a complex, the coils, the charms, and the treacheries of the serpent. Vigny abandoned the plan of a sequel to *Eloa*, the Satan Redeemed he had planned. Hugo wrote it for him in *La Fin de Satan*.

Sentiments and Ideas

THE HUMAN CONDITION

Vigny's poetry is governed by one idea, which is confirmed by *Le Journal d'un poète:* the rupture between man and the creator, the refusal to admit that the world, nature, God himself are as they are. *Eloa* may at first seem a tale inspired by Thomas Moore's *Loves of the Angels*, with its reputation derived from the richness of its poetry, the beauty of its images, the rhythm and the flow of its passages, the fluidity and the spirituality of some immortal lines. But beyond these poetic assets there is something else: the fact that Vigny's poetry is on Eloa's side, that this poetry is an eternal Eloa. *Le Déluge* and *La Fille de Jephté* tell of the same sacrifice of innocence. Above all, the poems in *Destinées*, published in part in 1843 and 1844, take up the eternal theme again with a maturity, a concentration, a force and a seriousness that are even stronger. The tercets of *Destinées—La Maison du berger, La Mort du loup, Le Mont des oliviers*—are a quadrupled rejection of need, of nature, of complaint, of God.

They have become the most lastingly luminous poems, the fixed stars of French poetry. This they owe not to the purity of their language, which is often questionable, but to that of remarkable lines that hang here and there like grapes of Canaan; and then to their deep roots in a man's heart: the two apologias for silence, *La Mort du loup* and *Le Mont des oliviers,* are truly a testament of the poet, who himself knew when to be silent, to preserve behind walls of granite that inner life attested to by his *Journal.* And finally they owe it to their transmission from man to man along the royal road of myth and symbol.

La Maison du berger, whose stanzas thicken like a forest, is not only a symbol but an architecture of symbols. Its three parts set up three pairs of contrasts: the railroad of society and the shepherd's cottage of the individual; politics and poetry; nature and woman. Confronted with society, politics and nature, silence. But for living things, for poetry, for woman, tenderness. The machine vulgarizes the spirit, politics stultifies man, nature ignores the heart; against them the poet is the wolf, keeping the silence by which, in *Le Mont des oliviers,* he replies to the silence of God. But the shepherd's cottage is freedom, poetry is the pearl of thought, woman is Eloa's pity, of which Eve kept the greater part, that very part that the poet restores to her when he turns away from inhuman, too divine nature:

> *Plus que tout votre règne et que ses splendeurs vaines*
> *J'aime la majesté des souffrances humaines*
>
> (More than the empty splendors of your state
> I love man's majesty before his fate).

But admiration for this architecture of symbols can cause us to misunderstand the purer beauty of the poem: here and there, and especially in the last stanzas, a wholly pure disinterestedness, a presence not of the eternal feminine but, on the contrary, of the fleeting feminine, of the moment for love because she will not be seen twice, of love silent and always threatened. That imponderable disinterestedness would later become the highest quality of poetry—precisely because of its fusion with symbolism; and throughout the course of oratorical romantic poetry Vigny seems, with Gérard de Nerval, alone in his ability to sustain its hidden life.

Vigny's world is a world without God, Vigny's conscience is the tragic conscience of a world without God. It leads him to despair, but to an active despair, in this silent man the very despair of the silent: one has no need for hope in order to undertake. The enterprise survives beyond hope, and a part of *Destinées* puts the human enterprise into symbols.

THE HUMAN UNDERTAKING

The poems of the human undertaking are *La Sauvage, La Flûte, La Bouteille à la mer,* and *L'Esprit pur. La Sauvage,* which is somewhat lacking in resonance, was no digression for Vigny. Alone among the romantics, he hated nature in all its aspects. In every conflict between man and nature, he stood with man. He stood with man against God. When the problem of Rousseau arose, he was against Rousseau; he was for the civilized man against the natural man, for the white man against the savage. It was inevitable that one of his poems should be dedicated to civilization, to effort, to effort for the sake of effort, even if, as in *La Flûte*, it does not succeed.

La Bouteille à la mer and *L'Esprit pur* go back to that seven-line stanza of *La Maison du berger* that is Vigny's most beautiful lyric achievement, as well as his first. *La Bouteille à la mer* is a poem of the human enterprise in that it is connected to what is most insubstantial and that it lives and dies for ideas. Let us not mistake Vigny's idealism for a banal word. It resembled not that of the poets but that of the philosopher. The twenty-sixth and last stanza of *La Bouteille à la mer* begins with this line:

> *Le vrai Dieu, le Dieu fort est le Dieu des idées*
> (The true, strong God is the deity of ideas).

The poetry, the work, and the life of Alfred de Vigny are strung on the heroic dialectic thanks to which this enemy of an imposed god, of a god neither sought nor wished, arrives at the platonic idea of a true, strong god, the realm of ideas, as space is the realm of bodies. The poet of *L'Esprit pur* is the man of ideas—better yet, the knight of ideas. Vigny's ideas retain the mark of the inner implement and the painful tension that created them. But it was his vocation to create them as a poet, to bring myths as the "fabulist," La Fontaine, brought fables. He sketched many admirable ones, too, in *Le Journal d'un poète*, which is a treasure chest of plans and poems. Unfortunately, what is called inspiration was precarious in him, his youthful ardor to fashion a composition in a single motion wore out early. The circumstances of life and his taste for silence did the rest.

Love in the Theater

From his youth on, Vigny amazed the romantics by his reserve and his modesty. No one, Dumas said, had ever seen him at table. Hence it is supposed that he alone never wrote directly intimate poems, that he never, like the others, sang of his loves, his hates, his sorrows, and his joys (or at least that he never published anything of the kind) and that he stylized everything. *La Colère de Samson* is no exception. It is a curse on woman, as splendid and as famous as the adoration in *Eva*. Nothing is more transparent than this Biblical poem, the beginning of which is of an astonishing Oriental color, on his betrayal by the actress, Marie Dorval. The seraph of shadow, the prince of silence and the ivory tower, was cast out with his inmost secrets into the public square by the public woman, stripped almost naked before the eyes of the men and women who had taken his place with her. This time Vigny replied not with silence but with the pillory. One is reminded of the Archilochus of the *Iambics* and the Hugo of *Les Châtiments*. Stylization and the habit of myth threaten here to make us impute to woman what was meant of one woman. *La Colère de Samson* must be regarded also and especially as the physiology of a certain kind of love and of love in the theater, just as at the same time, with the same storms, there were *Les Amants de Venise* and Musset's lines to George Sand, *Honte à toi, femme à l'oeil sombre.*

Father Thought

After the publication of *Destinées*, which redirected attention to him after his death, Vigny's fame did not experience the peaks and troughs of Lamartine's and Victor Hugo's. It remained even and pure. The grammarians might quibble over the language of his great poems, but nothing of their poetry has aged. This stoic poet, this maker of myths around ideas, filled the place, rendered the services, maintained the rank, of a moralist, at the same time that he was the most apt of the romantics for pure poetry. His proud, tender sensitivity in no way impaired an active mind that made him the Father Thought of romantic poetry. On the contrary, it endowed that thought with more human tenderness, that fatherhood with more force.

VICTOR HUGO

Through his father, Victor Hugo belonged to a peasant family of Lorraine (canton of Baudricourt), which his grandfather, a skilled artisan and a clever merchant, a carpenter and a forester, had elevated to comfort, and which his father and his two uncles, all three soldiers of the Revolution and officers of the Empire, had raised to honor and glory. Through his mother, Sophie Trébuchet, he was descended from Nantes burghers and shipowners. Born at Besançon on 26 February 1802, the last of three sons, he spent a nomad childhood following his father from garrison to garrison: Corsica, Elba, Naples. Two long stationary periods were important: the three years spent by the Hugo children in Paris in the big garden of the Feuillantines (1808–1811) and the two years in Spain (1811–1812), whither General Léopold Hugo had followed Joseph Bonaparte. From 1812 to 1818 the three boys did well in their studies in Paris, particularly in literature. At the age of sixteen Victor Hugo had written a tragedy, had been cited by the Académie for an ode, had been honored for his poetry at the Floral Games of Toulouse; at seventeen he founded the first of all the youthful magazines, the *Conservateur littéraire* (1819–1821), cleverly directed in the wake of Chateaubriand's political *Conservateur*. The quarrels between his parents, who had lived apart since 1812, made his adolescence painful and inspired him with the necessity and the desire to make a place for himself through literature, the only profession by which he knew how to live (he always practiced it with exemplary integrity but also a very shrewd sense of business). A wife and children (at twenty, just after his mother's death, he had married, for love, a childhood friend, Adèle Foucher), his family's political position (in 1814, out of hatred for her husband, his mother had proclaimed herself a royalist, and then the general had joined Louis XVIII), and the example of his two great elders, Chateaubriand and Lamartine, were at the root of his youthful royalism, a rationalized, career royalism that had no stronger grip on the heart of Hugo than on the heart of

France. As early as 1822 his *Odes* marked him as the official serious poet of the dynasty. But he sought also, with determination and perseverance, a high rank as a complete man of letters, producing everything, exploiting the current mode, succeeding in everything, superior in everything: the novel with *Bug-Jargal* and *Han d'Islande*, the theater with *Amy Robsart* and *Cromwell*, creative criticism with his prefaces, classic poetry with the *Odes*, romantic poetry with the *Ballades*. At twenty-eight he was the leader of a school, or, more accurately, a leader; at the same time he published *Les Orientales* and *Le Dernier Jour d'un condamné* and gave the Comédie-Française *Marion Delorme*, the performance of which was forbidden by the government. In 1830–1831 the same triple ambition soared again with *Hernani*, *Notre-Dame de Paris* and *Les Feuilles d'automne:* a great time, a great turning point.

The battle of *Hernani* was the Austerlitz of romanticism. *Notre-Dame de Paris* was to become one of Hugo's most popular works because of its high color, and *Feuilles d'automne* marked his entrance into great personal, philosophical, and political poetry. At the same time his true political feelings showed themselves. They centered on Napoleon. *L'Ode à la colonne* was their birth certificate; the fourth act of *Hernani* was the certification of the imperial idea. In 1831, in a letter to King Joseph, he offered his services to the exiled Duc de Reichstadt (Napoleon II). The latter's death in 1832 left him politically at liberty and threw him back into an ideal Napoleonism (as Chateaubriand remained an exile in a decorative legitimatism), leaving him for many years most hostile to Louis-Philippe, who did him the favor of banning the deplorable *Le Roi s'amuse* in 1832 and whom he insulted in verses that remained clandestine. But, beginning in 1834, he made overtures to the young Duc d'Orléans and especially, in 1837, to the duchess, who was to cause him to be named a peer of France in 1845 and on whose behalf he was to speak out bravely, standing on a milepost, during the revolutionary days of 1848.

From 1831 to 1840 his literary life was dominated by the four collections of poetry, *Feuilles d'automne*, *Chants du crépuscule* (1835), *Voix intérieures* (1837), and *Les Rayons et les ombres* (1840), which, combined with the quasi-silence in the lyric of Lamartine and Vigny and the poetic failure of Sainte-Beuve, made him the prince of the lyricism of his time. His theatrical life was less happy: the great scheme of a theater of his own, of the history of France retold in a wealth of dramas for the people by a new Shakespeare, did not come to fruition. While *Lucrèce Borgia* (1833) was a success, *Marie Tudor* (1833) and *Angelo* (1835) were failures; the great triumphs were those of Vigny with *Chatterton*, Dumas with *La Tour de Nesle*. *Ruy Blas*, however, performed at the Renaissance Theater in 1838, had a great success and in sum remains Hugo's sole verse drama that did succeed. And, finally, his private life had not escaped the upheavals of the thirties: his closest friend, Sainte-Beuve, had broken with him after a notorious clash, a matter of a smashed marriage, in which almost all the fault was on the side of the critic. In his own home, discord and even sexual incompatibility with the woman who had already borne his four children were among the causes of his relationship, which began in 1833, with Juliette Drouet, former mistress and model of the sculptor, James Pradier. This relationship, which was to endure into old age and death, still stands out as a moving example and a magnificent monument of the renewal, the education, the creation of a woman by genius and love.

In 1838 Hugo visited Germany for the first time. His political concerns, of which *Ruy Blas* is the myth, would be made public in 1841 in his speech on his entrance into the Académie, in 1842 in *Le Rhin*, in 1843 in *Les Burgraves*, Hugo's second imperial play after *Hernani*, a sunset more beautiful than the sunrise but a dramatic Waterloo thirteen years after Austerlitz. Hugo's own life, when he had reached forty, had attained an imperial brilliance. His house on the Place des Vosges was a literary capital. His mask in marble had a Caesarean majesty. He saw far and well. In 1842 the death of the Duc d'Orléans gave rise to the prospect of a short-term minority, a regency. The parliamentary success of Lamartine, to whom a Cabinet portfolio and embassies were offered and who was holding himself in reserve for something better, and the recollection of Chateaubriand showed Victor Hugo the possible roads that a poet might take toward the heights. For seven years he kept himself available. He stopped publishing. He felt that *Les Burgraves* had lowered his stature with the crowd, which does not like defeats. In addition, 1843 was the dreadful year for a reason other than a failure in the theater. His daughter Léopoldine Vacquerie, newly married, the dearest of his children, the most completely her father's daughter ("That Léopoldine is the daughter of Caesars," Sainte-Beuve said in *Livre d'amour*), drowned herself at Villequier while her father was traveling in the Pyrenees with Juliette. It was the great sorrow of his life. Two years later, in 1845, on the anniversary of the death of the Duc d'Orléans and at the plea of the duchess, though against his own will, Louis-Philippe made Hugo a peer of France. But fate was implacable: Hugo was counting on embarking on a brilliant career in the Senate chamber of the Luxembourg when a scandal—a flagrant case of adultery with a Mme. Biard—doomed him to two years of silence, and he finally reached the speaker's platform only to demonstrate that he would never be an orator. Meanwhile, though he was not publishing, he was hastily writing manuscripts, beginning *Les Contemplations* with *Pauca Meae*, *La Légende des siècles* with *Aymerillot* and *Le Mariage de Roland*, *Les Misérables* with *Les Misères*.

The revolution of 1848 stunned him. But Lamartine's government and the establishment of universal suffrage at first gave that revolution the appearance of romanticism in power. The voters of Paris sent Hugo to the

Constituent Assembly and then to the National Assembly, where he took a seat on the right, supported Louis-Napoleon's candidacy for the presidency with his newspaper, *L'Evénement*, as well as his vote, and defended the Prince-President's policy, though unskillfully (Hugo was the opposite of a parliamentarian). His whole past, indeed, impelled him to become one of the representative men of the future empire: a genuine love for the people, an authoritarian philanthropy, the world politics of a Utopian and a dreamer were among the characteristics shared by Vicomte Hugo and the Prince-President. Louis-Napoleon would gladly have given the poet a ministry in his Cabinet. His advisers dissuaded him. Tremendously wounded in his immense pride and his immense ambition, Victor Hugo threw himself with a dark fury into the only party that he had not alienated, the extreme left, and, eloquent at last, embarked on a struggle without mercy against the government.

L'*Histoire d'un crime*, the story of Louis-Napoleon's *coup d'état* of 2 December 1951, which Hugo wrote in 1852 and did not publish until twenty years later, is only a propaganda novel. It is quite true, however, that Hugo bore himself with courage on that occasion. Disguised as a workman, he left for Brussels, the Duc de Morny having let him escape with a light heart, preferring to have him outside rather than inside.

The state of distress and anger in which he reached Brussels was expressed in the pamphlet, *Napoléon le Petit*, and in the early compositions of *Les Châtiments*, which he finished on the island of Jersey, where he established himself in 1852. In 1856 he moved to Guernsey. In this island solitude, where he was accompanied by his family and Juliette Drouet; where regular production, six hours' work every morning, had become the real substance of his life; where meditation on the sea and on God, on life and death, was a principal concern, he attained to a superhuman power of expression and creation. Having apparently purged himself of his rages in the volcanic eruption of *Les Châtiments* and settled into his exile, he added enough to the lyric pieces in his files to produce *Les Contemplations* (1856). He wrote his own *Chute d'un ange* in *La Fin de Satan* and *Dieu;* he became an epic poet in *La Légende des siècles;* he went back to *Les Misères* to produce from it the ten volumes of *Les Misérables;* he amused himself in *Les Chansons des rues et des bois* by strewing Béranger's jests among the stars; he wrote the novel of the ocean in *Les Travailleurs de la mer*, and the enormous fantasy of *L'Homme qui rit;* he made a powerful, wonderful prophet's life for himself on an island that commingled the images of Patmos, Saint Helena, and the Grand Bey. A divine sculptor had applied the chisel to the stone of his destiny.

With one line of *Les Châtiments* he had courageously blocked the road back for himself. He returned to Paris two days after the proclamation of the Republic, he wore the cap of the Garde Nationale during and indeed after the siege, he was elected a deputy from Paris to the National

Assembly with Louis Blanc and Giuseppe Garibaldi, and he soon resigned, having hardly any common language with the Assembly in Bordeaux—any more, for that matter, than he had with the Commune and
the parties that were forming and contending in the Republic. Elected a
senator from the Department of the Seine, he spoke rarely in the Luxembourg. He stood for two ideas there: amnesty, which he unwearyingly
demanded for those condemned by the Commune, and anticlericalism,
which made him a kind of ancestor in the religious wars of the Republic.

He continued to write after 1871: *L'Année terrible, L'Art d'être
grand-père, Quatre-vingt-treize, Religion et religions*, several fine pieces
in *La Légende*, including *Le Groupe des idylles* and *Le Cimetière d'Eylau*.
But these were exceptions: almost everything that he published was
drawn from the inexhaustible store of manuscripts written in exile, especially in the decade of the 1850s. He himself scheduled in his will the publication of his posthumous works, which was to extend into 1902, the
centenary of his birth, but which had not ended thirty years later.

Griefs had poured down on him. His two sons, the companions of his
exile, died in 1871 and 1873. His last daughter, Adèle, who survived him,
had lost her sanity during the exile and was locked away like her uncle,
Eugène. Juliette Drouet remained with Victor Hugo almost to the grave.
But his son's two children, Georges and Jeanne, were the joy of his old
age. Every literary and political figure visited him in his little house in the
avenue d'Eylau, where, as he had done all his life, he kept more or less
open house with the graciousness of a gentleman. Paris enveloped him in
a vast monumental glory.

He died at the age of eighty-three, like Voltaire and Goethe. His public funeral was part of the pomps and the ritual of the Republic, in which
it made the same display as the Day of the Supreme Being under the Convention. He was one of those strange men who, in his own expression,
intoxicate history. The half-century that followed his death was as rich
as his lifetime in impassioned discussions of the man, of his place, and of
his glory. "At last he has stopped blocking the horizon," the poet who
was to succeed him in the Académie said in 1885. Leconte de Lisle never
made as complete a mistake as he did that day.

Hugo's Place

In the world of the great poets there seems to be for the personal equa-
tion of Victor Hugo, if not a disproportion, at least a gulf between his
genius and his character, a certain impossibility of building a proper
bridge between them. This gulf can be better understood by comparing
Hugo's situation with Lamartine's. Hugo's literary work has survived al-

most in a mass, like an Iberian peninsula. In contrast, Lamartine's has vanished in great part: an archipelago, Cyclades, Sporades, on the site of an engulfed Aegean island. All things considered, Hugo's work is greater, better attuned to the measure of the centuries, than Lamartine's. There is a *situation* for Hugo that is superior to Lamartine's. On the other hand, there is a *presence* of Lamartine that is greater than Hugo's, a presence of genius, a familiarity, a friendship, an atmosphere, a daily recourse and succor. Lamartine offers twentieth-century France a genius of place, Hugo a place of genius. Perhaps we should be led to make the same distinction between Balzac's situation and Stendhal's presence, or what were for a long time Musset's situation and Baudelaire's presence.

A novelist like Balzac, a dramatic poet like Shakespeare or Molière, Corneille or Racine, adapts himself completely to a maximum of situation and a minimum of presence. Their created characters are present for them. Balzac's personality often (and no doubt wrongly) leaves the sensitive as cold as does Hugo's. But what is important to us in Balzac is old Goriot or Mme. de Mortsauf; it is not M. Honoré. Hugo, on the contrary, is a personal lyric, the greatest of personal lyrics, whose personality, rightly or wrongly (and more often wrongly) does not generally arouse interest and never stirs dreams.

Hugo's Destiny

Through a strange fortuitousness this emperor of style lacked all style of life, except in the realm of love. He had a style of destiny, which is not the same thing—the style, moreover, of a belated destiny, which he received in 1851 and in which, later, various lucky chances collaborated: isolation on his island, the fall of the Empire, the triumph of the Republic after 16 May. For him 2 December was a Sinai; 16 May gave him the apotheosis of 1885. But, as it was not borne and produced by a style of life, this destiny was too great for him. Today it irritates us more than it serves him. It is a prisoner of ceremony. There is a Lamartinian cult; there is no Hugoesque cult, only a Hugoesque pomp. The malevolent have no trouble compounding pomp into another term, and all that factitious part of Hugo's destiny has taken on the aspect that Tristan Corbière saw when he called him an epic national guardsman.

A Theatrocratic Personality

Here we would substitute for the word epic only the word theatrical. A great epic poet, Hugo was not a victim but a conqueror of the epic.

On the contrary, he can be seen as a victim of the theater. This is not only, nor chiefly, because he did not succeed very well as a dramatic author: the lines of *Hernani* and *Les Burgraves* provide him with enough extenuating circumstances for us not to insist on that. But there is this, which is more important. This great lyric poet went into the theater less to create parts than to play a part: the part of a conqueror, when romanticism had the theater to conquer. His first play could not be presented without a manifesto, which was the preface to *Cromwell:* a manifesto is a proclamation, and a proclamation is made from a platform, and one does not mount a platform without having made sure of music. Sainte-Beuve bore throughout his life the humiliation, the rage, of having had to play the foil then and of having been caustically rebuked for it by Heinrich Heine. Precisely because the theater is a loudspeaker, because the opening night of *Hernani* did more for Victor Hugo's glory than his purest lyricism, Hugo saw in the theater a means of "speaking" more loudly, the natural and necessary field of his poetic glory, the training ground, the course for his political genius. The collapse of *Les Burgraves* did not check his theatromania: it exaggerated it by diverting it to the legislature. And then the refusal of a ministry by Louis-Napoleon, or rather by the Prince's advisers, was for him the equivalent, the pendant, the sequel to the failure of *Les Burgraves* seven years earlier, which had exiled him from the theater. Perhaps equally unjustly. *Les Burgraves* was a great original work, and the Republic, which had had in Lamartine a great Minister of Foreign Affairs, could and should have tried Victor Hugo as Minister of Public Instruction. But in the end Hugo would have been a theatrical minister, as he had been a theatrical peer and a theatrical deputy. Once, when someone was making a noise while he was speaking, a colleague said: "Let him act out his play!" Such was indeed the common feeling.

Play, however, is not too accurate. The theater consists in dialogue. And Hugo, in the theater as in life, was the man of monologue, of harangue, of interruption, of lyric charge in which the speaker is alone or the other stands mute or limits himself to the quickly hushed "but . . ." of the dummy at whist. The apostrophes of Milton, of Saint-Vallier, of Ruy Blas; the monologue of Charles the Fifth, the Four Days of Elciis, the Satyr before the assembly of the gods, or the man who laughs before the peers of England—that is the attitude to which Hugo's natural movement invincibly leads him. He is the Delmar of *L'Education sentimentale:* "An English brewer, he cursed Charles I; a student of Salamanca, he damned Philip II; or, a right-thinking father, he raged against the Pompadour, that was the best! Just to be able to see him, the street boys waited at the stage door. . . . Everyone said: 'Our Delmar.' He had a mission; he was becoming Christ."

Obviously the genius finds it more difficult than the second-rate actor

to become a god. Hugo almost achieved it, however, in 1885, and, as
Royer-Collard said of M. Pasquier when he was made a duke, it did not
take anything away from him.

Olympio's Monologue

His vocation for the monologue and the restrictions entailed by it had
already given the man and the poet something of the exile and the is-
lander. By condemning him to an eighteen-year monologue on an island,
Napoleon III ratified that vocation and conferred on Victor Hugo a rank
with a range quite different from what the Emperor's uncle, Joseph, had
bestowed on Léopold Hugo by making him Comte de Siguenza. He
raised his poetic genius to the second power: the monologist who had
been only a count became a duke, a prince, a burgrave, what you will.
The four days of Elciis resounded and astounded like the days of the
creation. Grandeur and boundary.

When Lamartine demanded that Napoleon's tomb bear these three
words, "To Napoleon alone!" he showed the difference between a genius who is alone and a genius who is not alone. There could no more
be a solitary Lamartine than a solitary Louis XIV. But there is a solitary
Hugo. There is a Hugo who talks alone and before whom a part of posterity is seized with the same ironic unease that surrounds the man who
talks aloud to himself in the street. When Hugo verges on the absurd,
he takes the same road by which we all go when we speak alone, when
we are alone, when our social editors and adapters stop functioning. His
monologue among the living, then, is like his monologue among the dead
when the table-tapping of Jersey spoke for him and in him. This sovereignty of the monologue is all the more striking when it is juxtaposed,
though it does not blend, with a social personality of dialogue, that of a
man of intelligence, a perfect gentleman, a delightful conversationalist,
an attentive and generous friend, an exemplary son, an affectionate father, a lover as sensitive as he was tender. All the more striking, too,
when Hugo's monologue, which is indeed the monologue of the theater,
is the monologue for an audience, the monologue that presupposes the
speaker surrounded by the element, the aliment, and the magnet of a
crowd, of crowds, of peoples, of creatures, of the living and the dead,
of God. So, when Hugo wrote *Choses vues* for himself alone, not for a
theater, without the intervention of Olympio,[1] when he was Hugo alone
for himself and not Hugo alone for others, when, then, his monologue is
pure, we see him as lucid, as clear-thinking, as subtle as when he was talk-

[1] A creation and spokesman of Hugo (see p. 185).—Translator.

ing in 1830 with Sainte-Beuve, in the Académie with Royer-Collard, on Guernsey with the young Paul Stapfer. This was the man he was, this was not the genius, Olympio, who lived within him, the genius now the superior, now the inferior, of the man, who does not meet the same measurements, who makes do with him as well as he can.

Now, no literature is more sociable, more social, than French literature, or has better joined forces with the spirit of society, or is less tolerant of the monologue in the street, in books, in the theater. The same paradox that made Napoleon a French emperor made the Hugoesque monologue speak French and set Napoleon and Hugo to direct the greatest extension, the greatest advance of a French quality. They were given to us much more than produced by us: hard to absorb, to digest. It was this difficulty of digestion that Lamartine, in his speech on the *Retour des cendres*, prophetically signaled to the average Frenchman of the golden mean. The return of the ashes took place twenty-five years after the departure of the living man and eight years before the return of the heir. But, if there was a latent, brooding Napoleonism in France in 1840, was there, will there ever be, a French literary Hugoism? After 1843, had Hugo not been transformed literarily into a function of Hugo alone? Had not exile, after 1852, wrapped him in the visible cloud of that solitude and the dazzling symbols of the monologue? Had it not diminished him as a presence by providing a pedestal to his position? The end of the monologue's influence, of its excitement and its permanence, and the grains of that sociability that constitutes the timeless secret and the binding force of French literature, therefore, diminished the presence more and more. The position remained indestructible, monumental.

The Monumental Poet

Monumental in the style of the monument peculiar to Napoleon: the Arc de Triomphe. That arch is an artificially fashioned monument, without precedent in the architectural tradition of France, without relation to the stature, the reality of the man, and the architect Eugène-Emmanuel Viollet-le-Duc has described it without mercy. And yet it exists, it is an ancestor, it is incorporated into Paris as much as the Notre-Dame to which Viollet-le-Duc immolates it. Victor Hugo had made himself its poet in the ode of 1823, with its prophetic epigraph, *Non deficit alter*, and again in that of 1837. In the end he imposed himself on it after having imposed his father's name on it, near it he spent the last years of his life and beneath it the first night of his eternity. His work occupies the same place, human in its detail and its meaning, inhuman in its proportions, in its voice, in its Napoleonism, in its monologue, in its disturbing and formidable *Victor Hugo alone.* Hugo's monologue is a great gate of poetry as the Arch is a great gate of history. But the monument, without human proportions, gains by being alone of its kind in Paris, by not throwing the human architecture of a capital out of joint. Paris tolerates it, accepts it, incorporates it, digests it. But a lesser city, a lesser vista? The Hugoesque monologue, similarly, would have engulfed and crippled a literature less ancient and less vigorous, less endowed with counterpart and counterweight. What was this monologue?

The Youthful Years

THE POET WITHOUT A MESSAGE

It took shape slowly, in large part favored by events, and it would have been hard to foresee it in the poet of the early years.

From 1822 to 1830 romantic poetry was three great poets, Lamartine, Vigny, and Hugo, quite obviously ranked apart from and above the others. Hugo's precocity was such that there is hardly need to take into account the differences in age—he was twelve years younger than the first, five years younger than the second. Now, if we compare the author of *Odes et ballades* and *Les Orientales* with the authors of *Les Méditations* and *Poèmes antiques et modernes,* we are struck by the fact that, of the three, he was the only one who did not carry what must be called, since French has no word to match the English term, a message. In the poetry of Lamartine and Vigny a new and profound spirit insinuated itself into the young and the women in order to permeate them, to soften them, to dissolve them, to conquer them. Set beside their deeply felt and whispered poems, Hugo's seem contrived and declamatory, the work of a studious, honorable, ambitious young man, precociously mature and poised, who had a career to make and who would make it, for he had excellent principles, as the saying was in those days: political and religious principles, even poetic principles. Nothing was more reasonable, more sensible, than his idea of the ode, and his ambition, which was that of a great disciple: "He thought that, if the movement of the ode was based on its ideas rather than its words, if, in addition, its composition was founded on any basic idea that was suited to the subject and whose development relied in all its stages on the development of the event that is described, replacing the worn-out, false colors of pagan mythology with the new, true colors of Christian theogony, the ode could be injected with something of the interest of the drama and also be made to speak in that austere, consoling, and religious language that was needed by an old society that was still trembling as it emerged from the *saturnalia* of atheism and anarchy."

These lines from his preface of 1822 are completely clear. It was a question of doing rather than saying something new, of furnishing a model of the ode inspired by a single "idea," of developing, carrying over into verse the spirit and the substance of *Le Génie du christianisme*, of telling the society of the Restoration not what the poet felt the need to say, like Lamartine and Vigny, but what that society felt the need, or, rather, the desire, to hear, what it would ask of the theater and the speaker's platform, and what the ode, in anticipation of the theater and the platform, which would be ill suited to the twenty-year-old beginner, would exert itself to provide through its own very intelligently understood means. Already it was a situation of a poetry rather than a presence of a poet.

THE MASTER OF TECHNIQUES

If there was any message in this poetry, it was a technical message. Telling Restoration society—good society, of course—what it wanted to be told meant asking it what that message was and then repeating it, not bringing it one. But if this impoverished young poet, who had to support with his pen a precociously and bravely founded family, worked over his themes, he was not unaware that in the matter of technique he was the equal, or rather the superior, of any one of his rivals. At twenty-two he knew his language, he had a universal and profound feeling for verse, much more than Lamartine and Vigny would ever have. The ode to Lamartine and the ode *Mon Enfance* have a skill that French lyric poetry had not known since Malherbe. What Hugo called the idea inspires and fills out their well-proportioned bodies without ever overstepping or unbalancing them. It is great rhetoric, sound rhetoric. Hugo was already the man who could speak of poetry as Leonardo spoke of painting to the Duke of Milan: "In painting I can do anything as well as anyone."

Hence *Les Ballades* and *Les Orientales*, uprooting in time and uprooting in space, which are less the work of a conquering poet than of a technician at liberty. It might almost be said that, with *Cromwell*, which they preceded and followed, they make a kind of trilogy, the trilogy of attempt, professionalism, technique. *Cromwell* is famous for its preface: but all Hugo's production until 1829 has the appearance of a preface, of a poetic introduction to poetry, a dramatic introduction to drama, of an overture. The lyric entrance of the real Hugo dates from *Feuilles d'automne*. And then the four collections—*Les Feuilles d'automne*, *Les Chants du crépuscule*, *Les Voix intérieures* and *Les Rayons et les ombres*, from 1831 to 1840, came to constitute a poetic *Histoire de dix ans,* a whole, a dome on four columns, the first peak of the true Hugo-esque monologue, Olympio's monologue among the living.

THE GREAT ESSENCES OF 1830

In *Feuilles d'automne* there is a second ode to Lamartine, written in June 1830, as a tribute to *Les Harmonies,* which is as beautiful as the first and which, born of a generous emotion of deference and admiration, shows us clearly what Hugo could envy in Lamartine. Lamartine's poetry, in Hugo's view, is a great ship between the two spheres of the sky and the sea, moving forward amid applause, hailed by the excitement of the crowd after having, like Columbus, found its world and awakened a universe. But Hugo's ship, he said, battles alone against the teeth of the tempest. The world that it seeks flees before it. There is no fecundity in that element through which it toils day and night. One is the ship of Columbus, the other is the ship of Jean-François de La Pérouse.[1] And it would be pleasing if this were chiefly a lyric, decorative theme. But it is to be observed that a quarter of a century later, writing from his exile to thank Alexandre Dumas for having dedicated a play to him, Hugo went back to the same image, recalling the friends who had gone to see him off at the pier in Antwerp when he sailed for Jersey, remembering Dumas' gesture of farewell as the ship stood out to sea, and Dumas going off in his dazzling dialogue and himself in the habitual monologue of Olympio, "in the gloomy oneness of the night."

Now, Lamartine and Dumas (and Balzac, when Hugo was writing *Les Misères* and, later, *Les Misérables*) were the sole rivals to whom Hugo gave any thought for the purpose of understanding their secret, of establishing a line of comparison between them and himself, of recognizing in them a superiority on one point to which he could not attain. He seems never to have felt this sentiment with respect to Sainte-Beuve; his mind did not contemplate the idea of a quality that he had to envy, either as a critic or a poet. He might have taken inspiration from *Joseph Delorme* in *Feuilles d'automne,* as he was to be inspired by Leconte de Lisle in *La Légende des siècles,* or by *Emaux et Camées* in *Les Chansons des rues et des bois,* in the manner of one who repossesses his own property, who could have invented that just as well as they and who in any case uses it better. Perhaps, after all, the author of *Les Misérables* had the same thoughts (wrongly) on the subject of Balzac. But the poet and orator did not think them about Lamartine, nor the man of the theater about Dumas. He saw in them great countries from which he was separated by natural boundaries, by a kind of boundary that he sensed in himself; he set limits to himself in recognizing them.

---

[1] An explorer under Louis XVI.–Translator.

That the same image should be imposed, drawn from Hugo's unconscious to serve him after twenty-five years, is at least a valuable illumination. If we reread the Ode of 1830 and 1854 again, we see in it a confrontation between what might be called two princes of dialogue and a
prince of monologue.

THE VOCATION FOR MONOLOGUE

Dialogue with the crowd. Between Lamartine and the crowd, between
Columbus' ship entering the harbor and the people thronging the pier,
the accord was made. With this crowd the poet had a common language,
which was not always divine but whose baser parts were elevated and
inspired by the divine part. It is lyrical and oratorical, in the fullness of
the two natures, in the equal footing of these two natures with human
nature. On this subject there is a curious dialogue between Sainte-Beuve
and Pierre-Simon Ballanche, a precursor of romanticism. "How is it,"
Ballanche asked, "that M. de Lamartine is so popular at the same time
that he is so lofty?" Sainte-Beuve replied (or said in 1845 that he had
replied): "That is because M. de Lamartine always starts from a universal
moral sentiment and a morality of which everyone has a germ in his
heart and virtually the expression on his lips. Others rise as high, but they
do not do so in the same line of ideas and feelings common to all. He is
like a swan rising out of the midst of the crowd that watched and loved
it while it walked and swam alongside: the crowd's eyes follow it into the
sky where it soars, as if it were a swan with the gift of song and flight,
while others are instead wild swans, or unapproachable eagles, which
launch their equally sublime flights from the top of a deserted forest or an
unvisited peak. The crowd sees them from the distance, but without quite
understanding where they come from, and it does not follow them with
the same sympathetic and intelligent interest."

Others became The Other in 1845. But Sainte-Beuve's image almost
superimposes itself on that with which Hugo himself described the same
contrast in the ode in *Feuilles d'automne.* Let us leave the ships and the
swans. Here, next to Lamartine's vocation for the dialogue, is Hugo's for
the monologue—a vocation all the more remarkable in that he had all the
gifts that would have brought him to that dialogue if a force as irresistible
and absolute as the ocean's had not at once diverted them into the monologue.

Are we dealing, in effect, with a monologue born of obscurity, of the
difficulty of expressing himself wholly, the monologue to which Ballanche was compelled, or that Quinet of whom Cousin said: "He is one
of those to whom God has said: 'Thou shalt never straighten thyself
out!'"? Quite the contrary. Of all French writers Hugo seems to us
the author at once most lucid in his expression and the rhetorician most

powerful in cumulative effect. Not only is he lucid; he redounds and over-powers with lucidity.

Are we dealing with a monologue born of isolation, extreme individuality, a kind of "not like the rest" in the manner of Gérard de Nerval or Baudelaire? Not at all! As much as Lamartine and more than Vigny, Hugo found his poetic subjects in the most ordinary emotions, ideas, impressions, in the daily bread of human life: love, family, children, country; and the great political and religious themes are proclaimed by him with a loudspeaker that only amplifies, envelopes in limitless images, what the average man thinks, that transforms the sparrows of the street into wild swans and unapproachable eagles.

Are we dealing with a monologue born of unawareness, of forgetfulness of others, of a monstrous egocentricity? Still less. In his daily life Hugo was a courteous man, polite, witty, prudent, keenly attentive to his literary and financial interests and very skilled in their management, immune to that magic of chance in which Lamartine and Dumas lived, a shrewd observer, an expert in all things, and profoundly interested in life.

Are we dealing with a monologue born of abandonment at the desk to the phrase, the pace of the inner speech, the steeds of thought? Absolutely not. Hugo was always the artisan poet. Cousin said of him to Sainte-Beuve: "Hugo upsets all one's ideas about the lyric poet. One is accustomed to defining the lyric poet as a light thing. Instead of that, one finds in Hugo a calculated, complicated thought that works on everything." And Sainte-Beuve replied: "Yes, he makes an ode as one would make a lock! An expert lock, but still a machine." The green of envy, and of the Institut, aside, these remarks are not devoid of aptness. Hugo is a great *homo faber*, and *homo faber* is always taken more or less out of himself by the lure and the need of the material to be worked. Aside from literature, Lamartine possessed only one skill, which, furthermore, he had learned: that of diplomacy, a moral and political skill. Hugo's extraliterary skills, in contrast, were manual skills, the same as those of his grandfather in Nancy, drawing and woodworking. Cousin and Sainte-Beuve symbolize for us two intellectual natures that were amazed by the nature of an artisan. And it was just the technician's, the artisan's, nature that dominated everything in Hugo between 1820 and 1830. What is that artisan's nature if not submission to the material, a mind attuned to and guided by the material, in dialogue with it, attentive to it? Sainte-Beuve saw the art of a glass stainer in *Les Ballades*. "These are Gothic windows . . . in the poetic phrase one sees the break in the rhythm like the break imposed by the window frame on the painting, and there is nothing bad in the fact that one sees it." *Les Odes* and *Les Orientales* open the studio of a decorative painter. This great artisan, this master of the workshops of romanticism and Parnassus never lost contact with substance and precision: the contrast with Lamartine's insubstantiality and imprecision is always complete.

These, then, are the conditions that would alienate Hugo from the monologue, and that indeed did more or less alienate him from it until 1830. But more and more, after 1830, he was led, constrained, condemned to the monologue as a thinker—the Thinker.

The Thinker

When someone stopped him in the street and said: "Always something to think about!" Lamartine replied: "But I never think: my ideas think for me." It was quite true: like a fountain with four spouts, they gave him thought, rhythm, facility, eloquence. Of Victor Hugo it might equally be said that words wrote for him. But his ideas did not think for him. It was he who thought them; and above all it was he who thought. There is no reason to make fun of the name that he gave himself: the Thinker. Not in the sense of Maine de Biran or Amiel, obviously, but in a real and powerful sense. Auguste Rodin's Hugo, formerly in the Palais-Royal, and even the man who stood naked before the Panthéon, a Hugoesque reality that seemed to have risen from the vault to bear testimony to the poet, explain and annotate him more clearly than those critics who saw from their sash-windows that Hugo had no ideas. By this word and function of thinker, Hugo, with a true experience of the real, meant to convey the strength of the inner life as he experienced it in himself, like an element: an inner life as remarkable, in the realm of *homo sapiens*, as Hugo's technique in the realm of *homo faber*. His monologue was made of that inner life, and, besides, a monologue that has style cannot be made of anything else.

Let us remark parenthetically that the legend that made Victor Hugo a man of words who did not think was created by men who were themselves devoured by hack work, like Emile Faguet, or by social life, and within whom there was virtually nothing left. "There he is alone with himself," Alfred Capus said of one such; "in other words, really alone!" The very opposite of Hugo's enormously peopled solitude. No philosopher has ever fallen into this journalist's platitude on the subject of Victor Hugo.

This climate peculiar to his inner life, this monologue that was the condition of his genius, was depicted by Hugo in a remarkable composition that, as the formulation of his secret, holds in his work almost the same place as *La Nuit de décembre* in Musset's and *La Vigne et la maison* in Lamartine's—both real experiences, as we know, and not fictions. This is *La Tempête sous un crâne* in *Les Misérables*. It could be said that there were indeed countries in his brain, as with Pantagruel and *Le Satyre*. Musset and Lamartine portray their solitude in a dialogue between themselves and their poetic souls; Hugo expounds his in a monologue. A virtual transcript of the record of the birth of the Hugoesque monologue might be found in it: Jean Valjean yielded "to that mysterious power that bade him: *Think!* as two thousand years earlier it bade another doomed man: March! . . . It is certain that one talks to oneself; there is no thinking being who has not experienced that. It might be said even that the Word is never a more splendid mystery than when, inside a man, it goes from thought to consciousness and then returns from consciousness to thought. It is only in this sense that words often used in this chapter must be read—*he said, he cried*. One tells oneself, one talks to oneself, one cries out to oneself, without a rupture of the outer silence. There is a great tumult, everything in us speaks except the mouth. For all that they are neither visible nor palpable, the realities of the soul are none the less realities." Realities . . . There exists an inner reality of Victor Hugo as there exists an outer situation of Victor Hugo. They are two potent gods.

The Four Volumes of the 1830s

LES FEUILLES D'AUTOMNE

It is this inner reality of Victor Hugo that puts so great a distance between *Feuilles d'automne* and the poetry that preceded it. Everything of the future poet, the poet of a half-century, is already contained in the forty poems of the fragile volume that carries as its first epigraph *Data fata secutus*—and that indeed would follow them to the very end. Among these destinies there is precisely that sober hue of a tree that, at twenty-two, already feels its autumn in its responsibilities, in that inner weight that is revealed in the opening poem and that is made explicit in the second, *A Louis Boulanger*, and in so many others, the *Rêverie d'un passant à propos d'un roi*, *Ce qu'on entend sur la montagne*. Many of the poems in this volume are addressed to individuals—Boulanger, Sainte-Beuve, a nephew, a friend, the poet's wife or daughter. But it will be observed how little the poems seem to concern them, passing over their heads, asking of them only the opportunity for a monologue, lacking that appeal and that direct grip that, in Lamartine, go directly from man to man and sustain the spirits of a dialogue above a poem; the two poems most characteristic of this monologue are *La Pente de la rêverie* and *La Prière pour tous*.

La Pente de la rêverie has the same quality of an official report as *La Tempête sous un crâne:* official report, dated 28 May 1830, of a totalitarian vision of the world, of a hallucination of abundance, in which human history is seen and sensed in the manner of a Gothic cathedral, at once in its totality and in the infinite detail of its sculptured stones. By way of this *Pente de la rêverie* one enters the soul of the poet as one walks through the limbs and the head of a bronze colossus. Here for the first time Hugo found his eternal theme. Three moments on a rainy spring day in that apartment in the rue Jean-Goujon where he had gone in search of country and green. His children, Léopoldine and Charles, were playing in the garden, the birds were singing, the Seine, Paris, the dome of the Invalides were spread out before him. There is the first level, the first life, the first Hugo as family man. Then this level fades. It is succeeded by a second, his friends, literary friends, painter friends—in other words, the school over which he ruled, the world of letters, of ideas, of glory, that family according to the spirit in which the family according to the flesh was merged. Such are the first two Hugos, the normal character of a poet, which are to be encountered more or less in every normal poet, which have nothing of the *Hugo alone*, which could even be virtually his opposite. Abruptly then, on another level, as a new face of the earth is seen from the summit of a hill, there is the third Hugo, the visionary Hugo, lacking any common measure with his predecessors, Hugo the unique, Hugo alone, or, better, Hugo a people, Hugo peopled, Hugo an element, a Hugo in whom physical barriers yield, the lock between body and brain is loosed, the production is no longer obstructed by attention to fact; the whole memory of a human past, present behind the lock like water behind a dam, flows out, inundates, merges with the centuries, the generations, the Solyma Mountains of Asia Minor, the Tyres, the Carthages, the Romes, and human history and cosmic continuity drink the life of a man like a drop of water. This theme of the impersonal plane that replaces the personal was to reappear in the last poem of *Les Contemplations*. By then, in the solitude of exile, it had become Hugo's daily vocation. But this vocation peculiar to Guernsey was already present as early as *Feuilles d'automne*, which Hugo wrote between the ages of twenty-six and twenty-nine and in which the prophet, the visionary, first spoke.

La Prière pour tous, banalized by the dragging of extracts from it through children's anthologies, is directed toward the same point as *La Pente de la rêverie*. If it is compared with the odes of the 1820s, this poem of 1830, clearly shows the change of climate precisely because it seems to belong to the same family of themes,—the themes of *Magnitudo Parvi*.* Léopoldine, whom Sainte-Beuve called the daughter of Caesars, already assumes, as if she were on the other side of the grave, the aspect of intercessor and angel between her contemplative father and the throng of the living and the dead.

* *The Greatness of the Small*—Translator.

And with what poem, dated November 1831, does *Feuilles d'automne* end? With the first poem of *Châtiments,* twenty years before the *coup d'état* of 1851—the map of Europe brought to life, blazing, streaming with the names of cities turned to diamonds for the setting of the rhyme, peoples avenged, kings pilloried, marked off, blazoned at the shoulder, iron collared, and the last line announcing the birth of that Muse.

> *Et j'ajoute à ma lyre une corde d'airain!*

> (And to my lyre I add a string of bronze!)

The final poem in *Les Voix intérieures* was to conclude the 1837 volume on the same note. To the new muse, the young Fate that sensed her destiny and wanted to come forth, to go free, the poet's finger signaled: "Stay yet a while, it is not time."

> *Aie au milieu de tous l'attitude élevée*
> *D'une lente déesse, à punir réservée,*
> *Qui, recueillant la force ainsi qu'un saint trésor,*
> *Pourrait depuis longtemps et ne veut pas encore!*

> (Bear thyself in their midst apart from all,
> A goddess slow to sound the judgment call,
> Who, storing strength like sacred treasure still,
> Long since could do what is not yet her will!)

LES CHANTS DU CRÉPUSCULE

Feuilles d'automne had taken the new course; the line continued straight and solitary through the three other volumes, *Les Chants du crépuscule, Les Voix intérieures* and *Les Rayons et les ombres.* They are the four sections of a single poem, the four stages of a single life.

In *Les Chants du crépuscule,* civic, national, human bells rang out over Paris through the pierced towers of the ode. No other of Hugo's volumes of verse, unless perhaps *Les Châtiments,* has more of a political character. The early poems of love for Juliette sound their silver tone here, but the future peer, the rival of Lamartine, the annunciatory poet and prophet, rises to his full stature.

LES VOIX INTÉRIEURES

Beginning with *Les Voix intérieures,* this annunciatory poet and prophet takes on a new name, he calls himself Olympio. It was in 1835 that Victor Hugo conceived the idea of a major book of verse that would be called "Les Contemplations d'Olympio," the birth certificate of which is embodied in the dialogue of 15 October 1835, which is called *A Olympio,* properly placed in the volume of *Les Voix intérieures* (all Hugo's books of verse have magnificent but very appropriate titles) because, like

La Vigne et la maison, it is composed of two alternating inner voices, that of the poet as man and that of the poet as prophet, of the present poet of Paris and of the future poet of Guernsey.

> *Voix pareille à la sienne et plus haute pourtant,*
> *Comme la grande mer qui parlerait au fleuve.*

> (A voice like his and yet a louder voice,
> As of the ocean speaking to the stream.)

Like *La Pente de la rêverie,* here again in the volumes of the 1830s is a key poem, a hinge poem on which the gate of Hugo's destiny slowly turns and that is paraphrased in another place by the preface to the last of the four volumes, where a poem popularized the name of Olympio and of which the volume's title also indicated a theme of an unevenly matched dialogue between the past and the future: *Les Rayons et les ombres.* This portrait of the ideal poet, drawn in this preface of 28 April 1840, is already the very portrait of the author of *Les Contemplations,* the portrait of the poet of Guernsey. "He would make a religion of conscience, like Juvenal, who felt a witness in himself night and day; a religion of thought, like Dante, who defined as the damned those who no longer thought; a religion of thought, like Saint Augustine, who, unworried lest he be called a pantheist, called heaven 'an intelligent creature.'" Juvenal and Dante were among those pre-Hugos who would be reincarnated in the exile of 1851 and in *William Shakespeare.* Saint Augustine is designated here as a precursor genius to the theologian of *La Bouche d'ombre* and *Dieu.* What was to be the poetic mission of this poet composed of Juvenal, Dante, and Saint Augustine? The epic trilogy of Guernsey. "What this poet, this philosopher, this intelligence would thus accomplish in the whole body of his work with all his dramas, all his poems, all his thoughts together would be—let us say so here—the great mysterious epic of which each of us bears a song in himself, of which Milton wrote the prologue and Byron the epilogue: the Poem of Man."

LES RAYONS ET LES OMBRES

Les Rayons et les ombres provided the musical overture to those Contemplations d'Olympio whose then unknown destiny required the complicity of solitude and exile. The opening poem of *Les Rayons, Fonction du poète,* is *Les Mages* without the jewelry of proper names; the second, *Le Sept Août 1829,* is the eternal dialogue of those two majesties, the king and the poet. Even in the third, *Regard jeté dans une mansarde,* the popular sentimental poem mounts to the oracle's place: here is Hugo's war on Voltaire, the war of the prophetic century on the critical century, of the man of God on the man of Satan. There is also a bit of padding, assigned to the part of *Ombres,* and even the famous *Guitares,* but such as it is and in its very diversity the volume seems to be that one of the four that, being nearest to *Les Contemplations*, resembles it the most, best makes us feel the profound unity of the poet as he expresses it again in the decisive preface: "Nothing is apparently more varied than his poems, nothing is at bottom more unified and coherent. Taken in its synthesis, his work is like the earth: there are products of every kind, a basic idea for all the conceptions, flowers of every sort, a single sap for all the roots."

The Poetic Interregnum

We know how the sap seemed to dry up between 1843 and 1851. The disaster of *Les Burgraves*, the death of Léopoldine, the choice of a political career thinned the lyric vein for eight years, during which there was one brief poetic recovery, the autumn of 1846, when the poet wrote the verses of *Pauca Meae*, as well as *Aymerillot* and *Le Mariage de Roland*.

In November 1849, leaving a session of the Assembly, it was under the title and in the intimacy of *A Olympio* that he observed:

> *Parmi ces hommes fous et vainement sonores,*
> *Grave, triste, et rempli de l'avenir lointain,*
> *Tu caches, ou tu dis les choses du destin;*
> *Car le ciel rayonnant te fit naître, ô poète,*
> *De l'Apollon chanteur et de l'Isis muette.*

> (Sad, sober, with the far-off future full
> Among these mad men and their empty roar,
> You hide or tell the tally of fate's store;
> For, poet, radiant skies made you be born
> To Isis' silence and Apollo's horn.)

Wonderful personifications, like that of Proserpine in *Les Contemplations!* Between that Apollo of the poet and that Isis of the thinker, to which exile would provide their structure and their depth, there is a hiatus, the lack of a mediator, of a bond, of a third term, of what would have made an orator in the Assembly, a Lamartine in familiar lyricism, a Dumas in the theater: the absence of the bewitching Venus and the insinuating Mercury. But what an Apollo in *La Légende*, what an Isis in *Dieu!*

Les Contemplations

The ten thousand lines of *Les Contemplations* balance, in Hugo's work, the ten thousand lines of the four volumes of 1830–1840. It is the former that is generally considered superior, but that superiority is open to discussion, and the tetralogy of the 1830s, after all, is poetically its equal. Its unique place results from its function as a poetic journal or memoir, spread over almost a quarter of a century. In its broken form, it corresponds to *Mémoires d'outre-tombe* or *Confidences*. The poems of *Autrefois* are dated back only to fill in the gaps, to restore certain moments of the past through imaginative memory, and also to arrange these moments in such a way as to extend through the political life of the exile of Guernsey a unity that it did not have. Whence poems of literary criticism like *Réponse à une acte d'accusation* and especially of political criticism like *Ecrit en 1846*, which was written in 1854, love poems that are nosegays sent from Jersey to beauties of another time; and too, the poet who becomes the prophet, Jerusalem that becomes Patmos.

> *Si j'appelle Rouen, Villequier, Caudebec,*
> *Toute l'ombre me crie: Horeb, Cédron, Balbeck.*

> (If I call Rouen, Villequier, Caudebec,
> The dark replies: Horeb, Kedron, Baalbek.)

The two-towered poem, the Notre-Dame of exile, which ends with *Ce que dit la bouche d'ombre* and *A Celle qui est restée en France*, would carry, in sum, the same message as the four-towered poem of the 1830s, if, however, two new unexpected and eccentric elements, not posited in the horoscope of 1840, had not intervened on Jersey to lift that poetry above itself, to situate it in life itself on a superhuman dividing line analogous to the one that Hugo thought he had found in the theater with *Les Burgraves:* the sea and the dead.

The Sea and the Dead

At the age of fifty Hugo exchanged the inland air for the sea air. He was to spend eighteen years on two islands. To start with, it was a physiological revolution. Until then he had been a city man, a pure Parisian, and he, Boileau, and Baudelaire were readily called the three great poets of Paris. Everything that he wrote was written in Paris. During his short vacations in the country he rested: the opposite of Lamartine, who wrote virtually nothing in Paris and all whose poetic work was dictated by autumns in Burgundy or by summers on the Tuscan sea. Immediately, and with a profound acceptance, Hugo's health, his life, his poetry, and his thinking embraced the climate of salt and iodine, of space and storm.

Before the element with which he was to live for eighteen years, the poet took cognizance and possession of his inner world as of another element. That path of revery that he had followed twenty years before on the Champs-Elysées abandoned its character of a path on land to become a measureless bed beneath the sea. Solitude made the occasional visionary a habitual visionary. The mystic state of *La Pente de la rêverie* was amplified and deepened, reached out to hell and heaven with *Ce que dit la bouche d'ombre*. And Korah who became Proserpine, symbol of that transfigured poetry, is a poem out of *Les Contemplations*.

Hugo felt that his inner element was powerful enough to stand up to the other element, to debate with it, to listen to it, to answer it, to challenge it. As it strengthened his rib cage, the sea accustomed him to this roaring dialogue. Much fun is often made of the poem called *Ibo*, of the alleged contradiction between its idea and its rhythm, of the prophetic delirium that runs through it. And very wrongly! Written to the dolmen of Rosel, *Ibo* is again a hinge poem, the poem of a transfiguration, and in the compact energy of its short strophe is the very moment when the figure of Hugo passes from the portrait by Pierre-Jean David d'Angers to that by Rodin.

> *J'irai lire la grande bible,*
> *J'entrerai nu*
> *Jusqu'au tabernacle terrible*
> *De l'inconnu,*
>
> *Jusqu'au seuil de l'ombre et du vide,*
> *Gouffres ouverts*
> *Que garde la meute livide*
> *Des noirs éclairs,*
>
> *Jusqu'aux portes visionnaires*
> *Du ciel sacré,*
> *Et si vous aboyez, tonnerres,*
> *Je rugirai.*

> (I will read that great testament,
> Nude I will go
> Even into the holy tent
> We do not know,
>
> Across the sill of dark and void,
> Those double pits
> Where ghastly guardians are deployed
> And black light spits,
>
> Up to the visionary gates
> Of sacred sky,
> And, thunder, if your loud voice grates,
> Then roar will I.)

In the author of *Les Châtiments* this is no boast, for *Les Châtiments* brought the roar into poetry and this roar of Jersey has the roar of the sea as its bass and its *obbligato*. Some of the poems in *Les Châtiments* were written in Brussels. But their prophetic torrent and their tempest, their physical character, the measure of their cry would not exist without the dialogue and the combat of the human voice and the sea, similar to the dialogue and the combat of Jacob with the angel. Exile created a more or less Manichean Hugo, imposed on the author of *La Bouche d'ombre*, of *La Fin de Satan*, of *Les Misérables*, the presence of evil like the presence of the sea, as if it were still another element, an element embodied for the exile by the December government, by force at the service of political crime, by the reign of Bonaparte, against whose shouts the exile felt his lungs powerful enough to roar in answer. The cosmic and metaphysical theme of *Ibo* raises to the second power the political theme of *Les Châtiments*, the power of the roar that answers the howling of the dogs.

With the sea, the dead. In 1853, when Hugo had just finished *Les Châtiments*, Delphine de Girardin was visiting him in Jersey and introduced the Hugo family to table tilting. The first voice that spoke to them from beyond the grave was Léopoldine's. The historic dead followed, and for months they conducted their dialogues with Hugo in thousands of Hugoesque verses. Hugo's conscious posed the questions; his unconscious answered, telepathically and through the intermediary of his son, Charles, and other relatives. This natural explanation, which is the true one, may seem as superhuman as the supernatural explanation. The poems of the Hugoesque by-product, attributed by Hugo to the tables, are a unique phenomenon in the history of poetry and even in that of humanity. Hugo himself was never content with a natural explanation. If he put a stop to the séances and the dictations, in fear of overwhelmingly violent inner upheavals (perhaps he was thinking of his brother who died mad, and of his children, only one of whom, Sainte-Beuve's goddaughter and also mad, was to survive him), he never doubted that the dead, the voices of God, God himself had spoken to him. He himself wrote on photographs of himself in ecstasy: "Victor Hugo speaking with God." Whence the echoes of those conversations in his poems, the second volume of *Les Contemplations*, from *Pauca Meae* to *Au Bord de l'infini*, the book of death and the dead. The visionary poet was now an inhabited poet, a poet-world. His poems, like his novels, would take on the aspect of worlds, in his image. His triple epic and *Les Misérables* would be worlds. Just as the last poem of *Feuilles d'automne*, marking a date, had placed the first milestone of satiric poetry, so *Les Burgraves* and the epic poems of 1845 placed the first milestones of epic poetry. But how is it possible to think that this poetry would have cut so many roads through space after 1853 without that reinforcement, that discovery, and that presence of the sea and the dead?

The Giant Years of Poetry

Hence the remarkable years of Jersey and Guernsey from 1851 until about 1860. By then the whole generation of the century had died, like Balzac; had fallen silent, like Vigny; or else, like most of the rest, in a world that was no longer theirs, was overstaying its time with outdated productions, like Michelet, or piling up hack pieces, like Lamartine. Then it seemed that the whole heritage of that food of giants that was the share of the romantic generation, the unique generation, fell to Hugo, as the heritages of Europe had fallen to Charles the Fifth, and that Guernsey became the seat of a universal monarchy (against which the old French reactions did not neglect to fight); that, when in 1850 he left the tomb of Balzac, where he had delivered a magnificent oration, Hugo had taken with him, to make it part of his own, the cosmic part of that genius.

Hugo's poetic production during these nine years was almost double what had preceded them and what would follow them: *Les Châtiments, Les Années funestes*, the greater part of *Les Contemplations, La Fin de Satan, Dieu, La Légende des siècles, Les Quatre Vents de l'esprit*, the greater part of *Toute la lyre* and of *Océan*.

To these must be added *Les Chansons des rues et des bois*, published in 1865 but almost all written in 1859, the year of the operetta, *Orphée aux enfers*, which was to give the Empire's ten final years their style, the style of a good time, of the gods of Olympus amusing themselves. Hugo had always been extremely sensitive to literary trends, and, if politics had evolved differently, what a poet of presence the poet of exile on the rock would have given Paris! It might be said of his work in exile that, while the epic "pourâna" belonged to the mysticism of 1848, the truly Second Empire poetry was the "punishments" of absence and the "songs" of presence. In all Hugo's poetic work, Alphonse Daudet, who remained the former secretary of the Duc de Morny right to the end and was the spokesman for the twenty-year-olds of 1860, accepted and liked only these two books, these two watersheds of the imperial poetry.

At the Crossroads of Four Worlds

But, in the face of the peak and the substance of Hugo, *Les Chansons* is only an excursion, half a voyage to Cythera, half a voyage to Paris, and both journeys, in the days of *La Belle Hélène* and *La Vie parisienne*, were the same. The Hugo of exile, the Hugo chained to solitude, to prophecy, to the seas, to the dead, to words, was to be seen in the image of the four winds of the mind, of the four horses of the sun, at the crossroads of four worlds that corresponded equally to his idea of a universal monarchy and an infinite effulgence: the world of words, fed on lyricism; the world of visions, the epic subject; the philosophical world, the stage of a struggle between light and darkness; and the political world, which the satiric genius in him had curiously navigated.

THE WORLD OF WORDS

No enemy challenged his monarchy over words. In France, Hugo is to words what Descartes is to reason or Voltaire to intelligence, what elsewhere Michelangelo is to marble or Rembrandt to light. He got everything that he needed from them for his thought and they got everything from him that they wanted for their beauty. Never was that sovereignty of words more absolute, less limited than in the 1850s. One is reminded of Louis XIV after Nijmegen, of Napoleon in 1811. The lyricism of *Stella, Les Mages, A celle qui est restée en France* glitters with words like a summer night's sky with stars. The poem called *Dieu*, which undoubtedly marked the highest point of Hugoesque giantism, becomes frightening with them. If triangles had a god, Montesquieu said, he would be a triangular god. In this poem we literally see the master of language make God with language:

Car le mot c'est le Verbe, et le Verbe c'est Dieu

(For language is the Word, the Word is God.)

Saint John's word was Logos, not language. But Hugo alone was entitled to misconstruction and this play on words. He gave it being as Christ did *Petrus petram.*

THE WORLD OF VISIONS

And that would not carry much weight if the author of the pun were not also the author of *La Pente de la rêverie;* if the master of words were not also the master of visions; if *La Vision d'où est sorti ce livre,* which begins *La Légende des siècles,* had not been a real vision; if the peculiarly Hugoesque poetic life were not the marriage, the unexpected exogamy, of the Word and the *Chose vue.* Hugo did not create epic vision, but he did create the visionary epic. *Le Sacre de la Femme, Le Petit Roi de Galice, Eviradnus, Le Satyre, La Rose de l'Infante* are so many balances between two forces, the inexhaustible force of words and the unfailing, unartificed force of the evocative vision. To the inborn mastery of devices, of refinements, of pairings, of etymologies, of a language at the zenith of its virile potency, Hugo joined naked vision, the vision of the Biblical prophets. For Hugo the epic of Guernsey had only one precedent, the Bible, from Jeremiah and Ezekiel to Saint John. That is why *La Légende des siècles* should be taken only as one panel of a triptych, of which the two others, both of which are earlier, derive directly from the phophets: *La Fin de Satan* and *Dieu.* The *Jésus-Christ* of *La Fin de Satan* would be raised to exalted rank indeed when it was described as the only tolerable and beautiful transposition of the Gospel into French. But did Hugo win his wager with *Dieu?* Did he bring to life for the reader what was certainly and deeply alive for him? It seems that here that balance between words and vision that is maintained elsewhere is shifted in favor of words, that the words, "this body given air by the voice," tragically and passionately mass their body to express what has no body.

It was ten years since Hugo had given up the theater, given up the projection of his visions on the stage, which could not bear the vision of *Les Burgraves.* But on his islands it was he himself who became a theater, it was his inner world that became a dramatic world. As Napoleon's last word was *Armée*, Hugo's final line in his agony of May 1885 was

> *C'est ici le combat du jour et de la nuit*
>
> (This is the battleground of day and night.)

THE WORLD OF THOUGHT

This dramatic battle, this Manichean dialogue, this struggle of God against matter, of soul against substance, of good against evil, of life against death, this wholly Hugoesque *Noir et blanc* became on Guernsey the thinking of Hugo, the thinker's thinking: it was the awareness of this battle that constructed a philosophy for him. Good and evil were not precise ideas; questions crowded Hugo's consciousness, that inner poetic world that lived, that found its third dimension, only through light and shadow. But, if reality is spirit; if God becomes real or accomplishes his purposes only with difficulty; if the problem of evil exists; if substantiality is a weight to be lifted; if the religions of East and West and the philosophies from Anaximander's to Henri Bergson's have indeed felt and thought that this was the case; if this is a consequence of humanity's inner experience as the laws of physics are a consequence of its outer experience; if Hugo lived in the meditation and the expression of these truths; if he gave them a language, a substance, a glorious body; if, however obvious or probable they may be for philosophers, he made them perceptible to those who are not philosophers; if philosophers admitted and admired them in him, how would it be possible, in his lonely dialogue, in those storms, in that sea within a skull, in that presentation of God and the world, not to recognize the reality of the thought and the dignity of the thinker?

THE WORLD OF THE NATION

Finally the exile of December 1851, the author of *Les Châtiments*, assumed his definitive political stature. The First Empire had made his father a general and a count, the Restoration had given the son an official investiture, Louis-Philippe had raised him to the peerage. The very ingratitude of Louis-Napoleon toward the poet of Napoleon raised Hugo higher still. The refusal of a ministry separated the vengeance seeker from the ingrate, Archilochus from Lycambus. It was not great, but it was human. And this human quality was immediately succeeded by the superhuman quality that was in Hugo's poetic nature and that he carried over into his political pronouncements. His poetry profited by it when it was in verse. His glory did not suffer by it when it was in prose.

The Fruitless Years

The marvelous years virtually ended in 1860. The quarter of a century that Victor Hugo had yet to live added to his prestige, to his glory, to the rise of his name, rather than to his work. It added, and it imposed a burden. If Hugo had died in exile in 1860, leaving behind him in sum almost all his existing poetic work; if the funeral of 1885 had been a Return of the Ashes in 1870, bringing back Hugo dead with the return of the Republic, at the very moment at which he returned alive, and enclosing the oath of Jersey in the tomb, would he have enemies today? Similarly, if one of the muskets aimed at Lamartine in 1848 had brought him down on the steps of the Hôtel de Ville during his oration for the flag, what a magnificent memory he would have left! For the one as for the other the age of sixty was the dangerous point, the useless point.

> *Que te sert, ô Priam, d'avoir vécu si vieux?*
>
> (Priam, what use to live to such great age?)

The poetic works that were written after 1860—*L'Année terrible*, *l'Art d'être grand-père*—brought Hugo glory in the Paris of the 1870s; to his poetry they added only a fitting old age, as the few pieces in *La Légende des siècles* that date from this period would have done if there had not also been *Le Cimetière d'Eylau* and *Les Sept Merveilles du monde*.

It is childish to wonder whether Hugo is the greatest poet in the language. But he may well be called, in every sense of the word, the greatest phenomenon in French literature. His present situation, with that of Balzac and for the same reasons—their character as makers and bearers of

worlds, as Atlases, as shepherds (on headlands capped in clouds)—is probably the highest and the most solid of any nineteenth-century writer. In
part his future will be determined by what literary landscape the twentieth century, when it is over, will have added to the mass of the nineteenth and the earlier centuries when they have become like changes in
the shoreline, under new promontories and new cloud caps. Ronsard lost
rank in the seventeenth century not only because of the evolution of the
language but because the seventeenth century had the strength to do
something else, to do it equally well, and because the demotion, the loss
of Ronsard, analogous to the loss of the Rhône, was a condition of that
outcome: a half century after Ronsard's death *Le Cid* arose. But nothing
in the half century after Hugo's death threatened him with this profitable demotion. Nothing threatens the nineteenth century with it. André
Gide put a good deal of sense, and good sense, into his reply to the question who was the greatest French poet: "Victor Hugo, alas!" The shaded,
just, and genuine opinion of a writer of the generation whose duty it was
to dim Hugo, as Corneille's generation had dimmed Ronsard, and of
which in 1935 both itself and we had to admit that—alas!—it had not
dimmed him.

CÉNACLES; STUDIOS; ARTISTS

The Cénacles: Deschamps, Nodier, Hugo

A new literary movement often needs hermetic environments in which it tests itself *in vitro*, finds its watchwords, its rallying point, its personal ties: *salons*, cafés, beer halls, depending on the fashion of the time. Romanticism had its *cénacles* and its studios.

Cénacle is an esoteric word that in this context means the circle of a poet who entertains. The first *cénacle* was that of *La Muse française*, a magazine of verse and prose that lasted a year, from July 1823 to June 1824, and that had as its chief editors the Deschamps brothers, Émile and Antony, respectable poets who did not give their magazine a name that suited their poetry, since almost all their verse was translations from the Spanish, the Italian, and the German. *La Muse* was a very eclectic publication. The last of the classics, Charles Brifaut and Pierre Baour-Lormian, wrote for it. It did not include Casimir Delavigne, whose glory, with *Les Messéniennes*, matched Lamartine's in 1820, but it did contain three *langue d'oc* writers born before 1790—Alexandre Soumay, Alexandre Guiraud, Jules de Rességuier, Flower-Game poets. Hugo and Vigny also wrote for it. Above all, all these people met in the Deschamps' home.

When *La Muse* ceased publication in July 1824, the Deschamps *cénacle* became less useful for a few weeks. Charles Nodier, an unusual man of Besançon, learned, imaginative, the author of pleasant stories, had just been appointed librarian of the Arsénal. He opened a *salon* there that was presided over with much grace by his wife and especially by their daughter, Marie. For ten years the Arsénal evenings were the magnet of all the romantic writers, and particularly the young. Poets, painters, enthusiasts, foreigners thronged there, argued there, danced there. This free, open society was a counterpart and a contrast to the society of the closed *salons;* Musset was its spoiled child, its prince charming. But it cannot be said that these encounters in a transient hotel had any literary influence.

The real romantic *cénacle* met in Victor Hugo's red drawing room in the rue Notre-Dame-des-Champs. It was from there that the doctrinal literature of romanticism issued in 1827 in the form of manifestos and prefaces—especially the preface to *Cromwell*. Sainte-Beuve, Vigny, Dumas, Musset, Balzac, the Deschamps, Turquety, Boulay-Paty, artists like Eugène Delacroix, Eugène Devéria, Louis Boulanger, David d'Angers were assiduous in their attendance. And there was nothing closed about this society: any poet and above all any admirer was welcome. The important activities of the *cénacle* consisted in readings of new works. In July 1829 Victor Hugo read *Marion Delorme* in his home, and eight days later Vigny invited the poets to hear a reading of his *Othello*. On 30 September 1829 there was the celebrated reading of *Hernani* to some sixty friends, the usual complement of these gatherings. A restless, bitter, captious writer, Henri de Latouche, then published in *La Revue de Paris* for October the sensation-making article on *La Camaraderie littéraire* in which he denounced the peril of the closed circle and mutual admiration. Great discussions followed. And after 1830 the friendships came apart. The mutual quarrels of Hugo, Vigny, Sainte-Beuve, the sarcasms of Musset, the rivalries of the theater, political disagreements shattered the *cénacle;* romanticism was more brilliant than ever but it was no longer, in the precise and technical sense of the word, a school.

Painters and Poets

In one respect, however, this word "school," *schola,* retained a meaning that was important. Romanticism was the first literary revolution in France that could not be separated from a revolution in the plastic arts. There was a mixed school, a common spirit and art, in the generation of romantic poets and romantic painters.

Delacroix's *Le Radeau de la Méduse* [The Raft of the *Medusa*] in the 1819 *Salon* and *Les Massacres de Scio* [The Massacres of Chios] in the 1824 *Salon* had introduced a new style of painting with much fanfare. But it was the *Salon* of 1827, the same year as the preface to *Cromwell,* that raised the question of plastic and poetic romanticism, not so much because of Delacroix' *Christ au jardin des oliviers* and *Marino Faliero* as because of two canvases that are now disregarded but that aroused tremendous enthusiasm among the poets—Devéria's *Naissance de Henri IV* and the twenty-one-year-old Boulanger's *Mazeppa*. The *cénacle* opened its doors to the artists and Boulanger became a sort of official painter to Victor Hugo. Very soon a few young men created the romantic vignette, engraving, and lithograph: Alfred and Tony Johannot, Jean Gigoux, and particularly Célestin Nanteuil. And Hugo himself was not the least of the draftsmen of romanticism.

The rue du Doyenné

A final *cénacle* symbolized and consecrated this union of art and poetry at that time. In contrast to its predecessors, it was not a transient hotel, a place of confrontations and encounters. It was a common school with a unity, a zeal, a doctrine that were to survive romanticism itself. This was the group of the rue du Doyenné centered on Théophile Gautier and Gérard de Nerval and on the banner of what was later to be called the doctrine of art for art's sake.

The old rue du Doyenné, on the site of the present-day Place du Carrousel, serves as a reference point in this connection, because Gautier, Gérard, and their friends lived there together; because it was more or less there that what has been called the first Bohemia took shape—the life and customs of free, intemperate, bellicose artists. Poets and painters were mingled together there and the dominant style was the "arty"—the bourgeois was the monster, the fantastic, exaggerated scapegoat that "the infamy" was for Voltaire or that Pitt and Saxe-Coburg were for the Revolution. This provocative dress of romanticism, this playing to the gallery, had nothing in common—quite the contrary—with the M. de Lamartine who was a great drawing-room figure, the Comte de Vigny who was a man of the world, the Victor Hugo who was an irreproachable family man, the Alfred de Musset who was the star of the period's café society, the Joseph Delorme who was an impoverished intellectual. But the studios and the rue du Doyenné provided the devoted battalion for the opening night of *Hernani*. In romanticism they occupied more or less the same place that the conquerors of the Bastille held among the patriots of the Revolution; they provided romanticism with those eccentrics and those failures without whom there would never again be a living literary school.

Pétrus and Philothée

Pétrus Borel was the incarnation of the attitudes and the rebellions of this total romanticism, less in his person (about which there is a certain lack of anecdote, and this kind of glory is kept alive only by anecdote) than as a flag-bearer of romanticism, in view of which he had hit upon the felicitous designation of himself as a lycanthropist, and in a work written with the deliberate intention of showing off his truculence, the famous indefatigable and exclusive truculence of the rue du Doyenné. What has damaged Pétrus is the fact that every generation has its own Pétruses and the original, the founder of the race, has been forgotten, overshadowed. But anyone who enjoys Lautréamont (Isidore Ducasse) and Alfred Jarry should give a thought and an hour of reading to Pétrus. *Feu et flamme,* by Philothée O'Neddy (Théophile Dondey), if it were not consistently one grade below the void and the wind of rhetoric, would give us some idea of what the great poetic production of the truculent school might have been: it has a Satanism that brings Baudelaire to mind and a use of rare words that presages symbolism.

But the real masters of the rue du Doyenné were Théophile Gautier and Gérard de Nerval—or, as they signed the things that they wrote in collaboration, G.G.

Théophile Gautier

Like Pétrus, Gautier had hesitated between poetry and painting, and he had carried over into the literary field as much as possible of the usages, the ideas, and the style of painting.

The usages: let us not think in terms of any excesses. Gautier was a good literary day laborer all his life, very orderly, very much devoted to a family that he had very early to start supporting, very much a man of bad luck and the victim of his own goodness of heart and innocence. Within these limits of prudence and safety, he was a first-rate dauber. "The dauber" he said, "ruled the poet in us, and we were very much preoccupied by the interests of color." In time as in dignity, he will not be envied his title as the leading dauber in French literature: that is not a trifle.

He earned the title by his paradoxes. These paradoxes were obviously somewhat conventional and domestic, but still they had a style, a continuity, and they were exciting, especially when they emerged in Gautier's talk rather than in his books and his articles, where he was writing under the supervision of the editor-in-chief and the constant reader. Printed or oral, there is a Gauteriana that is still quoted, discussed, alive. In matters of artistic and literary craftsmanship, there is always a "Gautier said . . ." that excels in starting discussion and in which, perhaps, there survives what is best known of the artist who wrote the equivalent of a hundred volumes.

He earned the title, too, by his good humor, the extremely French way in which he reconciled enthusiasm and scepticism. The style of that ironic sympathy with which we speak of the school of the rue du Doyenné was created by him in *Les Jeune France,* a lively, friendly, and incisive picture of the life of the young romantics of the extreme left and at the same time a faithful transcription of the liquidation of the group. In the Daniel Jovard of *Les Jeune France* Gautier created a more solid, more substantial literary type than the shadows cut out ironically and externally by Musset—his Dupont and Durand, Dupuis and Cotonet: in Gautier it is real painting, with the third dimension and a model.

He earned the title by his ideas. Gautier was romanticism's deputy to artistic ideas. Art was enough, as in Malherbe's day. In 1830, when he was nineteen, Gautier published his first volume of verse, the verses of an artist's album, sharp impressions, colored, in which nothing goes beyond the preconceived frame, and which absolutely and deliberately turns its back on that romanticism of ideas, that political romanticism that was to overflow in the great outpourings of Lamartine, of Hugo, of Vigny, even of Sainte-Beuve (that Sainte-Beuve who at that same time became a Saint-Simonian and joined secret societies). At the height of the July sun, it was a fine paradox for Gautier to write: "To the Utopian, economistic, Saint-Simonistic, and other utilitarians who ask him what is the rhyme and reason of all that, he will answer: 'The first line rhymes with the second, when the rhyme is not bad, and so on.' 'What is it for?' 'To be beautiful. Isn't that enough?'" A way of life in which the whole reason for being of certain men, of certain callings, is beauty for itself and for itself alone was formulated by Gautier in two novels, the first of which was well known and had important literary consequences: *Mademoiselle de Maupin* and *L'Eldorado, or Fortunio*. Like the country squire who called God the gentleman upstairs, and in sum in contrast to Hugo, for whom the poet was God, Gautier would write: "Perhaps God is only the world's greatest poet."

Finally, he earned his title by his style. It is a platitude to call Gautier's style a painter's style. But this is a limitation as well as a virtue. Gautier is rightly considered the romantic writer who, next to Victor Hugo, best knew the language and used it with the most impeccably sure touch. But that assurance can as well be called facility, and a facility that he abused, when he embarked on description, in a reproduction that was not creative—in the form, as he said, of good literary daguerreotype. Stylist, poet, novelist, traveler, it was always on the border of creation that he came face to face with his limitations.

Let us add that this romantic painter tried too to be an oratorical romantic among his contemporaries. His two great pieces of romantic poetry, *Albertus* and *La Comédie de la mort*, remain as distinguished monuments of an abundance that is often healthy and an eloquence that is chilled. In the short poem, on the other hand, Gautier excelled through his use of the picturesque and his luminous and well-directed emphasis not so much on beautiful words as on the most apt words, classic virtues in the manner of Boileau. It is not surprising that he was felicitously inspired by painters, that his *Terze rime*, his *Ribeira*, and *Le Triomphe de Pétrarque* are splendid masterpieces, that the poems that he brought back from Spain, *España*, are heavily copied from Spanish nature. His *Emaux et camées*, pleasant, slender little pieces, have long been the subject of misunderstanding, praised for qualities of Parnassian plasticity that they do not possess: simple, well-engraved visiting cards left with the Muse from time to time by a poet who does not want to terminate relations, they must not be offered the sacrifice of the full, the alive, the adventurous character of Gautier's true poetry, that of his youth.

Gautier is great and talented, but, in verse as in prose, the end is soon reached. The painter lacks music and vision. This circle of ideas limited to letters, to art, to black on white, to line and color, is not devoid of automatism, of monotony, of the ready-made and of the contrived. Gautier is a good burgher of the republic of letters, the drinker of *apéritifs* and the Homais of the literary Landerneau.* This is said with clearer conscience because it is hoped that it will be understood in terms of praise and sympathy. He who has no feeling for Gautier, no friendship for Gautier, lacks a certain element of good-burgherdom, of familiarity, of habit, of civic republicanism in the republic of letters.

Gérard de Nerval

But having said that, we can observe without an excess of regret that today Gérard de Nerval's reputation outshines Théophile Gautier's. Gérard's spirit was that of music rather than of painting, of mystery rather than of expression, of inner rather than of outer poetry. But above all, in contrast to Gautier, he was a complex person and master in whom one is always making new discoveries, who is rich in abrupt turns and in insights into the infinite. So unlike Balzac in his novels, Gérard de Nerval seems truly a character out of Balzac, whereas Gautier seems not at all that but a character out of Flaubert or the Goncourts. If Gautier is the good burgher of the republic of letters, Nerval is its divine traveler.

There is first of all in Nerval the man of the rue du Doyenné, the friend of Gautier, the pure artist and the perfect story teller. No one in 1832 could tell stories with more grace than the author of *La Main enchantée*, a mixture of historical enchantment and clowning in the exact line of style of *Les Jeune France*. Ten years later Nerval went mad, with an illuminated, mystical, tender madness that allowed the artist in him to continue, so much so that the novel of that madness, *Les Filles du feu*, and particularly *Angélique* and *Sylvie*, is one of the masterpieces of

---

* The name of a Breton town that is idiomatically typical of the hinterland.— Translator.

French narrative. The evocation of the Valois in *Sylvie* and *Angélique* literally created the poetry of the Ile-de-France. *Sylvie* is to the fantastic what *Paul et Virginie* was to the exotic. *Angélique* and *Aurélia* are still more closely touched by the spirits of illusion and madness. The outside world becomes for Gérard a projection of the inner world, life is submerged and transfigured by dream, and the transmutation of creatures of flesh into creatures of dream becomes the alchemy proper to this poetic personality gently and divinely unbalanced.

The creatures of flesh were one creature—an actress, Jenny Colon, whose affair with Gérard has remained mysterious enough for its reality to be replaced piece by piece by the substitutions of dream. The dreamer then becomes the initiate. A whole part of Gérard's work—*Aurélia, Le Voyage en Orient, Les Illuminés*—is like a representation in series of the Eleusinian mysteries; that is, the adventures of the soul on earth through symbols that are beautiful and that look on man with eyes that are not only familiar but benevolent. Nerval's madness had horrible intervals, ended by his suicide. But only the gentle and lucid intervals or moments of that madness put the pen into the poet's hand, passed into his books, clothed themselves in that fine, delicate, and tempered prose. He is the sole writer in whom madness, or, rather, the memory and the shadow of madness, is presented in the aspect of a muse, an inspiration, and a friend.

And here at last in the poet of the Ile-de-France is the enchanted horn of the German forest. This brother of Novalis (Friedrich von Hardenberg) is the only romantic who knew Germany well and understood her, in her language, in her legend, and in her music. He was at home in *Faust*. He made the best translation of it, which Goethe admired. He had the feeling of the German *Lied* and ballad, very different from the artist's ballad in the style of Victor Hugo. A whole northern essence that runs from Paris to Vienna and has the Rhine for its axis can claim Nerval as its poet.

He had traveled that country, and the subtle, poetic simplicity of his accounts of his travels on the Rhine and in Austria can stand with his pictures of the Ile-de-France. But, beyond Germany, the visionary, the initiate, was summoned by the Orient. *Le Voyage en Orient* is not a series of authentic notes: it is imagined in part, reworked, fabricated in the manner that was to be that of Barrès, but always by an intelligent and impeccable artist. The Orient of Nerval remained always fresh, musical, fairylike, a poet's Orient still more than a traveler's, an Orient that he saw as he had dreamed it.

When at last madness came to Nerval, touched him delicately and capriciously, insinuated half tones and twilights into his thought, submerged it sometimes in the fluid state of primitive mentality and mystic ecstasy, he wrote the dozen sonnets of *Les Chimères*, which have no common standard with the rest of his verse or even with his literature, and in which the Eleusinian cluster of French poetry rises in the hand of an antique initiate. They have precisely that kind of obscurity and that style of clarity of those guides of the other world, among its meadows and its symbolic fountains, that have been found engraved on sheets of gold in the tombs of the Pythagoreans. Their music can never be exhausted, and a strange miracle has willed that this radiant music be enclosed, as with Mallarmé, in the strict plastic form of the sonnet. At the height of romanticism, *Les Chimères* pointed the way to symbolism and pure poetry, as it showed Nerval, in the other world, the way of the initiate.

Bertrand

It is virtually only in this group of pure artists, of the great chimerical ill-starred and also of the forerunners, that Aloysius Bertrand can be classified. He was a Dijonnais, at least by adoption. His prose poems of *Gaspard de la nuit*, precious and often perfect in their form, could be published by his friends only after his death. He too pointed a way, a promised land, the prose poem of Baudelaire and Mallarmé. It might be said that the immanent genius of French poetry, which sought to prevent a certain paradoxical immateriality from penetrating it too early, turned away Gérard and Bertrand with the same disciplinary brutality that it later imposed on those other precocious arrivals, Verlaine, Lautréamont, Arthur Rimbaud, Tristan Corbière.

VII

THE ROMANTIC THEATER

Revolution and Theater

The major task of the romantic revolution was to take over the theater as the political revolution had first had to take over the executive power. For more than a century, in fact, every literary commencement had been made with a tragedy, and tragedy had been the glamorous older woman that the young had aspired to possess in order to make their way in the world, in poetry, in prose—to succeed. The Revolution had prevented Chateaubriand and Mme. de Staël from sowing their necessary tragic wild oats. Their five-act tragedies in verse were merely postponed, and they had to write them later. In the first decade of the century a tragic poet whose plays were no worse than others but had been the butts of critical ridicule was to kill himself in despair near Belley, where his nephew was at school. He was Lyon des Roys, the brother of Lamartine's mother. When, later, she found manuscripts of tragedies in her son's desk and he went off to Paris with a *Saül* to read to François-Joseph Talma, the great actor, the poor woman's agony can be imagined. Fortunately *Les Méditations* and diplomacy drew him away from the theater, to which he would not return until he was more than fifty, like Chateaubriand with *Moïse;* his *Toussaint Louverture,* a tragedy about the Haitian Negro leader, had no successor.

The romantic revolution was not a revolution without doctrines. From the publication of Mme. de Staël's *Littérature,* and without taking into account pre-romanticism, which went back no one knows how far, it had been prepared for in a quarter of a century of manifestos. Now, three-quarters of these manifestos, this literature of dogma, criticism, polemic, dealt with the theater. We know the importance of Schlegel's *Cours de littérature dramatique,* translated in 1814 by a cousin of Mme. de Staël. Literary opinion was for or against Shakespeare, for or against the Spanish and German theater, for or against tragedy, for or against the classic unities. Soon the bookseller Ladvocat began the translation of the *Chefs-d'oeuvre des théâtres étrangers,* which was to become for the romantics a veritable dramatic *Summum.* Until 1815 the word "theater" had a French meaning in Europe; after that year it was understood in a European sense. Romanticism made its appearance in this broadened interpretation, in this breath of fresh air.

The Beginnings of the Romantic Theater

It did not lack a foundation in time any more than this asset of space. There is a whole history of various attempts made by Lemercier, Raynouard, Delavigne to loosen the iron collar of tragedy. Stendhal's *Racine et Shakespeare,* an echo of the debates of those days, easily predicted in 1825 the advent of a historical drama taken from the chronicles. The master of melodrama, Guilbert de Pixérécourt, had accustomed popular audiences in the first thirty years of the century to gloomy heroes, brigands, corpses, violent emotions. "Woe to the French theater," Geoffroy wrote, "when a man of some talent who knows stage effects takes it upon himself to write melodramas." But the Comédie-Française, very advanced and active in those days, was better at gauging the theatrical wind than the Académie at gauging the poetic wind. On 11 February 1829 it presented *Henri III et sa cour,* a prose drama with a remarkable feeling for the stage, hastily pulled from Louis-Pierre Anquetil's history, which Alexandre Dumas had just discovered. On 24 October of the same year, it presented an *Othello* in verse by Alfred de Vigny—*Le More de Venise*—which was real Shakespeare quite accurately adapted, and a few months later it opened 1830 with *Une Fête sous Néron,* by Soumet and Belmontet, in which a highly spectacular final act, a matricidal Nero, playing in spite of himself the part of Orestes like Saint-Genest the part of Adrien (the world is small), had a triumph with one hundred performances. It seemed as if the romantic drama already had its *Britannicus,* and Victor Hugo had not yet entered. At least into the theater. For books and published plays had served many years as the diligent procurement department of the stage.

The Theater of Books

A good part of the romantic theater in those days was a historical theater in prose, the potential and even the necessity of which had long been felt. As early as 1747 had not Charles-Jean-François Hénault, historian, poet and parliamentary president, demanded to know why French history had not been recorded in the manner of Shakespeare's historical plays? The English poet's *Henry VI* gave him the idea of a *François II* in prose, an effort that had no sequel until the Restoration. At that time a strange theater of written historical scenes arose everywhere, often played in chateaus (like Comte Pierre-Louis Roederer's): a theater of books and amateurs that was the neighbor and close kin of the *Proverbes* of Carmontelle (Louis Carrogis) and Théodore Leclercq. It testified to that period's general taste for history, initiated by Chateaubriand and fed on the great collections of memoirs, documents, bookshop researches, and especially Walter Scott's novels, which began to appear in 1820. When Stendhal wrote that "the nation is thirsty for historical tragedy," he was expressing the ideas of Louis-Charles Delescluze's *salon*, which was more or less the source, from 1820 to 1827, of Charles de Rémusat's *L'Insurrection de Saint-Domingue*, a *Cromwell* by Mérimée (not published), Mérimée's *Théâtre de Clara Gazul* in 1825, Louis Vitet's *Les Barricades* in 1826, *Les Soirées de Neuilly* by Dittmer and Cavé in 1827, *Les Scènes contemporaines* by François-Adolphe Loève-Veimars and Rumier in the same year. Hugo's *Cromwell* of 1827 was part of this theater of books, as was Alfred de Musset's *Spectacle dans un fauteuil* of 1832. Alexandre Dumas was to say of *Henri III et sa cour*, with justice and an unaccustomed modesty: "I will not call myself the innovator of a form, because in fact I innovated nothing. MM. Victor Hugo, Mérimée, Vitet, Loève-Veimars, Cavé, and Dittmer innovated with me and better than I. I thank them for that: they have made me what I am."

Cromwell

Why is the date of one of these plays, Hugo's *Cromwell*, written in 1827, so important in the history of romanticism? For three reasons. Because of its quality: this three-thousand-line play, which cannot be acted, is curious, entertaining, well written, still interesting to read. Because of its subject: this theme was in the air; in the political air, filled on the eve of 1830 with interest and perturbation by the precedent of the English revolutions, and in the literary air, into which it had been launched by Guizot's translations of *Mémoires sur la révolution d'Angleterre* and already taken up by Balzac and Mérimée as the theme of their first plays. Because of its preface, which was taken to be what it was not, an introduction to the romantic drama, and which contains ideas wholly individual to the point of view of Victor Hugo, like his strange theory of the grotesque. It had the importance of a manifesto quite simply because one was expected and Hugo expected it from Hugo. It remained for him to make his entrance into the real theater, as he would have done in 1829 with *Marion Delorme* if the censor had not forbidden it because of its anything but flattering portrayal of Louis XIII. This was too bad: the Louis XIII play would have been Corneillesque as *Une Fête sous Néron* was Racinesque and as *Othello* balanced *Zaïre*. Add to this the fact that the wanton in love and reformed was then a daring new idea, which went hand in hand with that *Dernier Jour d'un condamné* that the young author had just published as an attack on capital punishment. Would Fantine and Jean Valjean ever escape from the highroad of crime? Not yet. But, to take the place of *Marion*, Hugo wrote in a single month the most audacious, the most amazing, the maddest, the most beautiful play and fulfilled Geoffroy's prophecy from top to bottom: this fulfillment was *Hernani* and its battle of 25 February 1830.

The Battle of Hernani

Hernani was a battle, a conflict in which everyone spoke and took sides. It was not a victory. *Hernani*'s character as a dramatic event consisted in the tempest of poetry and lyricism that it unleashed on the theater, not at all in a dramatic revolution of which Hugo perhaps thought himself the hero but of which he was only the herald, and which took place barely if at all. Hugo, who had been in Spain and who even called himself a Spanish viscount, mixed into this extraordinary play the poetry of *Les Orientales* (which, in part, was *Les Hispaniques*), the phantoms of the Empire, political prophecy, Schiller's *Robbers*, the enchanted horn of the Hartz Mountains, the recollections of the bridegroom and the "drunken grape harvester" that Lamartine saw in him on his wedding night, the reference to Corneille, to *Le Cid*, seen as the inaugural play of a new dramatic form by a poet—I had almost said a First Consul—who was not yet thirty years old. The golden tide of gratuitous lyricism, the fire in the blood of invincible youth, the clarion of a generation on the rise made that opening of *Hernani* endure in literature like a *Marseillaise*. It was the poetry of the theater; it was not the reality of the theater. The reality of the romantic theater introduced by *Henri III et sa cour* triumphed with *Antony* at the Porte-Saint-Martin on 3 May 1831, a day of victory as *Hernani* had been a day of battle.

The Triumph of Antony

Dumas' success with *Antony* was a fantastic success. Much more than half the theater audience is made up of women, and in *Antony* Dumas created the tragic, fatal romantic hero about whom women are mad. If *Hernani* loosed a tempest of poetry on the theater, *Antony* inundated the stage with that torrent of dramatic movement that holds all the spectators breathlessly captive in the hall, not merely that minority that feels and lives poetry. *Hernani* dissolved like a golden cloud that leaves the spectator astonished. *Antony* was concentrated on its closing line, "She repulsed me, I killed her," the arrow of which was carried off in their own flesh by the spectator and particularly by his wife. In those days the romantic theater lived on antitheses. The antithesis of banditry and honor in *Hernani* remained verbal and void in the face of that antithesis of "the world as it is" and passion, an antithesis that romanticism established in literature for a quarter of a century, that was to be destroyed by *Madame Bovary*, and that was the reason for the novelty and the triumph of *Antony*.

The Triumph of La Tour de Nesle

La Tour de Nesle (1832) all but followed *Antony*. Perhaps the romantic theater was then at the peak of its creative impulse. To speak frankly, Dumas did not create in *La Tour* the drama of cloak and dagger that had conquered the stage of the Théâtre-Français in *Hernani*. But everything henceforth would come to pass as if the play and even the novel of cloak and dagger consisted in rewriting *La Tour de Nesle* and submerging it in anonymity beneath the platitudes and the repetitions. Nonetheless it has resisted. In 1934 it still drew all kinds of audiences. The drama of cloak and dagger, of which Corneille had thought (*Le Cid* is the movement of a blade, and *Don Sanche* already evoked *Hernani*, perhaps corresponding to the plane on which the romantic theater found the clearest road, the road of a pure dramatic movement), would have been more admired by Aristotle than *Oedipus the King* and *Iphigenia in Tauris* with those cascades of recognitions, incests, parricides, and infanticides. And the Corneille of *Rodogune* would have hailed Dumas as the magician of the craft.

If Dumas wrote verse badly, he wrought a superior prose in *La Tour de Nesle*. J.-J. Weiss had the courage to say that in *La Tour de Nesle* there is a style, "a managed style." Buffon's definition would have to be altered. The theatrical style here is the movement that the actions give the words and that the words give the actions. It has the dazzle, the movement, the swiftness of the sword. What happened to it is what happened to Athalie's dream or Théramène's narrative, devoured by platitude and parody, of which they had to be cleansed in order to be admired. An even better expert on style than Weiss made no mistake about this. That was Victor Hugo. *La Tour de Nesle* taught Hugo that drama could be written in a prose that would be the equal of verse, and *La Tour de Nesle* of 1832 inspired his *Lucrèce Borgia*, not to speak of *Marie Tudor*, another very great lady.

The Romantic Creation

What Victor Hugo created in *Hernani* and *Marion Delorme* was poetic drama and comedy, which would be repeated by the Auguste Vacqueries, the Théodore de Banvilles, the François Coppées, the Mendèses, the Jean Richepins, the Edmond Rostands, and which until 1914 would remain for the Parisian public the official equivalent of what classic tragedy had formerly been. They and the posterity of *La Tour de Nesle* are dead, while the posterity of *Antony* is still alive.

In effect *Antony* created that simple and supple dramatic reality that is called the play, the modern play in prose, which twenty years later, with the next generation, would become the common definitive language of the theater. *Antony* might be called the play of both Dumases, and it was in the son's theater much more than in the father's that it was carried forward. Furthermore, in his drama Dumas presented not only its practice but also its theory. In the fourth act he dared, and successfully, like Molière in *Le Misanthrope*, to join scenes of literary talk to the action and, like Molière, to make them contribute to the action. If dramatic genius and the sense of the dramatic future were enough to make a dramatic masterpiece, *Antony* would belong next to *Le Cid, Andromaque, L'Ecole des femmes*. Now *Antony* is no longer performed, no longer read, it no longer lives. For a dramatic creation lives only if, through a chance as exceptional as the birth of twins, it is accompanied by a parallel and equal creation of a style.

Dumas and Hugo

Aside from the success of *La Tour de Nesle*, an exception that proves the rule, this style, these styles were lacking in Dumas. In 1831, the same year as *Antony*, solid workmanship and picturesque ideas did not prevent *Charles VII chez ses grands vassaux*, a verse play in which he sought to prove himself in high art, from trailing among what had already been seen, memories of *Hernani*, of *Andromaque*, of *Horace*. It is the misfortune of the romantic drama that only these two great characters, Hugo and Dumas, each represent a half of its genius: Dumas its theatrical genius, Hugo its genius for style. "Ah!" Dumas said, "if I could write verse like Victor or if Victor could write drama like me." The opposite of classical tragedy, where again they were two, but where each of the two reigned equally in both domains.

As Dumas attempted to Hugoize in *Charles VII*, Hugo was to try to outdo Dumas on his own ground in his prose dramas. In vain. The "I am your mother, Gennaro!" in *Lucrèce Borgia* is the same explosive as "She repulsed me . . ." but with the difference that in *Lucrèce Borgia* the powder was wet. Both were to work furiously, Hugo would seek to have a theater of his own and in 1848 Dumas would bring the dream to reality with his Théâtre Historique. It is certain that during the eighteen years of the July monarchy he occupied in it the place of a French Shakespeare, romantic and modern, who shattered himself to bits by falling from the probable into the true and from the possible into the real.

Le Roi s'amuse seems to have been written expressly in order to knock him to the ground. But *Ruy Blas* (1838), which was and which remains Victor Hugo's main dramatic success, and *Les Burgraves* are still two substantial elements, and the most brilliant. The implausibilities of *Ruy Blas* do not prevent it from being full of movement and dramatic ideas, and its fourth act created the whole style of verse comedy for a half century. *Les Burgraves*, like *Hernani*, marks an important date: the date when the public, which for fifteen years had been waiting for the promised Shakespeare, took official cognizance of his absence beneath that superhuman envelope of bronze and stone and antiquity that descended, to the accompaniment of a great clamor of brilliant verse, on the stage of the Théâtre-Français in February 1843, like that of Eviradnus, but that did not conquer, that left the throne to a practical, vulgar wisdom and, like Barbarossa, withdrew again into the solitudes. The torrent of poetry set loose in *Hernani* grew here to the dimensions of the Rhine, the sound of the horn became that of a tremendous German ballad that dissolved into shapes lacking any common criterion with the nature of the theater. *Les Burgraves*, which no one has been able to stage again, even in Orange, holds a monumental position in the world of the Théâtre-Français. It is a cenotaph that resembles the tombs of Charlemagne and Napoleon, the porphyry urn in which there is nothing but that possible idea of a French romantic Shakespeare, one of those stone altars that Alexander caused to be built when he had to retreat and the conquest of India was denied him by his soldiers; it is the Moscow of the Grand Army of the drama, in a word Victor Hugo's most authentic act of Neopoleonic disproportion. A little more and one would be reminded of the Nimrod of *La Fin de Satan*.

Vigny

With *Le More de Venise* (1829) Vigny had been the introducer of the real Shakespeare on the French stage. Having written a novel on Louis XIII, in 1831 he offered a prose drama on the same period, which was then in fashion: *La Maréchale d'Ancre*, which dragged and had no success. But in 1835 *Chatterton* was a triumph, in which, with a felicity almost equal to that of his *Moïse*, Vigny blended all the living character of romanticism into the theater: the great romantic theme, the poet's destiny, the poet's mystery, the poet's claims, a pathetic situation, a touching heroine who stirred all women's hearts to a tender maternal sentiment, the unique wedding of a "drama of ideas" and a great emotion. If *Antony* and *Chatterton* were the two greatest successes of the romantic theater, it was because these successes were made by the same woman of the century, the woman of thirty, at the same time when she was finding her novelist in Balzac; they offer to this woman, in the most romantic manner possible, on the one hand the type of the strong man who defends woman in his love and his honor, on the other the type of the child man whose gift, whose genius, whose grace woman defends. *Chatterton* summoned woman into battle against society, *Antony* summoned her into battle against "the world." It is almost two sides of the same play in the same theater.

Musset

But, of all the great romantic poets, the one whose name has most often evoked that of Shakespeare is Alfred de Musset. The theater of Dumas, of Hugo, of Vigny was intended for audiences. Musset, whose trifling one-act play, *La Nuit Vénitienne*, had been hissed in 1831, thereafter wrote drama only for reading, like Byron, like Mérimée, like Hugo after 1842. Born of books, the romantic theater returned to books: from *Clara Gazul* to *Le Théâtre en liberté*. Musset published all his plays in the *Revue des deux mondes*. When François Buloz became director of the Comédie-Française, he insisted on testing on his audiences the theater that had been successful with his readers. In this he was assisted by Mme. Allan-Despréaux, who insisted on doing *Un Caprice* because she had seen it performed with success in Russia. This light persiflage was very well received. Most of the other plays followed. Three or four were kept in the repertory, like the best of Pierre de Chamblain de Marivaux. It has been argued that Musset was the only romantic poet who made a success of his dramatic writing. Perhaps this can be sustained. But he did this dramatic writing for himself, like his poetry and his prose, and its conjunction with the stage and the public would have been precarious anywhere else but in the Comédie-Française and before "society" audiences.

Musset's verse theater has no dramatic importance. *A Quoi rêvent les jeunes filles* contains some of the most beautiful verse that he ever wrote. But these two acts can be considered only a poetic sonata. *La Coupe et les lèvres* carries a superb oratorical poem throughout five acts, and certain of its apostrophes have remained famous. Like that of *Hernani*, the impulse of *La Coupe* springs from the inevitable *Robbers*. The adventurer hero, Frank, has the bad luck to allow a loose woman to drive the first nail of debauchery into his left breast. It is a temptation to look on *La Coupe* as an anti-*Marion Delorme*, and it will be noted that the rehabilitation of the wanton is attempted by the chaste poet of 1829 and her condemnation is pronounced by the debauched poet of 1832. But in Musset that is as far from the theater as *Rolla*. And we shall say nothing about his third verse comedy, *Louison*, written much later and of no account.

But finally, all things considered, *Lorenzaccio* remains the most Shakespearean of the romantic dramas. It is too much so, and one is quite aware that it would not exist if Shakespeare had not written *Hamlet*. But it would exist still less if the author had not instilled in Lorenzo, an admirable man stricken, like Frank, by debauchery, something of that bitterness and that remorse of a fallen deity that were to make the style of his life. And above all there is the life of the style.

In *On ne badine pas avec l'amour* and in that *"On ne badine pas avec ses masques"* that is *Lorenzaccio*, like Dumas and Hugo in *La Tour de Nesle* and *Lucrèce Borgia*, Musset created a prose of the romantic drama (which, however, would barely survive the 1830s), a prose that took on every quality, sometimes solid, flashing, and naked as a blade, sometimes rich, resonant, indefinite as woodwinds. That it lasted so little, that it did not stand up against the sovereignty of verse, is remarkable. Hugo wrote no more prose drama after *Angelo*, which is not good. Dumas, who was to occupy the theater until his death, would stop taking pains with his style soon after *Kean*. And *Lorenzaccio* had no successor in Musset's work.

In addition, *Lorenzaccio* was never staged before the end of the nineteenth century, and, in spite of the adaptations and the cuts, it failed. In contrast, *On ne badine pas avec l'amour* and *Les Caprices de Marianne*, because they had only two acts, because their comic parts are exquisite, because their subjects are close to the heart of art and man, have remained two of the jewels of the Comédie-Française. These two romantic plays have held the place of a classic in the theater. They convey accurately and purely the sound of what the classics called the human heart. The best play that Victor Hugo wrote after his withdrawal, the only one that he was to detach from his *Théâtre en liberté* in order to publish it during his lifetime, was *Les Deux Trouvailles de Gallus*, in which, it seems, he wanted to refashion *On ne badine pas avec l'amour*. Now, despite all the poetry, the brilliance, and the wit in which it abounds, *Les Deux Trouvailles* was a total failure when the Comédie-Française tried to perform it. Comparison of Hugo's and Musset's plays, none of which was written for the stage, and of their two fates on the stage is an excellent lesson for us in what is and is not likely to survive in the theater.

The Golden Mean

No fifth name shared with Hugo, Dumas, Vigny, and Musset the honor of having essayed the great Shakespearean adventure of romanticism. All the salt and substance of that word "adventure" must be preserved in order to honor the audacity and the extremism of *Hernani, La Tour de Nesle, Chatterton*, and *Lorenzaccio*. But no more is there any dramatic period without its honorable and intelligent play-makers who have the vocation of the golden mean as others have the vocation of adventure, and it would have been especially unjust if the golden mean of July had not had its own.

The golden mean in the theater was called Casimir Delavigne. He sampled all forms, if not with invention, at least with skill, with a feeling for his subjects and his means. *Louis XI* (1832) and *Les Enfants d'Edouard* (1833) were two triumphs, of which the first is explicable by the existence of a character and a part, the second by the theme of *Les Deux Orphelins* and the combination of this melodramatic foundation with a sound historical one. Delavigne was no fool, and, when it was required, he knew how to summon up some master scenes, some lines that would make four thousand hands applaud, to the assistance of his general output, which was stubborn convention, watery language, and moth-eaten versification.

The End of the Dream of a Great Empire

Romantic drama came to the same end as the ideal cathedral that, it was said, would have to have the steeples of Chartres, the front of Reims, the nave of Amiens, and the chancel of Beauvais. Here it was a matter of the verse of Hugo, the workmanship of Dumas, the humanity of Musset, and the philosophy of Vigny. But the four winds of the drama blew rather in different directions. The disaster of *Les Burgraves* in 1843 was the end of the dream of a great empire. Yet the success of François Ponsard's *Lucrèce* in the same year had no more meaning and consequence than reason, and the end of drama did not imply the return of tragedy. Rachel's genius brought attention back to Racine, but it had no effect on contemporary production. On the other hand, the frustration of the great empire did not put an end to the romantic drama, which under various guises more or less lived on until the beginning of the twentieth century. All the benefit of it went to comedy, plays in prose, middle-class demi-tragedy, which, from 1850 on, would reign over the theater like the middle classes over society, and which, moreover, in the days of the political golden mean, had already known a success almost equal to that of the drama.

VIII

STENDHAL

Stendhal's Literary Isolation

To be just twenty years old when *Le Génie du christianisme* had just appeared and *Delphine* was in its flower and its glory put a young writer into a generation that counted, into a sensitiveness that was taking shape, into the romantic army roused by the morning bugle. But the drive of French literature proceeds by oppositions. What was equally important and equally fine at the age of twenty was to consider *Le Génie* so much Hebrew, Germaine Necker's writing so much Swiss, to gamble one's life and taste on quite another picture, to sustain the sensibility of the eighteenth century with a revolutionary independence, to say *no* to phrases and *yes* to analysis. And this was a thankless task then. In that morning of the century the phrase filled the horizon, the written phrase with Chateaubriand, the spoken phrase with Mme. de Staël. It contained poetry as the sea contained life, and poetic romanticism was to be born of the romanticism of eloquence. The public became scanty for an anti-phrase and anti-phrasemaker analyst who had neither the young nor the women on his side. Such was the destiny of Stendhal. "If it comes in, I leave," Royer-Collard said in the Académie on the subject of a word that he did not want to allow in the dictionary. "When the phrase leaves, I will go in," Stendhal thought, knowing very well that it would take a long time to leave—about 1885, he thought. It never went away, but Stendhal entered. The phrase and analysis, those two powerful gods, came in the end to be worshiped equally and sometimes by the same devout, like Taine and his disciples.

His Refusal of One of the Two Natures of Prose

Stendhal is perhaps the sole example that exists in French literature of so abrupt, so radical a disproportion between the two faces of the literary life, between the face that is exposed to the sun of the living and the face that receives the sun of the dead. A precious geography! these slopes and these exhibitions are intelligible, full of enlightenment, eminently suited to making clear the contours and the climate of the literary country of France, that co-existence and alternation of the synthetic, intuitive phrase on the one hand and the analytical, critical word on the other, of Bossuet and Voltaire: all as closely connected to the French genius as the existence of a north and a south in France.

His Misunderstanding with the Society of His Time

Chateaubriand, an old Breton in the old France of the old world, contributed this that was new: to know what he was and to know how to make it known. Henri Beyle (Stendhal) was a new, a very new man, who wanted to be new, who was seventeen years old when the nineteenth century began—who, at the age of ten, alone in his royalist family had voted for the death of Louis XVI—who entered into life without in any way abdicating the nature of his class, the middle class, who was burdened with no preconceived idea, no inherited veneration—a pupil of the first central schools of the Revolution—a sharp mind, quick, alert before a clean slate, impatient to live, to love, to feel, to savor; the man of society for a new society, that society without noblemen or priests or real women of the world that tried to take shape under the Directory and did not succeed, that was a stew without a hare: Henri Beyle, who was its man, sought that society all his life, found fragments of it, wrote for it—that is to say, for a shadow, while Chateaubriand and Lamartine were writing for a real society, for a society of flesh and spirit, of conventions, which succeeded. Stendhal is the expression of his time but not of "the society of his time." Stendhal's defeat among his contemporaries seems natural, necessary, in a country where there was the Académie, where such terms as society and the world had drawing-room meaning, where literature was a category of that society. He would have succeeded in Weimar or Milan: so he became a naturalized Milanese.

The Disciple of Napoleon

And it is perhaps here, among so many paradoxes, that he is at his strangest. Beyle, who, if the Empire had lasted, would probably have published nothing and been discovered whole, like Saint-Simon, in posthumous papers, is the only writer who was strictly and literarily the colleague of Napoleon, or, rather, of Bonaparte. Fifteen years younger, he personified by his age the generation that followed him and asked only to be shaped by him—the situation of those who come fifteen years later, that of Sainte-Beuve or Musset with respect to Lamartine, or of Banville with respect to Hugo. Like General Bonaparte, Stendhal was a blank page, without inherited prejudices either religious or political and ready for the new order. This descendant of the Guadagnis recognized in himself a French-Italian nature, like Napoleon. Napoleon made phrases when it was necessary for the people, but his real style is that of his correspondence, and nothing is more alien to phrases. Like Stendhal's style, it says only what it says, and it means only what is. When Stendhal plowed his way through the Civil Code as a training, he was steeping himself in one of the typical schools of the Napoleonic style. His views, his ideas, his French rule, "tools to those who can use them," his civilian psychology, like a former soldier who has no illusions about the military, were shared with Napoleon. For him Napoleon was just Napoleon, not, as for Chateaubriand, "Napoleon and I." He was the literary disciple of Napoleon.

Nothing could be more unlike Stendhal or elicit more sneers from him than that attitude of the romantics that consisted in being the Napoleon of something before a mirror. There is a level on which Stendhal could be said to have furnished to the First Consul that contemporary in letters that Racine was to Louis XIV. From *Racine et Shakespeare* to *La Chartreuse de Parme*, Stendhal's work is a kind of return to zero, to the point of a failed or deviated departure in 1800, to the clarity, the precision, and the frankness of a military generation. But from 1809 to 1815 the potential Stendhals were under arms: literature was the domain of the emigration, the rear guard, the Restoration, and the women.

Italianism

Hence Stendhal did not become part of literature until quite late and by chance, through notes on painting and music and, in 1817, through his first personal book, *Rome, Naples, et Florence*, more or less drawn from his journal: impressions of Italian society, written at the beginning of a seven-year stay in Italy, chiefly in Milan: to him the country of candor and passion in talk and in love, which he was constantly contrasting to the composure and the vanity of the French, the country, too, of a pursuit of happiness that was more sensitive and more picturesque than in France. Stendhal's Italy is the most living and above all the most lived of the romantic Italys. He called himself a Milanese and perhaps he would have established himself permanently in Milan if the Austrian police had not forcibly put him back into his own country in 1821.

Stendhal and the Letters and Music of His Time

He had started living in Paris in the shadow of *Le Génie du christianisme.* He returned there in the shadow of *Les Méditations:* a kind of luck that was peculiar to this anti-romantic. He found his life there, however, and even in romanticism, what Stendhal at that period called *romanticismo* as distinguished from the French *romantisme* in order to distinguish the pre- or para-romanticism of 1824 to 1828, which recalled the ephemeral society of the Consulate more than it evoked that of 1830, which was clear-sighted and even ideologist, which excelled in its curiosity about and knowledge of foreign literatures, which examined and acclimated Shakespeare, which found its natural place in the *salons* and its general function in criticism, which was to debouch at once into Nodier, into Mérimée, into the *Globe* group, and to which Stendhal gave perhaps its most fitting manifesto with *Racine et Shakespeare.*

Between the two parts of *Racine et Shakespeare,* in 1825, Stendhal had published a pungent and brilliant *Vie de Rossini* that cannot be separated from his two critical pamphlets. His passion for Italian music, his conversations in La Scala and the *salons* of Milan had made him alert to the constant renewal of musical taste, which changes with every generation and which, in a single box in the auditorium, is different in the grandmother, the mother, and the daughter. He had seen how swiftly a whole generation had been conquered by Rossini's music. He relived this movement in letters and carried these views over into Parisian literature. Romanticism seemed to him the taste of the men of his time, classicism the taste of their great-grandfathers. In these two brochures he brought off the same subject that was to make the title of an unsuccessful work of Doudan: *Les Révolutions du goût.*

The Theoretician of Love

From 1821 to 1830 the *salons* and the pleasures of Paris took the place of those of Milan; Stendhal was still the eternal pursuer, almost always disappointed, of happiness and love: a man for whom life was above all women, music, conversation, but who had had, in the manner of Montaigne, a vocation: that of knowing himself, describing himself, keeping a record of himself. Whence his book, *De l'Amour*, which is one of several of these records, too much padded out with trivial pages, which are many and which need be read only once in their entirety in order to select forty pages to be reread eternally.

Observer and Novelist

Outside a circle of friends who were sometimes ironic, none of his works had any success. Stendhal was too far removed from the great highway along which romanticism was to hurl itself and its torrential poetry. Those critical, humorous reflections, these pages taken from his journals, would continue with *Les Promenades dans Rome* of 1829 and those very vivacious *"Promenades en France"* that Stendhal called *Mémoires d'un touriste* in 1838. Chiefly they would go on in thirty volumes of posthumous works, intimate notes, recollections, journals, that would hardly have enlarged that circle or that would have remained eternally buried in manuscript if, in an unexpected fashion, at the age of forty-four, a novelist had not come to the surface in Stendhal.

The Novels of Experience

Every novel implies an experience. But it might be said that Stendhal's five novels were experiments—that is, ways of diversifying his personal experience, pen in hand. At the center of each of his novels there is a young man who is more or less like Stendhal but who develops in another environment, follows another line of circumstances, has a different destiny. Stendhal found this character in two ways. First he changed some secondary quality of his own character into a dominant trait. Then he imagined a change in conditions—a lower birth than his own, into the poor class, like Julien, or else a higher birth, into the rich class, like Lucien Leuwen. Around this central character, this fractional Beyle, or this reconstituted Beyle, he assembled a certain number of living people, many of whose characteristics were borrowed from his experience of mankind but never copied from reality any more than he copied from himself—always excepting, of course, the autobiography of Henri Brulard, which is not a novel but authentic memoirs, a valuable point of reference from which to measure the fictionalization of Stendhal's experiences. Finally, he made of the novel a *chronicle* in the highest sense of the word —that is to say, the picture of an epoch: *Chronique de 1830* is the subtitle that he gave to *Le Rouge et le noir*. But *Lucien Leuwen* is a "chronique du juste-milieu"; the subtitle of *Armance* is *Quelques Scènes d'un salon de Paris en 1827*—in other words, "chronique des salons parisiens"—and what is *La Chartreuse de Parme* if not the broadest and most complete of those "chroniques italiennes" of which, furthermore, Stendhal wrote two volumes?

So, to borrow expressions or constructions from the greatest of Stendhal's disciples, Taine, it might readily be said that Stendhal's novels take as their three dimensions the social race of the hero, the human environment in which he lives, and the point in time—the *chronos*—in which he is treated.

ARMANCE

Armance, Stendhal's first novel, was written without the beginner's awkwardness (besides, he was forty-four years old). It is an elegant narrative, subtle and penetrating, even too subtle. Its true title might better be *Octave*, from the name of its hero, Octave de Malivert. Like Stendhal, Octave had studied for the Ecole Polytechnique, had read Condillac, was quite cultivated, had delicate feelings, analyzed himself like a mathematician, had great intelligence and heart. But, in contrast to Stendhal, Octave had been admitted to the Polytechnique, was a Parisian, belonged to a great family of the Faubourg Saint-Germain, was imbued with that family's view of honor and its traditions without sharing its ideas. In addition, he is recognizable as a "last of his race," and Stendhal wanted to make the reader (who found this too difficult and preferred not to understand) guess that Octave was physically incapable of perpetuating that race, that as a lover and even as a husband he could find no solution to his problem but suicide. All of Stendhal is already in *Armance*: a young, interesting hero and portraits of women traced with considerable love and at great length—Octave's wife, Armance, and the woman in whose *salon* the "quelques scenes" take place, Mme. de Bonnivet.

LE ROUGE ET LE NOIR

Le Rouge et le noir, Stendhal's central novel, bears a title that would almost seem to symbolize the gaming table of all his works of fiction. Certainly he himself had told us that, by red and black, he meant the military and ecclesiastical careers, each of which plays its part in the destiny of Julien Sorel. Yet the title has a false bottom, and one of its bottoms, the lower one, is obviously a gaming table. Now, a life always includes a gamble and, as Pascal said, a wager. Our character, our unique and intemporal personality, our elementary root being given, we have the feeling that it could be staked on happiness or unhappiness, wealth or poverty, good breeding or bad breeding, the employment of our gifts or the waste of them, that at many times that we can recall it has depended on no more than a trifle which way we went, that our red or our black was a matter of hazard or chance. Once a color has come up there is no longer time to go back, except if one is a novelist and appoints an imaginary, or, rather, a half-imaginary, character to deputize for oneself and relive one's missed, crossed, or avoided destiny. This is exactly the situation of Stendhal as novelist. For example, having prepared in Grenoble for the Ecole Polytechnique, Stendhal went to Paris at the age of seventeen to take the entrance examination, arriving the day after the *coup d'état* of 18 Brumaire in which the Directory was overthrown. He did not take the examination, we do not know why—probably because it was his first time in Paris and all that interested him was to discover it. He knew that his whole life would have been changed if, in that Brumaire of the Year VIII [November 1799], he had had the strength to go and answer to his name, pass his examination, and enter the school. Never mind! his heroes would enter for him. In three of his four French novels (*La Chartreuse* is Italian), Octave in *Armance*, Lucien Leuwen, and Fedor in *Lamiel* are graduates of the Polytechnique. And they are noble and rich to boot. Stendhal went to the school in dream, hit the lucky number in dream. His own life became all life. And that is how one becomes a novelist. The primary cell of the novel is the conjunction, *if*.

But the *if* of "if I had gone to the Polytechnique" or "if I were rich," for a man who was twenty years old under the Consulate—that is, under the system of "tools to those who can use them"—is a superficial if, an if itself governed by a deeper *if:* "If I really wanted to, if I had had, if I had the strength!" The presence, the degree, or the absence of strength is what makes a destiny. The gamble includes a direction, or a card from the bottom, which is strength. And that is why Stendhal was naturally to find his great theme and his great work in the novel of strength, *Le Rouge et le noir.*

For Stendhal there was an official publication of strength, *La Gazette des tribunaux.* Throughout a whole generation, from *Le Rouge et le noir* by way of Balzac's *Vautrin* to *Les Misérables*, the courts, the prisons, the penal colonies, the scaffold were to offer novelists examples of human strength. Reading the *Gazette*, Stendhal was struck by the story of a compatriot from the Dauphiné, the seminarian Berthet, sentenced to death and executed for having fired a pistol at a lady of the upper middle class in the house where he was employed as a tutor. It seemed to him that Berthet had admirably expressed the strength of an ardent, needy, poor young man in Restoration society, in those explosive years of 1829 and 1830. In *Armance* Stendhal had just written the novel of the lack of strength, above all of virile strength, in a subtle, delicate descendant of great families, a poor imitator, an inheritor. *Le Rouge et le noir*, the portrayal of strength, the character of Julien—here were the opposite, the antithesis of *Armance*. "Le Blanc et le Bleu" (blue in the sense of the republican wars) would make a joint title for both novels. Today we should say the heir and the scholarship boy.

Except that the subtitle of *Armance* was *Quelques Scènes d'un salon en 1827*—that is, a restricted and precarious little world, while the subtitle of *Le Rouge*—*Chronique de 1830*—meant France, the whole France of 1830. And the promises of this subtitle were kept, so that *Armance* is infinitely surpassed by *Le Rouge*, the key novel of an epoch and a country.

France in 1830, the provinces and Paris! It was an old idea with Stendhal that the provinces gave Paris its fresh supplies of strength. The first part of *Le Rouge* is a picture of provincial society and environments; the second is a Parisian picture, which, however, Stendhal brought off less effectively: the emphasis remains on the provinces. Julien Sorel is the provincial delegate to strength, to the strength of a mountaineer, the delegate of talent to a career, of the poor classes to the conquest of the world. A double conquest.

First the conquest of places, of fortune, of power. Under Napoleon, Julien would have been with the red—that is, a soldier, a colonel at thirty and, at forty, Général Comte Sorel, if he had not been killed. Under the Restoration he could "arrive" only by way of the Church, with the black. He would be a seminarian.

Then the conquest of women, conquest through women.

Julien's two mistresses, Mme. de Rénal and Mathilde de la Mole, are as alive and as famous as Julien. But Stendhal wanted them to share Julien's fate, existing through him and for him.

This same fate, this same drive, is tied up in the novel with the portrayal of society under the Restoration: provincial society, with M. de Rénal and Valenod; the world of the Church with the abbés of the seminary, the Bishop of Agde, Frilair: *Le Rouge et le noir* is the first great nonreligious but clerical psychological novel (Stendhal was a total stranger to religious feeling) that was ever written, and no precursor for it can be found, perhaps, except in that remarkable seventeenth-century *Le Rouge et le noir,* Marivaux's *Paysan parvenu;* and the fashionable and political society of Paris, in which Stendhal was less successful and left more to be done by his successors.

LAMIEL

Julien's strength was not without a violence of temperament, a furnace-like intensity that led him to the scaffold. In the sketched-out but unfinished novel, *Lamiel,* Stendhal amused himself (for it is an amusement, and it contains elements of the bawdy novel in the style of Paul de Kock) by imagining a kind of feminine Julien Sorel, of the people, resolute and strong like the masculine, who does not end on the scaffold but who can find a lover after her nature only in a convict. On the other side of *Le Rouge, Lamiel* occupies a place inverse to and symmetrical with that of *Armance:* Octave de Malivert, or the lack of strength, which feminizes a man—Lamiel, or the excess of strength, which masculinizes a woman. It is understood, moreover, that among these paradoxes of an intelligent novelist the success of the triptych is the middle panel; that full, powerful, normal portrayal of the strength of a man, of a country, of a time, that *Le Rouge et le noir* is; the vast work that was not understood by its own time, that found its public and its responses only twenty years later, and whose living influence is not yet drained.

MÉRIMÉE

The Heir of the Eighteenth Century

The men and women who knew Prosper Mérimée have left us many and most contradictory portraits of him. Among the many characteristics that we may choose in these, let us remember that he and Stendhal were two men, despite their differences in age, in ways of living, in appearance, despite the difference between the pure Parisian and the provincial in Paris, who form a pair to personify the man of the eighteenth century who was paying a visit to and had his habits in the romantic nineteenth century. There is, however, a difference. Stendhal will be remembered in connection with Mérimée because Mérimée needs that. Mérimée will not be remembered in connection with Stendhal because that adds nothing to Stendhal's importance. And there is a twentieth-century viewpoint that would have much surprised the author of the little book, *H.B. par un des quarante.* It is H.B. who in his turn would say of this Forty in 1934: "One of my followers!" In addition, Mérimée had in his lifetime more or less what Stendhal would have liked to have: a free, intelligent, pleasurable life—and security, and an equal footing in that Paris of July from which Beyle could get only an *exile* in Civitavecchia—and an expert, solid literature, approved and enrolled by the Institut, and simply a literature that, without pathos, with a clean style, found immediate triumph and deserved it.

The Parisian

It deserved it in a country where, if sometimes genius succeeds only on credit, work well done always succeeds for cash. A Parisian, the son of comfortably situated artists, Mérimée had from the outset the gift of workmanship of an artist of Paris, the gift that a Marivaux, a Beaumarchais, or a Scribe brought to the theater. He made his appearance, more-over, at the age of twenty-two, in 1825, with a very accomplished book of closet drama, *Clara Gazul,* and a dry *Cromwell* that has not been pre-served and that Stendhal liked. But that lucid and ironic reserve that was Mérimée's profound characteristic from his adolescence on prevented him from exposing himself to a crowd, from espousing it in order to pos-sess it, as it is necessary to do in the theater. It was elsewhere that he utilized his gifts as an intelligent artist and an impeccable fabricator.

The Traveler

He traveled. All of romanticism was worked over, plowed up by travel and changes of country. Mérimée made travel yield its content of interest and structure, of spirit and creations.

It was not that he covered so much of the planet, or even of Europe. A few quick journeys into England, Spain, Italy, Greece, nothing of the long voyages of Custine or Ampère or Xavier Marmier. But he prac-ticed a profession that kept him constantly engaged in creative travel in France: he was an inspector of historic monuments, a function that he more than anyone put on its feet when it had barely been born, in which he was a very able official, teamed here with Eugène Viollet-le-Duc, the architect, as he is elsewhere with Stendhal, gifted with an incomparable feeling for archaeology, one of the leading figures in that great movement of French stocktaking that marked the reign of Louis-Philippe. At the same time he was a great cosmopolitan in spirit. He had a talent for lan-guages, read Russian as well as Spanish, could make his way in any idiom, carried a remarkable atlas of Europe in his memory. He did not hesitate to fabricate false folk songs in *La Guzla,* but it was primarily because he was curious, because he enjoyed seeing a country live according to its individual or strange customs, in its native costumes, with its peculiar ways of eating, evaluating honor, or loving. And for him travel in space was augmented by voyages in time. Archaeology is the intersection of two roads. He wrote erudite books on Roman and Russian history, more because of his academic ambitions than out of historic vocation, for these are the most mediocre parts of his work, and his collaboration brought no luck to Napoleon III's *Vie de César.* Nonetheless he found in history the third dimension of his travel style.

The Birth of the Short Story

Out of this character of a traveling artist, this contact between a sure classic intelligence and a curiosity about all the turnings of romanticism was born a literary form that had not existed before Mérimée, that he carried to perfection, and for which he can be linked (a third time) only with Guy de Maupassant: the short story.

Mérimée wrote a novel in the style of Walter Scott, *Chronique du règne de Charles IX*, and another book of novel length, *Colomba*. Now, rather than a novel, *Colomba* is a long short story, composed in the fashion of the Mérimée short story, whose principal masterpieces the author had already written before this year of 1840. And from *La Chronique* to *Colomba*, in fifteen years, one does indeed pass from one world of narrative to another, one has seen Mérimée give birth to the short story, very far removed from the eighteenth-century tale, except for certain stories by Diderot. The viewpoint of the short story generally includes, as a focus, the presence or the passage of a traveler, of a witness who narrates, of a spectator who observes, of an artist who paints. In the novel, even if it is not a saga novel, the novelist throws himself into the water, embraces a current, reaches a wrecked ship or builds a pontoon bridge. . . . But the author of the short story remains on the shore with his easel and his canvas, or, if he leaves it, it is only to go to the willows of Galatea, and *se cupit ante videri*. Mérimée's short stories are much less comedy or tragedy or human idyl than scenes of cosmopolitan life, the album of a traveler who, like Baudelaire, would everywhere have seen the same boring spectacle of immortal sin if that spectacle had not first been remembered by Mérimée for his own and the reader's pleasure, if afterward the agnostic Mérimée, whose parents had not even had him baptized, did not remain alien to any idea of sin, which he even managed by a deliberate and ironic feat of strength to eliminate completely from his Spanish story, *Ames du purgatoire*.

The philosophy of Mérimée's short story was still that of Voltaire's tale: men are sorry mechanisms or comic jumping-jacks; ideas, morality, sentiments are relative to climate, period, customs; and Montaigne's pages on the diversity of customs would furnish the seed for stories in the manner of Mérimée. Ledoux, the slave dealer of *Tamango;* Lieutenant Roger of *La Partie de Trictrac*, the Corsicans of *Mateo Falcone* and *Colomba*, José in *Carmen* have their own honor, their own morality, like the tailor in the rue Saint-Denis and the national guardsman. Tastes and colors . . . Now tastes and colors are so many kinds of historic monuments. If one is an inspector of historic monuments and an artist, one can make an admirable collection of them, and Mérimée's short stories are in effect a museum of human passions.

The passions mean first of all love. Mérimée would seem to have had little occasion for self-pity in the matter of love. But he seems in his stories to be trying to take vengeance on it. Whatever form it takes in various climates, it ruins and kills the man. Mérimée's stories, like Maupassant's, almost always are bound to the fall of a humanity that destroys itself, or, rather, that would destroy itself if the monument inspector, the curator of the museum, were not there to haul it back, to enlighten it, and to do you the honors of it. Society, readers, and, in his last fifteen years, the imperial court, all curious of these honors, thronged round Mérimée. He had glory, he brought off his life as he brought off his work.

His stories have not budged; their prose, at once without style and without a lack of style, has traveled through time on a steady course. Much more than Balzac's novels, they brought a form to a point of perfection and offered it for imitation. But that is because the form is a much shorter one, sooner reached, than that of the novel, a form that is not a world and that coincides not with an enlargement and a discovery of the world but with a reduction, a classification, and a utilization of the world.

Colomba

Only once did Mérimée exceed the limits of the short or long story. Colomba appeared in 1840. It had one of the most deserved successes that a novel has achieved. The novel and romanticism, for the author of Clara Gazul was still being classed with the romantics. And Colomba is a masterpiece of narration, of technique, of absolute conquest of the reader without excessive means. Without excessive means! In 1840! Even three years before Lucrèce there was a presentiment of the returning classic. Colomba was the novel of an island, like Paul et Virginie. And the novel of Napoleon's island in the year of the Return of the Ashes. A story of a traveling Englishman gave it the frame of irony that contributed best to keeping it as much as possible short of romantic emphasis. The reader was dealing with a well-bred author, who, in contrast to Balzac and Stendhal, knew how to spare the reader the slightest touch of boredom.

Today we see only one defect, a beautiful defect, in Colomba: it has endured. The authenticity of its detail and its manners and customs has been challenged. But it is not for not resembling the real Corsica, which does not trouble us, that we complain of it. It is for too much resembling the Corsica of Colomba, real or false but in any case become a commonplace. We see in it the type of the too perfect book, evolved into an example, the interpretation and illumination of which are no longer renewed: the very opposite of La Chartreuse de Parme, which a year earlier had had no success.

Here we encounter again the distance between Stendhal and Mérimée. Stendhal worked in perfection less than Mérimée. But primarily he wrote novels, and between the novel and the short story there is the same difference as between what is a world and what is in the world. And besides he reigns, while Mérimée is still on the steps of the throne. One is a Stendhalian: it is a recognized nationality that is found in passports. One is not a Mériméan. Mérimée compels us to admire him but invites us to classify him. The exile of Guernsey did the courtier of Compiègne the disservice of repeating *L'Enlèvement de la redoute* in *Le Cimetière d'Eylau*. He crushed him under the charge of his eighty squadrons. What would you have us do? There is prose, but there is also poetry. *Colomba* is the incomparable island, but let us board the boat and we shall reach *La Chartreuse de Parme*, and *La Chartreuse* is the continent, and the continent is Italy. Mérimée's name evokes for us at the same time the rare quality of the content and the close presence of its limits.

X

ALFRED DE MUSSET

The impassioned dialogue that the first third of the nineteenth century initiated between the spirit of the eighteenth century and romanticism had its principal outlet in prose. But poetry did not escape it. Alfred de Musset was caught up in it altogether.

Like Mérimée, he was born into the Parisian upper middle class. His emotions and his senses were often the victims of women; his intelligence was never gulled by men. He had the gifts of analysis and lucidity.

Prince of Youth

And of precocity. A brilliant student who had seen or sensed everything in his parents' *salon*, in the group that surrounded the man of letters who was his father, he plunged into poetry at the age of twenty with his *Contes d'Espagne et d'Italie*, which must not be spoken ill of even today. It was youth calling to youth in a sacred poetic springtime. No book was better suited to the idea of a new wine of poetry in a year of the comet, the idea of a naked Bacchus in the tun. Spain and Italy—sun, mantillas, fiery eyes, duennas, judges, old men's noble faces, blood on the meadow, lovers in beds—that Spain and that Italy were called upon to give the wine its alcohol, to show what could be seen and drink what was to be drunk. The trinkets, the imitations, the carelessness, the technical games with verse form earned the author the mockeries of the critics. But from one day to the next the young had learned by heart a half dozen of his apostrophes, his flaming outcries, his belligerent pictures, his portraits of women to be possessed—and to die for or from. A masquerade-ball dancer in the costume of a Renaissance page, for a few months Musset held the post of prince of the romantic young, or simply of the young.

He held it, but he did not stop with it, and he did not insist on it. He was the only one of the romantics who never concerned himself with striking or adorning a pose, and this would seem all the more remarkable in that he had as great a gift for oratory as anyone. Primarily he was a man of the world who did not like the style of the *cénacle* or the ingenuousnesses and the extreme populism of romantic circles. He much preferred the company of wealthy young wenchers, the poetry of the elders—Mathurin Régnier, Molière, even Voltaire. Like Byron. He who was so little concerned to resemble Byron was the one French poet whose style and life were somewhat reminiscent of him. After July 1830, in *Les Secrètes Pensées de Rafaël*, he washed himself clean of romanticism and the dregs of that Bacchic parade that he had led.

Not he himself, who wrote at whim and who was all in circles, but his immanent genius seems to have wanted this Parisian poet, with Mérimée (who had some qualities of a quiet, water-drinking Musset) the only genuine and traditional Parisian of romanticism, to become for a half century the poet of Paris. And Paris was women, Paris was the theater. But another genius, an evil genius shuffled the cards.

His Theater

The theater is a discipline. Musset disliked all disciplines, beginning with that of rhyme, which he treated as a private enemy. In 1830 he had brought an Italian tale, *La Nuit vénitienne*, to the *Odéon*. It was hooted. God forbid that he should ever again expose himself to the judgments of pedants in boxes and salesclerks in galleries! Like Byron, he would bring the theater to life only for himself alone; the play would be played in an armchair. Hence in 1832 the drama of *La Coupe et les lèvres* and the romantic comedy, *A Quoi rêvent les jeunes filles*, poems of youth and women in brilliant verses that were consummated in *Le Spectacle* with the poem of *Namouna*, with its celebrated stanzas in which Don Juan, Musset's spokesman and symbol, idealized that constant woman-chaser produced by Paris in the thousands. Tyrolean drama and Italian comedy, imitation of Schiller and breath of Shakespeare, heartless wanton and abandoned virgin, debauchery in the left breast and flowering idyl, the antithesis of the two kinds of love would never again be absent from Musset's poetry. The problem of sensual youth, distorted into the antithesis of youth and the senses, would remain his problem long after he had lost all reason to endure it.

Rolla

Hence *Rolla*, which the *Revue des deux mondes* printed on 15 April 1833, provided youths of eighteen for a half century with a thrill to the senses, the heart, the soul. Paris, like every capital, was not lacking in a tremendous amount of prostitution, and *Rolla*, the story of Marie, a fifteen-year-old girl sold to a man by her mother, is a poem of prostitution. The debauched Rolla seems to us today a factitious creature, housed and fed by the worst rhetoric. And of course the poem was a wild success as long as there was a class in rhetoric where it could be read under the desk.

A Revolution in Love

The year 1834 marked a revolution in romantic love. Only one poet of the group was then well known and esteemed for his love affairs, which were adjudged illustrious: Ulric Goettinger, as a famous apostrophe of Musset's shows

> *Ulric, nul oeil des mers n'a mesuré l'abîme . . .*
>
> (Ulric, no ocean eye has plumbed the pit . . .)

But suddenly the leaders of the romantic movement began to emulate Ulric. It was approximately in 1834 that Victor Hugo became the lover of Juliette Drouet, Vigny the lover of Marie Dorval, Musset the lover of George Sand. As in the time of *Les Méditations*, these love affairs had great literary consequences, and none had more notorious consequences than the affair between *Lui et elle*.

Their journey of love to Italy, her infidelity, the reconciliations and the ruptures were at the origins of the four *Nuits*, which were three dialogues between the Poet and the Muse in the nights of May, April, and October and, in the night of December, a dialogue between the poet and his double. For a long time Musset was simply "the poet of *Les Nuits*." There seems to be no reason to revise this judgment. If one has kept (but not all have kept it) a feeling for oratory, for development, for spoken verse, clear and compact as prose, illuminated by poetry at its crest, like the wave beneath the sun, one will rank *Les Nuits* very high. If one prefers to follow Paul Verlaine's advice and wring the neck of eloquence, one must strangle the four sublime swans.

Classic or Romantic?

Those who are not brave enough for that will lay merciless hands on *L'Espoir en Dieu* and the *Lettre à Lamartine*, long-famous pieces whose modest and undeniable sincerity, like that of all Musset's lyric poetry, is bullied and drowned and buried by oratory. The basis of Musset's genius, his true vocation in another time, was the dramatic form, and his well-balanced verse often requires the tone of the theatrical speech. For a long time the public ear would welcome this kind of verse, which was to be, for example, that of Emile Augier's verse comedy. Beginning with Baudelaire it was wounded and exiled by the exigencies of pure poetry. When Musset was received into the Académie, Nisard, not without a certain pedantry and obviously combatting someone, described him in a welcoming speech as the most classic of the romantic poets and indeed a true classic. There is a whole doctrine of classicism in Musset. And something of it, after all, can be retained. First of all, in his character as the poet of unhappy love, the author of the most sincere, the most reserved, the most naked, the most desperate love poetry of his time, in *Le Souvenir*, in *Les Nuits*, in so many shorter poems of *Les Poésies nouvelles*, he occupies among the romantics the position of a witness to the human heart analogous to Racine's position among the classics. Further, he took little or no part in romantic illusionism; he was indeed the child of his century, not its giant or its prophet; unlike George Sand or Hugo, he did not lay his raptures to the credit of God's cause. He recognized weakness and evil in himself as weakness and evil: the poet was singly, ordinarily, classically a man. Finally, he had neither a politics nor a philosophy, he was a man of letters, a poet in the old style, like Malherbe and Boileau; the freedom of his utterance was not on God or the state but on customs and letters. He was a young-bourgeois, with the hyphen in order to make it plain that it was a question not only of age but of ideas and condition. All the same, later on and to subsequent generations he seemed more bourgeois than young. The generation of the Second Empire, Baudelaire and Flaubert, formed itself to a certain extent in opposition to him. To the question, who is the most outmoded of the four great romantic poets, the usual answer would be Musset. But, if the epithet is justified, it is not without its compensations. More or less withdrawn from fashion and trend, Musset has been carried, like a classic, toward an eternal left center of French literature. In fact he has lost readers and hearts. Between the spirit of the eighteenth century and romanticism he established a connection, a society, it might almost be said a golden mean: he was less the child of the century than the child of the July Revolution the little Parisian who grabbed his pistols and ran out to stand before Delacroix's *Liberté*—in this case, literary liberty. This child of July is the sole great poet of the nineteenth century whom nothing, absolutely nothing, allows us to call a great man and who, any more than a Jean-François Regnard or a Piron, has left nothing, absolutely nothing, of a testimony, or, as they say, of a message; and not, alas, for lack of the desire.

XI

BALZAC

Social Nature

"Social nature, which is a nature within nature," Balzac wrote in *Modeste Mignon*. This observation contains the discovery, the genius, the fiction, and the key of Balzac.

As the illuminating preface of 1842 to *La Comédie humaine* explains, the subject matter of this *Comédie*—that is, social nature—is animal nature plus something else. "The social state has hazards that nature does not permit itself, for it is nature plus society." The duality of the sexes counts for little or nothing in natural history; it counts tremendously in social matters. Social nature encompasses in a triple reality men, women, and things: that is, tools, furnishings, houses, cities, modifications of the planet by man. Historians, Balzac said, have shown us little or nothing of this social nature. As examples and as his forerunners Balzac cites what Abbé Barthélemy did for the Greeks and what Alexis Monteil did in his *Histoire des français des divers etats*. Walter Scott incorporated a history of the Scots of the various estates into the novel, and, Balzac said, raising the novel to the philosophic level of history, joined in it "drama, dialogue, portraiture, landscape, description, the marvelous and the true, those elements of the epic." In the domain of the novel it was Walter Scott's fiction that summoned Balzac's to life. Indeed, Balzac became himself, was born into Balzacism, only after having put into a novel in the manner of Scott the most Scott-like subject in French history, the war of the west under the Revolution. In order to write *Le Dernier Chouan*, he went in 1827 to Fougères itself, the setting. Thus he took palette and knife in hand, gained assurance of his technique, established himself in the portrayal of surroundings and in his rivalry with the official registers.

The Entrance of the Official Registers and of Women

Scott was a historical novelist. Now it was a question of applying Scott's technique and chronicle to the contemporary novel, of substituting, in the novelist's competition with the official registers, the open register of births for the closed register of deaths. And of introducing the register of marriages or of women. "Constrained to conform to the ideas of an essentially hypocritical country, Walter Scott was fraudulent, relatively to humanity, in his portrayal of women." His fiction lacked, as well as woman, the portrayal of the passions. Balzac ascribed this *lacuna* to Protestantism, which admitted no possibility for woman after the Fall. The flowering of the English novel in the nineteenth century leads us to suspect that the reason was less simple. The fact remains that from a certain point of view Balzac's novels mark the entrance of women and the approach to women.

That there was a connection in the seventeenth century between the novel and feminine writers, that in the eighteenth century *La Nouvelle Héloïse* had loosed a torrential enthusiasm and tenderness in the hearts of women, that love between the sexes had provided the daily bread of the novel—none of this diminishes the originality with which Balzac introduced into the novel the autonomous world of women and the novel into the world of women. Sainte-Beuve corroborated this, and, partly because his own *Volupté* left women indifferent, he never forgave Balzac for it.

The romantics explored the dictionaries. Three women much older than Balzac, who were the living and also the imaginative memory of the Revolution and the Empire—Mme. de Berny, Laure d'Abrantès, and, later, Mme. de Castries—were for him the living, intelligent, tender, perspicacious dictionaries of their time. His remembrance of things past, his presentation of things present, his exploration of human nature were undertaken with the required feminine collaboration. Like Goethe's nature, *La Comédie humaine* had its "mothers." But above all it had a father.

A Mystique of Fatherhood

Balzac, the greatest creator of living creatures who ever existed, looked into the face of the mystery of creation and plumbed it in its depths. We know how prominent a place was held for him by "Faustian natures," devotees of alchemy, of discovery, of work, a Glaës or a d'Arthez. But the *natural* form of creation is what provides the material for the official registers. It is fatherhood. In the work of every writer of genius there is always one creation that has the function of a profound message and that serves as a primary cell. In Balzac everything takes place as if this function had been that of *Le Père Goriot*.

Not only because *Le Père Goriot* already includes the majority of Balzac's key characters—Vautrin, Rastignac, Bianchon, the Nucingen household—but also because le Père Goriot is primarily the title character and the mystery of fatherhood. Montaigne said that he would rather have fathered a child in trafficking with one of the Muses than with his wife. But the second of these traffickings is the carnal symbol of the first, as tradition makes the couple of the Song of Songs the symbol of the union of God and his Church. *Le Père Goriot* could have been created only by the father of Father Goriot, the "Christ of fatherhood," by the genius of paternity and the paternity of genius. "When I became a father," Goriot said, "I understood God." This is an extraordinary remark that takes us to the source of Balzac's creation. The presence of God, the acquiescence of God are as obvious, as necesary, as absolute in Balzac's work, full like a day of the Creation, as the absence, the nonexistence, of God in the work of Marcel Proust, the day-to-day record of a world that is disintegrating. Competition with the official registers is the external, conventional description that implies, internally and in reality, collaboration with the Creator and that *"Imitation de Dieu le Père"* that is latent in *La Comédie humaine*.

Goriot is a victim of fatherhood because he is a father in the flesh, a father of individuals, a father from selfishness. The phrase, "Christ of fatherhood," means his passion, what he was made to suffer by the two daughters for whom he made himself a sacrificial victim. He loved his daughters totally, overpoweringly, he was the slave of their wills and their passions, and that is why he died desperate and destroyed. In a letter to Mme. Hanska, Balzac said that *Massimilla Doni, Louis Lambert* and *Le Chef-d'oeuvre inconnu* represented "work and execution killed by the overabundance of the creative principle." And the insistence with which he returned to this theme shows the degree to which he felt in this a peril in his own nature. Similarly, in Goriot the human and moral function of fatherhood is done to death by the abundance of this creative principle, which is a terrible gift for man if no discipline intervenes to reduce it, to contain it, and utilize it. If Balzac's production did not turn out badly, as Goriot's did, if the creative principle made the work and the execution live instead of killing them, it was because they were saved by two gifts as remarkable in him as that of creation: the work was saved by the gift of speciality; the execution was saved by the gift of will power.

"Speciality"

Balzac used the word *speciality* in a sense almost the opposite of its current meaning but in its true etymological and philosophical meaning. The gift of speciality is the gift of seeing behind things the species, the ideas that are at their origin—in other words, since Plato, the gift of the philosopher. In *Le Père Goriot* the gift of speciality is something as superhuman as the style of fatherhood is in Goriot himself. Through speciality Balzac saw and expressed in Goriot a *mystique* of fatherhood, a fatherhood that finds its authority above, in divine thought and creation, and, lower, in social nature, in everything to which the father's cries in his agony attest: "Send the police to get them, by force. Justice is on my side, everything is on my side—nature, the law. I protest! The nation will perish if fathers are trampled underfoot. That is clear. Society and the world depend on fatherhood, if children don't love their fathers everything collapses."

The Vauquer boarding house was described and constructed by Balzac not only as a node of humanity but as a node or a crossroads in the domain of speciality. Vautrin and Rastignac are drawn to it, driven by the same current as Goriot. If Goriot's fatherhood is seen as a symbol of the creative fatherhood of genius, Vautrin will appear as an enormous satanic parody of it. The substructures of *La Comédie humaine* are Christian substructures, those of a world in which the devil and hell exist. Among the visions that Balzac brought into the literary universe there is the social hell, the lower depths of capitals, the lower depths of human nature, the prisons. Prison has its hero as Milton's hell had him in Satan. In the instant of Vautrin-Collin's arrest, "prison with its customs and its language, with its sharp transitions from the pleasing to the horrible, its appalling grandeur, its familiarity, its degradation, was suddenly embodied in that question and by that man, who was no longer a man but the type of a whole degenerate nation, of a savage and logical people, brutal and supple. In a moment Collin became an infernal poem that depicted every human feeling except one, that of repentance. His expression was that of the fallen archangel who forever seeks war." There we are in the laboratory of speciality. It would afford a penetrating view of the system of *La Comédie humaine* to align end to end, in a Repertory of Balzacian Thèmes, all those in which images or realities of angels appear, from the angelic poem, *Séraphita*, to *César Birotteau*, in which the perfumer is curiously, it seems, designated as an "angel," the angel of commercial probity as Goriot is the Christ of fatherhood. To be an angel, pure or fallen, is to be an archetype. From a distance the gift of speciality is confused with the gift of thinking angelically.

Will Power

When *Vautrin* was revived, in 1917, Souday wrote that in Vautrin there is Balzac himself in the prison of his toil, "barely taking part in the pleasures and the pomps of that life that he never loved so much as through the intermediary of the heroes of his novels." Since Rastignac and Rubempré are for Vautrin what Anastasie and Delphine are for Goriot, it might be possible to say as much insofar as the analogy of Balzac and Goriot is concerned. But perhaps Balzac's deputy could as well be Rastignac himself, who is Balzac's exact contemporary, since *Le Père Goriot* takes place in 1820 and Rastignac is twenty-one years old, having been born, like Balzac, in 1799. "To the two of us!" is Balzac's own challenge to Paris. Without considering Louis Lambert, who is autobiographical, César Birotteau and Balthazar Glaës are other representatives, or, rather, other parts, of Balzac. In general, a character in *La Comédie humaine* is Balzac-like, in this personal sense, when he appears in it as the witness of a creative will.

Balzac wrote his first manuscript at the age of fourteen: a *Traité de la volonté* that one of his teachers confiscated and destroyed. It is a remarkable thing that, in the two great founders and teachers of French literature, the one in the theater and the other in the novel, Corneille and Balzac, criticism is held in check and in meditation before a mystery and a *mystique* of will. But in Corneille we can confirm only a result, a dazzling peak whose base and origins remain in shadow, while in Balzac, as in the interior of a colossal statue, we can travel through a nature from top to bottom.

First of all the nature of a novelist. Balzac was totally devoid of facility and improvisation; he carried his works in his head for years, wrote them with prodigious effort and tension, piling up outlines, drafts, redrafts, revised proofs. If will power occupied such a place in his world, it was first of all because it occupied the same place in his creation of this world. He saw everything in this will in which he was so rich, as the mystics see everything in God, with whom they are filled.

Then, and as a consequence, the nature of the work. In *Le Médecin de campagne*, when Genestas meets Benassis, he looks at him "accustomed, by the relations that he had maintained with the men of energy sought out by Napoleon, to discern the characteristics of persons destined to great things." This is a remarkable observation, which could have been made by Stendhal about Napoleon, but it is much finer that it should be made by Balzac reproducing Napoleon and faithful to the device that he had written on a statuette of the Emperor: "What he began with the sword I will complete with the pen." Like Napoleon, Balzac recognized and sought out men of energy destined, like himself, to great things. Out of them he built the Grand Army of the novel.

Balzac's characters, or at the very least the most notable part of them, seem made out of concentrations, weaknesses, contrasts, balances, will, as the paintings of a great colorist are made out of the language of colors or as Michelangelo's work is made out of the language of movements. It is in relation to their strength of will that men of letters are conceived and grouped in that novel of literature, *Les Illusions perdues*, between on the one hand d'Arthez, the hero of will, and on the other hand the journalist, Lousteau, or the facile and feminine poet, Rubempré, of whom his sister, Eve, says: "In a poet there is a pretty woman of the worst kind." Balzac recognized this pretty woman in the Canalis—that is, the Lamartine—of *Modeste Mignon*, with the reservation that this time she is of the best kind. How a will can be crushed is the story of *Le Colonel Chabert*. The mysterious balance of an ordered and "d'Arthezian" artistic will and the corrupted will of a mercenary in the same family tree is provided by the two Bridau brothers. The levels of will in the three honest subordinate Touraine brothers, the Birotteaus—the soldier, the priest, and the business man—show three states of the same being, the same will, structured and disciplined, modified in three ways by different environments (Birotteau I would undoubtedly have been one of the heroes of *Les Soldats de la République*, the first of *Les Scènes de la vie militaire*). The degradation of the feminized and dissipated man, Lucien de Rubempré, who can no longer live except by the will of someone else, Vautrin—whose function and mission it is to will for two—can be fully understood only as one of the central episodes of this epic of will.

The Positive Novel

This prominent function of will in Balzac must be viewed in connection with, and almost as a synonym of, the novel of a world that is being built, of something that is being made, of a height that is being scaled again, a *positive* novel in an even stronger and fuller sense than the strongest and fullest that has ever been given to the word, the meaning of Auguste Comte. Here Balzac would be in opposition to almost all the other French novelists of the nineteenth century, the post-1850 realists and naturalists for whom the novel is the phosphorence of a decomposition, the consciousness of what is coming apart.

The realists, however, had one representative in Balzac's generation: Henry Monnier. In order to grasp in the fullness of its action this opposition of the two natures, of an energy that is concentrated by will and an energy that is dissolved or degraded by caricature, one must follow the manner in which Balzac was able to return to and recast Monnier's subjects by turning them from the negative to the positive. Here are two instructive instances of this, which we shall stress because they take us to the heart of the laboratory where nature set up Balzac's experiments.

Henry Monnier drew the caricatures and the types of his *Les Employés* from his experience as a government functionary. He created that French administrative comedy that Georges Courteline was to carry forward. When Balzac came back to this theme of *Les Employés* in 1877, he took over a great part of Monnier's invention and introduced Monnier himself under the name of Bixiou. Through him and others, the comedy of bureaucracy—a bit heavy and congested, however—runs full stream through *Les Employés*. But Balzac would never have sat down to write a novel of gratuitous humor and comic demolition about a ministry. A ministry and a bureaucracy are constructions, Balzac, for his part, was a constructor of the breed of Colbert and Napoleon. He would write a constructor's novel. The subject of *Les Employés* is the Rabourdin plan, and a hundred years after the book the major points of the Rabourdin plan still held first rank among all the projects for administrative reform in the *video meliora* of the professionals of government. Balzac gave the Rabourdin plan life by linking it to the Rabourdin household. He had Rabourdin's creation destroyed by the infinitesimally little men of the ministry and by the world of Henry Monnier. But for the builder-novelist the novel of a ministry could be only the novel of an interest of the state, and the central character an incarnation of the interests of the state. The novel of the functionaries could equally well be called "Les Bourgeois," the lower middle class of the Saint-Paul quarter, the circle from which such men are drawn. Compare Monnier's burghers with Balzac's "shipworms." The shipworms that gnaw away the dykes of Holland are figures virtually comparable to those of such gentlemen as Gigonnet, Mitral, Baudoyer, Saillard, Gaudron, Godard and company—shipworms, moreover, who demonstrated their power in the thirtieth year of this century. It is no longer even a matter of Henry Monnier: even Flaubert's bourgeois is no more than a silhouette beside the three dimensions and the full flesh of Balzac's, especially beside his *strength* as it erupts in his own revolution, that of 1830; Balzac was there at the right moment to intercept that strength not at its beginning but at the instant of its most powerful and most original explosion. Balzac's bourgeois is Monnier's plus a certain number of things, in the very first rank of which is power. Let us observe that *Madame Bovary*, a novel of the degradation of energy, ends just at the moment when the subject would become properly Balzac's, when Homais is doing a tremendous business and has just received the *Légion d'honneur*. The real legion of honor for the bourgeois is the legion of *La Comédie humaine*.

His *dignus intrare* in *La Comédie humaine* can be linked to a moral dimension as it is ordinarily linked to a social dimension. After having revolved the subject of *César Birotteau* in his mind for years without deciding to undertake the story of a commonplace shopkeeper, in which he still saw only something for Henry Monnier, Balzac suddenly entered into Balzacian truth on the day when he discovered its key idea, that of a martyr of commercial probity as Goriot is a Christ of fatherhood. That means that the real subject of *César Birotteau* is the transformation of the negative to the positive, of the ironic silhouette to the fleshed model, with the same contrasts and the same counterbalances as *Goriot*. Birotteau and Pillerault implied the other side of the commercial morality of Nucingen and Tillet: "*Nucingen* and *Birotteau*," Balzac wrote, "are twin works." He is dealing here, however, with *La Maison Nucingen*, written immediately after *Birotteau* in order to further and complete the counterbalance.

Henry Monnier created Joseph Prudhomme. In a very curious letter to Mme. Hanska, Balzac decided that Monnier had not got enough out of him, that Prudhomme represented the whole century, and he sketched the outline of the play that he wanted to write about a Prudhomme of his own: for he saw him not in the novel but in the theater, where, fifteen years later, in 1852, Monnier himself would not only put him but play him. The comparison between Balzac's Prudhomme and Monnier's implies exactly the same criteria and the same contrasts as the comparison between their *Employés*. There is, moreover, something in Balzac's outline that leaves one stupefied. There the story of the Prudhomme family is virtually that of the family of Adolphe Thiers, the statesman and historian. Nothing is missing: the mines of Anzin, the love affair with the mother-in-law, and the marriageable young man named Adolphe. Now, in 1830 the brilliant young minister, Talleyrand's pupil and favorite, had nothing either in his appearance or in his character of that big and little Prudhomme that M. Thiers would become in the eyes of his critics after 1871. It might be said that Balzac, with his seven-league boots, anticipated him by forty years, as for that matter he anticipated everything: the hyperbole of the genius of construction.

The basic essences of *La Comédie humaine* soar far above the region where literary types are formed and where Monnier created Joseph Prudhomme. Balzac did create one type, however, and only one: Gaudissart. Today the name of Gaudissart is used not so much for a traveling salesman as for the loud, joke-playing traveling-salesman type, which has become as rare, for that matter, as the Tartarin type in the south of France. Apparently, in order to make Gaudissart a type, general opinion had to reduce him to the scale of a caricature in the style of Monnier. The real Gaudissart, that of *Birotteau* and *L'Illustre Gaudissart*, is really a Balzac character: a creator, a force in social nature, the inventor of modern advertising, who, though he might be gulled by the Touraine brothers as Balzac himself was by Monnier, is still an "ace." He, like the others, is part of that whole hand of aces held by Balzac.

The vision of the "dominating trait" that Balzac's fiction suggested to Taine, that investment of a character by a single passion—avarice in Grandet, the *mystique* of money in Gobseck, fatherhood in Goriot, lust in Hulot, envy in Cousin Bette, collections in Cousin Pons—these are so many concentrations of energy that, at a privileged moment, express and release themselves in acts of will. All these passionate natures are constructive natures, and, let us note, solitary natures quite as much as Vautrin and Glaës. For them the apogee of construction is construction in solitude, as the most disproportioned monument of man is a pyramid in a desert. Criminal solitude or angelic solitude, each is equally the solitude of a random will, which, in the shape of a passion, takes itself for its object, as in Corneille. And perhaps this parallelism derives from the fact that both Corneille and Balzac lived in the same solitude. Granted that Balzac had affairs, that he received twenty thousand letters from admiring women, that his conversation was a flood—just the opposite of the *larvatus prodeo* that Corneille might have borrowed from Descartes. But, as might have been the case with Corneille, the solitary passions of Balzac's heroes are symbols for Balzac's solitude, his nocturnal solitude in his living workshop, his "speciality" center, his Cyclopean forge. In the substructures of *La Comédie humaine* there is a crypt: "Comédie individuelle," autonomous will, pure energy, gratuitous gift of genius.

Let us remember the dialogue between Gobseck and Derville in *Gobseck:* "There are a dozen of us like this in Paris, all silent secret kings, the masters of your fates." Gobseck or the usurer, as rich and as hard as Grandet, a Parisian besides: "One goes to the usurer only when one cannot go elsewhere." That is why the quintessence of Paris is to be found at the Café Thémis, near the Pont-Neuf: the usurers meet there, "a fantastic image in which the power of gold is personified." Balzac's creative and intuitive genius surpassed everything, transcended the official register, when he made Gobseck, born in 1740 (eighty years old in 1820, a burgrave of Paris), the son of a Jewess and a Dutchman, and for twenty years a sailor and corsair; a corsair of the world changed, by a promotion that is an alchemy, into a corsair of Paris; the father, in that alchemist's world, of the prostitute, Esther Gobseck, out of the same necessity that makes Eugénie Grandet the blank page of another register of gold, the daughter of the Saumur burgher formed by another avarice, the avarice of the French provinces, whose language is as different from Gobseck's as that of the Jew, Nucingen, is from that of the Birotteau of Touraine— the poetry and the symbol of *La Peau de chagrin* and the *Etudes philosophiques* regretfully abandoning Gobseck to the *Scènes de la vie privée*— and then that figure of twelve secret silent kings of Paris . . . the thirteenth comes back, and again he is the first and the only one: he is Balzac.

When Balzac wrote the novel of fatherhood, *Le Père Goriot*, of which he said that it was "so genuine that everyone can recognize its elements in himself, perhaps in his heart," the novelist was so great and plumbed so deeply only because he had viewed fatherhood through his "speciality"— that is, he had put it into the world of essences, made it coincide with God the creator, with the "fatherland," which belongs to the same species as fatherhood and which will live or die with it. The elements of *Le Père Goriot* that Balzac could recognize in his own heart were the fatherhood that bound him to *La Comédie humaine*, that "goodness" that Lamartine saw as the principal feature of his physiognomy, a creative goodness in the ancient meaning of the word *good*. "There is nothing selfish in my life," Balzac wrote to Mme. Hanska; "I must relate my thoughts, my efforts, all my feelings to a being that is not myself, otherwise I have no strength." Since it had given him the essence of fatherhood, it would hardly be understandable if the gift of speciality had not also provided Balzac with the essence of motherhood. It is in *Le Lys dans la vallée*.

La Comédie humaine implied the collaboration of women, a motherhood of genius. It had one of its sources in Mme. de Berny, the Dilecta. Mme. de Mortsauf does not identically resemble Mme. de Berny, but she does incarnate Mme. de Berny's spiritual motherhood. If the dignity of Auguste Comte had allowed him to read novels, it can be supposed that *Le Lys* would have been for him one of the great books of the religion of humanity, the book of spiritual motherhood. Sainte-Beuve thought that Balzac's sole purpose was to rewrite his *Volupté*. While we will not say that *Le Lys* is to *Volupté* what *Les Employés* is to Henry Monnier's offices and burghers, at least it is along that road that their hierarchic relation must be sought. *Volupté* as a novel belongs to the family of *Obermann;* it is an admirable utilization of a personal adventure, but, like the work of Henry Monnier, it does not go beyond the range of a critical intelligence. *Le Lys dans la vallée* adds the creative dimension that is a kind of heroic dimension.

A Mystic Philosophy

When one reads *Le Lys dans la vallée*, as when one reads *Le Père Goriot*, one feels that *Les Etudes philosophiques* is a necessary part of *La Comédie humaine* and almost its Acropolis. Balzac is the only one of the great novelists whose fiction is governed by a positive philosophy, by a conception of the world. He derives it not from the philosophical tradition but from the mystic tradition. Few things, few styles, few vocations give us less the impression of a mystic than the person and the fiction of Balzac, and it is in quite a contrary fashion, as a materialist and a leader, a top leader of "brutal literature," that he has been characterized, described, admired by two generations of critics—Sainte-Beuve and Weiss and, after all, Taine. But in a Balzac the vast weight of the matter is there to balance an equal amount of spirit, of love, of speciality. And, if one compares one of the mystics who are at the origin of Balzac's conception of the world—Saint-Martin of Touraine or Swedenborg of Sweden—with philosophers, one sees that the superiority of the mystic, for the imagination, consists in giving to thought, if not a body, at least a support, and how much his divine realism is opposed to the divine realism of the philosophers. From *La Peau de chagrin* to *Séraphita,* by way of *La Recherche de l'absolu, Les Etudes philosophiques* forms a spiral that goes from the earth to the sky, that has as its base the fevered materiality of Paris and that reaches its peak with the angelic poem of the fjord. This romantic epic is richer, more complex, and more obscure than the two philosophic epics of Lamartine and Victor Hugo. But it comes from the same source and it goes in the same direction.

It is the mystic source and the direction of the new "Christianity." There has been much discussion of Balzac's statement in the preface to *La Comédie humaine:* "I write in the illumination of two eternal truths: Religion and Monarchy." It is true that, under family and feminine influences as much as from conviction, Balzac was at the same time a legitimist and (in a way as a successor) an admirer of Napoleon, and that he conceived France monarchically. But even more, although he was not a believer, he conceived *La Comédie humaine* as *La Divina Commedia* was conceived, in Catholic terms.

No more than Saint-Martin did Balzac feel Catholicism as a shadow, a dilution, the aroma of an empty vial. In this he was the opposite of a Chateaubriand and a Renan. His direction, on the contrary, was that of a hyper-Catholicism, an immoderate Catholicism. In the preface to *La Comédie,* he reminds the reader of Louis Lambert's letter "in which the young mystic philosopher explains, in connection with Swedenborg's doctrine, how there has never been any but the same single religion since the beginning of the world," and he calls *Séraphita* "the Christian Buddha's doctrine in action." *La Comédie* did not embrace that average Christianity brought into favor at the same time by Chateaubriand, by "enlightened priests" and by eclecticism, but on the contrary an eternal, more intense Christianity, a burning, mystic and paradoxical focus of religions, a center from which the gift of speciality perceived them, distinguished them, and classified them. Balzac would not say, as did Voltaire's verse, "let each in his own faith and peace seek light," but rather: "let each in his own faith share common light." In his faith and also in his work. For the master of social sciences that Balzac proclaimed himself to be, "Christianity, and above all Catholicism, being, as I said in *Le*

Médecin de campagne, a total system for the repression of the depraved tendencies of man, is the greatest element of social order."

Social order was one with the order of the world. Balzac viewed religion as a police force only because he considered it primarily a *mystique*. *La Comédie humaine*, too—and first of all—is a *Divina Commedia*. Balzac is filled with God, with good temper, and health, spontaneously—I had almost said shamelessly—because he is full of being. He saw himself as a passage of God in his creative force across rebellious matter, not only across the passions but across a Passion. Balzac would agree with Descartes that God is primarily Will, with Bergson that God does not act easily, that life, thought, creation are heights to be climbed. There is no point of view from which the human comedy seems more intelligible to us than the point of view of God.

Therefore it is a great absurdity in dealing with Balzac to take *La Comédie humaine* from the other end, that of its materiality. Balzac said as much, and even excused it: "In view of my having accumulated so many facts and described them, it has been imagined, quite wrongly, that I belong to the school of the sensualists and the materialists, two aspects of the same thing, pantheism. But perhaps it was possible and even necessary to make this mistake."

Two generations of critics did indeed make it: Balzac's materialism is a commonplace with Sainte-Beuve, and the novel of good society exhausted itself in providing an "idealist" counterpart; the generation of 1850 made Balzac the leading figure of "brutal" and sensual literature, with condemnation from Weiss, with admiration from Taine. Handbooks of literature have retained this label. It is a completely barren point of view. Ferdinand Brunetière had already displaced it in the second phase of his opinions on Balzac. No trace of it would be found in contemporary criticism, from Ernest Curtius to André Bellessort.

The fact is that the world of *La Comédie* is the hugest that has been created by art and that it is difficult to encompass in a single glance, to understand in our terms of day and night this empire on which the sun never sets. Once the basic ideas, those that are explained by the gift of speciality, have been understood, the most incomplete image that could be given of this world would consist in regarding Balzac's vocation as an attempt by nature, half a failure like all attempts by nature, to incarnate a century—the nineteenth—in France. Human comedy, yes, but one that shows itself within the limits of a French comedy and an ageless comedy.

The Museum of a Century

Balzac's father, who was in every way a character out of his son's novels, had always believed that he would live a hundred years and this would make him a millionaire as the sole survivor of the Lafarge insurance scheme. He did not make too great a mistake, for he was eighty-seven when he died, in perfect health, as the result of an accident.

Balzac inherited this timeless vocation. One of his youthful novels, *Le Centenaire*, was planted in him by this genius of his family. The heir of the centenarian was the old antiquarian of *La Peau de chagrin*. And *La Peau de chagrin* epitomized the dilemma of his destiny: a balanced, calm, long life or a short life consumed by passion and genius. But everything worked out as if the dilemma's terms had been reversed: the short life of a half century was Balzac's, the life of a century, the treasures of the antiquarian, the insurance fortune, belonged to *La Comédie humaine*.

La Comédie humaine is the testimonial and the living museum of a French century. And, to be honest, it contains much more than that century: it has its roots in the generation of 1789, in the French Revolution, and particularly in the economic revolution, the redistribution of property. It recounts especially the history of Balzac's generation, which, born at the turn of the century, was twenty years old in 1820 and came to its great chasm in 1850, the year of Balzac's death. But a chasm for men, not for things—for Balzac, not for the history or the comedy of his century. It has often been observed that *La Comédie humaine* predicted and pre-shaped the society of the Second Empire. The generation of 1850 was a Balzacian generation. And Balzac continued to explain, to penetrate, to magnetize the France of the generation of 1885. Balzac's world and the nineteenth century, which began in 1789, ended in 1914. With the generation of 1914, *La Comédie humaine* assumed the form of a historical novel or cycle.

Outstanding Characters

La Comédie humaine can relate to the century precisely because Balzac's generation was the propeller shaft of its century. His purpose was to express that generation, to transplant it into a book: an ambition that every novelist has more or less inherited and that Balzac was the first to have experienced. "A generation," he wrote to Hippolyte Castille, "is a drama with four or five thousand outstanding characters. That drama is my book." He reduced this number to a thousand, more or less, but a thousand representative persons—more precisely, outstanding ones. Or, rather, made outstanding or typical by the art of the novelist, who created prominence like Rembrandt in his quality of an alchemist of light.

No more than Rembrandt did Balzac accept the typical or the outstanding ready-made, just as they stood exposed in the light. For the Duc de Saint-Simon (the most Balzacian of French writers before Balzac, as Proust was to be the most Balzacian after Balzac), the outstanding characters of his comedy of Versailles were those whose prominence was officially established by the political order that gravitated round the king; the outstanding were the most important. Between the Duc de Saint-Simon and Balzac, everything occurred as if there had been a transition in the generation preceding Balzac: that of the prophet of the new society, the Comte de Saint-Simon. The parable that earned the Comte de Saint-Simon a year in prison at the time when Balzac was writing his first books voided the court system representative of the nation in travail. The thousand reformers of Saint-Simon, who were leaders, led to the thousand of Balzac, who were types.

This recollection requires what Balzac called, in the same letter to Castille, the resources of the Arab tale, the help of the entombed Titans. This meant subterranean characters, giants, who are to good and evil like the characters of a painting in shadow and light. Going further than Saint-Simon's parable, Balzac's sought out those who held and tightened the knots of power in the shadows, men of money, of passion and of action: the Vautrins, the Grandets, the Gobsecks, the Nucingens. Then came those who arose in the open, the Marsays, the Rastignacs, who, in *Les Scènes de la vie politique*, were to be part of one of the last ministries of Louis-Philippe, the first as Premier and the second, having married Mlle. de Nucingen, as Under-Secretary of State. They would have their great days under the Second Empire. Then came the types of life and the passions, the rise and fall of men and women, the opposition of complementary natures, that inventory of human situations that seemed to have been made by a man of the law assigned to an inventory of holdings. But always this contrast between the entombed Titans and the luminous gods, the clouded and the radiant, who, the former carrying the latter, govern the whole *Comédie* and whose type would be furnished by such pairs as the antiquarian and Raphaël in *La Peau de chagrin*, or Vautrin and Lucien de Rubempré, or Goriot and his daughters; and it all came to pass as if the real and pure entombed Titan were Balzac in his nights of toil.

Balzac's Geography

A geographical nomenclature for *La Comédie* is provided by the *Répertoire* of Christophe and Cerfberr. But a nomenclature is not a geography.

The whole complex and expository science that today we call physical, political, human geography could be applied to the country, the nature within nature, that is "La Comédie Balzacienne." When Balzac said in the preface to *La Comédie humaine:* "I have tried to give an idea of the different regions of our beautiful country," the pictorial content of the sentence was on the lowest level. What was important was what was explained by what followed: "My book has its geography as it has its genealogy and its families, its places and things, its persons and its facts, as it has its book of heraldry, its nobles and its citizens, its artisans and its peasants, its politicians and its dandies, its army—in a word, its whole world!"

Like that of France herself, this geography has its poles, private life and public life, provincial life and Parisian life, physical life and mystic life. Between these poles lie roads that are the novels in their stories and their continuity. *La Comédie* includes a whole highway geography: the mountain roads, which are those of social rise and fall, the long and broad roads, which lead from the provinces to the capital.

The geography of the mountain roads (which goes as far as the *mystique* of Dante, since for the author of *Séraphita* destinies are purifications) can be plotted only on the spot or, rather, from the air, with detailed observations. Here is one instance: it is known that Balzac wanted to make Mme. de Beauséant the type of the great lady. To the majority of readers of *Le Père Goriot* he did not seem to have succeeded. The heaviness and pedantry of her advice to Rastignac when he was making his first appearance in society, her "We women . . ." had a great deal to do with the reproach of the critics that Balzac "did not know how to make a duchess talk." Rastignac's rise seemed to have been begun with the assistance of a badly adjusted pulley. But all that becomes right again, and singularly moving, when one reflects that Balzac did not invent this tone, that these are lessons, the style of the lessons that he was given by Mme. de Berny and that he was to ask others to repeat. Balzac's mountain geography was derived from his experience of a life, from the experience of his life, always under the pressure of an immense ambition. The same is true of his geography in the other dimensions. Stendhal, perhaps, had preceded him in his intuition both of the Paris-province pairing and of the traffic between them. But he had not preceded him in his materiality, his geology, his writing as well of the French provinces as of Paris. Balzac's provinces, Balzac's Paris—what magnificent weight those words still carry today!

La Comédie humaine Is a Judgment

This presentation of *La Comédie humaine* as an expression of a country and a century, however, is only partial. The essential of this work is that it is *human*, that it represents, as Taine said, "with Shakespeare and Saint-Simon the greatest storehouse of documents on human nature that we possess." But it would be making a great mistake again to see in *La Comédie humaine* only a human document. Like *La Divina Commedia*, it is a judgment. Like *La Divina Commedia*, it has its *Inferno*, its *Purgatorio*, and its *Paradiso*—that is, the physical passions, moral purification, spiritual speciality. There are few characters in Balzac that cannot be assigned to one of these three stages.

Thus *Pierrette* and *Les Illusions perdues* are in part novels on the training of higher staffs. They served at least as much as Zola's Z. *Marcas* (which to Gambetta and his friends seemed to prophesy the "new classes" of the Grenoble speech) to explain the formation of that organization of interests, of legalists, of triumphant "shipworms" that was ready to go to work after 1830 for Cointet of *Les Illusions*, the future Minister of Commerce, and for Petit-Claude of Angoulême, who was to become "the rival of the famous Vinet de Provins and of Pierrette." The fate of Vinet, who raised himself by the martyrdom of the orphaned Pierrette, acquires an extraordinary symbolic force in Balzac, and the sentence that concludes *Pierrette* is neither merely stylistic nor a commonplace ending: "Let us admit among ourselves that Legality would be a wonderful thing for social knaveries if God did not exist." It cannot be said that, in spite of the successive recastings of *Louis Lambert, Le Livre mystique* is one of the most successful parts of *La Comédie*, but there are few titles that have been more insistently demanded than this. At the risk of a redundancy, let us not conclude this examination of *La Comédie* without mention of it.

There remain the technical questions—technique of the novel, technique of style.

Balzac was not always free to give his novels the dimensions that he preferred: contracts have their exigencies. That is why *La Comédie* abounds in passages of padding. But one must look at wholes. The base of Balzac's technique is that of Walter Scott, who, through him and the romantics, dominated the French novel until 1850: solid, slow depiction of backgrounds, long expositions, tightly knotted plots, sometimes slowed down, sometimes accelerated, natural yet literary dialogue, more power than flash, and the qualities of the reporter generally yielding to those of the novelist. *Les Contes drolatiques* were not only a gymnastic of language but also a gymnastic of narrative that did not yield all the results for which Balzac had hoped.

We know what flyspecks the purists have found in Balzac's style. "Balzac wrote badly" is not only a stubborn tradition in the universities but also a point of departure for the reaction of Flaubert and the artistic writers. This question is hardly raised any more. Flaubert's style too had its enemies, artistic writing its failures. Balzac's style is a style of labor and movement that is attuned to the labor and movement of his workshop of novels. He turned his back on the analysis and the narrative of Stendhal and Mérimée; he belonged to the oratorical and synthetic tradition. When he wrote to his friend that he had wanted to write *Le Lys dans la vallée* in the style of Jean-Baptiste Massillon, which would have caused him unmeasured effort, we understand very well what he means and the family of French style to which he referred. A force of nature necessarily assumes a style of flux, a marching style. Balzac's pace in his style is less flowing than Massillon's, less impeccable than Rousseau's, less expert than Chateaubriand's, less graceful than Lamartine's in his prose (here was the real successor to Massillon!). He advances in a stamping of horses and marching men, forceful and not musical. And the ear itself, in the end, knows that it is the Grand Army that is going by.

GEORGE SAND

Rousseau's Daughter

Both because of and to a degree in spite of the fact that the author of
La Nouvelle Héloïse was hardly a novelist, when one reads Rousseau
against the whole biography of French literature one senses to what an
extent the revolution that he initiated affected the novel. It was he who
brought the most important literary revelation of modern times: namely,
the fact that every man—and, even better, every woman—has a novel inside
him, is pregnant with a novel.

Her novel . . . the singular has no meaning of limitation here. A pleasant
stroke of luck arranged that Rousseau should thus become the patron of
the granddaughter of his patroness, Mme. Dupin. When Rousseau's spiritual daughter, his posthumous justification, Aurore Dupin, had given
birth to the two novels of transplanted or ideal or chimerical autobiography with which she was naturally pregnant, *Lélia* and (in the manner
of *La Nouvelle Héloise*) *Indiana,* she was launched on an infinite vocation
as a novelist, she reached and occupied the Promised Land with its huge
grapes of Canaan (but the biggest grapes do not always make the best
wine), of which Rousseau on his peak had had the view, the illusion, and
the desire.

The Woman and Her Work

George Sand herself said that she was "a fool." What she said must not
always be taken literally. But it is a fact that, gifted in an extraordinary
way for thinking, for producing, for putting life into eloquence, into
characters and into stories, she had no personal spirit, she does not attract
the reader, especially today, to her sources, her inner world; she rings
hollow. If the quality of a great artist is measured by the imagined world

that he adds to the real world as a supplement or that he sets up in competition with it, it does not take long to circumnavigate the world of
George Sand. She left no "message," and she does not make us dream.

The Romantic Document

And yet few novelists have put so much extended or modified autobiography into their work. All her love affairs were consummated by
novels—that is to say, they blossomed into literature. Not a factitious literature. *Lélia* and *Indiana*, it is true, can be taken as the written substitutes, the literary warmth, of a cold nature (a circumstance that is not
rare in literature). But, with this reservation, or with this conclusion, one
always feels the fire of passion that made the lava overflow and run in a
regular, harmonious, and flawless prose. She exaggerated, and nowhere
more than in the novel of love does Talleyrand's remark find justification:
"What is exaggerated does not count." The exaggeration of her early
novels has been ascribed to romanticism. When (like Gautier with his
Jeune France) she wrote a parody novel of romantic love in *Cora*, it
would be unusual. Unhappily George Sand lacks wit: she is serious, tragic,
or she stops being.

But, of all the great novelists of this period, it was she who most resembled the great romantic poets. The poetic power of *Indiana* explodes
like the poetic power of *Notre-Dame de Paris*. Not only is the novel
tropical in its evocation of the country in which it is set, tropical in the
excess of distracted passion that runs through it, it is tropical in the temperature of its poetry. It must not be forgotten to what extent the years
from 1830 to 1840 were charged with lyricism: George Sand's novels had
their part, as much as, for example, Edgard Quinet's *Ahasvérus*, in that
landscape of lush poetic vegetation.

The Technical Gift

Not only did George Sand make poetry flow through the novel; she
erected her poetic inspiration, her unsatisfied feminine ardor, her protests
against the marriage bond, her challenges to society, into real and solid
novels. All that Ovid thought became verse; all that George Sand thought
took without effort the shape of novels that, undertaken always with the
"thank God!" of inspiration or a happy chance, always without a preconceived plan, are ingenious and interesting novels, constantly varied in
composition, sustaining interest according to the best recipes (she was

born a quick-lunch operator and immediately became a *cordon bleu*),
with parts that dragged and parts that lagged, drawing on the reader's reserve of patience, but no more than in Balzac and much less than in
Dumas. Has Dumas written a more spirited novel with a more skillfully
evolved plot than *Les Beaux Messieurs de Bois-Doré? Mauprat* and *Le
Marquis de Villemer* were read with so much enthusiasm not for their
preachments on marriage, for their thesis, but for their technique, which
can still be admired today, like the chestnut timbers, the forest of the
rafters in a deserted mansion.

A Deserted Novel

Deserted . . . the novel collapsed because of the artificiality of its characters and above all because of the conventionality of its ideas. The artificial characters in George Sand are principally the men. The heroes of
her novels have even less luck with her than did her lovers. Sometimes,
moreover, they are the same, for instance in the autobiographical novels,
Lucrezia-Floriani and *Elle et lui*, in which, respectively, Karol is Chopin
and Laurent is Musset. But the historian would hardly be able to find the
one or the other in a psychological biography of the musician or the poet.
The women are more alive, and in *Pauline*, for example, there is a feminine portrait of great subtlety.

Lamartine said, "My ideas think for me." George Sand could have said
that her novels thought for her. But, when her novels think, they forget
to live. The socialist novels, like *Le Compagnon du tour de France* and
Le Péché de M. Antoine, are no longer to be borne. At that time she was
no longer writing her novels in the tropical atmosphere of exuberant romantic poetry, but on a barren soil, in the shacks of arid ideas inhabited
by Michel de Bourges and Alexandre-Auguste Ledru-Rollin. In order to
escape that insipid environment she had to emigrate; the historical mysticism, the Wilhelm Meister-like idealism of *Consuélo* and *La Comtesse de
Rudolstadt* still display the power of that novelistic imagination, and good
judges who have come upon them by chance still read them today with
admiration.

The Lady of Nohant

The most-talked-about works of George Sand, those to which immor-
tality has long been promised, are the rustic trilogy of *La Mare au diable*,
La Petite Fadette, and *François le champi*, written from 1846 to 1849.
Though they are somewhat old-fashioned, there is no occasion to chal-

lenge that opinion too strongly. *La Mare au diable* is a masterpiece of delicacy and narration, but diffuse: Maupassant and Paul Arène would have made it a short story, more perfect, in perhaps thirty pages. We will not reproach George Sand, any more than Mistral, for having idealized her peasants, but rather for having made them speak an artificial language, like the stage language in plays that are too well written. It is too clear in them that the good lady of Nohant is a lady.

A Style

George Sand's style has long been called the best style of the novel. Like the greater part of romantic prose, it is oratorical in nature, with a riverlike movement, slow and strong, that carries the load of narrative admirably and dialogue much less so (we know that George Sand's numerous attempts in the theater did not succeed, or succeeded only with the help of a craftsman in the field). This dialogue has no grip, no features; it does not bite the paper. George Sand was the soul of facility, of regularity. She almost never reread what she had done; she wrote the last word of a novel, and, if there was still an hour left in the working day, she started another. If Balzac was a force of nature, George Sand represents its facile, generous gift. It must not be forgotten that, if George Eliot and Colette came after her, she was the first woman to make the career and the manifold, abundant work of a novelist consubstantial with the nature of a woman. With the same limitations and the same weaknesses, she practiced on people that transplantation of motherhood that Mme. de Staël dedicated to ideas. As an initiator of great feminine literature in the West she is on a par with the prophetic Germaine. Have their literary sisters so much widened the circle whose two halves were drawn by these two women of genius?

XIII

THE POPULAR NOVEL

The Serial Novel

Sainte-Beuve's article of 1838 on *La Littérature industrielle* has remained famous. He denounced the introduction of industrial practices into literature, and the article itself, furthermore, is not without industrial purpose, since it was written for *La Revue des deux mondes* on behalf of Buloz and against his enemies, Balzac in particular. There is a magazine industry as there is a theater industry, and in sum the interests of literature accommodate themselves to the interests of these industries. The July monarchy introduced the serial-novel industry, which has been variously viewed.

It was in fact born of the magazine industry, the inaugurator of which was Dr. Véron, the founder of *La Revue de Paris* in 1829. Véron was the first to have the idea of giving his readers novels that would appear in parts in successive issues, and the formula, "to be continued in our next issue," was his invention. Buloz, of course, imitated him. Besides, they published novels of literary worth, especially Balzac's. What the magazines did on a fortnightly basis was done on a daily basis by Emile de Girardin when he launched *La Presse* in 1836. The success was such that the major newspapers imitated him. A portrait of the serial novel would overflow our frame. We will deal only with a few characteristic names, of which the elder Dumas and Eugène Sue are the most important.

Dumas and Maquet

Alexandre Dumas' vast production of fiction, more than five hundred volumes, however, first appeared, like Balzac's, as much in bound books as in serial form. Until 1839 Dumas was above all a dramatist, and he had written only three meager, mediocre, and neglected novels. Then he began his collaboration with Auguste Maquet, who brought him a novel about the Cellamare conspiracy, which Dumas made four times bigger as *Le Chevalier d'Harmental*. It was Dumas' first big success as a novelist. The collaboration between Dumas and Maquet lasted twelve years. It is a whole novel in itself and it ended in a lawsuit.

Except for *Le Comte de Monte-Cristo*, the ideas of the novels, the outlines, and the first drafts were Maquet's. Dumas took the *maquette* [rough model] of Maquet and worked the model over, embroidered it, played with it, put life into it. This was the procedure for *La Reine Margot, Le Chevalier de Maison-Rouge, Joseph Balsamo, Le Collier de la reine, La Dame de Monsoreau, Ange Pitou, Les Quarante-Cinq, Le Vicomte de Bragelonne*. It was Maquet who discovered in the *Mémoires de d'Artagnan* the subject of *Les Trois Mousquetaires* and sketched it out. But it was Dumas who had the idea for *Monte-Cristo* and wrote it first without being able to achieve more than travel notes, which were the favorite form of his genius. Maquet had to come to the rescue, snatch *Monte-Cristo* away from the musing demon, and construct a skeleton. After they separated, in 1852, Maquet produced nothing more than honest serials, and Dumas nothing but trash. That median date of the century, when Balzac, Sue, and Frédéric Soulié had died, was also the date of the death of Dumas-Maquet, who, like Emile Erckmann and Alexandre Chatrian under the name of Erckmann-Chatrian, made one indivisible novelist.

Brunetière considered Dumas, as a novelist, a jolly Negro who enjoyed nothing so much as making a fool of the whites. Regardless of this matter of the two Negroes, which has the same music-hall tinge as the story of the two deaf men, Dumas-Maquet can be regarded as the master of the oldest and the most universal conception of the tale—something intended to make people forget life in invented stories. Balzac wanted to write the *Thousand and One Nights* of the West. But it was Dumas and Maquet who did so, and this required a drop of African blood. The genius of the narrative in *Les Trois Mousquetaires* is the equal of the genius of the action in *La Tour de Nesle*. And in Dumas there was a genius that sustained them both: it was the genius of life, that flame and that movement that in the life of Dumas-Maquet belonged indeed to the author of the *Mémoires* and the *Impressions de voyage*.

Eugène Sue

Eugène Sue, who had been a physician in the navy, came home from his travels with the sea novel, which he created (*Atar-Gull* is perhaps his masterpiece, dedicated to James Fenimore Cooper, whom he imitated) and handed down to Edouard Corbière, the father of Tristan. His experience of life suggested a good novel, *Mathilde*, an interesting and almost Balzac-like story of a young woman. Financial exigencies made him write a serial novel, as an experiment and under the handicap of the strangest absurdities. This was *Les Mystères de Paris*, the publication of which in *Le Constitutionnel* filled the whole of France with a Pantagruelian thirst for each succeeding installment. In it Eugène Sue adapted *Notre-Dame de Paris*, with its truculent pictures, its angels and its monsters, its confessions of melodrama, to contemporary Paris, so that Hugo could get his own back only with *Les Misérables*. This was the period of the agitation against the Jesuits. "Where do you come from, black men?" "We come from under the earth." And in the House of Peers Cousin had declared: "I proclaim myself the enemy of that corporation: let befall me what may!" In *Le Juif errant* Eugène Sue wrote the novel of what the Jesuits could do, and, as they said in 1830, it was Gothic and like a catapult. It was *Le Journal des débats*, the newspaper of the enlightened middle class, however, that published *Le Juif errant* as a serial. And it is obvious that Eugène Sue knew how to put together a novel and that the genius of "to be continued in our next" had never gone so far since Scheherazade. But if, with Dumas-Maquet, we continue to be amused by what they wrote, with Eugène Sue we are hardly more amused than he who wrote and those who, from issue to issue, followed him. In fact the Second Empire suppressed this serial novel by levying a tax of five centimes per copy on any newspaper that published any of it; it came back to life under the Third Republic, in which, still flourishing, it occupied the lower depths of literature. At least Dumas and Sue left their mark on literature by creating types like d'Artagnan and Gorenflot, Pipelet and Rodin, and the influence of Sue's types on those of *Les Misérables* is definite.

Other Popular Novelists

Frédéric Soulié invested a genius for plot equal to Dumas' or Sue's in *Si Jeunesse savait* and *Confession générale*. Unfortunately none of his characters survives, and yet it is in such a legacy that the semi-immortality of novelists who are no longer read consists: take Henry Monnier.

Better still, there is a novelist who himself has become a type: he is Paul de Kock, who created the bawdy novel, tossed it off by the hundred for an avid public, and still has readers, since he is always being reprinted. When a certain kind of middle-class humor, moderately salacious, appears in real life, it always makes us say: "That's out of Paul de Kock."

There are two disciples of Balzac in whom real merit is to be recognized: Léon Gozlan, whose *Le Notaire de Chantilly* not undeservedly wound up in the courts, and Charles de Bernard, whose best-known work is *Gerfaut* but whose best is the scenes of provincial life in *Le Gentil-homme campagnard*. Should the amazing improviser of Marseille, Joseph Méry, be called a disciple or a rival of Dumas? He introduced Marseille and its humor into the Parisian novel, and at least out of his work one short story should survive: *La Chasse au chastre*, the prototype of Tar-tarin.

The Physiologies

It will be noted that in this vast literature for a popular audience there is almost no trace of the people, or only in conventional and stylized fashion. A much more faithful drawing of the people will be found in publications of a para-fictional kind that were much in fashion round 1840: the *Physiologies*, of which there were about a hundred and fifty, at which almost every novelist and journalist had a fling, and which were illustrated by Honoré Daumier and Gavarni (Sulpice-Guillaume Chevalier). The nine volumes of *Les Français peints par eux-mêmes*, which were undertaken by the publisher, Curmer, to provide an inventory of French society along the lines of *La Comédie humaine*, are themselves collections of *Physiologies*.

Children's Literature

This generation of novelists born with the century, this 1830-1850 period of production, was overflowing with creative zest and it surrounded the monument of the human comedy with a veritable romantic comedy. It even called into being a new kind of novel: literature for children, encouraged by *Le Journal des enfants*, which Loève-Veimars founded in 1833 and which, in its first issues, launched one of the most popular works of this kind: *Jean-Paul Choppart*, by Louis Desnoyers, very soon followed by *Robert-Robert*. It was for children that Jules Sandeau was to write *La Roche aux mouettes* and Alexandre Dumas the delightful *Histoire d'un casse-noisette*. Beginning with this period, every generation of adults would have its literature for children and adolescents, which would leave its mark on the next generation. The generation of 1820 had Desnoyers, that of 1850 would have Alfred Assolant and the Comtesse de Ségur, that of 1885 the same countess and Jules Verne.

So the inauguration of the novel by the generation of 1820, from which it was taken over by the generation of 1850, can be compared only with the inauguration of the theater by the generations of Corneille, Molière, and Racine. It was a dominating form, an absorbing one, which created a need, which imposed itself on the actors and the public, to which even Taine, Renan, and Charles Renouvier thought themselves obliged to sacrifice, and which established virtually a new realm in literary creation.

XIV

THE NOVELS OF THE POETS

Romanticism and Autobiography

Among other new aspects that came into French literature with Rousseau there was this: that, until the end of romanticism—that is, until the middle of the nineteenth century—every great writer, every great poet, at least once in his life, would write his novel—more often it would be his novels. The reign of romanticism was also the reign of the novel; one wrote one's novel as, in the classic period, one wrote one's tragedy. But, if none of the great romantic poets omitted to write a novel, none left a deep impression on the form. None strode out ahead and opened a breach. None was not more or less in the rank and file.

In principle, the sole novel that every writer potentially has within himself is the more or less disguised autobiography. Such was the case of Rousseau, of Chateaubriand, of Mme. de Staël, authors of *Mémoires*, who wrote their novels in the same ink as these memoirs. Such is to a certain extent the case of Alfred de Musset, of Sainte-Beuve, whose *La Confession d'un enfant du siècle* and *Volupté* idealized a personal destiny or adventure.

The situation of Lamartine, of Hugo, of Vigny, of Gautier, in relation to the novel is different. What they encountered on their paths was not only the temptation or the summons of the fictionalized autobiography but the presence of the epic and the existence of the historical novel.

Lamartine

Lamartine's case would seem instructive here. Lamartine was born in a time and lived in a province in which the epic poem had retained its status, in which the example of Chateaubriand naturally showed a reli-

gious young poet the duty of writing *Les Martyrs* in verse. Let us add
that he genuinely possessed the epic genius. Now, he began very late to
write novels, when he was almost sixty years old. Abandoning the idea of
writing his epic episode of *Les Pêcheurs* in verse, he put it into prose,
the prose of *Graziella*, a much less autobiographical novel than its place
in *Les Confidences* would lead one to believe. *Raphaël* is closer to autobiography, as is *Antonella*. But *Le Tailleur de pierres de Saint-Point* and
Geneviève, histoire d'une servante, sentimental and touching novels in
which there are very beautiful pages and in which there is an abundance
of speeches that cry out to be put into verse (the verse of *Jocelyn*), belong to that vein of the popular epic, for the thatched cottages "pathetic
and primitive in their bread and salt," of which Lamartine had dreamed
of writing an episode in verse under the title of *Les Ouvriers*. Obviously
Lamartine was not a novelist. But he was a great epic poet, who in forty
years had lived a life that the epic of the Middle Ages had taken three
centuries to live—that is, the transit from the epic to the epic novel, from
verse to prose, not out of a desire for novelty but by default, the slowing
down of a wheel that no longer turned, out of the aging of a form that
was decaying in its mechanism and its function.

The Hugo of Notre-Dame

Twelve years younger, Hugo in this instance belonged to an already
totally different epoch. He no longer depended on the classic traditional
epic that was finishing out its final generation of life, but rather on a
young, hale, truly romantic son of that epic, which was the historical
novel. He was twenty years old when Walter Scott's influence began,
he read Scott and imitated him. In the brief interval between Lamartine
and Hugo, then, there was Walter Scott. In contrast to Lamartine, it was
the historical novel that was to shine on Hugo's epic, to penetrate it, and
to transform it with *La Légende des siècles*, "a legend heard at the gates
of history," like the novels of the author of *Waverley*.

Before writing Walter Scott well, Hugo at twenty wrote him badly
in *Bug-Jargal* and *Han d'Islande*. This, moreover, was the height of the
brief fashion for the terrifying novel, and *Bug* and *Han* were resolutely
of that school. But in *Notre-Dame de Paris*, which dates from 1831, he
brought off one of the models of the school, within the limits of the
school, and with its gaps.

The limits, the gaps, of the historical novel are its lack of humanity,
the conventional attitudes of the characters, pretexts for well-made narratives, accurate costuming, and dazzling settings. The characters of
Notre-Dame—Esmeraldo, Frollo, Quasimodo, Phoebus, Louis XI—have

exactly the same kind of costume reality as the characters of *Ivanhoe*. But on the other hand *Notre-Dame*, contemporary with Delacroix, is perhaps the masterpiece of historical portraiture. The cathedral of Paris, the Paris of the fifteenth century, the Court of Miracles, the palace—in the prodigality of omnipotence all this exploits the limitless means of painting, of design, of etching. Many editions of *Notre-Dame* illustrated by the best romantic artists and their successors appeared during Hugo's lifetime. None of his illustrators could even approach the amazing sketchbook of the poet. A masterpiece in the painting of backgrounds, *Notre-Dame* is a masterpiece of style, one of the creations of French prose, and often a masterpiece of the art of the narrative. With its presences and its absences it has remained the type of the novel of romanticism.

Alfred de Vigny

There was, moreover, a reason for this, which was that *Notre-Dame* was written three years after Alfred de Vigny's *Cinq-Mars;* that, if the colors are pallid in Vigny's historical novel, in compensation the narrative art, the construction, of the novel can stand with their model, which was Walter Scott; that Vigny was the first in the field, that his novel had a splendid success, and that Victor always enjoyed to an extreme degree the genius of imitation: the genius of doing what others did and doing it better.

The two poets had comparable success in the novel, and a certain parallelism was to continue in their careers. Each having tasted the success of a great and beautiful historical novel, neither intending to abandon the historical novel—since at the end of his career Hugo was to write *Quatre-vingt-treize* and Vigny was to leave behind him the beautiful unfinished posthumous novel, *Daphné*—they followed in other ways the progress of their time toward the living modern novel, the author's testimony of himself, of his time, of the problems and the men of that time. They followed it, or, rather, they wanted and tried to lead it as poets. Hence, for these poets, the novels of their destinies with Alfred de Vigny, the novels of their time with Victor Hugo.

A soldier and a poet, with all the pride and sensitivity that made him infinitely vulnerable to all the affronts that are the occupational hazard of both careers, Vigny wrote the novel of the officer in *Servitude et grandeur militaires*, the novel of the poet in *Stello*. To be honest, *Cinq-Mars* also belonged to the category of the author's testimony of himself, since Comte Alfred de Vigny, who was filled with the consciousness and the pride of his nobility in every sense of the word, wanted to make this the novel of the nobility's defeat by Richelieu's harsh genius and the servants of the institution of monarchy. An officer of the old royal army, ignored by his superiors, the victim of misfortune, taking refuge in lonely honor, morally obligated to resign after the Revolution of 1830, which completed his uprooting, in the three episodes of *Servitude et grandeur militaires* he wrote the story of officers similarly sacrificed, the unfortunate heroes of passive obedience. In contrast to Balzac's Philippe Bridau, Captain Renaud is one of the rare military types that have persisted, in any case the only one of whom it can be said that he added anything to the spirit of the military career. It was in Vigny's destiny to arouse these enthusiasms and these fervors, and *Stello* gave the poets an analogous position, not socially but poetically and ideally. *Stello*, in other words, was the drama of the poet, the mystery of the poet, under three forms of government that equally despised and sacrificed him—Thomas Chatterton in the constitutional state, Nicolas-Joseph-Laurent Gilbert in the monarchical state, André Chénier in the democratic state. *Stello*, also three historical stories with a thesis, has aged much more than the contemporary novel, *Servitude et grandeur*. Its fictionalized history and its equally fictionalized great historical figures of the seventeenth century and the Revolution seem terribly false to us. But, by transposing the first episode of *Stello* to the theater under the title of *Chatterton*, Vigny achieved the greatest public triumph of his life, as well as the glory of having served for his generation as the champion of the poet's rights and the scribe of his sufferings.

Vigny hardly ever stopped fictionalizing himself, and the author of the *Journal d'un poète* could take his place in the posterity, mentioned earlier, of *La Nouvelle Héloïse* and *René*. Hugo used himself very little as material: at most a few pages of his early loves in *Le Dernier Jour d'un condamné* and *Les Misérables*, Walter Scott having inspired him up to *Notre-Dame*. After 1843, when he gave up the theater—or, rather, the theater gave him up—Balzac, Sand, Soulié succeeded to Scott, and Hugo decided to write a Balzac-like novel of his own time: this was *Les Misères*, the idea of which he had conceived in 1830, which he wrote from 1845 to 1848, and which remained in his desk drawer until 1862, when he went back to it, filled it out, consolidated its Balzac-like element, skillfully added a little more salt to it for the mass public, though there was already no lack of that in *Les Misères*. The result was *Les Misérables*.

The triumph of *Les Misérables* was immense and immediate, and it is still going on. It was through *Les Misérables* that the poet maintained contact with the crowds, a contact renewed in force by the film version. It deserved this popularity. Here, at the forge of a Cyclops, Hugo hammered out the novel of Paris, the novel of adventures, the detective novel, the novel of human pity, the heroic novel. Certainly *Les Misérables* would no more have existed without the July monarchy than *Notre-Dame* without Walter Scott. The fact is that Hugo was carried along by his time.

But his creations have no resemblance to those of anyone else, even those of nature. It does not shock us that his characters are all of a piece, that Javert is all policeman, that Thénardier is all the wicked man, that Marius and Cosette are all youth: their life outside time is a life. And it was in part as a result of this procedure that Hugo achieved that unique success in the novel—the creation of a saint, Monseigneur Myriel. He incorporated into the novel that theme that Lamartine had entrusted to the epic: the rise of a soul, the liberation of man the galley slave by the spark of goodness, of sacrifice; and in truth *Les Misérables* turns its back on the heroes of novels in order to become almost a novel of heroes. Another paradox: novels are women; the success of novels is made by women. Now *Les Misérables* is a novel without women: I mean without other love affairs than the incidental and the conventional, like those of Marius and Cosette. In this respect Hugo's masculine genius viewed the novel in the terms in which Corneille viewed the theater. The heroic novel is a virile novel. And yet Hugo, a great lover, wrote the most beautiful love letters in the world by the thousand.

Love has a bigger place in *Les Travailleurs de la mer*. But *Les Travailleurs*, like *L'Homme qui rit* and *Quatre-vingt-treize*, is again a novel of heroism: a novel of the sacrifice of Gilliatt, a novel of a Jean Valjean out of a tale of fantasy, a Gwynplaine, in which *Han d'Islande* is blended with *Les Misérables*, a novel of the clash of grandeur between the old rebel Breton royalist, Lantenac, and the young republican, Gauvain. And always in the famous episodes or descriptions, the color and the etching of a style that reaches the limits of the language's strength, as Valjean reaches those of physical strength when he raises the cart, those of spiritual strength when, after the storm within the skull, he gives himself up.

Musset and Gautier

Of the great poets of romanticism it is Musset who, with Lamartine, holds the lowest rank in the novel, despite *La Confession d'un enfant du siècle*, which confesses nothing remarkable and does it in a declamatory style. His short stories, pleasant and no more, are similarly quite inferior to his plays.

The same cannot be said of Gautier, a strange and various novelist, in whom the brief flaring romanticism of the school of 1830 was personified. In a totally opposite manner his fiction is the counterpart of Vigny's; Vigny is the novelist of the destiny and the rights of the poet; Gautier, with more simplicity and skepticism, is the novelist of the destiny and the rights of the artist. With him the word *artist* took on a meaning that it has never yielded. *Les Jeune France* (1833) is the confession of a child not of the century but of the year, the year 1830, a child who had "believed in Pétrus" and cleaned off the stigma by taking a cure of irony. In *Mademoiselle de Maupin* (1835) Gautier wrote the novel of the artist who, without difficulty but with belligerence and defiance, sacrifices morality to beauty, and in *Eldorado*, which later became *Fortunio*, the novel of a dream of success, sensual pleasure, and beauty—the last of his books, he said, in which he could remain free and not submit to cant (he used the English word) for money. All this is quite unremembered, and he is read hardly at all any more . . . except for *Capitaine Fracasse* because it is redeemed by its style, by that healthy, succulent prose of Gautier, and also because it is the good picaresque novel of a poet who had a fraternal understanding of the poets of the time of Louis XIII, in which *Fracasse* takes place.

So, then, all the romantic poets faced the question of the novel, wrote important novels. As for the forerunners and the poets of Parnassus,* either they avoided the novel, like Baudelaire and Leconte de Lisle, or they attempted it without conviction—like Banville, who at least wrote only one novel; Mendès, who wrote a shelf of them, but commercially, and Coppée, who wrote whatever was asked of him in prose and verse alike.

The real Parnassian novel was the antique novel that derived more or less from that titular tetrarch, Flaubert. Anatole France was as much a Parnassian when he wrote *Thaïs* as when he composed his antique verse drama, *Les Noces corinthiennes*, in imitation of Goethe. The most—the only—popular work among Parnassian novels was *Aphrodite*, written by an heir of Parnassus, Pierre Louÿs, who never went beyond his heritage, except for his sales figures; and that does not mean much. Hailed as a masterpiece by Coppée, it has held that rank for shopgirls, and that, in sum, is a logical fate for it.

* See Part III, Chapter V.—Editor.

LAMENNAIS AND RELIGIOUS LITERATURE

The Problem of Religious Literature

The religious failure of the Revolution, the Concordat, above all *Le Génie du christianisme* raised the problem of a Catholic literature at the beginning of the century. The defense of the faith, the reconstruction of society on Christian foundations, the reaction against the philosophy of the eighteenth century, the counterrevolution—would it be a powerful intellectual and literary movement that would sustain them, assist them, further them, make them alive and active on the heart and the mind? Would the clergy regain that post of leadership in Christian letters that it had occupied with the great men of the Church of the seventeenth century? Or would the genius of Christianity remain, as it was with Chateaubriand, a lay genius? Would it appeal to the senses or to reason? Would Christian thought seek to seize power through the counterrevolution as the philosophers' ideas had seized power through the Revolution? Fierce and contradictory replies came to all these questions. It will be observed that there were three great epochs of original Catholic literature in France: the first filled the seventeenth century, running from Saint Francis of Sales to Massillon; the second ran from the Revolution to 1870; the last began with the separation of Church and state and still continues.

It is the survival of one beaten man and two orators—Felicité-Robert de Lamennais, Charles de Montalembert, and Père Jean-Baptiste-Henri Lacordaire—that makes us prolong the second period into the Second Empire. But in a literary sense its sap, its originality were almost drained by 1833, after the ban on Lamennais' journal *L'Avenir*.

Against Indifference

Two books at two different periods brought glory to Lamennais: the *Essai sur l'indifférence* in 1817 and the *Paroles d'un croyant* in 1834. In their two titles there is all of Lamennais. Indifference—in other words, tepidness, the empty, susceptible mind—was for him evil and despair. He denounced it with horror in society because for him personally it was impossible. And his fierce vocation for belief took on an aspect all the more tragic as the object of that belief changed, reversed itself, and vacillated further.

He was a Breton, living among believers, for whom belief was the only air that he could breathe and who, after a gloomy youth harrowed by doubt, made his first communion at the age of twenty-one, immediately wrote his books of Christian polemic with his brother, a priest, and was thrust into the priesthood by the example of that brother and the influence of a Christian militant, a hero of the emigration, Abbé Carron. He strove desperately for faith, he was always separated from it by a gap that was sometimes imperceptible, sometimes a chasm. In such case Pascal was wont to say: "Have masses said and take holy water." More daring—in sum, more romantic—Lamennais wanted to say the masses and bless the water to the same end. Pale and trembling, he said his first mass in 1815, at the age of thirty-four. Then he wrote to his brother: "I am and from now on can be only extraordinarily unhappy." There were three successive faces of that unhappiness and those torments.

WILLED CERTAINTY

An excellent method of reinforcing his faith was to turn his back on his doubts, on himself, and do battle for it. Lamennais made himself the soldier of the Church against the times, and particularly against liberalism, seeing tolerance as a weakness of will, an indifference to all opinions, a lack of life. The *Essai sur l'indifférence en matière de religion* exploded in 1817 like a kind of *Génie du christianisme* of the Restoration. The close grain of its style, the precision of its development, the flights of its eloquence won universal approbation. He was hailed as a new Bossuet.

THE APOLOGETIC

The first volume left the way open and prepared for an apologetic that was begun two years later in the second volume and that did not have the same success. It was, however, equally personal. This individualist hated individualism: to give religion the basis of a universal accord, to force the doubt and the pride of individual opinion to bend before the opinion of all, to replace the continuity of tradition with a sort of ecumenical mass in time and space, such were the goals of an apologetic as different from that evolved in this period in the lectures of Denis de Frayssinous as it was from Chateaubriand's; it disappointed and it had no effect.

DOMINATION

To act on men, on souls, was the whole aim of Lamennais' will and passion, and to act as a leader, not only a spiritual but an intellectual leader. The immediate personal leader, the bishop, was the enemy. The author looked for authority only to the remote, impersonal leader. the Pope. An Ultramontane against the hierarchy, a plotter (in the sixteenth-century meaning) against the civil power, a clerical against the clerks, a royalist against the king, he launched under the Restoration the series of his prosecutions, and also an intense effect on an admirable young generation.

One example inspired him: that of the religious reform of the seventeenth century. He was not a Jansenist; far from it. But the first childhood reading that had shown him himself was that of Pierre Nicole's *Essais*. He inherited a fine Jansenist library. He was an admirer of Jean Duverger de Hauranne, Abbé de Saint-Cyran; was not Port-Royal a Christian creation, an edifice of souls, persecuted by the clergy and the state?

The most moving memory that he has left is that of the Breton Port-Royal that he established on his family property of La Chesnaie, on the banks of the Rance, through which a train of devout youth passed: Maurice de Guérin, La Morvonnais, Monseigneur Philippe Gerbet, Louis-Antoine de Salinis, Lacordaire, Montalembert. A part of the young clergy turned to him. After 1830, pamphlets and the Breton Port-Royal were no longer enough for him and his disciples. The periodical *L'Avenir* provided an organ for a new doctrine. The salvation of the Church would lie in its alliance with freedom, especially freedom of schooling. Once to the right of Charles X, Lamennais moved now to the extreme left of Louis-Philippe. He did not despair of aligning the Church and the Pope in the same position.

Lamennais is no longer read; his writings are too closely bound to their time. But his name, his memory, remain alive because he founded the theories and fixed the attitudes of Christian Democracy. The suspension of his paper in 1831 and then the condemnation of his doctrine by the Pope in 1832 were followed in 1834 by the *Paroles d'un croyant*.

The Prophet

The *Paroles d'un croyant* were inspired in part by the *Livre des péle-rins polonais* of Adam Mickievicz (*L'Avenir* had supported the Polish cause with zeal). This imitation of the form of the Gospels and the Apocalypse, these Biblical verses of a Parisian prophet, these anathemas against kings and priests, seem rather cold to us today and leave us completely indifferent. But at the height of romanticism, in the year of Quinet's *Ahasvérus*, the effect was tremendous: the printers wept as they set the type. Rome thundered the bull *Singulari nos* against Lamennais, against all his work after the *Essai*. And he, from his side, thundered the separation of Church and Lamennais.

It was also the separation of Lamennais and his friends. None of his disciples followed him. All the editors of *L'Avenir* had made their submission. Lamennais threw himself entirely on the side of the people, became a republican, paid fines and went to prison, was praised in words by his new party but aroused no enthusiasm in it, remained for it the *sacerdos in aeternum*, achieved only indifferent success with the works that followed, was elected to the National Assembly, where he functioned in obscurity, and disappeared into the shadows after 1851; in compliance with his despairing wish, his body was buried in a pauper's grave in 1854.

Sacerdos in Aeternum

In 1826, at the time of his first sentence—a fine of a few francs for his attacks against the declaration of 1826—Lamennais cried: "I'll show them what it means to be a priest!" It recalls the Abbé de Saint-Cyran's remark: "Here are six feet of earth where there is no fear of the Chancellor or of anyone else." And in a certain powerful sense, redoubtable and solitary, there were indeed two men in France who showed what it meant to be a priest: Saint-Cyran and Lamennais. Lamennais showed it in 1817 against society, in 1826 against the bishops, in 1834 against the Pope. He showed what a lone priest was, a separated priest, a priest without the Church. And the greatest service for which the Church is his debtor is precisely this, which he performed for twenty years and which his example still rendered the Church after his death: "Tremble," Bossuet said, "at the mere word *separation*."

His Influence

When Lamennais, Lacordaire, and Montalembert gathered on the benches of the Assemblies of the Republic, it was plain that in spite of everything the ideas of *L'Avenir* had borne fruit, and even today the freedom of the schools is still his victory. But what matters to us here is not the political but the literary mark that Lamennais was able to leave.

There is one reminder of it in the young and pure school of La Chesnaie. There is above all this, that from 1830 to 1835 the great influence that the romantics exerted on religion was that of Lamennais. He heard confession from Victor Hugo and, probably, in Juilly, from Sainte-Beuve, whom he wanted to take to Rome with him. *Volupté* was written in the shadow of Lamennais, as *Le Centaure* was written in the shadow of *Volupté*, and it was in that shadow too that the first idea of *Port-Royal* emerged. The influence of Lamennais on Lamartine was very strong at the time of *Jocelyn*, and after 1830 Lamartine's religion in sum, in the Jesuit style, resembled what that of Lamennais was in a severe style. Hugo was again to give him a great deal of thought in *Les Misérables*. The progression of all of them toward the left, their deaths on the left were those of Lamennais. It was perhaps in memory of his former confessor and his will—"I wish to be buried in the midst of the poor and in the manner of the poor"—that Victor Hugo wanted to be taken to his funeral in the pauper's hearse. The prophetic note of the *Paroles d'un croyant* had foreshadowed *Les Châtiments*. George Sand wrote her novel, *Spiridion*, round Lamennais if not about him, and it made a great impression on Renan. Now we come to the other Breton clerk.

The two greatest writers that the clerical sector gave the nineteenth century, Lamennais and Renan, did not remain in the Church. The great Catholic journalists were laymen. What was left for the clerics was eloquence, which has a great effect but defends itself poorly against oblivion.

Lacordaire

Two names, however, have earned literary survival: that of a Dominican, Lacordaire, and that of a bishop, Félix-Antoine-Philibert Dupanloup —in other words, a romantic and a classic.

In contrast to Lamennais, Lacordaire became great only after his submission. It becomes apparent on a reading of his work that he would have offered little aside from Christian doctrine, Christian lectures, Christian dogma; he remains the type of those souls that cannot live without powerful, illuminated, decorative, and definitive certainties. He could come to faith, militant faith, and remain in it only by the inner exigence of an infallible authority to which he submitted and in which he participated. He had been converted after his twentieth year. The formula of his conversion, as he phrased it in 1824, is important, and its argument was to have sequels enough: "Society is necessary. Therefore the Christian religion is divine, for it is the sole means of bringing society to perfection." But his Burgundian gift for oratory was balanced by an active and ardent inner life. Born in 1802, he knew by heart the sickness of the romantic century; he was its spokesman in the Church. He began the dialogue between the Church and this eternal sickness.

The dialogue is what used to be called the conference. "The incomparable author of the art of consultation," Pascal said of Montaigne. Lacordaire, a master of the conference rather than of the sermon, seems to have restored to this word all its former meaning, to the extent that this could be done by a monologue and in the name of an authority. He *conferred* the Church on the century. It is the audience that makes the preacher, Bossuet said. The audience of the July monarchy, the romantics, made their preacher, who addressed himself not to man, not to the confessional and conventional believer, but to the man of his time as he was, as Lacordaire felt him in himself, as he had battled or befriended him in himself. In the metal of this eloquence there are many elements that are questionable, outmoded, artificial, but there is also the presence of this gold: the scattered fragments of confessions from which Lacordaire was drawn only regretfully by the exigencies of the oratorical form.

All that is no reason to reread him very much—he is too bound to his time and to the urgent necessities of oratorical action. His funeral orations, his factitious hagiographies of Saint Dominick and Saint Madeleine show us, alas, conventions as the opposite pole of confessions, more than balancing them. But he had one gift: that of language. There are few orators of whom one can quote so many phrases struck like medals, so many forceful antitheses and illuminating definitions.

Dupanloup

From his catechisms of the Madeleine about 1840 to his presence and his bearing at the breach at the time of 16 May, Dupanloup was the greatest figure in the French clergy and, worthy of a portrait by Hyacinthe Rigaud, the Bossuet of the nineteenth century. But only up to the point of literary genius. His work is indispensable only to the historian of the Church. An exception might be made for his three volumes on education, which hold a high place in the rich literature of Catholic psychology, and especially for the published fragments of his *Journal intime*. This

Journal, which ought to be published in its entirety, this daily conversation of a great man of action with himself and with God, is a unique book in clerical literature: a great intelligence and a great life of action find their source here in a secret fountain that has the dimension of a human face.

XVI

THE FORM-MASTERS

In the World of the Professors

The intellectual form-masters of our age: that is the name that Sainte-Beuve liked to give to three professors of the Sorbonne: Guizot, Villemain and Cousin—that is, Doctrine, the Académie, the School. Born almost at the same time—Guizot in 1787, Villemain in 1790, Cousin in 1792—contemporaries of Lamartine, these three brilliant pupils, these precocious prize winners, were at once the representatives and the professors of their coevals. We say the professors and not the masters. A generation sometimes finds its masters in itself but always finds in the preceding generation the professors by whom and against whom it takes shape. The case of the generation that in 1820 drew its great young professors from itself seems unique.

Unique but explainable. The Revolution had virtually abolished literary studies for fifteen years. The political republic had interrupted that republic of the universities and preparatory schools that, in France, has always occupied a position alongside the republic of letters that is the incarnation of a kind of Council of State in the parliamentary institution of the mind and that introduces a hundred thousand children and young people into a civil service or a national guard of humanism. The reconstruction had been slow; it was the work of the imperial university. By 1808 excellent courses in rhetoric had been reinstituted in the secondary schools of Paris. The enlistment of the middle classes of the mind, the conscription of the bachelors, resumed with regularity. But the influence of the barren years made itself felt. The masters that they would have shaped were lacking in 1820. As the Revolution had sought its generals, so first the Empire, then the Restoration, called on the young to provide the professors. What happened with the writers was what happened with the professors. A new start was made with fresh staffs. The need created the organ: a young generation just out of the schools occupied many of the command posts of the mind.

It occupied them with dogmatism. First of all, because youth is a dogmatic age. Second, because the romanticism that more or less governed the trends of that period was caught on all sides in a torrential and impassioned movement. Finally, because that young generation, as was its function, reacted in every way against the preceding epoch, against the spirit of the eighteenth century, against an analytical and critical age and generation.

Moreover, a new style had been born at the end of the eighteenth century: the eloquence of the professorial podium, inaugurated in 1786 with the opening and the succes of the *Lycée,* and back in favor under the Directory and the Consulate. It had its laws. Certain theatrical qualities, an atmosphere of contemporary allusions, the gift of knowing without seeming to have learned, the art of teaching others well what one had just learned well or badly oneself, an easy manner, an eloquence midway between the parliamentary and the religious made for rapid and dazzling successes.

The Father of the Form-Masters

If the professorial podium was the mother of the form-masters, they had an eminent father, Royer-Collard. A descendant and a disciple of the best Jansenists of the eighteenth century, secretary of the Commune of Paris until 10 August, proscribed 2 June, a member of the Royalist Committee and a correspondent of Louis XVIII under the Directory and the Consulate, professor of the history of philosophy in 1811 at the Sorbonne, where his teaching determined the whole career of Cousin and where he had Guizot appointed to the chair of history, a great and courageous citizen, Royer can be defined in every field as a dogmatic liberal whose liberalism never blunted the edge of his dogmatism and whose dogmatism never made him recreant to the slightest call of threatened liberalism. Beginning with the charter of 1814, this dogmatic liberalism (philosophy of common sense, system of vested rights, suffrage based on the ownership of land, supreme right in the king, who would not only reign but govern) was personified in the party of the doctrinarians, of whom Royer-Collard was the chief and the orator. The Duc de Broglie gave the Doctrine the support of Staëlian liberalism and the spirit of Coppet. Guizot, who occupied an important political situation from 1814 on and who had followed the king to Ghent, was its journalist and its hope. The Doctrine, its principles, and its men were to come to power in 1830, the time of those whom Molé called the pedants and Sainte-Beuve the form-masters.

In the fields of history, philosophy, and literature, dogmatic liberalism
was to give the form-masters spirit and influence their common mark.
This spirit and this influence were spread by eloquence. The three form-
masters were eloquent men. From 1816 on, language in all its forms in
Paris took on an admirable magnificence that recalled the great years of
the seventeenth century. In this ambiance of brilliant *salons* and a new
parliamentary eloquence, it was natural that, the Christian pulpit lacking
great orators, the university podium should attract, charm, and dominate
a public of every class and every age. It was the Doctrine's propaganda
medium. In 1830 it seemed to have been engulfed by its own victory, for
the three form-masters assumed high office and stopped teaching. But
their government was a sequel to their professorship, and written eloquence was the continuation of spoken eloquence. Of this government
and this eloquence we need remember only what was particularly important to letters and what history, philosophy and criticism kept of Guizot,
Cousin, and Villemain.

The Inventories

Pursuing projects already begun in the eighteenth century, the early
years of the nineteenth century and the Empire were a period of stocktaking. A whole descriptive literature, often luxuriously illustrated (from
1798 there had been buyers for the publications of Ambroise-Firmin
Didot, Hellenist, bookseller, and printer, which were extremely costly),
was dedicated to the past and the present of France. What did *Le Génie
du christianisme* do but provide a banner and a *mystique* for this spirit
of panorama and synthesis? An intelligent publisher, who was not on the
wrong track, proposed that Chateaubriand write a "Génie de la France"
as personified in her provinces. The project came to nothing, and this
was indeed a loss. What book would have suited Chateaubriand better in
1803 than this "Tableau de la France," this "Génie de la France?" Certainly this new Génie would not have gone out of fashion like *Les Martyrs* and even *L'Itinéraire*. Chateaubriand's feeling for history and description, his individual movement with its substantial phrases and its lofty
ideas would have been in their rightful domain. For lack of the great
architect, more modest draftsmen attacked the task. Aubin Millin undertook a project of this kind in 1804. His *Voyage dans les départements du
Midi de la France* in five volumes, which began to appear in 1807, still
holds an honorable place in a good library. The *Musée des monuments
français* that Marie-Alexandre Lenoir, not satisfied to bring it together
in Paris, put into beautiful books was to cause Michelet to say "It was
there and nowhere else that I first had the living feeling of history."

History as Dissertation and History as Chronicle

It was in fact in the form of history that this spirit and this business of French stocktaking entered into literature. Before the birth of the noted works of the generation of 1820, they were prepared for with intelligence by the historians of the first twenty years of the century. Two roads of history were opened with them.

First, in the face of the remarkable changes that had turned France upside down for fifteen years, the public demanded an explanation, a connection, and, to use the word then in fashion, "considerations." Like the war of 1914, the Revolution was followed immediately, and from its beginning the literature of emigration was already accompanying it, by a historical point of view. In 1801 Pierre-Louis de Lacretelle (the elder), who was later to teach history at the Sorbonne, began a *Précis historique de la Revolution.* The connection between the monarchy of Richelieu and Louis XIV and the Jacobin and Napoleonic centralization was judiciously made in 1818 by Pierre-Edouard Lemontey in his *Essai sur L'établissement monarchique de Louis XIV.*

In the second place, the revival of the Middle Ages, which recalled at that time the revival of antiquity in the sixteenth century, naturally had as much repercussion on history as on poetry, and more. From Geneva and Coppet—in other words, from the mother house—came *L'Histoire des républiques italiennes* of the shrewd but unevocative Sismondi in 1809. And in 1811 Joseph-François Michaud published *L'Histoire des croisades,* written with fervor but conscience on the basis of sources of which he published a part in *La Bibliothèque des croisades,* and also on the basis of journeys to places that he described pleasantly in the seven volumes of his *Correspondance d'Orient.* Michaud was, moreover, a poet, and, like a cedar in the Valley of the Wolves, his *Croisades* grew in the very shadow of that Knight of the Holy Sepulcher, François-René de Chateaubriand.

Thus a history as dissertation and a history as chronicle took form. Under the Restoration the former found a veritable leader in Guizot, the latter its chief in Barante, and the union between them its great representative in Augustin Thierry.

Guizot

A Calvinist born in Nîmes, driven out of France at the age of six by the Revolution, which guillotined his father, Guizot got all his schooling in the city of his refuge, Geneva. A writer from his adolescence (he had to live, and in his family living meant having a pen in hand), he brought the pure spirit of Mme. de Staël into literature as early as 1808, and he was launched on a Staëlian career as a European literary critic when in 1812 Royer-Collard suggested to Fontanes that Guizot be named to the chair of history at the Sorbonne to replace Lacretelle. "But I do not know history," the young man said. "Precisely so," M. Royer replied; "you will learn it by teaching it." That is what he did, and it is quite visible. As was still being said in 1828, it was history "without facts, without dates, without names." And Royer-Collard, who always observed with a terrible clear-sightedness the disciples whom he had emancipated, said later of the minister what was already true of the historian: "What he learned this morning he seems to have known from all eternity."

Except that it must not be forgotten that Guizot rose very early and that he knew much. He learned history not only by teaching it but also by reading a great number of historical texts, and especially memoirs, while he directed for publishers the great collections in which these texts were published and translated. It was on the solid rock of accomplishment that by his two series of courses, those of 1820 and those of 1828, he provided history with a date, an act, and a work.

A date. He had brought into general history that Staëlian art and system of *Considérations*, which were nothing but the principle of the intelligibility of facts, of categories of the mind applied to the changes of historical time. At the same time the same thing was being done in Germany by Hegel, with more creative genius but with less sense of reality. The *Histoire du système représentatif*, the *Essais sur l'histoire de France*, the *Histoire de la civilisation en Europe*, these were not, like Hegel's *Philosophie de l'histoire*, the history of the Idea, but it was the animation and the classification of history by certain great ideas—that of feudalism, that of representative government, that of the middle class, that of the balance beween the growth of association and the growth of freedom. There is still a Section of General and Philosophical History in the Académie des Sciences Morales. We hardly know now what it is. But, if Guizot, in the chair at the Sorbonne that he held from 1812 to 1830, with the interruptions caused by politics, did not create the phrase, he gave the example of the actuality; he established it with a veritable institutional power.

An act. A man of politics, Guizot did not separate the history of the past, which was to be explained, from history to be lived, to be made, to be carried on. He sought in history instruction for the present. As there was the doctrine of the throne and the altar, there was also for him the doctrine of the podium and power. When the podium was not available, it was replaced by the couch of the doctrinarians, Royer-Collard in the middle and Guizot and the Broglies beside him. The Doctrinarians had a doctrine of government based on a certain very serious conception of human nature, in which Royer's Jansenism was attuned to Guizot's Calvinism and Necker's religiosity; based on a certain idea of the history of

France, conceived as a progress toward an enlightened, supervised liberalism; based on an admiring sympathy for English institutions, a Genevan loyalty to a kind of Anglo-French duality of political wisdom. The July Revolution, conceived strictly as a French 1688, was to provide the crown, the corroboration, and then the headquarters of these views. The revolution of 1848, like 16 May 1877, would lay bare a misunderstanding between this group and the nation, would make apparent what was alien—half from across the Jura, half from across the Channel—in these ideas, what the average Frenchman did not assimilate.

A work. If the great doctrinarian's *Leçons* have grown old, it is because they have been absorbed, assimilated in so far as they were assimilable. But what can survive of his is that great *Histoire de la révolution d'Angleterre* begun in 1827, when his time made him find this subject most appropriate (in addition, he had been working on it for many years while he translated English memoirs of the period), which he did not finish until after 1848. Rich in political sagacity, it is full of masterful narrative and great scenes in the classic manner. Jacques de Thou, his predecessor as a historian, would have felt at home with it.

Picturesque History

The fact was that in the interval Augustin Thierry and Prosper de Barante had won readers and applause for a history that was to the fashionable book, the novel, what oratorical and philosophical history was to the professorial chair. Marchangy and the troubadour school had made the stories of the Middle Ages fashionable. Between these fictionalized narratives and critical history Barante and Thierry created picturesque history, with portrayals, narrations, backgrounds, which were not fictionalized because the chroniclers included all their elements and which offered the reader, especially the woman reader, pleasure without fiction through their evocative style, pleasure to equal that of reading Walter Scott.

BARANTE

In *L'Histoire des ducs de Bourgogne*, of which the first volume appeared in 1814 and the last in 1826, Barante had found a rich subject. It was a rich and picturesque period, the epoch of the four dukes of the house of Valois, and almost all their history could be found in four chroniclers—Jean Froissart, Georges Chastellain, Enguerrand de Monstrelet, and Philippe de Commines—whom Barante had only to order into good French. The work can still be read with pleasure, and it has hardly any errors that are not in its sources. Its major flaw is that, while it is inadequate to take the place of a history of the dukes written in a critical fashion on the basis of monographs and documents, Barante's work had enough merit to prevent the birth of such a history.

AUGUSTIN THIERRY

The most celebrated historian of his time was Augustin Thierry. He deserved his fame for the solidity and the splendor of his style, both worthy of a disciple of Chateaubriand; for the dramatic interest of his narration, which rivals Walter Scott's; for his philosophical idea of modern history, which is that of a contemporary of Guizot; for his generous and deep populist pity for the suffering, which is that of a forerunner of Michelet. And there we have many great names, beside each of which his is always second. Second too in time after Barante, since *La Conquête de l'Angleterre* was begun in 1825, a year after *Les Ducs de Bourgogne.* Thierry was long popular among teachers as the master of a decorative historical narrative whose influence was to be found later in Flaubert's *Salammbô.* But no one reads him now, and no one is wrong. His *Histoire de la conquête de l'Angleterre par les normands* has been devastated from foundation to rooftree by the progress of criticism. Its foundation is the explanation of modern history by wars between races, by the centuries-long subjugation of one race by another, the local and general revolutions that liberated the slave race, all that fiction of Henry de Boulainvilliers in which Guizot still believed and to which Numa-Denis Fustel de Coulanges put an end. Its rooftree is those beautiful pediments or metopes of narrative than can be salvaged from this ruin for the museums of style called "selected pieces": the myth of the *Histoire de Jacques Bonhomme,* the *Histoire de la commune de Vézelay,* the *Récits des temps mérovingiens.*

The History of the Revolution

There is one way in which Guizot, Barante and Thierry are alike: their attention is fixed on the present; the history of the past is or will be a useful, and utilized, introduction to the history that they are called upon to live as statesmen or as reformers. Guizot's history courses were an introduction to the new order inaugurated by the French Revolution, his *Révolution d'Angleterre* was an introduction to the government of 1830. Such was not the case of *L'Histoire des ducs,* but Barante, a doctrinarian statesman, was to complete his career as a historian with an *Histoire de la Convention* and an *Histoire du Directoire,* mediocre artifacts of old age. Thierry, the Saint-Simonist, was induced to become the historian of the oppressed races by the same impulse that drove him toward the social reformers. The foundation level of history at that time was the French Revolution, as for Herodotus it was the war of the Greeks and the Barbarians. The generation of 1820 was singled out for this history in a special fashion. This was the case of François Mignet, of Thiers, and of Michelet, the institutional historian, the statesman historian, the professorial and prophetic historian.

Mignet and Thiers

The two friends from Aix, Mignet and Thiers, had set off to conquer Paris with no other preconceived idea than the will to succeed. Before they were thirty each had written a *Histoire de la Révolution*, and both were successful because they wrote without prejudice—this earned them the designation of fatalists—and because Mignet's book was for twenty years the best and most reliable summary. Both have been demoted today.

It was otherwise with the *Histoire du Consulat et de l'Empire* that Thiers, then out of office, began to publish in 1840 and that he took almost twenty years to write. For a half century it was the most famous historical work in France, indispensable to any serious library, the school of statesmen. A soldier of Napoleon, Général de Pelleport, writing his memoirs at the beginning of the Second Empire, said: "One of the greatest regrets that I can feel today is the thought that I may have to die before having read Thiers' history of our immortal campaign in Russia. Indeed, only the true and serious historian of the armies of the Revolution and the Empire will be able to report completely and impartially, without falling into fiction, that great phase of our victories and our reverses. What can we tell, we who were actors in parts of that long drama?"

When, in 1863, Thiers entered legislative life as an opposition deputy, the Emperor's message to Parliament hailed him as "our great national historian." And after 1870 a part of his sovereign prestige came to him from his great historical work. This glory did not endure. He has been found dull and stereotyped. Detailed studies have overthrown him on many points. And the vocabulary of contempt has been drained on his style, devoid of splendor and line.

This denigration is unjust. As the picture of a reign, Thiers' history has never been supplanted. Nor, especially, as a history of the state by a statesman. Thiers was eighteen years old in 1815. He knew the men of the First Empire well. Some of these men formed the backbone, of which he was part, of the July monarchy. He had access to an immense oral and written documentation. He overdid his accounts of battles, but it is the civilians, not the soldiers, who make fun of these accounts. When it comes to the Emperor's government and policy, Thiers is no ivory-tower historian: he knows government, diplomacy, administration, ministries, and offices. The clarity that he gives his subject is like the clarity of his speeches, and, if it is a clarity intended for the ignorant, it is not the limpidity of ignorance. People who say today that they have nothing to learn from Thiers evoke a smile. The *Histoire du Consulat et de l'Empire*, in short, has aged in the same degree as the work of Albert Sorel: it is a normal historical aging, which could not turn back the intelligent reader. When one thinks that Frédéric Masson's work on Napoleon dethroned Thiers' history for the generation that preceded the First World War, one is no longer so proud to belong to it.

Nonetheless Thiers was remarkably lacking in genius. In that company of the three historians by birth, the two born in Aix in 1796 and 1797 and the one born in Paris in 1798, all the genius belonged to the third: Michelet.

Michelet

There was a mission peculiar to this epoch, as much in France as in Germany, of which Michelet seems particularly the representative: it consisted in conceiving history as an absolute, in feeling and expressing a *mystique* of history. It was in this that Jean-Baptiste Vico, better than Hegel, served him as discoverer. Michelet at first felt his vocation as philosophical, and he always knew himself and was recognized to be an artist. An art of bringing the past to life, a philosophy of humanity as something that endures, a *mystique* of peoples that create themselves and that simply create—it was with these powers, these divinities of his own, that Michelet's soul harmonized and vibrated. When one speaks of a page of Michelet, one generally applies the adjective, "moving." Without a challenge we apply the adjective to the pages he wrote in the archives that were his profession and that, according to him, fed his history of France. But it is irritating that this history should thus begin with an illusion of Michelet about himself and about the object of his history, that this *mystique* should start with a mystification. Common sense, in fact, tells us that any general history of France implies detailed monographs and that it can be written only at second hand. A history of France written properly according to all the sources would require the lifetimes of a hundred men. This *mystique*, like all *mystiques*, lives in the world of intuition. In the field of history the word "intuition" seems to have been created and put into the world for Michelet. His *Histoire de France* and *Histoire de la Révolution française* have almost nothing of a sustained, contained, restrained narrative, master of itself and determined to enlighten the reader. They assume the knowledge of the history that they tell. And so, in short paragraphs, in strong feelings, in indignations, in enthusiasms, in images, in lines of fire, in showers of stars, Michelet's visions and reflections come one upon another. Whatever he said of it, his history is not a resurrection: it is a landscape under a barrage of lightning. This climate does not suit everyone's nerves.

Obviously Guizot does not have Michelet's genius. But a reader who knows nothing of the history of the English and French revolutions will come away from a reading of Guizot with clear ideas and precise information on the first, and from a reading of Michelet with a passionate interest in the second, confused insights, and the desire to learn its history from some other source.

A REPUBLICAN BOSSUET

A professor at the Ecole Normale, the Sorbonne, and the Collège de France, professor too to the granddaughters of Charles X and the daughters of Louis-Philippe, Michelet wanted to be something more: the teacher of the people. This chief general of the university aspired to the highest decoration. He got it. His career can be compared to that of the man who, in the century most despised by Michelet, most accurately achieved the antithesis of Michelet: Bossuet. Michelet was as deliberately of the people as Bossuet was of the Church. Michelet's plan for his historical monument is like Bossuet's: a universal history written in many fragments and at many periods (in other words, *La Bible de l'humanité*, which is an anti-Bossuet *Discours*, the *Histoire romaine*, the *Histoire de France* and the *Précis*), generally as the result of a lesson and in the spirit of a lesson; then, as the transverse arm of the monument, the *Histoire de la Révolution* and the related books, which, like Bossuet's *Histoire des variations*, are the book of battle, the book of defense of a faith, the book of propaganda history. These two men, who, rightly or wrongly, are considered not as our greatest historians but as our greatest classic artists of history, were led to build dissimilarly to a similar end. The metaphor of graduation speeches, according to which each little Frenchman, the crown prince of universal suffrage, is the object of the same educational efforts (in a republic) as the heir to the throne in the time of Bossuet, is obviously not without its comic aspect. But it will be taken seriously to the extent to which Michelet is present, to the extent to which this printer's son, this Parisian who wanted to be of the people, who was of the people in mind and feeling rather than in fact, inaugurated a history of which peoples are the heroes, exerted an influence on thousands of spirits, had not only audiences, august or not, as Bossuet had, but also disciples, created a current of faith and enthusiasm that is still strong. In contrast to Guizot, to Macaulay, to Tocqueville and to Renan, Michelet entered little or not at all into their European republic of the mind. He has only all the more importance in their French Republic on that account, even in *the* French Republic. Neither the history of radicalism, which is the only permanent republican party, nor the *mystique* of the tide to the left can be understood without constant reference to Michelet; he was the educator of the republicans who were twenty years old in 1870 and who, between the war of that year and the war of 1914, maintained his feeling, his enthusiasms, his limits, his affirmations, and his negations.

A ROMANTIC ARTIST

It is less to the nature of his *mystique* than to his remarkable qualities as an artist that Michelet owes his brilliance. His history was born and developed over the same time as that great romantic portrayal of history that disappeared more or less with the end of the nineteenth century. Taine compared him with Gustave Doré. And it is true that, like Doré with the great books of mankind, he romantically illustrated its annals. But Doré was a meteor without a morrow. Michelet's style, his phrasing, his art, like his historical preaching, had great morrows. In the nineteenth century, the existence, the action of a Charles Péguy justified Michelet still more.

He was not only the great animator of history. He was its great person. This great person will never be known, with his burning undercurrents, his carnal geology, until the day when his vast *Journal* comes out of the archives and out of secrecy. The personality of Michelet will emerge. But for the moment he is still the man who, having written, "France is a person," became the mystical realization of the phrase.

He thought and lived France as a person in her body, in her continuity, and in her soul. In her body: it is the geographical picture that serves as the introduction to the second volume. In her continuity: it is the history of France. In her soul: it is the messianic Michelet. Of no writer less than of Michelet can it be said that he left the idea and the being of France as he had found them.

LE TABLEAU DE LA FRANCE

The *Tableau de la France* meets Francis Bacon's definition of art: man added to nature. The *Tableau* is France conceived as a work of art and expressed by a work of art. To understand the extent to which Michelet was the first in this respect, it is enough to compare the *Tableau* of 1833 with the various *Eloges de la France* more or less inspired by the *éloge* of Italy, by the *Georgics*. There is nothing between the one and the other.

The *Tableau* created a habit and a style for the bonds between the man of genius and the soil that produces him. Obviously nothing is more open to question than the mass of hasty and contrived comparisons with which it abounds, and, like his enemy, the Englishman, Michelet never stops finding, in a journey through France, the red-haired feminine curmudgeon who enables him to generalize about a province. For instance: "Same critical spirit in Franche-Comté; hence Guillaume de Saint-Amour, the opponent of the mysticism of the begging orders; the grammarian, [Pierre-Joseph] d'Olivet, etc. If we wanted to cite some of the most eminent of our contemporaries, we could mention MM. Charles Nodier, [Théodore] Jouffroy and [Gustave] Droz." But these hypotheses, these fantasies set things in motion. To suppose order, an order, between things that neither precede nor follow one another naturally is often to prepare the way for a science.

However, it is not a science for which the *Tableau* prepares the way, but "literary—that is to say, vague—truths" (the phrase comes from Taine himself), those of which Taine would make one of the frames of his criticism. Leaving the "moment" to history, the *Tableau* creates a composition of "race" and "environment."

The picture of Champagne in *La Fontaine et ses Fables,* one of the most brilliant and most widely read pieces that Taine wrote, a sort of literary introduction to his method, comes authentically from the school of Michelet. Similarly, the *Tableau,* through the intermediary of Taine's *Champagne,* more or less sired the *Lorraine* of Barrès. When Ernest Lavisse ranked the pages on Lorraine in *Un Homme libre* very high and saw them as a great piece of historical psychology, it was to a degree because Lavisse recognized the seed of Michelet here, the progeny of this *Tableau* whose brilliance he too had felt so strongly. What in Lavisse had passed into the work of the professors produced for Barrès an immense, wholly literary posterity, to which we belong.

A picture of Michelet's work should be written like the *Tableau de la France* itself, with the same insight into complexity, the same voyage of discovery in a vast work where there may be irritating or ridiculous parts but where there are no more dead parts than in the work of Victor Hugo. Does not *La Bible de l'humanité* give us the idea of a tremendous human criticism, at once literary and historical, that would have been to Sainte-Beuve's what the chain of the Alps is to a line of modest hills? Michelet's beginning of the *Histoire du XIXᵉ siècle* is little read. And yet what a revealing book the *Origines des Bonaparte* is! Above it is that *Origines du droit français* that is, so to speak, the Mont-Beuvray of the history of France. Certainly there exists a frenzied Michelet, the Michelet of the *Jésuites,* of *La Sorcière,* of *La Femme.* But the tetralogy of *La Mer, La Montagne, L'Oiseau,* and *L'Insecte* is rich in miraculous pages. What is important is that it was written by a historian, that the connection between natural history and the history of man was made and felt by such a poet. Like that of Hugo and Balzac, the work of Michelet is a climate,

an element, and an ailment, in which one does not so much journey as
seek to renew or to strengthen oneself, as in the mountains or at the sea.

Quinet

Born five years after Michelet, Quinet formed an alliance with him
beginning in 1840, and they became the two champions of the lay struggle against what was then called the Jesuits after having been called the
Congregation fifteen years before. In contrast to Michelet, Quinet never
found the form in which he could give durability to the generous, new,
creative ideas of which he was full. Although the prose dialogue epic of
Ahasvérus, a symbol of mankind on the march, was his best-known work,
he failed in this as much as in his verse epics. His great work on *Révolution*—philosophy as much as history—exerted a great influence on the
founders of the Third Republic. More than in Michelet's work, all the
elements of a republican philosophy can be found in him. His ideas became
facts: this is the most honorable of the reasons why his books are no
longer read.

1848

On the eve of the revolution of 1848, histories of the French Revolution were demanded and devoured by a great public. That was why
Michelet interrupted his history of France after Louis XI in order to start
publishing that of the Revolution, the first volume of which appeared in
1847. But in the same year, and all at once, the eight volumes of Lamartine's *Histoire des Girondins* appeared. No other historical work had so
immediate a success, like a thunderclap. There are two approaches to
judging the *Histoire des Girondins*. One is as a work of history, and then
its existence is absolutely zero. The other is as an intelligence and reality
of revolution that continues or is renewed, and then it is an important
book. Tocqueville was shocked in 1848 to see the people and the political
leaders act out the scenes of the Revolution as actors play a tragedy that
they have learned. The *Histoire des Girondins* is the script, what is called
in the theater the "sides," of that tragedy. From this point of view it was
"dynamic," like *Les Provinciales*. However few illusions we may have on
its historic value, it remains a fascinating book; it is part of that infinite
tide of eloquence that Lamartine loosed from the speaker's platform. In
this swarm of phrases, of images, of portraits, as often as in Michelet, one
comes upon sentences or pages that have been illuminated by the passage
of genius: "I do not think; my ideas think for me." At his own risk they

also wrote history for him, while waiting to do so with him, and even though neither of the two crafts was theirs.

In the same year, 1847, there began to appear the third of those histories that so imperiously called for a new revolution, that of Louis Blanc, already the author of that long pamphlet, *Histoire de dix ans*. The *Histoire des Girondins* was not Girondist, but Blanc's *Histoire de la Révolution* was absolutely from The Mountain of the Convention: it pushed ahead like a mountaineering expedition, with an ardent conviction, a grand style, but declamatory and out of date. From this history, and from a whole literature of the left and the extreme left, in which Pierre Lanfrey's anti-Bonapartist *Napoléon* must be mentioned, there arose, more or less in subterranean streams, perennial sources of republican idealism and *mystique* that would come to light again twenty years after 1848 and would provide the *mystique* for the radicalism of the Third Republic.

XVII

SAINTE-BEUVE

The Three Great Names of the Century

It is not an exaggeration to say that Sainte-Beuve has taken in criticism the rank held by Victor Hugo in poetry and by Balzac in the novel, that he occupies as eminent a place, that he gave his area of literature a revelation of the same kind. It will be observed that Hugo, Balzac, and Sainte-Beuve were the three shelves of the library of the nineteenth century that still hold together, form a solid entity in rows that time has but little affected. This is all the more surprising, as far as Sainte-Beuve is concerned, in that four-fifths of his work was journalistic copy—in other words, the most fleeting and fragile of forms; alone among all the journalists he has lasted.

The reason is that he was a journalist only as Molière was an actor, but a critic as Molière was an author. He filled half the field of criticism, as Molière filled half the field of the theater. For this half he had all the technique. He experienced it in its externals and in its problems, and, since the other areas of criticism, the criticism of life, the criticism of drama, did not have their Sainte-Beuve, he has remained the unchallenged prince of the form. Literary criticism became the garden of Sainte-Beuve as the Théâtre-Français is the house of Molière.

Romantic Formation

His alliance with time began early. He belonged to that potent generation in which precocity was the rule. He acquired an unusually solid background in French, Latin, and Greek under the best masters in Paris. At the age of twenty-three he published a book of criticism that was the work of a master, in which he established values that have not been shaken: the *Tableau de la poésie au XVIᵉ siècle*. Furthermore, when he died at the age of sixty-four he was still a student, he had just taken his last lesson and analyzed Homer with his professor of Greek, Pantassides, a native of Epirus. For each of his articles he took six full days of work in order to satisfy a more exigent master: himself. Clemenceau, at the beginning of his career as premier, was interrupted one day in the Chamber by an imbecile who told him: "We are no longer in school." The old man retorted: "I am always in school: I was there yesterday when I was listening to my opponent, M. [Jean] Jaurès." Sainte-Beuve was of the same race. And yet, like M. Jourdain at school, he regretted the fact that he had not yet been there enough. In the beautiful articles in which he bestowed his powers on the "young criticism"—by which he meant Taine —he envied its having been able to acquire a massive foundation of philosophic and scientific knowledge in a lay cloister at the age at which he, living in the world, was running about collecting copy.

What he gained in those years, however, was much more fertile, more living, better endowed with vitamins than the acquisitions of the great *normaliens*.* About 1830 he went to war in a youthful school, among the twenty-five-year-old generals of that army of the romantic revolution: war in poetry, war in the novel, war in love. His love affair with Adèle Hugo left a mark on him and a mark on literature almost as strong as that of the Venetian loves of Musset or that of Balzac's love for Mme. de Berny.

Furthermore, it left a mark on criticism, on the genius and the underbody of the critical spirit in France. As between Hugo and himself, Sainte-Beuve experienced what was meant by inequality between persons, what was the difference between the lion and the fox, what the *Know thyself* of the critical mind ordered him to abdicate, and what compensations, what clandestine joys, intelligence was reserving for him, as well as the eternal dualism of literary natures, the debate between Neptune and Minerva on the pediment of the eternal Parthenon.

The Barrès of *Un Homme libre* spoke with anger of those who wanted to sacrifice Sainte-Beuve's youth to the maturity of the *lundiste*.† Sainte-Beuve would have approved. He resigned himself with difficulty to the vocation and the solid glory into which he was thrown by a fate that had not consulted him. He suffered from being only the representative of the public among the masters, from feeling that he himself was not a master and a creator. He had very little inner awareness of the range and the strength of his creative criticism. Rather, he knew that critical faculty as a state of inhibition; inhibition of a poet, of a novelist, of a moralist.

---

* The Ecole Normale Supérieure and the Ecole Polytechnique have been the training ground of French intellect since their foundation.—Translator.

† Sainte-Beuve's most famous essays were known as *Causeries des lundis* ("Monday talks"): hence "the Mondayist."—Translator.

Three Inhibitions

Of a poet. He had heard and found as a poet one of the most original voices of the movement of 1830: intimate, popular poetry, the diary of the emotions of a delicate, sickly, humiliated plebeian, not so much a "Jacobin Werther on horseback with a carbine," as Guizot called him, as a cultivated Julien Sorel who would soon seek a Mme. de Rénal in Mme. Victor Hugo: an 1830 newspaper scandal! The *Poésies de Joseph Delorme*, to which he united prose reflections of a marvelous delicacy, deserve to retain the love of a certain group among the young and support Barrès. *Le Livre d'amour*, also a diary, the diary of his love for Adèle Hugo, goes even further than *Joseph Delorme*. But in the *Consolations* and the *Pensées d'août*, the style of his unharmoniously hammered verse, like chips of rock and wood, was decidedly repellent. Sainte-Beuve spoke the poetic language of his time badly—he had no ear; Lamartine, Hugo, Musset automatically doomed him to frustration.

Of a novelist. *Volupté* is the novel of a cultivated Parisian Obermann, and above all of a critic, an observer, a caresser, a voluptuary of the skin, forever prowling outside the houses, the loves, the forces, the action, and the lives into which he was not to enter. Its wealth of inner life would always, in every generation, earn this book a few dozen zealots (the Amiel side). Its style has a compounded and labored harmony, like that of Sainte-Beuve's verse, but in prose he found the road clear and new. It does not surprise us that Amaury became a priest in 1830, as he would have entered Port-Royal in 1650. Sainte-Beuve would be the most "clerical" of the great writers of the nineteenth century if Renan had not existed. He gets inside authors as he was able to penetrate women's hearts, through his genius as a confessor.

More than poetry and the novel, his vocation, to which criticism brought him back over an indirect road, was that of a moralist. He knew himself to be of the substance of which the great French moralists were made from Montaigne to Chamfort. The greatness of his criticism is due not so much to the poet who died young as to this tradition of the moralist who has traveled a long road and will travel another. This is the ancient, indigenous salt that made his weekly criticism incorruptible and that is to be found in its original form in the bodies of so many of his "thoughts," from those of Joseph Delorme to those of the *Cahiers*. As much as and more than a view of literature, a study of authors, Sainte-Beuve's criticism should be taken as an investigation into mankind and women, into himself and others, into the natures of minds and the mind of human nature. The whole human content of French literature culminated in this humanism, as the world of sounds, words, and rhythms culminated in Victor Hugo. The moralist in Sainte-Beuve is superior even to the critic: the critic was often wrong, the moralist never.

Criticism of Contemporaries

Even better than authors he knew men; even better than men, man. But himself? Undoubtedly, and particularly in his fiction, but, in sum, hardly more than average human nature allows, setting us up as the lawyers but rarely as the judges of ourselves. He had judges, in his lifetime, and harsh ones. Posterity has often been still more harsh. Beneath his mask he made judgments and felt hatreds. That he was spiteful, envious, hypocritical is certain. And yet, if in his secret literature he sometimes wrote of his contemporaries, and especially his colleagues in the Académie, the opposite of what he wrote in his public literature, let us first ask ourselves whether we should like that secret literature suppressed, and then let us pose to ourselves the delicate problem of criticism of contemporaries, which was no more resolved in Sainte-Beuve's time than it is today.

The criticism of the living, he himself said when he was young, is the most difficult and the noblest side of the craft. And a side also in the sense of a side in a game. How did he handle this side?

Let us leave aside dramatic literature, with which he did not concern himself except to study as a moralist the classics of the seventeenth century. In his world of acting he sensed a different world from the world of writing, one that depended on another perspective; he rejected the servitudes without greatness of the craft as Jules Janin practiced it. And, besides, the theater as theater did not interest him, although he attended once every week. In the seventeenth century he would have stood with Nicole against Racine, with Bossuet against Molière.

But criticism of poets? He himself was an original poet, his *Tableau de la poésie au XVIe siècle* represents an important sum of poetic discoveries and intuitions. But in 1842, in his considered article on *Mademoiselle Bertin*, he made an effort to classify the poets of his time. He distinguished (1) the group of the first-rate; (2) the group of those "who have not fulfilled their promise and whom, therefore, public acclaim has not consecrated"; (3) the vulgar. Now in the first class there were only three: Lamartine, Hugo, and Béranger. Musset belonged only to the second, and Vigny was not mentioned, nor, more properly, was Gautier. One day Gautier admitted: "To think that I believed in Pétrus!" It was fine to have believed for a few years in Pétrus Borel; it was extremely serious to have believed all one's life in Béranger. In none of his work did Sainte-Beuve ever mention the name of Gérard de Nerval except once, using the verb, "to Ronsardize," and adding, "as the good Gérard de

Nerval used to say." He hailed the early work of Banville, but he refused to write an article on Baudelaire. He did justice to Marceline Desbordes-Valmore, the elegiac poet, but primarily among the likes of Amable Tastu and Blanchecotte.

It is still more serious that he passed over the novel and looked far down on Balzac and Stendhal as manufacturers who were not of his literary world. He spoke better of Flaubert and Eugène Fromentin. But, in a word, it never happened that he went first, that he summoned opinion from afar. Le us add that he entered the Académie in 1844, five years before the *Causeries des lundis*. Now, the Académie is a deplorable place for criticism of one's contemporaries. The house rules oblige one to speak of one's colleagues only with a solemn face: he praised the poetry of Pierre Lebrun, who had his article in the *Lundis;* he went down as far as Jean-Guillaume Viennet. And read in the *Lundis* the sorrowing, or, rather, the sorry, article on *Poésie et les poètes en 1852.* . . .

But the importance of these errors, limitations, or pettinesses must not be exaggerated. Even when he was unjust to men or erred on merits, Sainte-Beuve was still a great critic, less of ideas than of thoughts: "Where is one to classify," he wrote, "a writer in whom one can be sure of never encountering *elevated* thought, nor *delicate* thought, nor *judicious* thought?" He was the critic of those authors who are because they think. To speak ill of them in the country of Descartes would be unlucky. He did not often act in bad faith, and, while he made mistakes, he did not seek to deceive. Nonetheless it helps in knowing more about Hugo, Lamartine, Balzac, to know how and why a part of their genius made them antipathetic to great literary minds. Even when it is neither just nor judicious, Sainte-Beuve's criticism of his contemporaries rarely lacks a certain power of enlightenment. Besides, what criticism, however narrow, however unrighteous, does not shift the needle of truth in one direction or another when it is honed by ill will? Nor let us forget how much he had suffered from having practiced in his youth the opposite criticism, that "criticism of beauties" that had become an advertisement around Hugo. Heine's page on the Sultan of Darfur and his crier had cruelly wounded him. Like Vautrin, he had that mark to efface, even with vitriol.

The limits of Sainte-Beuve's judgment were natural limits, and like the boundaries of France they circumscribed a harmonious country. The case of Baudelaire, who should have been his poet and to whom the successful man refused a hearing, remains an exception. The tragedy for Sainte-Beuve, for this moralist, this analyst, this great classic, was to live among writers whose natures personified his incapacities, especially those whom he called the strong men of the marketplace—Hugo, Balzac, Dumas. "I too very willingly admire power, but for that I must know that I am dealing with real power of mind, and not just any strength of no more than a robust health and a robust character. Which is worth more, Gen-

ghis Khan trailing behind him all the hordes of Asia or M. de Turenne *
at the head of thirty thousand men?" Then it was the turn of the authors
with infinitely open hearts, the men of sentiment, illusion, and charlat-
anry, sons and daughters of women—the impossibilities of the intellectual,
Lamartine, "the most sublime and the most charming among the idiots";
George Sand, "an echo that understudies for a voice"; Michelet, "a lout
playing the dandy." Next came the decorators and the orators, the social
surface, the literary crust, official authority, the "form-masters" of 1830—
Villemain, Guizot, Cousin. Two kinds of minds were of his family—the
moralists and the eighteenth century: Stendhal primarily. But Sainte-
Beuve was completely devoid of the feeling for the province or for the
cosmopolis, and this academician was selective in his associates. Stendhal
irritated him by his insolent tone as much as Gautier irritated him by his
reminder of the red shirt. Later it was Mérimée, but with him Sainte-
Beuve would have given better than he would have got: "Mérimée holds
himself in too much: he is too aloof out of principle and finally he has
become that way by nature." In the world of minds Sainte-Beuve remained a suspicious bachelor.

It can be argued that, with the exception of certain deliberate and
forced tipping of the scales which can be found even in the *Lundis* (for
instance, in the article on *Fanny*), Sainte-Beuve expresses with exactitude
and skill his own taste and the average taste of decent people, and theirs
alone, during the one or even two generations of which he was not very
perceptibly either in the van or to the rear. In good time he took into
consideration the fact that the tropical temperature of romanticism would
not allow him to play the part of a Boileau with the leading figures. But
from the very beginning he had held himself absolutely aloof from the
romantic manifestations that were at once the most explosive and the
most challengeable: those of the theater. For him the theater of Hugo
and Dumas was as if it had never existed, and the battle of *Hernani* was
fought beyond his horizon. In romantic poetry he was not a prophetic
but an enlightened critic. He contributed to giving Marceline Desbordes-
Valmore the rank that she was to hold. He fired the morning gun of romanticism with *Le XVIe siècle*. He sounded its retreat in 1843 with
La Fontaine de Boileau. To the extent to which romanticism can be compared with the political revolution of 1830, he was its Guizot.

That generation was the last that, in spite of momentary tumults like
those of the studios and the Young French, allowed regular and solid systems, in which the tone continued to be set by the average mass of respectable people, those respectable people with whom the romantics integrated themselves when their entrance into the Académie indicated that

---

* Henri de la Tour d'Auvergne, Vicomte de Turenne, a great military leader of
the seventeenth century, Marshal of France, conqueror of Alsace.—Translator.

the school had been assimilated. Sainte-Beuve remained stubbornly in accepted literature, in the neighborhood of those nice people on whom he left, like a house guest's visiting card, that *Fontaine de Boileau*. For him Mme. Récamier's *salon* was more important than the *cénacles*, and it was to carry him to the Académie at the age of forty. From then on there was a pronounced distortion in his criticism. Not only was the theater excluded from it, for the theater required a special application, in which it was necessary to take everything as it came and to speak about everyone, in which one could select neither the authors, who were imposed on one, nor the hall, whose perspective had to be understood. But again a major question arose after 1830, a sphinx before which Sainte-Beuve found in himself nothing of the spirit, the powers, and the boldness of an Oedipus: the novel, which overthrew the consecrated hierarchies, shoved itself into the foreground, interrogated, and disturbed all the respectable people as well as the respectable women. In dealing with the novel, that universal suffrage of literature, Sainte-Beuve found his limitations as Guizot had found his with respect to the people. He did not understand the revolution. He had not followed. He said of this third estate, with mistrust: "What is it?" In Sainte-Beuve criticism of his contemporaries was always criticism without Balzac and after 1837 without Victor Hugo: a horrid great wound made in the poor hedge. But what does it matter that it was without Balzac when it was done by another Balzac, when it was a "Comédie Littéraire" of France?

A *"Comédie Littéraire"*

Sainte-Beuve was the only critic who had a profound and intricate feeling for what in other days was called morals, the literary *ethos*. He knew what a successful man of letters was, what a spoiled man of letters was, the glories and the miseries of literature, the general society of letters and its private societies. He was the Montesquieu of its republic, and from this "literary comedy" that is the *Lundis* one can derive an "Esprit des Lettres" more supple and no less rich than Montesquieu's *L'Esprit des lois*. Certainly he advanced the art of literary portraiture further than anyone else. But above this art of portraiture there was the art of the movement among the portraits and there was the shared, opulent, and crowded nature that constantly produced their models. More than minds he cared about families of minds, and more than families of minds the mind of the great literary family. A Sainte-Beuve can be born only in a country of social literature, where literature not only is the expression of the society but shapes an autonomous spiritual society that has its own perpetuity and its own laws.

This perpetuity and these laws were felt by a Nisard, a Taine, a Brunetière, as well as by Sainte-Beuve. But Nisard saw them in the guise of canons, Taine in that of physiology, Brunetière in that of architecture, Sainte-Beuve in that of geography.

A geography—that is to say a *datum* in which, certainly, reason operates but where experience and discovery have their share, where nothing is foreseeable, where nature has never acted logically, where it offers its hazards to man, who adds to them, who determines them, or who settles into them. Criticism consists in espousing this geography, following it, reflecting it by collaborating in it. At the age of twenty-five the Sainte-Beuve of the *Pensées de Joseph Delorme* foresaw and sketched, in a page in which the course of criticism is compared with the course of the river, the Sainte-Beuve of the *Lundis*.

A geographer and an intelligent observer. In 1830 a professorial criticism was dominant. This young citizen of Paris, this Latin Quarter bachelor, replaced it little by little with a *critica pedestris*, which circulated through French literature like the citizen through his city, like the poet, Delorme, in that suburb that he discovered and painted with little strokes. He might have his prejudices, his manias, his envies, his prudent hatreds (those of someone who does his fighting under an umbrella, which he, like Louis-Philippe, never forgot), but he knew all the houses, all the people, all the families—a living chronicle of the ageless city.

Such was already the character of his first work, that of his twenty-fourth year, the *Tableau historique et critique de la poésie française au XVIe siècle:* a book as important in its own kind as the *Défense et illustration de la langue française* that Joachim Du Bellay published at the same age. For in it Sainte-Beuve discovered Du Bellay and Ronsard ignored or misunderstood, as Du Bellay and Ronsard had discovered Pindar, and he made this discovery a point of perspective on all literature, since, according to him, romanticism took up their tradition again. The young critic enlarged the dimensions of great poetry in time, backward to Ronsard, forward to Hugo.

Ten years of contemporary criticism followed. This was no longer a matter of geography, of a stroller among the houses. It was necessary to plunge in again, to take part. Not only to enter the houses but, as the Sainte-Beuve of *Volupté* said, to enter the women's apartments. A time of *portraits* . . . Henri Harpignies, the painter, said that painting landscapes was more enjoyable than painting portraits because "landscape does not keep raising objections." In any event, the landscape is the concern of the geographer or geophile painter, the stroller. It was in Lausanne that Sainte-Beuve was to become definitely the great literary landscape artist. His hegira to Lake Geneva in 1837 marked the great turning point.

Sainte-Beuve saw the geography of French literature as Michelet in his *Tableau* saw France from the height of the Dôle; he recognized in it, like

Jean-Baptiste-Armand-Louis-Elonce Elie de Beaumont and O.-P.-A.-P. Dufrénoy in their *Explication de la carte géologique,* a pole of divergence and a pole of convergence.

Port-Royal

He searched out and built a Massif Central for it, *Port-Royal. Port-Royal* is the greatest book in literary history and criticism. Certainly it is not lacking in artifice. It goes without saying that the author does a great deal of forcing in order to center the whole seventeenth century on the illustrious abbey, and, if its portraits are the great charm of *Port-Royal,* they can be redone in a very different sense, as Abbé Henri Bremond did not overlook. But, since the seventeenth century is the capital century, try to find another literary capital for it than Port-Royal and you will fail. And, once selected, a capital influences by its attraction and its facilities. It becomes populated. Sainte-Beuve populated it; Montaigne, Balzac, Descartes, Corneille, Racine, Boileau, Molière, Nicolas de Malebranche, Bossuet, through the bonding agency of Sainte-Beuve's genius, allied to the genius of the place, naturally become in it the *Conscripti* of the two great families of autochthonous *Patres,* the Arnaulds and the Pascals. In Port-Royal French literature acquired its *corpus* of importance, it dealt with the fundamental and dramatic problems of human nature, it placed on the balances of its scales the great moral and religious issues. Conversely, religion began a connection with the interests of the language and of literature. From Port-Royal, French literature seems like a battlefield of ideas on human nature, which it remained until the eighteenth century, which was still to be seen in romanticism, the very thing that Sainte-Beuve's moralist character constantly sought in it, constantly extracted from it. It is enough, furthermore, to follow his inner history from 1830 to 1840 to feel him carried toward Port-Royal and to know that the author of *Volupté* had his own problem of Port-Royal within himself.

On his return from Lausanne he established himself in the world round him. The Mazarin Library, of which he was appointed curator, provided him with a sinecure among books. The first two volumes of *Port-Royal* and the friendship of Mme. Récamier won him entrance into the Académie. By finishing *Port-Royal* and by writing a second *Port-Royal* on another literary period, if one existed that was worthy of being set off against the first, would not Sainte-Beuve, with wisdom and maturity, achieve the double monument of French literary history, its Massif Central and its Parisian basin?

The Lundis

We should hardly dare to say that revolutions made other dispositions. They simply constrained him to go the long way round.

Eleven years after his hegira to Lausanne, the Revolution of 1848 caused, or Sainte-Beuve believed that it should cause, his hegira to Liège. His course of 1848–1849 in Liège very nearly gave him, like that of 1837, the occasion for a great panorama of literary life in France, this time in the period of Chateaubriand, from 1800 to 1848—in other words, the history of the preromantic and romantic generations, reviewed, relived, explained from the *templa serena* of a foreign land by a man who had known very well the actors and the works, a *Port-Royal* of the nineteenth century and of romanticism. Apparently all that came of it was the unfinished attempt of *Chateaubriand et son groupe littéraire*. But the fragments of the whole range of the work were to be found more or less, as Sainte-Beuve himself said, in the *Lundis*.

The Revolution and the Second Empire confirmed his plan, his program. They made 1850 the median break in the century, in literary life, and in the whole of French life; 1800–1850, the interval between the two *coups d'état*, from the return of Chateaubriand to the departure of Victor Hugo, was the image of circumscribed, finite French continuity, and, for Sainte-Beuve, a kind of mature literature, like that of the seventeenth century, a mature literature that Sainte-Beuve associated with all the other mature literature since Malherbe.

Thus, on a suggestion from Véron, the editor of *Le Constitutionnel*, in 1849, the *Lundis* were born and there began and continued for nineteen years (except for an interruption when Sainte-Beuve was teaching in the Ecole Normale) that rigid discipline, deliberate and unremitting, of the long weekly article, the unique concern of the whole week, composed in six days of assiduous exploration of an author.

The method and the presentation of the *Lundis*, however, did not break with those of the *Portraits* or even with those of *Port-Royal* and *Chateaubriand*. *Port-Royal*, especially in those parts of it that are best known, is made up of fragments, of vistas on the seventeenth century, of portraits of writers of the first or second rank—the whole free, discontinuous, in a manner that was already very *lundiste;* and from edition to edition, expanding with notes, reflections, digressions, Sainte-Beuve was to "Mondayize" more and more. Similarly, *Chateaubriand et son groupe littéraire*, another picture of an absolute, supple group into which not only the friends but the contemporaries of Chateaubriand could enter, offers us the great landscape of the sources where the *Lundis* took shape and from which their course runs. If Sainte-Beuve left it unfinished, he said, it was because its continuation is in the *Lundis*, with other watercourses, and be-

cause the single stream was succeeded by the reservoir. Observe that continuation beginning 18 March 1850, with the article on the *Mémoires
d'outre-tombe*, and even earlier, in the second *Lundi*, that of 8 October
1849, with the article on Lamartine's *Confidences*. In the preface that he
was writing for *Chateaubriand* in September 1849, when he had already
contracted with Véron for the publication of the *Lundis* at the beginning of
October, Sainte-Beuve said: "Detached from every active part and almost
from every tie, observing literary matters and men closely for almost
twenty-five years, having no reason not to see them just as they are, I can
say that I am running over with truths." It was these "truths" on the generation of 1820 that he was to serve up after 1849 to the readers of *Le Constitutionnel*.

Let us leave aside the question of envy, the capital sin of which Sainte-
Beuve is generally accused. But in 1849 the great romantic poets, almost
all of whom had virtually stopped producing, could have seemed like a
group in the process of liquidation. It was even good that this was so,
since it could only encourage the generation that was twenty years old
in 1848 and enable it to make a fresh start and do new things. And, since
the romantic poets, like their sire, Chateaubriand, had professed to be
political guides, it appeared most plainly in 1849 that this ambition had
miscarried, had been one of the causes of the revolution of 1848. This
revolution—"a vast catastrophe of which we are all part and all victims,"
Sainte-Beuve wrote in 1850—was now considered by all fair minds as a
misfortune, and the infantry, the citizen national guard, of these fair
minds was composed precisely of the readers of *Le Constitutionnel*. Lamartine's unpopularity had begun. There was a world, a public, for which
the word poet had become a mockery. Sainte-Beuve could not fall so low
as that, but the investiture by Véron, the twenty-five years that made
him run over not only with truths but with rancors, the public movement
that bore him up, even what was expected of him, were all to make the
Sainte-Beuve of the *Lundis* more or less a leader of the anti-romantic reaction.

And, what is more serious, of anti-poetic reaction. Obviously, throughout the course of the *Lundis*, Sainte-Beuve would acquit himself as he
must toward poets and present them kindly, especially if they were second-rate and could be used against someone. He would even discover
Théophile Gautier when it was a matter of backing the academic candidacy of a romantic who had joined the Empire . . . But his ill will toward
Lamartine and Vigny was not to abate. His unease and his reserve with
regard to Baudelaire are known. And we will sum up everything in the
irreparability of these two things: first, the absence of Victor Hugo,
exiled, for reasons that we know, from the *Lundis;* and, second, in the
article of 28 January 1850 on Alfred de Musset, this prediction: "What
will remain of the poets of these times? . . . One of the poets of whom

most will remain: Béranger. . . ." Two months later, the *Mémoires d'outre-tombe* were completely sacrificed to *René*. In Sainte-Beuve there was a bourgeois who was to feel at home in *Le Constitutionnel*. And the author of *Port-Royal* ended up to a certain extent in Béranger's boots, a fact with which we shall not too much reproach him, since it was almost the case with Renan himself.

Aside from these and other reservations (and nothing that has to do with Sainte-Beuve is without reservations), the *Lundis* are the work of the surest reader who ever lived. In the authors of three centuries, from Rabelais to Lamartine, one can always be sure that the quotation that he chooses is the best, the characteristic that he stresses is the most typical, and one must attempt a subject after him in order to see that, in the manner of the ancients, he rose the earliest and plucked the finest fruits. Then too the word *Lundis* must not be allowed to make us forget the word *Causeries*.

When he has pen in hand Sainte-Beuve is indeed the best talker of French literature, as pleasant as Voltaire, as powerful as Diderot. He knew this very well when, like an old serpent shedding his successive skins of romanticism, Catholicism, sentimentalism, mysticism, he discovered for his final and truest form the analytic spirit and the sensibility of the eighteenth century.

What then does it matter what "theories" have been ascribed to him or by what theories he characterized a moment or a phase of his eternal mobility? Physiology, natural history of minds: let us not leave these labels stuck on him; magician and not theoretician; reflecting and not thinking; observer and not professor; doubter and not doctor; son of Montaigne, the most authentic in the nineteenth century. But, beneath all the talk and the mind, always the serious and the substantial: never, as in Montaigne or Diderot, thought for the sake of amusement, or gratuitous games.

His mistakes, like theirs, teach us. His gaps do not embarrass us, since they were filled by his successors. Through him and through him alone criticism became the tenth Muse; moreover for this a poet was needed, the touch of a poet.

Montaigne's most authentic descendant, Sainte-Beuve is like him a dialogue in a man. Dialogue of Montaigne and Port-Royal, dialogue of the eighteenth and the nineteenth centuries, of classic reason and romantic ties. A dialogue with prejudices and affirmations, loves and hates, but always carried on on the level of "conversation" not only with the reader but with himself, of questioning in the face of problems incessantly renewed. From this point of view, the *Nouveaux Lundis* do not seem so inferior to the first. Perhaps Sainte-Beuve was not altogether the senator of the *Lundis*, but in a word the *Nouveaux Lundis* are indeed the *Lundis* of a senator. History, politics draw new illuminations from them; the

thinking of the literary critic ripened into the thinking of a social critic.
It is a fine thing that he concluded his life as a writer, more or less, with
a book on Proudhon, on a last dialogue, of remarkable loftiness, between
the cultivated bourgeois, the heir of letters, and the plebeian writer.

A Summum of Wise Letters

All things carefully considered, just as the *Essais* form a sum, a compendium, of literate wisdom, the *Lundis*, or, rather, that bookshelf of
which the *Lundis* is the center, has given us a *summum* of wise letters.
Two sums that carry on good literature ancient and modern, blending
the Socratic sense of doubt, the humanist sense of liberal reason, the constructive sense of acquired civilization. Anatole France is praised for having called Sainte-Beuve the Thomas Aquinas of France. The phrase was
that of the Comte d'Haussonville in his book on Sainte-Beuve in 1873,
from which the author of *La Vie littéraire* borrowed it without ac-
knowledgment, and he is nothing the loser for that. But rather we will
put the fifty volumes of that *summum* under the sign of the two Saint
Thomases—Thomas the Apostle who had the capacity to doubt and
Thomas the doctor who knew how to build and who, simply, knew.
These are the two "roads that march" of criticism, of that criticism whose
capital Sainte-Beuve erected at their junction.

PART THREE

The Generation
of 1850

I

THE GENERATION OF 1850

Morrows of Empire

No literary generation would have less reason to be called a generation without masters than the generation that was twenty years old at the middle of the nineteenth century. The men of fifty could supply them in abundance. Poetry, the novel, the theater, philosophy, history had been furrowed and turned over by giant plows; the young men were children in the days when the arms of the sowers cast seed as far as the stars. They had grown up under the eyes of an assembly of masters, in the Homeric sense of the assembly of the gods, in the epoch of the Napoleons of literature, as those literary Napoleons themselves had come to maturity from 1800 to 1815 under the Consul or the Emperor.

But the analogy does not end there. The great empire of romanticism too had known the destiny of the empire of one hundred and thirty departments. If *Ruy Blas* was the Ligny of the theater, it had been followed by the Waterloo of *Les Burgraves*. Political romanticism foundered with Lamartine's Republic. The Collège de France of Michelet, Quinet, and Mickiewicz can be compared with the cemetery of Saint-Médard; and it was inevitable that the convulsive Jansenists should have Voltaire's fate. The lyrical silence of Lamartine, of Hugo, of Vigny, of Gautier, even of Musset, after 1840, had already hollowed out a void. Debility seemed to have reduced romanticism to the defensive along a major front: one is reminded of those difficult years, of that plateau that began for Napoleon at Essling and Wagram. Talleyrand and Fouché—that is, Sainte-Beuve and Mérimée—sensed the coming of the end, the hour about to strike for them. In literature 1850 was another 1815: Balzac died, Lamartine was removed, and nature had prepared a comfortable Saint Helena for Victor Hugo within sight of the shores of France. For twenty years Hugo would fulfill the function of decorative exile and witness that had been Chateaubriand's under the July monarchy.

Like Napoleon, that generaiton had fallen because of obvious and glaring defects, defects of genius and superhuman ambitions. With Balzac himself it had enthusiastically exhausted the book binderies. It was natural that it should be the object of a judgment by its successors. Perhaps never since 1815 has a literary generation been observed in such clear and conscious reaction to its predecessor generation.

A reaction of intelligence against genius—in other words, what the Talleyrand–Napoleon and Sainte-Beuve–Hugo dialogues had been. Hence a critical reaction. Constrained to a general critical effort against its predecessors, this generation seems to have brought all the currents of literary production under the aegis of criticism.

A Generation of Criticism

It was in this manner that its two great poets, Leconte de Lisle and Baudelaire, were differentiated from romanticism and from such disciples of romanticism as their predecessor, Banville. In contrast to the poetry of *La Légende des siècles*, the evocative, antique, and "barbarous" poetry of Leconte de Lisle took a critical view (relatively critical, of course, but is there any other?) of history. And Baudelaire's poetry was distinguished from romantic poetry in that it was not an effusion but a criticism of the human heart. If it acknowledged any ancestors in the preceding generation, they were Joseph Delorme (therefore Sainte-Beuve) and criticism. Even today, particularly today, we contrast Hugo and Baudelaire as two *essences* of poetry, and there are admirers of Baudelaire who deserve the suffix of "Hugolators." It is genius and intelligence, effusion and criticism, that confront each other.

With the birth of the problem play in the theater, the criticism of life replaced the portrayal of life and its utilization on the stage. The most typical case is perhaps that of the novel. The realistic novelist devotes himself to critical observation, while in Balzac or George Sand the observer is absorbed, drowned in a creative tide. When Flaubert succeeded Balzac, it was the succession of a critic to a poet. "I am increasingly interested in criticism," Flaubert said in a letter of 1854. "The novel that I am writing (*Madame Bovary*) sharpens this faculty in me."

But above all the spirit of criticism concerned criticism properly so designated, gave it a worth, a range, and a fertility without equal. It is striking and instructive to contrast, under the Second Empire, the absence of Victor Hugo on what he called his rock, in the manner of Chateaubriand, and the presence of his contemporary, Sainte-Beuve, of the garden of Sainte-Beuve, who after 1850 became the Sainte-Beuve of the *Lundis*. He acquired that endowment, that uncontested sovereignty of a form that is so rare in literary history. And his successors grew up under his eyes: they were Renan and Taine.

A Generation of Technique

The great men born at the beginning of the century had surged up in a remarkable explosion of genius. It cannot be said that genius was lacking in the generation of the twenty-year-olds of 1850, but it bore or sought its genius with discretion, and what it valued most highly was talents, technique: poetic techniques in the masters and the emulators of Parnassus; subtle techniques of the novel and the "throes" of style in Flaubert and the Goncourts; technical revolutions in the theater in Dumas, Eugène Labiche, Benjamin Crémieux, Jacques Offenbach; technical subtleties, born of the necessity to deceive the censor, in newspaper articles. It was the same with the art of this epoch as with its furniture: because of the attention devoted to technique rather than character, it lost its warmth and became obsolete much more quickly than romantic art.

The Great Schoolmen

The great rhetoric of romanticism, of the philosophical or historical movements connected with romanticism, was rejected. As early as January 1848, six months before the revolution, Sainte-Beuve had labeled Cousin a "sublime fraud" in his notes and had written (for himself, of course): "Men like Cousin, the doctrinarians and their disciples and in general all the platform phrasemakers and philosophers, are destroying France." Sainte-Beuve, whom they had relegated to the background, under the Second Empire took the revenge of a critical observer and a naturalist of the mind against these platform phrasemakers and philosophers. Above all he ranked as a school among the young who were reacting against phrases and platforms, the Taines and the Renans.

But this reaction against the professorial crew was the work of new schoolmen and in no way that of anti-schoolmen. The generation that was twenty years old in 1850 had come from the hands of those professors. It produced much better studies than those of the romantic generation, which had been given, under the Consulate and the Empire, an education of bits and pieces: "a confused hodgepodge," Sainte-Beuve wrote, "in which the remains of the old disciplines were merged with fragments of precepts, incoherent flotsam of every shipwreck; connections were made at random, by means of a seam of philosophical and philanthropical phraseology in accord with the thinking of the moment." Before students could be taught, the university of Fontanes had to fashion masters. It was only beginning in 1825 that the colleges and also the seminaries (reorganized by the Church at the same time that the state was reorganizing the university) offered the whole of youth a solid humanistic training, even better than that provided before the Revolution and destined to last throughout the nineteenth century.

Hence the generation that really profited by this training was that born around 1830 and aged twenty in 1850. It had no resemblance to the generation of the great self-educated romantics. It had not random masters but teams of masters. The monarchy of the professors, the regiment of Cousin, had created successors and opponents. When the natural revolution of ages and the political revolution coincided, toward 1850, to bring to light the active new generation, it was natural that there should be strong and active elements of that generation in the ranks of the students of the Ecole Normale. Was not the Ecole Normale the eldest daughter of the lay church of the form-masters, the seminary of the clergy of Cousin? This was the source of the importance of the great, the unique *normalienne* generation of 1848–1850. It was the great generation of students who made their way, as over a bridge, across the generation of the great professors.

These students were young men who knew much, and the greatest of them, Taine, was supposed to know everything. They were ambitious; they wanted life and they would know it. It was not fortuitous that one of them, Marcelin Planat, founded *La Vie parisienne*. Dropping the oratory and the transcendentalism of romanticism, they were, furthermore, the first intellectual generation to discover Stendhal and Balzac, to digest them as a way of life and human experience. The morning gong of the rue d'Ulm told these middle-class young men what Comte de Saint-Simon's servant was instructed to say to his master every morning: "Get up, Monsieur le Comte, you have great things to accomplish." Those who lost their free Thursdays and Sundays were entitled to a book by Balzac, which was provided for them by their unpenalized colleagues. Their Julien Sorel was Lucien-Anatole Prevost-Paradol, who, under the pseudonym of Lucien Sorel, published his first book in 1851: *Conseils à un jeune homme, du choix d'un parti*. He wrote: "No fear can make me draw back from emerging from my mediocrity and entering the world, which must be taken by storm." Taine was to write on Balzac and Stendhal the two articles that showed that they had rounded the cape and found their public. Sainte-Beuve's dismay at these articles was enough to show that he belonged to the earlier age.

The Rupture of 1871

It will be observed that in the generation of 1789, as in the generation of 1820, there was an intermediate point, in effect a pass that it crossed and that led it to a new level. Or, to alter the figure, a springboard on which it balanced. From this point of view each of these generations could be divided into two half-generations. For the first it was the emigrants' return in 1802 and for the second it was the mass invasion of places of prominence by the poets, the professors, the journalists, at about 1832—what Sainte-Beuve called the breach in the center. The generation of 1850, which normally ended between 1880 and 1890, had an analogous median point, but it was not a pass or a springboard or a breach; on the contrary, it was a drainage ditch, a hole, a high-banked lane of Ohain, from which the generation emerged, if not broken, at least bent—this was 1871.

In 1871 the Renans, the Taines, the Flauberts, the Goncourts, the Dumases—all those whose youth had begun with Louis-Philippe's retreat—were about forty years old; the ordeal that the war and the Commune inflicted on that still young generation was probably the most terrible that any literary group as a whole had endured since the sixteenth century. In contrast to the romantics, it had been led, except among the professional entertainers of the theater, to pessimistic conceptions of the world. Philosophy, the novel, poetry, in their presentation of life seemed to follow the descent of a reality that was disintegrating. It was with a strong tendency to answer affirmatively that it asked itself Renan's question: "Who knows whether truth is not sad?" The affirmative answer was corroborated by 1870 and 1871, which multiplied its burden of gravity, of anguishes, of responsibilities.

Of gravity. It was the only generation that had as its leaders not heroes of imagination but men of philosophy and science, Renan, Taine, Marcelin Berthelot, the chemist and politician. The insolvency of the temporal and religious powers after 1870 invested them under the Republic with a spiritual power that had nothing in common with what it had represented under the Empire or with the conformist, tendentious, semi-official professors of the July monarchy.

Of anguishes. Taine lived in anguish, even if Renan protected himself against it with a canon's wisdom. Arthur Schopenhauer's pessimism found the ground ready for it. The spokesmen of that generation, Parnassian poets and realistic novelists, were unanimously and profoundly pessimists. It was with a "pessimistic epic of human nature" that Emile Zola strove to succeed Balzac.

Of responsibilities. Here again the contrast to the preceding generation is clear. In 1852, in his famous article on *Regrets*, Sainte-Beuve observed that the leaders of the generation that had compromised and lost the cause of political freedom in 1848 considered themselves simply victims of evil and evildoers. Criticizing what was being done then in teaching and responding to various remarks, Cousin grew angry: "I believe in absolute truth," he cried, ending the conversation; "I believe in the good." And Sainte-Beuve adds: "Apparently he called good what he had done and evil what others did." The generation tested by 1871 believed in its responsibilities. It abounded with examinations of conscience written in verse and in prose. This was itself, this was that answerable generation of the *Essais de psychologie contemporaine* that first asked itself and then caused its heirs to ask it the question posed by Paul Bourget in *Le Disciple.*

This is the bilateralism of the Revolution—in the total meaning that the word would assume in 1830—and of the spirit of the eighteenth century. On one side enthusiasm, poetry, the creative tide of worlds. On the other side analysis, clear insight, the study of what the classics called the human heart. It would be inadequate to say that the generation of the children of their century comprised two families of minds. One must speak of two nations of minds. In the one, the children of genius, the Lamartines, the Balzacs, the Hugos, the Dumases, the Sands. In the other, the children of thought, the Sainte-Beuves, the Mérimées, the Tocquevilles. Between them, the hybrids, the Gautiers, the Nervals, the Mussets. Between the two, above all, those normal relations between nations that are dialogues, wars, marriages, travels, and an ideal Coppet, a place for meetings and confrontations; and 1850 representing the defeat of the nation of genius and the victory of the nation of intelligence. But the problem remained unresolved, the bilateralism continued, and it was not long before the two parties had new names.

The Appeal to the Scholars

In this fashion, for a time, the events of 1870 exceptionally enhanced the authority of letters, the standing of the great writers. It was generally admitted that the cause of that catastrophe was a moral cause, that France was ill, and that her illness required physicians. There was no lack of those! It might almost be said that a good part of the post-war literature was a literature of consultations. Flaubert himself, the son of a physician, said when he saw the ruins of the Tuileries: "To think that this would not have happened if people had understood *L'Education sentimentale!*"

Renan and Taine left their scientific workshops in order to become the physicians of France, Taine definitively so with his *Origines de la France contemporaine.* Dumas the younger, who was already a director of feminine consciences, brought problems into comedy and the platform into the theater. Even more the philosophers, who could more reasonably see their proper field here: Renouvier's republican plan was directly opposed to Taine's conservative plan. These consultations increased and clashed all the more as France was not yet settled in her political system or, with more reason, in her religious aspect, as politicians and scholars called upon her to choose their sides under penalty of eternal disgrace.

In this republican period of the generation of 1850, a place and a function without equal were accorded to Renan and Taine as heirs of Sainte-Beuve, delegates of the critical spirit and intelligence to the world of letters. On this score too this generation, which departed this life at the end of the nineteenth century, could be called the type of the generation of masters. It provided them as it had acquired them. Renan's death in 1893 was immediately followed by a reaction against him; the reaction against Taine was postponed a little longer. But there was no influence of this kind against which sooner or later there was not a reaction, a contradiction, an attempt at replacement. This is the necessary and normal play of generations. A master is as much an influence against which one shapes oneself as he is an action by which one is shaped. It is up to the grandsons, then, to observe and to judge whether the sons profitably replace the fathers and to cast their votes as between the two preceding generations. It seems that the grandsons' judgment after 1914 was favorable to the generation of Taine and Renan and that they envied their grandfathers masters of such scope.

The Juniors

It will be noted that, more than either of the two preceding generations, this generation included a considerable group of juniors, who were twenty years old between 1860 and 1870 and who were to constitute the appropriate crew of the Third Republic in its first thirty years. These were the Parnassian poets, Coppée and Sully-Prudhomme, and also Verlaine and Mallarmé, These were also the novelists of the school of the Goncourts and Flaubert: Alphonse Daudet, Zola, Maupassant. With one major exception (that of the forerunners of symbolism, Verlaine and Mallarmé), which proved the rule, it is striking to see how they clung more closely to the generation of 1850, from which they had sprung, than to that of 1885, toward which they were moving. The Parnassians made little or no deviation from the lessons of their tetrarchs.

Alphonse Daudet was singularly marked by the spirit and the customs of the Second Empire and the times of M. de Morny. Zola, who had written: "The Republic will be naturalistic or else it will simply not be," would have gladly been, and to a certain extent was, the novelist of the Third Republic. But, on the one hand, he was born a disciple, a disciple of Flaubert and Taine, and, on the other hand, he had condemned himself to portray in *Les Rougon-Macquart* only the society and the way of life of the Second Empire. The generation of 1885 intended to react against him for the same reasons as against Renan, confusing them in a single generation. And these juniors, all of whom died rather prematurely, vanished at the turn of the century at the same time as their elders: Coppée outlived Leconte de Lisle hardly longer than Daudet survived Goncourt and Zola survived Dumas.

The withdrawal of Victor Hugo and Lamartine after 1851 must be associated with the withdrawal of the form-masters, Guizot, Villemain, and Cousin—a retreat, however, that was academic, comfortable, and anything but barren of books, above all anything but barren of regrets, to repeat the word with which Sainte-Beuve's famous article recorded their resignation. The essential point is this, that their time had passed and that their influence on minds had fallen to zero. These eloquent men, these men of principles, these doctrinarians, these dogmatists, these established figures became ancestors: against them there was not even a reaction—only indifference.

The signal for this indifference was given in a striking manner by that Ecole Normale that they had created, the eldest daughter of the form-masters. For the first time, in its great student bodies of 1848–1850, the Ecole Normale provided literary life with a major contingent. Now the Ecole Normale was just the opposite of a school for creators (which, by the way, is a contradiction in terms). It was a school for the critical mind. It gave the generation of 1850 the framework of a critical team destined to restore the task and the function of Sainte-Beuve: criticism of ideas in Taine, political criticism in Prévost-Paradol, criticism of morals in Edmond About, literary criticism in Weiss and Sarcey, historical criticism in Fustel de Coulanges. It will be observed that in the same generation the two other great schools delegated two other masters of criticism to the same task: Renan from the Seminary of Saint-Sulpice, Renouvier, the founder of philosophical criticism, from the Ecole Polytechnique.

What a magnificent beginning, and a task full of promise. But we have mentioned the high-banked lane of Ohain encountered by the romantic impulse. Must it be believed that every literary generation will run into one of its own in midcourse?

When the generation of 1850 disappeared between 1880 and 1893, between the death of Flaubert and that of Renan, it seemed in the end again to have scaled the heights. In no way did it, like the others, leave the impression of a bankruptcy, a liquidation. At the very time when its successors were preparing themselves to supplant it, its masters were still masters, Renan and Taine counted for much. The techniques of the novel had barely moved. Those of the theater had been clumsily replaced. Those of poetry had not been shaken without effort. And there was a general illusion that the era of revolutions seemed over. In fact, the generation of 1885 would be the first in a century that did not live through a political revolution, changes of systems of government, and that would have to find in itself, as at the time of the Dreyfus case, the anguishes and the tragedies that were denied it from without.

HISTORY

The Effect of the Movement of 1820

The movement of 1820 had created an important and majestic form: history in all its aspects. In the Académie des Sciences Morales et Politique, the fifth academy, which the Institut de France owed to the July monarchy and which was composed of sections, there was a section for Histoire Générale et Philosophique. This name, archaic today, is most accurate evidence of the climate in which history lived and developed under the July monarchy. It is like a portrait of M. Guizot. Moreover, it applies to all the noted historians of the period, to Michelet as much as to anyone else, and more.

This general and philosophical history was in addition an informed history. Under the influence of Guizot, indeed, vast publications of historical texts had been undertaken, the *Documents inédits sur l'histoire de France*, to which private initiative added the publications of the Société de l'Histoire de France. And many others. More than any other discipline and any other literature, history was a workshop, a cooperative, an intellectual industry, which was organized at that period. Its evolution does not resemble that of the other literary forms. Its generations succeeded one another less swiftly, worked more in continuity, less by contradictions, polemics, and substitutions.

Therefore the generation of 1850 was virtually a continuation of the generation of 1820 in history. Since history, in contrast to poetry and the theater, is a form suited to maturity of years, and since the historian, who is constantly learning, is less enfeebled than enriched by age, it is not surprising that history under the Second Empire, still represented in part by the historians of the preceding epoch, in no way evidenced a reaction to the former generation. Such a reaction would be looked for in vain in the two great historians who built a part of their work on historical ground—Renan and Taine. Renan was an artist of history like Michelet.

As much as Taine the philosopher rejected and denigrated Cousin, to the same degree he proclaimed himself an admirer and disciple of Guizot, whose anti-revolutionary, conservative, yet liberal history—Anglophile and oratorical, to boot—he continued in the *Origines*. The production of the *Histoires de France* in the manner of Michelet, superficially written by one man alone, from the most remote times to the present, was continued by Cléophas Dareste de la Chavanne and the popular Henri Martin. Guizot himself, in the leisure of his political retirement, brought to fruition one of his old ideas by writing a great *Histoire de France racontée à mes petits-enfants* and also an *Histoire d'Angleterre*, intended for the same public, both worthy of reading and respect within the limitations of their titles.

With these reservations, it goes without saying that, in disciplines as flourishing as that of history, a generation always adds something new and that the generation of 1850 was no exception.

Psychology in History

To the title of "general and philosophical history," which designated the first rank of historians—that is, those of the Institut—the generation of 1820 could have added, as a third adjective, "picturesque." The generation of 1850 was to add instead "psychological." At the very least as far as its two great names, Renan and Taine, were concerned. Religious psychology in the first, and revolutionary psychology, the psychology of Napoleon and indeed the psychology of the French state, in the second—these were great innovations, and, if their results do not always seem durable to us, their idea and their method are. Saint-Sulpice should be viewed in France as the headquarters of the understanding of souls, and the grafting of philology on to this clerical pyschology contributed to producing the fruit of Renanesque history. Similarly, if Taine the philosopher was predestined for philosophical history, it must not be forgotten that he was in addition an admirer of Balzac and a disciple of Stendhal. Hence the Balzacian character of the psychology of the Jacobin, the Stendhalian character of the strings of minor details.

The Preferred Studies

General and philosophical history was fittingly represented by the Orléanists, liberal noblemen or wealthy citizens kept out of power by the Empire, who sought an excuse for their inactivity by pursuing historical studies. Thiers (until the liberal Empire) and Guizot are illustrious examples. So are the descendants of Mme. de Staël, the Broglies; the rich and accurate historical work of Prince (later Duc) Albert, and the d'Haussonvilles—the *Eglise romaine et le premier Empire* and *L'Histoire de la réunion de la Lorraine à la France* of the first, in expectation of the great work of the second on *La Duchesse de Bourgogne*. All of them members of the Académie Française, of course. The Duc d'Aumale himself, in 1869, began the *Histoire des princes de Condé*. This middle class of history had breeding and integrity. It would not be possible to say as much of the historical adventure with which the house across the street compromised itself: the *Histoire de César* by Napoleon III.

But history often advances within a profession more modest than that of a prince or a statesman between posts—namely that of a professor. In 1830 history had been furthered by professors: Guizot, Michelet. It would be the same again after 1850.

The Professors

There are two kinds of professorial histories: general, oratorical history, the daughter of the podiums of the Restoration, and history in detail, the daughter of workrooms in the rue Monsieur-le-Prince or the rue Cujas. Beginning in 1855, the latter was encouraged by the Sorbonne. The dean of the Faculty of Letters, J.-V. Le Clerc, summarily discouraged doctoral candidates from theses on general philosophical considerations and guided them toward specific and learned subjects. These official guidelines contributed to the orientation of historical research toward precision, toward critical and technical pains which were less familiar to the preceding era and the academic school.

The interest of these limited researches was that they made it possible to revise historical commonplaces in the texts. General and philosophical history had few defenses against commonplaces, which it had no time to examine and which it utilized, just as they stood, in its construction. On the right and the left, from Guizot's side as from Michelet's, it was fed on what Flaubert called accepted ideas. The generation of 1850 wrote into the historical agenda the study of the dull or obscure parts of history, which are often its most important parts, as well as the examination of accepted ideas.

Adolphe Chéruel had been Michelet's student and Flaubert's professor at the Collège de Rouen. With his substantial labors on the first half of the seventeenth century, he placed the counterweight of the competent scholar on the scale against the frivolous, petulant, and comical agitation of Victor Cousin. Camille Rousset, an exceptional professor of history, opened the archives of a public body, the military administration under Louis XIV, and drew out of them the great *Histoire de Louvois*, which was easily unseated by a new one and which frankly resorted to the hagiographic method customary in such monographs, but which offered us a solid model of detailed work in favor of the new professorial school. This same Rousset provided the model for a brilliant re-examination of accepted ideas in his book on *Les Volontaires de 1791–1794*. The government made him slightly ridiculous by reviving for him the post of historiographer of France, which he held from 1864 to 1877: its fruit was books on the wars of Algeria and the Crimea. One would not include among the authorized reviewers of accepted ideas Lanfrey, the author of an *Histoire de Napoléon Ier* (1867–74), a heavy and hate-ridden pamphlet worthy of his *Histoire politique des papes* (1860).

Fustel de Coulanges

The master of pure history in this generation was Fustel de Coulanges, a fellow-student of Taine at the Ecole Normale, whose life was all in his teaching and his books, two registers that are completely separate. The maxim in which he expressed the duty of the historian as "a lifetime of analysis for an hour of synthesis" is to be understood only if it is limited to his written work. The analysis was the continuous toil of the scholar who dissected the texts and of the professor who taught his students how to dissect them. The synthesis was, or was to be, a few books in which, without references, like an expert's report that is based only on his own thinking, he would expound the general results of his labors.

His first years of teaching, in Strasbourg, produced one of these books in 1864, *La Cité antique*, the work of a successor to Montesquieu, which remains one of the masterpieces of French historical literature.

Of historical literature because only history was able to subject him to serious reprobation. The ancient Greek and Roman cities were linked by this book to the abstract concept of the City. The historian examined this city—that is, basically, the worship of the gods of the city superimposed on the older worship of ancestors in the family. These two beliefs were harmonized and reciprocally shored up each other in a belief that formed the religion of the state and that supplied the key men to ancient society. As these beliefs developed, revolutions broke out. When these beliefs disappeared, the city disappeared.

A synthesis marked by purity and admirable intelligibility, which was crystallized wholly around Greek and Latin historical texts. But too pure and too intelligible. First of all, reflection suggests to us that the habits of historic continuity are opposed to such a logical progression of events.

Although Fustel held philosophy in utter scorn, here he behaved like an ideologist in the style of his contemporary, Taine, except that with him it was not the "minor details" that marched in close order, it was the texts. And historians' experience has shown them, first, that in Fustel the philological feeling for texts left something to be desired; second, that he was lacking in caution before these texts and their authors, that he put a text of Thucydides on the same footing with one by a compiler of some minor epoch or with an epic legend used by Livy, Pausanias, or Apollodorus. It is not surprising that *La Cité antique* no longer carries any historical weight: but has even Theodor Mommsen's *Roman History* itself retained its own? *La Cité* survives on the literary level of Montesquieu's *Considérations* and Tocqueville's *Ancien Régime:* it is still very great.

Fustel intended to write a four-volume history of French institutions up to the Revolution, which, similarly, would have been the synthesis of his teaching of modern history. In 1875 he published the first volume, which ran from ancient Gaul to the fall of the Merovingians. Contrary to accepted belief since Boulainvilliers and fortified by German scholarship, he reduced to the minimum the importance of the Germanic element. Whence, in those years of the 1870s that still smelled of gunpowder, a hail of javelins of erudition from the other side of the Rhine, which violently upset Fustel, led him to a different historical method—namely that of placing before the public itself the content and the discussion of the texts—and caused him to recast this whole volume of synthesis into several volumes of analysis, the last of which were published after his death by Camille Jullian and which, admired by historians as masterpieces of method and analysis, were admired on trust by the great public, for which, however, they were almost unreadable and which knew nothing of them but their conclusions.

Fustel's importance derives primarily from his quality as a professor and his function as a historical innovator between 1870 and 1885. Then there is the reform that he brought about in the style of historical exposition and that has earned him a prominent place in a history of literature. His own style has the sharpness and the precision of a medal; it is purged of those epithets and abstractions, of that oratorical moralism, of which the form-masters of 1820 had sown the bad seed. Under his pen the common written language becomes a common light of reason. In both meanings of the word he is the type of the *intelligible* historian. The *Quelques leçons à l'impératrice* on the history of France, which he wrote for the monarch's wife and her ladies in waiting and which was interrupted by the war of 1870, is probably the masterpiece of the fashionable "lecture" in the French language, which any society woman or any child could understand and in which the specialists recognized their master. Finally, Fustel's historical work was aimed—victoriously, in sum—against two "accepted ideas" of the seventeenth century: *La Cité antique* against that accepted idea of the Revolution that the ancient city can be compared with the modern state, that Sparta can be used in Paris and Plutarch in deliberative assemblies; *Les Institutions* against that other accepted idea of the Germanic conquest as the mother of the modern world. Fustel's theories did not escape the fate of all historical theories; what is important is that the accepted ideas that were the objects of his criticism could not reappear. In history, criticism alone leaves a net profit and a definitive result.

La Cité antique was not an isolated work under the Empire. More attention was given to ancient history than in the previous period. Victor Duruy's *Histoire des romains*, obviously less a work of genius than Mommsen's, is still a work full of reason, a skillfully built monument. Gaston Boissier popularized acquaintance with the history of Rome in his judicious, malicious, and lively books. *Cicéron et ses amis* was long regarded as a model of exposition, a classic for the baccalaureate by the same right as *La Fontaine et ses Fables, La Cité antique, Les Moralistes français*. To demote these works is not forbidden; it would be even less forbidden to replace them. And they have not been replaced.

After 1870

Historical studies, linked with the teaching of history, gladly accepted an official patron, as Guizot had been under the July monarchy. Under the Empire this post was filled by Duruy, who was not a specialist of detail but who encouraged the specialist groups. The creation of the Ecoles des Hautes Etudes put a "seminary" at the disposal of the young historians. Contemporary with Fustel's teaching, it inaugurated a school of precision in the study of texts. The university historians of the Third Republic owe much to these influences.

From a literary standpoint the most remarkable of them was Ernest Lavisse, Duruy's secretary and the imperial prince's tutor. Under the Third Republic Lavisse continued a *cursus honorum* which recalled that of the great professors under the July monarchy. But he was in fact a great professor. He had an aptitude for the total viewpoint, an art of historical ideology, that recalled Tocqueville. For ten years after the war of 1870, his works dealt with the history of Germany and Prussia. A great French history of Frederick the Great, set in the center of Europe and of the eighteenth century, would have been one of those magnificent subjects in the manner of Sainte-Beuve's *Port-Royal* with which a historian adds to the civilization that he describes. Lavisse wrote two charming volumes on Frederick before his coronation, their accuracy assured, in the manner of Duclos, by excellent studies in Germany, but he did not persevere in the project; schoolbooks to be written and publications to be directed prevented him from leaving his monument, which was supplied for him after a fashion by his *Louis XIV*, which was his contribution to the collective *Histoire de France* that he supervised. This *Louis XIV* is bursting with intelligence—intelligence of history rather than intelligence of men—But it is still a long way from Michelet.

Lavisse was twenty-eight years old in 1870, and he did not die until several years after the First World War. Albert Sorel, who was born in the same year of 1842, died in 1906. They made a fine healthy pair, balanced and contrasting, in French history between those two wars.

From a certain point of view that history is a French-German dialogue. Germany before 1870 had been brought to a national consciousness in part by great historians—Leopold von Ranke, Mommsen, Heinrich von Treitschke. In addition, its arsenal of historical work in the universities was unequaled. The work of reconstruction and reform could hardly proceed in France without an analogous attention being given to history, without a bastion of French history, without laboratories of French history, capable of matching the German bastions and laboratories; and in addition a maximum of good faith and critical approach was sought. The Ecoles des Hautes Etudes, *La Revue critique*, *La Revue historique* served as laboratories, and Lavisse and Sorel were the leaders of the research.

In contrast to Lavisse, and like Taine after 1871, Sorel was a man with a single monument, which, under the title of *L'Europe et la Révolution française*, was a diplomatic history of Europe from 1789 to 1815. Like Lavisse with his project of Frederick the Great, Sorel established himself at a crossroads of Europe. The object was to develop a young generation that would understand Europe, and Sorel, also a great professor, strove to shape it; he held a chair that would soon be the most brilliant in the Ecole Libre des Sciences Politiques, founded at that time in order to create political minds and a political state of mind. There he taught, before he wrote them, all the chapters of these eight volumes, which are volumes of synthesis, or, rather, of theses: the continuity of national and international politics among all governments and in all states—a justification of Napoleon, who had received from the Revolution a France that was too big and whom this inheritance forced into the continental blockade and its consequence, the distant wars of Spain and Russia. The work is written with much art and ingenuity. Sorel's influence was considerable on the whole generation of diplomats who entered upon their careers between 1885 and the First World War. His charming style blends Tocqueville's idioms with the austere elegances of the doctrinarian historians. The early volumes are burdened with artificial and old-fashioned portraits. As a whole, it is perhaps the masterpiece of great academic and diplomatic history. One reads it with the same respect with which one walks through a series of embassy drawing rooms lined with Gobelin tapestries.

But this great book on Europe was not altogether a great European book. Sorel's systematic theses were not followed at all in England and Germany. The Sorbonne historians challenged them, in little-read works, devoid of literary and academic brilliance, but perhaps more solid. Sorel's usual disciples were diplomatic historians, imbued with the tradition of the Quai d'Orsay, like Albert Vandal, or technicians of tradition, like Jacques Bainville. He grew old without being supplanted.

The same generation of academic historians produced two serious works of major history for the mass public: *L'Histoire de la Monarchie de juillet*, by Paul Thureau-Dangin, which appeared between 1884 and 1892, and *L'Histoire du second Empire*, very vigorously written by Pierre de la Gorce. At the same time there were the abundantly informative but poorly organized *Napoléon et sa famille*, a hagiographic Vendôme Column, by Frédéric Masson, and more reliable works, though inspired with the same Bonapartist fire: Henry Houssaye's *1814* and *1815*.

III

THE TETRARCHS

The Four Masters of Parnassus

There is a risk of being misled by the term Parnassians, which was coined in 1860 by poets who would not yet be thirty years old in 1870 and which served as a banner to a school that flourished in the first twenty years of the Third Republic. These young poets were in reality the successors of the four masters whom they called the tetrarchs: Gautier, Leconte, de Lisle, Banville, and Baudelaire (who is the subject of the next chapter); the three last were all about thirty years old in 1850. Now, movement, invention, and poetic genius were inherent in the tetrarchs. The *Turba magna* of their successors was the sequel. Hence it is the generation of 1850 into which that poetic peak called Parnassus is really incorporated, that peak that was recognized and named only belatedly and that occupied a place between the romanticism of 1820 and the symbolism of 1885.

Emaux et Camées

To be exact, among the tetrarchs there was one, Gautier, who began his fortieth year in 1850, who had little by little given up poetry for the labors of journalism, and who served on the general staff of romanticism. It would be almost impossible to see in the Gautier of 1830, of *Albertus* and *La Comédie de la mort*, a forerunner of Leconte de Lisle or even of Baudelaire. But in fact in 1852 Gautier published *Emaux et camées*, a simple little book that he would later inflate a little. As much as and even more than the content, the title served as a verbal emblem of an objective and decorative poetry. The picturesquely rhymed quatrain of nervous, cambered octosyllables was in those days a discovery, which influenced Baudelaire, the Hugo of *Les Chansons des rues et des bois*, and the school

of Parnassus. By virtue of his colorful conversation, his technical paradoxes, Gautier was the only romantic who was still listened to; in short,
he, who alone had represented the bond between poetry and painting in
romanticism, who alone had undressed the Muse to stand nude in a studio,
passed in 1852 into a generation in which this paradox of yesteryear was
becoming common practice. Hence the importance of this little book of
verse that undoubtedly earned Gautier the dedication of *Les Fleurs du
mal*. We will agree that, once its function as a liaison officer had been
completed, this *Emaux et camées* turned remarkably pale.

Among the tetrarchs Gautier figures as a guest of honor and an ancestor. The three great poets of the generation of 1850 are the three other
tetrarchs, to whose names those of Louis Ménard and Louis Bouilhet must
be added; both were born in 1822. These five names exhaust the list of
significant poets in that generation, a distinct and homogeneous group
from which Baudelaire's genius detaches itself to fly higher.

Against Personal Literature

Homogeneous by virtue of the same rejection, the same *No!* against
what great romantic poetry had deployed along its whole front—namely,
the lyric exploitation both of natural feelings and of private life. The
homes, the loves, the marital infidelities, unilateral or reciprocal, of the
romantic poets had nourished their poetry and, imposed by them, belonged to literary history. It was in the same way that under Louis XIV
and Louis XV the loves of the prince, his going forth and his lying down,
had their place in the life of the court and in the public interest. And
besides it was still a question of the prince, since the most illustrious of
these poets intended more or less to govern their country. Had not Lamartine in 1849, barely removed from power, published those volumes
of *Confidences* on which the women of the provinces threw themselves,
although Paris did not greet them without surprise and irony? The generation of 1850, in fact, cut short these displays or engaged in them only
according to the ancient mode, with extreme discretion and under the
pressure of a rare emotion: the apparent exception of Baudelaire would
prove the rule.

The Poetry of 1850

It was a generation, if not of learned poets, at least of educated and
technical poets. The romantics, coming into the modern age first after
the rupture of the Revolution, had shared the good fortune of firstcom-

ers, which, according to Jean de La Bruyère, was that of the ancients and which in the seventeenth century was that of the writers who came immediately after the regularization of the language. They had taken forceful possession of the general feelings at ground level and for love, death, pity, the family, the nation, they had at first held the new place of the echo poet. Now it was necessary to go under the ground, to exploit the poetic lode by digging into it with tools, hence to refine with technique, to move from general sentiments to more particular and rarer sentiments, to what Sainte-Beuve, face to face with Baudelaire, called with suspicious disquiet Kamchatka.

Thus in part this poetic generation closed off the great public. The imperial epoch took no interest in poetry, but above all poetry took no interest in the epoch: it was the question of the chicken or the egg. These poets would spend twenty years emerging, finding an audience and glory: the opposite of the eruption into light before the age of thirty that the romantics had experienced. Contact between great poetry and the great contemporary public was broken off.

These poets had no leaders, formed no school, had little to do with one another. In contrast to the romantics, the younger Parnassians, and the symbolists, each more or less played his unlucky part alone. Yet, at a distance and because of the effulgence of his last years, Leconte de Lisle appears before us with the stature and the grand manners of a general on inactive duty.

Leconte de Lisle

He was a republican of 1848 who, after the defeat of his ideal, took refuge in poetry, in antiquity, and in memories.

The collapse of liberty, which threw Hugo into messianism, reinforced Leconte de Lisle in an absolute pessimism. At the age of thirty he had learned from life the lesson that it is loathsome to be a man, shameful to think and to live. There was in him no other philosophy but despair, less shaded and less human than Vigny's, and its anchors were pride, misanthropy, hatred: "I hate my times."

Aside from this hatred, from the need to emigrate that it implied, he had no compelling reason to be a poet in the lyric sense in which in his time the word was understood when one "sang." But for him the world of verses was an admirable world, animated by his own life. The instrument in his hands was sure, strong, and subtle. He would use it not to lead great causes or to declare great passions but to expound great themes.

These great themes were those of the ancient religions. Leconte de Lisle was not at all a religious poet, but on the contrary fiercely antireligious, the only great French poet, perhaps, who hated Christianity.

But he was the poet of religions, the potent and sonorous custodian of their empty monuments, the curator of a poetic Guimet Museum.* He had an admirable knowledge of the great Greek poets and made beautiful prose translations of most of them, which are made unrecognizable today by the barbarization of the proper names. (Jean Moréas accused him of playing Homer on a Malagasy drum, and there was something to it.) But chiefly he used the Greeks in the Hellenic myths and the paraphrases of his *Poèmes antiques,* which sound rather of the zither than of the drum. Let us add that the Second Empire was the period when the translation of so-called primitive—Hindu, Scandinavian, Finnish—epics began. The author of *Poèmes barbares* carved out large panels of epic narrative into which he put as much barbarity as the French Alexandrine can hold—in other words, not much. He touched on Asia only from without, as a librarian. His Greece of white marble, blue sky, reason, truth, proper names, seems schoolboyish to us today. And it is remarkable that this poet of myths created no living myth, had neither his *Centaure* nor his *Satyre.*

Coming from Reunion Island at the age of twenty, after a voyage in the Netherlands East Indies, he retained, if not a nostalgia for it, at least childhood memories that inspired him to admirable personal poems, the only tropical landscapes that exist in French poetry, and to recollections of Pacific *fauna* that made him a remarkable painter of animals, the Antoine-Louis Barye † of French literature.

Ménard and Bouilhet

Louis Ménard wrote very little verse, and a hundred beautiful lines of *Les Rêveries d'un païen mystique* are not enough to bring this original and ingenious Alexandrian out of the shadow of Leconte de Lisle. But among these Parnassians of the great period, a quite gifted and honorable provincial poet, in his proper place here, must not be forgotten: Louis Bouilhet. Sainte-Beuve saw in him a disciple of Musset: wrongly, although there was some connection between the epic strophe of *Melaenis* and that of *Namouna.* The real connection (without imitation), on the one side, is with Leconte de Lisle, since *Melaenis* is a great archaeological poem of robust form and in *Les Fossiles* Bouilhet was the sometimes felicitous painter of antediluvian animals and of the landscape of the Mesozoic Period; on the other side, it is with Flaubert, of whom he was the compatriot, the friend, and the adviser, and whose archaeological prose

* A remarkable museum of Oriental religions founded by Emile Guimet, industrialist and scholar, and bequeathed by him to the nation.—Translator.
† A contemporary sculptor of animals.—Translator.

balances the archaeological poetry of Parnassus; in that respect this group of erudite, decorative, and solid art forms a mass.

Théodore de Banville

Let us not imagine that the pleasant, brilliant, and happy genius of Théodore de Banville was so far removed. Certainly, if the literature of the Empire presented a face that was pessimistic on one side and frivolous on the other, Banville can be taken to a certain extent as its delegate to a certain frivolity. His bright optimism affords a perfect contrast to the radical pessimism of Leconte de Lisle. And, again in contrast to the latter, a zeal for form is linked in Banville with an Ovidian facility. Born five years after Leconte de Lisle, he began ten years earlier, in 1842, with *Les Cariatides*, a title that was already Parnassian. With the *Odes funambulesques* he invented a spirit of unmotivated lyricism, of punning rhyme, of contemporary allusion, that made him the Offenbach of poetry and that did not fade until it had engendered a whole school over two generations.

And he too, like a good tetrarch, made his excursions into the past. *Les Exilés* is a series of epic fragments of great pace; *Le Forgeron* could be called the only living Greek myth, created and creative, that Parnassus left; and, with the *Trente-six Ballades joyeuses à la manière de François Villon* and *Rondels composés à la manière de Charles d'Orléans*, he brought the ballad and the rondeau back into poetry, as Sainte-Beuve had brought back the sonnet. Furthermore, it is easy to imagine him in the fifteenth century, a great rhetorician and court poet attached to the Knights of the Golden Fleece, the lords of the best wines in Christendom.

Banville's excursions into the past were a diversion and not, like those of Leconte de Lisle, an emigration. Leconte de Lisle hated his times; Banville adored them while he mocked them. In addition, this generation required a very great poet, one who powerfully, tragically, lived and felt and portrayed his time. He was not lacking: his name was Baudelaire.

BAUDELAIRE

Heroic Poetry and Inner Poetry

Romantic poetry is a heroic poetry, and the romantic poet cultivated heroic attitudes and heroic settings. He lived, if not in perpetual self-satisfaction and a perpetual noble self-presentation, at least under the conditions, the responsibilities, and the exigencies of his glory. Lamartine and Victor Hugo rather generally assumed the pose of statues to be erected at their graves, and, like their ancestor, Chateaubriand, they were artists in destiny, in their own destinies. It was the same, at bottom, with Alfred de Vigny and Alfred de Musset, who needed illustrious loves, who voiced their sufferings and their revulsions in such oratorical proclamations as *Rolla* and *Chatterton*. Their miseries were the miseries, if not of dethroned kings, at least of orators reduced to silence. When Chateaubriand asserted that he was weary of everything and wished only a cell in which to await death, a friend murmured: "Yes, a cell on a stage." This was essentially the style of the romantic cell, even if it was called *La Maison du berger*.

But in opposition to this outpouring of the poet's self to the world there existed, in other poetic natures, a turning of the poet toward the interior; in opposition to that conviction of greatness, an awareness of suffering; in opposition to that deliberate illusion of magnificence, a realism of vice and sin; in opposition to that splendid instrument on which a resounding skin was drawn taut, the dark heart of man, which, according to Pascal, is hollow and filled with filth; in opposition to that cell on a stage, a confessional in the shadows. It was more or less for this function that the genius for balance and contrast inherent in a healthy literature designated Sainte-Beuve's *Poésies de Joseph Delorme* in 1829 and Baudelaire's *Les Fleurs du mal* in 1857.

Sainte-Beuve the Forerunner

When *Les Fleurs du mal* was published, Sainte-Beuve said, *"Joseph Delorme* is yesterday's *Fleurs du mal."* To which a florist who sells day-old flowers at half-price would reply that Sainte-Beuve was putting the right figure on his work. But he intended only to emphasize his own character as the precursor, and there too, in sum, he was being only fair to himself.

In 1829 his originality was as unquestionable as it was unrecognized. He was a clear-sighted and sorrowful poet, who found his poetry only in that clear-sightedness and sorrow, who did not project it around him in ornamented illusions. He himself, with a melancholy that soon turned to bitterness, contrasted his position as a sacrificed, uneasy, little-loved poet to the Olympian effulgence of Victor Hugo, his habituation to shadow to that intimacy with light. Baudelaire was to admire very much, and with reason, the poem entitled *La Veillée*, written 22 October 1828 and dedicated to Victor Hugo, in which the fascinating contrast of these two destinies is illuminated.

But, if it would be absolutely unjust to say that this poet of sorrow was a sorry poet, at the very least it can be admitted that this clear-sighted poet was not a very great poet. So it is that *La Veillée* begins with thirty-four lines that are beautiful, that seem to be its sunlit aspect, warmed moreover by Hugo's radiance, while the eighteen final lines, a low-lying cold north, complete it in a despairing platitude. And it is this platitudinousness, so frequent in Sainte-Beuve, that has put off so many readers, that from the appearance of *Les Pensées d'août* discouraged this original poetry, caused it to disappear in public indifference, relegated it in effect to the condition of yesterday's flowers.

Baudelaire's Poetry

Today's flower is yesterday's flower plus efflorescence. Baudelaire's poetry is Sainte-Beuve's poetry plus poetry. I mean the matter of that poetry plus the radiance and the genius of pure poetry, the aliment of light reserved to the gods, which Sainte-Beuve never tasted. This manner and this radiance will be found in *Les Fleurs dul mal*.

The material common to Sainte-Beuve's and Baudelaire's poetry consists in four elements: an inner Christianity, a critical intelligence, the secret life of a great capital, Paris, and finally an alliance with prose.

An inner Christianity, opposed to the Christianity handed down to the romantic poets by Chateaubriand and the spirit of *Le Génie*. Opposed in this, that the Christianity of the romantics was a Christianity without the consciousness of original sin—that is, a Christianity stripped of its substance and reduced to its shell. Now Sainte-Beuve sketched the poem of original sin, that illness of the will, in *Joseph Delorme* and wrote the novel of its analysis in *Volupté*, and that was not all. Since he was at the same time a great critic, a great scholar in the natural history of the mind, in *Port-Royal* he went in search of original sin in that doctrine and that Jansenist group that were, so to speak, its principal seat or its laboratory in France. It will be noted, moreover, that Sainte-Beuve's Port-Royalism barely survived the early death of his poetry and that after the second volume of *Port-Royal* the spirit of the eighteenth century, which Baudelaire would always regard with horror, triumphed more and more in the critic. But in Baudelaire the view of man as sinner, originally, naturally, and appallingly a sinner, "the boring vista of immortal sin," remained unshakable. Sin had marked nature: Baudelaire detested nature. "Nature can guide us only into crime." The naturally good man was an insensate dream of the eighteenth century, exaggerated by the Hugos and the Sands. "Woman is natural: that is, abominable." Every genuine civilization was a reaction against nature, a mitigation of original sin. And "all the prevailing heresies are only the consequence of the great modern heresy: the elimination of the idea of original sin." For the first time since Racine there was a genuine and full-bodied revival of the poetry of sin and the sinner.

A critical intelligence. We have two volumes of critical essays by Baudelaire. Everyone agrees that his criticism, with Sainte-Beuve's, is among the most penetrating and the most intelligent of the nineteenth century, as acute, as far advanced when he is judging *Madame Bovary* as when he is dealing with Richard Wagner or Delacroix. But as a poet he applied this critical intelligence principally to himself. *Un Voyage à Cythère* remains the typical poem of an atrocious clarity of vision. *L'Examen de minuit* is the examination of conscience of the very life of Paris. Baudelaire found the phrase, "confessional of the heart," and for him this phrase well described a reality. His lucidity on man is of the family of Pascal's lucidity, which would have seen the poet as the most intelligent of the damned. Nothing, in any case, is more remote from the potent illusionism and the golden wedding of the romantics.

A keen perception of Paris. If Victor Hugo was the poet of the externalities of Paris, of its commemorations, of the great currents that swept its citizens and stirred its history, if Sainte-Beuve discovered the landscapes of the working-class quarters and the city of the people, Baudelaire drew out the soul of all these, a sophisticated and perverse soul, the soul of the city's nights, the soul of its disgusts. Was not *Le Spleen de Paris* the original title of *Les Poèmes en prose*? Paris became Baudelaire's glory slowly, during a half-century, through successive discoveries, through the awareness that the great city gained of its secret, of its poison, of its poet.

Finally, an alliance with prose, an alliance that was something original and that must not be taken as a degeneration. Did not Sainte-Beuve owe his poetic defeat, at the very time when French verse had its maximum of music and sky, above all to the prosiness, or, rather, to the prosinesses, that he mingled with his poetry, that we have learned to appreciate in a certain fashion but that offended the ears of his contemporaries by their corrugations and wounded the friends of strong, pure poetry, then at the saturation point? There is similarly a banality in Baudelaire, or, rather, there is the problem of Baudelaire's banality; what some call platitudes or lapses in his verse is regarded by others as a deliberate bareness intended to produce the same effect as the unhewn sections that Rodin left in his marbles. Consider for instance the banalities strewn through the admirable poem, *Le Cygne*. Some readers are shocked by its ending in this platitude:

> *Ainsi dans la forêt où mon esprit s'exile*
> *Un vieux Souvenir sonne à plein souffle du cor!*
> *Je pense aux matelots oubliés dans une île,*
> *Aux captifs, aux vaincus! . . . à bien d'autres encor.*

> (So in the forest of my soul's exile
> Old Memory sounds the fullness of its horn!
> I think of sailors left upon an isle,
> Of captives, beaten men! . . . and many more.)

Others admire the very fact that the poem does not end, that its last lines are only hinted dreams in a language and in images that are themselves only sketched, and to them the final line has a tremendous music. They believe that the Parnassians, in conformance with their rules and the habits of their school, would have put this lush stanza at the end:

> *Andromaque, des bras d'un grand époux tombée,*
> *Vil bétail, sous la main du superbe Pyrrhus*
> *Auprès d'un tombeau vide en extase courbée,*
> *Veuve d'Hector, hélas! et femme d'Hélénus!*

> (Andromache, from a great husband rent,
> Vile body in the hands of Pyrrhus' pride
> Beside an empty tomb in rapture bent,
> Widow of Hector and Helenus' bride!)

And they think that, by rising to poetry and sonority only to debase itself in the stammered prose of a dying melancholy voice, the poem becomes more consubstantial with the picture or the myth of the strayed swan on the dry dusty pavement of Paris. All Baudelaire's prosinesses could give rise to similar discussions.

The truth is that there is a Baudelairean connection between a naked prose and a pure poetry incorporated together into verse; that each has long offended and unsettled conformist ears, habituated to traditional harmonies; that, as is usually the case, readers have not only become accustomed to this dissonance but have recognized in it a more subtle and more delicate art than that of consonance, which for example is that of Gautier; that, if in addition a defect can become beauty, that, if defect and dissonance are indistinguishably mingled here, the fact remains that Baudelaire, a poet far superior to Gautier, did not know his language and its grammar as Gautier did; he would not have written the terse dedication of *Les Fleurs du mal* to Gautier if he had not been the first to recognize this infirmity.

Les Limbes Turned Fleurs du mal

There are fanatical Baudelaireans who refuse to acknowledge the slightest failing in the beauty of Baudelaire, the slightest flaw in his metal. But I think that even among them there will be no defenders of the ridiculous, rococo title of *Les Fleurs du mal*. It seems to have been suggested by the booksellers as being more "commercial." It is infuriating that the poet did not drive these money-changers out of the temple and that he did not stand firm on the title that he had chosen first: *Les Limbes* (*Limbo*), which would have far better shown the Catholic nature of the poems.

According to a theological tradition that had already given Delavigne the subject of a poem (the only good poem that he ever wrote), Limbo is a sort of fourth realm in the topography of the next world: not Paradise, not Purgatory, not Hell; a place barren of joy and sorrow, reserved for children who died before baptism, infidel pagans, heretics of good faith and morals—a tradition, however, that the Catholic Church has never hallowed, that the catechism ignores, and that has never taken a precise form. Baudelaire's Catholicism, less religious than philosophical and literary, needed an intermediate, special, original realm in which to live between God and the devil. The title *Les Limbes* showed the geographical localization of Baudelaire's poems, made it possible to understand better the order that Baudelaire wanted to set up among them, which was the order of a journey and, more exactly, a fourth journey after Dante's three journeys through the *Inferno*, the *Purgatorio*, and the *Paradiso*. The poet of Florence survived in the poet of Paris.

Les Limbes (let us temporarily restore this title) of 1857, to which later editions of *Les Fleurs du mal* added nothing fundamental, was divided into six parts in which Baudelaire carefully classified poems written without any order during fifteen years, and he wanted these six parts to represent the six periods of a "poetic alchemy" of destiny, or, rather, the six stages of a journey from life to death through a Catholic country and landscape, denoted and bounded by the first poem, *Au Lecteur.*

The initial section, *Spleen et idéal,* contains more than half the whole. It represents in effect Baudelaire's reality, his human condition. And also his professional condition, that of the poet. The poet's condition! We know what a monumental aspect was bestowed on this problem by romanticism, Lamartine, Hugo, Vigny, Musset, through lyricism, the theater, and politics. It was natural and necessary that the first poem in *Spleen et idéal* should be *Bénédiction,* that *Chatterton* to the third power of which *l'Albatros* was a first draft, placed here at the back of the picture. The fourteen poems that follow, up to *Châtiment de l'orgueil,* could then have been called "La Comédie Poétique," in the sense of *la Divina Commedia.* Then there is the poet contemplating forms, contemplating *La Beauté,* and, beginning with *La Chevelure,* the poet among women, contemplating woman—that is, to go back to predecessors (for Vigny represents in a way Baudelaire's Old Testament), *La Colère de Samson* after *Chatterton* and *La Maison du berger.* Angers, adorations, humiliations, lusts, sensualities of furs or scents that add their harmonies to the terrible note of the black Venus or the public Venus—then the other, the guardian angel, the muse and the madonna, the very good and very dear, she of *Confession,* of *Chant d'automne,* of *L'Invitation au voyage;* those love poems that constitute almost half of *Spleen et idéal* conclude in the season of the *Sonnet d'automne,* which the first poem of *Spleen* follows with *Tristesse de la lune;* then, with some disharmonies caused by the necessity of finding places for all the poems written in fifteen years, the twenty last poems of *Spleen,* concluding with *Le Goût du néant, Alchimie de la douleur, L'Héautontimorouménos, L'Horloge,* that final poem that is the poem of absolute despair and that provides a precise counterweight to the first, *Bénédiction.*

The first cycle by itself would constitute a whole. But a second circle begins, in the manner of Dante's circles, his *bolge* (pits). This is the eighteen poems of *Tableaux parisiens.* There is a Comédie Poétique for the poet. And, for the man accustomed to the "most sinuous of capital cities," there is also a Parisian comedy, which must not be taken more in the comic but in the tragic sense. The old capital of the great poet of Paris lived for him, lived in him like a woman, like those ripe women, heavy with memories, with pasts, and with sins, whom alone he loved. *Les Sept Vieillards, Les Petites Villes, Le Crépuscule du matin* are badly named *Tableaux parisiens:* they are the heart of Paris, its secret, its *mystique.* Baudelaire hated nature, but here he re-created a capital as a nature.

A capital, a crowd, is an occasion for flight, flight into anonymity in the midst of men and in the midst of women, those trees of the forest, anonymity in which one forgets this man or that woman. But that flight and that loss can be found as well outside men, without men. In the third cycle Baudelaire, the poet of Paris, is succeeded by Baudelaire, the poet of artificial paradises, which, with the help of Thomas De Quincey, he described at length elsewhere. Here he retains only one of them, the only one that has any poetic titles of nobility: wine. Baudelaire wanted to make a cycle, an autonomous section of his book, out of the five little poems on wine, on the same ground as the hundred poems of *Spleen et idéal*.

The voyage was becoming more and more perilous, was drawing down more and more reproof, though it was invited, from the "hypocrite reader, my likeness and my brother." The normal life of the romantic poet, the secret life of Paris, the sin of drunkenness were succeeded by Evil for the fourth cycle. The title of *Fleurs du mal* is especially reserved to twelve poems, the twelve apostles of the devil, the most daring in the book, those same poems that the courts compelled Baudelaire to eliminate: *Une Martyre, Lesbos, Femmes damnées*. And *Un Voyage à Cythère*, which is the eleventh, seems to us the most audacious and the strongest form that a great poet has ever given to a confession, to a prophet's robe torn apart from top to bottom. After the circle of wine, the circle of vice, of clairvoyant vice, of desperate vice, of punished vice.

Since the poet rejected romantic illusionism, cowardly pretense, ignorance and its masks, all that is vice in vice, since he opted for "conscience in evil," what circle, then, could be drawn below the circle of evil? The circle of revolt. After having opted for evil, the poet would opt for the leader of evil, for the devil. There are only three poems in *Révolte—Le Reniement de Saint Pierre, Abel et Caïn, Les Litanies de Satan*—and Baudelaire wanted them too to form a circle, a cycle. These are the boundaries between Limbo and Hell, in the way in which the artificial paradises looked toward Paradise. And it is enough to read these three poems and to look Baudelaire's mask in the eye to be convinced that all of this is frighteningly genuine and that, when Brunetière called Baudelaire a Beelzebub at a restaurant table, it was Brunetière alone who was at the table, like a grotesque waiter.

Only a sixth cycle was still possible: Death. The final section, of six poems, is entitled *La Mort*. They justify the original title of the whole volume. Baudelairean death is not a hope of heaven, or a purification by ordeals, or a plunge into hell. It is the journey into Limbo earned by *Les Amants, Les Pauvres, Les Artistes*. It is *La Fin de la journée*, it is *Le Rêve d'un curieux*. It is, finally, *Le Voyage*. This *Voyage* puts the full stop to these poems of a voyage through the human world, along the borders of the human world, beyond the human world. The human condition is appalling, but it is not the only condition. Over the wreckage of life and far from humanity, forward!

O Mort, vieux capitaine, il est temps! Levons l'ancre!
Ce pays nous ennuie, ô Mort! Appareillons!
Si le ciel et la mer sont noirs comme de l'encre
Nos coeurs que tu connais sont remplis de rayons!

(Up anchor, Death, old captain! It is time!
This land has drained us, Death! Get under way!
Though sky and sea be blackly inked with slime,
You know our hearts are full with light of day!)

And thus *Le Voyage* goes back to *Bénédiction*, the final circle returns to the first, as in Nerval's poem the thirteenth hour comes back in the guise of the first. The journey of *Les Limbes* riding a crest between heaven and hell is over. Such was the message entrusted to Baudelaire. A poet, he had no more to say, no other book to write than *Les Limbes*. He would have lived longer if he had simply added other poems to his unique book, of which his papers, his intimate diaries, are the commentary and in which since 1900 Paris has recognized its *Divina Commedia*.

V

THE SUCCESSORS

The Parnassians

Some twenty years after the tetrarchs—more or less in 1840—the covey of their disciples was born: Léon Dierx in 1838, Sully-Prudhomme in 1839, José-Maria de Hérédia and Coppée in 1842, Catulle Mendès in 1843, Anatole France in 1844. Their beginning coincided with the end of the Empire. These, properly speaking, are the Parnassians.

They took this name—or, rather, the little newspapers gave them this name—because the collective anthology of verse that was published in 1866 by Alphonse Lemerre, the bookseller who was making his start as the publisher of the younger poets, was called *Parnasse contemporain*. The admission fee to Parnassus in those days was very low: all that was needed was to rhyme correctly and to take a public stand against facility, sentimentality, and banality. In other words, against nouns and against bad habits, but not against persons. These young poets were extremely respectful, very properly behaved and dressed, usually employed in some office: for their first anthology they requested verses from Auguste Barbier himself, the author of *Les Iambes*. Worshiping M. de Lamartine, they were therefore reduced to seeking opponents among his provincial disciples and the Muses of the hinterland. Poets of the romantic generation, the Parnassians rejected hardly anyone but Béranger. Hugo was still their divinity and it was the Parnassians themselves who set up their predecessors as the tetrarchy in order to pay them homage.

They were great disciples. They introduced no flashes of lightning, no new excitement. It would be regrettable if they had not existed, but, if they were missing, certainly nothing major would be missing from French poetry. Among them there were pupils of great schools, those of Leconte de Lisle, of Banville, and of Baudelaire. Many of the Parnassian poets, moreover, belonged to two or three of these schools: Coppée and Mendès worked under the influence of any tetrarch as he appeared.

That is not a criticism. First of all, it is necessary and sound that great poets should create schools. Second, the tetrarchs, themselves often pupils of Hugo or Sainte-Beuve, had inspired many other poets besides their successors. The influence of *Poèmes antiques* was not absent from *La Légende des siècles*, nor that of *Emaux et camées* from *Les Chansons des rues et des bois*. In sum, the successors of Parnassus that are remembered by posterity owe the fact to their originality, which was genuine.

It would be easy to differentiate in Parnassus among the currents of decorativeness, sired by Leconte de Lisle; of fantasy, sired by Banville; and of intimacy, sired by Baudelaire.

THE DECORATORS

Contemporaries of the period in which the favorites of the drawing rooms were great historical contrivances, themselves contributors of other great historical contrivances to the theater, the Parnassians had a keen sense of archaeological setting. Coppée and Mendès each wrote his own little *Légende des siècles* in the form of an epic narrative. Only one original form came out of all this: Hérédia's sonnets.

No form is more favorable than the sonnet to the poet in love with technical perfection. Therefore Parnassus was a great proving ground of the sonnet, of which Hérédia became the master to such a degree that after him the sonnet fell into slumber, where it has remained. This artisan of art understood the sonnet like a book binding or a suit of armor: but a splendid binding for a trite text, an armor of rhymes as empty as those of Eviradnus, under the helmet of which a (library) rat nibbles. The historical Roman, Castilian, Japanese sonnets of *Les Trophées* lived; they dazzled the cultivated from 1880 to 1900 with their novelty. Later they took on for provincial youths, in the time of Francis Jammes, the august and hollow shape of the emissaries of the state in the museums of their native towns. When the platter of the sonnet appears bearing the rhyme, which might have been Hugoesque, of *ombre* or *sombre* with *scombre*, the reasons for Hugo's scorn of the sonnet become clear. And reading Hérédia also makes it clear why the sonnet could hardly emerge from the perfect circle into which it had been sealed by Ronsard, under whose auspices Sainte-Beuve had revived it. Those sonnets of Hérédia that have remained the most beautiful, the only ones that move us beneath their perfect forms, are the Greek and Renaissance sonnets, or the simply human sonnets, those that rise simply, as a breast breathes, in four waves and end with a smile directed toward a human face, for that face alone, not like that smile for the photographer that is the scourge of the modern sonnet.

The fantasist Parnassus sired by Banville is not lacking in charm. It is an exquisite talent to be witty in verse and put wit into rhymes. If Mendès strove in vain for this gift, it was not lacking in Coppée. It was the principal heritage passed on to poor Albert Glatigny. Emile Bergerat also shared in it in his *Lyre comique*. Like Hérédia with the sonnet and Banville with the ballad, Léon Valade drank from a little glass all his own, the triolet. But the real heirs to Banville came a little after the generation of the successors: they were the delightful Gabriel Vicaire (twenty years old in 1868), who must not be shut up in his *Emaux bressans* alone, and the breveted balladeer, Laurent Tailhade (twenty years old in 1874), who spewed his flood of insult over his contemporaries out of the mouths of amazingly sculptured archaic gargoyles.

In spite of its proclamations on objective poetry, in spite of its utopian decorative aspirations, its clowns who wanted to fashion hoops to be rolled among the stars, it was in the poetry of intimacy and confession, in the footsteps of Baudelaire, that Parnassus found its way clear.

In 1868 François Coppée called his second book of verse *Intimités*. The best of Coppée is indeed in an intimate, delicate poetry, generally full of insight, not too hypocritical, the poetry of a *petit bourgeois*, of a minor employee, of a minor lover, of a minor poet. We have noted that Béranger was the only poet liquidated by Parnassus. But it liquidated him only by supplanting him. Coppée's popularity, like Béranger's, derived from the French *mystique* of the word "little," from the religious accent that invests this word when it appears in the title of a newspaper or a political speech. Furthermore, it is to the title of a Coppée book of 1872, *Les Humbles*, that political language is indebted for a word that it abuses and in which Jules Lemaître very reasonably found something hypocritical and depressing. Coppée's innumerable narratives, in the style of *La Grève des forgerons*, formed a kind of *romancero* of the little man, with virtually no originality, since it was already all in Sainte-Beuve; with the help of these tales Coppée pushed back somewhat the frontiers of imbecility. But he remained a good Parnassian, even a great Parnassian, by reason of a perfect form, of constantly renewed resources of craftsmanship in which one senses the expert hand of the Parisian artisan (he was, however, of Belgian origin). It is not with the same meaning that we should call Coppée, like Baudelaire, a poet of Paris; nevertheless the name suits him exactly.

Sully-Prudhomme is still the most substantial poet of this Parnassus by inheritance. No one, obviously, is less Baudelairean than this placid conformist, this reserved and prudent burgher, this pure rationalist. And yet he, like Baudelaire, reacted against the romantic convention. He turned inward. He was a psychological poet, a kind of Parnassian Théodore Jouffroy: precise, meticulous, timid, uneasy. The numerous verses that he dedicated to an unrequited love scarcely move us any more and they earned him only a minimal position among the love poets. But many of his verse efforts represent in their detail, their line, and their sharpness the model of psychological dry point. The poem called *La Justice* is a beautiful dialogue between the soul and itself and it contains admirable sonnets. One cannot say as much for his epic, *Le Bonheur,* his biggest endeavor and his most complete failure.

Romantic Connections

Anatole France must be counted among the Parnassian poets. *Les Poèmes dorés* is one of the good products of the school. Besides, he was long an assistant to Lemerre and it was he who in 1876 took on the task of selecting the poets to be included in the third and final *Parnasse contemporain.* And finally the ties of the librarians and the scholars, the engineers of Parnassus, with a literature of the plastic and expert novel and story should be recalled especially in connection with M. France. Between *Salammbô* on its right bank and *Thaïs* on its left, the historic river of Parnassus flows like the Rhine flanked by its castles.

But she might better be linked with some other name. Let us not forget that from 1848 to 1885—that is to say, as long as the two coveys of the tetrarchs and their successors were on the wing—Hugo was there, producing and above all publishing. The survival of romanticism imperceptibly accompanied the life of Parnassus, and to what extent can it be said that this or that writer was a Parnassian or a romantic?

Nevertheless, no one would think of including among the Parnassians Paul Déroulède, Richepin, or Clovis Hugues, who, born between 1846 and 1851, were among the twenty-year-olds of 1870 and who, perhaps under the influence of the patriotic poetry of the time, would represent a romantic, declamatory, and oratorical idealism under the Third Republic: national in Déroulède, social in Hugues. As for Richepin, who occupied a more important place and who is almost as ignored today, he was above all an eloquent and learned *normalien,* a descendant of the Latin *rhetores* and the French rhetoricians. He did indeed invent something with *La Chanson des gueux,* in which he took possession of that aspect of the romantic heritage that is called the truculent; he was a passable poet of sensuality in *Les Caresses;* and he fell flat when he sought to wear the cast-offs of a country-fair Lucrece with *Les Blasphèmes.*

If one wanted to go from all these demimasters or semidemimasters to the subdisciples, one would never come to the end of listing poets. The tetrarchs and even the successors were fathers of large families. By virtue of the attention that it directed to professional problems, by virtue of its technical integrity, to which it gave a place of honor, Parnassus contributed to making poetry, if not a craft, at least an exercise both attractive and, in sum, easy. What writer of the first thirty years of the twentieth century has not made his start with a collection of more or less Parnassian verse? In those thirty years the French made sonnets with as much facility as the Italians in another time. Minor lyricism, like pedantic tragedy in the eighteenth century, flowed full tide.

VI

FLAUBERT

The Heritage of Balzac

Flaubert was in Constantinople when he learned of Balzac's death. He was about to be thirty years old. Paris was preoccupied by the problem of inheritors of that Alexander the Great. Flaubert did not think, apparently had never thought, that he might be the heir. When he himself died thirty years later, doubt was no longer possible. But the hegemony disappeared with him. Balzac had a successor, Flaubert had none.

Flaubert's work is not a world as Balzac's is. It is not established, as *La Comédie humaine* is by its title, in a literary body, a cosmos. It runs in various directions, it attempts various experiments. If Flaubert's work, like Balzac's, had a general title, it would be Montaigne's: *Essais*. And the *Essais* of the house in Croisset *instituted* in French literature, as did those of the tower in Périgord.

A fortune and a family, a heritage and an inheritance, a strongly middle-class tranquility and independence, remote from business and marriage, in the province that was at once the most individually solid and the closest to Paris, enabled Flaubert to marry literature, to carry out his *Essais* with an abundance of deliberation and patience. These *Essais* were completed after his death in an unexpected way by two important annexes: the manuscript works of his youth and his correspondence.

In the work of his youth what is uniquely important is the autobiographical collections, which are the direct autobiography of *Mémoires d'un fou* and *Novembre* and the disguised autobiography of the first *Education sentimentale*. Written between 1840 and 1845, they show us Flaubert in command of an easy, powerful style, inspired by the romantic oratorical style; endowed with a remarkable aptitude for dramatizing, for poeticizing the most commonplace events of his life, of a life; and, in the first *Education*, possessed of an art and a humor of narrative that foreshadowed the true novelist. No one doubts that, if Flaubert had published that *Edu-*

cation and frequented the wineshops, the realistic drinkers surrounding Gustave Courbet would have accepted and supported him. But this great bourgeois, this true bourgeois was always appalled by bohemianism and "sets"; in Paris he knew only the Café Anglais, Brébant, Tortoni, and similar places; he visited Pradier's studio and not Courbet's.

La Tentation de Saint Antoine

It was his ambition to write a *Faust*, or, rather, a "Second *Faust*." Like Georges de Brébeuf's *La Pharsale* two hundred years before Flaubert, Quinet's *Ahasvérus*, published in 1833, had long been admired in the provinces; it was a compendium of history, religions, philosophies, panoramically developed with grandiloquence, myths, moving characters, the wandering Jew of the legend seeming to have been created by Providence itself as the godfather of this planetary survey. In 1845 a *Temptation of Saint Anthony* by Pieter Brueghel in a museum in Genoa suggested to Flaubert that the procession of the famous hermit's temptations, fed by a procession of readings, and become a procession of mythological, historical, philosophical, and pandemoniacal visions, would look even better. In one year of effort he easily produced a tremendous work of remarkable vigor, imagination, luxuriance, and style. Bouilhet, who had become his artistic conscience, was undoubtedly right in advising him against its publication while at the same time he pointed him toward the subject of *Madame Bovary*. But the vast *Saint Antoine* remains the finest blaze of what might be called provincial romanticism, far superior in interest to the revised extract of it that Flaubert published much later.

The Grotesque Province

From the slack and solitary springboard of the provinces, Bouilhet also pointed him toward observing the provinces, and away from provincial art toward provincial life. Bouilhet, furthermore, knew what he was doing. Flaubert was surrounded by a literary generation born in Rouen about 1820, by former schoolfellows with whom he had a common language, of whom the most important, next to Bouilhet, was Alfred Le Poittevin, uncle of Guy de Maupassant, Le Poittevin whose *Une Promenade de Bélial* was so much in tune with the works of Flaubert's youth. As children, these Flaubertians of Rouen, who are known to us through the *Correspondances*, had set up in the hospital there a theater of which Gustave was the Shakespeare and in which he produced a strong and mysterious creation, *Le Garçon*, a precursor of Alfred Jarry's *Ubu*. At that time the provinces were enthusiastic not only over *Ahasvérus* but also over *La Caricature* and *Le Charivari*, periodicals born at the same time that Henry Monnier was creating that uncle of the Garçon, Joseph Prudhomme. These publications, if they did not enter Flaubert's house, were taken at least in the homes of his friends, where he read them. They helped him to cultivate an acute sense of the grotesque, which he employed in his conversation and which Bouilhet advised him in 1849 to apply to provincial life in a novel. But this grotesque was a sad grotesque in the author of *Novembre*. And, besides, every grotesque is sad.

Madame Bovary

The triple sense for oratorical lyricism, realistic observation, and the sad grotesque, distilled through the great journey in the Orient that rejuvenated Flaubert, through habits of deliberate work, of re-examination, of erasures, of casuistics of style which abruptly supplanted the forceful facility of *Saint Antoine*—all this was at the origin of *Madame Bovary*, which Flaubert took five years to write; an official transcript, a journal, sometimes daily, of part of that work is provided for us in his invaluable letters to Louise Colet.

Madame Bovary was prosecuted by the imperial government. But Dupanloup called it a "masterpiece for those who have gone to confession in the provinces," and so it was too for those who had not confessed, since it can be called the most celebrated French novel. Nor has any other become a landmark, and that for various reasons.

The novel is women; it is written usually for them, often about them, sometimes by them. They were Balzac's major audience. In Emma Bovary Flaubert created the type of the Frenchwoman who was closest to the Frenchwoman who read novels.

The novel in France is the provinces. The life of the provinces. France contains not only Brittany, Provence, Béarn, etc. There is one province, one and indivisible, the French province. Flaubert established the synthetic image of it in *Madame Bovary*.

Every man meets Madame Bovary many times in his life. Every pretty woman meets Léons and Rodolphes. These characters are multiplied by the reality around us as by a hall of mirrors, and yet it is within fictional life that the character remains of whom the novel that is life seems to present only reflections. There is a level on which the novel dominates the official registers: general agreement has recognized this level in *Madame Bovary*.

The province is politics. Flaubert is the sole French writer who, in

Homais, created a political type, who created him with intuition as Balzac had described in advance the society of the Second Empire. Of the pharmacist Homais, scientist, anti-clerical, intelligent in his job, limited in his ideas, one may say: *vires acquirit eundo*. He was a generation early: the France of the Third Republic, turned radical, made Homais the "left" type, who, attuned to a literary masterpiece, balances the "right" types of Tartuffe and Basile.

The importance of *Madame Bovary* can be compared with that of *Le Cid* and *Les Méditations* in this sense—that, just as Corneille raised the tragedy confected by Alexandre Hardy to the highest literary level and Lamartine did the same thing for the classic elegy that overflowed from the eighteenth century, so Flaubert lifted to the level of style that realism that the school of Henry Monnier and Champfleury (Jules Husson) cultivated not only without style but against style. First of all, style in characters: Emma Bovary is Champfleury's provincial woman plus a style; Homais is Monnier's Prudhomme plus a style. Next, style in writing. In the pains that Flaubert devoted to image, to harmony, to the sentence, to esthetic detail, he reacted maximally against the tendency to facility of reproduction that became part of realism, that led the self-educated and the populists into it; he placed himself at the opposite pole from Restif de Bretonne and Champfleury, and that opposition became part of the very geography of the novel.

Salammbô

Leonardo and Valéry cast out "the rubbish of no one knows what great undertakings." Flaubert abandoned the successes of successive enterprises carried to their conclusions; he was the man of rational experiments. *Madame Bovary* was succeeded by an "experiment" in pure historical background, the Carthaginian evocation of *Salammbô*. *Salammbô* is a flight to Carthage; Flaubert's own flight from his time, from modernity, from himself; a flight from the subject, which led him to a paradoxical determination on a pure style. This pure style created a school for a half century, it aroused the enthusiasm of the mandarins, it was their *Conciones*. From the beginning of the twentieth century it began to age, to ring hollow, and *Salammbô*, wrongly, has become unreadable for some in later generations. But, first of all, the place that it occupies should inspire respect. Second, it is not pure style to such a degree that it does not include an excellent picture of the Oriental woman, of the African, even the Carthaginian, character; the archaeological setting is a fabrication but the political life is believably imagined, guessed, portrayed.

L'Education sentimentale

Flaubert's third novel, *L'Education sentimentale*, was a complete failure with the public and the critics of the last months of the Empire. Even as late as 1935, university criticism as a whole spoke of it almost unanimously as Flaubert's mistake, the paradox of realism, a picture of wasted lives in a wasted work. Novelists, on the other hand, held it in great regard; its influence on naturalism was profound; today a whole section of literary opinion views it as Flaubert's masterpiece, ranking it above *Madame Bovary*. Roughly, this latter view is the correct one.

It was the book that, even more than *Madame Bovary*, required the genius of realism. The principle is that of Henri Murger and Champfleury: take as the subject the author and his friends; thus, with Courbet, *L'Atelier du peintre* came after that *Enterrement d'Ornans* that is *Madame Bovary* (let us risk the grimace that Flaubert would make at this comparison). But what transformations, what stylizations! First of all, if Flaubert used in Frédéric Moreau his own life, his personal experience, his love for Mme. Schlesinger, he was careful not to make his hero a writer like himself; he took him away from literary mechanisms to offer him to pure, ordinary, average human experience, to the "just like the rest of us" on which every visionary, however great, always falls back in the end. Second, from the group of the painter's studio (all the characters in *L'Education*, Maxime du Camp said, really existed), the painter creates the group of the painter's generation, which was twenty to thirty years old in 1848, a generation in bankruptcy, it thought, in the Revolution and the *coup d'état*. Flaubert's great novel thus became a document in the manner of Balzac. Finally, the character of Marie Arnoux, in whom Flaubert immortalized the only prolonged passion of his life, is very rightly considered one of the purest and most perfect portraits of women in fiction. But around her, around Frédéric, there are at least a dozen characters portrayed with unmatched technique, sureness, and success.

Thus *L'Atelier du peintre* deserved to become the painter's school, the school of the most important area of the novel between 1870 and 1900. Undoubtedly the author of *L'Education* himself owed something to the Goncourts, who, beginning in 1860, had stylized the realistic novel. But the Goncourts had everything that was necessary to make their school dangerous, Flaubert everything that was necessary to make his beneficial. The style itself moved down a step toward simplicity and reality. He virtually abandoned that music, those oratorical cadences, that contributed to the aging of *Madame Bovary* and *Salammbô*. He achieved a perfect balance between a rigid style and a flowing style.

Indeed, the lack of success of *L'Education* added to its worth and its influence. There was a school of the conformist novel, and a very distinguished school it was, that of Octave Feuillet and *La Revue des deux mondes*, which flattered the reader and especially the woman reader, which aimed for the consensus of writer and public, of novelist and subscriber. But art progresses only through disharmonies. The last page of *L'Education*, which evoked outcries for thirty years, inflicts a healthy discomfort on the reader, sustains the atmosphere of the novel in a nonconformism. And what it says is true: desires are often what is best in a whole life. Through his *Correspondances* we know Flaubert well enough to understand that this was his own case, and it is as good as any other.

Bouvard et Pécuchet

The misunderstanding that existed—not between the critics and the author, since this was a posthumous book—but between the readers and the literary heirs of Flaubert was aggravated by *Bouvard et Pécuchet*. Like *La Vie de rance*, *La Chute d'un ange*, *Dieu*, *Bouvard* is that limited work that an author is called on to produce by an exigent destiny, for himself, almost against the public, and that the public will long regard as a mistake. Flaubert had always thought that it was his mission to write the book of human stupidity. He had an awareness of stupidity to an exceptional degree, as one has an awareness of color, of wines, or of women. He recognized it everywhere, marveled at it everywhere. He had composed a summary index of it in 1847 in the *Dictionnaire des idées reçues*, a collection of middle-class stupidites of which he said: "Anyone who has read it must be afraid thereafter to open his mouth lest he say something that is in it." *Bouvard et Pécuchet* was the moving, living dictionary, the story of two retired office clerks on a voyage of discovery—discovery of science, the arts, life. And hence a dictionary of human ignorance and stupidity on parade before these two reviewing-stand cronies as the dictionary of ancient religions and philosophies paraded past the hermit in *Saint Antoine*. The ancient parade is decorative and magnificent because it is distant, the modern parade is grotesque because it is seen close and because Flaubert takes pride in resembling Saint Polycarp (his birthday was on the saint's day), of whom it is written that it was his custom to break into flight crying: "O God, into what century have you thrust me to live?"

His plan was not perfectly clear, and in addition the novel was not finished. Roughly, it may be said that he wanted to provide a synthesis and a summary of everything that is automatic and grotesque in the intelligence and the life of the average middle-class person, the man in the street, the conformist in society. As naturalism was to make the novel consist principally in the portrayal of a mediocrity of caricature, it is understandable that *Bouvard et Pécuchet* served as a Bible to a naturalist group in which it was known by heart. There is something of an inside joke in it, a posthumous return by Flaubert to the theater of his childhood. "I am turning into an old fool, a sheik," he often wrote; he did so as a great man of letters.

The case of this book is not the same as that of *L'Education*. Nice people have the right to remain stony in the face of *Bouvard*, to refuse to follow Flaubert in his dark design. As a novel the book does not exist. Its characters have one dimension less than those of *Madame Bovary:* a visible loss in a Euclidean space.

Trois Contes

Two of the *Trois Contes* can rank as perfection itself: *Un Coeur simple,* the story of an old servant, taken from the Flaubert family chronicle, and *La Légende de Saint Julien l'Hospitalier,* inspired by a Norman stained-glass window, itself artistry in stained glass, perhaps the most exquisite apex of the style, or, rather, the styles, of Flaubert (this is all the more extraordinary because the *Trois Contes* were written easily, without any of the famous agonies). There is more bric-à-brac in *Hérodias,* in which Flaubert took the death of John the Baptist as the pretext for a picture of Judea in the first century.

Les Correspondances

The first *Tentation* and the *Voyage d'Orient* divide Flaubert's literature into two opposing parts: on the one hand, a literature of youth and personal confession, of romantic and romanticized autobiography, which remained in the author's files; and then, when he returned from the Orient, a rigorously impersonal literature, the writing of *Madame Bovary* having served for Flaubert as a depersonalization treatment at the same time that it was a detoxication for his romanticism and a treatment against facility in writing and the euphoria of producing. This does not mean that the author of the second *Education* is not in his book. But, when he wrote the first line of the story of Delamarre, of Charbovary and his cap, he closed the door of Croisset on the author who said "I." Thrust out at the door, "I" came back after his death through all the windows. This is *Les Correspondances.*

It may be called the most important correspondence of any man of letters of the nineteenth century. It shows us all the undersides of Flaubert's work. And it also shows us one of his new styles, the style in a state of freedom, sentences in the schoolyard abruptly following sentences in the classroom, the flood of ideas, of images, of absurdities, of clownishness, of obscenities, the sap of the province, the Norman vintage. The novel of Flaubert and the Goncourts, supported by those vast substructures that are the *Correspondances* of the one and the *Journal* of the others, shows us and explains to us with great clarity, and in a manner that is not to be found elsewhere, the bond between the novel and life.

Once published, *Les Correspondances* contributed importantly to keeping Flaubert in the first rank, to delaying or softening the inevitable reactions that arose against his art and his influence. It gave the artist the extension of the man. André Gide said that for years it was his bedside book. It should be kept as a breviary of literary honor.

TAINE

Top of the List

In the last thirty years of the nineteenth century the four syllables "Taine-et-Renan" had the same indivisible sound in the language of letters as Tarn-et-Garonne in ordinary speech. They were the names of the two masters, associated and complementary, of a generation, the name of a scholarly magistracy. The function that had been fulfilled in the romantic generation by the great poets, the Lamartines and the Hugos, was served by these two encyclopedic minds—critics, historians, and philosophers—both the supreme fruits of the two great French clerical families, the ecclesiastical training and the university formation, Saint-Sulpice and the University. In addition, though they were as opposite as Montaigne and Pascal, as liquid and solid, whatever might have been excessive and dangerous in the domination of one of them was tempered and brought into balance by their coexistence.

Of the two minds, the more subtle was Renan's, the more solid and better furnished was Taine's. Vigorous, organized, centered, Taine can be viewed as the greatest Scholar (to use the English word) of the nineteenth century. At the top of his class when he entered the Ecole Normale —the *cacique* was the students' term for it—he remained the *cacique* of French university training in the same way in which Hugo would be the *cacique* of poetry and Bossuet the *cacique* of the episcopate. With extraordinary method and facility, he plunged himself into all the disciplines in the Ecole Normale and emerged from it at the age of twenty-two as philosopher, critic, historian, at large. Among all these disciplines he chose the greatest: he chose to be a philosopher.

The Philospher

In philosophy there was a generation, Cousin's, to be overthrown and replaced. Against it, from his school years, Taine had found and revived the spirit of Condillac, of the eighteenth century, of the ideologists, the spirit of the generation of Stendhal; as a result of this he failed the examination for admission to teach philosophy, his thesis on *Sensations* was rejected, and he was subjected to scholarly persecutions. His persecutors contributed to the endowment of his first book of philosophy, *Les Philosophes français du XIX* siècle, with the youthful, lively, and mordant tone of a pamphlet.

It is one of the rare living literary books, pleasant to reread, in French philosophy, and in it one senses the companion of About and Prévost-Paradol, of Sarcey and Weiss. A spirit worthy of the eighteenth century was utilized to call attention to a philosophy of the eighteenth century, that of the ideologists. *Les Philosophes* begins with a charming portrait of Laromiguière, the conclusion of which contains in embryo the theory of the *ancien régime* on the classic spirit. "It has been said that the function of the French spirit is to clarify, to develop, to publish general truths. . . . If this is the case, ideology is our classic philosophy; it has the same scope and the same limits as our literary talent; it is the theory of which our literature was the execution."

This classic philosophy that Taine intended to assimilate was analysis. Analysis of words, which consists ("every abstract is an extract") in always translating words into things in order not to be their victim, Cousin's verbalism acting here, for young critical minds, as a drunken slave. Analysis of things—that is, transformation of "the large masses of objects that are perceived by common experience into a particularized and detailed catalogue of facts that are every day more broken down, more numerous."

But at the same time that he intended to assimilate this philosophy, he knew and felt in the mighty European experience of the nineteenth century what would enable him to go beyond it—to go beyond the spirit of analysis by completing it with the spirit of synthesis (this is the theme of the last chapter, the dialogue between M. Pierre and M. Paul); to go beyond French ideology by way of English associationism, that of the John Stuart Mills and the Alexander Bains, and, beginning in 1857, this contributed to giving Taine's thought its Anglo-French aspect; to go beyond attention to detail and the spirit of exactitude, which analysis teaches, by way of the spirit of the great Hegelian syntheses, which he read at great length in the original during a whole year of provincial solitude; finally, to go beyond the limpid and transparent style of the eighteenth century, the elegant delicacy of Laromiguière, by means of enthusiasm, oratory, and color: *in philosophia orator.*

Like Cousin, after all, whom he thus rejoined at the end of a long divagation, and of whom, like all his generation, like Renan himself, he admired only the style. For us today the stylist in Cousin has vanished, as the philosopher had vanished for Taine, and there remains only a remarkable and very living character out of a comedy. But there is another point on which Taine might almost be paired with Cousin. This is his lack of understanding of the inner life as principle and source of philosophy. *Les Philosophes* begins with an execution of Maine de Biran, treated as a simple visionary. Taine had no idea of the importance of Maine de Biran's influence in the philosophy of the nineteenth century. He had never given the word *philosopher* its deepest meaning, which is Biranian. One of his disciples, Paul Bourget, wrote, and specifically in connection with Taine: "The various translations, whether laudatory or hostile, that have been given to the word *philosopher* amount to this: a philosophic mind is one that forms ideas of things as a whole; that is, ideas that no longer represent this or that isolated fact but rather whole series of facts, entire groups of objects." A most Tainesque definition! A philosopher is a man for whom the inner world exists, for whom the outer world is to be explained only as a reference to the inner world. Taine's philosophy collapses, like Cousin's, for lack of that solid within. The reaction against Taine was to be a reaction of the within, a Biranian reaction.

Although the whole of Taine's philosophy is already recognizable in the conclusion of this book of 1857, *Les Philosophes français* is only a polemical introduction to the great work on which he labored for ten years, *L'Intelligence* (1870), and which was foreshadowed in his study *Stuart Mill, le positivisme anglais,* from which he derived much more than from French positivism. *L'Intelligence* is Mill rethought by a Cartesian mind. For Taine it was a matter of seeking the elements of knowledge, which are signs—that is, extracts, or real abstracts; of going, on the one hand, to experimenters and physicians for knowledge of their physiological conditions, and of pursuing, on the other hand, their reconstitution in ideas and laws until the entire mechanism of intelligence appeared and the law was formulated to which the others were subordinate: the conservation of energy, real identity, the eternal axiom.

L'Intelligence (which Taine was intending to follow with *La Volonté* when the war of 1870 and the Commune turned him to history) had great consequences. It marked a revolution not in philosophy but in psychology. It gave a whole generation, from 1872 to 1900, an interest in experimental psychology. This captivating abundance of argument, this constant and facile (too facile) illumination, these well-chosen and well-brought-out little details, these examples and anecdotes of the world of dreams and hallucinations, even the smell of sulfur around a book rebuked by the spiritualism of the pulpit—all this seduced the imaginations of the young philosophers, sent them into the clinics and the laboratories, gave them the impulse through which they went beyond this illustrious book, outmoded today, this bridge that collapsed once the troops had crossed it.

The Critic

Not only had Taine got this philosophy and this psychology under way at the age of forty-two (1870), the philosopher had also become one of the masters of literary criticism, designated by Sainte-Beuve as his successor, the man of whom he was thinking always and only when he spoke of "the young criticism." The three volumes of *Essais* are filled with force and suggestiveness, and the articles on Saint-Simon and Balzac were events. *La Fontaine et ses Fables* can rank as the most living and colorful illustration of the philosophical determinism that governed Taine's criticism. But in the great *Histoire de la littérature anglaise* this determinism and this mechanicalness often turned empty; literary taste, difficult to acquire when one is dealing with a foreign language, was lacking and was too often replaced by harangues and especially by theories: "My general idea," he said of this book, "was this: to write generalities and to particularize them through great men, to disregard the small fry. The purpose was to arrive at a general definition of the English mind."

This brings us to Taine's habits and limitations as a critic and historian of literature. His adviser in the Ecole Normale, Etienne Vacherot, judged him thus at the age of twenty: "Understands, conceives, judges, and formulates too quickly. Too fond of phrases and definitions, to which he too often sacrifices reality without the faintest idea that he is doing so, for he is completely honest."

Formulas and definitions are to Taine's criticism what crinolines were to the gowns of his time. Their artifices soon went out of style. For a long time writing about Taine as a critic meant forgetting all that was new and powerful in his best pages, all that revealed a remarkable genius for interpretation, and discussing only the skeleton of this interpretation, his two theories, the two formulas, which were, first, the determinism of race, environment, and time, and, second, the definition of a writer or an artist by his major faculty. The first theory is an arbitrary and ingenuous contravention of didactic philosophy in the realm of sentiment, taste, plurality, and complexity. As for the procedure that consists in focusing a writer or a work on a major faculty, it is related to the same passion for "definitions," assisted in addition by the recollection of Balzac, that read-

ily creates a character like Grandet or Hulot around a major characteristic or a single passion.

The Artist

But with the *Voyage aux Pyrénées* an artist had come to light in Taine.
Until this time sensations had meant nothing to him but the subject for a
thesis in the spirit of Condillac. As he entered his forties, they made some
inroad into his life with their brilliance and their flower, and much more
inroad into his style, which was amply and felicitously fed on images.
His sylvan childhood in the Ardennes was given back to the Parisian professor, and he exchanged the drawing pencil for the painter's palette. In
1862 he wrote: "When I look at myself as a whole, it seems to me that
my state of mind has changed, that I have destroyed in myself the talent
of the orator and the rhetorician. My ideas no longer form ranks as they
used to do; I have flashes, intense sensations, impulses, words, images—in
short, my state of mind is much more that of the artist than that of the
writer." It was true. Taine's experience as an artist represents the opposite of the prematurely dead poet survived by the man. It is the story of
the artist in his prime, momentarily obscured by the school and emerging
again after the school, beneath the school.

This artist, however, is to be found only quite rarely (except for the
admirable pages on Rubens and Rembrandt) in *La Philosophie de l'art*,
which is his only professorial book, the text of a few lessons given at the
Ecole des Beaux-Arts, where he taught esthetics and the history of art
for twenty years. Here Taine appears as a real and even a great professor.
The audience that listens to him is made to perform a movement opposite
to his own, the opposite of the movement of the *normalien*. To artists
who know what the world of art is, or who learn it in the studio, he re-
veals another world, that of general ideas. Within the framework of
these general ideas he parades the ranks of picturesque minor details with
order and discipline. Speaking in the great semicircular auditorium beneath the fresco of Paul Delaroche, he carried its rhythm over into his
lectures, he made his podium one of the typical places of French history.
Nowhere else does the theory of race, environment, and time seem more
inoperative and oratorical than in this *Philosophie de l'art*, a simple men-
tal exercise that classifies facts. Those who heard it and read it were
plunged into a healthful bath of general ideas, but for them there could
be no question of living in those frigid waters.

The luck of a friendship, that of Planat, the founder of *La Vie parisienne*, served the artist far better by inspiring in him that picture of the
customs of the Second Empire, *Thomas Graindorge*. Obviously Graindorge has aged because of his oratorical content. But, since the society

that he represents has undergone the same aging, since in addition this is the book in which Taine, so reticent and fearful when it came to revealing himself, put the most of himself, *Graindorge* retains an attraction. It became the peak of the Stendhalian Taine, the Taine with little or no system, the Taine of small pure facts—of the *Carnets de voyage*, of the *Notes sur l'Angleterre*, those well-written books that flowed from the pen of a genuine traveler who traveled, and far superior to the *Voyage en Italie*, which is too gorged, too much the professional journey undertaken to refresh the store of general ideas. All of Taine the artist is found again in his solid, brilliant, and valuable *Correspondance*, much more alive than Renan's and, with Flaubert's, the best literary correspondence of his time.

The Historian

But Taine's greatest work of art is his historical work. In *Les Origines de la France contemporaine* he erected one of the greatest monuments, at once oratorical, evocative, and dialectical, that has ever existed in French literature. A historical monument? That is something else.

When the defeat of 1871 and the Commune led him to attempt a historical diagnosis of the illness of France, which frightened him, Taine was not entering a new realm of study; for twenty years, apart from *L'Intelligence*, he had written hardly anything but books of history. The year before the war, in fact, he had been a candidate for the chair of history in the Ecole Normale, in competition with Fustel de Coulanges. The five volumes of *Les Origines de la France contemporaine* in no way broke with his usual concerns and his earlier studies. But he made use of documents that he had examined little or not at all until then, those of the archives; he gave his work a civic compass and function; he exerted an influence on new circles.

His uncountable collection of small details, brought together in support of directives and general ideas that were not absolutely preconceived but that had taken shape very quickly in his mind, soon became a file constructed to uphold a thesis, a thesis that was not itself a thesis for anyone, that was a thesis against, that of a severe and sorrowful physician for whom health had never been visible in the face of France except in a precarious condition that augured nothing good. None of the ideas that were contending for supremacy in France in 1875—legitimism, Napoleonism, republicanism—escaped his terrible diagnosis. The *ancien régime*, the Revolution, Napoleon became three artisans of the same disintegration, three precursors of what Barrès, a disciple of Taine, was to call a disassociated and decerebrated France. In the end the reader told himself that, while everything was going badly now, M. Taine offered some ground for consolation by showing us that everything had always gone very badly and that people had survived just the same, even survived well. *Les Origines* is the book of a great pessimist who resembles that historian for whom the decay of Rome began with the assassination of Remus by his brother. But it is also the book of a great bourgeois, a great orator, and a great classic.

Embarked or re-embarked on middle-class life through his marriage, he had pledged to the middle class the loyalty, though somber, of the convert. Here he must be likened to Guizot, from whom everything separated him as far as the style of thinking was concerned but who was his master in everything that concerned the style of living. He had learned in the Guizots' home, he said, what a family was, a middle-class family, an English-style family. For Taine as for Guizot there existed a political nature, the political nature that he found with the Guizots, that France had not brought off and that England had. All the characteristics peculiar to France, whether they were monarchist, Napoleonic, or republican, were struck down with the same verdict of doom insofar as they differed from those of the neighboring island, were thrust aside by the monotonous but strong recurrence of a sorrowful contempt.

This great book in defense of the middle class is a class book in the social sense, but it is also a book of great class in the literary sense and most certainly Taine's literary masterpiece; more generally, the greatest monument of oratorical continuity since Livy—*molus animi continui*. Elsewhere the profound artist that Taine is might have been restricted or out of his element as a result of his subject. Here he had free rein, like Michelet.

And this book of great rank brings together in a supreme pyrotechnical display all the resources and all the power of the classic genius. Never more classic than in that theory of the classic spirit, which, located in the heart of the *ancien régime*, has remained the most famous, the most discussed, the most suggestive of Taine's ideas. It is clear that here he was doing battle with himself, that the artist bore his schoolroom culture with bad conscience and observed it with distrust, that he never falls more wholly into the circle of the classic spirit and culture in their rational, constructive and oratorical form than when he imagines that he is fleeing them. In *Les Origines* he found the subject that best suited a classic artist's genius: portraits to be made, or, rather, constructed. His portraits of the philosophers of the eighteenth century, of the men of the Revolution, and of Napoleon are astonishing structures, undoubtedly the only pages that show us what Balzac could have done if he had been cast in the classic mold of the Latins and the eighteenth century: ideas to be filled in, a discourse to be developed, and, to give this discourse warmth, a passion that merged the political passion and the personal passion of the bourgeois, almost of the landowner: an incomparable source of life!

It is chiefly through the tremendous influence of *Les Origines* that Taine's presence continues. He furnished a conscience, an ideology, images to all the parties of the right. Barrès and Maurras come in part from *Les Origines de la France contemporaine*. For a half century this work never stopped finding an audience; it is the great book of French reaction. In contrast to the philosophical historian, the pure philosopher has lost his force, the literary historian has been surpassed, the critic's theories have aged. But, looked at again in the history of ideas, Taine holds a high place: a place even in the urban sense of the word, crossroads, landmark, open spaces, porticoes of general ideas, monumental staircases among the various disciplines.

RENAN

A Crossroads of the Nineteenth Century

One of the best critics of this period, Pierre Lasserre, had decided to dedicate the last part of his life to a *Port-Royal*—that is, to a great strong work, central and cyclical, like that so appropriately made by Sainte-Beuve the backbone of his total work. To this end Lasserre had begun a vast *Renan*, which death prevented him from pursuing. He was right. In his own person, Renan stood like Port-Royal in the middle of a century as the embodiment of a complex world in which the roads of that century crossed, in which the revolutions of science, morality, politics, religion took on an expression, a literary resonance; were made palpable, current, popular; created a style. As in Port-Royal, all this took place in a world at once clerical and lay, in which the drama not only of religious ideas but of religious conditions was enacted. As in Port-Royal, the great spiritual and literary interests that had come together were sustained in a human temperature by an intimate literature of correspondence, of memoirs, almost of confessions, the extreme flood and ebb of the tide that had begun with Saint Augustine.

THE BRETON CLERK

To be honest, this *Port-Royal* of the nineteenth century must be enlarged somewhat in time. At the center of Port-Royal there had been an Auvergnat mountain, the two Auvergnat families, the Arnaulds and the Pascals. In similar fashion, the corresponding mountain of the nineteenth century would be a Breton mountain: Chateaubriand, Lamennais, Renan, who constituted the Christian drama after the Revolution as Port-Royal had been the Christian drama of the old order.

Renan had been naturally, delicately, shaped, almost laid down, by one of the purest religious districts in the world, Trégorrois, with its chapels, its private cults, its sacred fountains, its Breton saints unknown to Rome, among whom there is a Saint Renan, and that clerical capital that is Tréguier, peopled by good priests ("I have never known other than good priests," Renan said, perhaps with a satisfied glance at the mirror that showed him one). A stroke of chance, watched for or contrived by the solicitous affection of his sister, Henriette, enabled this future priest of Tréguier to go, at the age of fifteen, in 1838, to the Parisian seminary that was directed by the great stimulator, Dupanloup, and then to Saint-Sulpice. It was then that philology and the criticism of Biblical texts took him away from the Church. From 1845 to 1848 three turntables revolved in the young Breton's mind, and their movements coincided with the major movements of the century.

THE PHILOLOGICAL CLERK

The first was a movement synchronized with a contemporary German movement: philology, which came out of the specialist's library to become an educational discipline, a criterion for truth and falsity, a vocation of integrity and intellectual conscience, a *criticism*. Sainte-Beuve's criticism had been shaped by humanism. Renan's, which went as far in other moral domains, was shaped by philology. Taine, for his part, set up a criticism based on philosophy. Here we are in the midst of a revolution not of taste but of the critical spirit.

THE LAY CLERK

Then came a transformation, a secularization of the clergy. Renan had called his mind a secularized cathedral. Habits learned in the Church, a life of the spirit become a mission, a broadened, strengthened, activated service of God, as the conception of God, furthermore, had become in Renan, the words and the ideas of a millenary religion filling out, refreshing, poeticizing a modern Voltairean criticism, a ductile religion that became as with Plato a myth in the artist's hands, Christianity put into contact with science as Chateaubriand had put it into contact with poetry or Lamennais with the Revolution—these were the changes that Renan brought about in the atmosphere of the nineteenth century and that earned him a whole posterity under the Third Republic.

THE CLERK OF SCIENCE

Finally, with Taine and Marcelin Berthelot, he represented a generation that had believed in the full power, the full beneficence, and the full future of science. A skeptic and a master of skepticism, but of a full —that is, a living—skepticism, like Montaigne (his maternal ancestors came from Bordeaux), he was only the more loyally bound to positive science; he transferred to it a part of the absolute faith of the priests of Tréguier.

The Experience of a Life

This important youth of Renan's, this starting point of a man and a generation are known to us through a whole experience that he recorded: his letters to his family, especially those to his sister; his diaries of thoughts and readings; his private writings, among which there was even an autobiographical novel, *Patrice;* the huge work into which, in 1848, he cast his youthful experience and his new faith, *L'Avenir de la science,* all long left in manuscript and published only in his last years and after his death. The *Souvenirs d'enfance et de jeunesse,* completed by the *Feuilles détachées,* were belatedly organized into a splendid literary work, perhaps a masterpiece of the literature of memoirs in France, the image of this life in its general landscape, in its clerical idea, in a slightly smug self-satisfaction, and in a *nunc dimittis* that in sum is only what follows a successful career, modest but fulfilled vows, a happy journey on earth among devoted people and the colleagues of the Institut. This canonical career has all the outer forms of the clerical life. But Renan made it expressly clear that the Christian nucleus had dissolved for him when he wrote: "Sin? Good Lord, I think I am eliminating it."

History

Renan, a reasonably sure philologist, not overly adventurous, without genius, had a healthy, delicate, subtle idea of science, of the precision instruments that it includes. Now, he remarkably exceeded this idea in his great historical works, in that *Histoire des origines du christianisme* and that *Histoire du peuple d'Israël* that were to remain as his monuments and whose fate has not conformed to either his own expectations or the high evaluation of his contemporaries.

Renan wrote in 1848: "The most important book of the nineteenth century should be called *Histoire critique des origines du christianisme.*" When he began it, he was right in eliminating the essential word, which is "critical," and which, on *La Vie de Jésus,* would have seemed an irony.

No critical work would have enjoyed in 1863 the lightning-like worldwide success of *La Vie de Jésus,* which in six months sold more copies at seven francs than, five years before, *Madame Bovary* had sold at only two francs: sixty thousand.

It was the most popular of Renan's books, and the only popular one. In the domain of timeliness and success it can be compared in its century only with M. de Barante's *Histoire des ducs de Bourgogne* and the *Histoire des Girondins*. It was extracted from the Gospels by a skilled artist as the *Histoire des ducs* had been from Froissart, Chastellain, Monstrelet, and Commines. It resembled the *Girondins* in its store of gold, its azure, its ornamentation, its orientation toward the feminine public (it must not be forgotten that the only two imaginative authors who had any influence on Renan's youth were Lamartine and George Sand). But in addition Renan was a philologist, a Hebraicist, and represented the science of the Institut and the Collège de France with the same authority as Etienne-Marc Quatremère and Jean-Louis Burnouf. His duties gave him the keys to German exegesis, which was discussed in those days without being known and of which virtually nothing had yet reached the great public. And now this famous German exegesis was suddenly flooding in through the bright window of a fresh mind that, moreover, had gone to study on the spot, in an official capacity, the geography of the Gospels, as M. Taine had taken the train to Champagne and described its chalky landscape in order to understand and make others understand *Le Meunier, son fils, et l'ane*. Besides, this was no longer a matter of the negative criticism of the eighteenth century but of a positive life of Jesus. It showed how things might have happened on a human level. It did so in a spirit and for minds that were to convert it into the way in which things very probably had happened, in which "a professor at the Collège de France said" that they had happened—that is, into a rationalist gospel by a member of the Institut, who substituted himself, as was fitting in the century of illuminations, for the credulous gospels attributed to mythical characters. Christianity and its founder were secularized with honor by a great Orléanist mind in an operation analogous to that of 1830, and the last page of *La Vie de Jésus* virtually formulated the postulate of a quasi-divinity as there had been quasi-legitimacy. Immediately translated into many languages, this fifth gospel penetrated everywhere on the heels of the four others: no literary event more suddenly became a world event.

And yet, whatever its popular audience, whatever the influence in depth of the cheap reprint issued in hundreds of thousands of copies by Michel Lévy, the enlightened public on all sides showed an astonished reserve in its greeting to the book of which everyone was talking and that set off as many thousands of family and household battles as the first translations of the Bible had ignited in the sixteenth century.

Although on 24 June 1863, the date of its publication, Sainte-Beuve devoted an enthusiastic, somewhat puffing paragraph to it in *Le Constitutionnel*, it was only two and a half months later that he made it the subject of a *Lundi*, much more reserved and singularly accurate in its foresight. Three friends—or, as Renan was to say, three lobes of his brain

—went to visit the critic and told him their opinions under the guise of asking for his. The first was a Catholic, who was not too unhappy, for he declared that "the first effect of this book will be to strengthen and redouble the faith of believers." The second was a skeptic, who found that this Jesus who was no longer God and who was other and more than man had nothing in common with historical, moral, or human reality; the third simply did not like to see such questions raised, was impressed only by what "time has assembled and accumulated round these ancient and ageless establishments," and saw the book as a sin against historical time.

Renan's most famous book has become his most outmoded and unreadable. This is not the case with the volumes of *Les Origines* that followed *La Vie de Jésus* and in which Renan was no longer face to face with a single book to be paraphrased and fictionalized, but rather face to face with the Roman world in which Christianity was preached, that he knew through long voyages and of which, especially in *Saint-Paul* and *Marc-Aurèle*, he provided a lively and suggestive picture. But his documentation has aged too much to be able to delude us today; his psychology of the Apostles, and especially of Saint Paul, seems to us arbitrary and brittle. The once-famous psychology of Nero in *L'Antéchrist* has become for the modern reader as literary a fantasy as Renan's Christ. His Marcus Aurelius, who is the traditional Marcus Aurelius, remains solid and splendid nevertheless, and this final volumes of *Les Origines* undoubtedly will long seem the summit of Renan's historical work.

L'Histoire de peuple d'Israël is less celebrated and less read, perhaps wrongly. For twenty years Renan was at the center, almost was the center, of Semitic studies in France; his knowledge of the literary and epigraphic texts was unmatched, and his intuition of the psychology of the Semite was very sure. He understood the men and things of the Old Testament and brought them to life with novelty and genius, while the New Testament and the Gospels crushed and surpassed that literary intelligence devoid of *mystique*.

Greatness and Failure of Criticism

In Renan philological criticism and intelligence, both strong and healthy, appear to have done their work separately. The arduous searching out of texts, the study and knowledge of them were irreproachable in him. He assembled and possessed all the materials necessary for a critical history. But this critical history, this history dealing with the accessible part of reality, was always overshot by him with a history of the possible, a picture of the probable, an imaginary reconstruction. For him, according to his own admission, it was a matter of saying: "Here are one or two ways in which it is conceivable that the thing happened." Unfortunately, things have never happened as one might conceive that they could have happened, and between the first and the second of these possibilities it is usually a third one that reality has chosen.

Montaigne's Part

Nevertheless there remain a considerable and living work and presence of the author of the *Dialogues philosophiques*. The parts of Renan's work that were most famous in his lifetime, *La Vie de Jésus* and the two pages of *La Prière sur l'Acropole*, have lost their light. But they lost it only after a tremendous brilliance. What subsists of Renan, what, though it has no strong influence, still deserves consideration, is his function as a protagonist, his almost Socratic function, at the center of the great dialogues of the nineteenth century, which are still in part the dialogues of the twentieth: dialogue on God, dialogue on religion, dialogue on science, dialogue on the future of mankind, dialogue on capital and culture. On all these points he comported and maintained himself like a modern Montaigne, opening breaches, posing problems, feeding their imponderable drive with gray matter, giving them the vehicle of the lightest, the most diaphanous, the most familiar style, the closest to moving thought that has been written in French since the *Essais*.

Literary Style and Style of Life

It is notable that this justly famous style of Renan's was a belated style, that he discovered it only on the threshold of his fortieth year, that his fluidity and his simplicity emerged only after long treks through dense, heavy country. There are three styles in Renan. The first is his scholarly-review and Institut style, which for a long time was sluggish and colorless. The second is his studied, Saint-Sulpice style in *La Vie de Jésus*, written with enthusiasm in Syria in one of those "masked balls of the imagination" that Flaubert distrusted and that can no longer be borne. But it seems that, like Flaubert's in his first *Tentation*, Renan's style had sown its wild oats in *La Vie de Jésus*. Beginning with *Les Apôtres*, there appeared a historical style of unequaled limpidity, which found all its transparency and its belated youth in *Marc-Aurèle*. The *Dialogues philosophiques* created a style of thought, the *Souvenirs d'enfance et de jeunesse* a narrative style, both of which, and especially the latter, will always rank among the most exquisite discoveries of the French speech.

Two of the *Drames philosophiques, Caliban* and *Le Prêtre de Némi,* reveal in Renan an animator of ideas, a platonic creator of myths. *Caliban,* a political sequel to Shakespeare's *Tempest* as *Télémaque* is a political sequel to the *Odyssey,* remains perhaps the masterpiece of "marginal" literature, and the symbol drawn by Renan from *The Tempest*—Caliban as the people and Prospero as the aristocracy—is linked to the mythology of the Republic, as *Télémaque,* during the eighteenth century, was linked to the ideology of the monarchy. *Le Prêtre de Némi* presents with a great nobility the difficulties encountered by the advent of reason, common sense, and humanity. The same favorable judgment cannot be made on *L'Eau de Jouvence,* a mediocre sequel to *Caliban,* or on *L'Abbesse de Jouarre,* a senile error aggravated by a preface no less so.

And yet this word, "senile," when one is dealing with Renan, would have to be taken, perhaps, in no more pejorative a sense than the word, "juvenile." Renan, who came to his literary style only late in life, virtually created a style of intellectual old age in his life and in his thought. This drinker of the water of sacred fountains became an Anacreon of the intelligence under the Republic. His life was complete; his work was finished; his ideas were settled, after having been conquered, but "settled" did not mean "arrested"—they retained a mobility like Montaigne's, a movement of dialogue; the flower of doubt gained this trophy of certainties. Paris recognized itself in this old man who knew the art of conversation, and yet Brittany won him back. He became a Breton again, the Breton of the Celtic Dinner, at the moment when the most irreverent of his disciples, the young Barrès, was beginning to be a man of Lorraine. *Huit Jours chez M. Renan* represents a necessary stage for every reader, even if he be Eugène-Melchior de Vogüé.* And all in the style of the eve of a departure, the eve of a reaction that broke out as soon as Renan was dead, the style of a ripe olive about to fall. Of the three great Bretons of the nineteenth century, one did not know how to grow old and went in despair to a pauper's grave. This was Lamennais. But the two others had everything of the style of old age. Chateaubriand, before his tomb of Grand Bey, took its severe, its Doric mode; Renan, before the Pantheon, its Ionic.

---

* Diplomat, historian, and literary critic, one of the first to introduce modern Russian literature into France.—Translator.

REALISM

The Rupture of 1850

The rupture in the French novel when one goes from the generation of
1820 to that of 1850 is one of the sharpest that exists in literary history.
The novelists who had grown up with the century and who were twenty
years old in 1820, poets like Hugo and Vigny, fantasists like George Sand,
creators of worlds like Balzac, *minores* like Gozlan and Charles de Bernard, storytellers like Dumas, serial writers like Sue, all brought into the
novel an unequaled power of creative imagination. No matter how they
tried to use their recollections and their surroundings, the effort made
their inventiveness only the freer and the better equipped. Their watchword was that of their leader, Balzac: competition with life itself. Toward 1850 this competition abated. Face to face with life, the novelists'
condition changed from that of competitors to that of employes. That is
realism.

The Two Realisms

When it is stripped of the theories that were attempted, on the one
hand by Champfleury and Philippe Duranty, though with moderation,
and on the other by the Goncourts, when works and men are examined
freely, it becomes apparent that principally realism consisted (1) in an
act, that of telling real stories—in other words, stories that had happened
to the author, to the author's friends, and (2) in an insolvency, that of
the novelistic imagination. The one, moreover, is only the corollary of
the other. The novel of the eighteenth century had already passed this
way with Abbé Prévost and especially with Restif de la Bretonne, who,
by reason of his origin, his class, his way of living, his talents, and his

works, may be taken as the ancestor, and the recognized and esteemed ancestor, of the realists of 1850.

As the imaginative novel of the preceding generation had had only one prince, Balzac, the realistic novel of 1850 had only one, Flaubert. Its following was less powerful than among the twenty-year-olds of 1820, but these novelists communicated to us, and we have kept, with respect to the minor realists, certain class prejudices. On the one side were the bohemians or former bohemians, sons of the people, Murger, Champfleury, Duranty. On the other were the upper-middle-class men, the Goncourts and Flaubert. The two classes belittled each other, despised each other—for Flaubert was certainly of his class! And the Goncourts as well. Thus a distinction can be made between a popular realism that came first in time and a realism of the middle class (*middle-class realism is an invitation to evasion*), first in order of importance.

The realist movement, which had an ancestor in the preceding generation with Henry Monnier, was born after 1845 in a circle of poor writers and artists (including Courbet). They wrote in the little newspapers and hung about the cafés. The first trait recalls the Jeunes-France of 1830, the second foreshadows the decadents of 1885.

Murger

The first of the realists in date was Henri Murger, whose *Scènes de la vie de Bohème* was in fact the most famous picture of that environment. He was the son of a Parisian concierge. In his secondary school he had studied just enough to learn syntax and to feel imbued with a literary vocation. And, what is more, his novels smell of a porter's cubicle in the rue Montmartre, of the tenants' newspapers and letters. But he loved to talk, to write what he had said, as he had said it—and that was rather laboriously; he had a feeling for reproduction, like a good copying clerk, and the realistic humor of the Paris streets. A colorfully written little paper, called *Le Corsaire de Satan*, in which almost all the writers of this school (and even Baudelaire) got their start between 1847 and 1849, first published the *Scènes de la vie de Bohème* and the *Scènes de la vie de jeunesse*, which appeared later—in 1851—as a book. These are realistic books because all their characters really lived. Yet the concierge's son remains a sentimentalist. He made a cult of the scent of mignonette, and, if he removed the novel from fantasy, it was to turn it toward romance. The great success of the *Vie de Bohème*, moreover, was made for him by middle-class men and women rather than by "bohemians." Buloz made no mistake on this score and went out of his way to get contracts with Murger for the *Revue des deux mondes*, in which thereafter his chief novels appeared and to which he provided that industrial merchandise that came back to light after 1918: serial Bohemia, tours of proper Bohemia prepared and embellished for the nice people. His health having made it necessary for him to live part of the time in Marlotte, he received orders for rustic books, which were not bad at all; one was *Le Sabot rouge*, a novel of remarkable peasant realism, perhaps his best book and in any event the most truly *realist* in the modern meaning of the word.

Champfleury

Murger was a semi-realist whom a fortunate subject and success enabled in spite of himself to break a pioneering realist trail. As much in sharpness and originality of realism as in talent, Champfleury was to seem greatly superior to him. This will be recognized in a comparison of *La vie de Bohème* with his *Aventures de mademoiselle Mariette*, a documentary picture of the same circles and the same people. The son of small shopkeepers, he too came from the people, but from the people of the provinces, like Restif, whose temperament and malice he shared. The twenty novels that he published in twenty years (1847–1866) provide one of the most solid pictures of provincial life by one who felt it, who had lived it. In general they are a chronicle of Laon, as in *Monsieur Nicolas* Restif provided part of the chronicle of Auxerre. Authentic characters from them can be found in the official registers, the files of lawyers, and the recollections of families in Laon. But one can understand why residence in Laon should have been almost forbidden, under harsh penalties, to the author of *Les Bourgeois de Molinchart*, and that the prefect of the Department of the Aisne and the judiciary should have given him warnings. The writing of this book, one of Champfleury's most important novels, which was published shortly before *Madame Bovary*, may be regarded as very characteristic of Champfleuryism. When the author was a child, a hunted deer fled out of the forest into the city one day and took refuge in the toy shop owned by Champfleury's mother, Mme. Husson (the family's real name). That was a great event in a child's life, and a more important one than the Revolution of 1830. The deer likewise entered the early pages of *Les Bourgeois*. It set off a series of middle-class stories that captured the various levels of society in Laon, that paraded a cast of quite entertaining individuals, and that ended with a long episode of provincial adultery, the competition of which made Flaubert momentarily uneasy. If *Les Bourgeois* remains the most amusing of Champfleury (it betrays the influence of Paul de Kock, who was his principal reading in school), *La Succession de Camus*, the story of an inheritance, is undoubtedly the best constructed, the strongest. And in *Monsieur de Boisdhyver*, a novel of clerical morals, Champfleury raised himself quite far in the direction of a great subject. Sainte-Beuve, who had encouraged him only modestly, really enjoyed only his most shrinking violets: *Les Souffrances du Professeur Delteil* and *Le Violon de faïence*. When the stories of middle-class provincials that he knew had run out, when his whole family, his whole street, his whole chronicle of Laon had been squeezed of their last drops, Champfleury had to stop, to take his documentary habits and his inventories of reality elsewhere, to occupy his last fifteen years with works of caricature of history, French *faïence*, and cats.

Duranty

Murger represents a sentimental realism, Champfleury a documentary realism, Duranty an intelligent and doctrinal realism of a man of letters. Duranty knew how to write, whereas Champfleury never lost the championship of France for grammatical errors throughout the Second Empire. Duranty was doctrinaire, splenetic, and secretive: he was said to be an illegitimate son of Mérimée, and indeed he seems to have effected a transition between Mérimée and the minor naturalists like Henri Céard. He was not lacking in envy. In *Réalisme*, an ephemeral magazine to which he had given this title and which he and Champfleury edited, he wrote of Flaubert's realism as a middle-class distortion as loathsome as the deformation that this same realism suffered with Murger in Buloz's magazine. Inferior as a storyteller to Champfleury, he was his superior as a psychologist; *Le Malheur d'Henriette Gérard* is one of the most penetrating, most intelligent novels of provincial life that had been written since Balzac, but in the tone of Stendhal rather than that of Balzac, and altogether at the opposite of Flaubert's epic tone. The same qualities were in the rural novel of *La Cause du beau Guillaume*, but the subject appeals to us less. That Duranty's name has never gone beyond a narrow circle of enthusiasts is one of the most unjustified of literary mischances.

The Goncourts

But the brothers Goncourt would have been highly scandalized if anyone had told the eternal weepers of the *Journal* to their faces how lucky they were as novelists. Yet after all it was luck that caused *Renée Mauperin* to become an almost-famous novel and *Henriette Gérard*, which is much better, to remain unknown. But this luck must not be considered unexplainable. In literature there are not only books; there are collectives, careers, that make the laws for the public and the critics.

The Goncourts came into the novel by way of history, into the anecdotal novel by way of anecdotal history, into the contemporary document by way of the document of the eighteenth century. Behind them, when they began as novelists, they had ten years of collecting trinkets, of admittedly excellent books on the art of the eighteenth century, the society, and the customs of the times of Louis XV and the Revolution, a minute knowledge of sixty years of history that had earned them the respect of Michelet and Sainte-Beuve. For them the eighteenth century was not merely the great century but the only century. That epoch, which was not at all in fashion and which they helped to bring into fashion, had delighted in leaving a wealth of detailed testimony of itself, of true stories like those of Restif, of chronicles and gossip like those of Louis-Petit de Bachaumont; *Bachaumont's* memoirs inspired the Goncourts to conceive the ambition of doing for their epoch what he had done for his. Whence the *Journal* that the two brothers began on 2 December 1851.

Now the novels grew out of the *Journal*, the documentaries out of the document, like branches out of a trunk. All these novels too were made out of true stories. As with Murger and Champfleury, the Goncourts' realistic novel could as well be called romanced reality. It is well known, besides, that reality does not necessarily imply truth—and vice versa.

Charles Demailly, their first novel, which appeared in 1860 under the title *Les Hommes de lettres*, came out of the same design as *La vie de Bohème* and *Mademoiselle Mariette*. It is the picture of the literary life that the authors had known since 1850, drawn not so much in the form of a novel as in the form of scenes: writers, newspapers, men and women, a suitable neurasthenia (that of Jules de Goncourt) for a man of letters— nothing was invented and the key to all the names is handy. *Soeur Philomène* is a story of the Rouen hospital told to the Goncourts by Louis Bouilhet. *Renée Mauperin*, which was at first supposed to be called *La Jeune Bourgeoisie*, is a picture of the authors' family: the biography of the elder M. Mauperin is that of their father, Denoisel is Jules, and Renée is one of their childhood friends. *Germinie Lacerteux* is the story of their old servant, whose partly double life and erotic hysteria they discovered after her death; for *Mademoiselle de Varandeuil* they exactly copied one of their cousins. *Manette Salomon* was at first called *L'Atelier Langibout;* it is the counterpart to the documentary *Hommes de lettres*, a documentary of the artistic world. The *Journal* gives us the keys to it, and the conversations and the esthetic *dicta* of Chassagnol were virtually taken down verbatim in the studios. Finally, *Madame Gervaisais* is the exact story of the life, the conversion, and the death of one of their aunts.

These knickknack collectors of documents were also knickknack collectors of style. They did not create the documentarily written novel, since there was Champfleury, but they did create the artistically written novel—in other words, the celebrated artistic writing. They recounted, with some exaggeration, the tortures that they had suffered in establishing their style, and no one can challenge the incomparable task of creation that this studied style represents. Through their novels and the notes in their *Journal* in preparation for the novels, the Goncourts rank high in the history of style. Of good style? That is something else.

In any case, not of good novelistic style. This brush style, made of strokes that dazzle and that play their part without entering further into the line of a sentence than the chapters pretend to enter into a line of composition and a well-made book, made remarkable phenomena of their novels at the end of a half century. For today's public, as much as there is a style to be learned, there is a language to be learned, Goncourtese—and life is short. If it were essential to name two books that deserved to be rescued from oblivion, one would be *Manette Salomon*, the only respectable novel that has been written about the painter's life, which is still full of vigor, and the other would be *Les Frères Zemganno*, a novel that Edmond de Goncourt wrote alone, in memory of the collaboration, and that removes brotherly love and joint effort to the world of acrobats: it is new, ingenious, and, in its closing pages, filled with powerful feeling.

The Consequences

From the very outset realism was presented in an armor of theories. Its proponents went out to do battle principally when it was a case of defending Courbet, who had proclaimed himself the champion of realism and whose one-man show in 1855 was one of the artistic events of the century. In preference to Courbet's articles and pamphlets and even *La Gazette de Champfleury*, which had two issues, and *Réalisme*, which had all of three times as many, what would be read was the remarks of Pommageot in *Manette Salomon*, copied by the Goncourts from Champfleury. Some importance would be given to the polemic against *Madame Bovary* by *Réalisme*, a polemic that opposed the realism of the natural and of nature to the romanticism of the stylized and of style: today an increasing number of readers would side more or less with Duranty.

The flood tide of realism perturbed the powers, and there was a hail of prosecutions, of which Flaubert's, in which realism was denounced even in the text of the judgment of acquittal, was only the most famous. The Académie and the important magazines adopted measures of defense. These did no good. Realism endowed literature with certain additional permanent characteristics.

All the circumstances of life, of the author's life, of the lives of his contemporaries, became subjects for novels; the novel was the portrayal of human life, and any life is a human life and can be put into a picture. Henri de Villemassant said that everyone, even a chimney sweep, had an article in him. Everyone also has a novel in him.

The natural subject of the realist novel was to be popular or middle-class reality, both of which, moreover, offer more, in emotion as well as in absurdities, than the classes called upper. "Family life," Champfleury said, "sicknesses of spirit, the portrayal of the world, the curiosities of the street, country scenes, observation of the passions, all alike belong to realism." For Champfleury the book that came from the people appealed to the people, and that was literature. "The public of the twenty-sou book is the real public." In contrast, the realists who insisted on and pursued style, and who had independent means, and in addition the Goncourts and Flaubert, would write for the elite.

In short, the realist novel is the modern novel, which rejects the traditional and the ancient, which refers frankly and exclusively to today. The *modern* became a complete, exclusive system, like reason in the classics or the belligerent in the ultra-democrats. The word modernism, created by the Goncourts, is of great importance. It will be observed, however, that, if the Goncourts gave modernism its name, these cultivated gentlemen were no less the possessors of a tradition that at times turned them against the modern and that gave them the status of exiles from that republic: the Goncourts in their eighteenth century, like Flaubert in Carthage, needed their cures at the thermal springs of the anti-modern. It was, furthermore, through the great personality of Flaubert that all these problems were posed with a reverberation and an abundance that they did not have in his contemporaries.

THE HUMAN DOCUMENT
AND THE NATURALIST MOVEMENT

The Inter-Generation of 1860

Those who made the realist revolution and who were of the generation of 1848—Champfleury, Flaubert, the Goncourts—had as successors and, in part, as disciples that half-generation that had spent its youth under the Empire and reached the age of twenty about 1860, for which the realist revolution was a completed revolution and which was to succeed Flaubert under the Third Republic as Flaubert, the novelist of the Empire, had succeeded the Balzac of the July monarchy. Political ruptures coincided rather exactly with the ruptures in the history of the novel. Like its contemporaries the Parnassians, this half-generation was a generation, and moreover a very important one, of successors. And like the Parnassians they followed after tetrarchs, who were to be Champfleury, Flaubert, and the two Goncourts.

Alphonse Daudet

The most instructive instance would seem to be that of Alphonse Daudet. He had no more of the creator's temperament than did the Goncourts. He invented nothing. He needed constantly to lean on reality, on his personal histories, those of his friends and relatives, and until *Tartarin* he never could do more than romance real anecdotes. But he was well served by a feeling for life, by the depiction of ways of living, by a gift as a storyteller, and by his style.

The feeling for life in him was sympathy with life. He loved people; their destinies inspired in him a pity and a tenderness that might seem extreme. No one could be further than he from the ironic objectivity of Flaubert and the naturalists. *Jack,* which, however, is not his best novel, undammed as many tears as *David Copperfield.* A painful and unjustly broken destiny filled Daudet with sorrow and indignation. These same feelings dictated his admirable *L'Evangéliste:* a life destroyed by the fanaticism of a preaching woman, as Jack's was destroyed by the cruel frivolity of a mother. His third book is a masterpiece, superior even to *L'Evangéliste: Sapho,* the story of an artist's life ruined by a love affair, a detached and powerfully treated episode from *Femmes d'artistes.* The importance of *Sapho* derives from the importance that this problem, *L'Art et les femmes,* or *L'Homme de lettres et la femme,* had assumed in his life and in that of his family, exceptionally devoted to literature; from the importance that was also assumed in this literary family by the problem of middle-class defense, of the defense of the middle-class style of life, against everything that is included in the label of "Bohemia" (the dedication is a key: "To my sons, when they are twenty years old"); from Daudet's knowledge of and profound sympathy with artistic circles and the conditions of the artist's life, both from without and from within. This theme of artistic circles and the destruction of an artist by a woman, by a bad love affair, had been created by the Goncourts in *Manette Salomon,* of which *Sapho* is only a repetition, but a repetition far superior to the original. Most of Daudet's novels have the subtitle of *Moeurs parisiennes,* and, to be honest, this is hardly more than an advertising imitation of the subtitle created by Flaubert for *Madame Bovary: Moeurs de Province.* *Les Rois en exil* shows us clearly enough that it is not Daudet from whom a picture of the Parisian world from within is to be sought. But the fact remains that he is an admirable painter even of what used in other days to be called quite simply "manners," that is to say average, daily, real humanity, not the great human comedy but the comedy of little people, the clear course of life, illuminated by a ray of what we would call humor, thinking what Daudet owes to Dickens, if the term *hoax* were not better suited to Daudet's soil.

His Provençal soil: Daudet was from Nîmes—in fact, a member of the Félibrige,* and he brought the spirit of the Provençal storytellers into the novel and especially into the tale. *Roumanille* and *Armana Provençau* are at the origin of his *Contes du lundi* and his *Lettres de mon moulin,* which have become so popular, which have done as much as his novels for Daudet's fame, and which were long regarded as the best honey of a French Attica: in them, as in Courier's Atticism, we see today a certain artifice. The Provençal storyteller became the novelist of the south with *Tartarin de Tarascon,* or, rather, with the trilogy which is rounded out by *Tartarin*

---

* A literary school founded in 1854 by Mistral, Joseph Roumanille, and Théodore Aubanel to restore the Provençal dialect to its old poetic and literary standing.— Translator.

sur les Alpes and *Port-Tarascon.* They are destined to remain Daudet's most celebrated works. First of all, there is still a pure storyteller in them, and his weaknesses as a creative novelist no longer stand in his way. Second, only here did he create a type, and even types. Tartarin has become the Don Quixote of France. But it would be wrong to see in this personal creation of Daudet's a figuration and especially a psychology of the south. In *Tartarin,* as well as in *Numa Roumestan,* it is a south that the author has fabricated for caricature and export. In actuality, this contrast, this dialogue of north and south that determines the nature and the construction of France has not yet found its novelist.

Neither symbol nor psychologist of the south, but storyteller of the south, Daudet is in addition—and this time he really is—a stylist of the south. The artistic writing of the Goncourts has seriously impaired the durability of their prose. But when Daudet grafted that artistic writing on to a French swollen with the saps and juices of Provence, the success was perfect. Daudet's style brings to light, brings to life, brings pleasure. It sparkles, it gesticulates, it is physical. It has not aged, in contrast to the obsolescence of his novels. But while he experienced influences, those of the Goncourts and of Joseph Roumanille, he himself exerted none; he started no school. And, in sum, nothing of Daudet launched a school; he remains on his sunlit little hill, if not in isolation, at least in independence. Willy-nilly he must be made to enter an order, but he wears "isms" as awkwardly as Flaubert does. Realism was Champfleury and similarly naturalism was to be Zola.

Zola

Zola, like Daudet, advanced through the breach that had been opened by Flaubert and the Goncourts, but he was oriented more toward Flaubert, while Daudet had turned toward the Goncourts. Zola, moreover, was only ten years younger than Jules de Goncourt, eighteen years younger than Edmond Goncourt and Flaubert. Maupassant, ten years younger still, was the crown prince of the group. But it was indeed a homogeneous group, which established its problems, its people, its works in the very center of the French novel for thirty years, from 1857, the date of *Madame Bovary,* until 1887, the date of the Manifesto of the Five, and Zola held a great place in it, and not merely as the sixth wheel.

As far as Zola is concerned, one must go back further. For him, the problem of the heritage of Balzac was posed as it had been posed in 1850 for Champfleury and Flaubert. The realists of 1850 were only half heirs of Balzac; they had made no "human comedy." They had not carried on what might be called the monumental Balzacism. In this seeker of documents and that ascetic of style, the stuff, the will, the health, the temperament of Balzac were lacking.

LES ROUGON-MACQUART

They were not lacking in Zola. At the age of twenty-eight, he decided to do for his time, that of the Second Empire, what Balzac had done for his own: to fashion a cyclical work, with recurrences of the same characters, that would deal with all levels of society, a human comedy of the generation that the death of Balzac had left in the schoolroom.

At that time *La Comédie humaine* was the twenty volumes of the Houssiaux edition. The human comedy of the Second Empire, envisaged in ten novels, written like *La Comédie*, would similarly turn out to be twenty-five volumes over twenty years. On the other hand, Balzac had come only rather late to the cyclical idea of *La Comédie humaine*, and belatedly he had attached to it and organized within it novels that had been written for themselves alone. Zola made a plan from the beginning, and he was to follow it without much change. This plan was to include (as the belated idea of *La Comédie* could not include) a drive shaft for the vast machinery, called the genealogical tree of a family whose members would provide the chief heroes of the twenty novels: *Les Rougon-Macquart, histoire naturelle et sociale d'une famille sous le second Empire*. They numbered thirty-two; about a thousand characters under this rooftree made up the population of secondary characters in this city of a novel. Finally, Balzac's work was more intuitive than scientific. It mattered little to him whether he was in agreement with the science of his time. Now, it was science that would give *Les Rougon-Macquart* its dominant idea—that is, Taine the idea of determinism, Claude Bernard that of the experimental method (*le roman expérimental* was one of Zola's gaudy placards), Darwin and Dr. Lucas that of heredity.

Here was a remarkable construction, carried to its conclusion with solid determination and an enormous talent. But this novel of the Second Empire was in a way to *La Comédie humaine* what the nephew's monarchy was to the uncle's empire.

The plan of *Les Rougon-Macquart* had been made and the first volume (*La Fortune des Rougon*) had been written when the empire fell. *La Fortune des Rougon* did not appear until 1871, and *La Famille sous le second Empire* was published under the Third Republic. Zola had no reason to give up his project: a novelist is not a newspaper reporter, he needs a consolidated continuity in order to build, and *La Comédie humaine*, written under the July monarchy, took place, as far as more than half of it was concerned, under the Restoration. And, besides, in 1871 the same generation was still going on, and *Les Rougon-Macquart* did not begin to be the historical novel of an epoch that was past until about 1885. In his preface of 1871, Zola even wrote these lines, with an ingeniousness that was less habitual to him than ingenuousness: "The fall of Bonaparte, which as an artist I needed and which inevitably I always found at the end of my drama without daring to hope that it was so near, has come to provide me with the terrible and necessary conclusion of my work."

Nor was this inaccurate. *Les Rougon-Macquart*, whose genealogical tree goes back from Adélaïde Fouque, who died an insane centenarian in 1873, is the portrait of a family, of a society, of a humanity that are disintegrating, unraveling, becoming corrupt, poisoning themselves, the clinical record of a decomposition, and, in opposition to Claude Bernard's definition of life, the whole of the forces that struggle against life. They almost did not need the War of 1870 to bring them to *La Débâcle*.

NOVELIST OF THE PEOPLE AND SOCIAL IDEALISM

This descent to Avernus is the whole of *naturalism* as a school. But Zola himself goes beyond naturalism in his worker's optimism, in his religion of science. *La Débâcle* is not the last but the next-to-last volume of *Les Rougon-Macquart*. The last is *Le Docteur Pascal*, the novelist creator's symbolic figure of life, of the good and healthy scientist, trooper of truth on the march. Truth on the march . . . Just as the future author of *La Débâcle*, as an artist, needed Bonaparte's fall, the author of *Le Docteur Pascal*, which dates from 1893, seems to have needed what was to erupt four years later, the Dreyfus case.

From this, Zola's literary destiny acquired a monumental character incorporated into the first thirty years of the Republic. Shall we find the same aspect of a monumental whole in *Les Rougon-Macquart?*

As a monument it has not held up. The mass, which was arbitrary and ingenuous, has come apart. The novels of provincial life like *La Fortune des Rougon* and *La Conquête de Plassans*, portrayals of Aix just after the *coup d'état*, have never been taken into consideration. Zola, who was then earning his livelihood in modest employments, did not know "society" under the Second Empire, and his laborious, honest mechanisms, producers of the ready-made, could not invent it. He saw it artlessly, popularly, or through the keyhole. He had none of that living experience that women of fashion transfused into the young Balzac. The world of the state was a mystery to him. So were those of business and commerce. Balzac would have transported the Boucicaut and Cognacq couples in all their aliveness into his novels, where they would have found themselves on an even footing with the Guillaumes of *La Maison du chat qui pelote*. But what is *Au Bonheur des dames?* The shop and the merchandise without the merchant—that is, without the essential element. It is significant that Zola's first success was *L'Assommoir* (1877), that his career was divided into two parts: before *L'Assommoir* and after *L'Assommoir*. What is there to say except that Zola seemed to public opinion and to the intellectuals to be the novelist of the people, the novelist who did not flatter the people, since *L'Assommoir* is the picture of a people's disease, alcoholism, and finally and chiefly a people's novelist?

A people's novelist. The word "elementary" must be stripped of all the malevolence and the pedantry that are injected into it by the men of letters who use it; it must be taken in its solid and healthy, efficacious and positive sense, and then it can be said that Zola was a great elementary mind. His materialism is that of common sense. His pessimism must not be viewed as a radical pessimism, in the manner of Taine, but as a relative pessimism that is consummated in social idealism and a belief in progress. In this he differs both from the pseudo-realists, who are descriptive without a philosophy, and from the realists like Flaubert and the Goncourts, respectable citizens respectablizing with respectability. Zola's philosophy is extremely brief, but it is precise, it is popular, it embraces everything in the word "work." Zola had the religion of work as Balzac had that of will. Of his *Quatre Evangiles*, *Fécondité* was inspired by his becoming a father late in life, *Vérité* by the Dreyfus case, but *Travail* sprang from his whole deep nature, his whole life, his incapacity to conceive otherwise the reason for man's being. The last, *Justice*, could never be written, but Justice, as Proudhon has demonstrated, is the alpha and omega of every philosophy that comes from the people.

It is from this point of view of work that all Zola's fiction must be ranked and understood. Jules Lemaître called it a pessimistic epic of human nature. Pessimistic is not an inaccurate word, in the sense in which, as the philosophers say, nature sets up the known quantity. The known quantity was the society contemporary with Zola, it was the society of the Second Empire and that of the Third Republic to the extent to which it carried on that of the Second Empire. But above this known quantity Zola maintained a simple, manageable, popular ideal, identical with that of the Sandoz of *L'Oeuvre* who is the author's twin—the ideal that is marked by the title and the final page of *Germinal*, the last page of *La Débâcle*, the ideal that, from *Le Docteur Pascal* to the empty place (filled by Zola's final act) of *Justice*, corresponded to a social optimism, to what in sum was the ideal of the Third Republic.

EPIC NATURALISM

Epic, too, can be understood. Since Champfleury and Flaubert there had been two kinds of realisms: an analytical realism and an epic realism. Epic pages abound in *Madame Bovary*, and *Salammbô* was born of Flaubert's need for an epic. On the other hand, there was nothing epic in the Goncourts or in Daudet. Zola created epic naturalism in the wake of

Flaubert. His style is naturally epic: epic in its oratorical movement; epic in its commonplaces, its foreseeable adjectives, its superfluity of words, explanations, clarifications; epic in its preponderance of masses, groups, collective beings; epic in its adoption of a certain developed section of the people—the teacher, the worker, the reader in popular libraries; epic in its lack or paucity of qualities of refined culture, of the rare flowers of middle-class life.

Les Soirées de Médan

Beginning in 1875, a number of new writers who admired Zola—Guy de Maupassant, Henri Céard, J.-K. Huysmans, Léon Hennique, Paul Alexis—fell into the habit of meeting at first in his home in the rue Saint-Georges and then in weekly dinners in modest restaurants. After a dinner at the Trappe Restaurant, to which Goncourt and Zola had been invited, on 16 April 1877, the year of La Fille Elisa and L'Assommoir, the press fell into a habit of its own: speaking of a "naturalist school." In 1879, during a visit to Médan, where Zola had just bought a house, he, Maupassant, Huysmans, Céard, Hennique, and Alexis decided (on Hennique's suggestion) to publish a collection that would contain a short story by each of them on the War of 1870 and that would be called Les Soirées de Médan. This anthology appeared in 1880.

Primarily it was a kind of manifesto. Zola's short story, L'Attaque du moulin, was a serious effort that conformed to the laws of the national-defense story. But the five others, the younger men's stories, veered more or less in the direction of parody (some consideration had been given earlier to the title of L'Invasion comique) and seemed already to belong to what would later be called anti-patriotic literature, and still later anti-militarist. This created a scandal.

Maupassant

In addition, Les Soirées contained Boule de suif, one of the master-pieces of the French short story. Maupassant was not yet thirty when he wrote it, and, if he never surpassed it, it was because perfection cannot be surpassed. During ten years, with a regularity and a strength that did not, any more than in the case of Zola, preclude a furious expenditure of work, he was to produce two hundred and sixty short stories and seven great novels.

He owed nothing to Zola, his senior by ten years. But he was the son of a woman who had been Flaubert's childhood friend and he was a compatriot of Flaubert, and also he was the disciple and the spiritual son of the great Norman to such an extent that it would perhaps be impossible to find another literary instance of a relation between geniuses that was so full, so direct, so logical, of so sharp an original focusing within the same realm of human experience, the same scheme of Norman nature. Only schools of painting can match this phenomenon: Van Dyck and Rubens, Veronese and Titian.

From the very beginning Maupassant was the sure master of the tale in literature, the classic of the tale, superior to Mérimée in the solidity and the variety of the living beings that he shaped with a painter's colors instead of bringing out their features like the great draftsman of *La Partie de Trictrac*, superior to Alphonse Daudet not only in the abundance of his production but in a more masculine, more accented, more direct art.

This superiority in the short story did not follow him into the novel. His two masterpieces, which are *Bel Ami* and *Une Vie*—(that is, a man's life and a woman's life), have a splendid solidity, and obviously they overflow the frame of the novel of Parisian manners, but they lack necessity— that unquestionable necessity with which Flaubert's novels were bursting—and their appearance, their cut, their humanity are dated in the same way in which the very different novels of the Goncourts are dated. Maupassant entertained the characters of his novel with complete ease, like Zola. They did not live in him as in Flaubert and Daudet. He was only tangential to the divine part of the novel.

He clearly felt the differences between the two forms. He never made a short story out of the subject of a novel (this, however, occurs seldom); he never made a novel out of the subject of a short story (and this does occur with the majority of novelists).

Other Men of Médan

The median man of Médan was thirty years old in 1880—that is, they were all ten years younger than Zola. Maupassant, like Zola himself, stayed aloof, went beyond the rules, and his connection with Croisset was more important than his visits to Médan. In contrast, Huysmans, Céard, Hennique, and Alexis formed a quite homogeneous naturalist team. In them naturalism consisted not so much in clinging to the portrayal of reality as in a hatred of reality—and therefore in a caricatural outlook, governed by a radical pessimism—and in the exclusive portrayal of grotesque characters, seedy or shabby, which was especially successful when the characters were the twins of the authors, as was the case with Huysmans. The holy book of this group, which appeared, unfinished, in magazine installments in the same years as *Les Soirées de Médan*, was *Bouvard et Pécuchet*.

HUYSMANS

In one way Huysmans went beyond Médan and added a singular note. Like Zola, he had a style of his own, far superior and even opposite to Zola's in its quest for new expression, in a horror of platitudes that was integral with the naturalists' horror of reality, in a way of elevating to a method of transcendent humor what the Goncourts called artistic writing, of divesting it of its pedantry by divesting it of its gravity. The Goncourts never parodied the reality that they distorted; Huysmans proceeded in a constant parody, of himself first of all.

Granted salvation by a rich and parodistic style, Huysmans also received it, while still on earth, through his conversion. Certainly, religious sincerity and literary fabrication were interlocked to a point at which he himself could no longer distinguish one from the other. But finally, for Huysmans as for Zola, the net result was an *En Route* (which is the title of one of Huysmans' books). Huysmans' *En Route* is Christian, Zola's is democratic and social. The Fleming's and the Latin's *mystiques* were diametrically opposed, but in both of them naturalism, alive by reason of a certain poetry, was used only in order to be put into another element.

Did Huysmans also gain salvation by the content of what are called his novels? Except *A Rebours* (but not *Les Soeurs Vatard*, a novel of his family's affairs), except to a certain degree *A Rebours*, he never wrote anything but the biography of a dyspeptic and maniacal bachelor, sometimes on the hunt for a quiet restaurant (*A Vau-l'éau*), sometimes in the boredom of a miserable vacation (*En Rade*), sometimes in quest of the devil (*Là-Bas*), finally in search of God (*En Route, La Cathédrale, L'Oblat*). Unfortunately, while what such a character says and how he says it may rouse some interest, much less is stirred by what he is.

Unless he is a writer. The Goncourts wrote *La Maison d'un artiste*, and many others of their novels could also be included under the same title. Huysmans opened and inventoried the house of a writer. He came out of himself for a day only in order to create a robot of literature, Des Esseintes in *A Rebours*, the contemporary of that other robot named Hedely, in *L'Eve future*. It was *A Rebours* that made Huysmans famous. From 1886 to 1895 he modeled—or, rather, he confected—a whole little literary population. The mechanics of *A Rebours* continued working in Huysmans longer than is generally believed. Substitute love for literature, and, for Huysmans, return to the Stendhalian metaphor of crystallization.

JOURNEYMEN AND MINOR NATURALISTS

Hennique and Céard, also journeymen naturalists, wrote little. Hennique's *Benjamin Rozes*, the story of a lonely worm; *Francine Cloarec*, the story of a servant (realism's servant since *Germinie Lacerteux*); *L'Acci-*

dent de M. Hébert, the story of a cuckolding, all of which are parodies of middle-class life, could as well be taken as parodies of naturalism. Céard wrote two novels, *Une Belle Journée* in 1881, the story of a rainy day seen from a private room in a restaurant by a timid couple, and *Terrains à vendre au bord de la mer,* published a quarter of a century later, which is partly autobiographical and the close-knit transcript of an existence.

The school was regular and well equipped: after the journeymen naturalists, the minor naturalists, of whom the type, the worthy type, was Paul Alexis, a native of Aix, who found his reason for being not so much in *Madame Meuriol* as in the shadow of Zola and in the five words of the telegram that he sent from Aix in reply to an inquiry from Jules Huret: "Naturalism not dead letter follows." Must Paul Bonnetain be mentioned? Rather, let us come to a full stop with the pure naturalist novel of Louis Desprez, *Autour d'un clocher,* which appeared in 1884. But Desprez, who died a year later at the age of twenty-five, already represented the next generation of naturalism, that of the Manifesto of the Five.

THE REACTIONARIES

The literature of emigration reacted against the Revolution. Nothing could have been more normal. But that reaction, in the course of the nineteenth century, became simply reaction, in the spiritual, political, sibylline meaning of this word, which is understood in the smallest village. Under each succeeding system, reaction had an individual face. It developed, but all in the same reality, the same idea, the same leadership. A history or a picture of reaction in France would provide a curious portrait of French morals and ideas in the nineteenth century. The least part of it would be the literary part, which alone concerns us here.

Let us leave aside the reactionary literature of opinion, what came from the great journalists. But above this there were great reactionary writers, the Fathers of Reaction, and, to use a phrase that, if it was not created by him, was at least picked up by Jules Barbey d'Aurevilly, the Prophets of the Past. The phrase was applied to Xavier de Maistre, Bonald, Chateaubriand, and Lamennais in the book that Barbey published on them. In the period that followed them, these four prophets had four successors in Barbey d'Aurevilly, Arthur de Gobineau, Auguste de Villiers de L'Isle-Adam, and Léon Bloy.

Barbey d'Aurevilly

He was twenty-two years old in 1830, and few styles have as dazzling a romantic color as his. Yet he did not belong to romanticism. He spent that whole period in his Norman province, in a legitimist, clerical, circle, as anachronistic and picturesque as one could wish, from which, a curious meteor, he was hurled on Paris in 1851. He was replete with reading, memories, wit, style, all raised to and fixed on a perpetual military metaphor, musketeer and even Constable of France. This glory barely shone past the circle of his friends, but he knew how to keep it alive through the unmeasured potency of his language. And, if he is not much read today, he is still regarded, if not as a great man, at least as a great simple fellow, except that no one was less simple than he. This he owes to his novels, his criticism, his witticisms, and his attitude.

Barbey's novels remain as the best part of his work. To tell the truth, even when they run to two volumes they are, rather, stories, stories of his native region, and of the days of the Breton royalist risings, with remarkable and occasionally terrible recollections, and above all an incomparable style of enhancement, images, tricks, sonorities. *Un Prêtre marié, Le Chevalier des Touches, Les Diaboliques* are bursting with strangeness, passion, beauties, but extremely short on humanity. He had the makings of a Norman and Breton Walter Scott. Unfortunately, journalism, or, rather, literary criticism, engulfed him, and, in spite of the important admirers whom that criticism can still claim, the fact is to be regretted. To a painful degree Barbey was lacking in reason, judgment, and even good faith. His criticism is the vehicle for his witticisms, which were many and clever and of which a great number has come down to us, and for his attitude: that of the intransigent Christian, the avenger, the crusader against the eighteenth century, who, in his own words, views Catholicism as the old wrought-iron balcony best suited for spitting down into the crowd. Provided one stands at a respectful distance, it is a splendid spectacle.

Gobineau

It was not Catholicism that provided the balcony for Arthur de Gobineau. It was his ancestors—not those that he really had, who were of insignificant, even middle-class origin, but those that he imagined for himself, Nordic conquerors and feudal barons. Barbey had more style than ideas, Gobineau had more ideas than style. His theory of the life and death of races, expounded in the *Traité de l'inégalité des races humaines*, furnished Germany with one of the foundations of her racist ideology. But, like Barbey, Gobineau needed fiction in order to give of his best. The most fortunate result of his rash racism and his reactionary blue-blood genius was that they gave him the ideological carcass of the very beautiful novel, *Les Pléiades*. His long diplomatic experience in Persia and Greece was expressed in *Les Nouvelles asiatiques* and *Trois ans en Asie*, perhaps the truest view of the Orient that there has ever been in French fiction.

Villiers de L'Isle-Adam

This principal private secretary of Tocqueville, this minister plenipotentiary, this posthumous prophet will not be compared with that unlucky Bohemian, dying in misery, Villiers de L'Isle-Adam, who, moreover, was more authentically a descendant of the Grand Master of the Knights of Malta than Gobineau was of Ottar Jarl. And yet the work of this hallucinating and chimerical Breton remains much more precious to us than that of the prophet, Gobineau, or the constable, Barbey. He was one of the great poets in prose of French literature. He created a type, that Homais exaggerated by moonlight, Tribulat Bonhomet. His *Contes cruels* remains one of the peaks of the French story. *L'Eve future* is one of the novels prophesying the mechanized and Americanized French civilization of today, the prophecy of Daniel of the cinema. The four-act play, *Axel*, with its strange visionary power, can be called the highest myth of poetic idealism.

Léon Bloy

Léon Bloy lived in the same misery as Villiers—worse because it was also his family's. He transformed that misery into hatred against men. Few beings have known a comparable abyss of rage and felt more strongly the need to create in hell. But also in heaven. A genuine Catholic, and one of the most remarkable who ever existed in France, he had sublime intuitions that attained to the highest theology. The serene and visionary audacity with which he entered into the plans of God does indeed seem the bearing of genius. His style, which was that of one of the great prose writers of his century, is enough for everything. But at the very least, from the point of view of quantity, the preferred road of this style was that of invective. His capacity for outrage is one of the forces of nature; not only the anti-clericals of the Republic but also the lukewarm or academic Catholics, the comfortable burghers who gave the poor writer nothing, were lyrically submerged under tons of verbal matter that are worth removing—that is, reading: *Je m'accuse, Les Dernières colonnes de l'eglise*, and especially the volumes of Bloy's *Journal*. But in Bloy this reaction of insult results from an action of suffering. *Le Désespéré* and *La Femme pauvre* attest to incredible ordeals. The qualities of a damned man that exist in Bloy are compensated, or cauterized, by his qualities of saintliness, particularly when we consider that he effected conversions, that the world of writers contains men really converted by Léon Bloy.

The literature of reaction was above all a reaction of literature: that is, of a forceful personality against conformism, accepted ideas, the "commonplaces" of which Bloy wrote *L'Exégèse*. It is part of the salt of literary life. *L'Action française* would later provide a general doctrine of reaction; and the style of reaction, examples of which would be found in Léon Daudet, Paul Claudel, Jacques Maritain, is more alive today than ever.

THE THEATER

Dramatic Epic

If, in every sense of the word "poetry," and first of all in its etymological meaning of creation, the generation of 1820 was the most poetic of French literary generations, that of 1850 was the most dramatic since the retirement of Racine—that is, the generation that established itself most solidly in the theater, that brought to it the greatest charge of original and lasting creation. We will not say that this superiority can be explained by three reasons, but we will mention three conditions that encouraged it, three revolutions to which it was connected.

THE TECHNICAL AGE

A revolution in literature. With the decline of romanticism, the poetic forms ran dry. In poetry and in the novel it was the time of ebb, of narrowed aspirations, precise and more modest, in which great inspiration gave way to technique. Whence Parnassus and realism. The Second Empire was a period less of beauty than of craftsmanship. It was much concerned with good arrangement and with good materials. Now, there is no art more closely bound to delicate techniques than the theater, none in which the author has to forget himself more, submit more completely to his object, which is his characters, his public. The literature of the Second Empire produced good theater from the same source from which it produced *Les Fleurs du mal* and *Madame Bovary*.

THE CIVILIZATION OF PLEASURE

A revolution in morals. It is a commonplace to liken the society of the Second Empire to the society of the eighteenth century. Like the earlier society, it expanded outward. It was a society of light and splendors. Its pursuit of pleasure was greedy and open. The civilization of pleasure became a condition and even a problem of the epoch. The symbolic token of this civilization of pleasure was the entrance of a new character into Parisian life, which would flourish there for a half century and then vanish at as sharp a stroke as that of its entrance: the great accepted courtesan. Now the theater functions more or less as the center of any civilization of pleasure. Enough sobriety and tradition, however, were left in this society to observe and judge that civilization of pleasure, to *conceive* it as a moral and social question at the same time that it was being experienced as a natural destiny. Therefore the theater aspired to become a platform, the comedy of manners to function as a critic of manners. Comedy professed to offer to a more mixed and enlarged, a more superficial and fashionable society something of what had attracted listeners to the Christian pulpit in the seventeenth century and to the professorial podium under Louis-Philippe. The generation of 1850 was a theatocratic generation.

THE NEW AUDIENCES

A revolution in the public. Under the Second Empire, the ordinary public of the theater increased substantially. The railroads created a new Paris, the Paris of travelers, for whom an evening not spent in the theater was an evening wasted. The traditional public of the theater, the respectable people of Paris, was augmented by three new publics: that of foreigners, that of provincials, and that of the newly rich, for whom French literature was not so much what one read as what one went to see (and what "must be seen") and to hear on the stage. This augmented public, like the travelers to Venice in another time, made the fortunes of the courtesans of the new Paris. They occupied a remarkable place in the theater of this period (*La Dame aux camélias, Le Demi-monde, Les Filles de marbre, Le Mariage d'Olympe*). And, like the Dutch in their painters' pictures, this same public was to encounter itself, and chiefly to be encountered, very readily on the stage: the foreigners in *La Vie parisienne*, the provincials in *La Cagnotte*, the newly rich in *La Question d'argent*. This expansion in the public had not yet been matched by a debasement of the stage. The public of the European aristocracies was familiar with French culture; the provincial public read; the new fortunes were consolidated and social climbing became normal. The theater now faced a public that had quadrupled in number and undergone no marked diminution in quality.

Sarcey used to say that in his long career as a spectator he had seen only three dramatic revolutions: *La Dame aux camélias, le Chapeau de paille d'Italie* and *Orphée aux enfers*. And indeed these were three creations peculiar to the Second Empire, to the degree to which creation can be spoken of with regard to the theater: the comedy of manners, the new light comedy, the operetta.

The Comedy of Manners

DUMAS THE YOUNGER

That the comedy of manners was born of *La Dame aux camélias* is one of the most curious facts in the history of the theater and one of those that best show us that the theater has laws and habits of its own that must not be confused with those of written literature. Dumas had written it in a week, he insisted, under the impulse of an emotion: his genuine love affair with a courtesan who was dying of tuberculosis. He had put life, his life, on paper, like Lamartine when he wrote *Le Lac*. But this life of the author was that of a young illegitimate son of Alexandre Dumas, of a chip off the old block, accustomed since childhood to the ways, the language, the behavior of the theater, who wrote plays almost as M. Jourdain wrote prose; and this is obviously the most unusual way of writing for the theater. After three years, out of deference to his father's reputation, producers staged the plays of this monster of inexperience who had nothing else to recommend him. But immediately the public found that his plays were just like life and gave him a remarkable success that lasted until the beginning of the twentieth century. Meanwhile *La Dame* soon came to interest only an inferior public. This public was primarily that of the *Scènes de la vie de Bohème*, which appeared at the same time, which was born of the same confidences and personal adventures, which appealed to the same sentimentality, and which, as *La Dame* was at the origin of the comedy of manners, was at the origin of the realist novel.

But Murger left the task of creating this novel to Champfleury and Flaubert, while Dumas was his own Champfleury and even, in a certain measure, his own Flaubert.

Here Dumas was not the only one involved. Since 1849 and Augier's *Gabrielle*, there had been in the theater not so much a reaction against romanticism, about which the public cared extremely little, as that need for order that the Empire satisfied. *La Dame aux camélias*, which stirred pity for the courtesan, the flesh-and-blood prostitute, had been answered by Théodore Barrière with *Les Filles de marbre*, a sinister picture of the courtesan without mercy, the arid, avid prostitute who devours the son of the family for breakfast and his father for supper; it was the play most often performed in provincial theaters under the Second Empire. Women told one another that they must take their husbands and sons to see it in order to make them hate the courtesan, as they must take them to see

Trente ans ou la Vie d'un joueur in order to make them hate gambling. Now, probably in memory of Tiberge in *Manon Lescaut*, Barrière had introduced into *Les Filles de marbre* an honorable and virtuous logician and adviser named Desgenais. Dumas borrowed this author's spokesman—this Aristes or this Cleanth—from him and made him the logician of his plays, the man of the world, intelligent, intuitive, witty, devoted, heroic as the need might be, who led the dance, tore off the masks, drew the moral.

In 1855 he was Olivier de Jalin in *Le Demi-monde*. In 1864 he was to be de Ryons in *L'Ami des femmes*. Both are perhaps Dumas' most brilliant plays, of excellent craftsmanship, with solid dialogue, and, especially in the case of the first, of great importance to the comedy of manners. In *Le Demi-monde* Dumas uncovered and brought under the spotlight, baptizing it with a name that has clung to an important section of Parisian society that he knew as well as that of *La Dame aux camélias*, since it was his own, the half-world, or half-license, midway between the closed world and recognized license. Under various titles, he repeated many times this typical play of the contact and the conflict between two worlds, or two fractions of a world: the hereditary French world and the outside world, or, rather, the outcast woman who attacks it, unsettles it, shatters it: this is the theme of *Diane de Lys*, of *La Femme de Claude*, of *L'Etrangère*, even of *Les Idées de Madame Aubray*.

The fringes of fashion, the transitory and brilliant elements of Parisian society had their painter in Dumas. He professed to be as well their moralist, their preacher; with a mixture of arrogant pedantry, extravagant prophetic pretense, and businessman's cunning, he held forth the dramatic author as the successor to the director of conscience of the eighteenth-century faithful, to the household philosopher of the ancient Romans. Hence his dramas of ideas, drawn out and commented on in the explanations and oracles of the prefaces. Just as the real, if not realistic, play of *La Dame aux camélias* was born at the same time as Murger's real novel, Dumas' drama of ideas was born at the same time as Feuillet's novel of ideas. Between them there is this difference, that Feuillet's problems bore on moral questions (*Sibylle, Camors*) that arose for individuals in a society whose form and direction were established, while Dumas' problems were those of social and family questions in a society whose ill-made framework was to be enlarged or consolidated, rectified or remade: problems of marriage (*Denise, Francillon*), problems of illegitimate children (*Le Fils naturel*), problems of the feminine condition (*Monsieur Alphonse*), even problems of marital sex (*L'Ami des femmes*). Through its ideas the problem play naturally became something that was talked about and discussed in the town. It extended the domain of the theater in a direction toward which it had always looked—and, after all, *Tartuffe* and *Les Femmes savantes* are problem plays. But the artificial and artful form that the problem play assumed in Dumas and the changes subsequently undergone by the social structure contributed to making both the thing and the phrase obsolete. Dumas' theater vanished into oblivion.

AUGIER

Vanished perhaps more quickly than the theater of Emile Augier, whose temperament, however, was less curious and less creative. Dumas had created the modern play. It was he and no one else who stole the spotlight from Scribe. He knew how to borrow a character or two from his contemporaries, but he did not borrow his technique, his exact science of representing an environment, like Flaubert, or a problem in this setting, like Feuillet. He excelled even in revivifying with his sure technique the play that someone else had botched or merely imagined (and his *Théâtre des autres* is not the least curious part of his work). Augier, in contrast, had made his start with verse plays in the manner of François Ponsard, and *Gabrielle*, a piece of shameless "Ponsardizing," had the success of a second *Lucrèce*, or that of *L'Honneur et l'argent*, with the same means and the same audience. The appointed heir of Ponsard, in the way in which Victorien Sardou was to be the appointed heir of Scribe, Augier was soon able to see with common sense, the very common sense of "the school of common sense," that the time for his verse comedy was over, and, at the crossroads where several signposts offered him several kinds of other comedies, he chose the direction that *La Dame aux camélias* was pointing for the new theater. *Le Gendre de M. Poirier*, in 1854, was the second modern play.

La Dame aux camélias laid bare a habitat, that of the half-world, or quarter-world, in contact and in conflict with another world, the middle-class world. In these spheres there were living people, Marguerite Gautier and the Duvals. That was enough to make a revolution in a Scribe-ridden theater. The play lacked types, a style, action, words (Dumas was to find the style, the action and the words later). It was *Le Gendre de M. Poirier* that provided them. Coming after *La Dame aux camélias* and after Sandeau's novel, *Sacs et parchemins*, from which he had derived the play, thus taking his advantage where he found it, Augier had the luck and the skill to create *Les Précieuses ridicules* of the modern play.

A sphere: that of the hard-working middle class that grew rich, in contact and in conflict with the aristocratic world, which it needed in order to raise itself and which needed it in order to support itself. Living people: Poirier and Gaston, who were really Poirier and Gaston as Marguerite was Marguerite, not the burgher and the marquess of the repertory. One of these living people, Poirier, had the good fortune to remain a type, a piece of luck that Augier was to find a second time in Giboyer and that always eluded Dumas (in Dumas there was barely the shadow of

because nothing is more traditional than a music-hall sketch and, especially for a theater director, either a music-hall sketch is traditional or it is nothing. *Un Chapeau* was something, in its way, which was that of creating a new tradition that would last for a half century.

Un Chapeau substituted a sketch of action for the situation sketch, or, rather, it superimposed it on the situation sketch. The comic situations were no more than paper hoops through which a whole parade of what was supposed to be the height of comedy leaped and ran, the kind of crowd that lined up to throw balls at a country fair: a revel. The bungled revel became the sacred revel, I mean the revel of sacred frenzy of a procession in Aristophanes, of pure movement and Panic frenzy. Replace the revel with a troop of provincials visiting Paris: there you have *La Cagnotte*. *Un Chapeau* and *La Cagnotte* were for a long time Labiche's most popular plays. But this comedy of pure movement was only a part of the theater of Labiche, who put his name on more than three hundred plays and was a kind of Molière or Dumas the Elder of the vaudeville theater. He was and still is savored as a caricaturing moralist, a true contemporary of Daumier and Gavarni, whose theater remains as a living and inexhaustible album of middle-class profiles.

Labiche's burgher is the same as the burgher of *La Caricature* and *Les Physiologies:* not too bright, leering, lucky in business, selfish, a real Sganarelle and an imaginary Don Juan, round as a five-franc coin with Sancho's proverbs inscribed on it, he moved through this theater under a hundred names, like Homais through the streets of Yonville. But it was not Homais who made *Madame Bovary* a success, whereas it was the burgher who made Labiche a success by bringing recognition to the stage of the Palais-Royal or the Gymnase: recognition of neighbor by neighbor, of wife by husband, of husband by wife.

Until the 1914 war the Palais-Royal did *La Cagnotte* every summer; *La Cagnotte*, the Grévin Museum, and sole Marguery were the three ritual attractions of Paris for the little provincials in the last half of the nineteenth century. But Labiche was the only dramatic author of the nineteenth century whose success in books matched his success on the stage. The ten volumes of his selected plays filled the gap in the libraries between Paul de Kock and Courteline as the type of French bawdry. Nor is there any reason to exile them even today: *Célimare le bien-aimé*, *Le Voyage de M. Perrichon*, *Les Petits Oiseaux*, *La Grammaire*, *Le Misanthrope et l'auvergnat* have retained their beneficence as an evening's reading between the light supper and the bedtime tea.

MEILHAC AND HALÉVY

The third dramatic revolution that Sarcey recognized was that of *Orphée aux enfers*, an operetta resulting from the collaboration of the

normalien, Hector Crémieux, and the German musician, Jacques Offenbach, or a mixture of Ecole Normale humor and lyric buffoonery. But
Crémieux did not retain the height of this success, and Offenbach became
the musician by appointment to Meilhac and Halévy. While Dumas had
himself profited by the revolution of *La Dame aux camélias*, and Labiche
by that of *Un Chapeau de paille*, Meilhac and Halévy exploited the revolution made by Crémieux and alone were counted.

So this revolution would apparently date from *La Belle Hélène*, in
1864, followed by *Barbe-Bleue* and *La Vie parisienne* in 1866, *La Grande
Duchesse de Gérolstein* in 1867, *La Périchole* in 1868. These are remarkable types of plays written in collaboration, plays in which, conformably
to the healthy perspective of the theater, a man alone no longer existed.

The collaboration, of course, of Meilhac and Halévy, which here seems
indistinguishable and equal, formed by the very dialogue of two intelligent
men. Later, when witty and sentimental works would appear under the
same signature, pure comedies like *Froufrou*, *La Petite Marquise*, *La
Boule*, *La Cigale*, Meilhac's function would be rather that of the man of
the theater, the inventor of movements, of words, of emotion, while
Halévy's would be that of the observer and the critic—secondary here,
however, since the plays signed by Meilhac alone are as good as those of
the two collaborators and Halévy alone never tried anything for the stage.
It will be noted, moreover, that Labiche never wrote any of his plays
alone. A dialogue of authors often precedes the actors' dialogue.

The collaboration of the authors and the musician. In the old music
hall, and even in that of Labiche, verses were prescribed not only by tradition but also by the government, which, until the Second Empire, allowed only song-and-speech plays in light theaters and forbade them to
encroach on the privilege of the theaters of pure speech. It will be understandable, therefore, that the verses and the music had only a very tenu-
ous, official place. The case was not the same with the comic opera, or
the operetta, in which the orchestra timed, determined, took over all the
movement of the play, and which, with Crémieux and Offenbach, succeeded Scribe's comic opera in the world.

The collaboration of the authors, the musician, and the actors. In
Scribe's comic opera, all the detail was determined by the librettist and
the musician, and the actors had only to interpret it, as strictly as they
would interpret a play. But, even in comedy, an actor of genius had been
known to invent, even to re-create the play: that was the case of Fréd-
érick Lemaître and *L'Auberge des Adrets*. In the operetta of Meilhac and
Halévy, the action was laid down only in its basic outlines, and these
basic outlines succeeded in being a literary work. Among them there are
intervals in which the music takes the foreground and the actors can also
modify, improvise, tighten, or expand: obviously, this is feasible only
with a superior and very homogeneous company, as that of the Bouffes-

Parisiens was then. *La Belle Hélène,* very badly received in its early performances, was in part revised on the job by the actors, who brought back the audience and transformed a disaster into one of the greatest Parisian and European triumphs of the period. The authors' genius is in no way diminished thereby. Quite the contrary! The elastic play, the play that asks to be put into final shape, is a form that has its difficulties and its successes. The miracle is that it carried on, that after 1920 *La Belle Hélène* could still be seen triumphantly produced in Paris, in Stockholm, and elsewhere.

The collaboration of the authors, the musician, the actors, and the public. In this kind of *commedia dell'arte,* everything comes off as if the audience became a link in the chain, took part, and was transformed from passive to active public: that is the revolution of movement, like that of *Un Chapeau de paille.* The literary operetta of Meilhac and Halévy could not be understood without the audience, the manners, the echoes, the pace of those ten years of the liberal Empire that had their highest moment in the Exposition of 1867. *La Grande Duchesse de Gérolstein,* the play of that very year and Exposition, was Paris in Germany, and *La Vie parisienne,* which prepared the way for the Exposition the year before, was the Germanic foreigner in Paris. And even *La Belle Hélène,* in the heroic idiocy of Achilles and Ajax, did not hesitate to recall the generals of the Empire in the charades of Compiègne. Like *Le Mariage de Figaro* before the Revolution.

Offenbach and his music were carried off by 1870. But in 1869 Meilhac and Halévy had succeeded with a gay comedy with a touch of tears that was to be a success for thirty years, *Froufrou.* These animated pictures of Parisian life, brilliantly phrased, light, clever, were good for a generation. Meilhac and Halévy provided another foreground for the Exposition of 1878; Meilhac alone saw to the needs of that of 1889. His last play, *Ma Cousine,* was a success in 1890.

All these things were dazzling in their craftsmanship: Racine's "little matter and much art" had its triumph here. But, in this generation of technicians, the reputation of the greatest craftsman of his time went to Sardou.

Sardou

This reputation would be justified if Sardou had invented anything for the craft. But he invented nothing. About 1860 he conceived the idea, accurate essentially, that the whole craft of the theater was in Scribe. On the other hand, Scribe had been completely cast aside for ten years. He could serve as a professor without becoming a competitor. And the public has no memory. Sardou practiced his scales by reading two acts of a play by Scribe, but not the third, which he imagined for himself and which sometimes was better than the master's work. After training on fancy cakes, he gave the Gymnase *Les Pattes de mouche* in 1860 and the Vaudeville *Nos Intimes* in 1861: marvelous successes.

In *Les Pattes de mouche*, a letter plays the dynamic part of the Italian straw hat in Labiche's sketch, and it is chased through the interior of a Scribe comedy. It is no more clever, and it is enormously clever. *Un Chapeau* was a tour of Paris in Paris. In *Les Pattes* it is a world tour on a water glass, *Le Verre d'eau* of Scribe. The virtuosity of *Nos Intimes* is not superior, but almost as good, and Sardou applied it this time to an excellent comedy of manners. Thus, as early as 1861, he had written his best play.

He was able to repeat the same success in 1865 with *La Famille Benoîton*, in 1872 with the political comedy *Rabagas*, in 1880 with *Divorçons*. He was able to construct historical dramas like *Patrie!* (1869) and historical comedies like *Madame Sans-Gêne* in 1893, his final triumph. The great dramatic generation of the nineteenth century was concluding with a flourish. All that has been forgotten. Of the four or five great names that filled the theater between 1860 and 1890, Sardou was the most purely durable. A great constructor but not a great inventor, Scribe's heir remained an heir. And here was the consolation prize: an heir who himself left no heir. He had succeeded Scribe; no one has succeeded Sardou. Since 1893, the official post of prince of the craft has been vacant.

Barrière and Pailleron

The names of Dumas, Augier, Labiche, Meilhac-Halévy, and Sardou do not exhaust the theater of that happy era. The successes of Théodore Barrière (whose collaborator was Lambert Thiboust) under the Second Empire matched those of Dumas and Augier when, with too great facility, he brought to the stage the greed of the frigid professional courtesan in *Les Filles de marbre*, and those of Labiche with *Les Faux Bonhommes*, a bright, hard, and strong picture of three species of middle-class selfishness furnished with the fine names of the music-hall sketches of those days—Péponet, Bassecourt, and Dufourt—and with *Les Jocrisses de l'amour*. This moralistic vigor was lacking in Edouard Pailleron, a pleasant author of serial comedies, a fortunate specialist in *ingénue* parts for the Comédie-Française (*L'Etincelle, La Souris*), but also the author of *Le Monde où l'on s'ennuie*.

The case of *Le Monde où l'on s'ennuie* is quite instructive. Ever since its triumphant opening in 1881, it has been part of the regular current repertory of the Comédie-Française. Its ritual reappearance in the summer program recalls *La Cagnotte* at the neighboring theater. Now the play is thin, the workmanship is very clever but utterly without originality (the path of *Les Pattes de mouche* toward the chestnut trees of Figaro), the characters and their sentiments have no great relationship to modern mankind. Whence comes the loyalty of the public?

From the fact that, as a picture of a world, the play has never been supplanted. As Stendhal's *Armance* was subtitled *Un Salon en 1827*, *Le Monde où l'on s'ennuie* is "un Salon en 1881." A literary drawing room; Molière was not ashamed to put two of these on the stage, in *Le Misanthrope* and in *Les Femmes savantes* (without counting *Les Précieuses*). Pailleron took from Molière what he needed and what he could. He did it in Molière's own house: and the Comédie-Française alone could have given the play the strength of an institution as it does for its actresses on long leave of absence. Drawing rooms were Pailleron's natural environment: three years earlier he had already depicted a drawing room for the Gymnase in *L'Age ingrat*. The son-in-law of Buloz, he was the brother-in-law of a *salon*, and a *salon* hates a rival *salon*. Pailleron wrote the comedy of the literary *salon*, as Robert de Flers and Gaston-Arman de Caillavet were to write the comedy of the Académie in *L'Habit vert* and Edouard Bourdet the comedy of publishing in *Vient de paraître*. Three successes arising out of the same causes in a country, perhaps the only country, in which literature exists as a way of life, in a literature in which comedy was founded by *Les Précieuses ridicules*. It was fitting that this dramatic generation should establish the literary play of manners in the Comédie-Française, and Pailleron had that chance. He did not have it again in 1894 with *Cabotins*. *Ma Cousine* and *Madame Sans-Gêne* had made the full stop for this group, and there was nothing more to be done about it. The words, the stage, the chance belonged to another generation, another arrangement, another throw of the dice on the eternal board.

PHILOSOPHY

It Goes to the University

Between 1850 and 1885 the life of philosophy was divided even more sharply than the other forms of literary continuity into two periods that corresponded to the two political systems.

One of the lasting results of Cousin's influence was to domicile French philosophy for a long time, and indeed even until now, in the Ecole Normale. Cartesianism, from Descartes to Leibnitz, by way of Spinoza and Malebranche, has never been a philosophy of professors, and no more was it the doctrine of the philosophers of the eighteenth century. Professorial philosophy appeared, or, rather, reappeared, in Germany with Friedrich Augustus Wolf and received a great splendor from the fact that Kant and his three famous successors, Fichte, Friedrich Wilhelm Joseph Schelling, and Hegel were also university professors. For the first time since the thirteenth century, the tradition of the great professors of philosophy was revived on Mount Sainte-Geneviève by Victor Cousin, who rediscovered the public of Abelard. Cousin established philosophy as a way of university life and a history of systems. All that was lacking here was philosophy as philosophy. The Napoleonic university and Cousin's "regiment" could provide only a dreary caricature of German professorial philosophy, even when in 1831 the latter lost its crown with the death of Hegel.

As long as Cousin lived, and as much under the Second Empire, when the colonel of the philosophical regiment was pensioned off, as under the July monarchy, which was his period of active duty, officially philosophy was not only domiciled at the Ecole Normale; it was domesticated there. The reaction of 2 December 1851 tightened its collar. The colonel was succeeded by the corporal: Taine's setback in the examination for teachers of philosophy, the dismissal of Vacherot, excluded from the Ecole Normale after *La Métaphysique et la science,* the temporary suspension of the class and the examination in philosophy fenced off the paddock in which the distributors of professorships intended to isolate professorial philosophy. Whence the discredit of what was called official philosophy.

Under the July monarchy, Cousin's government had not prevented a great original philosophy from establishing itself: the positivist philosophy of Comte. In opposition to a philosophy of the realm of letters, Comte, the *polytechnicien*, a true heir of Descartes, had set up a philosophy of the realm of the sciences. The same tradition, the same opposition continued under the Second Empire, whose philosophy, in sum, contains three names: Antoine-Augustin Cournot, Renouvier, and Taine—that is, two *normaliens* and a *polytechnicien*.

COURNOT

Normally, Cournot would belong to the preceding generation: born in 1801, he was a contemporary of Comte. However, a *normalien* in the scientific section, a professor of analysis, who was moved into the upper administration from 1836 to 1862, he first wrote nothing but mathematical works, not releasing the result of his philosophical reflections until 1851, in three great works published at ten-year intervals beginning in that year: *Essai sur les fondements de nos connaissances et sur les caractères de la critique philosophique, Traité de l'enchaînement des idées fondamentales dans les sciences et dans l'histoire, Considérations sur la marche des idées et des événements dans les temps modernes.* They found almost no audience, and, being extremely modest, Cournot did not seek any. Almost all his glory as a philosopher is posthumous.

Few men of his time more quietly stirred up more ideas, generally unfinished, since he was satisfied to touch on them and move on to others. There was only one that he explored and dug through to the end and that he indeed made his domain: that was the idea of chance. Out of this negative term he patiently extracted the positive content that incorporates it, on the one hand, into the order and the reality of the world and, on the other, into the laws and calculations of mathematical probability. The definition of chance as an irrational meeting of independent causal series led Cournot's mind to a pluralism and a probabilism, and in sum to a way of thinking that overflowed, changed, unseated more or less all the contrary systems. No philosophical thinking was more different from Comte's than the thinking of this other mathematician. To read Cournot, which was an irritant for logical minds, was a pleasure to philosophers who liked Sainte-Beuve and Montaigne, those who enjoyed baths in ideas. His three great works, composed of numbered and rather disjointed paragraphs, are like pages of notes taken during his scientific and historical reading and classified in a succession in which chance, the philosopher's familiar demon, took a part. Little by little a collective view of the real can be distinguished in them (contingency and hierarchy of phenomena, innovation in their intersections and their successive levels), but it is not attempted formally, and it remains in an unstable balance, subject to new approximations, reserved for the adjustments and revisions of an invincible probabilism. In addition, Cournot lacked qualities of form that would have assured him of a real audience, and he remains a philosophers' game bird.

RENOUVIER

The same can be said of Renouvier. It is out of homage to the eternal nourishing snows of thought that we place him in a history that in principle deals only with inhabited, cultivated, and flourishing lands. Born in 1815, like Comte a Provençal and a *polytechnicien*, he belongs through his formative years to the July monarchy. He was one of those who, with Pierre Leroux, strove in 1848 to create a republican world of the spiritual, and on the request of the minister Lazare Carnot he prepared a *Manuel républicain de l'homme et du citoyen* whose revolutionary tone created a scandal and caused it to be filed in the red section of the spectrum. The *coup d'état* sent him back to philosophy with all the more good fortune in that he brought Hugo to poetry. In the ten years between 1854 and 1864 he published the four *Essais de critique générale*, which remain the best and the most substantial part of a work whose quantity was vast. Here he made an original synthesis of Kant and Comte, which after 1870 became an integral part of French philosophy. A positivist in principle like Comte, although he called himself his adversary, he based himself like Comte on science and especially on mathematics, calling the "law of numbers" the key; he applied this thinking not, like Comte, to the object of science, but to its subject—that is to say, to representation and its laws; in other words, to the problem of Kant. But he modified the Kantian positions on certain points: rejection of the noumenon, resolution of antinomies by the law of numbers, flexibility of categories that abandon imitation of metaphysical species to become simply general laws, or even categories of the general facts of representation. The title, *Essais de critique générale*, is admirably appropriate to these four basic volumes on logic, psychology, the philosophy of nature, and that of religion. They are essays in the manner of David Hume: in Renouvier there is a plan to return to Hume, the reaction to the "going beyond Hume" that is at the origin of the *Critique of Pure Reason*. He applies a critical method that examines everything in a logical spirit. And this criticism bears on the general and the universal, like Kant's. No one has valued criticism more highly than Renouvier; no one has used it more forcefully for more important purposes; no one has better explained its rights, its duties, and its limitations. Unfortunately his abstract, prickling style, like pieces of broken bottles, much harder even than Comte's, has restricted his influence to a domain of which the professional philosophers alone possess the keys. To take the full measure of the anti-literary nature of this *polytechnicien*, it must be noted that he found the subject of the most beautiful historical novel that anyone had ever imagined and, having decided to write it under the title of *Uchronie*, discovered a means of making it unreadable.

Returning to political speculation after 1871, Renouvier resumed his task of establishing the republican world of the spiritual, at the same time continuing to develop his critical philosophy in numerous works, the most remarkable of which is *L'Esquisse d'une classification systématique des doctrines philosophiques*. His complete retreat into his house in Perpignan and the austere obscurity of his style allowed him to exercise, without clamor and in depth, an influence on the world of professors of philosophy that was tremendous and that is to be encountered in Sorbonne theses, in the growing position held until about 1905 by Kantianism, in the creation of a lay morality, and in the Dreyfus movement.

TAINE

Similarly, it was only after 1871 that Taine's influence began to be felt among the philosophers, an influence due solely to *L'Intelligence*. What they retained of *L'Intelligence* was not the Condillac part, which turned to dust where it stood, not the English part, which Théodule-Armand Ribot went to investigate *in situ*, but the psychophysiology, case studies in illness. At the same time Auguste Comte's influence penetrated the University in 1877 with Espinas' thesis on *Les Sociétés animales*.

Ravaisson

The first years of the Republic marked a decompression and a rejuvenation of university philosophy. Cousin had died in 1867, quite forgotten by his old regiment. A part analogous to his, but this time based all on persuasion and good will, was played by one of his former disciples, who early quarreled with him: a contemporary of Renouvier, Félix Ravaisson, who never taught philosophy but who had revitalized Aristotelianism between 1836 and 1842 with a great charm of style, a depth of thought unknown to Cousin. In 1868 Ravaisson wrote a *Rapport sur la philosophie au XIXᵉ siècle*, impartial and penetrating, which ended in a dogmatic conclusion, thirty pages of which Bergson said that generations of philosophers had known them by heart. A memory, however, that was not without use, since Ravaisson held that very influential position, the chairmanship of the board of examiners for aspiring philosophy teachers.

Lachelier, Fouillée, Boutroux

In contrast, Jules Lachelier taught philosophy at the Ecole Normale from 1864 on. In his teaching there he revived the true philosophic method thrown into disorder by Cousin—that of a Descartes, a Ravaisson, a Biran. After the brief tenure of Alfred Fouillée, Emile Boutroux occupied the chair in 1877. These three philosophers maintained for thirty years in the world of high philosophy a style of thought of which their rare publications gave only an imperfect idea. They put the accent of the mind on immaterialism, on finalism, and above all on liberty. Out of this came a series of celebrated theses, which began in 1872 with Fouillée's and ended in 1889 with Bergson's. In this Renouvier was of valuable assistance to them. The elaboration of a theory of psychological freedom, in opposition to the determinism of the scientific philosophy of the English and of Taine, called forth the major effort of this generation of philosophers after 1870.

A Syncretism in Depth

This university philosophy, in which Plato, Aristotle, Descartes, Leibnitz, and above all Kant were admirably included, might be called the Saint Martin's summer, or, rather, the sole effective period, of eclecticism. Once Cousin had vanished, there appeared this free, inner and meditative syncretism of culture that the celebrated colonel's haste, verbalism, and imperialism had derailed in 1830 and sterilized for forty years. In his *Essai sur la métaphysique d'Aristote*, Ravaisson had presented the sole example of a great system recogitated from within. Renouvier had provided a second example with his study and his criticism of Kant. A syncretism in depth, a true society of systems of the mind, was thenceforth possible. A citadel of philosophic minds flourished in the last thirty years of the nineteenth century. It was certainly still a philosophy of professors, but in the spirit of free dialogue. The regiment was demobilized. Philosophy had returned to civil life and blended into the subtle essence of civilization.

Alliance with the Sciences

But this was only half of its conquest and of its life. The major event of this philosophic team, aided by the influence of Comte, Renouvier, and Taine, it will be seen, consisted in its entering into resolute and complete contact with the sciences. This was a return to the idea of philosophy as the great philosophers, who had also been great scientists, had conceived it: reflection on the objects and the accomplishments of the sciences, collaboration between philosophical research and scientific research, the mutual dialogue and stimulation of two disciplines that were really only one. The scientists, similarly, embarked on the philosophy of their science: a Claude Bernard, a Marcelin Berthelot. The philosophers turned toward the new sciences that grew out of philosophy—psychology and sociology. Here again appears the scientific character of this generation, its advance toward positivity.

PART FOUR

The Generation
of 1885

THE GENERATION OF 1885

The generation of 1850 disappeared at the end of the nineteenth century, replaced little by little by the generation that will be called here that of 1885 to 1895. There were a liquidation and a renewal very similar to those of 1850 to 1860, which bore directly on the values and the accomplishments of 1850 to 1860: that is, the personalities of the leading figures, the cult of science, formal and plastic poetry, realism.

The Deaths of the Leaders

The two great leaders, Renan and Taine, died—Taine in 1892, Renan in 1893. Taine was in a state of stoic pessimism before an era that he did not understand and for which he predicted the worst of fates; Renan was at the end of the very relaxed life of an indulgent intelligence. It was just their high rank as recognized leaders that emphasized the problem of their legacy in the minds of all, or, rather, the problem of new values, anti-Renan and anti-Taine in position, that might be fated to succeed them.

The Criticism of Science

The values that Taine and Renan had created and brought into acceptance were stamped with the image of reason and science. Now these values were not absolutely precarious, because their turn always came again; they were relatively precarious, because they had their part in an eternal human dialogue in which skepticism, the intuitive, and the irrational debate with reason, in which religion and philosophy, those inner experiences, debate with science, the system of outer experience. It gen-

erally happens that, taken as a whole, each generation is more or less appointed to one of the voices in this dialogue.

The history of this dialogue between fathers and sons after 1885 would
be worth a book of its own. In the single year of 1889, which was that
of one of those world's fairs by which, it seems, there was a desire every
eleven years between 1855 and 1900 to underline the end of an appreciable
third of a generation, there was the instructive coincidence of the publication of Renan's *L'Avenir de la science*, *Pensées de 1848*, Bergson's *Essai
sur les données immédiates de la conscience*, and Paul Bourget's *Le Disciple*.

L'Avenir de la science was a new book only for the bookshops. Kept
until then in manuscript, it had been written by Renan in 1848 in Paris,
at the same age at which Bergson in Clermont in 1887 wrote the thesis
that took the road that we know: the age of twenty-eight. The interval
between the two books, forty years, is the same as that separating Taine's
Philosophes françaises from Cousin's course of 1817. The dialogues between generations of philosophers were articulated in time as Plato would
have articulated them in space.

Les Philosophes françaises, moreover, was a book of direct personal
attack. There was nothing of the kind in Bergson's *Essai*, just a firm and
quiet *no* from psychology and philosophy to the system of values that
Taine's *L'Intelligence* had applied to them—that is, to external analysis
and ideological synthesis. It would have only small importance for the
historian of literature if this philosophical reaction did not serve as a
sign or a symbol of a movement that was then current everywhere. A
few months after Renan's death, an article by Brunetière, *Après une
visite au Vatican*, provoked a tremendous battle on the value of science,
and the extreme poverty of that article showed clearly that this agitation
had arisen only out of the ripeness, the timeliness, of the problem at the
moment when it was posed and had nothing to do with the anything but
competent individual who stated it. Berthelot, in a sense Renan's co-author
in *L'Avenir de la science* (since this book was the transcript of their conversations in 1848), entered the arena like an old athlete, with the same
spirit and the same outmoded arguments of the young of 1848.

Now Brunetière and Bourget had been friends in their youth and in
their thinking, like Renan and Berthelot. They were almost forty years
old in 1889 and they did not exactly belong to the generation of 1885. But
Le Disciple, that question mark of 1889 between religion and science, that
uneasy book by a novelist between two generations, too young to belong
to the one and too old to belong to the other, came to seem, by reason of
its accord with the uneasiness of the times and by reason of its success,
only the more like a book of enlightenment, a key book at this turning
point.

Materialism and Immaterialism

A great generation of historians and of positive philosophers, the twenty-year-olds of 1850 had brought a literature of inventories to perfection in poetry and in the novel. Parnassus turned to a poetic inventory of the past, realism to a descriptive inventory of the present. Documentary poetry and documentary fiction. Here again it was a matter of plastic, solid, material values. Not a philosophical materialism but a sort of immanent materialism was erecting a strong and well-made base under this generation.

After 1885 this immanent materialism was succeeded by a kind of immanent immaterialism. It was not only or especially a question of Bergsonism, which was to lead, in *La Perception du changement*, to an immaterialism as subtle as Bishop Berkeley's. It was a question of poetry, of what had risen out of music to envelop, dissolve, and vaporize poetry. Reaction against Parnassus, in the time of symbolism, was as precise a slogan as reaction against romanticism in 1850.

Could an analogous direction be observed in the novel? In this generation the novel was to remain a consolidated form. The previous generation had posed the problem of the inheritance of Balzac. This problem existed little, if at all, for the generation of 1885. It had abandoned hope of having its Balzac. It recognized that, all things considered, Zola had not taken his place, that Maupassant's short stories were only the local voting list of the novel, a broken mirror in which it did not recognize its reflection. Bourget and Anatole France were intelligent novelists, and almost the entire novelist crew after 1885 would also belong to the class of intelligent novelists (even Pierre Loti, the autobiographer and intimate diarist, would not be an exception). But, when a novelist is called intelligent, that means also that he is not very creative. In this generation immanent immaterialism in the world of the novel was evidenced by a lack of that brutal material, that virility of a cerebral mule driver that were shared by Balzac, Flaubert, Zola, and Maupassant and that seem more essential to the natures of novelists than to those of philosophers and poets.

The same relative deficiency appeared in the theater. The materiality proper to the theater consists not in this creative virility but in the techniques of the artisan with which the generation of 1850 had been exceptionally endowed and that waned after 1890.

The Problem of Masters

Who were the masters of this generation of 1885? It will be observed
at the start that the reaction against Renan and Taine did not have that
quality of a collective movement that the reaction against romanticism
had assumed along the whole front of the generation of 1850. The philosophy of that sardonic old man, Ecclesiastes, illusionless and kindly, that
of the balance of opposites, which had been the final form of Renanism,
could hardly seduce the young of any period, and it is understandable
that Renan, regarded as "negative," was escorted across the borders of
the Republic of Men of Good Will after 1893 by the young "positives"
of action, of today's duty, of the merits of energy. As for Taine, he long
retained the prestige of his work. If *Le Disciple* erected a question mark
in front of Taine, *L'Etape*, thirteen years later, gave him a sign of adhesion.

The function of master, after Renan and Taine, was fulfilled by France
and Bourget, who belonged to an intercalary generation, and by Bergson
and Barrès, who were part of the generation on the march. France, when
he is not a pure artist and a pure storyteller, puts Renan into myths;
Barrès and Bergson do the same with Taine; and Bergson would not have
to be excessively removed from the philosophical domain to be diffused
into literary influences. There was nothing comparable to the great universal figures of the generation of 1850.

The originality of the generation of 1885 in French literary geography
was derived principally from its straight and narrow path, very different
from the lane that its predecessors had traveled. The generation of 1820
had had to go through a political revolution, the revolution of 1830; the
generation of 1850 had been more or less dislocated by the War of 1870:
both, in other words, by the great common occurrences of the life of the
nineteenth century, revolution and war. The generation of 1885 experienced something special that was neither revolution nor war, that had no
resemblance to anything that preceded or followed it: this was the Dreyfus case.

The Dreyfus Case

The Dreyfus case was not only an intellectual event but the event of
the intellectuals. It compelled intelligence to take sides for one or the
other of the values of which this generation was already the battlefield:
either that pragmatic truth of adhesion, of sensibility, and of interest that
governed religious, national, and social beliefs, or else impersonal truth,
based on objective investigation, which is the familiar domain of scholars,

professors, magistrates. An artistic providence created the Dreyfus case in order to afford them an arena. New young groups, which were produced specifically by the Dreyful case and which remained marked by it, appeared in both camps. Here we are compelled to do what we did not have to do for the revolution of 1830, the *coup d'état* of 1851, the war of 1870, or any of the famous events that were matched by a literary break or turning point and that are sufficiently well known to allow us to proceed by allusion. A more reinforced and more complete picture is necessary. The Dreyfus case was not sufficiently integrated into political history and the memory of later generations to let allusion suffice. We shall make every effort, however, not to go beyond the literary aspect of this case.

We should observe first of all that the generation of 1885 was the first literary generation in which groups of Jewish writers had figured in any considerable number. It is true that the preceding generation had already included Ludovic Halévy, Hector Crémieux, and Catulle Mendès, and there were important newspapers and bookshops controlled by Jules Mirès, Millaud, Michel Lévy. In the generation of 1885 an extraordinary place was occupied by the young Jews of the Lycée Condorcet, *La Revue blanche*, the Ecole Normale. Their families for the most part had achieved some wealth in the rise of Parisian business under the Second Empire, and they brought into letters an intelligence that was precocious, sharp, brilliant, eager, that was urbane—that is, doubly Parisian in that it was Alexandrian as well as Parisian.

With this same generation anti-Semitism appeared. Edouard Drumont's *La France juive* appeared in 1886. Subsequently this powerful pamphleteer gave a popular anti-Semitism its newspaper and its public. It was this diffused anti-Semitism that, in 1894, when leaks had been discovered in the Ministry of War, focused suspicions on an Alsatian officer, the only Jew in the office of the General Staff, from which the documents transmitted to a foreign power had apparently been taken. He was Captain Alfred Dreyfus, who was convicted despite his protestations of innocence. Three years later his family and friends, on the basis of illegalities committed in his trial, raised the question of a review. The most prominent and the most active among them was a celebrated member of the Chamber, Joseph Reinach.

Joseph Reinach, in fact, belonged, with his two brothers, Salomon and Théodore, to the most learned and the most brilliant family of Jewish intellectuals, known for their university achievements between 1875 and 1880. In addition, he had married the daughter of his uncle, Jacques de Reinach, a Frankfurt banker, a Panama buccaneer, the Nucingen of the opportunist Republic, who committed suicide in 1892. He enjoyed a tremendous and not wholly undeserved unpopularity. He aroused not

only the natural clamors of the anti-Semites but also the distrust of the
nicest people, who did not at all discount the legend according to which
a Jewish syndicate, headed by Reinach, had been created in order to free
a coreligionist sentenced in 1894. In addition, the first appeal on behalf of
Dreyfus was made by a Jewish writer, Bernard Lazare, and unanimously
denounced by the Chamber in 1896. A former General Staff officer, Lieutenant Colonel Picquart, had also expressed well-founded doubts of the
captain's guilt; two Senators, Scheurer-Kestner and Ludovic Trarieux, had
declared that the trial had been improper. But the nation trusted its military leaders, who underwrote the justice of the verdict of 1894.

The "Intellectuals"

In a letter in Le Temps of 6 November 1897, Gabriel Monod, professor of history at the Ecole Normale Supérieure, explained how he had
been convinced of a judicial error in the verdict after a study of the information supplied by Scheurer-Kestner and a lawyer, Leblois, who was
an intimate of Picquart. The anti-Semitic press calumniated Monod, and
the students of the Ecole Normale launched a public defense of their professor. The intellectual and literary aspect of the Dreyfus case may be
dated from this letter. Monod was a professional in historical criticism;
the Ecole Normale, defined by Nisard as the school of precision of the
French mind, was at least a school of criticism. Now Monod's antagonists
were to answer him not in the arena of criticism but in that of oratorical
and literary ideas. They said: "He is a Protestant, like Scheurer-Kestner.
Both of them have 'Protestant reactions.'" In order to assert the guilt of
Dreyfus and confidence in the leaders of the army, French and Catholic
"reactions" would have to oppose these "Protestant reactions." Besides,
they said as well, the normaliens were book-learners, new men, stock-
brokers: six months before Monod's letter, La Revue de Paris had published Les Déracinés, by Barrès, in which the stock exchange led to crime.

Barrès and the Case

Barrès was then writing L'Appel au soldat. He was to say in his memoirs:
"I have needed no other ideas than those in which I have bathed since
birth. Thanks to them, I have always known absolutely what was the
truth. My nationalism was only their expression, their cry, and their

thrill. When the Dreyfus case came, my father was dead. I believe that everything that I said then came from our home. Lavisse was not mistaken about this. The day when I went to see him about my application (for entrance to the Ecole Normale, of which he was then the director), he told me: 'I can see in you everything that I saw at Nancy. I will not vote for you.' I told him how much I thought it must pain him to be marching with the enemies of the army. My mother wrote me an unforgettable letter. Having read my Rennes article on Picquart, she told me, she had gone again to my father's grave to reread it there." That showed why the memorandum had been written by Dreyfus.

At the end of 1897, Dreyfus' brother discovered and denounced the real author of the document imputed to Dreyfus and the principal source of his conviction: a Hungarian *condottiere* named Esterhazy. Zola, whom Scheurer-Kestner had convinced that Dreyfus was innocent, joined the battle. On 20 November 1897 he wrote an article for *Le Figaro* in which, in a turgid and unpleasant manner, he called for a review of the 1894 trial. That night he dined at the Durand Restaurant with Bourget and Barrès, who wrote in his *Cahiers:* "One word impressed me very much in the mouth of Zola during that meal . . . He said of his proof: it is scientific, it is scientific. Those are the same words that I have so often heard in the same sense from fools—not liars, but the illiterates of public meetings."

Zola's Intervention

In the three years since 1894, indeed, Zola had just published *Lourdes* and *Rome* and had just finished *Paris*, which in time followed *Le Docteur Pascal*. It was a literary setback: here his science of religion was the equal of his religion of science. *Lourdes* was written by Homais, *Rome* by Bouvard, and *Paris* by Pécuchet. He had irritated the Catholics, to whom the reign of the new spirit had restored confidence and vitality. For years his articles in *Le Figaro* had been material for columnists' jokes, and all the young writers had riddled him with sarcasms. This was a fighter that attracted blows.

He attracted blows, but with his noise and his weight he unleashed a tremendous agitation, to which other ground swells replied from the opposite side. A war of religion, a storm unknown since Jansenism, broke out. Several years earlier Drumont's newspaper had replaced *L'Univers* as the journal of the minor clergy, which rediscovered in *La Libre Parole* the messianism of Henry V and a favorable atmosphere for denunciations of the bishops. In *La Croix* the Assumptionists revived the passions and the violences of the League.* The Jesuits thought themselves obliged to take the same side, and their real or supposed presence in any matter always brings the passions of both sides to a boil.

On 4 December 1897, Zola and the partisans of a review of Dreyfus' trial were defeated by a vote in the Chamber, where the Radicals and the Socialists joined forces against them. On 13 December *Le Figaro* did the decent thing and divorced Zola, who was reduced for a while to publishing pamphlets, a *Lettre à la jeunesse* and another letter *A la France*. These were verbose repetitions that accomplished nothing. Meanwhile, Ernest Vaughan, a former collaborator of Henri de Rochefort, who had founded *La Lanterne*, a violently anti-Empire weekly, established a newspaper, *L'Aurore*, which was quickly won over to the fight for review. Its political editorials were written by Georges Clemenceau; though he was still hesitant, he knew how to shout louder than Drumont. It was in *L'Aurore* that, on 13 January 1898, Zola published his letter addressed to the President of the Republic, *J'accuse*.

J'accuse identified eight military men responsible for the torture inflicted on an innocent man. Among them were two Ministers of War. It was because he named names that this time Zola made the lightning flash. Two hundred thousand copies sold in a few hours, questions asked in the Chamber, prosecutions. *J'accuse* is in no way a literary monument. But, for the first time since the first of *Les Provinciales*,† a handbill sold in the streets sounded the trumpet for a war of religion.

Three weeks after *J'accuse*, the 5 February issue of the official Jesuit review, *La Civiltà Cattolica*, declared: "The Jews have invented the allegation of a judicial error. The plot was worked out at the Zionist congress in Basle, convoked ostensibly to discuss the deliverance of Jerusalem. The Protestants made common cause with the Jews for the creation of a syndicate. The money came from Germany. . . . The Jews allege a judicial error. The real error was that of the Constituent Assembly, which granted them French nationality. That law must be repealed." On the other side, after the publication of Zola's letter, *L'Univers Israélite* began presenting the case as the fruit of a plot by the Church against the intellect and concluded: "It is then up to us—Jews, Protestants, Freemasons, whoever seeks light and liberty—to stand shoulder to shoulder and fight so that France, in the words of one of our prayers, may keep her place among the nations, for a black crow has already dug its claws into the head of the Gallic rooster and begun to pluck out its eyes." The reference to the

---

* The Sainte Ligue, formed in 1576 by the Duc de Guise in order to defend Catholicism against the Calvinists and seat the Guises on the throne by overthrowing Henri III. The League, allied with Philip II of Spain, was destroyed by Henri IV.—Translator.

† Eighteen letters written by Pascal in 1656–1667 to defend Port-Royal against the Jesuits.—Translator.

Freemasons was premature, for at that time they opposed a review. Thus spake the organ of the illustrious Society of Jesus and the official journal of French Judaism, directed by eminent and sober men. The promises of such literature were fulfilled.

Emile Duclaux, director of the Institut Pasteur, followed Monod in insisting on the necessity for a review. These were still only lonely voices. *J'accuse* sparked the movement of the revisionist intellectuals, or simply the "intellectuals," a word used at first as a label of contempt by the anti-revisionist journals. The intellectuals included, among others, the chemist, Grimaud; Anatole France, Ernest Desjardins, Gabriel Séailles, Darlu, Michel Bréal, Louis Havet, and Gaston Bonnier, the botanist.

The centers of intellectual revisionism were primarily in the Ecole Normale, where the dominant influence was that of the Socialist librarian, Lucien Herr (who was credited with the conversion of Jaurès to socialism), abetted by Monod, C. Andler, and Paul Dupuy; among the young *normaliens*, Péguy first of all, Paul Langevin, a physicist; Jean Perrin, Albert Thomas; among their elders, Léon Blum and Victor Bérard. It was this university group that brought what was called Dreyfusism out of the Dreyfus case and the "Dreyfusard" movement. In addition, two *salons*, those of Mme. Emile Strauss, born Halévy, and Mme. Arman de Caillavet, became the centers of a Dreyfusism that was more social than doctrinaire and that recruited protesters among writers and what was called the Right Bank.

On 24 February 1898, the day after the Court of Assizes for the Department of the Seine had sentenced Zola to a year in prison for *J'accuse*, a meeting was held in the home of Senator Trarieux at which Dreyfusism acquired an incarnation in the creation of the League for the Rights of Man and the Citizen. Thus Dreyfusism identified itself with the principles of the French Revolution, with civic education, with the republican spirit. The old phrase, "Gospel of the Rights of Man," took on a new meaning and a new necessity. The principal founders were the scientists Grimaud and Duclaux; Professors Paul Meyer, Giry, Auguste Molinier, Paul Viollet, graduates of the Ecole des Chartes; Professors Séailles and Georges Lyon; the philosophers Desjardins, Havet, Emile Bourgeois, Lucien Herr, Gabriel Réville; the physicians Richet and Paul Reclus; Arthur Fontaine; Renan's son and son-in-law (Berthelot, who cherished his peace, remained aloof). The League's by-laws were drafted by a Catholic, Paul Viollet, who came from the Jansenist tradition, a fact that is important to the historian of ideas in France (Royer-Collard would have been the rock of Dreyfusism). Viollet and his most prominent cofounders, however, were to resign from the League when it degenerated into an anti-clerical body.

The Creation of Leagues

The League for the Rights of Man, then the general headquarters of the militant intellectuals, should not be separated here from the "sympathetic" intellectuals brought together by petitions of protest against the trial of Picquart by a military court; they included Sully-Prudhomme, Sardou, Lavisse, Gaston Paris, and hundreds of professors, scientists, and men of letters (Marcel Prévost, Edmond Rostand, André Picard, Capus, Georges de Porto-Riche).

The establishment of the League for the Rights of Man preceded by six months the discovery of the forgery by Lieutenant Colonel Henry which was the turning point of the case. (It should have turned automatically toward a review but the pride of the Minister of War, G. Cavaignac, turned it instead toward civil war.) Four months after Henry's suicide, the anti-Dreyfus intellectuals formed the League for the French Fatherland (December 1898). It included more than half the members of the Académie: twenty-two academicians, including Brunetière, Gaston Boissier, Bourget, Victor Cherbuliez, all the academic dukes in a body, a few professors—Paul Janet, Charles Hermitte, Alfred-Nicolas Rambaud, Petit de Julleville, Emile Faguet, almost all from the preceding generation. Its real founder, Vaugeois, aided by Maurras, who brought Mistral into it, came from the League for Moral Action, which was pro-Dreyfus from the start. Later he was to found L'Action française.

The three leaders of the League for the French Fatherland, anti-revisionists and traditionalists, were Coppée, who was as popular as the upper deck of a bus and who was counted on to perform for anti-Dreyfusism the services rendered to revisionism by Zola; Jules Lemaître, the deputy from the anti-revisionist salon of Mme. de Loynes, who wanted to have her own Anatole France just like Mme. de Caillavet's revisionist salon (women played a large part in the case); Barrès, who, with Maurras and Vaugeois, gave the League its spiritual substance. The League's part at the time of Emile Loubet's election (he was president of the Senate and later President of the Republic), its disaster in the election of 1902, and the Gabriel Syveton scandal drained the League of all this spiritual substance. It could not hold on even to those cells of minores who on the other side made it possible for the League for the Rights of Man to survive as a political organization, an appendage of Masonry.

The two leagues were briefly the general headquarters of the ideas of this period. Their rosters of membership, which are most eloquent, help to classify those ideas and constitute the map of an intellectual generation. Here are the principal features of that geography:

The rejuvenation of the old line of religious divisions, a rejuvenation linked, in addition, to the life of the Third Republic; to the entrance of

Jews into French intellectual life; to the policies of the Catholics and the rightist parties between 1871 and 1890, which revived for the country one of the problems of 1830—that of the "priests' government"—and which propagated, especially under the monastic robe, the species of the government priest; to the opposing policies of the republican leader groups, which, beginning in 1880, generally entrusted the spiritual welfare of the University and the management of the great schools for teachers to liberal Protestantism; to the duty that the traditionalist and Catholic families evicted from political and administrative positions felt incumbent upon them—the duty to remain landowners, social leaders, and soldiers and to create for themselves a conception of life that corresponded to that way of living; to the good moral conscience and the literary expression that, flourishing in a large and cultivated elite, helped to erect ideologies that legitimatized, illuminated, and idealized these spontaneous conceptions of the world, the mind, and France; and, finally, to the release of inherited religious drives, to the voices of the dead. For four years the family, the conscience, the schools, the state were the forums of such dialogues, of such clashes. Never had any generation had so magnificent an opportunity to clarify and contrast the ideas of France.

The outcome of the battle (or, rather, the outcomes) was no less instructive than the battle itself. There is no longer any obscurity in the Dreyfus case, which was resolved and concluded in 1906 by the investigation of the Court of Cassation, the judgment of this supreme tribunal, and the complete rectification of the judicial errors committed with regard to Dreyfus, Picquart, and Zola. The political conclusion of the matter was no less clear: the destruction of the nationalist party, the victory of the republican defense, the victory of the republican attack with the laws restricting the religious orders and the separation of Church and state.

But in 1906 the separation had been accomplished; the great journalist who was the artisan of revision, Clemenceau, was Minister of the Interior; Dreyfus and Picquart were back in the army; later Picquart would be Minister of War; the general elections, three months after the court's decision, put Clemenceau into power; the parties of the right (as they say) pulled themselves together, or pulled their pieces together. How, for its part, was the intelligentsia going to react?

Anatole France and the Dreyfus Case

Only one writer acquired the rank of a master, and indeed a good master, from the Dreyfus case: that was Anatole France. For fifteen years his position in France and in Europe would be an important one. People thronged to his house; his anecdotes were repeated everywhere; interest was keen in his Socialist development, his messages; his memorable conversations were recorded and collected. And yet the place of Taine and Renan remained unfilled.

Primarily it was not filled because Anatole France, Parnassian and stylist, did not belong to the generation of 1885 as Taine and Renan had belonged to the previous generation. It was not filled because the belated adherence of M. France to the ideas and doctrines of socialism, which he had not so much experienced as a man as he had defended them as a citizen and presented them as an artist, brought nothing new into intellectual life; the splendid maker of phrases had found an admirable one to describe Zola's part in 1898: "a moment of human conscience." In the same way Anatole France would be a link in the literary chain, upholding something and adding little.

The Dreyfus case, which came to fruition in victory for the parties and the forces of the left, did not bear similar fruit for the ideas of the left, for social justice, the rights of man, democracy, free inquiry. The hopes placed in Jaurès, in the Dreyfusard generation of the rue d'Ulm, the attempt at a return to Michelet and Quinet fell short. Anatole France's speech before the statue of Renan in Tréguier gave off only a cold light.

Barrès, Maurras, Péguy

In the camp of the defeated, in contrast, the rebound was instantaneous. Barrès remained a creator of values: the best years of his influence were those between 1902 and 1914. Out of the ashes of the League for the French Fatherland was born *L'Action française*, and the influence of Maurras balanced and prolonged that of Barrès. This strange reversal, this victory of the unexpected, had nowhere a clearer explanation than in Péguy, the more so because out of this Dreyfusard generation of the Ecole Normale, which provided so large a part of the political personnel of the twentieth century, Péguy was the only creator of movement in the literary and moral domain to emerge, and because Péguyism is the very transcript of this turning point of Dreyfusism. Finally, the even more unforeseen consequence of the separation of Church and state, of the triumph of laicism in the state, was a Catholic revival and spectacular, often singular, literary conversions: those of Brunetière, Péguy, Renan's grandson; the Catholic diversions of Barrès; the Thomist movement. The ground of objective truth on which the intellectuals of 1897 conquered juridically, morally, and politically in the Dreyfus case was thus a worse ground for literary ideas and the literary spirit than the ground of organic, inherited, passional truth whose complete geography and geology have been recorded by Barrès from *Un Homme libre* to *Les Cahiers*. The former ground, however much more satisfying to the intelligence, more suited to civil, moral, and political usage, is like Berthelot's ideal nutrient—it lacks vitamins, those that vitalized a *Cahier* of Barrès, and that a Jaurès, however eloquent, could not even guess at. The most important attempt that the Dreyfusard generation made before 1914 to balance the literary ideas of Barrès with its own vitamins was probably Romain Rolland's *Jean-Christophe*, and that was not to be a complete success.

Jean-Christophe is a novel. It will help to make clear to us the minimal extent to which the generation called realist, that of 1850, and its naturalist successors were supplanted in the novel by the generation of 1885. Maupassant had died in 1893. The years of the Dreyfus case carried off the leaders of the novel—Goncourt died in 1896, Daudet in 1897, Zola in 1902. Perceiving the void that they left, one would say that this generation had used up its novel in living, with the Dreyfus case, as the generation of 1789 had used up its novel and its poetry in action. The Dreyfus case is probably the only victorious competition that the official register in its turn has ever offered to *La Comédie humaine*. The two years that elapsed between *J'accuse* and the trial at Rennes have remained famous in the history of the crises of French publishing; no books and especially no novels were sold, the public wanted only newspapers: Zola's trial, Picquart's imprisonment, Henry's forgery, General Chanoine's treachery, Félix Faure's death, race results at Auteuil and Longchamp, Dreyfus' return, the Rennes military tribunal surpassed *La Comédie humaine* in force of meaning and "philosophical studies" and *Les Mystères de Paris* and *Le Juif errant* in dramatic interest.

II

THE NOVEL

The novel after 1885 is evidence of a diminution in literary creation, which, however, it expressed in a very positive manner, transforming the insolvency of the novel into the novel of insolvency, utilizing this ebb as a motive power, expressing itself through the forms, more intellectual than vital, of the personal novel, the novel of analysis, the problem novel, and the myth novel that were revivified by the important writers and novelists of this period: Loti, Bourget, France, Barrès, Gide.

The personal novel, which is a disguised autobiography, has been an old tradition of French literature since Rousseau. The realism of Champfleury and the Goncourts carved out its great "slices of life." Naturalism opened a limitless, wearisome, constantly traveled road to it and in sum democratized it: the little writer narrated his little life, his job, his army service, his schooldays, his restaurants, his mistresses. But it happened that a great writer, even though starting with the same inventory, infinitely transcended it; and by virtue of the nature of his style and the nature of his life, this was the case with Pierre Loti.

Loti

Loti was a Protestant sailor from that old French Holland, the region of La Rochelle and Rochefort, and, like many Protestants, like Constant, like Amiel, he started early to keep an intimate diary. His life as a sailor, his natural concern to retain some recollection of all the parts of the world to which his job took him, strengthened, fed, and enriched this taste and this habit of diary-keeping. He read little and experienced no literary influences. Having written at first only for himself, without concern for a reader, he clung, even after he acquired readers, to all the habits of style created in this loneliness. He did not strive after words, he always used the same ones, and this made his language extremely poverty-stricken. But, with these few words, he portrayed this whole world, basically uniform and always falling back to the same foundations, of the sea, the light, land, the senses, ordinary, simple emotions. Toward the age of thirty, he began to arrange (more than he later admitted) the notebooks of a stay in Constantinople in order to use them as the basis for *Aziyadé*—the story of a young officer's love affair with a Turkish woman. This was followed by *Le Mariage de Loti*, a Tahitian diary, and *Le Roman d'un Spahi*, taken from a Senegalese soldier's diary. The old theme of *Graziella*, the easy novel of easy loves, the nomad novel of nomad loves, the anecdotes of ports and the picturesqueness of the colonies, rigorously free of romantic imagination and Lamartinian rhetoric—such freshness, in that era of method, such artlessness, standing out against the artifices of naturalist description and the sterilities of the fashionable novel, soon assembled round Loti a part of the public that was to give *Le Pêcheur d'Islande* one of the memorable triumphs of the French novel.

It is not because *Le Pêcheur d'Islande* is the most famous of Loti's books that one endorses the facile paradox that it is not his finest book. But it stands a little apart from the rest of his work. This time Loti wanted to write a novel, and it has hardly anything more to do with pages from a diary. He who had lived among sailors and loved them wrote the novel of a sailor, the Breton loves of a Breton sailor. A novel, a narrative, a description imbued with the most simple, the most modest, irresistibly penetrating poetry of pure language and classic bareness, the rhythm of a popular song or a ballad. Published in the year that followed Victor Hugo's death and *Germinal* and therefore at the crest of naturalism, *Le Pêcheur d'Islande* was a kind of physical decompression that everyone could feel. It transcended Loti's literary personality to vibrate with the immaterialism that was the proper message of that generation and that 1889 would confirm with more emphatic features in Bourget's *Le Disciple*, with intelligible symbols in Bergson's *Essai*. At least once Loti showed too that he was a compatriot of Fromentin, the novelist and painter.

Mon Frère Yves, also a portrait of a sailor, forms a more relaxed, more casual pendant to *Le Pêcheur d'Islande*. It had an equal success, but it has not lasted as well. *Madame Chrysanthème* and *La Troisième jeunesse de Madame Prune* are not lacking in attraction, and in fact almost all the pages of description of Japan taken from Loti's journal have an unmatchable fineness of vision and of easy transposition. But one must not look here for the slightest Japanese humanity: this is not the Japan of Loti, which is, just as he saw it, small and caricatural; it is the Loti of Japan.

Beginning with *Matelot*, a third sailor portrait, which offers nothing new, the novels or half-novels more or less drawn from Loti's journal become tedious. *Ramuntcho* is a Basque chore; *Les Désenchantées*, for which women readers provided the best sales that Loti ever had, arises out of a trick by two Frenchwomen who disguise themselves as Turks to keep it going, in the same way in which the author disguised himself as an Arab for the photographers. An exception must be made, however, for one Turkish book in which Loti recaptured all the emotion and poetry of *Le Pêcheur d'Islande:* this is *Fantôme d'Orient*, the story of a voyage to Constantinople in order to try to find Aziyadé again. Gérard de Nerval would have admired it, and it is the most Nervalesque work written since the drama of the rue de la Vieille-Lanterne.

But Loti exercised no more influence than he received, unless perhaps in arousing vocations for literature among seamen. He stands alone, very simple, attuned by his best works to elementary, constant, and classic forces in French literature. He had nothing to do with his time except to show that he did not understand anything of it, and his time had little to do with him. Yet it was just the oppressive weight of naturalism and the idealist and symbolist breath of fresh air that helped him from the outset, and considerably, to gain a tremendous public. Has it survived? The truth is that many readers today get through him quickly and the sophisticated affect to reject all his work except *Au Maroc* and, especially, *Vers Ispahan.*

Bourget

The young Loti's sudden glory was exactly contemporaneous with Bourget's (Bourget was born two years later, in 1852), for it was also between 1885 and 1888 that the author of *Essais de psychologie contemporaine* published *Cruelle Enigme, Crime d'amour*, and *Mensonges*, which set everyone to talking and infatuated the fashionable and educated public. After a half century they had hardly any readers left, but the historian of literature can never reproach them for having supplied nothing new, for not having marked a date in what Brunetière called the evolution of their kind. At most they suffer from being too consciously and deliberately the anti-Zola of their time that the elevated public demanded.

Zola, who was matter made man, had created the physiological novel in *Les Rougon-Macquart*. Bourget answered him with the psychological novel—that is, the novel that analyzes states of emotion, crises of conscience, inner debates demanded by dramatic events. Bourget incorporated as much of drama, as much of theatrical technique into his novels as Zola incorporated of epic poetry into his. But in both the machinery is cumbersome and strained. In Bourget there is a materialism of technique even more apparent than Zola's.

Zola was a temperament without culture. It would be extreme to say that Bourget was a culture without temperament, but in any event he was an intelligent novelist, who had demonstrated great skill, in the *Essais de psychologie*, in handling complex literary ideas. Both were disciples of Taine; Zola took from him what the average took while Bourget took what the literate took; neither took what the philosophers took.

Zola's public was a lower-middle-class public, or middle-class, what was called "the new levels," what is now called democratic. There are very rich people in his novels, in *La Curée* and *L'Argent*, all of them newly rich and wicked, and their wealth has shameful origins. There are no people born rich, no heirs, or, if they do appear, they are extras and they are flawed, like Renée Saccard. Nor are there any women of fashion in his books, and not many among his readers. Bourget, on the other hand, was to write the novel of the comfortable classes for the comfortable classes, the novel of their sentimental complications, their "ideas," their heritage. Certainly something of Bourget was already to be found in Feuillet. But it is noteworthy that Bourget's world is no longer in any way Feuillet's: it is very much the world of the Third Republic, and Bourget's success came much less through the French aristocracy than through the cosmopolitan and Jewish *salons* of 1888, which were wide open to literature. Adultery is not the shocking rarity with him that it is with Feuillet; it is in fact the driving shaft of the novel.

Zola's novels are novels of the left. "The Republic will be naturalist or it will simply not be." Bourget's fiction would be fiction of the right. The same invincible leverage pushed both into the novel of ideas—religious, social, and political ideas: Zola at the end of his life and very awkwardly, in *Les Quatre Evangiles*, Bourget almost from the beginning, and very skillfully, first of all in *Le Disciple*.

In *Le Disciple* the psychological novelist wrote the novel of a psychologist, or, rather, of two psychologists, the master and the disciple. Bourget knew what a psychologist was, better than the author of *Le Docteur Pascal* knew what a scientist was: yet Taine, who had more or less served as Bourget's model, made him some sharp observations on the matter in a letter; and above all the disciple, who seduces a girl for the sake of his work, in order to document himself, as the novelists used to say then, is crammed with implausibility. And *Le Disciple* was not at all a lasting book. For all that, its publication, its date (1889) and its success constitute a major literary event. They mark the entrance of ideas and systems into the current novel. *Le Disciple* added thought and weight to this literary form; it enriched its ledger and its means.

Cosmopolis (1893), one of Bourget's best novels, can also be called a novel of ideas, ideas on the permanence of race. But it was only in 1902, under the influence of *Des Déracinés* (*Un Homme libre*, published in 1889, had not been alien to the thinking of *Le Disciple*) and the Dreyfus case, that he resolutely settled on the problem novel as the highest manifestation of the fictional form, and his four most solid novels—*L'Etape*, *L'Emigré*, *Un Divorce*, and *Le Démon de midi*—flanked by two short stories, *L'Echéance* and *Le Justicier*, do indeed constitute the backbone of his maturity.

They are lacking in air, in question marks, in flexibility. They are rigid novels with conservative theses. For Bourget the law and the prophets were *Les Origines de la France contemporaine*, and everything followed as if his problem novels were myths intended to animate Bonald's conservative philosophy and Frédéric Le Play's *Réforme Sociale*, to make them understandable to the heart and the senses. The novelist became a lawyer: the lawyer for heirs in *L'Etape*, the lawyer for hierarchies in *L'Emigré*, the lawyer for Christian marriage in *Un Divorce*, the lawyer for the existing order against the rights of the individual in *Le Démon de midi*. The novelist had entered an organic period completely opposed to the critical period of the *Essais de psychologie*, though just as fully governed by his talent.

A talent that was also that of the lawyer, since it was the oratorical talent. Two writers of this period were endowed with an oratorical style, Brunetière and Bourget. Bourget's style, often heavy and pedantic, is always redeemed by its massive, continual movement, its logical connection, its solidarity with the convincing word. It is a demonstrative style, and in any event everything in Bourget takes place as if he thought that this demonstrative style demonstrated something, as if a "demonstration" in the soldier's sense could resemble a geometrical demonstration. But that matters little. All that we ask of him is the literary impression, the appearance and not the effect of conviction. As the epigraph to his *Tite-Live* Taine had chosen: *In Historia Orator*. In his *Origines* he himself had been that orator. In Bourget's problem novels, in the original style of his theses, the reader perceives an *in fabula orator*.

This oratorical technique is doubled by an equally remarkable technique of the novel. The connections among the occurrences in a Bourget novel are as solid as the connection of his demonstrative style. With a scholar's background that made him incapable of success in the theater, he can be regarded as that writer who has incorporated into the novel most of the technical elements proper to the theater and made them become thoroughly assimilated. Perhaps with a certain monotony. The center of his skillful turns of plot is always provided by the chestnut trees of *Figaro*. Published in *La Revue des deux mondes*, *L'Etape*, *L'Emigré*, and *Un Divorce* were so divided as to be publishable in six installments, and with as much technical skill as Dumas employed in the division of a play into acts.

Let us not forget that, like Anatole France, Bourget belonged to an intermediate generation between that of the Empire (1850) and that of the Republic (1885), that he reacted against the Council of Ten of his *Essais*—that is, the ten masters of the generation of 1850—only by remaining their respectful disciple and even their imitator. The names of Taine and Dumas had for him a meaning that they would have lost in part for a twenty-year-old of 1885. For Loti, who was the same age, that meant nothing, since, in contrast to Bourget, he came into letters brand-new and virgin of reading.

The fortunate longevity of Bourget, who was eighteen years old in 1870, made it possible for him to live on long after the War of 1914. While this great craftsman of letters continued a very regular production well into his old age, *Le Démon de midi*, published in 1914, put the final touch to the best of his work. His fictional form and substance belonged to the past. The immobility of his ideas, the repetition of the same commonplaces, damaged the social critic, infected the novelist with their mechanicalness. But for thirty years Bourget stood as an original testimony to the French novel as it had been established by Balzac and George Sand. With sustained power he continued to fill this plastic form with eloquence, thought, the feeling for social interests and polite society. His well-made novel was the contemporary of the well-made play, his technique belonged to the golden age of good techniques. The later loss of what that age had been able to sustain cannot be viewed from any point of view as a gain.

Anatole France

Eight years older than Paul Bourget, Anatole France was over forty in 1885; with Coppée, Sully-Prudhomme, and Hérédia he belonged in actuality to the generation of the Parnassian successors. He was lazy, timid, a bit backward. He felt that his was the vocation of the reader, of the lover of books, rather than that of the author. *Le Crime de Sylvestre Bonnard*, which appeared in 1881, and *Le Livre de mon ami*, which appeared in 1885, are indeed narratives, delicate narratives, but done in the shadow of books, calling on the world of books at least for their characters, their recollections, their language. Almost all the Parnassians were librarians: but France, born in a bookshop, was more especially the spiritual delegate of the school to this profession. French literature, moreover, is filled with these men of taste, of feeling, whom books prevent from fully entering into letters, as the trees make it impossible to see the forest. Anatole France had all that was required to keep him one of these men.

He escaped this danger, at first by the awareness of this kind of life that he gained, the confession of it that he made, and the style that he gave it. He escaped, too, because of the exacting supervision and control exerted by the intelligent woman who disciplined this lazy man, suggested themes to him, made him work, and gained thereby an unhoped for reward. Finally, he escaped because of the complicity of the last epoch that still knew inherited traditional riches in portfolios, literary and other, passed down from father to son. In his style, his cadences, his imitations, his centos,* his parodies, he set a curious full stop, or provisional full stop, to classical literature. He had the gift of making his native Paris a second Alexandria, Greek and Jewish, erudite and cultivated, the Alexandria that exists potentially in French classicism and that produced a late-season fruit on the Parnassian branch.

Most of France's books are novels and tales. Is he a novelist? The question was raised about 1892 by the Egeria, Mme. de Caillavet, who made up her mind that M. France could write as good novels as M. Bourget. Women of fashion having been responsible, to hear them tell it, for Bourget's writing *Un Coeur de femme* and Maupassant's writing *Notre Coeur*, France's *Le Lys rouge* was a kind of heart of the same color, the same style, or greater style. It cannot be said that *Le Lys rouge* was a failure. But this story of a Parisian drawing room in 1892, this oratorical estheticism, this chess game of Parisian adultery played on an ancient (in the antiquarian's sense) board managed to be much more dated than *Notre Coeur*, which is also anything but an eternal work.

From a certain point of view, France was indeed a contemporary of Bourget, and, in the world of the novel, the ideas of the one and the myths of the other enjoy an unending reciprocal resemblance. In both cases, creation is subordinated to ideas, which it is a question of demonstrating, of making palpable and acceptable through fictions. In Bourget the thesis is bound to the technique of dialogue. In both cases it is a matter of an ebbing of the novel, in harmony with an epoch that savored the values of intellect.

In 1889, Anatole France, then literary critic of *Le Temps*, was visiting Mme. de Caillavet and met the master *in partibus* of the house, the philosopher, Victor Brochard, whom he was very soon to succeed. Brochard knew Greek philosophy from the inside, and lived it. He contributed to the Hellenization of Anatole France, he helped to habituate him to wisdom, or to ancient wisdoms, to set him up in a modernized debate among Epicureans, skeptics, and Christians, which also, it might be said, included Renan, whose *Origines du christianisme* was at that time a kind of required reading for erudite *dilettanti*, and the Alexandrianism of the Jewish literary *salons* of the end of the nineteenth century. Style alone could save these attitudes, and the eclectic, composite, artificial, anthological, and contaminated style of Anatole France, a cento of Chateaubriand, Flaubert, and Renan, could not have been more appropriate. Hence, in 1890, *Thaïs*, the story of a sinful woman redeemed and a hermit damned, a sort of drawing-room cameo, or, already, a *Lys rouge* in mosaic, in which so many collaborations were masterfully fused and whose success in the

* A cento is a composition made up by assembling passages from various works of others.—Translator.

cultivated world was remarkable. Six years later Pierre Louÿs' *Aphrodite* was published: the 1890–1896 interval was just the time when *Salammbô* and *La Tentation* finally found their public and started a school.

Thaïs in 1890 and *Le Lys rouge* in 1894 were the work of an artist and artisan who would have been made obsolete by the reaction against dilettantism that followed the death of Renan. Fortunately it came about that France was able to revive that Greek wisdom more than merely on the outside and that he embodied it with admirable suppleness in characters, or, rather, in one character with several names who was to become a type. As early as the end of the nineteenth century, two expressions became the usual ways of designating Anatole France. He was called the Good Master as Rousseau had been called the Citizen. Or he was called M. Bergeret as Chateaubriand had been called René. The Good Master meant Jérôme Coignard, who was created first for *La Rôtisserie de la Reine Pédauque* and who later provided his model for *Opinions*. The M. Bergeret of *L'Histoire contemporaine* got even more use. As in *Thaïs* and *Le Lys rouge*, an expert gardener made a graft, a graft of wisdom learned by living on a willing character, and the graft was done so well that the character was accepted as a type, that M. Bergeret, paraded through the provinces and Paris, snowballed imperceptibly, became first an effigy of a man and then a man.

Neither Coignard nor Bergeret was capable of indefinite survival. The real Coignard was already out of his element when he went from *La Rôtisserie*, where he had his little nation round him, into *Opinions*, where he was no more than a peg on which M. France hung the hats of his ideas. It was the same when M. Bergeret left the provinces for Paris, where he vanished in the Dreyfus case. Bergeret could grow hardly anywhere else than in that rich, slow soil of the province and the provincial originals, the real soil of the novel as mud is that of wheat. If *L'Histoire contemporaine* is compared with *Le Lys rouge*, France's provincial novel with France's novel of Parisian society, it can be seen to what a degree the "provincial manners" win out here over the "Parisian manners."

If there is a point at which France really came close to the true novel, it is in the first three volumes of *L'Histoire contemporaine*. It may be surprising that this pure Parisian could create so corporeal a province. One wonders where he learned to know it. But it must be observed that this province of France is primarily a province of Anatole France, populated by his own relatives, and first of all by Bergeret, whom he met each morning in his shaving mirror, the character who first made him laugh every day; the ecclesiastics, to whom the author of *La Rôtisserie* gave an attention natural enough in an old Renanian and a spoiled priest; the librarian, the archivist, the bookseller; and the story of Mme. Bergeret is nothing else than the story of Anatole France's life with his first wife, told with a cynical precision that has since legitimatized all the versions of *Anatole France en pantoufles;* and Mme. de Gromance is the woman of *Le Lys rouge* on whom France slyly took certain vengeances; and the drawing rooms where France was a constant visitor were not lacking in public officials and generals. That does not prevent the seams from showing in many places. The Ducs de Brézé, for instance, could have been associates of Feuillet or Marcel Proust. M. France himself knew only their literary butler, Arthur Meyer. Besides, it is quite possible to create types from completely false characters. Everything in *Crainquebille* is factitious and false. Here the rue Montmartre is seen by the same artist who depicts the streets of Alexandria in *Thaïs.* Yet *Crainquebille* became the single very popular work of Anatole France, and vegetable peddlers are called Crainquebille as street boys are called Gavroche.

The philosopher, midway between the new Academy and the garden of Epicurus, who was educated in a Paris drawing room as those of Athens were educated in a gymnasium, expressed himself in novels as those of Athens and Alexandria preferred to express themselves in myths. But in fact, in his time and in the hands of intelligent writers like him, writers who had ideas, the novel turned to myth or half-myth. Only once did France write a whole myth, *La Révolte des anges.* It is probably his masterpiece, and it has gone unrecognized. It is clear that France wrote it for himself, to deliver himself of his most secret thoughts, to express himself fully, just once, on religion, on the intellect, on life, on God. By parody he went back to John Milton and perhaps further, and more unconsciously, to the Gnostics and their remarkable metaphysical epics. *La Révolte,* like *Les Dieux ont soif,* is the novel of a clear-thinking old age, the consummation of long-contemplated works that had at last to be written. In the same way the son of the bookseller, Thibault (the real name of Anatole France), that author of *Le Catalogue Labédoyère,* a specialist on the French Revolution, had to write a novel about the Revolution. *Les Dieux ont soif* is written with absolute mastery. It is primarily through these two works of his last years that Anatole France will one day return to favor.

His present rejection is a necessary phenomenon, common in the generation that follows the death of a great writer. It was legitimatized in part by the disproportionate place that he had taken in the first quarter of the twentieth century, not only as the recognized leader of French literature but as the most brilliant of Europe's literary personalities. He owed this primarily to the worth of his work: the origin of this popularity was healthy. But he owed it as well to the prominent place that his part in the Dreyfus case had given him in the Republic of Reason, where, in sum, he had received Zola's legacy after 1902 as the overseer of the "human conscience." He owed it to the sympathy that was earned all over the world by his "avant-gardism" at a time when almost all French values were national or nationalist. It was Romain Rolland who received this heritage after 1918; there is a straight line that runs from Zola through France to Rolland. But in addition, the Great War having inevitably been presented in its propaganda as the war of civilization against savagery, Anatole France seemed consequently, as the result of his position, of the very body and meaning of his work, of the surfeit of culture represented by his synthesis of Alexandria and Paris, to be the symbol, the guaranty of the accomplishment, the memory, the tradition of what is called by the general name of civilization. Thus he has been favored, defended, magnified by both sides, like Voltaire in 1820, when he was admired by the liberals for his anti-Christianism and by the Jesuits for his poetry. France grew smaller later, was demoted by both sides at the same time, again like Voltaire and the eighteenth century between 1830 and 1850. Nor does the time yet seem to have come when a return to Anatole France might excite imaginations and be of service: this will inevitably occur, provided that—though he himself foresaw the contrary—the future allows the survival of the phenomenon called literature. The good master, who was not so good, had a death in the manner of Chateaubriand's: above all his communism, like the viscount's Carlism, consisted in a "Drop dead, society" that included a "Drop dead, literature." This is where one does not want to die alone.

THE NOVEL (*Continued*)

Without leaving and impressing an isolated presence like those of Balzac and Flaubert, this midway and fully exposed generation nevertheless distinguished itself by a rich and sustained production, varied experiments, an aptitude for filling every frame, for adapting the form of the novel to all kinds of ideas, messages, or influences. Renan in *Patrice*, Taine in *Etienne Mayran* had felt ill at ease and not too original in fiction, and they had left their autobiographical novels unfinished. In contrast, their successors had established themselves there with complete flexibility. Every source of ideas flows at a given moment into the easy bed of fiction, of myth. Renan had his successors in France or Lemaître, Taine his in Bourget or Edouard Rod. Literature ran to the novel, carrying with it the product of its destructions, as a river runs into the sea. We recall what had occurred in poetry in the preceding era, when the Parnassian successors put no matter whom into a position to express no matter what in quatrains or sonnets.

The gain, however, was much greater for the novel than for poetry. Thanks to the autobiographical novel (Jules Vallès or Eugène Fromentin) on the one side and to the naturalist novel on the other, this generation seemed to be the first that had realized the universal character of the novel and the fact that everyone has subjects for novels in him and around him. Obviously this state of mind is not too favorable to the birth of an unexpected and creative Balzac. But equally obviously it enhances the general and average vitality of a literary form. This will be made clear by the multiplicity of the branches that the literary novel grew during these thirty years.

The Naturalist Tradition

The telegram from Paul Alexis, "Naturalism not dead," expressed a truth in 1890. Naturalism had endured as a system of vision, of expression of reality, doubled, moreover, by epic naturalism and documentary naturalism.

By epic naturalism we mean not the tradition of the epic style that in Flaubert and Zola was opposed to the artistic writing of the Goncourts but the kind of cyclical and monumental undertaking that took in the tradition of *Les Rougon-Macquart* as Zola took in that of *La Comédie humaine*. Two of these undertakings were noteworthy, that of Paul Adam and that of J.-H. Rosny.

The tremendous and profound production that Paul Adam amassed is little read today, and his career gives the impression of a failure. Nevertheless *Le Temps et la vie*, a fictional biography of Adam's family since the Revolution, of which he completed four volumes, was an original monument. And above all Adam influenced a large body of post-1918 literature through his dynamic style, his modernism, his colonialism, his anti-humanism, his sporting spirit. He was at least a step toward a new Balzacism.

There were more life and still more presence in J.-H. Rosny, probably the most opulent novelistic temperament of this period. Rosny's start was magnificent, and the author of *Le Termite, Daniel Valgraive, Nell Horn, Les Xipéhuz,* and *Vamireh* seemed destined in the last years of the nineteenth century to occupy in triumph the place that the author of *Le Docteur Pascal* and *Les Quatre Evangiles* never succeeded in filling: that of the novelist of a lay world of reason and science—reason that was adventurous and poetic, science that was subtle, promising, bold, a lightning storm of hypotheses that did not smell of the elementary school and that were those of what was called an informed man. Neither in the domain of style nor in that of imagination were any of the normal resources of the novel lacking to him. What was lacking was that will to create, to invent, that break between the artist and his past that was so complete in a Flaubert and that was not to be found again in Daudet until *Sapho*. He repeated himself early, and after about 1912—after, that is, *La Vague rouge* —his production grew principally in quantity.

Documentary realism was flourishing and solid. The documentary novel was to be made into a catalogue that would almost take on the proportions of an encyclopedia. Georges Lecomte in *Les Cartons verts* (government) and *Les Valets* (members of Parliament) and Léon Frapié in his novels about schoolteachers were to provide examples of this. A whole library of the kind was to be created, and we know how such novels continued to pour out, how they filled the mail of the Académie Goncourt, which at first had favored them. It was after 1914, however, that the documentary novel was to have its most vigorous and most original specialist, the most endowed with precise experience: Pierre Hamp in his cycle of *La Peine des hommes*.

It was documentary naturalism that could also claim Gustave Geoffroy, the author of a detailed novel of the life of the Parisian working girl, *L'Apprentie* (1904), and Lucien Descaves, who was prosecuted in the days of naturalism for *Sous-Offs* and whose *La Colonne* (1902) and *Philémon* (1913), novels of a veteran of the Commune, have a rich depth of Parisian recollection.

One of the curious novelties of the novel of life would be seen in the novel of The Life, by which we mean the life of the outlaws and the underworld, written in an ironical and accessory spirit of sympathy, the initiator of which seems to have been Jean Lorrain. Charles-Henry Hirsch, with *Le Tigre et Coquelicot* (1905) and *Eva Tumarches et ses amis*, popularized it. But it was represented above all by two poets: the perfect Charles-Louis Philippe of *Marie Donadieu* (1904) and of *Bubu de Montparnasse* (1906) and, after the 1914 war, Francis Carco.

The hazards of literary development and the accepted ideas of those who bought novels caused the novel no longer to be called documentary as soon as it turned to the middle class and its betters; then it became the psychological novel, or the imaginative novel, or the chronicle of society. It is not very easy to see why the portrayal of the middle class should belong to a different category of the novel from that of the portrayal of the poor, and indeed Zola created a scandal by treating both in the same fashion and putting them on the same scale. It can be granted, however, that wealth and the middle-class way of living facilitate emotional and intellectual complications of the kind that fits the tradition of moral analysis in French literature and that contributes to the creation of a special category of the novel for their beneficiaries.

The Middle-Class Novel

The novel of the rich had been tried without mercy by Paul Hervieu in *Peints par eux-mêmes*, a novel in letters that recalled Laclos, and in *L'Armature* (1903), a novel of money conflicts in fashionable society. Thereafter the theater took him over altogether. It was not the same with Abel Hermant and Marcel Prévost, both born in 1862, both novelists of the great school, primarily because the first was a *normalien* and the second was a *polytechnicien*, and both men whose superficial incursions into the theater left them a position and a function as important novelists.

Only the smallest part of Abel Hermant's prolific and uneven output still sees the light and deserves this lasting importance. First of all there are the conversational novels, *La Carrière* (1894) and *Transatlantiques* (1897), whose satiric zest marked an era. There are also the incomparable *Courpière* (1901 and 1905) and *Les Confidences d'une biche*, which dates from the time of the Dreyfus case and offers a harsh picture of the great world and the half-world of that period, establishing the novelist in his function of social moralist, in which there are complicity and rancor, something of the pedantry of the *normalien* tutor at the nobleman's table, an insight into insolence, and an amazing art of portraiture. It is a novel of classic power and sobriety like *La Discorde*. The part of his work to which Abel Hermant gave the greatest care and that he preferred was the disguised autobiography in three parts of *La Journée brève*, which he published after the Great War. Readers have not confirmed this preference. But there is ground for hesitation. Something of the passion with which this novel of an ideal image of the author was written survives in those three volumes, which obviously were not written for the crowd but which were written, and undoubtedly too written. There are still Hermantians in letters—rather rare, but their spirit is likely to last a very long time. All the author's novels that are important are more or less keyed— disguised biographies as *La Journée brève* is a disguised autobiography. Nothing does more for a posthumous chapel than the hunt for keys, the knowledge of which would establish degrees in Hermantism as it does in Stendhalism. And this chapel would be served by the admirers of style. This style has a somewhat imitative elegance, but the traditional republic of letters would be ill indeed if there were no admirers of it.

The precise, sure technique that Hermant put into his style, his dialogue, his portraits, was employed by Marcel Prévost in the workmanship of his novels. They earned him a solid and lasting success. His readers, especially the women, were replenished without diminution for more than forty years. His novels would no longer be consulted now, as Hermant's would be, for recollections that would be useful to social history, but, to the extent to which the French middle class includes a society of women, a republic of women, as well-grounded recollections to serve the history of that republic. In all the more than thirty of his novels, what does not deal with it is factitious and what does deal with it is alive. Not only, in 1894, did *Les Demi-Vierges*, like *Le Demi-Monde* of Dumas, introduce a felicitous new word; it was one of the discoveries of the novel. It could easily be made part of a trilogy with *Les Vierges fortes* and *Les Anges gardiens*, or, rather, of a tetralogy, for *Les Vierges fortes* has two parts, in which the best of Prévost is to be seen: interesting characters, a story told with a skillful slowness, a moral that is in the end traditional and that the author takes pains to draw by dangerous means that please the reader. As the author of *Le Demi-Monde* had his theater, the author of *Les Demi-Vierges* added to his novel a little office for the guidance of feminine consciences, out of which came *Lettres à Françoise*, who is the respectable French girl. They are pleasant and wise.

The novel of Hervieu, Hermant, and Prévost is obviously respectful of everything that is respectable. But nonetheless these are, or were, writers of the left, of the lay school. All three were militant campaigners for revision in the days of the Dreyfus case, and their novels are what is called agnostic. Although at least one of them, Marcel Prévost, was educated by the priests, questions of religion have little or no importance for them. They are at the opposite pole from Feuillet and Bourget. But it was the Catholic direction of these two that was taken by the greater part of the middle-class novel or the novel of good society.

René Bazin and Henry Bordeaux wrote their novels of social and religious defense on cognate themes. On two or three occasions Bazin had the luck and the intelligence to write novels whose themes were in the political and social air and to do very well with them: the threat to landed property in La Terre qui meurt (1898), the Alsatian question in Les Oberlé (1901), the problem of lay and religious teachers in the west in Davidée Birot (1912); he was serious, lofty, and moving, with a poetic feeling for the things of the soil and the things of the soul. Bordeaux dealt with more imaginative matters, but his best novels are those in which there is a man of the law, a thesis to defend—on the family (Les Roquevillard, 1906), the memory of the dead (Le Barrage, 1927), religion (Le Chêne et les roseaux) and even the reconciliation of the races in Syria in the ingenious and tendentious novel of the French occupation, Yamilé sous les cèdres.

Bazin and Bordeaux as novelists were borne on a strong current of this decline of the nineteenth century, a current attested to chiefly by Brunetière, Bourget, Barrès, which, to use a phrase familiar to Brunetière, might be called the movement of the utilization of Catholicism. Whatever their personal experiences, they made Catholicism felt and known as a system of conformisms and external structures much more than as an appeal to the spirit. A contemporary of Bourget, the Waldensian Edouard Rod, on the other hand, put the emphasis on inner tragedy and Protestant anxiety in his austere novels (the two called Michel Teissier, in 1893 and 1894, Le Ménage du Pasteur Naudié in 1898). The place that Calvinism was to hold in Rod was apparently taken for Edouard Estaunié by a hereditary Jansenism. But here we shall abandon the strictly religious area. Estaunié became the novelist of a mystery, a secret, an anguish, an inner tragedy, that no longer concerned a revealed religion. Through him the novel became a myth by means of which the hidden truth of man and things was opposed to their appearance, to what we think they are, to what we think we are. L'Ascension de M. Baslèvre (1921) and L'Appel de la route (1923) are excellently titled: a novel of the rise of a cold, automaton-like man, a high official, to whom the spiritual presence of a woman breaks through, and a novel of an attraction that obscurely summons a respectable provincial family to a horrible tragedy. The effort of these novels seems to amount to the search for a laic equivalent to grace. At the same time the author who gives such an impression of inner life does not give the impression (except in the two more or less autobiographical novels of his youth, *L'Empreinte* and *Le Ferment*) that he is writing personal novels.

The Personal Novel

Nevertheless the personal novel was in full cry at this time. At least in appearance it is the easiest form of the novel, since it consists in creating or confecting one's double, in which it is up to the reader to decide what is artifice and what is truth. Each personal novel occupies the position between this artifice and this truth that is appropriate to it: it has its level as it has its style.

The type of the vocation for the personal novel is to be found, for example, in Huysmans, who could never do anything but fictionalize his own experiences by delegating them to doubles of himself, Folantin or Durtal. An equally typical example of this vocation can be found in Jules Renard. Now that we have the astonishing *Journal*, we connect Renard's novels with this perpetual and manic concentration of the writer on himself and on others through himself.

It is surprising that in this *Journal* Jules Renard never speaks of Jules Vallès. Was he embarrassed by the existence of Vallès, whom certainly he did not imitate but with whom he shared a common character as writer and as man? The story and the style of *Poil de carotte* were already those of *L'Enfant*. Children of the left, like Henri Brûlard, and the same anti-social literature, explosive in its foundations, as Flaubert said, in the roots, as Barrès said, the seat of the family and of middle-class society. To derive a Brûlard, a Vingtras, and a Poil de Carotte from ordinary autobiography is a master stroke of literary experimentation like the experiment that converts the air that we breathe into liquid. And criticism, that Department of Highways and Bridges of literature, marvels that there are three of them among whom, in the geography of the nineteenth century, a road follows so natural a slope of the land.

Renard wrote perhaps only one real novel, a masterpiece: *L'Ecornifleur*, the story of an observer with a hard, clear vision who lives as a parasite, a literary exploiter, and a social critic in a middle-class family; the egg of analysis laid by the immanent genius of French literature in a good middle-class caterpillar in which it grows and that feeds it without knowing that it is itself being destroyed. In *Ragotte* and *Nos Frères farouches*, it is peasants, Renard's servants and neighbors at Chitry, who occupy the position of the Vernets in *L'Ecornifleur* and who are similarly used, exploited, analyzed, taken apart, cut up into an unbelievably hard and sure lace, transparent and light, of attitudes, words, ideas. This old word for "scrounger" has remained in the language of France virtually solely because La Fontaine applied it to the fox, and Renard, the old fox of a novelist, was well aware of the fact. The fifteen volumes of Renard's work will remain one of the most perfect official transcripts of one of the most devilishly—in every sense of the word, including the capital initial—clever observers that the French literature of analysis has ever let loose among men.

This matter of a literature of fiction that ripens in a private diary has already been encountered in the Goncourts and Loti. It too is linked to the profile of French literature. A comparison of Renard with the Goncourts and Loti on this score gives us the measure of what, in these latter, remains of a conformism of caste that had disappeared in Renard. The case of Barrès, in sum, is also bound to the same monumental family of literature. And with even more reason the case of André Gide.

André Gide

A whole part, which is the central part, of André Gide's work carries on that scarcely or not at all fictionalized journal that was the book he wrote at twenty, *Les Cahiers d'André Walter*. *L'Immoraliste* and *La Porte étroite*, which Gide called "narratives," are half-novels in which a personal experience is put into order, neither more nor less than in *L'Ecornifleur*, but here the adventure is entirely one of inner tragedy. Under a Nietzschean title, *L'Immoraliste* crushes the analysis of a personal case that would better deserve a name between egoism and egotism, the need for sensual happiness in conflict within a man with the joys of the home and the sacrifice of a woman, that need for happiness that triumphs amid the ruins of tenderness, and the opposition driven in, widened to twice its depth, by the nonconformism of the sensual need, the Protestant form and tradition of the home. *L'Immoraliste* is the broad door, the open door on the world of *Les Nourritures terrestres*, El Kantara. *Les Nourritures* becomes also a kind of logbook or diary of *L'Immoraliste*, as Gide would later write *Le Journal des Faux-Monnayeurs*. Here we are, then, at the very core of the diary novel. *L'Immoraliste* was the novel delegated to the broad door of *Les Nourritures; La Porte étroite* can be taken as its counterpart, its complement, or its ideal sequel. All this has formed a secret garden, carefully cultivated, of which we have the key today and which has become one of the most visited, one of the most "public" gardens in literature. But this publicity was belated. Until the Great War Gide's work was known only in literary circles; the sudden glory attained in 1893 by the three ideologies of *Le Culte du moi*, with their utilization of Catholicism, forms a singular contrast to the stubborn obscurity that, until he had passed the age of forty, clung to André Gide's work, which, more-over, has in a way come to us by way of Protestant Switzerland.

In Gide as in Barrès there is a major literary element that does not exist at all in Jules Renard. In a sense they are much more men of letters, much closer to Anatole France, than Jules Renard. In effect, what flourishes on their need for intimate journals or notebooks is not only novels that are three-quarters autobiographical but myths.

Barrès' *Trois Idéologies* charmed with their myths. And he created Lorraine itself as a myth. Gide wrote pure myths, more subtle and more sparely allegorical in *Le Voyage d'Urien* and *Le Promethée mal enchaîné*. In 1913, he conceived *Les Caves du Vatican* as a myth, a myth of carica-ture, a great Daumier in the manner of *Bouvard et Pécuchet*, in which the hard insight like Renard's that he had revealed in the little book of *Les Paludes* stood naked. The profound theme of *Les Caves* seems to be that of a mature man who runs after his youth, as they say—and not only after mine, he added—and who does so in two rhythms: first, by depre-ciating and caricaturing in three-quarters of his "farce" everything that he sees in the world that is automatic and growing old (except himself, and this is a weakness: Flaubert wanted to be involved with *Bouvard et Pécuchet*); and then by focusing his idea, his ideas and his memories of youth on the curious and suggestive portrait of Lafcadio, and this he did so well that Lafcadio became one of the heroes in whom the post-war young saw and more or less loved themselves. The success of *Les Caves* in the generation that was twenty years old in 1914, the adoption of Lafcadio by the post-war young, was one of Gide's decisive successes. At the same time, all his earlier work suddenly came to light and a tremendous influence was launched.

Gide devoted several years to *Les Faux-Monnayeurs*, the only one of his narratives that he was willing to call a novel. This strange and rich book caused amazement, amazement mixed with reservations. At that time Gide had been seized by a singular passion for newspaper items, an interest that had already manifested itself in his *Souvenirs de la cour d'assises;* he built his novel round two such items, which had interested the newspa-pers about 1910: a gang of young Latin Quarter delinquents who had been counterfeiting coins, and the suicide of a secondary-school student in Clermont, which had been rather inaccurately reported in the news-papers and even in a question by Barrès in the Chamber. And the con-struction was not successful. But this central construction was covered with stories, figures, portraits, events drawn more freely from disguised reality and autobiography, dialogues, newspaper bits; all this resulted in a remarkably intelligent whole, but one that was almost exclusively intelli-gent, and obviously that is not the quality most necessary to a novel. The book must not be separated from Roger Martin du Gard's *Les Thibault*, which was written almost in league with *Les Faux-Monnayeurs* and which offered completely opposite qualities and defects, thus providing a contemporary, contrasted, and friendly couple that is among the most curious in the landscape of the novel.

Among a "restless" youth (from 1920 to 1930 that was the ritual, Homeric epithet), *Les Faux-Monnayeurs* had a remarkable reception. In a way on which we shall not pass judgment here, it contributed to focusing for a time what Barrès called the sensibility of the young. Gide's fiction played its part in the history of the French novel only very moderately. But it functioned very powerfully, like that of Barrès from 1890 to 1902, in a history of influences. Like myths, *Les Faux-Monnayeurs* acted as a function of ideas: the vocation of the myth maker that Gide had attempted at the time of *Le Voyage d'Urien* was indeed that to which his nature impelled him and by which, after strange and dramatic detours, he achieved the best of his current influence.

Ernest Psichari's *Le Voyage du centurion,* the autobiography of a young Catholic officer and the story of a conversion and an African campaign, is a book that testifies to the Catholic literary movement that followed the separation of Church and state. Louis Bertrand's *Jean Perbal,* the last volume of which appeared under the debatable title of *La Nouvelle Education sentimentale,* and which would undoubtedly have an abundant progeny, might well remain one of the most instructive and most interesting evidences of the life of an intellectual, a *normalien,* a writer, during that generation. This fictional autobiography, which had little success, is much superior to Bertrand's other novels, even to *Mademoiselle de Jessincourt.*

The Artistic Novel

The personal novel, in which the author's eye is in principle turned inward, would always in principle be the opposite of a novel in which the author, turned toward the object, would be concerned only with esthetically representing that object, transposing it delicately into his own sensibilities and into those of others: in other words, an artistic novel. The artistic novel is a solid tradition of the French novel, and in sum it goes back in the nineteenth century to Gautier on the one hand and to Mérimée on the other. Its problem was thoroughly lived through by Flaubert, whose influence, it must not be forgot, was preponderant from 1885 to 1914 and much greater than Balzac's.

The artistic novel, however, makes an excellent marriage with the autobiographical novel; this garment can seem as transparent as any other on the author's body. Anatole France became and throughout all this period remained its chief and its patron, and, when Barrès became apprehensive about M. France, it was indeed an opposition of two natures of the novel, like two kinds of politics. A similar antithesis was to be observed, beginning on the benches of the Ecole Alsacienne, between André Gide and his classmate—the first in the class—Pierre Louÿs.

There is indeed an artistic novel that is a kind of novel of the first in the class. *Aphrodite* would be almost its type. In a literature that includes *Salammbô* and *Thaïs*—in other words, Corneille and Racine—*Aphrodite* is like a tragedy by Voltaire. It is strange that it has survived, for a certain public, like a kind of nudist novel wearing jewelry and taking place in a Marseille of another day; the best novel of Pierre Louÿs, rather, would be *La Femme et le pantin*, with its fine lean narration, no more tricked out, in sum, than all the French *olé-olé!* novels that call themselves Spanish and that we are not qualified to refute.

With Henri de Régnier and Maurice Maindron, Louÿs was one of the three sons-in-law of Hérédia, and the noble house of the scholarly *conquistador* could be taken in this generation as the very home of the artistic novel. *La Double Maîtresse* and *Le Passé Vivant* can count as masterpieces of the form, and the second of these novels would perhaps provide the psychological key to the form—the psychology of the gift of living in sympathy with the past. Régnier's novels, however, are very uneven. Less style and more life will be found in those of his wife, Marie de Hérédia, who took or resumed her name of Gérard d'Houville from one of her Norman ancestors: her *Séducteur* is the most lively and colorful evocation of Cuba, and *Tant pis pour toi* was too quickly forgotten. Maurice Maindron's historical novels, and especially those that take place in the sixteenth century, *Saint-Cendre* and *Blancador l'avantageux*, carry the reader into a veritable erudite antiquarian's shop.

The rare novels of Elémir Bourges came from an equally industrious but more modern workshop. *Le Crépuscule des dieux* is a strange transposition of a theme from *Les Rois en exil* to the tragic level where bookish and musical influences intersect, those of the English playwrights of the sixteenth century and that of Wagner. This great museum piece, like its counterpart, *Les Oiseaux s'envolent et les fleurs tombent*, has since grown tarnished. But that is not the expression that would be used to indicate that René Boylesve has not retained all the respect that he received in his lifetime. Not much will be made of his licentious novels like *La Leçon d'amour dans un parc*, and the mere title of *Le Parfum des Iles Borromées* may discourage the delicate from any desire to open it. But Boylesve, like a fruit of the long autumns of his native Touraine, ripened right to the end. The novels of his last years were to be almost his best, and his *Madeleine* is one of the most sensitively observed women in the novel of this period. *L'Enfant à la balustrade* deserves to stand as one of the most finely spun stories of provincial life.

The graft of the rich provincials on the wealthy middle class and the social pleasures of its neighborhood of Paris, the Sixteenth Arrondissement, can be observed in the style and the art of a Boylesve. The novel or the artistic tale of his contemporary, Marcel Schwob, would afford one of those contrasts that are the very life of Paris. Schwob's erudition has much less resemblance to the rich *armada* of the Hérédians than to the antiquarian's warehouse in *La Peau de chagrin*. Sea lanes and land lanes brought the rare pieces that were worked in *Le Roi au masque d'or* and *Les Vies imaginaires;* the style is pure and beautiful, but these tales have grown chilly, almost as chilly as all that allegorical jewelry that symbolism found in the legacy of Parnassus and that it sold at a loss: Bernard Lazare's *Le Miroir des légendes*, Gustave Kahn's *Le Conte de l'or et du silence*. Three Jewish antiquarians of the Left Bank.

The Country Novel

Furthermore, the artistic novel is always a product finished in Paris, or a finished product of Paris, and the psychology of the apparent exception provided by Flaubert would easily keep it within the rule. But there is a whole category of the novel that is not very artistic—very often fortunately not—and that really belongs to the provinces. This is the country novel, which has finally acquired the unpleasing name of regional or regionalist. Ever since the last quarter of the nineteenth century it has been so flourishing that nothing would be easier than the drafting of a fictional map of France, as crowded as its gastronomical map. It does not make the mouth water, however, and so we shall refrain. Almost all these country novels resemble one another as if they came out of a cake-pan. The most important, perhaps, are those of Eugène Le Roy, the novelist of Périgord: *Jacquou le croquant* and *Mademoiselle de la Ralphie*. The areas that have afforded the greatest abundance of such novels are Quercy, with the hard-working and gnarled Léon Cladel, the novelist of country priests, Ferdinand Fabre, and Emile Pouvillon, a pleasant storyteller and no more; Brittany with Charles Le Goffic; Burgundy with Gaston Roupnel's *Nono;* the Bourbonnais with Emile Guillaumin's *La Vie d'un simple*. This category does not include the group of the storytellers of Provence, which was an advance guard in the field and whose masters, Alphonse Daudet and Paul Arène, belong to the previous generation.

The Society Novel

The regional novel must not be confused with the provincial novel, the novel based on the provinces. It might almost be said that, since Stendhal and Balzac, the novel in France has been the provinces, the novelist emigrated from the provinces to Paris, as, on the contrary, the theater is Paris and virtually nothing but Paris. The purely Parisian novel, the novel of Parisian life, is often lacking in body and leads a meager life beside the novel fed on the provinces (with perhaps one exception). The classic of the society novel, Feuillet, was himself a provincial, and the landed proprietors of his Norman countryside provided him with the foundations of his work. From Feuillet to Proust, society people have reproached novelists for portraying them with an ingenuous and uninformed self-sufficiency, and it is advisable not to take too literally the title of Hervieu's novel, *Peints par eux-mêmes*. Nevertheless some society people wrote their own novels. First of all there is Gyp. Under this pseudonym the Comtesse de Martel wrote some forty books, dialogues and novels, which had a great success and created a category, or revived it, but it would be most embarrassing to try to mention one title of hers that has endured: one might suggest *Leurs Ames*, an anything but flattering, though picturesque, account of fashionable behavior, or *Bijou*, a curious portrait of a cruel young girl. Rather than the Comtesse de Martel, the most exact and the most interesting of the novelists of the aristocracy at this time would be the Comte de Comminges, who wrote under various pseudonyms and even under his own name, and whose humor had a subtle quality.

The Novel of Paris

To be accurate, here we are dealing with a novel of society and country estates rather than of Paris. It will be observed that the strictly Parisian novelists like Hervieu, Henri Lavedan, Fernand Vandérem were drawn into the theater by an irresistible force, a force that is natural to the "peasant of Paris," and *La Vie parisienne* is not the title of a novel.

We have said that there was one exception. Would this be Henri Duvernois, the author of *Faubourg Montmartre* and *Edgar?* Not altogether: primarily Duvernois was a storyteller, a narrator of the chronicle of Paris, but the chronicle of the irregulars, in the style of the Capus of *Années d'aventures*. Subsequently he too took the road to the theater. The exception is Proust. In Proust, for the first time, Paris had a novelist entirely its own, its own Balzac. But, although in reality Proust belongs to this generation, his presence and his influence are so bound to the next generation that in good conscience there is no choice but to enroll him in the generation of 1914.

And besides there is Paris and Paris. The provinces begin or end on the Left Bank. The Parisian novel of the Left Bank will not be confused with the Parisian novel of the Right Bank. Jean de Tinan, the author of *Penses-tu réussir* and *Aimienne,* those delightful autobiographical reportages, died very young; he had started out to create the style of a literate Bohemia, which degraded itself and sank to the level of Willy (Henri Gauthier-Villars); but the Ecole Normale of the rue d'Ulm shaped the climate of the principal vineyards on that bank. Ever since the generation of 1830, of About and Sarcey, it had not been lacking in novelists, even, and especially, when, like Hermant and Lemaître, they transported the house tradition to the Right Bank. Now, at the beginning of the twentieth century, this environment produced its fitting, authentic, and autochthonous novel: *Jean-Christophe* by Romain Rolland.

Jean-Christophe inaugurated those saga novels of the twentieth century, all of which sought to encompass the experience of a life in a whole. In contrast to the majority of the others, *Jean-Christophe* is centered not on an autobiography but on a biography, or, rather, on parts of the biographies of German musicians, which Rolland brought together by means of a skillful and felicitous acetylene weld. The musician, Christophe, is alive, he is moved and he is moving, and this pre-1914 French-German hero had the well-earned good fortune to arouse tremendous sympathies in the whole of Europe. With this modification of the German musician Rolland did much more than merely record his individual experiences. He stylized the experience of an intellectual in the special sense that the Dreyfus case had given to this word: a highly cultivated *normalien,* an idealist in the style of Jaurès, a believer in civilization with that feeling for the common treasure of mankind natural to a *normalien* humanist who is the incarnation of the high vocation of the rue d'Ulm: to write of great men. *Jean-Christophe* constitutes a kind of sequel to that *Vie des grands hommes* (Tolstoi, Beethoven, Michelangelo) begun by Rolland in Péguy's home, and his German musician is presented in that domain of greatness, reconsidered from without. Rolland's Germany is a Germany of the mind: a Germany of a scholarship student. And his France as well. Even the episodes of great emotion (there are very beautiful pages in *Le Buisson ardent*) are bathed in intellect. None of the ten volumes of *Jean-Christophe* embodies this Left Bank accent better than that called *La Foire sur la place:* a picture of Parisian intrigue seen from Mount Sainte-Geneviève, described, judged, and rebuked from the height of a pulpit, and a picture that becomes very interesting as soon as one has descried in it the sign of the necessary misunderstanding between the two banks: it would be such a loss if there were only one Paris!

France has become rather unjust to *Jean-Christophe,* which goes unread today, partly because the considerable body of literary work that followed (*Colas Breugnon, L'Ame enchantée*) was disappointing, partly because the significance of Rolland's reputation as an "intellectual" has overshadowed his significance as a novelist; partly, finally, because other saga novels have thrust it into obscurity. But in any event it was the first, and something of *Jean-Christophe*—quality, flaws, and Left Bank—will be found again in the other saga that had its origin in the rue d'Ulm, Jules Romains' *Les Hommes de bonne volonté*.

It is to this street on the Left Bank that we must also relate the work of the Tharaud brothers, at least through the work of Jérôme. In contrast to Rolland's oratorical flow, Jérôme and Jean Tharaud were painstaking technicians who left nothing to chance, who were lacking in invention, but who were admirable organizers of the material that inventors (the streets are full of them) provided for them, and who could be called the masters of the finished product. Their trilogy of Carpathian Jews, *L'Ombre de la Croix, Un Royaume de Dieu*, and *La Rose de Sâron*, is a masterpiece of evocation, narration, and rendering.

The regional novel was naturally enlarged, after 1885, by the colonial novel. Here again one could make a map or, rather, a literary globe, where Robert Randau for North Africa, Marius-Ary Leblond for the Indian Ocean, Jean Ajalbert for Indochina, and for everything within the jurisdiction of the Colonial Ministry, Pierre Mille, the father of *Barnavaux*, would not stand alone.

CRITICISM

The generation of 1850, with its vigorous covey of *normaliens*, should have been a great critical generation, and the leading figure among these *normaliens*, Taine, had been designated by Sainte-Beuve as his successor. There were some disappointments.

Advance and Retreat of the Normaliens

Taine's great articles, which so powerfully counterbalanced the *Lundis*, his *Saint-Simon*, his *Balzac*, his *Stendhal*, were youthful efforts that he very soon strove to surpass, first with a hasty *Port-Royal*, *L'Histoire de la littérature anglaise*, and later with his great philosophical and historical work. The two other leaders of the company, Prévost-Paradol and About, had ambitions that could not be gratified by the chores of book reviewers. Sarcey, who was a great dramatic critic, was notably disastrous as a literary critic.

The Currency of Sainte-Beuve

At the time of Sainte-Beuve's death, and far removed from him, there was an intelligent and informed critic who deserved consideration. He was Emile Montégut, the critic of *La Revue des deux mondes*, who knew English literature well, who was also, in the field of contemporary literature, wise and even brilliant, and who had no lack of individual ideas. In *Le Temps*, which Sainte-Beuve had joined in the last year of his life, his collaborator and eventual successor was Edmond Scherer, a Protestant theologian of French nationality but wholly foreign blood and education: English and above all German-Swiss. Certain domains of French literature, such as poetry, remained absolutely closed to him, and he made a fool of himself as soon as he put his hand on them. But his criticism of ideas is full of interest; the eight volumes of his *Etudes sur la littérature contemporaine* belong after Alexandre Vinet as a fitting monument of that honest, intelligent, limited Genevan criticism to which Sainte-Beuve was sympathetic and to which in 1830 he accorded his *dignus entrare* for high criticism.

Contemporaneously with Sainte-Beuve in *Le Moniteur* and then in *Le Temps*, with Scherer in *Le Temps*, with Montégut in *La Revue des deux mondes*, readers in the 1860s also had at their disposal the criticism of Alfred-Auguste Cuvillier-Fleury in *Les Débats*, Armand de Pontmartin in *La Gazette de France*, and Barbey d'Aurevilly in *Le Pays*. There is nothing to be said, nor any longer to be read, of Cuvillier. Pontmartin was a gentleman of the old Comtat Venaissin,* a legitimist in literary criticism as elsewhere, who was not lacking in dash and still less in pretensions, and who gathered his articles into more volumes of *Samedis* than Sainte-Beuve could furnish of *Lundis*. This criticism based on party and personal ties can hardly be taken seriously, but it has its amusing pages, not too unworthy of a compatriot of Joseph Roumanille, and at least he has left a rather delicious picture of the men and manners of letters in Paris, seen by a clear-eyed provincial, which is called *Les Jeudis de Madame Charbonneau.* Dash . . . not to be taken seriously . . . amusing: such qualifications should be raised to the third power for Barbey d'Aurevilly, whose innumerable collections of articles, entitled *Les Oeuvres et les hommes*, fling magnificent insights, prejudices, and absurdities into a torrent of life and images. Between a Scherer and a Barbey, obviously, a fancier of criticism could sample all its degrees of climate and all its species of flora. But in any event, all of this could serve only to emphasize, in 1869, the emptiness of the place that Sainte-Beuve had left.

In fact it has never been well filled since, and Sainte-Beuve's critical heritage is like Victor Hugo's poetic heritage or Balzac's in the novel. Nevertheless, among the young men who were going to make their appearance after 1870 and take their places in the movement of 1885, there was a Sainte-Beuve currency that was highly honored everywhere, a solid group of prominent critics whose deaths raised questions of succession as difficult as that posed by the death of Sainte-Beuve.

* The modern Department of Vaucluse.—Translator.

Brunetière

Two twenty-year-olds of 1870, two witnesses to this intermediate generation, who would be young elders in 1885, held positions of the first rank in a revival of serious criticism: Brunetière and Bourget.

If he had kept the proper distance, Brunetière might have been the true successor of Sainte-Beuve, to whose supple and lively course, furthermore, his own straight line offers us a perfect contrast. Unlike the majority of the other critics, he never wanted to be anything else but a critic— adding to the criticism of books, moreover, that of ideas, of manners, and of laws. He created a paradoxically lofty idea of criticism for himself: an imperialist. Sainte-Beuve had given three professors of 1830 the name of form-masters. Brunetière had taken up that vocation with fanaticism. To it he brought inflexible will and courage. He had always only one platform, *La Revue des deux mondes,* which he managed to enter through the smallest door and where he gave Buloz to believe that he would be a second Gustave Planche *: he knew how essential it was to a critic's authority that he be domiciled in a residence of his own. Like the form-masters, he had been a very great professor, having done much better than Sainte-Beuve at the Ecole Normale. Like the form-masters, he more or less ran the Académie Française. Like the form-masters, he aspired to a part as a politician, even as a doctrinarian, but this ended in frustration, in the eternal misunderstanding in France between "Doctrine" and the country. And more than the form-masters, as much as Taine, he brought new ideas and new forces into criticism.

First of all, he was the only critic after Sainte-Beuve who gave the impression that he knew French literature from the inside, like a village, as a citizen knows his city, or, better, as a teacher serving the town hall as secretary knows his community. He had his friends and his enemies there. He called Fénelon "that scoundrel!" and he went through the files on Baudelaire in order to find something that would make it possible to forbid him to remain in Paris. But he had even more ideas than enemies, and even more than ideas he had one idea. Indeed, he had only one idea, and this is admirable in a critic. And it was an old idea, Voltaire's and Nisard's: namely, the primacy of the seventeenth century, the seventeenth century defended against the eighteenth, against romanticism, against everything in the seventeenth century that foreshadowed the threat of the eighteenth and of romanticism—the seventeenth century conceived of and respected especially in its two pure states, Boileau and Bossuet: that is, the classic and the oratorical, the norm and salvation. In terms of these norms he diagnosed the eternal maladies of French literature: the burlesque, the

---

* Brunetière's predecessor in *La Revue.*—Translator.

precious, the fantastic, to which he later added the romantic and naturalism. There is something of Molière's physician in Brunetière. In the great century he was perhaps called Gui Patin.*

From this idea of the primacy of the seventeenth century it was natural that he should derive the ideas of the reasons for this primacy: the seventeenth century believed in categories and applied distinct, clear-cut, and rationally defined categories; the seventeenth century was Christian and French.

From then on Brunetière was the critic of categories. He had a vigorous and original idea of categories; he believed in them as in Platonic ideas of literature, but as a critic: that is, he did not think that literature's interests were bound to their rigidity; he believed, on the contrary, that the function of criticism consisted in seeing them and following them in their development. Liberated from a somewhat artificial apparatus and Darwinian metaphors, the hypothesis of the evolution of categories, which he developed in a book thus titled and which he applied to criticism and to tragedy, has been much less a failure than is generally thought; it remains a useful working hypothesis.

The literary point of view of the Christian seventeenth century and of classic literature established on Catholic values became in the end a dogmatic point of view with Brunetière. This literary critic presented the first instance of a literary conversion: converted by Bossuet, as others have been converted by Bloy or Claudel. Particularly through Brunetière, in the very last years of the nineteenth century and the time of the Dreyfus case, the seventeenth century was made the core of a kind of body of ideas of the right and was armed with a militant goad.

The seventeenth century in France was French literature before it had been exposed to the great alien influences, those of the north. And in the influences then active on literature, the Italian and the Spanish, Brunetière saw virtually nothing but the enemy. In contrast to Sainte-Beuve, Brunetière had had little contact with the classics of antiquity. In contrast to Taine, he had little contact with foreign literatures. He gave criticism a specifically French character, French in a middle-class way, defiantly French in an aggressively reactionary spirit. He was a type—a character out of the Land's End of literature in the substantial fashion in which in Balzac a character is from Angoulême or Issoudun or the antiquarian's warehouse. But these recrudescences of the seventeenth century must not be allowed to make us forget that he was long the running critic of *La Revue des deux mondes*. Therefore he had to be a critic of the present, to say his say on the literature of his time. And contemporary criticism accounted for at least a third of his work. Here he was much inferior to Sainte-Beuve himself. (I do not speak of Taine, who never

* A seventeenth-century satirist and physician.—Translator.

dared to express himself on his contemporaries.) He had more intelligence than taste; he was absolutely devoid of sensuality—at least in esthetics; and although his conscience and his intelligence had made him an excellent magazine editor, he seems to have been badly upset by literature that was not all finished but was in the process of being made. His "naturalist" novel was extremely short: principally it was a defense of the "novel of *La Revue*" by the "new Planche." His frenzied campaign against Baudelaire damaged only Brunetière. And his counsels to creators produced only the "prose tragedy" on which he had laid down the law to Paul Hervieu. The reactionary character and the lack of views in his contemporary criticism in the end did him even less good with the broad public than with authors.

Obviously he is read less than Sainte-Beuve today. In order to read him as he should be read, with interest and profit, it is necessary to like his style, so singular, so personal beneath its apparent imitation of the seventeenth century, not only oratorical but oral, gesticulated, in which all the author's passions and manias retain all their life, a dynamic style that points a finger like a gimlet and is always ready to attack something or someone; its antique robe is embroidered with the word *Argumentabor*.

Bourget

Paul Bourget, identically contemporary with his friend Brunetière, made his mark in the criticism of his time with the important *Essais* and *Nouveaux Essais de psychologie contemporaine*, which constitute a date. Ten studies on ten authors of the previous generation: Baudelaire, Renan, Taine, Flaubert, Stendhal (as far as he was known in 1880), Turgenev, Dumas, the Goncourts, Leconte de Lisle, and Amiel, analyzed, examined, judged by a *disciple*, by a successor, who cast up the balance of the intellectual and moral legacy that they had handed on to him. The interest of these *Essais* is virtually exhausted, and the author's massive style does not contribute to their being reread. But they accustomed literary opinion to think in terms of generations. To be twenty years old in 1870, to draw in 1882 a picture of the twenty-year-olds of 1850, to initiate, though with respect and admiration, a kind of liability action against the writers of the Second Empire, as Taine on the whole had done with regard to the philosophical section of the generation of 1820 with *Les Philosophes français*—all this, for Bourget, meant the establishment of an important example for the next generation to follow. It meant the provision of a useful commonplace to criticism. The two volumes of *Essais* (in the first edition) are, indeed, the only important part of Bourget's critical work:

the rest belongs, if not to the novelist, at least to the conservative doctrinarian.

The Return of the Normaliens

The case of Sainte-Beuve aside, the generation of 1885 was perhaps the generation best staffed with solid and original critics, in a healthy equilibrium between the elder and the junior. From the elder, the twenty-year-olds of 1870, the vintage of Brunetière and Bourget, it is possible to separate those who, fifteen or twenty years younger, had been formed by the literary movements and revolutions that occurred after 1885. This is the one generation of *normaliens* that has held the scepter, or the ruler, of criticism.

SARCEY

The great surge of 1848–1850, destined to make Sainte-Beuve stand out, had been caught up in the current of more ambitious destinies, with which it did not do too well. It had only one pure critic, Sarcey, and Sarcey succeeded only in a special niche of criticism, the dramatic; besides, he did not acquire any authority until about 1880—that is, twenty years after his launching in journalism. He was the master of this criticism, which he based on these few simple, brief, perdurable ideas: that the theater is the theater, that as a result it is not books or literature or poetry; that fifteen hundred people facing the stage in an auditorium constitute a new entity that it is the critic's function to measure, whose reactions it is his duty to understand and share; that it is by sharing them that he will guide them (and Sarcey's newspaper pieces were the only ones that had any influence on theater box offices); that there exist not rules but a certain number of empiric necessities that the author cannot contravene except under penalty of failing in his purpose—that is, of not pleasing, since pleasing, as in the days of Racine and Molière, is still the law and the prophets. Sarcey did please. He had spirit and life, he was abundantly rich in that springboard called enemies—and this "professor and journalist" left a body of work behind. On certain subjects—Corneille, Molière, Regnard—he refurbished the knowledge of the classic theater, studying it no longer from the literary point of view but from that of dramatic technique. On the other hand, being a representative of the generation of Dumas and Augier, he did not really understand the inevitable dramatic revolution that followed them. He was part of the resistance against the *Théâtre libre*. He was always more reserved than the public about Shakespeare; he was resolved to understand nothing of Ibsen; at times he justified the legend that he was the official apostle to the Philistines.

WEISS

Les Débats was the counterpart of *Le Temps*. Over more than forty years, from 1830 to 1870, Jules Janin, "the prince of critics," took pride in the fact that he had provided it with two thousand two hundred and forty weekly articles. Two thousand two hundred forty paper bags of wind, of imbecilities, of fakes. The house in which Geoffroy had founded dramatic criticism regained its lost tradition when a school friend of Sarcey, Prévost-Paradol, and About, disillusioned with political journalism and aspirations to high office, launched his career as a drama reviewer there at the age of sixty. He was J.-J. Weiss, whose brilliant campaign lasted three years, full of prejudice, of personal fantasy, with little doctrine; the pure spirit of the Second Empire but enlivened with intelligence, honesty, and a taste for the theater. Sarcey was the critic in the audience, who gave the reader the reaction of the audience itself; Weiss was the critic in the wings, the smoking room, and the lobby, the voice of one who knew the theater, a man of intelligence filled with recollections and views. In 1884, when illness prevented him from attending the theater, Weiss was replaced by his young associate and quasi-disciple, Jules Lemaître, who had less originality and vigor, perhaps, but more judgment, more insight, an even clearer and more charming style, a more pleasant confidence, and who was to remain with *Les Débats* for fifteen years.

LEMAÎTRE

Jules Lemaître was probably not the best critic of his time, but he is still the most read, and on the whole rightly so. No one, perhaps, was given a more express mandate to represent the traditional average Frenchman, circumspect and circumscribed. The son of a teacher, educated in the little seminary of Orléans and then in the Ecole Normale Supérieure, professor and poet, reader and contemplater, he supplemented the experience of letters with an experience of Paris, society, and life when the most talked-about of the courtesans of the Second Empire, who was old enough to have been his mother—and who was in any case the mother of his mind—attached him to her fortunes. All the layers of these superimposed destinies fused in him as if to form a cameo. An adequate poet, the exquisite narrator of *En Marge des vieux livres*, the author of a dozen plays, some of which deserved and received great success, a moralist, and even a lost sheep at the head of a political party, he transcended the pure practice of criticism in all directions. He made it a game. But he remained essentially a critic, and it is only for that reason that he has kept his place in the libraries. The two great bodies of this work are *Les Contemporains* and *Impressions de théâtre*.

In principle *Les Contemporains* would seem to derive from Bourget's

Essais de psychologie contemporaine. Lemaître was one of those emancipated *normaliens* promised early to literature, the solid culture of which constitutes a foundation, a past that they respect but that no longer interests them very deeply and that they are impatient to hurdle in order to enter the present. Lemaître was competent to understand, to feel, to judge at least the leaders and the successes of the literature of the present. He characterized them with balance, delicacy, wit, and without using Sainte-Beuve's long cathode ray. His level was that of Sully-Prudhomme and Paul Bourget: nothing revolutionary, therefore, and he never discovered anyone, or else his discoveries were unlucky. But even when it was a question of writers whom he did not enjoy, like Zola, his articles were intelligent, luminous, witty, and such words as "subtle" and "exquisite" came naturally into the reader's mind. Such things as his flaying of Richepin and Georges Ohnet stand as masterpieces of the literary pamphlet, to be kept beside Sainte-Beuve's *Pontmartin*. His *Renan*, which made him famous overnight when it appeared in *La Revue Bleue*, shows his limitations well: Renan or Taine was too much for him. But the essential thing, in order to triumph, was make the reader and especially his wife "get beyond" Renan: a Renan for the ladies who invited Renan to dinner.

Of the four books that, beginning in 1907, Lemaître had to write as a lecturer in order to read them to fashionable audiences, three remain trapped within this kind of limitation: *Rousseau, Chateaubriand*, and especially *Fénelon*. He established Racine as Sainte-Beuve established Port-Royal. He accomplished a composite with the collaboration of the genius of French literature, the seventeenth century, a feeling for men and women and—what Sainte-Beuve lacked—a feeling for the theater.

FAGUET

Like Brunetière, Emile Faguet knew French literature from the inside. He built fewer great highways through it, but he beat more little paths and raised a considerable amount of small game: ideas, suggestions, constructions. His books on the eighteenth and nineteenth centuries, his *Politiques et moralistes du XIXe siècle* threw questionable judgments onto the market, but the important thing was that they could be discussed. He made these periods the subject of four or five books of criticism that was always lively, though partly because it ran counter to life. He himself thought his greatest ability lay in the art of "preparations" in the anatomical sense: that is, laying out and dismembering an author for the examiner. But a dead author. One must view with distrust the clever string of ideas into which he dismembers a Calvin, a Rousseau, a Royer-Collard, a Tocqueville, a Proudhon. It is impossible to find anything more opposed than these anatomical preparations to the natural history of the mind as Sainte-Beuve understood it. Faguet's criticism of his contemporaries has not kept. And the intemperate prattle of his last years, his five hundred lines *de omni re scibili* a day, made readers unjust to the good books of his rich maturity, his living ideas on the classics, and his solid work as a professor.

The Decline of University Criticism

After 1914, this *normalien* generation, or rather these two generations, found no replacement. Must the blame fall on the reforms of 1902, which changed the character of the traditional Ecole Normale? For a long time a useful, even brilliant part was played in criticism by the professors of rhetoric of Paris, of whom René Doumic is an excellent example. But rhetoric disappeared from the scholastic vocabulary in 1902, and with it a whole order to which it had been connected. Above all, the twentieth century began with a crisis in humanism. Values and habits of judgment based on the classical disciplines, backed by the professorial chair, illuminated, as from an oil lamp, by the gentle light of culture and taste, all were frightened and jostled from various directions: literary history, criticism by essayists and moralists, revival of religious values, needs and habits of journalism, spirit of revolution.

LITERARY HISTORY

Literary history has always had an alliance with literary criticism; Sainte-Beuve's major monument is a work of literary history, *Port-Royal*. And Brunetière at the Ecole Normale was what he was in criticism: a stimulator of ideas in the field of literary history. Beginning at the end of the nineteenth century, Brunetière's best student, Gustave Lanson, the author of a *Histoire de la littérature française* that was a fund of vigorous personal judgments in the strict spirit of the traditional university, set himself to exceed this youthful work and even to react against it. Officially qualified to *direct* after the separation of 1902, occupying a place like Cousin's in this "direction" of the teaching of French literature, he established a workshop of methodical literary history, which brought on, primarily for himself, a great burden of work, performed great services, and renewed knowledge of French literature in innumerable areas on the basis of the original texts. Enjoying the favor of the Ecole Normale and the Sorbonne, this literary history attached to inventory and investigation of detail has been accused of clouding the faculties of judgment and taste in those young masters of the university who until its inauguration had been so ready to be young masters of criticism. This accusation, fed by the religious and political controversies of the years after 1902, gave birth to the pejorative term of Lansonism. The attackers thought that they descried a relation of cause and effect between the new methods of literary history and the decadence of the criticism of judgment and taste in its previously licensed practitioners. The legend circulated that Lanson was an enemy of the light, a clipper of wings. If indeed Lanson, whose personal work is considerable and deserves great respect, was a kind of director of infantry in the army of criticism, the road is still open, even in the University, to the intelligence and the engineers, the commanders who assign the tasks of the cavalry and the air force. Perhaps these noble arms have left something to be desired in the twentieth century. Let them accuse only themselves, not the infantrymen.

ESSAYISM

What is a feeling for letters without a feeling for manners, for men, for life? Purely literary criticism in the country of Sainte-Beuve will always be lacking in one dimension. Now there has been a certain Ecole Normale and University tradition of this pure criticism, this cold criticism, which could already be glimpsed in Taine (the Goncourts compared him with a perfect hunting dog that has no nose) and seen to the full in Brunetière and Lanson. It is understandable that criticism, in the broad and living sense in which Sainte-Beuve understood it, could and should extend its domain as it had previously done in the sixteenth century, taking Montaigne's way—that is, in the world of the *Essais*, or of the essay. A moralists' criticism, an essayists' criticism, to which Lemaître and even Faguet were not entirely strangers, will always make a writers' criticism complete; it did so in the generation of 1885, and in the first quarter of the twentieth century it seemed more or less to replace the writers' criticism.

For twenty years Rémy de Gourmont was its most important figure. To be honest, this libertine librarian was a descendant of Bayle rather than of Beyle, and the formula of *Le Dictionnaire historique et critique* is certainly what would have best suited his learning, his imagination, his winding roads, his unforeseen emergences. Like Bayle, he can be seen in union with an epoch. The immanent genius of French literary geography was just what gave Gourmont the climate of 1889, logically erected him at the junction of naturalism and symbolism, with Huysmans' *A Rebours* as his place of worship and the Flaubert of *Saint Antoine* and *Bouvard* as an ancestor. He had a very keen nose for stupidity; he sensed stupidity, which attracted him; and he turned beams of cruel light on the conventional, the official, success. But it is precisely the critic in him that is especially interesting as a destroyer and a negater. The creative zest and sympathy of a Diderot are remarkably alien to this spiritual son of the eighteenth century. His two *Livres des masques*, portrait galleries of the symbolist catch-all, of a symbolism in which Philothée O'Neddy would be hung in the same section with Sainte-Beuve and Victor Hugo, testify to his failure in criticism of contemporaries, which here became a clan criticism. No more did he elevate or degrade anyone in the past. His fictional and theatrical works do not count, and it might be said of *Sixtine, roman de la vie cérébrale*, that he was qualified to write it but that he did not really write it. There is another dead side in his books, an arid, overrefined, refrigerated eroticism, the eroticism of the devil at the witches' sabbath. For all that, the fifteen volumes that contain his criticisms, his essays, his thoughts on books and men and his time have held up admirably as a library shelf, held up in the manner of the *Lundis*. They owe this to the almost constant presence of the intelligence, to a gift for analysis and, to use his word, to a dissociation of ideas, a harsh, scornful inspection of accepted ideas, a subtle sense of undersides—the undersides of language, of thought, of literature, of emotions, and of morals. Anatole France and he came to be congenial in the end, and the literature of both is in effect a literature of the full stop, a nutrition of extracts, an experience on the margins. Except that France would have little part in today's dialogue, while Gourmont would still be taking part; France would have nothing to tell us, while the corner of Gourmont's dissociations is still dear to us because it has never been supplanted.

Before the Great War there was, especially, a Gourmont-Gide dialogue, which turned bitter, and which potentially contained a strange religious war between a disciple of Huysmans and a Protestant. Gourmont and Gide, who were contemporaries, belonged equally to the symbolist, anti-scholastic training, and the critical spirit of both likewise derived from a libertarian essayism. Gide's novels, like France's, are myths, which flower on an intellect, and also, like Loti's, personal episodes that flower on the disquiets of an intimate journal. They could as well be called experiments—experiments, that is, in Montaigne's meaning: essays. Gide's five or six volumes of literary criticism are compacted in a multiformed and subtly shaded mass of essays. No one today represents better than he what might be called the French complex of the essay since Montaigne.

It was precisely this climate of the essay that modified the positions of criticism, the bid-and-asked that it satisfies and that is as far removed as possible, paradoxically and instructively removed, from Brunetière's, and equally distant, too, from what France and Lemaître, in opposition to Brunetière, called their impressionist criticism. It is no longer a matter of an objective criticism, which ascertains values and "importances" in itself, then measures these importances against criteria (influence, necessity, beneficial result, social function, place in the development of a species). Nor is it any longer a matter of that impressionist criticism in the manner of Lemaître and France, which tells us enjoyably what the critic likes or dislikes with no more of impersonal reasoning than is to be found in a woman's "I adore it" or "I detest it." And it is no more a matter of belief in good taste, of the quest for this good taste, as these were practiced by traditional criticism. It is a matter of what we will take the risk of calling the criticism of sustenance.

CRITICISMS OF SUSTENANCE

Literary sustenance, in the sense in which Gide wrote *Les Nourritures terrestres*, which is a diary of sensual discoveries, a diary of decompression after a puritanical youth and an illness. One can similarly suppose a search for what, in books, can sustain the spirit. One can imagine (and one can observe) a criticism that gives the place of supreme value to the quality and efficacy of books in so far as they govern a sensibility, an intelligence, an action—that is, something in man—and not the evolution of a literature, which is something in the abstract. The founder of this criticism is to be discovered in Montaigne. The criticism is to be encountered again, long afterward, in the Sénancourist Sainte-Beuve of *Volupté* and in the Sainte-Beuve of *Port-Royal;* it was, however, to be almost abandoned by the Sainte-Beuve of the *Lundis.* Lemaître apparently adopted it as the guide for his preferences and judgments in the field of *Contemporains:* but for him and in his work the man to be nourished is only the average reader, the man in the street. The real master of this criticism in the generation of 1885 is the Barrès of *Un Homme libre* with his "intercessors." But Barrès stays too close to his own sustenance. He was made on the exact model of his familiar image of the tree, with its roots that take from the earth only what it needs in order to live, to grow, to give shade, and to rustle. In order for criticism to exist, there must be more play, more freedom, more flexibility, more vagrancy, exactly what we find in Gide, who is closer to Montaigne—to whom Barrès is extraordinarily foreign—close to the Sainte-Beuve of the *Lundis,* whom Barrès preferred to ignore in favor of the young Sainte-Beuve. The temptation and the danger of the criticism of sustenance are a pragmatism, or an egotism, that in the end provokes the loss of the sense of the objective, of the universal, of disinterested literature.

PRAGMATIST CRITICISM

Since, all the same, a criticism of personal taste and selfish sustenance does not go very far, it was natural and necessary that that quest and that technique of literary sustenance should transcend the individual, should release a force that was that of an institution and a discipline. It was because of the Dreyfus case that after 1896 the originality of the criticism of sustenance became not a humanism but a nationalism, that individual sustenances were consolidated into national sustenance, solitary pragmatism into a pragmatism of solidarity. "Thinking solitarily," Barrès said, "leads to thinking in solidarity."

Here we are no longer concerned with André Gide, who before the Great War represented only a criticism of solitary taste and sustenance: whence perhaps his minor position, on the outskirts, his limited public and influence until 1914. The foreground, not in purely literary criticism but in this general criticism by which the detail of literary criticism was renewed and governed, belonged on the one side to Barrès and Maurras and their groups and on the other to Péguy and his.

Barrès held the rank of a great leader here, aloof in the manner of Chateaubriand. Since he has contributed hardly more than a few intuitions to literary criticism, there is no occasion to take much account of him. But Maurras' part was quite different. For ten years he was a literary critic by profession, a reviewer of books and ideas. The Dreyfus case turned him more and more in the direction of politics; the nationalist movement between 1900 and 1908 gave him influence, a school; and the foundation of *L'Action française* as a daily newspaper in 1908 offered him a platform. The leaders of the group L'Action Française were men of letters—Maurras, Léon Daudet, Jacques Bainville. In the realm of timing, it was commanded (and recommended to the attention of letters) by a slogan of "Literature first!" In literary criticism Maurras was indeed the only writer of his time who really functioned as the leader of a school; the evidence lies in Pierre Lasserre's Sorbonne thesis on *Le Romantisme français*, in *La Revue critique des idées et des livres*, in the neo-classic movement, in Henri Massis' *Jugements*. But this criticism was always closely bound to a traditionalism, to the notion, the acute and militant emotion of a *French heritage* to be known, to be marked out, to be upheld, to be defended—a notion that in the beginning of the twentieth century played a part analogous to that of the *French spirit* in Nisard's criticism and influence, but this time with a political dimension, concerned to feed a doctrine, to establish disciplines, to make use of intelligence, to contribute to a restoration.

From the point of view of literary criticism alone it would be impossible to compare Péguy's influence with Maurras' in importance. In sum, there is not even one of the *Cahiers de la quinzaine* in which a work of pure literary criticism can be recognized. And yet Péguy and the group of the *Cahiers*, born like *L'Action française* in the atmosphere of the Dreyfus case, contributed important elements to the atmosphere of criticism.

Primarily through what might be called Péguy's entrance. We see from a distance that there was an entrance of Péguy in somewhat the same way that there was an entrance of Rousseau. He was the first (if not the only) *normalien* who came out of the rue d'Ulm with his popular essence intact, a rhinoceros hide that the spirit of the place could not penetrate, an earthy attitude that was hostile to a traditional humanism, an eye that rebelled at the lights of the workroom. That flat-bottomed tub, the *Cahiers*, has been likened to a fire ship moored beside the high-decked galleon of the Sorbonne. "Péguyism" contributed as much as the school of L'Action Française to the erection of the scarecrow of Lansonism and to the launching of an offensive against the official masters.

Secondarily through the team that made up the *Cahiers*, which otherwise went in various directions (like a stained-glass pattern, Proust would have said). This was where certain questions were posed that were vital nutriment, where a dialogue was begun that was important to criticism, where kinds and families of minds—Péguy, Daniel Halévy, Albert Sorel, Julien Benda—did battle, where, rising out of even greater depths, old French antagonisms were brought out into the light, like that between the schools of Corneille and Racine, of Rousseau and Voltaire, where a problem of Michelet, a problem of Hugo could be posed in new terms, in the sense and in the measure in which they dealt not with an idea of the beautiful or even of the true but with an idea of France. Through Péguy the criticism of sustenance communicated with the physical sustaining substances produced by the cultivator of the soil of France, with the grain of Beauce and the wine of the ancient Orléanais.* "Nothing noble," the middle-class heir, Barrès, says in *Un Homme noble*, "was ever thought outside an armchair." There are no armchairs in peasants' houses, and there was none in the office of the *Cahiers*, since Péguy could sit only on a straight chair. Péguyism gives rights of citizenship to a criticism of the straight chair, distinct from and even hostile to the criticism of the professorial chair and the academic armchair. If professorial and academic criticism—Brunetière, Lemaître, Faguet, and their followers—flourished until Péguy's entrance and fell into decay after Péguy, Péguy seems to have had something to do with it, all the same. Above all, he had something to do with the products, rather complex and turbid in other respects, that replaced it.

The criticism of sustenance implies a criticism of party, a choice of sides, partisan choices, the will to a faith, a "something first" that is not literature. Toward 1910, with the school of L'Action Française, it took a clearly defined political side, and the reaction of the left did not counterbalance this action of the right. And also and above all it chose a religious side, religious sides.

CATHOLIC CRITICISM

In 1894 Brunetière's *Visite au Vatican* had abruptly oriented the celebrated professor's previously rationalist and even Darwinian criticism and

* A province of old France, now the three Departments of Loiret, Loir-et-Cher, and Eure-et-Loir.—Translator.

the liberal magazine of the Voltairean Buloz toward the Church. The religious adventure of Bossuet's convert went through strange stages, however, and seems not to have involved that inner life before which he was always in a state of flight. But in the interim the Dreyfus case unleashed a war of religion and the old religious profile of France was rejuvenated by a downward thrust. Péguy's conversion rather precisely shows the meaning of this thrust. In a most unexpected fashion the separation of Church and state was followed by a religious revival that spread over the literary front and in which the values and the habits of criticism were caught up. In part this was the reason for the very lively function fulfilled in criticism and literary history during the first ten or twelve years after the Great War by Abbé Bremond, the priestly dowser wielding the divining rod over the literary desert. In the twentieth century *L'Histoire littéraire du sentiment religieux* remains the sole critical work that belongs to the climate of Sainte-Beuve, that maintains at the same time the monumental tradition of *Port-Royal*, the intact freshness of humanism, and the spirit of delicacy in erudition, the library that becomes a hive and the bee among its shelves. That the spirit of living criticism, familiarity with the literary values of other times, of today, and even of tomorrow should have been represented then by a priest was not an accident: it was a sign of the times. The criticism of the professor was opposed, or, rather, supplemented, by the criticism of the confessor, for which, moreover, Sainte-Beuve had more or less the vocation.

JOURNALISTIC CRITICISM

A whole part of literary criticism could as well be given the designation of news reports, or, if one prefers, of critical chronicle. The criticism is that of current literature and new books. This is a chapter of journalism. Not much consideration is required in order to recognize that it will never be able to constitute the highest level of criticism, that between what is current and what is lasting there are a necessary opposition and option—and that, if Sainte-Beuve had devoted his *Lundis* to reviewing new books, if he had not been one of those whom the Goncourts called with loathing the singers of praises to the dead, the *Lundis* would belong pretty much to the same week as M. de Pontmartin's *Samedis*.

That said, and whatever the inferior necessities of the newspaper, criticism by professional journalists acquired after the war of 1914 an importance that it had not always had. The withdrawal of university criticism into literary history automatically redounded to the benefit of professional journalism. Hence the place that Paul Souday took in literary criticism was connected from that time on with functions and reasons analogous to those that had assisted his adversary, Bremond. A wealth of reading, a store of learning very satisfactorily kept up to date, an old humanism of one educated by the priests, and above all a remarkable talent as a journalist and polemicist made Souday for ten years the most spectacular and even the most popular figure in criticism. He provided the form, the battlefield, the publicity for the conflict between right and left in literature and especially in criticism. He had the good fortune to write and to shine just at the moment when it was a paradox in letters to behave as an anti-clerical, an unshakably laic republican. His preferences provided an interesting counterweight to the propensity of the republic of letters for the right and for Catholicism.

Souday represented not a criticism of duration (his best articles could not fill a volume) but, and to the highest degree, a militant criticism. He maintained in criticism a militant spirit and tone that for various reasons declined somewhat after him and of which Fernand Vandérem, who represented them with him and willingly against him, long maintained the tradition. It was in large part Souday and Vandérem who made it possible to write a military history of the critical campaigns after the Great War, campaigns of right and left, campaign of pure poetry, campaign of the textbooks, campaign around Valéry. Souday had diagnosed his colleague as a "professional brawler"; the diagnosis had some application to himself. There are no brawls in journalistic criticism today. Lack of interest?

Or a crisis of autonomy in the republic of letters? Properly literary disputes, disputes in which the accent used to be placed on literature, are more and more absorbed into political and social disputes and devoured by them. When journalistic criticism relaxes from its reviews of new books, it no longer finds at the door the green suburb, the promenades of ideas, the gardens of Academe, the athletic fields of literary teams, but the industrial suburb, the final conflict, the atmosphere of conspiracies. After the Great War there was what was called the crisis of the concept of literature. But this crisis was still a literary crisis. As in 1830, in 1850, in 1885, the old concept of literary revolutions ending in "-ism" still existed. There are no more literary revolutionaries today, there are only revolutionary men of letters, some for whom the revolution lies on the right, others for whom it lies on the left. The massive appearance of the concept of physical revolution, political and social, in the consciousness of Europe has declassed the concept of literary revolution as a luxury in the French republic of letters. And, ever since, pure literary criticism has been without current material, without great problems and great debates.*

* The reader is reminded that Professor Thibaudet died in 1936, before the vigorous rejuvenation of French literature and literary controversy that followed the Second World War.—Translator.

V

BARRÈS

Representation

Barrès owed to his time his position as a representative writer whose inner life was important to the general and guiding ideas of the period, gave them body, warmth, movement, and style, was extended into the emotional, religious, and political life of a generation, expressed itself from the platform or the public square, created an action, entered the domain of the state, and all that without falling in quality, without becoming smaller from a literary standpoint, while on the contrary infusing a poetic, life-giving current into the attitudes in favor with the French theatrocracy: a type of literary existence that had begun earlier with Rousseau, that acquired its aura with Chateaubriand, that explained the parts played by Lamartine and Victor Hugo, and in which, in sum, Barrès, who was twenty-three years old at the time of Hugo's funeral, had no rival for a quarter of a century.

The Tree

The considerable and complex work of Barrès had as its expressive coat of arms an image whose banality is of little moment, since he had completely renewed it: that of the plant that grows and that finds its road and its light in the soil in which it was born—reflection, patience, living logic, connection from within among apparently divergent and hostile forms of life. Among these connections, these syntheses, the one that governs all the others, that Barrès found in his youth and that is already wholly embodied in *Un Homme libre* is the discovery of social life by taking the road of inner life, a collectivity encountered at the turning of an individuality, a "thinking solitarily leads to thinking in solidarity" not through renunciation but through the confirmation of that solitary thought.

Sous l'Oeil des barbares, which Barrès wrote when he and the generation that was his contemporary were twenty years old, is the hyperbole of that solitary life from which was born the paradoxical pride of a wounded adolescence that raises itself erect again in challenge. In this first part of the trilogy of *Le Culte du moi,* in which "cult" is not an empty word, a self open to cults and creating cults discloses itself and expresses itself. Beginning with *Un Homme libre* and especially with *Le Jardin de Bérénice,* this cult takes shape: cult of inherited values, and, more precisely, of the heritage assumed by a literary and mystical petitioner, which gives off an undefined effulgence.

The Inheritor

The heritage is personal, since the three volumes of *Le Culte du moi* may be described as the inventory of the inner treasures of an intelligent young bourgeois. But that would not have carried very far: Barrès would have had difficulty making a great literary career out of that, and very soon he would have acquired the official status of a former young man. The original title of *Le Jardin* was *Qualis artifex pereo!* The artist decided to pretend to perish in order that the man who survived him might enter into communication with those hosts of the living and the dead, that people that Bérénice symbolizes.

For, with this plantlike growth and this elementary materialism without which there can be no *artifex,* Barrès was not willing to conceive in terms of a lawyer's, an orator's, a sociologist's, a writer's abstraction that collectivity to which he intended to give himself and that he intended to enjoy. This morality required something physical, a body: not only Bérénice but a popular man, a Caesar, who in a monarchical country would be the incarnation of the nation. Hence the Boulangism of Barrès, the stubbornness of his latent Caesarism. Hence too, and even better, and with more patience and originality, his creation of Lorraine.

Themes of Lorraine and France

The literary origin of the Lorraine of Barrès is drawn from Michelet's *Tableau de la France* and Taine's *La Fontaine.* Its human origin is drawn from the tradition of a family of middle-class patriots and border soldiers. Barrès incorporated his construction of Lorraine into the basic ideas of his

time through *Le Roman de l'energie nationale*, the three parts of which
he published from 1897 to 1902 under the titles of *Les Déracinés*, *L'Appel
au soldat* and *Leurs Figures*—a strong trilogy, a fictionalized thesis that is
lacking in neither artifice nor bad faith, but after all the most living of
his works, which provided the French intelligentsia with subjects of discussion for thirty years.

What subjects? The theme of the opposition or the dialogue between
the provinces and Paris; the theme of the conflict in the city between the
inheritors and the new men, a conflict expressed by the two groups into
which the seven uprooted Lorrainers who "come to Paris" are divided:
the wealthy, who have inherited virtues, and the poor, who, compelled
to make their own lives, do it badly, falling into murder or into unlawful
occupations; the theme of the state, Varennes turning a Lorrainer against
the King, Panama making him disgusted with the Republic, university
education forcing him to uproot himself, to go to Paris in order to serve
a state of legalists; and *Le Roman de l'energie nationale* ending in a bankruptcy, an anguish, vain appeals. Let us add also themes of style, the picture of the philosophy class in the *lycée* of Nancy in *Les Déracinés*, the
valley of the Moselle in *L'Appel*, and above all, in *Leurs Figures*, the immortal pictures of the political assemblies at the time of Panama.

This is the central work of Barrès, written with enthusiasm at the age
of thirty. With intelligence and flexibility, later, he developed, he an-
nexed, he regulated an admirable literary career. He knew how to popu-
larize his ideas without vulgarizing them too much (unless perhaps in a
fabrication like *Colette Baudoche*). *Les Amitiés françaises* has aged
neither more nor less than Chateaubriand's *Amitiés chrétiennes*, for it
belongs on the same shelf and has enough honesty and essence to prevent
its being viewed as an imitation.

The Traveler

There was always a Barrès who was a traveler and a landscapist. His
Venice already coexisted with his Lorraine in *Un Homme libre*. His
Spain, which was new, has been outmoded. His *Mort de Venise*, a fire-
work of language, dropped back in blackened sticks. Yet he adored Venice and Toledo. In contrast, *Le Voyage de Sparte*, written as a chore
when he returned from a journey to Greece that had bored him, marked
a date nevertheless. Here, in an unexpected and truly created light, Barrès
posed the problems of criticism and of good faith that concerned the journey and his view of Greece: the departure, half genuine, half a school
assignment, half reality, half antiquity; the French traveler who, in
Greece, reflects on his pleasure and always sees *Le Voyage de Sparte*

ahead of him. The dialogue of *Un Homme libre* and *Les Déracinés* with, or, rather, against, the professors and the whole University, which is pursued again on the Acropolis, is a good date in the Third Republic. This battle on the Acropolis replaced Renan's outdated *Prière* as a standard theme. Much less of durable substance is to be found in the journey to the Orient, whose title, *Enquête au pays du Levant*, very well describes its largely routine content.

The Publicist

And yet, as with Chateaubriand and Lamartine, the great character of Barrès sustained almost all his tasks at its own high level. Preoccupied by the novel for the mass public, he succeeded with at least one, *La Colline inspirée*, in which themes of Lorraine and Catholicism are brought together masterfully. The monumental ballads of *Un Jardin sur l'Oronte* and *Le Mystère en pleine lumière* have moved us: will they endure the test of time?

Leurs Figures was at first the title of newspaper articles on Panama, which were compared with Saint-Simon, in part because Barrès had successfully imitated Saint-Simon, blending him with Michelet (Chateaubriand also practiced these techniques of composite style): the highly partisan reporting of the Rennes trial in 1898 and that of the sessions of a parliamentary committee, called *Dans le Cloaque*, are "observations" of high class. But the courageous and thankless labor of Barrès for five years on the *Chronique de Grande Guerre* was literally devoured by events, no visible profit was left: a labor for victory, which came, but literature was defeated in advance.

Besides, he enjoyed playing difficult games. Just as always happened to Chateaubriand, the political life of Barrès tied together, after a fashion, three resounding defeats, three bets on wrong horses: the defeat of Boulangism in 1889, the defeat of the conservatives at the time of the Dreyfus case, the defeat of Rhenish annexation and militant Lorrainism after the Great War. This poet appears to have lacked the Grévy style of good sense. Nevertheless, when historians studied Chateaubriand's political life closely, they had no trouble finding in it the persistence of an idea, a leading idea that survived the viscount. One day the political biography of Barrès will be written. There will be a chapter on Barrès as a Socialist (1892–1897). And perhaps it will be recognized that the idea born with Barrès in the marches of Lorraine was a kind of National Socialism, extremely anti-Semitic, in which, with some artifice, it will be possible to see as early as the end of the nineteenth century, in a French writer, many of the themes that surged up abruptly in Germany after Barrès' death.

The author of *Bastions de l'Est* had his war in 1914. He had his Germany in 1934. Furthermore, Germany is the foreign country in which he will always excite the most attention and the most commentary.

There is still great argument today on what Barrès called Lorraine ideas. Are there, as he thought, a French truth and a German truth, two ideologies that, like the two prayers, do not mix? Or else is there only a single truth in the political and moral order? Barrès never used the word "pragmatism." That does not make him any the less one of the founders and the most potent popularizers of that European pragmatism from which today the totalitarian *mystiques* derive the most implacable consequences. "Intelligence—what a little thing on the surface of ourselves!" That was said by this man, so intelligent, so little the intellectual, so hostile, in sum, to intellectualism!

Like Chateaubriand, Barrès gained immensely from his posthumous work. The doctrinarian of the soil and the dead is survived by a voice from beyond the grave. He did not have the time to write his memoirs, which he began the summer before his death. But their raw materials, his diaries, his *Cahiers*, published more or less completely, keep him on the horizon, like Victor Hugo after 1885, and one wonders whether anything prepared for display, in the manner of Rousseau or Chateaubriand, would have ever been as valuable as these notes from day to day, this journal of a soul, this record of a life whose effect on ours still goes on.

VI

THE DISSIDENTS

By calling the poets who were twenty to thirty years old in 1870 "successors," we implied that they were inheritors, that they belonged not to a creative generation but to the troop that kept the fire lighted for the half-generation that would relieve them. A mass poetic renewal was to appear only thirty years after the generation of the tetrarchs. But it was announced by those who might be called the dissidents of 1870, who were a half-generation of movement, contemporary with the half-generation of fire watchers; setting off toward the future while the fire watchers clung to the past but intersecting them in that railway station of poetry, *Le Parnasse contemporain*, where Mendès, Ricard, the subalterns were busy.

The Damned Poets

The first Parnassus anthology, in fact, included verses by Paul Verlaine, born in 1844, and by Stéphane Mallarmé, born in 1842, that did not wholly resemble the rest. In the basket of hens' eggs there were a couple of ducks' eggs. As soon as they were hatched, furthermore, the ducklings were pecked at. Verlaine did not collaborate again with Parnassus, and Mallarmé was expelled as the result of a very scornful report by Anatole France. They disappeared until 1885, Verlaine into his wanderings and Mallarmé into obscure jobs as an English teacher. One and two years after Verlaine, Tristan Corbière (1845) and Lautréamont (1846) were born. Rimbaud, who brought up the rear, was not born until 1854, but his amazing precocity made it seem that nature wanted to make up for lost time and insert this big boy willy-nilly into the group of the twenty-five-year-olds of 1870. Verlaine's famous essay earned them all the name of "the damned poets." In reality, they were a vanguard that was to render the same services to the poetic generation of 1885 that the tetrarchs had performed for Parnassus. Like the tetrarchs, and except for Verlaine and Rimbaud, they were not organized into a literary group. Their existences were totally separated; they represented a kind of absolute dissidence.

VERLAINE

It required many years after his death (this was also the case with Baudelaire) for Verlaine to be recognized as one of the great French poets. He could not have been at the time of Parnassus, which imposed certain demands of an oratorical and studio-light order on ears and tastes, and which preserved or more or less brought back the classic dogma that would have verses be beautiful like beautiful prose with something added. To this Verlaine gave a thoroughgoing *no*. He purified and dematerialized poetry. If Baudelaire stripped his heart naked psychologically, Verlaine did it musically. No language is closer than his to what cannot be said, more newly snatched from the grasp of silence and fullness. Even with the inevitable clumsy imitations of schools, he is already himself in a sonnet in his *Poèmes saturniens:*

> *Je fais souvent ce rêve étrange et pénétrant*
>
> (Often I have this strange and stabbing dream).

His verse has the inflection of voices that have stilled or not yet spoken. This verse is like nothing that had been done before he wrote, nothing that was to be done after. All other verse seems hard beside this rich sap. The man without will, the unresistant sinner that he was for so long were perhaps necessary for this snow to be formed and this unburdened matter of poetry to fall.

Inner music carried him, like Nerval, into the habit of popular poetry. It is indeed to this popular poetry rather than to a historical Parnassus that *Fêtes galantes* must be connected, a book in which, like the young men in *Sylvie*, he adopted the dress of the eighteenth century and the Italian *commedia*. These colors, these pink and purple, russet and rusty stains (in the inventory of his household as a young husband there was a Monticelli)— these are the garments in the magic closet. Love would be dressed in them in the following year with *La Bonne Chanson*. A mysterious recapture of the poetic heart of France, unknown to everyone then, perhaps even to the author! But young love and eighteenth-century gaiety were again crutches, a source, from which, during his hegira with Rimbaud, he escaped in 1874 with *Romances sans paroles*, the highest flight of Verlaine's rocket. Poetry stripped itself and dissolved into the ether. After *Romances*, shall we have to say what we were to say after *Les Illuminations:* that the water that leaped from the fountain did not fall back?

No. For Verlaine became a great Catholic poet. Here Verlaine is to

Baudelaire what Baudelaire was to Chateaubriand or Lamartine. An artist's decorative Christianity in the romantics; the Jansenist Christianity of a descendant of Racine in Baudelaire; but, in Verlaine, it is the popular Christianity of the pagan converted by Saint Martin, which the apostle to the Gauls handed down through the faithful centuries to the parish priest or the prison chaplain. Verlaine did not want or feel his Christian poetry to be Christian only, but Catholic, French, clerical, the poetry of a poor devil who had been baptized and converted, poetry that would be absolutely rejected by Calvinism and Jansenism. A biographer of Verlaine, having gone to question the priest who had been in attendance at the poet's death, was answered only with polite commonplaces and this one remark: "He was a Christian, sir." If not with the same authority, at least with the same grounds, we will say: "He was a Christian poet."

Poetry that was pure, popular, and Christian: it was by these three steps, taken in their time in absolute obscurity, without an audience, that Verlaine, who had started from Parnassus, moved forward to open the sluices of poetry that flowed, that would envelop Parnassus without, however, drowning it, but even adding to it an unexpected landfill that perhaps would be represented by the poetry of Mallarmé.

MALLARMÉ

Verlaine denied the art of Parnassus; Mallarmé distorted it, transposed it, or transfigured it. He too went off to conquer pure poetry, but let us not think now of any rich sap. To Mallarmé this pure poetry was to be the inaccessible diamond peak of a pure Parnassus. His glacier, in a harsh refusal, scorned any suggestion of a gentle hill. Beyond Parnassus he would base himself rather on Hugo (the only French poet of whom erratic fragments can be found in Mallarmé). He brought into the conscious and the dogmatic that law that governed Hugo's poetic unconscious and that Banville's liberated genius had followed with insight: let the words take the initiative.

"Let the words take the initiative"—the formulation is Mallarmé's own. The romantic ancestor, the tetrarch of Parnassus, and the hermetic symbolist played their three parts on the same line across the life spans of three schools.

The theater began with the chariot of Thespis, the steam engine with the lid that bobbed on the pot when the water boiled. In the same way, the cession of the initiative to the words meant at first no more than mere bridges of words thrown up between two previously chosen rhymed syllables. There was a minimum of this sort of thing in all French poetry. Then came Hugo. A poet arrived, who, as the spider ejects a thread from its body to connect two near-by solid points, was always to erect a bridge of images and logic between two beautiful rhymes, to endow with under-

standable crystallization the words constantly rained down on him by
the weight of their music. Words are at home in Hugo as bees are in the
hive, and they create an independent honey in him. Obviously their initiative was cut down in Banville: reduced above all to rhyme. But Banville
was the arranger, the amused, occasionally clownish theoretician of this
initiative. Mallarmé became its mystic.

In Mallarmé's pure poetry the initiative is yielded to the words as, in
the *mystique* of pure love, the initiative is left to God. At the beginning
of a poem there is indeed a scheme, a tone of emotion, a receptive void,
a flexibility, as at the beginning of pure love there is always the individual.
The incantation and the magic of words act on this scheme in order to
bring it into being; they are summoned by the poet and he abandons himself to their workings. But, while words overflowed in Hugo into a
mighty river and spread in Banville into a quiet stream, in Mallarmé they
dripped in an unhuman climate and slowly formed the stalactites of a
miraculous poetry.

Impotence? It is easily said. Every great trembler is a great lover. As
Thales, the geometrician, was capable of running a business, so Mallarmé
was capable of proving himself a facile poet: an influence, a change in his
life, a command would have loosed a rope dancer of rhyme in him, an
unlimited reporter in verse in the style of Raoul Ponchon. *Vers de cir-
constance* shows us his capacity. But the fear of language, respect for
words, had a meaning to him, like the fear of God, respect for God, to a
mystic. And besides there was an unhealthy horror of the trite. He symbolized his poetry in Herodias, the virgin who withdraws from reality,
from any exchange, any stipulation, and from the Other, like Narcissus.
Words meant most for him not in their connections but in their secret
affinities, in their allusive movements, in their inappropriateness to special
language and their capacity for pure language. The lot that Abbé Bremond assigned to the "fine point" of Saint Francis of Sales in the matter
of mystic states must also be assigned to Mallarmé's fine point in the matter of pure poetry: the words, the music, the rhymes are there in order
to designate and to refine, in the same way as an extreme poetry, a poetry
of extremes, extremist, attenuated, after which there is nothing more.

A poet "sings" something. And the epic poet always begins by telling
us what it is. Asked of what it sings, Mallarmé's poetry is as speechless
and powerless before us as Cordelia before Lear. It sings, or it tells, only
of itself. It lives and grips by the essence of its words. Flaubert dreamed
of a book without a subject that would attract by the sheer virtue of its
style. Thus the last part of the nineteenth century put out a few feelers
toward the unbreathable limits of the literary atmosphere.

And now this fragile little book, the two thousand lines of this "im-
potent" poet, long relegated by the voice of the public to the world of

the "incomprehensible" and the "obscure," is one of those that have most surely rounded the Cape of Storms, the cape of posterity,

jusqu'au Reflet du pâle Vasco

(as far as pallid Vasco's image).

Measure the power of enchantment that is preserved and evidenced today by these nine syllables borne on the acrobacy of rhyme, which, having cut their way through time, have come to carry tremendous meaning, have become universally clear and profound, have *succeeded*. In this microcosm, in this drop, in this unique vibration, the whole destiny of Mallarmé's poetry will be seen, its unique function, the minimum of verbal matter on which it balances its naked foot in order to leap into the air: the initiative yielded to the word and, as with a machine gun, retrieved from the words; the demotion of one poetry, the dawn of another, the transformation of the purpose, the substance, and the taste of poetry through the leaven of a buoyant work.

RIMBAUD

A third extreme position, on a borderline, was taken by Rimbaud. Since the action of these dissidents consisted, to the extent permitted by necessary human connections, in consciously or unconsciously attempting an absolute new beginning of the world of literature, it was natural that a place among them should have been occupied by that age whose function it is to assure renewal and to make a clean-cut break with traditions: childhood. The author of *Poètes de sept ans* was a child or an adolescent whose work was consummated when he was eighteen years old and who seemed at that age to have forgotten his poetic life as by day a sleepwalker forgets his nocturnal life. It is worth noting that in the famous *Lettre du voyant* he assigns to the poet exactly that function that nature allots to new generations.

In the work of this adolescent poet the verse is less important than the prose. The poems in verse are brutal and vulgar, powerfully colored, and there is no lack of traces of Hugo or others. Rimbaud did not intend them to be published, he would give the manuscript to anyone without a second thought, and what remains for us was preserved by astonished friends, including Verlaine. Rimbaud's real work of genius is the two little books of prose poems, *Les Illuminations* and *Une Saison en enfer*. The latter—alone among his works—was printed through his own efforts, but he immediately lost interest in it and left it in the printshop in order to roam the world. The spare, electric prose of *Les Illuminations* waited a half century to be given its rightful place: visions of journeys, of countryside, of walking trips, of drunkennesses, that could rank as the masterpiece of poetry if poetry were measured (as it is not impossible that one day it may be) by the sum of coherent novelty that it creates. In *Une Saison en enfer*, worthy of its title, Rimbaud hurled onto paper, in a burning, naked, striking language, the desperate confession of a being without love and without joy, whose furious experiments had failed: loathing for Europe and its laws in the poet who had seen enough of it and who had withdrawn into a state of nature, into the brutal light. Such a testament silences any literature. Rimbaud was to be regarded later as having erected the Pillars of Hercules of the literary world with *Les Illuminations* and *Une Saison*. And, after all, this geography is accurate.

CORBIÈRE

Some of the verses interpolated into *Une Saison*, which are better than those in the *Poésies*, have the simplicity of popular songs. Rimbaud, like Verlaine, was responsive to their quality. Similarly, the Breton, Corbière, who died before he was thirty, left *Les Amours jaunes*, disjointed, violent verses, full of *no!* to all the poetry before them, to any restriction, sculptured with a sailor's knife, the onslaught of a primitive who makes his own language as well as he can with fragments of civilized men's and who, in *Le Cantique spirituel*, returns to all the harshness and roughness of a popular imagery.

LAUTRÉAMONT

Verlaine was the faun, Mallarmé the mystic, Rimbaud the child, Corbière the mystic. Among all these dissidents there certainly had to be an authentic dissenter from reason, a madman, his madness presented by genius. This was the case with Lautréamont. Although he never wrote a line of verse, Lautréamont brought an unaccustomed parcel of poetry into literature with *Les Chants de Maldoror:* a frenzied monologue in six songs, an oratorical surge, a proclamation of ferments of violence and violator, of sensual and sexual, of redskin and antediluvian in a creature of letters cast up from an austral world on to some unexpected shore of France. A pre-Columbian idol and a sea serpent, Maldoror has given French literature what England has asked in vain of Loch Ness: its monster. With him as with the four others, a limit of literary creation was reached—hyperbole!

Hyperbole

Hyperbolic literature is the name that we could as easily have used instead of "dissidents" to designate these attempts of 1870. They are the diametrical opposite of Parnassus, which stood on its technical position, which saw literature as a seat for its bottom, not a springboard for its drive, which created a studio, which turned out respectable staffs of average poets. These five poets in the shadow of the Parnassus of 1870 were like Charles Fourier and Etienne Cabet in the shadow of the golden mean. Theirs was a generation of twenty-year-olds whose time had not come, who simply took cognizance, who testified in prophecies before being plunged back into the flood that had brought them, and whose message, premature at that time, was to be heard again, at first fifteen years later in symbolism and later, and still better, thirty years after those fifteen years in the generation of the Great War.

VII

SYMBOLISM

The New School and the Old Schools

Victor Hugo was born in the year of *Le Génie du christianisme*, and this man was so closely bound to the continuity of the century that it seems that the poetic revolution waited for the year of his death to announce itself. "I am going to clear the horizon," he said.

He cleared it principally to the benefit of those poets born after 1860 who were later called the symbolist generation and whom one must be careful not to view too expressly as a reaction against Parnassus and against naturalism. Through their masters, Verlaine and Mallarmé, on the one side, and through Hérédia on the other, their connection with the Parnassians is evident. And one of the reasons why that date of 1885 is important is that in the preceding year one of the naturalists of *Les Soirées de Médan*, Huysmans, published *A Rebours*, a book that put the public at the disposal of the new poetic school and that, in a certain measure, played the preparatory part of a *Génie du symbolisme*.

Symbolism's *no!* was not very categorical, or else it was shouted with a certain confusion. It is not by what it denied that it must be defined but by what was new in its contribution. Now it produced three revolutionary drives that changed the conditions of poetic life in France. By reason of the fact of symbolism and the five pre-symbolist dissidents, a new poetry was opposed not only or chiefly to Parnassus but to the whole body of French poetry from Ronsard to Hugo.

FREE VERSE

The first and most serious revolution: the liberation of verse. The question of the origins of free verse is not complicated. It came from popular poetry, which, from time immemorial, has never shackled itself to rhyme or to syllabic scansion. The first deliberately free verse ever printed appeared in 1873 in *Une Saison en enfer*, in imitation of popular songs. There was a similar origin in Jules Laforgue. But side by side with this spontaneous free verse a deliberately planned free verse was to prosper, worked out with a calculated technique, an often arbitrary and abstruse dogmatism: in this field the initiator was Gustave Kahn. Be that as it may, the free-verse revolution changed the nature of the instrument put into the hands of half the French poets and created a rupture between the "normal" poets and the "free-verse" poets.

PURE POETRY

The second revolution: the advent of a pure poetry in contact and commerce with music. Symbolism, a contemporary of Hugo's departure, was also a contemporary of Wagner's arrival; he won the French public in a few years, and in 1885 one of the young symbolist magazines was called *La Revue wagnérienne*. The major aspiration of symbolism, according to the directive laid down by Mallarmé, was "to recapture the best in music." And, if it is possible to speak accurately of a reaction against Parnassus, it was above all in this sense that the poetic enemy of symbolism was precision in all its forms, by which we mean, as in music, the preciseness to be given to the reader or the listener, not that technical precision invested by the author in his work, which in music is rigorous, and which the theoreticians of free verse easily carried into pedantism. Hérédia, who in the precision of his sonnets sought to suggest, was still favored by the symbolists, while Sully-Prudhomme, the final purpose of whose poetry was precision and who strove to apply it to the inner life, was viewed by symbolism as the enemy incarnate, on the same ground as Coppée.

THE REVOLUTION

The third revolution: the idea itself of revolution. The purpose of the romantic and Parnassian revolutions was a conquest and an organization, a stable condition of poetry—freedom perhaps, but freedom within forms. The fine frenzy of romanticism did not last ten years, and Parnassus was always careful. But symbolism accustomed literature to the idea of indefinite revolution, an artistic Blanquism,* a right and a duty of youth to overturn the preceding generation, to run after an absolute. If the poets were divided into "normal," or "regular," and free-verse, literature was divided into normal literature and "advance-guard" literature. The chronic avant-gardism of poetry, the "what's new?" of the "informed" public, the official part given to the young, the proliferation of schools

---

* Louis-Auguste Blanqui, who participated in the revolution of 1848, was the ancestor of the political theory of permanent revolution.—Translator.

and manifestos with which these young hastened to occupy that extreme point, to attain for an hour that crest of the wave in a tossing sea—all this was not only a new development of 1885 but a new climate in French literature. The symbolist revolution, the last thus far, might perhaps have been definitively the last, because it incorporated the theme of chronic revolution into the normal condition of literature.

Decadence and Symbolists

It is possible that in an old literature this might be a sign of decadence. But it will be noted first of all that this was a question of a poetic climate and that poetry, precisely since symbolism, has been less and less the principal concern of literature. And it will be observed also that decadence as a word and as a fact was first inscribed on one of the banners of the new school and that one of its magazines was called *Le Décadent*. It was specifically in order to get rid of this name and to restore it to its natural state as a nickname that Jean Moréas invented the name of symbolism.

The symbolist impetus lasted some fifteen years, until about 1902. It was at its height of creative youth in 1890, when Jules Huret's *Enquête sur l'evolution littéraire* appeared in *L'Echo de Paris*. After 1902 one wondered what was going to take the place of symbolism. One of its prominent representatives, Henri de Régnier, was indeed admitted to the Académie in 1911. But that did not at all mean: "Symbolism not dead." On the contrary.

Some order could be brought into the overcrowded picture of the poets of this school by making distinctions—somewhat artificially, as is inevitable—among the militants, the allies, the representatives, the heirs, and the rank and file.

MILITANTS

The militants were the early symbolists who established the forms and stated the problems of the school. Their activity was linked chiefly to that of the "little magazines" that were really big, like Harpagon's money box, by reason of their content and that were one of the bright ideas of symbolism. Two of the leading positions in this field must be given to the editors of *La Vogue* (the first issue appeared in April 1886), Jules Laforgue and Gustave Kahn. Laforgue, who died at the age of twenty-seven, would probably have been one of the newest and most complete writers of his generation. What he contributed to symbolism that was essential was the alliance between the habits (or the methods) of popular poetry and the widest and most delicate contemporary sensitivity. Let us add to this the not too beneficial influence of his reading of Schopenhauer and Karl Robert Eduard von Hartmann. He has gone out of fashion but he has retained the loyalty of many. Gustave Kahn was an organizer and a technician in poetry. The history of symbolist technique should likewise not overlook either Stuart Merrill, an excessive champion of alliteration, or Robert de Souza, a poetic phoneticist. The most astonishing technical apparatus of this militant age of symbolism was the work of René Ghil, who aspired to depict, or rather to score, the evolution of the world and mankind in stonily schoolboyish free verse. All these militants were extremely serious, and, if one of the glories of poetry consists in these attacks, of which Mallarmé remains the hero, on a frontier,—they will deserve rescue from oblivion.

ALLIES

The influence of a school is measured by the allies or the sympathizers through whom it succeeds in infusing its color into the general complexion of a literature. Semi-symbolists hovered between symbolism and Parnassus and helped the imprecise musicality peculiar to the new school to enter into normal verse. They included Ephraïm Mikhaël, who was most purely Parnassian; Louis Le Cardonnel, a harmonious pagan who died a Christian; Albert Samain, whose median qualities made him the poet of his generation most read by the general public; the vibrant and burning Signoret, Pierre Quillard, Adolphe Retté, and, less Parnassian and more turned inward, Georges Rodenbach, a meticulous poet of Flanders, and Charles Guérin, a master of the elegy and even of the epistle.

REPRESENTATIVES

Let us define as official representatives of symbolism those poets who in the twentieth century, after the deaths of Verlaine and Mallarmé, figured as leaders and were recognized, in the manner of Gautier and Vigny, as veterans of the school or the movement.

About 1900 there was a tendency to couple the names of Henri de Régnier and Francis Viélé-Griffin, who helped to make free verse popular. Régnier seems to us the most complete, the most flexible, and the most varied poet of the symbolist movement. With a poor vocabulary, monotony of device, casualness, chance or padding in his themes, he exerts a deep charm through his sustained musicality, his remarkable gift for making the substance of words soft and sensual. An intelligent opportunism devoid of abdication and concession made it possible for him to go from a gracious freed—rather than free—verse to the finest and most solid forms of the sonnet and the stanza.

If Régnier moved through free verse as a courteous guest, Viélé-Griffin absolutely inhabited it, guiding and following its fortunes. Little odes, light sketches of spring in Touraine, secrets of love, tender, tranquil stories grow in gracious gradations that, with time, have passed.

THE HERITAGE OF MALLARMÉ

It is to genuine symbolism that Paul Valéry's work and remarkable career must be linked. Following Mallarmé, he conceived and practiced poetry as a series of explorations, experiments, games to be tried, obstacles to be overcome. The games were tried at first under influences—Mallarmé and Leonardo; then, beginning with *La Jeune Parque* after a long silence, in an independent and inventive fashion.

Valéry presents us with a man endowed with a dual faculty, or with two manias that thus far had been regarded as opposites. Two extremes met in him. On the one side there was the gift of pure poetry, which, in many forms, was the great discovery of symbolism. On the other side there is a singular sense of precision, the habit of conceiving every operation of the mind as a victory of the precise over the vague. He reminds us of the double harness of Bergsonian thought, but also of Leonardo's pictorial genius, of the necessary genius of music.

When the sense of poetry and the sense of precision exist together in the same mind, they would tend, it seems, to execute together the same work, a precise poetry. This is just the part that was played by the ingenious Sully-Prudhomme. Valéry played the opposite part. There is no precise poetry; there is pure poetry carried to its hyperbole and there is poetic form, poetic rigor, carried to the same hyperbole. The steam engine is used to make ice. It is the alliance of a pure poetry and a pure technique: a seemingly nonhuman position, for which Valéry would probably not have incurred the risk if there had not been the precedent of Mallarmé.

In the case of Sully-Prudhomme, as in that of a philosopher or a writer of prose, the face of poetry and mystery was the inner face, turned toward the poet, possessed in secret by the poet; the face of precision was the outer face, turned toward the reader, striven after with effort for his comfort and his pleasure: poetry was at the origin, precision at the goal. In the case of Valéry, on the contrary, the face of precision was the secret face that clung to the mind and the operation of the poet, and the face of pure poetry, of music, of accessibility and suggestion was the face turned toward the reader, the face that the reader perceived and enjoyed. Sully-Prudhomme's poetry is like a machine whose human driver is invisible. In Valéry's poetry the precise machinery is underneath, the human beauty above: this is the Hadaly of *L'Eve future.*

And indeed, reading Valéry's verse, one recalls the soft, elastic, incorruptible substance of Hadaly's naked arm. Valéry is one of those without whom one of the five or six extreme peaks of French verse would not exist. It was also, but it was not only, in the manner of a mathematician that he introduced new functions into poetry. And schools are not in vain: it required all the laboratory and all the sacrifices of symbolism to arrive at the *Cimetière marin* and *La Jeune Parque*.

One of the platitudes of critics hostile to symbolism consisted in reproaching it for being a school of foreign poets. That is also a title of honor. It must be observed that it was through symbolism that Belgium, which had had no French-language poets since the times of the Dukes of Burgundy, found herself once more incorporated into French poetry. Charles Van Lerberghe, Max Elskamp, Albert Mockel delivered their tributes. Maurice Maeterlinck's bare, mysterious, and musical *Lieder* were celebrated before his plays. But it was really within the ranks of symbolism, and as one of its greatest representatives, that the poet of Flanders, Émile Verhaeren, took his place.

IN THE RANKS OF THE SYMBOLISTS

With Viélé-Griffin Verhaeren was the recognized master of free verse. In the five collections of *Toute la Flandre* the favorite form is the set of irregular verses, oratorical, spontaneous, stressed on strong syllables, as habitually as Viélé-Griffin's groupings are lightened by the mute *e*. A symbolist both in his love of symbols and in his use of free verse, a fugitive from symbolism in his eloquent romanticism, Verhaeren flees it also in his stressed and consistent development, which is never satisfied with allusion and suggestion. This powerful and honest poet lacks resonance, opposes to pure poetry a poetry ballasted with heavy alloys, a civic and social poetry, too, which is never disinterested. He looked into the shadows as, in contrast, Viélé-Griffin's pastels turned paler.

The breadth of the symbolist movement is such that we can encompass in it an ultra-Parnassian like Signoret, a cicada drunk with music in the pines of Aix, as well as a poet as anti-Parnassus as Francis Jammes. The case of Jammes is instructive here. First Lamartine and then the Parnassians, by propagating their styles among the thousands of provincial poets, created and long kept alive a provincial style. Now Jammes was a provincial poet who would literally have been made impossible by the Parnassian system and who could have been brought to life only enveloped in and sanctioned by the symbolist climate. This poet, not so much of free verse as of freed verse given suppleness, is undoubtedly, with Lamartine and Mistral, the most original incarnation of the poetry of the provinces, and, through a fortunate rejection of Paris, a well-governed and subtly wary spontaneity, and the porosity and the freshness of an earthen jug, he was able, in his corner of Béarn, like Mistral in the middle of Province, to preserve the habit and the intimacy of its ways.

VIII

THE THEATER

Toward 1890 a new dramatic generation, destined to replace Augier and Dumas, Sardou and Labiche, Meilhac and Halévy, was called to the stage, and it was inconceivable that it should not keep the appointment. There was a great audience for the theater; the Comédie-Française and other theaters had a wealth of great actors who left no reason to envy earlier periods. And, furthermore, the new literary schools of the novel and poetry were ambitious to conquer the theater.

Was this conquest accomplished? Romanticism had had its theater from 1830 to 1840 and middle-class realism had had its from 1850 to 1860. But neither naturalism nor symbolism was to succeed in getting a foothold on the boards.

The realist novelists had long sought to repeat their bookshop successes on the stage, sometimes through their own dramatic writing, sometimes by having their novels adapted to the stage by literary day-laborers. In general, despite some financial successes such as Alphonse Daudet's *L'Arlésienne* and Zola's *L'Assommoir,* they did not succeed.

Nevertheless it is naturalism to which, with all good will and in deference to temporal coincidence, both Henry Becque's theater and the Théâtre Libre may be traced.

Henry Becque

It could not be said that the first play of the new drama, *Les Corbeaux,* was the work of the generation of 1885. It was performed in 1882, and its author, Henry Becque, barely known through several unsuccessful efforts, was forty-five years old. The intercession of Dumas and the liberalism of Emile Perrin had opened the door of the Comédie-Française to this play. The 1882 audience reacted violently. This gloomy picture of a family deprived of its head and at the mercy of businessmen was almost a disaster, in spite of the cuts made in it for the first performance and the esteem that the critics were not stingy in giving it. And it is worth noting that *Les Corbeaux* has always encountered virtually the same resistance, that it has been impossible to establish it permanently in the Comédie's repertory. But what will seem still more remarkable is the fact that a play so badly received by the public could produce a dramatic revolution as, thirty years before, *La Dame aux camélias* had done. Here attention must be directed to what it swept away rather than to what it brought in. Like an artillery shell that makes the first breach, it swept away conventions on which the theater had lived until then, conventions of composition, moral conventions, social conventions. Perhaps, indeed assuredly, it replaced them with others, but new conventions are not yet conventions. As for what the play contributed, it was a dramatic work in consonance with the businessmen of Balzac, the grotesque title out of Flaubert, the gloomy outlook of Zola. It had as well one of the best dramatic styles written in the nineteenth century. Finally, in sequence with *Turcaret* and *Mercadet*, it was the third panel in the triptych of the drama of business. And it will be observed that the first two had had no greater success with audiences than did *Les Corbeaux*.

Three years later Becque offered *La Parisienne*, the title of which rightly seemed to be in dubious taste, but the play had a decent success and even lasted. In contrast to *Les Corbeaux*, *La Parisienne* contained nothing revolutionary. It was well done, and perhaps false, like the old light comedies. It has been observed that in Becque there was a light-comedy writer who did not know of his own existence. Let us say a "Labichist." Tissier's line that brings down the curtain on *Les Corbeaux*, "Ever since your father's death you have been surrounded by swine," was already the opposite of an actor's speech in the manner of Dumas or even of Augier. It was a spontaneous remark in the manner of those made by Labiche's egoists. From a certain wholly technical point of view, *Les Corbeaux* was Becque's *Les Petits Oiseaux* and *La Parisienne* was his *Plus Heureux des trois*. But Becque had no spontaneity. After *La Parisienne*, he worked fourteen years on *Les Polichinelles*, of which he left only the equivalent of two acts. Like Alain-René Lesage, and again Balzac, he really wrote only one play.

The Théâtre Libre

No more than *Les Corbeaux* did the Théâtre Libre make any pretensions to the creation of a naturalist theater. It simply found that its position put it into touch with naturalism. André Antoine was a young working-class Parisian, employed by the municipal gas company, who, like thousands of other Parisians, had the passion of the theater in his fingers, his limbs, and his tongue. He formed a company of volunteers. Every month, in closed offices after hours, this company staged a play, which had only one performance, before a subscription audience whose dues covered the expenses. Considered as private meetings, these performances were exempt from censorship. This theater was naturally inclined to present plays that the censor would have forbidden in a normal theater, as well as experimental plays, even of pure poetry, for a restricted audience (what was called the *élite*). The Théâtre Libre naturally assumed the character of a proving ground for experiments in drama, analogous to the "little magazines" that were beginning their golden age. It was then that the literary and theatrical expression *avant-garde* became a part of the language and of reality. The advance guard represented by the Théâtre Libre included such naturalists or "Médanists" as Hennique, Céard, and Alexis; such fantasists as Emile Bergerat; romantics like Mendès; such men of the Provençal school as Paul Arène. Lavedan made his start there; there the same actors played Banville's *Le Baiser* and "slices of life" that took place in whorehouses. Finally, while waiting to stage Ibsen's *Ghosts*, Antoine put on Tolstoi's *Power of Darkness*. As for the realism claimed for the direction—which consisted, for instance, in often having the actors talk among themselves with their backs to the audience—it was more irritating than revolutionary. But the mere fact of Antoine's ardor, his conviction, his unselfishness impressed on actors and audience alike the idea that they must *do something* and set the theater free, though no one quite knew from what. The work of the Théâtre Libre was more or less the embodiment of the theater's drive and dynamism at a time when literature was being remade and a waning generation was handing over its powers to a rising generation.

At this time, furthermore, the naturalist formula was running dry, and the theater had naturalism behind it rather than before it. The "slices of life," which meant no more than anything else to Antoine, became studio pieces. Something new was needed.

The Symbolist Theater

Would symbolism, like romanticism earlier, provide it? The naturalist label having been rightly or wrongly fastened to Antoine, it was logical that the critical success of the Théâtre Libre should lead to the birth of a symbolist Théâtre Libre. It appeared in 1893 in the Maison de l'Oeuvre, where Aurélien-Marie Lugné-Poe served as the Antoine, and which served symbolism until the end of the nineteenth century as its laboratory of theatrical experiment, utilized also by the youthful groups of *Le Mercure de France* and *La Revue blanche*.

The majority of the writers called symbolists attempted the theater with poetic works that could not stand up at all on the stage. Henri de Régnier's *La Gardienne* was no more than a lyric dialogue, but Viélé-Griffin's *Phocas le jardinier*, Gide's *Saül* and *Le Roi Candaule*, and Verhaeren's *Le Cloître* and *Philippe II* can be counted among their authors' best works. But the footlights were cruelly harsh to them. Edouard Dujardin's attempt in *Antonia* was not a success. On the whole, the intellectual history of symbolism in the theater lies in what might be called the Maurice Maeterlinck experiment and the Paul Claudel experiment.

Let us observe at the start that these experiments originated in books and not in the theater. Nor is this an isolated instances. From Count Roederer to Louis Vitet and from Merimée's *Clara Gazul* to Hugo's *Cromwell*, the romantic theater had got its start by several probationary years of closet drama. But it poured like a torrent over the stage with *Henri III et sa cour*, *Hernani* and *La Tour de Nesle*. It cannot be said that the theater of the two symbolist writers did not break through, almost as much as that of the author of *Cromwell*: but this was something different.

THE THEATER OF MAETERLINCK

It is an exaggeration to view *Les Flaireurs* by Maeterlinck's compatriot, Charles van Lerberghe, as the initial impulse of Maeterlinck's theater. But, like *Les Flaireurs*, Maeterlinck's first dramatic works were written in a state of poetic vision in no way concerned with the stage and were caught up in the brisk movement of Belgian, or, more accurately, Flemish, symbolism: a theater of the inner life, a setting that could not be imagined otherwise than in terms of the painter Hans Memling. The title of one of the first of Maeterlinck's dramatic efforts to be staged, *Intérieur*, presented by the Maison de l'Oeuvre in 1894, is as symbolic as the play itself. It is the interior of a house around which the signs of a disaster take shape. And this whole theater can be called an inner theater. *La Princesse Maleine* and that *Pelléas et Mélisande* which, like *Carmen* and *Mireille*, was popularized and devoured by its music, stand as its masterpieces.

Except that this idealistic Fleming was also a very positive Fleming, very determined to allow all the right material things to play their parts, and, beginning with *Monna Vanna*, he was able to enter adroitly the physical substance of the stage. With Henri Bataille he is one of the two writers who came out of symbolism to have major dramatic successes. Maeterlinck's chief successes were *Monna Vanna* and *L'Oiseau bleu*, not to mention *Pelléas*, for the success of which he is indebted to Claude Debussy. But he found his successes in the area of facility. *Monna Vanna* is an inferior play, very certain in its effects, basically romantic, sound in its construction, but rather short, and its explicit and emphasized poetry lacks music and *chiaroscuro*. And *L'Oiseau bleu*, the greatest success of this period, can be called the masterpiece of the allegorical theater. But if the dramatic critic thinks that the passage from symbol to allegory, from symbolism to allegorism, represents an evolution, the unhappy esthete will retort, "You mean decay!"

After *Monna Vanna*, Maeterlinck's dramatic position was greater abroad than in France, and for many years *L'Oiseau bleu* enjoyed universal success.

During the Great War Maeterlinck wrote a very moving short play, almost a masterpiece, *Le Bourgmestre de Stilmonde*. But in the theater as in the rest of his literature, the Maeterlinck who matters is still the Maeterlinck of his symbolist youth.

CLAUDEL

Even more than Maeterlinck's early theater, Claudel's is a written theater, very remote from the stage and from France, written by a great lyric poet. Only two of his plays have risked the theater, and both belong to his prime (that is, to the few years before the Great War): *L'Annonce faite à Marie* and *L'Otage*. Only the second has more or less held the stage, where it was recognized and admired afresh by those who had read it. The second act, that of the pope, becomes tremendously powerful on the stage, but the last act is virtually unintelligible for the unforewarned spectator. Aside from this effort, Claudel's work should be treated as dialogue and lyricism, following the example of *La Tentation de saint Antoine* and *Axel*. It is only with a certain arbitrariness that we include it under theater.

It is encompassed between two masterpieces, Claudel's first drama, *Tête d'or*, which he wrote at the age of twenty, and *Le Soulier de satin*, written between his fiftieth and sixtieth years. In *Tête d'or*, there is hardly anything but the title character and, in this character, a heroic state of grace magnified by a poetry that has experienced the sunstroke of *Les Illuminations*. But on that day Claudel tossed on to our deck the biggest poetic mailbag that it had carried since the Hugo of Guernsey. Once this beginning had been made, he had his instrument in his hand, the Claudelesque line that makes us think of a translation, a translation of a text too powerful for the human voice. As for *Le Soulier de satin*, thirty-five years after *Tête d'or*, it is an evocation of the sixteenth century in Spain, in Bohemia, in America, which, like the *Second Faust* or the first *Tentation*, creates a kind of world, a Catholic, or rather a Jesuit, world, or better still an Ignatian world, universal like the apostolate of the Jesuits or the career of the poet-diplomat. This great Catholic artist's poetic materialism made him the poet of the materiality of dogma, of devotions, of the sacraments, of the images, of everything that religion, being human, can or should contain of the corporeal. The dramatic form in which his lyricism flowed spontaneously shows his attraction to the materiality of the stage. In another mode of life, with the career of a French writer remaining in France, he would perhaps have dovetailed better with that materiality and truly given symbolism its man of the theater.

Romantic Revival

ROSTAND

Naturalism and symbolism having given the theater only experiments, it was necessary to satisfy it with older experiments. This generation gave romanticism an after-life. It was more than a survival: it was a little revival of verse comedy and drama.

Five acts in verse: until 1914 that still had a certain prestige in ageless tragedy. The poets of the previous generation, romantics and Parnassians, once more had enormous successes with poetic theater in the closing years of the nineteenth century: Richepin, for example, with *Par le glaive* and *Le Chemineau,* Coppée with *Pour la couronne.* And Rostand put a brilliant full stop to this theater.

There are three possible points of view on the case of Rostand. That of his contemporaries and the theater audiences endowed him for fifteen years with the greatest glory that a poet had enjoyed in France since Victor Hugo. That of what might be called literature on the march vehemently rejected him at the same time and for the same reasons as Anatole France. That of literary history has reason to rehabilitate him.

That Rostand, like Anatole France, has nothing to say today to the twenty-year-old Frenchman or his ten-years-older sister is a fact, and if children clung to their grandfathers' tastes, there would be no literature. But Rostand, like France, brought intelligibility into French literature. Rostand represents something in it. He had a mandate. He exercised it brilliantly, and to the end. Thanks to him, verse theater had a magnificent burial and splendid funeral games.

His first attempts were those of a good poet of the end of the nineteenth century, a bachelor of theater arts who had made a brilliant entrance into the Comédie-Française with a theme that had no need to be new, *Les Romanesques.* Then on two occasions he starred with the poetic plays that young men dreamed of writing for Sarah Bernhardt: *La Princesse Lointaine* and *La Samaritaine.* And finally there was *Cyrano.*

There are perhaps six nineteenth-century plays that remain in the repertory of the public with the approval or the acquiescence of the cultivated,

and no one doubts that *Cyrano de Bergerac* is among them. A great actor
(which, to be honest, is more and more seldom to be found) will long
be enough to give this play full houses. *Cyrano* stood up into the future,
but it stood on the past entirely. There is a Louis XIII style, that of *Les
Grotesques,* which the author of *Marion Delorme* had, moreover, discovered quite alone, without waiting for Gautier, and of which *Ruy Blas* and
Le Théâtre en liberté stood as the masterpieces until *Cyrano,* which
definitively surpassed them. The stage, which had been arrested, led into
a trap or against a blank wall, for instance in Auguste Vacquerie's *Tra-
galdabas,* was brought by *Cyrano* into the light, where it emerged and
triumphed. Brunetière regarded the burlesque and the precious as diseases
that always threatened French literature, and he endlessly pursued them
with a menacing finger, as M. Purgon pursued Argan's medical independence through the illustrations of the maladies that lay in wait for him.
And these are perhaps defects, but *Cyrano* gave the burlesque and the
precious that magnificent destiny that Brillat-Savarin's *La Physiologie du
goût* assured to gluttony. The burlesque and the precious were snatched
aloft in a movement of rhythm and rhyme, in a physical surge, in a dramatic dress, all of which, obviously, added not to the theater's intellect
but to its joy, its health, its historic tradition. Granted that nowadays
there is no more humanity in *Cyrano* than in *Les Burgraves* and *Le Chapeau de paille d'Italie.* These are plays that could get along without it,
and that is all.

Humanity, history, the quality that makes the solidity of classic tragedy
were striven after by Rostand in *L'Aiglon:* a total error, which has
weighed more heavily on his memory than anything else. The same cannot be said of *Chantecler,* one of the most courageous attempts in the
French poetic theater. Only one hero was possible for Rostand: himself,
or, rather, The Poet. A great poet incarnated in a great actor, and animal
nature providing the poet with the help and the tricks that it had given
the crafty clerks who had set feudal society spinning around Renard the
Fox, who was their twin—the enterprise was bold and beckoning. Poetically it succeeded, and *Chantecler* is indeed the only truly great work
that Rostand wrote. Dramatically it turned out otherwise. Constant Co-
quelin died before he could play the title part. Rostand was overwhelmed
in a torrent of the worst publicity that ever submerged a poet. The enormous clumsinesses of the play recalled those of *Les Burgraves.* If *L'Aiglon*
was too much for Rostand, *Chantecler* was too much for the stage. But
Mallarmé admired that experiment on the frontiers of the theater. Naturally!

THE LAST VERSE COMEDIES

Rostand's successes naturally gave verse comedy a revival in fashion from 1910 to 1914. Mendès unavailingly became his aging disciple with *Scarron* and *Glatigny*. *Les Bouffons*, by Miguel Zamacoïs, and André Rivoire's *Le Bon Roi Dagobert* profited by this Saint Martin's summer. The theater in Alexandrines is one of the many heritages that vanished in the abyss of the Great War.

Ibsen's Influence; the Theater of Ideas

The real dramatic monument of the new generation was not bound up with the poetic movement and did not begin to rise until ten years after it, at the end of the nineteenth century, at the exact moment of the disappearance of those two pillars of the old theater, Alexandre Dumas on the stage and Sarcey in criticism.

The authors and the enthusiasts of the Maison de l'Oeuvre intended to supplant what they called the naturalist theater—though it was rather a mere wisp of a naturalist theater—not so much with a symbolist as with an idealist theater. Maurice Beaubourg's *L'Image*, the first modern French play that had any significant success in the Maison de l'Oeuvre, was published with a preface that concluded thus: "By me or by others the idealist theater will be created." In reality the great influence here was Ibsen's. Antoine had staged nothing by Ibsen except *Ghosts*, the play about heredity, which was the most in accord with the naturalist turn and especially with the reading of Zola. But the Maison de l'Oeuvre became the recognized Ibsen theater, especially for his new plays, which were presented in Paris almost simultaneously with their introductions in Scandinavia and Germany. The natural evolution that opened the road of succession to the Augier-Dumas theater, the failure of the naturalist experiment, the fresh current of symbolism reinforced Ibsen's influence, not on the public, which always rebelled against him, but on the authors, each of whom aspired to be the Ibsen of France. What came of this was not an idealist theater (the concept was stillborn) but a theater of ideas.

The play of ideas supplanted the previous generation's problem play, and, at least when it had a popular success, it retained many of the problem play's characteristics and even some of its methods. In addition, the chorus that the authors of the ancient Attic comedies placed on the stage to voice their own opinions, and the Cléantes and Aristes of Molière, had long since given comedy its core of ideas. The new generation's play of ideas assumed that precise, classic, and didactic form more often and more successfully than the spontaneous, poetic, in sum Shakespearean, forms of Ibsen and Shaw and, later, Pirandello.

CUREL

The master of the drama of ideas was François de Curel, one of those for whom the Théâtre Libre was created. He began there. Obviously, Curel's plays are not message plays, since as a rule he posed questions for argument without drawing conclusions. But his protestations must not be taken too literally when he defends himself against having put "ideas" into his plays and asks that they be taken simply as dramas of life—an adjunct to a hunting gentleman's fresh air. Ibsen raised the same objections against critics with respect to his own plays, and we know what talk means. In one of his forests Curel had a little hunting lodge whose shelves included the complete collection of *La Revue philosophique*. It can be considered, symbolically, the laboratory of his plays.

It is not quite clear what qualities of a man of the theater were lacking in Curel. His plays are solid, occasionally powerful; *Les Fossiles* and *Terre inhumaine*, the one at the beginning and the other at the end of his career, can be called masterpieces of workmanship. He wrote a good theatrical style, open, ventilated, solid. In *L'Envers d'une Sainte* and *L'Ame en folie* he created quite individual feminine characters, as living as those of any playwright of his time. He won his successes progressively against the resistance of the public, without making too great concessions to it, raising it to his own level almost by sheer physical force. And yet he soon became dated; inclusion in the repertory did not save him from that. He retained much more standing among people who read plays, and abroad, than among those who knew the theater. He acquired the aspect of a Sully-Prudhomme of the theater. This fate derives from the dangerous game that he played: the game of the theater of ideas. Ideas automatically succeed one another, whereas emotions are eternal. Ideas have their specialists, the men who live with them. They have hardly more to do with men of the theater than the mistresses of an evening. And *Le Repas du lion*, *La Nouvelle Idole*, *La Comédie du génie* truly make the stage resemble a night school. Anyone who said of Curel, "He is a schoolteacher!" would be doing him an injustice, but he would be understood, at any rate, and he would establish a basis for discussion that would have to do with Curel and with the theater of ideas.

HERVIEU

Such a discussion, undoubtedly, would end with esteem for Curel but would find its victim in Paul Hervieu. Hervieu had many successes, and he almost supplanted Dumas the Younger for the fashionable and upper-

middle-class public of 1895 to 1910. He brought to the stage very skillfully all the problems that had to do with the kind of marital and family
life characteristic of the comfortable middle class: marriage (*Les Ten-
ailles*), the family (*Le Dédale*), fathers and children (*La Course du flam-
beau*), adultery (*L'Enigme*). This was therefore a class literature, in the
social sense. What is more, Hervieu wanted to give class to this class theater. He demanded that class first of all from rhetoric—that is, a literary
style whose laborious fabrication made one wish for Scribe—and then
from the higher rhetoric, which was a conception that had been suggested
to him by Brunetière. The celebrated critic had told Hervieu that the
laws of the evolution of art forms should rank prose tragedy first. In
1843 it was verse tragedy. Hervieu wrote prose tragedy with less success
than Ponsard, but it was enough, and it was to have the same future.

BRIEUX

The expert for whom Hervieu's characters would have underlined the
loss of Scribe found satisfaction in Eugène Brieux, whose style was barren
of any pretentions. Brieux had a career as a thoroughly respectable dramatic author, preaching (as Diderot said) to the people, and all classes of
the people, on the problems of the day and occasionally of always: com-
pulsory secular education (*Blanchette*), venereal disease (*Les Avariés*),
motherhood (*Les Remplaçantes*), public charity (*Les Bienfaiteurs*), the
judiciary (*La Robe rouge*), education for girls (*Les Trois Filles de M.
Dupont*), what the woman of France should be (*La Française*)—a theater
that did too much good to be thought ill of and of which nothing remains
that can be thought anything of.

THE THEATER OF AGITATION AND MIRBEAU

It may be useful to single out the theater of agitation within the theater
of ideas. The theater of Curel and Hervieu, which laid questions on the
table of the stage without seeking to resolve them any more than life itself does, leaned toward dialogue, whence perhaps a certain coldness. The
play with a thesis belongs to the theater of agitation, and the "Kill her!"
that is the beginning of *La Femme de Claude* conspicuously underlines a
rather sharp aspect of the spirit of agitation. Most of Brieux's plays become plays of agitation.

The dramaturgy of dialogue and the dramaturgy of agitation could
be compared when the same season of 1887–1888 brought to two theaters
Curel's *Le Repas du lion* and Octave Mirbeau's *Mauvais Bergers*, in other
respects an extraordinarily bungled play. Both dealt with the same subject: a strike. But it was above all in *Les Affaires sont les affaires* (1903)
and *Le Foyer* (1908) that Mirbeau let loose on the stage his belligerence

of an anarchic journalist, incoherent and violent. *Les Affaires sont les affaires,* where, in Isidore Lechat, Mirbeau created a vivid and violent character of a money man set loose on the stage exactly as he is set loose on society, deserved its lasting place as one of the great plays in the repertory of the Comédie-Française, one of the rare plays that was still good thirty years later.

Théâtre d'Amour

This is the title under which Porto-Riche collected his plays into a book, and the title was obviously inspired by their subject. Porto-Riche did not belong to this generation any more exactly than Becque, having been born in 1849; at first he worked in the romantic style with bad verse plays, gained attention with an excellent one-act prose play, *La Chance de Françoise,* and in 1891 had a triumph—shared with the actress, Réjane —with *Amoureuse* at the Odéon. *Amoureuse* of 1891 has the same importance in the history of the theater as *Les Corbeaux* of 1882: It created a comedy—the comedy of the couple. In strict truth, here again Becque had preceded Porto-Riche, and *La Parisienne* had opened the way for *Amoureuse.* But in *La Parisienne* Becque wrote the comedy of a household, which is not at all the same thing—and a three-cornered household to boot. The inevitable lover appears also in *Amoureuse,* but in short Porto-Riche was the first to suppose that the life of a married couple, particularly its bedroom life, could furnish the whole matter of a play. The public accepted it, according him a triumph that was shared by the magnificent actress, and the play of the couple was founded.

Le Passé in 1897 and *Le Vieil Homme* in 1911 form a trilogy with *Amoureuse* only if one assumes the transmission line of a certain disguised autobiography of the author (*Un Homme léger* was the original title of *Le Vieil Homme*), the memories of a heart and a journey among women. Dominique in *Le Passé* is probably the masterpiece of what might be called the dramatic portrait—that is, of a complex character presented with all the psychological shadings of the novel of analysis and given life with all the best dramatic means: significant situations, real action, fitting or profound words, literary style, occasionally, however, more literary than natural. The two elders of this dramatic generation, Becque and Porto-Riche, were not only its masters but the masters.

A book attacking Porto-Riche was called *Le Racine juif.* This title is not inaccurate. Like Mendès, Porto-Riche was one of those Portuguese Jews of Bordeaux willingly delegated to a feverish sensuality. And it might be said that *Amoureuse* created a certain Jewish theater that soon found its affinities and its own soil in the group of Jews of the Lycée Condorcet who founded *La Revue blanche.* This theater favored a theory of vagrant love, polygamous and polyandrous, which Léon Blum, the group's dramatic critic, expressed in his book, *Du Mariage*, and which Tristan Bernard, the same group's humorist, illustrated in his novel, *Un Mari pacifique*. For some ten years Romain Coolus was its playwright, from *L'Enfant malade* to *l'Enfant chérie*. Among those who were twenty years old in these very last years of the nineteenth century, this theater, at once very Parisian and very Jewish, born quite naturally on the superficial dissection of a great capital, increased its forces with Francis de Croisset, author of the pleasant *Le Bonheur, Mesdames* (1905); Nozaire, more juvenile, who specialized in libertinage of the eighteenth-century model; André Picard, whose *Jeunesse* (1905) attracted notice, and Edmond Sée, whose *La Brebis* (1896) is one of the good plays of that close of a century.

Bataille; Bernstein

Since France is a country where the whole theater is Parisian, where, consequently, the dramatic seismograph can record none of those important interactions and conflicts that so visibly bind novelists to the various provincial inspirations, it becomes incumbent on us to try to differentiate among dramatic essences, when we can, on the basis of purely Parisian distinctions. Now the difference between Jewish and Christian authors is one of those that, beginning in 1890, criticism could employ in order to set up its categories. One is well advised, however, to employ as well a certain discretion, a certain subtlety. So it was that, beginning in 1900, two exactly contemporaneous authors held the first rank in the younger theater: Henri Bataille and Henry Bernstein. Now Bataille, originally a symbolist, the sophisticated poet of *La Chambre blanche*, would seem to repesent very well the tradition of the *Revue* of the same color, the tradition of the Jewish theater and of pungent sensuality. But of the two the Jew was Bernstein, who was a perfectly healthy stage author, even if his characters were not healthy, and whose theater could be called a theater of action more than a theater of passion.

Bataille made his start in the theater with the worst symbolist nonsense, with *La Belle au bois dormant*, and such final pre-war plays as *Le Phalène* inspired the critics to affix the label of "gamy plays." Between these two he wrote three original plays, of which at least the second deserves to endure: *Maman Colibri*, *La Marche nuptiale* and *La Vierge folle*. Like Porto-Riche, he created characters of women who have not been forgotten, and his Grâce de Plessans is all the more true because she is made up of contradictions that logic does not tolerate but that life admirably bears out. To be honest, he was lacking in major theatrical talents: that of dialogue and that of balance in the progression of his scenes. No one is a better illustration than he of the risks that were run by a generation that did not set off for the theater until it had given a kick or two to the old technique, and unsettled four S's of whom there was no assurance that they contained nothing good: Scribe, Sardou, Sarcey, and the stage. Bataille's artificial poetry did not afford sufficient compensation for this technical deficiency, and the plays in which he aimed the highest, like *Les Flambeaux*, a comedy of the man of genius, are naturally the worst failures. His pre-war social plays are artificial and of little account.

Bernstein, on the contrary, may be considered a master in the art of the "play," extremely skillful in spotting each season's subject to be made into a play, a very sure technician of the theater, well placed to maintain contact with the stage and with life. His main characters for a long time were corrupt people, violent and unrestrained. The platitude that made Bataille's the gamy theater was balanced by the platitude that made Bernstein's the brutal theater. The position of typical work and masterpiece held in Bataille's theater by *La Marche nuptiale* would be occupied in Bernstein's by *Le Secret*, in which an equally individual portrait of a woman is rendered not at all by literary means but by means of pure dramatic technique. In *Samson*, a play about the stock exchange; in *Israël*, a play about Jewish blood and the problem of race in Parisian society; in *Judith*, a Biblical play the first half of which rises as high as *Le Secret*, if not higher, Bernstein, perhaps alone among his many coreligionists in the theater, put on the stage the memories and the problems of the children of Abraham. And these subjects gave him extraordinary inspiration. In the first thirty years of this century his annual plays had few failures, and he took great pains to keep himself in the tide and the conditions of success. After the Great War he had no real self-renewal except with *Judith*. But he attempted it with skill and success in a series of subsequent plays, none of which was like the others or, even more, like the legendary brutal theater of Bernstein before the war: *La Galerie des glaces*, *Mélo*, *Félix*, *Espoir*. The public received them extremely well, even and especially the last, which is superior Brieux; they hold an honorable place; if they were welcome in a time of poor theater, they did not assert themselves with the same new vigor as *Le Secret*, *La Rafale*, or *Samson*.

The Life of Paris

The tradition of the French theater demands a constant recording of the life of Paris. In part the Parisian audience goes to the theater in order to recognize itself on the stage. Since the Second Empire, the title of *La Vie parisienne* officially belonged to a play written by Meilhac and Halévy for the Exposition of 1867 and to the magazine founded by

Planat, which had a literary existence until 1914. (Let us not forget that it was inaugurated with Taine's *Graindorge*). In the final fifteen years of the nineteenth century the magazine became quite brilliant, especially in a kind of fashionable dialogue, observant and ironic, of which Gyp was the initiator and which soon brought together, under pseudonyms, Lavedan, Maurice Donnay, Hermant, and Pierre Veber. Such dialogues, which ran successively through a dozen issues on the thread of a very loose association and episodic themes, were later commissioned from the same authors for large-circulation daily papers like *Le Journal*. It was a kind of written theater like that of 1820. This written theater flowed toward the stage in a natural movement. In no time *Les Transatlantiques* or *Le Nouveau Jeu* could be turned into a play and earn from the spectators all the success that it had had among readers. Hence arose what might be called a school of *La Vie parisienne*, a theater in which there were more dialogues than action, more caricature than observation, and from which the author, when he had talent, escaped at a certain moment into the comedy of manners.

Meilhac's and Halévy's comedy and Marcelin's magazine marked out the world of pleasure as their principal field of observation: if not to "get into it up to here," like Baron de Gondremark, at least to get into it, to move about in it, to inform the spectator; even, in order to let him see it all, to moralize on it.

Lavedan's theater was a kind of elder in this dramatic family. No one was in higher favor with the Parisian public of his time for dialogue, witticisms, feeling for the average spectator, and also and especially for a specious bilateralism. Lavedan gave the repertory of the Variétés some of its greatest successes—his dialogues, transformed into comedies, of *Le Nouveau Jeu* (1898) and *Le Vieux Marcheur* (1899), brilliant and crackling portraits, one of the rich young playboy, the other of the even richer old libertine senator. But he gave the Théâtre-Français plays for its members, in which morality was handed down from on high: *Le Prince d'Aurec*, *Le Marquis de Priola*, *Le Duel*, *Servir*, *Catherine*, well made, furthermore, and solidly established in the repertory of the house. This partly double theater, conformist at one end of the rue de Richelieu and libertine at the other, between the podium of Dumas the Younger and the "madness" of Regnard, will seem to the historian just as republican-middle-class-of-1900 as that of Meilhac and Halévy was imperial-middle-class-of-1867. The world is small.

There was the same turn, on the whole, in the theater of Donnay, who wrote *Lysistrata* (1892) and *Education de Prince* (1900), but whose effort toward an elevated theater branched off in the direction of the theater of love rather than that of the moral theater. In spite of a huge and brilliant output, Donnay remains the author of *Amants* (1896) as Porto-Riche remains the author of *Amoureuse*. Like Hervieu, Donnay took the side of the woman, passion, and the heart. Like Hervieu and Bataille, he tried, if not the theater of ideas, at least the difficult "intellectual play," in *Le Torrent*. His association with Descaves was in this respect quite fortunate in the social play, *La Clairière*, and in the best French-Russian play ever written, *Oiseaux de passage*.

Lavedan and Donnay alone gave *La Vie parisienne* an independent position in drama that is important in the history, the technique, and the normal function of the theater. Abel Hermant found great success in the theater with *Les Transatlantiques*. At first the subject of dialogues in *La Vie parisienne*, *Les Transatlantiques* marked a date in the Cosmopolis of Paris, for the same reason as that other *Vie parisienne*, the work of Meilhac, Halévy, and Offenbach, and the best of the dialogue reappeared and even improved in the play. But however fine this entrance of Hermant's critical and caricatural observation into the theater, it was only a visit. He could never make himself at home on the stage. The same is not to be said of another writer for *La Vie parisienne*, Pierre Veber, a very subtle and even creative humorist, who preferred, however, to use the theater for the easy successes of the old light comedy, and got them.

Alfred Capus, journalist, humorist, and dialogue writer, was not, strictly speaking, a writer for *La Vie parisienne*. Partly because he went beyond it, but not, unfortunately, as a man of the theater. He was wittier than anyone of his day, and in no way, like Aurélian Scholl, witty because he lacked intelligence, but witty because he had intelligence and because his Parisianism was grafted onto provincial stock: the real Capus was first of all the man of wit. Secondarily he was the original novelist of *Années d'aventures* and *Scènes de la vie difficile*. He had not so much the taste and the sense as the intelligence of the theater, and half the time he did brilliantly in it. Like Sacha Guitry, he won personal sympathies. He owed this to an original, spontaneous philosophy, impressed on him quite naturally by his life and his family's, a remarkable life that would be more worthy of recording than any of the Parisian literary lives of his day. Whence enough electricity to animate his plays for a season, to win them reasonable success and, in sum, the good luck of his first dramatic success, *La Veine* (1901), but not enough to keep them alive longer for anyone except those who reread them because they liked Capus.

The school of *La Vie parisienne* and Capus has shown a closer bond between books and the theater than in the earlier periods, unless perhaps at the time of the written theater of 1820. This observation is even more applicable to the careers of three authors who wrote well-known plays though they had no exclusive vocation for the theater: Georges Courteline, Jules Renard, and Tristan Bernard.

Courteline; Renard; Bernard

Courteline never wrote a comedy, any more than he wrote a novel, even in *Le Train de 8 h. 47*. Only one of his plays has more than one act: *Boubouroche*, which has two. *Boubouroche* and a few one-act plays were enough to entitle him to occupy the theater as a master, a master of laughter greater than Labiche, by reason of his dialogue, his style, and his movement. Like Labiche's, his comedy is bound to existence, to the way of life of the middle class, of its average member, but not, as in Labiche, the average citizen as seen from his own home. Courteline saw him, observed him, expressed him from the point of view of the place where he met him, which was the café. Like Rabelais, Courteline is a great French writer without women. There is only one in his theater: Adèle in *Boubouroche*, just as the cashier in the neighborhood café where Courteline and his court elected to domicile their evenings was sufficient to represent her sex. To *L'Ami des femmes* Courteline opposed *L'Ami des lois*, La Brige, the anti-clerical bachelor, as big as life. The two other best-known preferred arenas of Courteline's comedy were again settings without women: the barracks and the office—the barracks before the war and the office before the advent of the stenographer. If the war, the stenographer, and the decline of the neighborhood café did not unseat Courteline's comedy, it was because Courteline, like Rabelais and Molière, had built it on the rock. He has enemies, but they are enemies of laughter, young men who, like the old Fontenelle, have never admitted that it is possible to utter *ha ha!*

Jules Renard was one of the greatest writers of his time and, like Courteline, one of the rare writers whose complete works will perhaps hold up as an entity. In his *Journal* he wrote the most amazing and the most exciting transcript of the life of a man of letters in existence; it stands beside the Goncourts' *Journal*. His works of apparent fiction were more or less drawn from his *Journal*, or at the very least from his own history. And on these fictions he drew again, without diminishing them but adding the dimension of the theater, for dramatic works that have not lost an inch: *Monsieur Vernet* (1903), from *L'Ecornifleur*, and *Poil de Carotte* (1900). But in 1897 he wrote *Le Plaisir de rompre* for the theater—a masterpiece of cold, dry, disillusioned wit.

Tristan Bernard, in contrast to his contemporaries, kept a watertight bulkhead between his famous novels and a theater that was rich in quantity, in success, and also in collaborators; there is no equal of *Triplepatte*, a comedy of vacillation, and *Le Petit Café*, a play for the Palais-Royal that virtually revived the situation comedy.

PART FIVE

The Generation
of 1914

THE GENERATION OF 1914

The Mutilated Generation

Even if the war of 1914 had not taken place, that year would have marked the date of a new generation, and "twenty years old in 1914" would have a meaning in literary history, like "twenty years old in 1820." Furthermore, rather than "even if," one must say, "especially if." The war was able to give the twenty-year-olds of 1914 important positive characteristics. But above all, tragically, it robbed them of being and gave them instead a vacant place. In large measure the generation of 1914 is the absent generation, mutilated, much more even than that of the twenty-year-olds of 1870. Its great man, in his tomb beneath the Arc de Triomphe, is the great unknown writer.

If it had been able to play its normal part at its full strength, there are grounds for believing that this generation would have made a splendid troop comparable to that of 1820. "Twenty years old in 1914" was like a crossroads.

Historical Synchronisms

It will be observed first of all that the very first years of the twentieth century corresponded to a triple political revolution: the Dreyfus case, which did not leave France as it had found her; the consolidation of the Republic, after a third assault, which failed; the definitive creation, after 1904, of groups of alliances from which the Great War came. Between 1898 and 1905 the cape of a new political world was rounded.

But we will make the observation only to remember it and on the ground of temporal coincidences. In the matter of literature, these facts of the political sphere worked and exerted their influences mysteriously. Other events are of more direct interest to our readers.

The New School System

First of all, the educational revolution of 1902. To be twenty years old in 1914 meant that one had gone to school, spent one's formative years, in the first years of the twentieth century. Nine-tenths of the writers came from the middle class and, with or without scholarships, attended the secondary schools. Now in 1902 secondary education as it had been handed down from the Jesuits to the university of the eighteenth century and from there to the university of the nineteenth century changed its character. Latin, and especially Greek, were more or less dethroned, and ancient languages and the humanist schooling no longer constituted the necessary and outstanding mark of culture. Democracy ran at full crest through the teaching staffs. The term, "the modern humanities," came into favor. The word modernism, introduced by the Goncourts to indicate a form of literary art and employed by the theologians to designate a more flexible method of understanding the evolution of dogmas, would serve here to describe that element of the anti-ancient, the anti-classic, the anti-traditional that was insinuated into the education of the new generations. Modern languages took over part of the place hitherto occupied by the ancient languages. The young traveled, the typical *normalien* went off to see the world, children exchanged countries and languages. Outside influences of all kinds found easier access, more fertile soils.

This venturesome young generation that spoke languages, that had turned to sports, that had left home for pleasure and for the conquest of the planet abruptly found itself blockaded by the war. When fish are taken from great depths, they come to the surface with organs that have burst because of decompression. It was in this state of inner revolution that this generation entered on its third decade. The first generation whose adolescence had been deprived of traditional humanism was further deprived, by its youth, of traditional humanity.

Decompression

It carried and would carry to the end the marks of that decompression. Those revolutions of the self that appeared about 1920 were the condition of a self that had burst like the bladder of a fish. Gide, or the delicate self in opposition to the armored self, with that Lafcadio who from 1914 on was ready for the young of 1921 to recognize themselves in him, was still a semi-humanist compromise. But then came Proust, and the changing, fluid self; and then above all the torrential entrance of Freud, until that time completely unknown to the French public, with the unconscious self; and even Luigi Pirandello, with the acrobatic self. Here above all is what this generation drew from itself: a disquiet that was fitting to it, a search, a mobility that was looked to for everything, and that led nowhere. The novel of the punctured life belt, the useless organ of equilibrium, was Drieu La Rochelle's *La Valise vide*.

The awareness of the explosion naturally expressed itself in literature with words ending in "-ism." There was dadaism, there was surrealism—that is, an awareness of absolute ending, of absolute beginning, of absolute disorder, and of absolute liberation. What is important here is that, especially for surrealism, it was a matter of literary movements, which expressed themselves in a literature in which, as in every literature, there was the good and there was the execrable, invention and pose, in which there were neither more nor less miscarriage and almost-success than there were for the average Frenchman in academicism or in literature; this is important because, in this order (or this disorder) of absolute collapses and beginnings that followed the Great War, the totalitarian experiment that in other countries found its road in political revolutions was expressed in France in literary forms. France is the country in which not only a literary condition but the literary state, the republic of letters, exists, in which, in matters of revolution (this was the case under Louis-Philippe), literature readily assumes the function of an abscess of fixation.

This French generation did not have the great literary and intellectual influence in Europe that was exercised by its two predecessors, the generations of 1850 and 1885. Without any adequate French counterbalance, it was subjected to the action of the new *mystiques* created by its contemporary generations in Italy and Russia.

The Reserves to the Front

Happily, in literature as in agriculture, France can live in the condition of an almost closed economy, can partly compensate with her reserves for the failure of a harvest. Since the war years, it seems that nature (to the degree to which a literature is a nature) has oriented her toward a compensation of this kind. One of the most remarkable literary phenomena of the war was in fact the sudden emergence of an army of forty-year-olds into the light and into action; long stocked, as it were, in what were then called chapels, they moved into the front lines to share the moment and the destiny of the regular army of literature. Gide, Proust, Claudel, and Valéry were suddenly masters, and their influence was to continue for fifteen years. With them let us include Péguy, so much more influential after his death than in his lifetime, and still so modern today; Barrès, who is at the source of the new nationalisms; Maurras and Georges Sorel, so to speak the spiritual fathers of the totalitarian movements; Benda, who was over fifty when his new stand on the problem of the intellectuals brought him out of obscurity. This on a grand, a very grand scale, is what happened on a much more infinitesimal level when, thirty years after its publication, *Obermann* found a public and out of this there came *Volupté*.

Techniques

The revelation and the revolution proper to this generation were above all of a technical order: twenty years later, when these pages were written, they had not yet manifested all the literary consequences that they bore within them, and this, indeed, is in consonance with precedent.

When we think of the great inventions that marked the nineteenth century, created the mode of living of capitalism and big industry, we observe that, however broadly they extended man's domain, they did not add perceptibly to the common scope and exercise of his senses. We say "common," for the use of laboratory and observatory instruments that alter and infinitely extend the range of the senses is specialized in certain professions. In the midst of the flood of inventions that transformed mankind, the writers continued to study and to explain man, traditionally. It is remarkable that none of the great inventions of the nineteenth century left its mark on a literary work in the way in which, for example, *La Comédie humaine* was marked by the economic revolution of the sale of the national lands, George Sand by Socialist theories, Lamartine and Hugo by the street revolutions, Flaubert by the evolution of the middle class, Zola by textbook physiology, the Parnassians and Anatole France by libraries, symbolism by music. But when Balzac absorbed himself in railroads, he did so in order to write the novel of the stage coaches before it was too late (see the beginning of *Un Début dans la vie*). Flaubert was twenty-five years old when the rail line from Paris to Rouen changed the lives of the people of Rouen, beginning with his own, but the railroad does not appear in his novels, in which all traveling is done by coach or by ship. And, after all, for its user the railway is only a string of huge and swift stage coaches. Be that as it may, literature went through technical revolutions with hardly any attention to any techniques but its own.

The inventions of the twentieth century are different from those of the nineteenth. Those of the nineteenth century gave man new mechanical means; those of the twentieth give him new sensory means. The first transformed the planet, society, production, consumption. The second transformed the powers of the human body.

Between the techniques of the nineteenth century and those of the twentieth there are the same differences as those between the railway and the automobile, or, rather, between the two systems of motive power that are at the sources of the one and the other: the steam engine and the internal-combustion engine. If the railroad gave men's minds new habits, the automobile, which became part of the most general customs with the generation of 1914, gave the human body new reflexes. The railroad belongs to the world of the machine, but the automobile succeeded the bicycle in the world of tools. The railroad is a means of transport; the automobile is or has become an instrument of sport. And the automobile serves here only as a point of departure and an elementary symbol already surpassed. Aviation, even more, gives the human body a new power, as the cinema enhances the eye and the radio the ear.

And it follows logically that these changes concern above all the young; that is, those who have nothing to unlearn, who are on an equal footing with the new instruments, who were born with the new tools that their fathers had to invent.

This revolution in equipment, implying a modification and an extension of the body's powers, has posed two questions: that of the literature of sport and that of the relations between literature and cinema.

LITERATURE AND SPORT

As the generation of 1850 was the generation of the call to science, that of 1914 was in certain aspects that of the call to the body. About 1924 there was a whole group of young men (Henry de Montherlant, Prévost, Braga) who tried to integrate sport into literature and to create a species of lyricism of games and of the movements of the body. This came to a rather quick end. But one must look further, consider the literary atmosphere rather than the literary achievement. Now it is a fact that the body has occupied a greater place in the literature of the generation of 1914 than in the literature of the generations of the nineteenth century and that to a certain extent it has evicted emotional complications. If the height of art consists, as Benvenuto Cellini said, in creating a naked man and a naked woman, this generation has nimbly scaled that height. In addition, the intimacy between man and mechanisms, the rapidity of modern life, or, rather, its rapidities of every kind, have been introduced into style. This is not to say that they have unseated their opposites, since the minute introspections of Proust found the public of 1924 as attentive as did the elliptical mechanisms manufactured by Paul Morand, and since the progress of the saga novel is much more like that of the canal boat than that of the airliner. Literature is composed of these simultaneous existences of a yesterday, a today, and a tomorrow: let us not forget, moreover, that Proust's novel is part of the reserves of the preceding generation, that its good fortune is that it was written by a

man confined to a bedroom, and that there are disappointments in the
history of the saga novel.

As for the question of the relations between literature and cinema, it
is obvious that this generation was the first for whom the question was
raised, but it has not resolved it. The influence of the cinema, of its movement of images, on novelists and journalists is obvious. So is its influence
on the theater. When Mallarmé went to the concert, he wanted to find
a poet's profit in the music. In the same way the theater too seeks to find
its own profit out of its dangerous, powerful rival, to incorporate its
rhythms, to reckon with the reaction speed that its public has learned from
the cinema. But this indirect utilization has no resemblance to a direct use,
which would be an incorporation of cinema into literature. The sound
film is equally foreign to it, even more foreign than the silent film. And
so is broadcasting.

The Crisis of Continuity

Unequal in their importance, the decline of humanism, the massacre of
the young elite, the necessity of living on reserves, the revolutions in
equipment and in the human senses combined with a general and profound feeling of instability to divest this generation of the normal means
of enduring. They threw time off balance for it. As the Treaty of Versailles posed the problem of peoples without space, here was the problem
of generations without continuity, or, less brutally, of generations that
faced a crisis of continuity.

Social continuity is a memory and a habit. All memories and all habits
had been overturned. On the one side the rupture with the time before the
war, on the other the absolute uncertainty of the tomorrows, seemed to
put life, as the old language of the law had it, in jeopardy—and literary
life especially.

The Three Climaxes After 1914

We have observed that after fifteen years, on the average, each of the
literary generations since 1789 came to a turning point, a crisis, that divided it more or less into two generations. But these breaks were never
so deep as they have been since 1914; the median date of 1930 indeed has

a tremendous importance, like 1902, 1870, 1843, and 1802 for the preceding generations. For the moment, with due consideration for the time that still remains for the twenty-year-olds of 1914 and for the fact that we are compelled to close their ledger in 1935, we can say that these first twenty years are divided into three parts: the war and the years immediately after it, until about 1923; the literary inflation that lasted until 1930; and the literary deflation since 1930—in other words, the defense, the expansion, and the depression of the republic of letters.

In the first period, the republic of letters, like the other republic and in every sense of the word, was defending itself. It defended itself in this sense, that it overcame the crisis and even that it prospered, but, as we have said, by living on its reserves. What had already been written was read much more than what was being written. Writers of the preceding generation benefited by this change in perspective. The war literature, produced by the combatants and principally by others, gave rise to disappointments. Soon writers tried to escape from the war and, as the philosophers say, to transcend it. But a fierce travail was at work in men's minds; Bellona's plowshare was digging furrows like chasms for the seeds from which so much was hoped for. Wrongly, perhaps: indeed, the literary selection was not to be a selection based on quality, a selection among minds, based on the fact that the best writers would overshadow the mediocre writers, but a mechanical selection of quantity, a selection of bodies, based on the hazards of combat, of discharges, of ambushes.

Very soon the period of inflation began. Like the rest of the world, like the other republics, the republic of letters lived on the reserves of earlier generations, paper profits, publicity, custom, facility, and the belief that the facility would go on. When the time comes to write them, the memoirs of this period can be called "Scènes de la vie facile." The third decade of the twentieth century will prove to have been a Saint Martin's summer for Western capitalist society. Like the crisis of the franc, resolved by Premier Raymond Poincaré, the other crises to which attention was called here and there erupted only to be overcome. In that whole fragile literature, which multiplied in a swarm and was then swallowed up and forgotten in so short a time, profitable searches may one day be made. The 1920s may have their lovers, and not only among those who will be thinking of the time when they themselves were thirty. They have been compared with the Directory. But the Directory with a literature.

Their fate in literary history will depend on what follows them. Now this Directory, unfortunately, was not followed by a Consulate. From 1930 on, the literary deflation followed the other deflations and, like the others, it meant restriction. The pessimists speak of a great literary penitence. Will it continue?

Literature may very well be caught in the cycle of barren years on which we have entered, or, rather, re-entered. The call to the reserves, so rewarding yesterday, will arouse less and less echo. Here again a demographic necessity intervenes. The generation that will replace this one is that of the adolescents whom their fathers, the twenty-year-olds of 1914, are sending to school and college today, the generation of which a part was killed twenty years ago, before its birth, with its potential fathers. The literary recruiting officers have as much reason as those of the military to be concerned about this situation.

No matter from what direction we approach the literary situation of the generation that has not lived out its term, we find the crisis of continuity before us in one form or another: of a continuity that was linked to a minimum of humanism—that is, of common language and traditional body; of a continuity that preserves in the manner of a consciousness and that serves as a buffer to absolute beginnings; of a living continuity that is solidarity with the past and confidence in the future; of a continuity with which, even more radically than we, the youth of other great nations have broken the treaty. The newspaper and the film, which tend to oust literature properly so called—that is, books—imply powers of forgetting just as much as classic literature implied powers of remembering. But on one point at least, always on one point, a point that respects hope and the future, literature preserves a bond with living, ordinary, conscious, human, eternal continuity: that is the fact that literature is unpredictable.

IDEAS

In Quest of Root Ideas

The production of root ideas in eloquent literary form has been the central function of French literature since Descartes and Port-Royal. It gives them their forms, outlines their profiles, is first to testify for them. It is chiefly in this production of root ideas that the generation born between 1885 and 1905 has been more or less deficient.

In Bergson the previous generation had given France and Europe the root idea of a dynamic philosophy, in Barrès and Maurras the root idea of nationalism. These ideas had less literary brilliance but more external influence than those that in the generation before them had been embodied in the names of Taine and Renan. After the war there was a reaction against them, the inevitable reaction of all these turning-point periods. Thus people affected to see in Bergson the philosopher of pure intuition, in part in order to render easier and more necessary the definition that would arouse the opposing view: an intellectualist reaction. What better cause could one adopt than that of the intelligence! With strong support from laymen, the Church was then favoring a revival of Thomism. There was an inheritance to be claimed, like that of scientism after Taine and Berthelot. The new scientific discoveries and hypotheses came just in time to evoke the appearance of that equally new philosophy that, since the time of Descartes, had never been lacking in such case. And, finally, there had never been such a turning to the intellectuals, the great professors, with deference and hope, in the search for direction and light. But the hoped-for basic ideas did not come.

In the world of the intelligence, as was natural, the post-war period was a growth of reaction against nationalisms. Negative: nationalisms, it was thought, which had produced the war, should be destroyed for the sake of peace. Positive: there was a Europe to be built, an international culture to be established, a stalled bus that had no lack of passengers, but

none that could drive, and so it stayed beside the road; until 1936 root
ideas in Europe were all either nationalist ideas or class ideas. They found
their political expression in Italy, in Germany, in Russia. They found no
philosophical and literary expression in those countries. Today the insolvency of the great literature of ideas is a fact of Europe.

Insolvencies

During any given generation the literature of ideas admits of a lag behind the literature of poetry and imagination. The thinker embarks on
action and influence at a later age than the poet and the novelist: we can
speak, roughly, of a gap of some ten years. But this normal lag cannot be
compared here to the substantial overlap between one generation and
another as a result of which the generation of 1914 did not draw its great
makers of ideas from its own ranks but lived almost altogether on reserves from the previous generation. The authority of Barrès, of Bergson,
of Péguy, even of Georges Sorel remained a currency. The sole book of
ideas that was both a literary vehicle and an influence after the war was
La Trahison des clercs, by Benda, who was a contemporary of Barrès
and Maurras and who in 1925 re-created the identical positions of the time
of the Dreyfus case. It is true that the problem that is treated here, that
of the power of the intellect, has been for more than a hundred years the
central problem of the literature of ideas in France.

It was not, however, that public opinion or especially the generation
of 1914 and the anguished post-war young had abandoned interest in
ideas. Far from it! But it must always be remembered, first, that their
elite, their natural leaders, had been left on the battlefields, that Charleroi
had to be paid for with its Bergson and Verdun with its Barrès. Later the
new generation in France was faced with a choice of facts, of ideas, of
problems, that seemed to confront the intelligence with a reality that
could not be thought, the reality of the unthinkable. The method by
which the totalitarians, our neighbors, cut these Gordian knots was an
act of desperation, before which the republic of letters felt the same re-
vulsion as the Republic. In short, since the war the problem of the writer's
independence has become especially delicate.

The literature of root ideas is the summit of a mountain range on whose
slopes, at varying levels, there are history, the essay, criticism, and journalism.

History

In history there were two *lacunae*, which here again concern the vanguard.

First of all, there has been no reappearance of the great history of synthesis and reflections that was the work of a life and that represented a literary and academic career, the history of a Georges Sorel, of a La Gorce, of a Jullian. In the second place, history in the universities found it less easy to recruit the battalions of workers and great engineers who can assure the fruitfulness of its normal labors. The best of its effort went into collective works, the great textbooks, rather than into individual works, and the production of compendiums after the war enjoyed a great prosperity. Work done by a team, sometimes with propaganda guidelines, is not always favorable to originality and independence.

The revolution that took place in literary usages, the favor that the public showed to historical narratives, stimulated a tremendous demand from the booksellers, to which the best-known novelists, and above all the rest of them, responded with valor. This flood ebbed only slowly. It was, furthermore, the exaggeration and the unbalance of a movement that was interesting and reasonable in itself—the taste for biography, which emphasized especially the politicians and writers of the nineteenth century. Chateaubrianders, Lamartineans, Hugolians, Balzacians, Beylists, Nervalesques, Flaubertists, Gautierians, Huysmansards, Verlaineans (later, undoubtedly, turned Barrèsians), Proustians, Gideans, Valéryans formed congenial groups that produced a whole delicate literature suggestive of new illumination and elegant erudition.

This preference did not extend to more or less fictionalized popular biographies, which tumbled one over another by the hundred and made possible two or three original works behind which the others slipped by; this flood raged principally between 1924 and 1930.

It will be remarked that this movement of history, which in spite of everything remained superficial, was inspired by the political conflicts of the world of letters. The division between the historians—or, rather, the men who wrote history books—into historians of the left and historians of the right created one of the prominent features of the literary map. The success of the authors of the right—Bainville, Pierre Gaxotte—was much greater than that of those of the left. Perhaps chance willed it that in fact there was more talent on the right than on the left. But not in sufficient proportion to explain everything. First of all one would be much more inclined to observe that, in contrast to the Republic, the republic of letters was oriented toward the right; second, part of the public regarded books of popularized history from the right as a reaction against the university turn of mind. The conformism of the republican educational system provoked an obscure feeling of a need to counter it with an opposing conformism, which the republic of letters grew in its own soil.

Criticism: Essays and Observations

The essay has made a solid fortune since the 1914 war. It was abetted by the strange fashion (among editors more than among the public) of collections in which authors were asked, like students, to write on esoteric subjects, which they often managed to handle, delivering their messages, as the saying is, as well as they could.

Separate consideration must be given to that curious man, Charles Du Bos, who gave his essays the extremely apt title of *Approximations* and who indeed seemed in a state of perpetual approach to the authors whom he liked and the pursuit of whom he never completed. The chief of these portraits in progress was of course his own, and Du Bos' criticisms orbit around a vast intimate journal like planets round a sun.

Henry Bidou and Edmond Jaloux present remarkable types of the criticism of curiosity. Bidou's curiosity was universal, and literary criticism was only one of its provinces. Not, however, the favorite. This was a man who had read all the books and seen all the plays, and he admitted that he did not discover them with the freshness and the enthusiasm of the neophyte. No one knew better than he how to present a book, give a clear idea of it without passion, and, especially when he was dealing with a novel, analyze it accurately and completely.

In the usual meaning of the word, the curious man, with a nose for new books, would be Edmond Jaloux. The book that he called *Au Pays du roman* dealt with the English novel. But it might also stand as the emblem of his criticism. As he once wrote *L'Ami des jeunes filles*, undoubtedly he would one day write *L'Ami des romans*. He loved novels with a witty and unwearying curiosity and through them he discovered spirits and countries.

The author of these pages, writing in *La Nouvelle revue française*, represented a form of criticism that obviously has neither the virtues nor the defects of impersonality, but that seems concerned more with works than with persons and that perhaps would fall within that remark made by Gide, undoubtedly of someone else: "X is intelligent, but he seems to have met his ideas rather than drawn them out of himself." Let us say that he followed those lovely persons in the street, as Diderot more or less put it. Benda, the logician, condemned him as an intellectual Debussyan. But let us throw no further stones into his garden lest we frighten off the reader who is strolling in it and who, one hopes, will stay on.

The criticism of observation would form a subspecies of essay criticism. Let us call "observation" the brief summary essay, and the term is applicable to two critics of ideas and manners rather than of letters: André Suarès and Alain. Suarès, by calling his periodical notebooks *Remarques*, and the Norman observer Alain, by bearing observations as his trees bore apples, found words that suited their form. Suarès was an original master of the literary portrait, which he achieved through colorful strokes and observations. Alain deals only incidentally, but forcefully, with literary criticism in his observations. And his "I observe that . . ." can be considered a writer's revealing twitch. The criticism of Pierre Lièvre, composed of apt and subtle rare peaks, and very self-assured, comes within this category. And so does that of Denis Saurat in *Marsyas*.

The Magazines

The independent little magazines, in addition, are the privileged circle of a very independent criticism, all in observations, in remarks, in sharp jabs with a stick that is sometimes a pointer, sometimes a chastiser. It is in them, rather than in *La Revue des deux mondes*, that the lover of criticism makes his discoveries, gets on the scent, learns where the best strawberries and snails are.

Along our road we have already encountered the criticism of defense, without which there would be no schools: the criticism that naturalism vainly demanded of Taine and that its grandson, populism, found in André Thérive. Under the label of criticism of poets, Georges Duhamel supplied a criticism of defense for the unanimist poets before the war in *Le Mercure de France*. The fantasist school found its own, which was equally precious, in the charming *Divan*. The criticism of defense of the neo-classic poets, the conservative writers, and Pierre Benoit was directed with a master hand by *L'Action française* and *La Revue universelle*.

La Nouvelle revue française introduced highly diverse temperaments into criticism. Benjamin Crémieux, in his *XX*^{e} *Siècle* and his numerous articles, practiced an objective criticism that saw deeply and clearly into literature from a minimum of preconceived positions and that judiciously descried the trends of contemporary literature. But the dominating and original characteristics of this critical group, I think, would be found to be two.

The first is the unusual place held in it by philosophical critics. It seems that a philosophical education fulfilled here a part of the function that was served by a literary education in the criticism of 1900. Jacques Rivière was educated in philosophy, and the author of *Le Bergsonisme* introduced his master's points of view into criticism. In 1935, with varying temperaments, Gabriel Marcel, Ramon Fernandez, Jean Prévost, and Jean Paulhan represented varying forms of philosophical culture in the criticism of the rue de Beaune. They posed from within that conflict of reason and intuition that overflowed from philosophy into criticism after the war, as the battle of pure poetry demonstrated. In the second place, it is impressive to note to what extent the criticism of the NRF is an essayist criticism. And we know, besides, that its leader, André Gide, was of the family of Montaigne.

The critics' team of *Europe*, which, in contrast to that of the NRF, took a highly emphatic political position, was Socialist and internationalist. Jean-Richard Bloch and Jean Guéhenno were more concerned with social criticism than with literary criticism. But by that very fact the authors of *Carnaval est mort* and *Caliban parle* made an important contribution to the criticism of ideas. Then came the Marxist materialist group, composed principally of philosophers (Morhange, Politzer, Gutermann, and, more recently, Louis Nizan), who in two short-lived magazines, *Philosophies* and *L'Esprit,* began a revision of middle-class literary values in the spirit of communism with great help from historical materialism, like the help that Taine's philosophy afforded to the *Essais de psychologie contemporaine* or that Thomism provided to Maritain and Massis.

Journalism

The essay, which in sum is only a long article, was quickly led off and captured, however, by journalism.

Political journalism could be presented here only as a long string of transitory names. The criticism of manners and of life falls more within the framework of literature. The old style of the chronicle, devoured by the short account and reporting, is less than ever able, despite all efforts, to regain its former splendor. The most original product of the journalism of manners is what might be called the breakfast-roll article to which the reader is accustomed every morning: *croissants* by Clément Vautel, rolls by La Fouchardière, long rolls by Audiat.

The literary criticism in the newspapers naturally affords us a better handle. It is a necessary part of the current of literature. It is occasionally its adviser, constantly its secretary and archivist.

The *normalien* period inaugurated by the generation of 1850, which was brilliant, virtually came to an end in 1914. Not that *normaliens* and professors do not have an honorable place in journalism, but they represent in it nothing of the original tradition and importance. They are on a level with the other journalists. The profession and the necessities of journalism alone set the tone and the trend for criticism in newspapers.

In one respect, consequently, it has suffered. It has almost lost what was the flower of humanist criticism: relation to the classics, solidarity with the flow of French literature. A function and a platform like those of Sainte-Beuve, preserved by Taine, Scherer, Montégut, Brunetière, Lemaître, Faguet, have become almost impossible, and, if newspaper publishers must be believed, would no longer attract any but the most unreliable and diminishing audience. From the heritage of Taine, Scherer, Montégut, present-day criticism has much better maintained contact with foreign literatures, especially the English, which it follows with attention and discernment. Compelled to sacrifice more and more to information, to the moment, to summaries, criticism now contributes less in decisions and judgments than in qualities of the moralist and the psychologist. Its virtues and its faults are governed by this fact—that it has become a province of journalism and is no longer in any way a dependency of the school.

Dramatic criticism, in even worse straits, has taken shelter in the same inn. It can retain its dignity and be of value only in the weekly article, which allows it time to reflect and to choose. The exigencies of day-to-day reporting have reduced to three or four the number of dramatic critics who have the traditional place on the newspaper page at their disposal, and to even fewer the number of those who still have the will to defend literature in it.

THE NOVEL

The Vitality of the Novel

Almost automatically the generation of 1914 found itself, as it has more and more found itself since, persuaded to devote itself to the novel. It will be the task of its successors to determine what it has contributed that will endure. But even, in 1935, it is possible to perceive what it has contributed that is new.

Let us observe first that it was less embarrassed, less burdened, in confrontation with the novel than in confrontation with poetry. In its essentials, in its collective life, the line of the French novel dates only from the generation of 1820, whereas the line of poetry goes back to the generation of 1550. The novel is a form that is still young and that renews itself without visibly draining itself.

Let us add that, in contrast to poetry, it is in continuous and necessary relation with other countries, that there is an International of the novel, that this life in space, this presence of the English or the Russian novel have thus far been beneficial to the French novel, have given it suggestions without subjecting it to limitations, especially in this generation of 1914, which travels more and which is more concerned with foreign letters than its predecessors.

Finally, never has literature been constrained to defer so much to public demand, to submit to the conditions of success. Now, the public wants novels. It will be seen later whether the generation of 1914 is a generation to be prized, but it can be seen already that it is the generation of prizes. And important prizes are won only by writing novels. In the generation of 1914 everyone was fit to write a novel, just as everyone was fit to be a soldier.

Skeptical critics have not neglected to observe that, in the same way, everyone was fit to write a tragedy in the eighteenth century and that that was precisely what did tragedy to death. But the analogy does not hold up. Tragedy was a mold, it came after Latin verse and, in the scholastic system, represented a higher rhetoric: every rhetorician had his tragedy in his schoolbooks. It is in his very life, in contrast, that every modern man is capable of having his novel. The transposition of a living experience into a novel can furnish as many novels as there are transposed experiences. There is a theoretical limit, it is true, but before it is reached there is room for many living, real persons, in contrast to the Cimmerian black of tragedy.

In the novel of this generation, as in its poetry, distinctions must be made not only among the values that it demotes but also between the contribution made by those of its elders whom we have called the reserves of 1914 and its own contributions.

The Dispossessed Values

The dispossessed values were those values of connection and construction that play in the novel the part that language plays in poetry. The techniques of construction and plot underwent not only changes but very perceptible diminutions. In this respect the novelists of the previous generation had sent themselves to the school of Balzac, Flaubert, Maupassant, the builders, and those who survived continued. Certainly this tradition is far from being lost. It was to their irreproachable and intelligent technique that the Tharauds owed the best of their renown. Another technique earned an amazing start for one of the novelists of the generation of 1914, Pierre Benoit. The manner of arousing the average reader's interest has not, on the whole, much changed, and in the novel as in the theater a good traditional technique is an adequate condition of success. But it is less and less a necessary condition. It satisfies a stabilized situation of the novel. It was not by progress in its technique that the novel advanced after 1914 but by a progress or a change in significance, in suggestion. It has evolved not on the outside but underneath. Here again, the novel appears as the opposite of the ancient tragedy, sealed and congealed in a form that it could not break without ceasing to exist. The novel is the most flexible of forms, the most mobile, the most industrious, the most inventive.

The Novel and Time: Marcel Proust

Still in contrast to the classic tragedy and its twenty-four hours, the novel has time. Its duration is virtually consubstantial with that of a human life, and Boileau himself would not dare to reproach it for taking its characters in the cradle and leaving them when they are graybeards, or in their coffins. The novel takes place, or can take place, in a real, living time span, in the very measure of the span of a man's life. The remarkably varied, vivacious, and vigorous span through which the French plant passed between 1789 and 1840 is found again in those novels of Balzac that have the density, the variety, and the significance of a deep geological section. Reread Taine's page on English time—the Oxford morning—and there you will find the theme of the novel of Thackeray, Dickens, and George Eliot. Now, the previous generation had bequeathed to that of 1914 a philosophy of the duration of time, the Bergsonian philosophy, whose action in depth was considerable, not so much by itself as because it was combined with other actions, other movements, with a feeling for the dark and dangerous inner side of man, a mobility, an unrest, a revolution—revolutions, upheavals of every kind. It was natural that, precipitated into a new time span, the generation of 1914 should be precipitated into a new novel.

The first shock, the one that until 1935 has had the most consequences, was given by the novel of Proust. *A la Recherche du temps perdu* seemed at first an unforeseen and unclassifiable work in literature, a break, an adventure. Let us add that this paradoxical heroicizing of snobbery, this author who made himself a sacrificial victim to snobbery, immediately galvanized into action against him all the sound men, the Left Bank, the vital forces of normal literature. The meteoric ascension of Proust must be understood as something quite different from and opposite to the advent of the five damned poets. What the Five contributed was not, perhaps, absolutely new, because there is nothing absolutely new in literature, but at any rate they mined it out of what had not yet been brought to light, of what until then had belonged in literature to the shameful and the hidden. But Proust's *Temps perdu* is a *Temps retrouvé*. These searches through the author's memory were in harmony with searches through the dense memory of literature in a tradition that went back to Montaigne, that traveled by way of Saint-Simon, that was not alien to the Sainte-Beuve of *Volupté* and to which a good conscience had been given among the philosophers by Maine de Biran and Amiel on the one side and Bergson on the other. In all these authors it consists in familiarity with one's own continuity, the talent of living in the continuities of others, and a style that is the man, a style of continuity that is the man of continuity, comprehensive, penetrating, tortuous (exception being made here, of course, for Bergson, a *normalien* for whom style was only an intellectual instrument of exposition and precision, not the matter of a creation). Thus, from the moment when a certain feeling of familiarity with Proust had been established, one recognized that one had been waiting for him, that in him the French novel was making one of its natural and necessary journeys upstream and that like the greatest, like Balzac,

Flaubert, Maupassant, or Renard, Proust would not leave it what he had found it.

Like Balzac . . . Time in Balzac is a historical time, the French continuity of a half century expressed and reflected in *La Comédie humaine*. What Balzac had done for historical continuity Proust did for psychological continuity. But he is a novelist because he can emerge from his psychological continuity, because he has the gift of coinciding with the continuities of others, of seeing and expressing in them even more complexities, ruptures, varieties, than there are in his own continuity. Here he has traveled very far. There is a Proustian world, individual and peopled, as there is a Balzacian world, and much more than there is a Flaubertian world. There is a Proustian comedy of the years from 1890 to 1910. Perhaps Proust has helped since 1920 to clarify and fathom Balzac for us; for substance, for density, for terrible irradiations, Charlus has only one equal in fiction: Vautrin.

Since Stendhal the novel had been the provinces, it had been a certain conquest of Paris, a certain revenge on Paris by the genius of the provinces, like politics under the Third Republic. Even in Feuillet's novels of fashionable society, the originals of which were usually landed proprietors of the Cotentin peninsula, the novel of agrarian society is to be seen. But Proust's novel is perhaps the first complete example of a novel that is purely Parisian, as the theater is in France, and that strictly excludes the provinces. Combray and Balbec figure in it only as vacation places, just as the lower classes appear in it only as servants and its world is that of emptiness, futility, and money. That so much inexhaustible reality could be drawn from this narrow, arbitrary, and fragile setting is what it required much time to understand and what enhances the miraculous merit of Proust's work.

Nonetheless no one supposes that it could have been born before Proust's generation, that of *La Revue blanche*. This was the generation in which the Jewish groups, all urban, emerged into literature, and their manifestations in the novel (and, it goes without saying, in the theater) were to be exclusively Parisian. Proust was half-Jewish, like Montaigne and Bergson, with whom he shared that intuition of flux and continuity that seems to correspond to a graft of the Jewish plant on the Western trunk. Confronting aristocratic society, he faced, with ardor and trepidation, the problem of entrance and conquest. His ironic snobbery was composed half of his successes, half of his disappointments. It will be observed, moreover, that the problems of society were posed with the same solidity, the same profit, and the same healthy artlessness in Balzac: for the great plebeian, for the peasant blood of the Balssas,* the presence, the continuity, the memory of French society were primarily Mmes. de Berny,

---

* The real name of Balzac's Norman peasant family was Balssa.—Translator.

d'Abrantès, and de Castries. For Proust, read Villeparisis (actually the town of Mme. de Berny), Verdurin, and Guermantes.

Proust belonged too to the first generation that, to use a witticism of Barrès, made less good rhetoric and better philosophy. This was especially the case of the young Jews of the Lycée Condorcet. It can hardly be said that Proust was a philosopher. But when his psychology is compared with Bourget's, and when, consequently, the transit is made from one world into another, it is striking to see first of all how the psychology of the author of *Le Disciple* is that of a great rhetorician and then how Proust has integrated into the novel a whole domain, and even a style, that until then had belonged only to the philosophers. Taine compared Maine de Biran with a dark cave and made mock of the Périgord philosopher who had lured a few innocent minds into its shadows. What would he, who had already found Bourget sick, have said if he had seen the novel itself, with Proust, established in Biran's cave and from there exerting on a generation the influence that had been exerted on Taine himself by his beloved Balzac and his beloved Stendhal?

It was the discovery of a world, like that methodical exploration of caverns that dates from the end of the nineteenth century and for which it was necessary to create a word: speleology. But in fact in the novel— that is, in the only direction in which it succeeded—the generation that discovered Proust, or to which he discovered himself, is the generation in which everything followed as if it had taken for its watchword *the discovery of new worlds.*

And hence there arose two kinds of novel that were like a breath of air, the novel of the adventurer and the novel of venture.

The Novel and the Adventurer

The novel of the adventurer (which, however, can also be the novel of a sedentary, or of the house of the baobab in Tarascon) found, if not its models, at least its basic books in two novels that appeared in 1913 and that were received only with reservations: *Les Caves du Vatican*, by André Gide, and *Le Grand Meaulnes*, by Alain-Fournier (Henri-Alban Fournier).

The case of the first novel is very curious, because it makes it possible for us to distinguish between its two elements: a more or less comic novel of adventure, in the sense of unexpected and surprising events, which is not too successful, and a novel of venture (in the sense of an enterprise), which is not the same thing, and of the adventurer. It seems astonishingly perspicacious today because in its character Lafcadio Gide foreshadowed, as his spiritual father, the characteristics of the young man, and above all the young man of letters, of the generation that was on the rise. The generation of 1914 Proustized in the sense that it attended Proust's school of psychology, but not at all in the sense that it would have lived in the style of Proust's characters, beginning with the one who says "I," all of whom really belong to the end of the nineteenth century and the period of the author's youth. In contrast, this generation Gidized in the sense that the character of Lafcadio, like those in *L'Immoraliste* and *Les Nourritures terrestres*, for that matter, was projected far ahead.

Lafcadio, the adventurer of the gratuitous action, is a middle-class, cosmopolitan adventurer, born to money, for whom it is luck, or a career, to be an illegitimate child. The freshness of *Meaulnes*, on the contrary, comes from its popular origin, from its adherence to the provincial, to the elementary, to the village school. The adventure of *Meaulnes* is lost in poetry. *Les Caves* added to the deliberate fantasy of the years after 1914, but *Meaulnes* added to the poetry of this generation, a generation that, moreover, had in part to make its upstream journey of poetry in the novel.

The Novel of Venture

The novel of venture, which enjoyed so much popularity after the war, was appropriate to the entrance into a new world, the impatiences of youth, that decompression and that lack of *Sitzfleisch* that were to be the physical outlet of imaginations penned in by wartime disciplines. Benoit, Pierre MacOrlan, Marc Chadourne gave it a triumphant guise, but this became dated much sooner than the impetus that *Meaulnes* had given to the novel of the adventurer. It was natural that the psychological should win out over the physical and the inner novel over the novel of event.

The adventurer can run his course in a village. The venture, in contrast, needs space, the world. The novel of venture led into the world novel.

The World Novel

Here again the post-war decompression and detumescence must be reckoned with. Between the war and the financial depression the writer who did not spend a part of every year on the highways of the world for his books, for lecture tours, or for journalism made himself conspicuous. The itinerant author had had predecessors before the war, however, and, not

to mention Paul Adam, the Tharauds, with their flawless novels of discovery of Oriental ghettoes, had served as forerunners.

Let us cite another forerunner with a very different talent, Valéry
Larbaud, who, in almost the same year as *Les Caves du Vatican, Meaulnes,*
and *Du Côté de chez Swann,* published *Barnabooth.* And the fact that
these four novels appeared within a few months of one another, on the
eve of 1914, constituted perhaps the richest turning point that had occurred since 1830 in the history of the novel. *Barnabooth* created a style
of journeys as *Meaulnes* created a style of adventure.

Somewhat under the influence of that mandarin, Philippe Berthelot,
and with the distant image of Claudel, which was beginning to supplant
that of Loti, one flotilla of the novel tied up to the port of the Quai
d'Orsay. It was perhaps that common origin in the Ministry of Foreign
Affairs that long persuaded criticism to couple Morand with Jean Giraudoux. They did not resemble each other, but, if they did not belong to the
same literary climate, they were members of the same team and carried
the same luggage, and their respective influences operated alternately.

Few books have been more required, inspired, and adopted by a given
period, which was approximately 1925, than Morand's *Ouvert la nuit*
and *Fermé la nuit.* These were not novels of post-war Europe, they were
a synthesis, a construction of that Europe, more successful than the syntheses and the constructions that cubist painting was attempting at the
same time, but of the same order. Morand's novels never attained the success of his short stories, in part because they came later in time. But in the
novel as in the short story, and especially in the narrative of travel, he
created a style. This style was attuned to a swift cross section of civilization, to machines, to a state of the world, of a period, too, in which fashion
changed rapidly. Morand knew how to follow it or to guide it, like an
automobile designer at the annual show.

The Inner Adventure

Here we record not so much the writers as their influences. Giraudoux's worked simultaneously with Morand's in one of those counterbalances, those double exposures, that *Rouge et noir* that are characteristic
of the French literary climate: they intersected. Morand's world sense,
his connection and his over-flight of countries in space, the terrestrial
globe that he shook as if it were a cocktail—all this was quite foreign to
Giraudoux, who, as *Amica America* and *Siegfried et la limousin* proved,
might indeed be able to carry a suitcase everywhere but always had the
dust of the central plains of France on his shoes. That world connection

that Morand established in space was opposed, or, rather, associated, by Giraudoux with a French connection in time. There is obviously nothing remarkable in that, in principle, and for a hundred years we have faced the question of classic renascences, of the harmonious French linkage, and been burdened by its renewals and its rediscoveries. But with Giraudoux it was a question of a French bond that was not classic, for which there is hardly a definitive word, not even the word that is being used here, still less "modernism" in the sense of the Goncourts, but of which some idea can be gained by reflecting that the classifiers view Giraudoux as a restorer of that affectation that Brunetière tracked down and uprooted, a gardener fighting weeds, in the flowerbeds of French literature. Others, more astute, have been reminded by Giraudoux of the Middle Ages, the far side of the Renaissance. Indeed the usual hero, the preferred hero, the ingenuous and miraculous "he alone" of his novels seems to us very much a kind of Lancelot of the Lake. One speaks of Simon the Pathetic as one speaks of Percival the Gaul, and *Bella* must be compared with the exact things and persons that were at its origin in order to see to what extent Giraudoux is possessed by the genius of luxuriant romance, of invincible distortion, and of magic unrealism.

In Morand the outside adventure blends with the materiality of the journey; in Giraudoux the inner adventure blends with the play of imagination. The novel finds itself at a crossroads of those escape routes down which this generation of movement flung itself and that, in its way, the word "unrest" expresses.

When, however, at the outset of the generation of 1914 the soothsayers examined the auspices, it was the very opposite of unrest that the sacred fowl predicted to them for these young: a virile, precociously mature generation, a generation of energy and resolve that, after the victory against the enemy without, was going to win victory within over the old literatures, the tortuous Byzantinisms. . . . What promise was not seen in the war and post-war literature!

The War Novel

Let us remain with the novel. The war novel had three great successes: *Le Feu, Les Croix de bois* and *Vie des martyrs*. These successes were deserved. The three books have endured and will endure. But, in contrast to novels of adventure, they are much less creations than arrangements. Henri Barbusse, in his novel of a squad of soldiers, brought *La Débâcle* of 1870 up to date for 1914. Furthermore, he was right. The old wars were always fought and experienced by the same squads of peasant origin, just as the diplomats who organized the wars took them out of the same files in the office of Vergennes.* Zola had been the precursor. *Les Croix de bois* gave us tales written by a storyteller in the firing line, those pictures of war in loose formation that the authors of *Les Soirées de Médan* very properly considered the best way of presenting them. *Vie des martyrs* benefited by the great contemporary taste for Dostoevski. The war by itself renewed neither the form nor the substance of the novel. But after the war? The return home? The *Odyssey* after the *Iliad*?

The Novel of Homecoming

The novel of venture had become the novel of the adventurer. The war novel soon became the novel of the warrior, of the conqueror—who, in the ironic phrase of Roland Dorgelès, was the man who survived. Under those habits of bilateralism that we have already encountered, Montherlant and Drieu La Rochelle were invested with a kind of collective charge of representing the returned war veteran in the novel and elsewhere. The six-syllable compound, Montherlant-and-Drieu, became as commonplace as Giraudoux-and-Morand, and we shall not be foolish enough to drop it.

At that time Barrès filled the function of literary patron of the combatants. He offered the new generation a type that it could, if not replace, at least carry on, that of the representative, original, attractive character who imposes himself as the spokesman for the sensibilities of a period and who, with the talent of storytelling, of moving the public by his stories, remains the major character of his own novels under various names. Montherlant was pursued by this destiny. He called his Philippe or his Sturel Alban de Bricoule, he of *Le Songe* and *Les Bestiaires*. With tart eloquence he offered the imperialist image of a young Frenchman. Barrès came from egotism; Montherlant achieved it.

With more or less success, Montherlant was a builder. In *Le Songe* and *Les Bestiaires* he was striving to construct himself, to realize a being who would withstand lapse and collapse and for whom the problem—a bit simple, all the same, simpler than the problems of Barrès—was to reconcile sensual exigencies with this aim. He proved himself a novelist when he portrayed the opposite nature in *Les Célibataires*, the nature that cannot resist destruction. Drieu, perhaps more richly endowed than Montherlant, and also more capable of being interested by ideas, enlisted, on the contrary, in the post-war youth's party and practice of a dissolving reality. He was a dangerous incarnation of the young who were in the spotlight in 1924. The autobiographical titles of his novels—*L'Homme couvert*

* Charles Gravier de Vergennes was one of the archetypes of skillful diplomacy under Louis XVI.—Translator.

de femmes, Le Feu follet, La Valise vide—are characteristic, and the last virtually served as a symbol or a banner to a whole regiment.

A regiment, or, rather, a whirlwind of movements, of emotions at liberty, as people spoke then of words at liberty—what came out in Jean Cocteau's *Thomas l'imposteur* or Soupault's *Le Bon Apôtre.*

The Novel of Middle-Class Youth

These were the young over whom the war had passed, actually or figuratively. More resistance, of course, will be found among those who went through the war and who were thirty when it was a year old.

For their time, André Maurois and François Mauriac—the first with a more general vocation as a man of letters, the second with a more particular vocation for the novel—wrote the novel of the main body of the middle class, midway between the upper and the lower, and provincial enough to belong to the customary climate of the novel: in this order and for this public, they were the most widely read class novelists (in both senses of the adjective) of this time.

Education in France turned middle-class youth into what René Waldeck-Rousseau, the godfather of the separation of Church and state, called the two young generations: the laic and the Catholic. Maurois, a Jew and a student of Alain, analytical of mind, was a pure laic, and Mauriac was a Catholic novelist, the novelist of the Christian problems of the soul. This he was to a point of anguish and depth that cannot be compared with the position of the novelists who were literarily in order with the Church and whose novels bore not so much on its *mystique* as on its politics and its morality: Feuillet, Bourget, Henry Bordeaux. If, in the fleeting moment of 1935 when these lines are written, Mauriac is still the most noted French novelist, one of the reasons for the fact must be seen in that literary and intellectual discredit of the laity that strangely followed its political triumph and the separation of Church and state. Let us add to this the reaction against oratory, which made itself felt in the novel as elsewhere: Mauriac is urgent and moved, he rejects eloquence and the grand flourish. His position, his success, his influence, suddenly enhanced in 1924, belong completely to the ordeals, the directions, the causes of this time.

The Saga Novel

Maurois and Mauriac wrote the novel of good families, without exploiting an extensive field, going little beyond their experience in their fictionalization, barely leaving their Quesnays, their Peloueyres, and the like, familial and familiar territories that they could utilize as the founders of the discontinuous chronicle of a group. The novelists of the previous period, the Bourgets and the Prévosts, had and retained more Balzacism, more invention, more flexibility, and they were less bound to the little stories of their environments, in part because they lived them less. Was it in order to remedy this lack of substance, density, and variety, while still holding fast to the romantic momentum of their novelistic generation, was it in order to subject the novel to a cure of Balzacism that an unexpected number of novelists, at the critical date of 1930, pledged allegiance to that no longer discontinuous but continued, and long continued, chronicle of a compact group, the saga novel?

Not exactly. The saga novel had contributed one of the most famous works of the beginning of the century, *Jean-Christophe*. *A la Recherche du temps perdu* can also be linked to it. But Rolland's and Proust's novels were biographies, written more or less to the measure of an individual. When nature created in humanity something analogous to the saga novel, it did not use the individual: it used the family—that is, individual or contradictory creations thrown up from a single center and sharing in a single momentum. Beside and above the natural family, society created the group and proceeded by groups. Out of this, to which they joined the novel of the individual life in its multiplicities and its complications, came three groups of saga novels, all three in the process of publication as I write, which, if they are completed, will all three stand, by reason of their wholes, their contrasts, their rank in the saga, as the most important testimony of the French novel of this period.

INDIVIDUAL

The saga novel centered on an individual life (and this is the case for Rolland and Proust) has difficulty finding enough in the individual to give it force and keep it alive. Therefore Jean-Christophe and Marcel are much less interesting to us than the secondary characters, whose stories make the work truly live, and even in *Temps perdu* we see the character who says "I" really swallowed up by the immense Charlus. Of the saga novels now in progress, the only one centered on the life of an individual is the very uneven cycle that René Béhaine has entitled *Histoire d'une société*, and, like the two just mentioned, it falls within this observation.

FAMILY

The history of a family during a time span that can run from one to three generations is obviously the most normal framework of the saga novel, the one that is proposed to the novelist and almost imposed on him by the intervals of nature. Therefore it has supplied the generality of the form. The first impulse was given by Roger Martin du Gard's *Les Thibaults*, the beginning of which, *Le Cahier gris*, very deeply impressed readers and the author's colleagues, and the success of which had something to do with getting the current cycles into production. The sequel, and especially the long interruption, made for some uneasiness, and this first example has had something to do, too, with the relative reserve of the public with respect to these enterprises, a reserve that is, however, of no importance, given the fact that they need time and perspective in order to be judged.

Georges Duhamel may be called a very representative figure in the saga novel, since he has written two of them. His four *Salavin* novels, in fact, are a saga of the first kind, which is that of an individual, a "Life and Death of Salavin," a great monograph from below, that of the little mystic, as the naturalists had the little burgher and the little employe. *La Chronique des Pasquier*, one volume of which appears regularly in October of every year, is the story of a lower-middle-class family of little intellectuals, admirably attuned to French continuity, and the reader waits impatiently for it to produce its man of genius.

A similar family portrayed throughout a time span, with a very different art, by Robert Francis in his *Histoire d'une famille sous la troisième République* deserves the name of an extended novel rather than that of saga novel: everything—style, characters, inner life—is made fluid in it and moves in fact with a remarkable liquidity.

Will the four volumes of Jacques de Lacretelle's *Hauts-Ponts* be considered a saga novel one day? Probably. They take place within a limited and precise span: three generations of a more or less declining family— the first is evicted from its property, the second strives to get it back, the third loses it forever. The background is the Vendée, but only because some background was essential: the saga is intended only to focus the light of the novel on a psychological case that concerns a family, as in the same system of transpositions *Silbermann* and *La Bonifas* recounted the case of an individual.

The family is born of the couple. The novel of a family in *Les Destinées sentimentales* formed a sequel in the most natural way to the earlier novels of the specialist in novels of couples, Jacques Chardonne. It is, moreover, a quite well balanced saga, which criticism, perhaps, would place as well in the area of Mauriac as a novel of respectable families of the southwest and of their problems.

It would be easy to imagine a literary map of France in which each great region would be entitled to its saga. That would be too good. But, if the southwest was given its saga by a psychologist, Lyon and its area were given theirs by a storyteller, Henri Béraud, with the *Chronique de Sabolas*, a chronicle of Lyon life in the nineteenth century. In this novel the religious divisions yield to those of right and left: hence it is the *Chronique* of a half-Lyon, since Lyon, which would be well entitled to its own Mauriac and its own Chardonne, is first of all a religious capital. Between the saga novelist of Lyon and the saga novelist of the southwest it is tempting to emulate the Maurois-Mauriac contrast, laicism and religion, one of the sharp contrasts of France today.

MASS

We have enumerated five saga novels based on family life. It was natural and almost necessary that the theorizing poet, playwright, and chronicler of groups, Jules Romains, who in unanimism realized the idea, the feeling of the group, the author of *L'Etre en marche*, should write, when he attacked the saga novel, the novel of a group on the march, *Les Hommes de bonne volonté*. This saga is timed to the pace of the period and the generation of Jules Romains. One character, as in all the preceding sagas, is more or less the author's spokesman, but no more than any other does he assume a preponderant place in the novel. Unity, which has not yet appeared in the excessive diffusion of the characters, will undoubtedly be achieved in the course of the saga and presented as *unity found*, in the way in which *A la Recherche du temps perdu* concludes with *Le Temps perdu* and *Les Rougon-Macquart* with *Le Docteur Pascal*.

Somewhat in the manner of *Les Rougon-Macquart*, which offered the pre-1870 novel after 1870, these seven saga novels are still engaged in a kind of historical period. None of them, in fact, has yet reached the war years. The seven authors visibly emphasize and linger over the years that correspond to their own youth, and in this quest for a vanished time they seem to be in no hurry to reach the present. It is furthermore to be observed that, in the face of the instability of society, of the seasonal character of its manners and its position, novelists since 1930 have hesitated before what used in other times to be the daily bread of the novel: contemporary manners, the record of society. The time span of the novel thus finds itself, as it were, thrown back upstream. That always results from a current unbalance in literary continuity. The haste with which, when they are barely thirty years old, writers whose only experience is something of literature and nothing of life begin to publish their memoirs amuses us and also instructs us. It is a question not only of haste of production but also of uncertainty for the morrow, of the incoherence of life, of a growing necessity to live on reserves, of a crisis and an insolvency of creation. In spite of these difficulties, it would hardly be possible to doubt that the super-saga of these seven saga novels, the Tour de France of the seven cycle novelists, is a major aspect of the history of the novel, of the geography of the novel, for that slice of life that the generation of 1914 will fill out.

IV

POETRY

The sense of poetic movement remained for the generation of 1914 virtually what it had been for the generation of 1885: a more and more radical, more and more extremist separation between rhetoric and poetry. For the half century that separates us from 1885, this is an irresistible trend that opposes this period of French poetry to its whole prior course since the sixteenth century.

Poetry and Rhetoric

The alliance of poetry and rhetoric, however, is so much in the ageless French tradition that it can survive almost indefinitely on a track of parallel development or on a siding. In 1914, indeed, everything seemed as if this question of rhetoric had again been raised. The poetry of eloquence launched its final battles. It had its muse, Anna de Noailles, the last of the romantics of either sex, with whom as with Jaurès—to whom it would have pleased her to be likened—all the great commonplaces of the nineteenth century vanished. The poetry of eloquence also flew the flags of schools: the humanism of Fernand Gregh, the integralism of Adolphe Lacuzon, the paroxysm of Nicolas Beauduin. And nothing would officially forbid us to bring together under the name of meridionalism— the south is eloquent—the sonorous, declamatory, and oratorical poetry of Léo Larguier, Joachim Gasquet, and numerous men of Aix and Toulouse.

The case of unanimism will be more instructive—the group of poets of the Abbaye who were thirty years old or a little younger in 1914: Romains, Duhamel, Charles Vildrac, Chennevière. Romains and Duhamel had minds directed outward, and, as became clear later in the theater and the novel, the vocation of the orator and the education of the rhetorician. But at the same time they were intelligent and clear-sighted, they loved their time, and they took pains to harmonize fully with it. Whence the interest of the contrast between the early poetic manner of Romains, that of *La Vie unanime* (1908), and that which in the next year began to replace it with *Prières*. This was a transit from the oratorical flow to the elliptical suggestion and the stripped emotion. The poetic work of Romains, in the very proportion in which it became extremely deliberate, growing and becoming specific through the practice of technique, a *Traité de versification*, seemed by 1914 to be adaptable for use as the direction sign of a movement. The oratorical character survived more in Duhamel and Chennevière, whereas it was always quite foreign to Vildrac. But at last we have the opportunity to see how, within a group in the process of formation, which attaches great poetic importance even to the construction of the group (that was unanimism), oratory could vary and diminish, just as within symbolism and the twenty-year-olds of 1885 it could be seen waning steadily from Verhaeren to Viélé-Griffin.

Oratory and connected rhetoric are part of the tradition of French poetry. As early as the time of symbolism, the break with oratory had been a break with that tradition. And a break with tradition is generally made for the sake of an adventure. If the eighteenth century shows pure tradition—in other words, immobility—in poetry, it was reserved to the twentieth century to attempt the useful and legitimate experiment of pure adventure.

The Adventure

In truth, such had already been the function of those whom we have called the Five of 1870: Verlaine, Rimbaud, Mallarmé, Lautréamont, Corbière. *Romances sans paroles, Les Illuminations, Un coup de dés,* the Roscoff sea poems, *Maldoror* were so many departures for an unknown sea and safe returns.

> *Solitude, récif, étoile,*
> *A n'importe ce qui valut*
> *Le blanc souci de notre toile.*
>
> (Loneliness and reef and star—
> The white obsession of our sail
> Matches all the things that are.)

Between the adventurers who were twenty years old in 1870 and those of the war that followed there was nevertheless a difference, in favor of the earlier. Once when Clemenceau was being besought on behalf of a politician whom he did not like and in whose favor it was argued that he was like Robespierre, the Tiger retorted: "Yes, but Robespierre did not know that he was like Robespierre." Rimbaud did not know that he was like Rimbaud, and, besides, at the age of twenty he had completely stopped being like him. In contrast, the adventurers of 1914 knew, knew only too well, that they were like Rimbaud, and they talked a great deal about the fact. When the surrealist group made a flag for itself, it inscribed only one word: "Lautréamont!" That was already in the tradition. The generation of 1914, to the extent to which it had magnificent precursors, nevertheless did not know pure adventure.

But in the direction of quantity and publicity it achieved a great deal of the equivalent of what it lacked of purity. Adventure was at the root and in the marrow of this generation. The war added too, it did not create, its need for adventure. The *Correspondance* of Rivière and Alain-Fournier is a geological excavation in the soil from which those roots grew. And Fournier's *Le Grand Meaulnes* and Rivière's article on *Le Roman d'aventure* date from the months before the war. It might be said that, from the death of Guillaume Apollinaire to the decorative-arts exhibition, poetry, like the novel, lived in the atmosphere and the vague idea of adventure.

Poetry was captured by adventure at its root. As early as 1910, Filippo Tommaso Marinetti, who was French-Italian as Apollinaire was Italian-French, had prophesied at the same time as Apollinaire by means of the proclamation of futurism and the poetic play of words at liberty. The word at liberty was the height of the poetic adventure, and as well a result of the poetry at liberty of the Five and the verse at liberty of the free-verse symbolists. Into that musical liberty permeated with assonances, memories, libraries, refrains of popular songs, everything that could be collected on a European road, and, more simply, between the bar and the table in a café, Apollinaire infused enchantment, and also a personal magic. Such a magic usually accounts for much in the uneven success of these adventurers. It created, for example, P.-J. Toulet's fragile glory. Like the ballad of Banville and the sonnet of the Parnassians, traditional among the traditionalists, adventurous forms were invented or reinvented by the adventurers. After Toulet's *Contre-rimes* came Apollinaire's *Calligrammes*. One is reminded of Bacon's *sortes experimenti*, the experiment made at random in order to see whether, by chance, something might come out of it. It had to be thought of. Later it became quite easy.

Something more, however, is to be seen in the *Calligrammes*, poems in the form of designs, which have their ancestor in the *Bouteille* of the fifth book of Rabelais: a game in consonance with the pictorial experiments of the time, an attempt on a frontier where there is something not only of the *Bouteille* but also of the *Coup de dés*. The incomparable interest of a whole poetry since 1885, and even since the Five, is the fact that it added to French continental poetry what in the same era the colonial conquerors were adding to French territory and to the old colonies: not only real colonies but chaplets of uninhabited islands, atolls, and wildernesses, many wildernesses. The latter made for a greater France and the former made for a greater French poetry, for a place in the world, in the realm of the possible. If there was a Sancho poetry, Charles de Pomairols wrote, there was also a Quixote poetry:

> *C'est un très grand honneur de posséder un champ*
> *Fuir, là-bas, fuir je sens que des oiseaux sont ivres . . .*

> (It is great honor to possess a field
> To flee there, flee I feel the birds are drunk . . .)

Except that Apollinaire too, especially he, was a Quixote who knew that he was a Quixote, who strove somewhat pedantically to be a Quixote. If we wanted to enumerate, we could list the names of many poets, participants in these colonial adventures—for instance, Max Jacob, who succeeded more in the novel. Following Apollinaire, perhaps, adventurous experimentation found its principal hero in Jean Cocteau, after *Le Cap de Bonne-Espérance:* more intelligent, more supple, more pleasing than Apollinaire, less inventive, less inspired, less the navigator for the long voyage, but rather the coaster (with some hesitation in defining the term), lacking in Apollinaire's kind of hoax but not in charming impostures, and in sum, by the 1930s, the ancient mariner, still visible, of that bark of Pantagruel that had sailed the seas of the poetry of the 1910s and the 1920s, for whom we cherish a certain weakness.

An intelligent weakness, the reader will have no doubt, since it is a question of learning the secret of poetry's destiny from the oracle of the goddess. Unfortunately the reply is or would have been not too encouraging. Curious but unfruitful experiments. Shall we go back into our little vineyard and plant Alexandrines, watch the rich rhyme flower, pride ourselves on our formal beds of sonnets, dazzle the end of a vicar's garden with the blazing, well-watered setting out of a Hugoesque ode? No. All the same, the drive of poetry lies in invention, adventure by sea and air . . .

The Reserves

VALÉRY

Here, happily, by that good fortune that never forsakes French literature, the reserves of 1914 were in formation. It was with reserves that the then General Louis-Hubert Lyautey held Morocco at that time. The crew of forty-year-olds that compensated during the war for the partial absence of the new generation included two poets, Valéry and Claudel. It was extremely significant that Valéry, in poetic slumber for twenty years as Paul von Hindenburg was a general in disgrace and Henri-Philippe

Pétain was a little-known colonel, should take command of the colonial
expedition and the adventure. He was not free not to write *La Jeune Parque* in 1916.

Published in 1917, *La Jeune Parque* needed only a few months to make
its way, time enough for three or four hundred lovers of poetry to learn
it by heart as they had learned Racine and Hugo. This poem of the inner
life entered into memories as into an invincible parade ground and from
there it radiated slowly throughout poetry, injected into it the unexpected
influence of a bit of radium.

Here the reader was on the bank directly opposite from Apollinaire
and his group, from that facility and that almost automatic writing with
which, from Apollinaire and Max Jacob to the surrealists, some poets have
deliberately and desperately rejected continuity, rejected the necessary
and perduring hardness of matter. Each line of *La Jeune Parque*, in contrast, was won from a hostile silence, against a resistance that poetic
alchemy incorporated into the final product. According to Boileau's pre-
cept, easy, flowing verse was made with difficulty, and it was from the
difficulty that the solidity of the work was born. Further, Valéry opposed a kind of infusion to the diffusion and the confusion in which the
poets of adventure coursed: the infusion of the adventure and of the unexpected into the inner life. *La Jeune Parque* would be almost in poetic
conjunction with the titles of two famous philosophical works: *Mémoire
sur les perceptions obscures* and *Le Cheminement de la pensée*, the fullness of a naked consciousness as the fragment of the Apollo Belvedere is
the fullness of a torso alone.

During the next five years it was followed by poems that were collected
in *Charmes*. The two short periods of poetry, the one in youth and the
other in middle age, recall in Valéry's life those islands of which the young
Fate said:

> *Rien n'égale dans l'air les fleurs que vous placez*

> (Air has no equal to the flowers you place).

But, from the point of view that concerns us here, the important thing
is the tradition that this poetry established or re-established and the influence that it exerted.

The tradition is that of Mallarmé. There is no doubt that there are
great differences between Mallarmé's poetry and Valéry's, and more still
between their two minds, the one believing in Letters, the other in Science. And yet, thanks to Valéry, Mallarmé no longer seemed a meteor.
They shared a single domain. The fact that, like Rudyard Kipling's sea
serpent, they were two changed the situation. Valéry's first poems, those
collected in the *Album de vers anciens*, were almost, in the final years of
the nineteenth century, the only French poems that were written directly
and certainly under Mallarmé's influence, which had no technical effect

on any other symbolist poet. Rejuvenated by the thought and the music of *La Jeune Parque*, the Valéry of the 1920s exerted, in contrast, a profound influence on a part of French poetry. Lucien Fabre seems to have been his first disciple, and later a part of the younger poetry that remained loyal to regular verse forms was touched by Valéry's rays. Then came this paradox, that Valéry (like Anatole France, heaven help us!) may be said to have acted as a conservator. At a period when they were vacillating, he conserved the technical, rigorous frameworks of French poetry. As Mallarmé said, he refused to attack verse. He allowed those who were still defending it to do so in good conscience.

It will be observed that the symbolists properly so called, those who were twenty years old in 1885, the Laforgues, the Régniers, the Viélé-Griffins, had little influence on their successors of 1914, and that in the end it was as if, to the extent to which the generation of 1914 had any masters, those masters were the Five of 1870, Verlaine to a certain degree, Mallarmé by way of Valéry on the one hand and by way of the champions of the *Coup de dés* on the other, something of Corbière in his popular and marine imagery, Lautréamont through surrealism—and, finally, the extraordinary fate of Rimbaud.

CLAUDEL

Taken as the figurehead of a poetic ship, Rimbaud was more or less at the origin of *Tête d'or*, Claudel's first drama. Now Claudel was the second of the reserve poets of 1914. It cannot be said that he was unknown before that time. Quite the contrary: the correspondence between Rivière and Claudel would almost provide the gauge for us to measure the reputation that the poet of *L'Otage, L'Annonce, Cinq grandes odes* had gained in the eyes of a part of the silent young. But primarily the war set him among the four replacements. Later the time came when he had not only an intellectual trade but poetic disciples.

Claudel's verse line was in effect a great discovery, not only original, not only very fecund in his hands, but completely capable of providing a good poetic tool to certain others. Through a circumstance similar to that that made Valéry a "conservator," this Claudel technique proved admirably fitted to the hands of the young men returning from the war. Montherlant and Drieu La Rochelle, who for a while were the two Ajaxes of this *Nostoï*, employed it also to state poetically both their questions and their affirmations. In another direction, Claudel's influence being very strong on the Catholics, it will hardly be surprising to find the form of his verse being adopted by poets of Christian sentiment like Henriette Charasson.

There is one difficulty, however. Claudel's line is a form that is very peculiar to its author, deliberately invented by him to his own measure, in conditions that he himself has described for us. Now, if imitation and influences are part of the climate of poetry, it is all the more necessary that neither imitation nor influence be visible from without and even before reading. The strophe of *Mireille* and *Calendal* bore the brand of Mistral's invention so strongly that no southern poet dared to touch it after him. The case of Claudel's line, with its prominent signature, is somewhat the same. And yet in itself this instrument, capable of being successfully varied according to temperament, seems to be in good use. Very new when Claudel created it, almost a half century ago, its flow has achieved a good balance today between the very broad rhythmed passage of Saint-John Perse (Alexis Saint-Léger Léger), like an estuary, and that poetic trickle of little streams in which the generation of 1914 seems to have found its median instrument.

The New Verse

A median instrument, moreover, bequeathed by the previous generation, and it would be quite difficult to say when it originated: perhaps with Laforgue's *Derniers Vers*. The Abbaye group had pledged itself to it in a conscious and concerted fashion, and Romains and Chennevière demonstrated one kind of technique or employment of it in their *Traité de versification française*, first taught at the Vieux-Colombier in 1913. Perhaps nowhere better than in Léon-Paul Fargue's *Pour la Musique* is there a better example of its necessary and acute expression of a sensitivity. Like the free verse of the symbolist generation, of which it is the heir, the new verse has profited by the very uncertainty of its paternity, and, in contrast to Claudel's line, it does not carry anyone's authentic mark; there is no shepherd for the flock. To the same extent as regular verse it gives free play to each poet's originality and allows many to achieve a distinct touch. Pierre-Jean Jouve does not resemble Romains in it, André Salmon is not like Morand, or Paul Eluard like Pierre Reverdy, or Jules Supervielle like Henri Michaux. And yet this poetic domain exists, like Parnassus or symbolism. It balances the current domain of regular verse. If the scope of this book permitted, it would be easy to identify the dozen volumes—or, usually, slender books—that will stand surety for it in literary history. Better still, one can already draw from them the line that it is making on the horizon.

It has almost nothing in common with the symbolist line any more, in spite of a wholly external analogy of the poetic instrument. It is even more drained of oratorical and logical substance. For his movement the poet employs a very light stress on his words, which is best expressed by the word "allusion" in its full etymological meaning. An old theory of esthetics, expounded by Schiller, had it that art was the highest form of play. And that does not mean at all that neither art nor the play of children is serious. Now, very modern poetry, that of the diminished or meager line, has simply thrust one of the usual boundaries of poetry back farther toward play. It has given not only the language but the emotion more gratuitousness, as Gide said at the time of *Les Caves,* more detachment in the sense in which the young Fate "is detached" *Pour la musique,* Fargue said. But it is a properly poetic music, which has broken with that musical music whose lyricism has been sated since romanticism, and which symbolism, Mallarmé, and Valéry carried to a paroxysm that can no longer be exceeded. A poetic music in which the gap between impression and expression is reduced to the minimum. All this can survive.

But being able to survive is not enough. Something must be done with this ability. And the new poetry, the poetry proper to the active generation of 1914, independent of the reservist generation, has done little.

Since the generation of 1789, which had André Chénier, every French literary generation has had its great poet or poets. The generation of 1914 was the first that did not have its own. And yet, in contrast to the generations that found themselves in this position in the eighteenth century, it has been not at all lacking in poetic invention: on the contrary! Perhaps the exploitation of the poetic world has its own limits. Perhaps a moment comes when, as in the colonies, all the good land has been taken and the latest arrival finds nothing more available to him, in effect, than those wildernesses of which we spoke, a wilderness of stone or a wilderness of salt—where La Bruyère's "it has all been said" is like the "sold out" sign put up by the old colonial powers against the new. Conditionally, of course, for there is always war, there is always adventure . . .

Poetry and Prose

And from now on, even with reservations, one must not be fooled by typography. The Banville of the symbolist generation, Paul Fort, almost marked a turning point when he gave his torrent of verse the typographical appearance of prose. Today's prose is sometimes a masked ball—badly masked—at which poetry, all poetries have made assignation together. Even among the Five, it was not at all through his verse but through *Les Illuminations* that Rimbaud became a master of 1920, and *Maldoror* is in prose, in fact in oratorical prose. Fargue's verses in prose functioned exactly like poetry in the literary life of 1930. Cocteau's vocation as a poet is similarly fixed in prose to the end. It is in prose that poetic surrealism flows. Between prose and poetry there is an ever-increasing osmosis. Poetry has overflowed especially on the novel. It has often been observed to what an extent Giraudoux's condition is a poetic condition. It was in-deed sluice gates of poetry that, from the time of the war, had been opened by *Le Grand Meaulnes*. It would be curious and rewarding to make a poetic map of the contemporary era that would show the seats of poetry, the trends of poetry—and also the trends and the seats of anti-poetry (they exist); on such a map the places marked poetry would not at all imply, would less than ever include, writings in verse.

V

THE THEATER

The Theater of the Home Front

The theater was not in at all a bad state in 1914. Jacques Copeau's initiative at the Vieux-Colombier, in succession to Antoine, had stimulated a movement analogous to that of the Théâtre Libre. But with one difference. The Théâtre Libre was a theater, but it was also authors. Now it would be unjust to say that the Vieux-Colombier had no authors, but it is a fact that it did not go in search of them: Copeau's plans thus far did not go beyond a physical treatment, a sharpening of the instrument, a training for the actor and the public. Nevertheless a movement was stimulated that was undoubtedly going to bear fruit. On the other hand, the group that had made its start in the theater at the end of the nineteenth century was at the height of its powers in 1914, the theater was still loyal to the customs of the comedy of manners, and society was still accustomed to the manners of the comedy. The war overturned everything.

The ways of war could not be transposed to the stage, and no more could it any longer take the paths of peace. On the other hand, it was necessary to keep the theaters working. A vast audience of soldiers on leave, foreigners, war profiteers, allotment recipients asked only to be allowed to spend its paper money there. The industry met this demand as well as it could, or, rather, as well as this scarcely cultivated audience required. The normal theaters had to adopt this production standard in order to survive; they had to submit to the direction of industrialists—ticket brokers yesterday, merchants of entertainment today. It was a magnates' theater. By the time of the armistice genuine dramatic art in a body had taken refuge in little places on the order of the Vieux-Colombier, where costs were low and which found a few benefactors, sought out young artists, and worked with them. Rehabilitation came slowly, with difficulty, much impeded by the cinema. In the theater much more than in the novel, more even than in poetry, the generation of 1914 had been crippled, stifled, had had to make its way through perilous ravines from which it had not yet emerged.

A very natural tradition had it that the leading form, in matters of the theater, should be the verse theater. But, after the war, that category was part of the necrology. We will say nothing about it.

It had, however, its substitutes in prose. The public, especially the European public, was greatly interested by the eloquent theater of Paul Raynal, and *Le Tombeau sous l'Arc de Triomphe* served as a war play for the post-war period. Alone among his contemporaries, M. Raynal obeyed the orders of that prose tragedy the problem of which had been raised by the previous generation.

Comedy of Manners

The comedy of manners lost its leading position. The theater, however, would hardly be able to get along without it, and it was necessary that the manners of the day appear before its bar or behind its footlights. Having, immediately after the war, gorged itself on the newly rich, the comedy of manners soon sickened on the plethora and the facility of the subject. It sickened in quality, but not in success, as *Mon Curé chez les riches* showed. It was represented in 1935 by the intelligence and the skill of Edouard Bourdet, who found his way by interesting the mass audience in the distortions of literary manners in *Vient de paraître*, in plain manners in *La Prisonnière*, and *La Fleur des pois*. The spectator in the gallery would say of this comedy of manners, as he would say before the hero of *Monsieur Alphonse*, that the name was not stolen.

Comedy of manners means above all social comedy—in other words, a comedy of private life in so far as it is governed by external trends, conformities, nonconformities, fashions. The contemporary public is more interested in the comedy of private life in so far as it is closed and domestic: that is, the comedy of the family and the comedy of the couple.

Comedy of the Family and the Couple

The comedy of the family has shown much more evidence of running dry than the comedy of the couple, of which at an earlier time *Amoureuse* had created the type. The fabulous poetic success of *Toi et moi* appointed Paul Géraldy to attempt it in the theater. This is the concern of *Robert et Marianne*. We take this example because of its felicitous title: two given names. But with other given names, and more complicated titles, the comedy of the couple, which is that of marriage and the love affair, is to be encountered everywhere. It has become one of the stereotypes of the theater. All these couples—at odds, of course—end by looking alike to the old spectator, as all marriages look alike to the license clerk and all divorces to the judge. What Gautier said of the old music-hall sketch might be said of this form: that there should be only one of the kind, and from time to time it could be altered. These plays are generally ready-made in the authors' experiences, and they have no trouble becoming part of the spectator's experience. Besides, people go to the theater in couples, and hence their success.

But the post-war couple was an even more precarious and fragile couple than the couple of 1900. It became complicated not only in respect to situations but also in respect to the people in them. The post-1920 tart, one day, will join the light woman and the madam in a museum. Meanwhile she has her theater, the theater. She is an easy woman—I mean easy for the dramatic author, for whom she makes all kinds of combinations of the regular or irregular couple possible. Paul Nivoix' *Eve toute nue* (1927) and Jacques Natanson's *Le Greluchon délicat* (1925) are pleasant types of this comedy chosen at random.

The combinations of the couple, furthermore, go far beyond the barn-yard. It is indeed at the opposite extreme that one would place Stève Passeur's major success, *L'Acheteuse*, an impressive modern Lamiel. As for adultery, the theater has stopped taking it seriously. Fernand Crommelynck with *Le Cocu magnifique* and Emile Mazaud with *Dardanelle* could present cuckoldry, the ritual daily bread of the light comedy of sixty years before, only under the auspices of poetic farce.

Let us not too quickly assume the amorality of the contemporary theater. Today's public, more mixed, more passive, more amorphous, accepts situations that would not have been accepted in the time when there was a society. But in the same way it accepts being moved by means of eternal forms and fibers (if not theatrical devices). *La Souriante Madame Beudet*, by Denys Amiel and André Obey, and Charles Vildrac's *Michel Auclair*, following *Le Paquebot Tenacity*, had post-war successes no element of which was dependent on "manners" (this time in the sense that manners are the mode) or on the fleeting figures of the couple.

Unrest in the Theater

Those are permanent forms of comedy. Alongside them there are dramatic problems more peculiar to this generation.

The theater lives on conquests. It is imperialist or it does not exist. It seeks to take the best from other forms that defend themselves. For three generations, from romanticism to the war, the theater strove to roll back its frontiers in the direction of the poet and in the direction of the moralist. Romantic drama marked the maximum of its invasion of poetry, the comedies and the prefaces of Dumas the Younger the maximum of its invasion of the domain of the moralists. These two questions were in debate again before the war. The poetic invasion had its great days with Rostand, the moralist tradition was quite solidly represented by Brieux. With varying successes, all that was the life of the theater.

In proportion as something disappeared from literature, problems disappeared. The theater is looking elsewhere for its gains. Current problems concern not the theater's relations with poetry and moralism but its relations with literature and cinema.

More exactly, three aspects of the theater may be discerned, according to whether the author is stirred and disquieted by the theater alone, by the theater and letters, by the theater and cinema.

THE THEATER ALONE

In every period of the nineteenth and twentieth centuries, an important dramatic author emerged to personify what might be called, if not the pure theater, at least the theatrical theater. Scribe and Sardou were the most noted. In all honesty, what they lacked was to be actors and directors like Picard (let us go no higher) at the same time as authors, and to stage and play their own works. They also lacked a certain communication with the audience, with Paris, certain fortunate traces of loss of class, or, rather, of the acquisition of a new class in which theater people lived until the nineteenth century. Both, for example, were quite naturally members of the Académie, whereas the Other could not be and none of his contemporaries even raised the question whether he was. But even the Other lacked something, the same thing that Napoleon lacked. The Other was the theater, but he was not born to the theater. He had been trained to become the king's upholsterer. He did not have the theater as an inheritance, and from his conception on. "If only I were my son," Napoleon said. There was not one of these obstacles that was not raised against Sacha Guitry, who was the pure and exclusive incarnation of the theatrical theater of 1935 on the stage and in the audience, in the theater and on the street, in body and in soul. Therefore we shall choose him as an example in preference to some other excellent man of the theater such as Jean Sarment.

The tally of his plays exceeds a hundred. The personal magic of the actor-author usually wins them as much success in their novelty as oblivion when they descend to the rank of printed books. It does not seem, to be honest, that any of them will remain as part of a repertory. But something better may remain of them: first of all, a certain day-to-day chronicle of Parisian reactions over thirty years, what for instance is to be found in the early years of *La vie parisienne*, and also the sentimental history, or, rather, the little sentimental histories, of the author-actor that are born, live, and die in a state of theater.

The case of Marcel Pagnol is very different, but it too goes back to the theatrical theater. His gift for the theater seems to have been restricted (in the manner of Becque's) to two subjects that he carried inside him, as Piron carried *La Métromanie*, and that he had experienced personally: first, the destiny of a little schoolteacher who succeeds, a *Petit Chose* who becomes a *Monsieur Quelqu'un:* this was *Topaze*. And this Marseillais had also in him the play of his city, Marseille: that was *Marius* (of which *Fanny* is only the sequel, and also the rehash). Having gone from the theater to cinema, he has now to create a third and final comedy there.

THE THEATER AND LETTERS

All this theatrical theater has no connection with contemporary written literature. Exactly the contrary can be said of the theater of Henri-René Lenormand, who imported ideas into the theater with an honest and passionate intelligence, and who created a theater of his own with *Les Ratés, Le Simoun, Le Temps est un songe, un lâche*. His silhouettes of character are more like those of the novel than those of the theater and do not make it easier for his plays to succeed. On the stage he boldly plays the part of the psychological and psychoanalytical novelist, which will perhaps be remembered more by the literary historian than by the current public: Lenormand is probably the contemporary dramatic author who will soonest become the subject of a thesis.

THE THEATER AND CINEMA

The young author is more concerned today with cinema than with literature. Consciously or unconsciously, the influence of the new art has insinuated itself into a significant part of post-war dramatic literature. First of all, cinema, which is the art of movement, has given the average spectator a training ground; he has become accustomed to more rapid perceptions, and this has made it possible for the dramatic art to sweep away obstacles: the theater of the young authors no longer lives in the same time span as the theater of the old, and the last traces of long explanations have disappeared. In the second place, the language of facial expression has replaced or illuminated dialogue. Finally, there is a certain search for quality and novelty that is barred for the cinema by material considerations, the necessity of reaching a mass audience, above all the provincial audience: it is the theater, infinitely more flexible, more liberated from the materialities of machinery and even of money, whose task it is to make literary profit out of the capital of the vogue for cinema. It is impossible to imagine Jean-Victor Pellerin's *Têtes de rechange*, which was one of the best conceived and newest of the post-war plays, being born anywhere but in the shadows of cinema. In the same way it is possible to see roads of communication between cinema and theater that Marcel Achard and Jean-Jacques Bernard have been able to follow. The way in which they succeeded in putting accent and life into what is between the lines attests to the proximity and the fellowship of their theater with the silent art.

With the formerly silent art. Silent cinema was able to enrich the theater and also the novel with its suggestions, in the manner in which ancient or foreign literatures have helped French literature. The need for transposition and a new creation is the salvation of originality. Speaking cinema, in spite of its vast material resources, or because of them, has succeeded thus far only in degrading the literary quality of everything that it has touched. No doubt it has a literary future. In 1936 its only present is anti-literary. To cite a film in a history of literature is still impossible and even contradictory. Literature is a domain of what endures, at least of that for which one can without absurdity presume some duration. We do not have even an idea of what a lasting film can be, a film that after a few months will be anything but an almanac of another year. And then again there are precious almanacs of other years, like the *Armana Prouvençau!* As for the transposition of a literary work, a novel, a poem, or even a play, to speaking cinema, thus far, like the *Bibliothèque bleue*, its only importance is as a diminution of literature, in the way in which physicists are interested in the diminution of energy.

INDEX